The Drama:

Traditional and Modern

Edited with Introductions and Notes by

MARK GOLDMAN
University of Rhode Island
and
ISADORE TRASCHEN
Rensselaer Polytechnic Institute

ALLYN AND BACON, INC.

Boston

Library of Congress Catalog Card Number: 68–15224

Printed in the United States of America

🔱 *Preface*

The idea of this anthology is evident from the arrangement of the table of contents. Tragedy and comedy are the primary forms of traditional drama, and any introduction to the drama should begin with them. But as we point out in our introduction to modern drama, these are no longer the dominant forms. The very idea of form has itself become suspect now. In the past the sense of form derived from the generally held belief in a meaningful, coherent order, divinely inspired. But the weakening of this belief has led to a collapse of traditional forms, not only in the drama but in all the arts and this, as the reader knows, is merely part of the general collapse of forms: social, political, economic, religious, and others. The table of contents is thus instructive, pointing to the shaping idea of this anthology: the secure sense of form in the past, and its absence in the present.

It was our intent, in our introductions, to give the student a sense of the *spirit* of the drama, some sense of the *life* behind the traditional forms of tragedy and comedy and the new, experimental forms. In our remarks on tragedy and comedy we sketch out the underlying patterns of each, and the types of characters common to them. In the modern period the representative form is a fusion of tragedy and comedy. The old preoccupation with the distinctions between these forms has shifted to distinctions between the realistic and non-realistic presentation of their fusion. This has given rise, as the reader will see in our introduction to modern drama, to radical changes in plot, character, setting, and language.

Contrasting comments follow each modern play. These will give the student a sense of the variety of contemporary critical approaches. The fact that they offer differing interpretations should also be of value. They should disabuse the student of the notion of a *correct* interpretation, and they may free him to pursue his own *valid* interpretation. The student should certainly absorb professional criticism; but his own critical manhood depends on his eventually moving out of the house, so to speak.

The headnotes provide biographical data and some observations on the significance of the playwright. For further study the student may consult the bibliography appended to each headnote, and the bibliographies after each general introduction.

Our first obligation, we felt, was to choose plays which would excite students; this means, we admit, plays which have excited us. Those in the traditional section are classics. When we speak of tragedy we think of *Oedipus Rex*, and *King Lear;* and when we speak of comedy we can hardly do better than *Twelfth Night* and *The Misanthrope.* The plays in the modern section are among the best by each author. *Happy Days*, though the only play by Beckett available, is a minor masterpiece. The plays are examples of different kinds of modern theater: realistic, expressionistic, epic, grotesque, absurd. The fact that more than half of the anthology is modern reflects the remarkable renewal of interest in current drama. It would be academic in the worst sense not to recognize the validity of this interest; it is an instance of our general sense of urgency.

We wish to thank Miss Mary Gorham and Mrs. Martha Arsics for their assistance in preparing the manuscript of this book. To Mr. Wayne A. Barcomb of Allyn and Bacon we are indebted for encouragement and editorial advice.

MARK GOLDMAN

ISADORE TRASCHEN

◈ *Contents*

Introduction to

Traditional Tragedy

I

What is tragedy? What is the so-called tragic sense of life? What are the elements which make it a profound human expression? What defines the tragic hero, setting him apart from everyone else? These are some of the questions we will try to answer in this introduction. But the reader should be at once forewarned that, as with all literary questions, answers vary from person to person.

Sustained thinking on tragedy begins with the *Poetics* of Aristotle (384–322 B.C.), a series of notes taken down by one of his followers. According to this source, tragedy began with improvisations on the Dithyramb, a choral song in honor of the god Dionysus, who brought the cult of the grape to Greece. The song gave thanks to the god for the fertility of the land. As the ritual evolved it probably became both a thanksgiving for the harvest and a lamentation over the sacrificial death of the god (symbolically the death of the old year), and a supplication to the god to return in the spring of the new year and revive the land. These prayers have their equivalent in tragedy in the choral lamentation for the dying hero, who may himself be symbolically understood as the dying god of the old fertility rituals. Tragedy was clearly something more than an entertainment—though it was certainly that too: people came in a festive as well as religious mood. The Dithyramb was sung by men dressed in goatskins (tragedy is usually said to mean goat song) to represent satyrs, the goat-men of myth who followed Dionysus. From these choral beginnings tragedy evolved by the time of Aeschylus (525–433 B.C.) into an action with two actors as well as the chorus. Sophocles (497–405 B.C.) added scenery and a third actor.

II

Tragedy has a distinctive pattern or form, in good measure deriving from its origin in the ritual of the sacrificial death of the year-god. In developing this pattern we should think of it as a model; it will not correspond in every respect to particular plays. It is merely a guide, an ideal pattern. This pattern is a way, furthermore, of pointing up the *quality* of the tragic experience, the human experience that draws us to tragedy in the first place; and it is a way, more particularly, of defining the progression of that experience.

Aristotle says that a tragic plot should have a beginning, a middle, and an end. Accordingly, the pattern may be divided into these phases: (1) The Breakdown of Established Values; (2) The Descent into the Abyss; and (3) Transcendence and Transformation.

(1) *The Breakdown of Established Values.* The tragic action begins when events damage orthodox beliefs and values sufficiently to bring on a crisis. The crisis may be brought on by some fault of the hero; or by a god, by fate or some evil daimon visiting a curse on a great house; or by evil figures like Edmund, Regan, and Goneril. Religious breakdown is evident in Oedipus' cry; "If I was created so, born to this fate, who could deny the savagery of God?" or in Lear's questioning of the justice of the gods; moral breakdown is evident in Regan and Goneril's treatment of Lear. The hero's new, developing tragic sense conflicts with his traditional orthodox values. Hamlet suffers from the loss of the traditional values of mother and beloved, and his paralysis is in part owing to the fact that he cannot fully surrender them; Lear suffers from the loss of the traditional values attached to filial love and the authority of king and father, as well as from the loss of the benign, ceremonial, orthodox world represented in the opening moments of the play. The time is out of joint. Of course the hero retains some fragments of his old beliefs, but they seem largely irrelevant.

(2) *The Descent Into the Abyss.* Deprived of the consolations of the orthodox, the tragic hero confronts the abyss. He is bound to a wheel of fire, like Lear; or he tears out his eyes, like Oedipus; or he talks to ghosts and skulls, like Hamlet. The hero's descent marks the symbolic death of his old self, of his old values and beliefs. Significantly, Hamlet meditates in a graveyard, even plunges into a grave, and Lear speaks of being in the grave. The hero's "death" drives him to a new, a tragic sense of things. He discovers his limits; that, as Lear cries, he is a "poor, naked forked animal," born to suffer and to die. He

discovers that beneath the fair skin of appearance lies grinning reality: if not a skull, then woman's frailty. He discovers his tragic identity. In Aristotle's phrase, the *discovery* or *recognition* (*anagnorisis* in the Greek) marks a change from ignorance to knowledge. Sometimes, as in *Oedipus Rex*, the discovery comes through an ironic turn or reversal called the *peripety*. The messenger brought good news which turned out to be the worst possible news since it led to the discovery by Oedipus that he was the son of the man he had murdered and the woman he had married. The peripety in *King Lear* takes place in the opening scene. The bestowal of his kingdom on his daughters was to Lear a joyous occasion which turned out to be the beginning of his tragic fate. The rest of the play is one continuing discovery, as in *Oedipus Rex*. It is this that accounts for much of the power of both plays. When a change in the hero's fortune is accompanied by a reversal or a recognition we have what Aristotle calls a complex plot. The surprise evokes either pity or fear, or both. With such a plot the action up to the peripety is ambiguous: what is happening is merely the surface, the appearance beneath which reality is waiting to spring. Tragedies may have a *simple* plot, one without a peripety, as in Euripides' *The Trojan Women*. Here there is no surprise or ambiguity in the action.

Now the discovery enlarges the hero. His old, arrogant pride is gone, what the Greeks called *hubris*, an insolent self-confidence, a feeling that one's powers are unlimited, like a god's. He sees his condition now as an instance of the condition of all men. His pride turned him inward. Now he turns outward. He retains his integrity, but it is now grounded in universal sympathy. In the storm Lear declares: "Take physic, pomp/Expose thyself to feel what wretches feel"; and at the end Oedipus is troubled over his daughters' future, and is prepared to die to purge Thebes of the pollution.

(3) *Transcendence and Transformation*. The suffering and symbolic death of the hero are the preconditions of his new, tragic sense of life. In the familiar Greek adage, wisdom—tragic wisdom—comes through suffering. Suffering leads to a lacerated consciousness, a wounded probing of "the mystery of things." A figure like Hotspur in the first part of *King Henry IV* is not really tragic because he does not suffer; and for this reason he does not really change. Out of the hero's suffering come the great rages on the contingent character of the old values, such as religious belief, love, friendship, filial piety, and those meditations on the absolute character of fate which all the good will in the world cannot alter. In the eighteenth century, middle class sentimentality was so strong that in some versions Lear lived on with

Cordelia. This violated what we may well call the first law of tragedy, what Aristotle calls "necessity." The hero's fate is fixed, irrevocable, necessary. It cannot be adjusted or ameliorated. Though the hero is endowed with sympathy now, and though he has the affections of others, he is at bottom alone, alienated, fated. He has seen hell; after that, ordinary life is a freak show, a horror. He is outside of it; he has seen through it. He has, really, one single interest, to confront his fate. He comes to terms with it, and so begins to remake it. Though he must suffer and die, the new, hellish consciousness that suffering leads to, that it *is*, makes for his transcendence of his fate and his consequent transformation. He resolves the dilemma of free will and fate. Though fated, he is free to die meanly or greatly; in this sense his character shapes his fate. He does not submit to his fate pathetically, passively, self-pityingly; he transcends it tragically. We might say he dies nobly, but this grand Roman-Renaissance word has been reduced to Victorian stuffiness and sentimentality. And the word is in any case misleading for the Shakespearean hero. He is noble *and* gay—suffering is the source of true gaiety, a passionate gaiety. Hamlet is gay as he fingers Yorick's skull, and mad Lear too when, in a moving and brilliant pun, he declares to the blind Gloucester: "I shall be jovial." As Yeats puts it in *Lapis Lazuli*: "All perform their tragic plays,/There struts Hamlet, there is Lear,/That's Ophelia, that Cordelia,/Yet they. . . . If worthy their prominent part in the play,/Do not break up their lines to weep./They know that Hamlet and Lear are gay; Gaiety transfiguring all that dread."

In Greek tragedy the hero's transcendence is often realized through the mediation of a God, the *Deus ex machina*. This changes tragedy into what we may call a divine comedy, a resolution appropriate to the religious context of the Greek theater. Our ideal *tragic* pattern stops short of this divine mediation. The tragic hero relies on his own resources. He acquires his own kind of holiness, that which comes through deep suffering. His transformation penetrates the community. At his death everyone gathers round him, a natural act, symbolic of the ritual sacrifice of the old vegetation year-god we spoke of in the beginning. He is the scapegoat whose death restores the community. This restoration is possible because he has taken on a holy character, through suffering. The community partakes of his holiness. We, as audience, are affected too. Aristotle suggests that we are also purged psychologically. The tragic action arouses pity and fear; and in experiencing them we realize what he calls a *catharsis* of these emotions. As the reader will see in the introduction to modern drama, this psychotherapy is hard to come by in our own theater.

The tragic pattern begins with a downward movement; then, with the hero's discovery of his tragic condition, a reversal takes place; there is now an upward movement leading to his transcendence and transformation. This pattern is an instance of the archetype of death and rebirth. It is worth reminding ourselves of the relation of tragedy to this archetype because of the latter's pervasiveness. It is the pattern of the central event of Christianity, of the pre-Christian fertility religions which celebrated the yearly death and rebirth of their gods, of the movement from night to day, sleep to waking, winter to spring.

III

The tragic pattern accounts for the central experience of the hero. There are other matters, though, which should be considered. There is, first, the difficult question of evil. It may take the form of a curse by a daimonic spirit or god on a great house (the house of Atreus in the *Oresteia* and the house of Labdacus in the Oedipus plays), or it may make itself felt, as in Shakespeare, through human agents like Regan, Goneril, and Edmund. We might account for it rationally in some way, explain it in psychoanalytic terms, for instance. Yet such an explanation does not seem to be enough. How can we explain the serpent in the Garden of Eden or daimonic spirits! In tragedy, evil takes on an ultimate character; it is a given, a fact of life, a motiveless malignity, in Coleridge's phrase. We do not pretend to say what evil is, only that in the tragic universe it is there.

What, then, is its function? It is, first, the force which breaks down the order of things: established, orthodox beliefs and values. In so doing it promotes the temporary well-being of its agents. As a consequence the idea of justice, of divine justice, comes into question. Thus its second function is to assert the fact of injustice. This leads directly to the great and simple tragic question: why do good men suffer? The hero may have flaws, but he suffers in excess of any reasonable punishment. So Lear, after cataloguing those who have really done wrong, cries: "I am a man more sinned against than sinning." The hero's ultimate fate has little or no connection with his faults. Evil, then, is a function of the fatality of existence; it is the form of fate. Since evil, or fate, is in the nature of things in the tragic universe, tragedy is grounded in the *irrational*. If we were to say that the tragedy of Lear was occasioned by *naturalistic* causes such as passion and lust, we would be imposing our own modern, rationalistic, scientific cause-and-effect view (which scientists have to some extent now abandoned). Science had begun to make itself felt by the time of Shakespeare, but it had by no means replaced the sense of fatality stemming from ideas like original sin and man's depravity, and the general sense of the irremedial, fatal character of existence.

Now a *rationalist* view assumes that effect follows cause, that good is rewarded and evil punished, that justice operates in the universe in the form of some "transcendental police system," in Miguel de Unamuno's ironic phrase. It is true that there is some justice in the tragic universe; evil figures like Edmund and Iago do not come out well. But the good suffer, at times without having done anything, as in the cases of Hamlet and Job. The rationalist view implies an alternative to the tragic end, that if the hero had not been at fault, or if the evil figures had not been evil there would have been no tragedy. This view is implicit in Aristotle's notion of *hamarta*, generally interpreted as a tragic flaw like excessive pride or as an error in judgment. In this view the tragedy would seem to follow from the hero's flaw or error. We can say that the tragic action may be *set off* this way, as with Oedipus and Lear. But the *tragic* sense of life has it that unreasonable, unaccountable suffering is our natural condition. It is this fatal fact of life which drives one to a tragic view, and which grounds tragedy in the irrational.

The argument that the hero's suffering is unreasonable would not seem to account for tragedies like *Macbeth*, where the hero's evil act precipitates the tragedy. Here he seems to be getting what he deserves. Yet this is not really the case. What happens, what makes such a play a tragedy rather than a morality is that the hero's experience goes far beyond the orthodox equation of sin and suffering. As with the more or less blameless hero, the action develops a logic of its own. So it is, we notice, that the hero is not preoccupied with the fact that he has done wrong; his preoccupations are tragic rather than moral: life "is a tale/told by an idiot, full of sound and fury,/signifying nothing."

IV

A further matter of interest is the relation between the hero and the other characters, something we have touched on only briefly. For convenience the others may be crudely divided into three groups, the orthodox, the profane, and the materialists. By the orthodox we mean those who are governed by prevailing spiritual and moral values; examples would include the Chorus, Kent, Cordelia, and Edgar. By the profane we mean those who may be materialists but who are governed primarily by the negative, destructive force of evil, as with Regan, Goneril, and Edmund. We call them profane to suggest their unholy difference from the hero. By the materialists we mean those who are governed primarily by material considerations; they are generally social climbers, expedient figures like the time-serving Oswald, in *Lear*, though sometimes decent people like Creon and the messenger in *Oedipus Rex*. If we are not rigid or mechanical in our application of these categories, they can be useful. Principally, they help us to see the difference between the values of the tragic hero and the others.

Take, first, the hero and the orthodox. The tragic pattern revealed the conflict within the hero between his old orthodox values and his new tragic sense. But this conflict is revealed externally too. Through the chorus and the other orthodox the claims of traditional values are balanced against those of the tragic vision. The orthodox serve as foils; in this way they heighten the tragic commitment. For example, we frequently see them pleading with the hero to go no further in the direction of the unknown, the abyss—so Tiresias, Jocasta, and the Shepherd. The hero's distinction is measured by the fact that only he can stand the tragic vision.

In the conflict between the tragic hero and the evil, profane characters we have already pointed to the latter's function as the force which breaks down the orthodox order, and with it the idea of divine justice. Thus we may say that the profane character also breaks with the orthodox view. Both he and the tragic hero perceive the irrationality of existence. But the tragic hero suffers over this fact because he believes in life even if he cannot understand it. The profane character does not suffer because he has no conviction. Instead he uses the fact of the irrationality of things as an excuse for doing whatever he wishes; but it opens up only the possibilities of destructiveness. In this sense the profane character is a simple-minded rationalist. He is unable to see that life may still have meaning even if we cannot say what it is. Ultimately he is shallow; he serves hell but he has no sense of what it is.

There are, finally, the materialists. They fill out the world of the tragic action, more so in Shakespeare than in the Greeks or Racine. The materialist adjusts to the social arrangement; the tragic hero confronts the universal derangement. He is a kind of parody of the hero. Oedipus' tragic search for his true self is parodied by the messenger's search for self-comfort. The parody may be openly comic, as in the contrast between Hamlet's speculations on death and the gravedigger's businesslike remarks on the durability of corpses; or between Macbeth's hell and the drunken porter's version of it; or, in Greek drama, between the tragic trilogy and the satyr play following it.

As a general rule, then, we can say that the characters in Greek and

Shakespearean tragedy fall into the types outlined. Though the different preoccupations of modern drama make for different ways of seeing people, these types still may be found in some modern plays. In *Six Characters*, for example, there is the contrast between the tragic father and the materialist manager. Our interest lies in part in the conflicts and tensions which rise out of throwing these types together. The relations are rich, and the reader will easily discover others besides the few we have touched on. All this makes for a livelier, more rewarding reading.

READINGS:

ABEL, LIONEL, *Metatheatre*. New York: Hill and Wang, 1963.

ARISTOTLE, *Poetics*, tr. by Ingram Bywater, in *The Student's Oxford Aristotle*, ed. by W. D. Ross. New York: Oxford University Press, 1942.

CLARK, BARRETT H., *European Theories of the Drama*. New York: Crown Publishing Co., 1947.

FERGUSSON, FRANCIS, *The Idea of a Theater*. Princeton: Princeton University Press, 1949. Reprinted by Doubleday Anchor, n.d. New York.

HEGEL, R. W., *Hegel on Tragedy*, ed. and tr. by Henry and Anne Paolucci. New York: Doubleday Anchor, 1963.

HENN, T. R., *The Harvest of Tragedy*. London: Methuen, 1956. Reprinted by Humanities Press, n.d. New York.

KRUTCH, J. W., *The Modern Temper* (1929). New York: Harvest Edition, Harcourt, Brace and World, 1956.

MULLER, H. J., *The Spirit of Tragedy* (1872). New York: A. A. Knopf, 1956.

NIETZSCHE, F., *The Birth of Tragedy* (1872), translated by Francis Golffing. Garden City, N.Y.: Doubleday & Company (Anchor Edition), 1956.

SEWALL, R. B., *The Vision of Tragedy*. New Haven: Yale University Press, 1959.

STEINER, G., *The Death of Tragedy*. New York: A. A. Knopf, 1961.

For further titles, see readings after headnotes on Sophocles and Shakespeare.

⚜ *Sophocles*

Sophocles (496–406 B.C.) was one of the three great tragic playwrights of the ancient Greek theatre; the others were the older Aeschylus (525–433 B.C.) and the somewhat younger Euripides (485–406 B.C.). Sophocles wrote about 120 plays, but only seven are extant. Though Aristotle said Euripides was the most tragic of the playwrights, Sophocles is generally considered to have perfected the form of tragedy. His characters grow with the developing action; the chorus is integrated with the action; the plot is shaped with that rigorous sense of form popularly if mistakenly associated with all Greek tragedy; his innovation of a third character enriches the tensions at a particular moment; and, as in *Oedipus* particularly, the lines are heightened by a continuing irony. Aristotle admired the plot of *Oedipus Rex* (the Latin title for the original Greek, *Oedipus Tyrannus*); it had what he called a complex plot, by which he meant one in which the hero's change of fortune is accompanied by a reversal of the situation. Sophocles won eighteen first prizes in the competition of the Great Dionysia, the religious festival at which the plays were presented, but not for *Oedipus Rex*. He was born near Athens, in Colonus, the scene of *Oedipus at Colonus*, written some forty years after *Oedipus Rex*. *Oedipus at Colonus* presents the tragic suffering and redemption of Oedipus, and his apotheosis in the sacred grove of the Eumenides in Colonus. *Antigone*, written before *Oedipus Rex*, deals with material which comes last chronologically in the tragic history of the House of Laios. It develops the conflict between Antigone, Oedipus' daughter, who abides by the law of God, and Creon, who upholds the law of man, of the state.

READINGS:

BUTCHER, S. H., *Aristotle's Theory of Poetry and Fine Art*. New York: Dover Publications, 1951.
FERGUSSON, FRANCIS, *The Idea of a Theater*. Princeton: Princeton University Press, 1949. Reprinted by Doubleday Anchor, n.d., New York.
KITTO, H. D. F., *Greek Tragedy* (1939, 1950). Garden City, N.Y.: Doubleday & Company (Anchor Edition), 1954.

Knox, Bernard, *Oedipus at Thebes*. New Haven: Yale University Press, 1957.

Neitzsche, Friedrich, *The Birth of Tragedy* (1872), translated by Francis Golffing. Garden City, N.Y.: Doubleday & Company (Anchor Edition), 1956.

Norwood, Gilbert, *Greek Tragedy*. New York: Hill and Wang, n.d.

Whitman, Cedric, *Sophocles: A Study in Heroic Humanism*. Cambridge, Mass.: Harvard University Press, 1951.

Oedipus Rex

Sophocles

CHARACTERS

OEDIPUS	IOCASTÊ
A PRIEST	MESSENGER
CREON	SHEPHERD OF LAÏOS
TEIRESIAS	SECOND MESSENGER

CHORUS OF THEBAN ELDERS

Act I

THE SCENE—Before the palace of OEDIPUS, King of Thebes. A central door and two lateral doors open onto a platform which runs the length of the façade. On the platform, right and left, are altars; and three steps lead down into the "orchestra," or chorus-ground. At the beginning of the action these steps are crowded by suppliants who have brought branches and chaplets of olive leaves and who lie in various attitudes of despair. OEDIPUS enters.

Prologue

OEDIPUS: My children, generations of the living
    In the line of Kadmos, nursed at his ancient hearth:
    Why have you strewn yourselves before these altars
    In supplication, with your boughs and garlands?
    The breath of incense rises from the city
    With a sound of prayer and lamentation.

THE OEDIPUS REX OF SOPHOCLES: An English Version by Dudley Fitts and Robert Fitzgerald, copyright, 1949, by Harcourt, Brace & World, Inc. and reprinted with their permission.

                                                  Children,
I would not have you speak through messengers,
And therefore I have come myself to hear you—
I, Oedipus, who bear the famous name.
        [*To a* PRIEST.]
You, there, since you are eldest in the company,
Speak for them all, tell me what preys upon you,
Whether you come in dread, or crave some blessing:
Tell me, and never doubt that I will help you
In every way I can; I should be heartless
Were I not moved to find you suppliant here.

PRIEST: Great Oedipus, O powerful King of Thebes!
You see how all the ages of our people
Cling to your altar steps: here are boys
Who can barely stand alone, and here are priests
By weight of age, as I am a priest of God,
And young men chosen from those yet unmarried;
As for the others, all that multitude,
They wait with olive chaplets in the squares,
At the two shrines of Pallas, and where Apollo
Speaks in the glowing embers.
                                        Your own eyes
Must tell you: Thebes is in her extremity
And can not lift her head from the surge of death.
A rust consumes the buds and fruits of the earth;
The herds are sick; children die unborn,
And labor is vain. The god of plague and pyre
Raids like detestable lightning through the city,
And all the house of Kadmos is laid waste,
All emptied, and all darkened: Death alone
Battens upon the misery of Thebes.
You are not one of the immortal gods, we know;
Yet we have come to you to make our prayer
As to the man of all men best in adversity
And wisest in the ways of God. You saved us
From the Sphinx, that flinty singer, and the tribute
We paid to her so long; yet you were never
Better informed than we, nor could we teach you:
It was some god breathed in you to set us free.

Therefore, O mighty King, we turn to you:
Find us our safety, find us a remedy,

Whether by counsel of the gods or men.
A king of wisdom tested in the past
Can act in a time of troubles, and act well.
Noblest of men, restore
Life to your city! Think how all men call you
Liberator for your triumph long ago;
Ah, when your years of kingship are remembered,
Let them not say We rose, *but later fell*—
Keep the State from going down in the storm!
Once, years ago, with happy augury,
You brought us fortune; be the same again!
No man questions your power to rule the land:
But rule over men, not over a dead city!
Ships are only hulls, citadels are nothing,
When no life moves in the empty passageways.

OEDIPUS: Poor children! You may be sure I know
All that you longed for in your coming here.
I know that you are deathly sick; and yet,
Sick as you are, not one is as sick as I.
Each of you suffers in himself alone
His anguish, not another's; but my spirit
Groans for the city, for myself, for you.

I was not sleeping, you are not waking me.
No, I have been in tears for a long while
And in my restless thought walked many ways.
In all my search, I found one helpful course,
And that I have taken: I have sent Creon,
Son of Menoikeus, brother of the Queen,
To Delphi, Apollo's place of revelation,
To learn there, if he can,
What act or pledge of mine may save the city.
I have counted the days, and now, this very day,
I am troubled, for he has overstayed his time.
What is he doing? He has been gone too long.
Yet whenever he comes back, I should do ill
To scant whatever hint the god may give.

PRIEST: It is a timely promise. At this instant
They tell me Creon is here.

OEDIPUS: O Lord Apollo!
May his news be fair as his face is radiant!

PRIEST: It could not be otherwise: he is crowned with bay,
   The chaplet is thick with berries.

OEDIPUS: We shall soon know;
   He is near enough to hear us now.
      [*Enter* CREON.]
                                    O Prince:
   Brother: son of Menoikeus:
   What answer do you bring us from the god?

CREON: It is favorable. I can tell you, great afflictions
   Will turn out well, if they are taken well.

OEDIPUS: What was the oracle? These vague words
   Leave me still hanging between hope and fear.

CREON: Is it your pleasure to hear me with all these
   Gathered around us? I am prepared to speak,
   But should we not go in?

OEDIPUS: Let them all hear it.
   It is for them I suffer, more than for myself.

CREON: Then I will tell you what I heard at Delphi.
   In plain words
   The god commands us to expel from the land of Thebes
   An old defilement that it seems we shelter.
   It is a deathly thing, beyond expiation.
   We must not let it feed upon us longer.

OEDIPUS: What defilement? How shall we rid ourselves of it?

CREON: By exile or death, blood for blood. It was
   Murder that brought the plague-wind on the city.

OEDIPUS: Murder of whom? Surely the god has named him?

CREON: My lord: long ago Laïos was our king,
   Before you came to govern us.

OEDIPUS: I know;
   I learned of him from others; I never saw him.

CREON: He was murdered; and Apollo commands us now
   To take revenge upon whoever killed him.

OEDIPUS: Upon whom? Where are they? Where shall we find a clue
   To solve that crime, after so many years?

CREON: Here in this land, he said.

                                If we make enquiry,
We may touch things that otherwise escape us.

OEDIPUS: Tell me: Was Laïos murdered in his house,
Or in the fields, or in some foreign country?

CREON: He said he planned to make a pilgrimage.
He did not come home again.

OEDIPUS: And was there no one,
No witness, no companion, to tell what happened?

CREON: They were all killed but one, and he got away
So frightened that he could remember one thing only.

OEDIPUS: What was that one thing? One may be the key
To everything, if we resolve to use it.

CREON: He said that a band of highwaymen attacked them,
Outnumbered them, and overwhelmed the King.

OEDIPUS: Strange, that a highwayman should be so daring—
Unless some faction here bribed him to do it.

CREON: We thought of that. But after Laïos' death
New troubles arose and we had no avenger.

OEDIPUS: What troubles could prevent your hunting down the killers?

CREON: The riddling Sphinx's song
Made us deaf to all mysteries but her own.

OEDIPUS: Then once more I must bring what is dark to light.
It is most fitting that Apollo shows,
As you do, this compunction for the dead.
You shall see how I stand by you, as I should,
To avenge the city and the city's god,
And not as though it were for some distant friend,
But for my own sake, to be rid of evil.
Whoever killed King Laïos might—who knows?—
Decide at any moment to kill me as well.
By avenging the murdered king I protect myself.

Come, then, my children: leave the altar steps,
Lift up your olive boughs!

                              One of you go

And summon the people of Kadmos to gather here.
I will do all that I can; you may tell them that.
        [*Exit a* PAGE.]
So, with the help of God,
We shall be saved—or else indeed we are lost.

PRIEST: Let us rise, children. It was for this we came,
    And now the King has promised it himself.
    Phoibos has sent us an oracle; may he descend
    Himself to save us and drive out the plague.
                [*Exeunt* OEDIPUS *and* CREON *into the palace by the central
                door. The* PRIEST *and the* SUPPLIANTS *disperse R and L. After
                a short pause the* CHORUS *enters the orchestra.*]

🐚 *Párodos*

CHORUS: What is the god singing in his profound   [STROPHE 1.]
    Delphi of gold and shadow?
    What oracle for Thebes, the sunwhipped city?

    Fear unjoints me, the roots of my heart tremble.
    Now I remember, O Healer, your power, and wonder:
    Will you send doom like a sudden cloud, or weave it
    Like nightfall of the past?

    Ah no: be merciful, issue of holy sound:
    Dearest to our expectancy: be tender!

                                            [ANTISTROPHE 1.]
    Let me pray to Athenê, the immortal daughter of Zeus,
    And to Artemis her sister
    Who keeps her famous throne in the market ring,
    And to Apollo, bowman at the far butts of heaven—

    O gods, descend! Like three streams leap against
    The fires of our grief, the fires of darkness;
    Be swift to bring us rest!

    As in the old time from the brilliant house
    Of air you stepped to save us, come again!

Now our afflictions have no end,   [STROPHE 2.]
Now all our stricken host lies down
And no man fights off death with his mind;

The noble plowland bears no grain,
And groaning mothers can not bear—

See, how our lives like birds take wing,
Like sparks that fly when a fire soars,
To the shore of the god of evening.

The plague burns on, it is pitiless,   [ANTISTROPHE 2.]
Though pallid children laden with death
Lie unwept in the stony ways,

And old gray women by every path
Flock to the strand about the altars
There to strike their breasts and cry
Worship of Zeus in wailing prayers:
Be kind, God's golden child!

There are no swords in this attack by fire,   [STROPHE 3.]
No shields, but we are ringed with cries.

Send the besieger plunging from our homes
Into the vast sea-room of the Atlantic
Or into the waves that foam eastward of Thrace—

For the day ravages what the night spares—

Destroy our enemy, lord of the thunder!
Let him be riven by lightning from heaven!   [ANTISTROPHE 3.]

Phoibos Apollo, stretch the sun's bowstring,
That golden cord, until it sing for us,
Flashing arrows in heaven!
                        Artemis, Huntress,
Race with flaring lights upon our mountains!
O scarlet god, O golden-banded brow,
O Theban Bacchos in a storm of Maenads,
        [*Enter* OEDIPUS, CHORUS.]
Whirl upon Death, that all the Undying hate!
Come with blinding cressets, come in joy!

SCENE I

OEDIPUS: Is this your prayer? It may be answered. Come,
   Listen to me, act as the crisis demands,
   And you shall have relief from all these evils.

Until now I was a stranger to this tale,
As I had been a stranger to the crime.
Could I track down the murderer without a clue?
But now, friends,
As one who became a citizen after the murder,
I make this proclamation to all Thebans:
If any man knows by whose hand Laïos, son of Labdakos,
Met his death, I direct that man to tell me everything,
No matter what he fears for having so long withheld it.
Let it stand as promised that no further trouble
Will come to him, but he may leave the land in safety.

Moreover: If anyone knows the murderer to be foreign,
Let him not keep silent: he shall have his reward from me.
However, if he does conceal it; if any man
Fearing for his friend or for himself disobeys this edict,
Hear what I propose to do:

I solemnly forbid the people of this country,
Where power and throne are mine, ever to receive that man
Or speak to him, no matter who he is, or let him
Join in sacrifice, lustration, or in prayer.
I decree that he be driven from every house,
Being, as he is, corruption itself to us: the Delphic
Voice of Zeus has pronounced this revelation.
Thus I associate myself with the oracle
And take the side of the murdered king.

As for the criminal, I pray to God—
Whether it be a lurking thief, or one of a number—
I pray that that man's life be consumed in evil and wretchedness.
And as for me, this curse applies no less
If it should turn out that the culprit is my guest here,
Sharing my hearth.
                    You have heard the penalty.
I lay it on you now to attend to this
For my sake, for Apollo's, for the sick

Sterile city that heaven has abandoned.
Suppose the oracle had given you no command:
Should this defilement go uncleansed for ever?
You should have found the murderer: your king,
A noble king, had been destroyed!

                              Now I,
Having the power that he held before me,
Having his bed, begetting children there
Upon his wife, as he would have, had he lived—
Their son would have been my children's brother,
If Laïos had had luck in fatherhood!
(But surely ill luck rushed upon his reign)—
I say I take the son's part, just as though
I were his son, to press the fight for him
And see it won! I'll find the hand that brought
Death to Labdakos' and Polydoros' child,
Heir of Kadmos' and Agenor's line.
And as for those who fail me,
May the gods deny them the fruit of the earth,
Fruit of the womb, and may they rot utterly!
Let them be wretched as we are wretched, and worse!

For you, for loyal Thebans, and for all
Who find my actions right, I pray the favor
Of justice, and of all the immortal gods.

CHORUS: Since I am under oath, my lord, I swear
  I did not do the murder, I can not name
  The murderer. Might not the oracle
  That has ordained the search tell where to find him?

OEDIPUS: An honest question. But no man in the world
  Can make the gods do more than the gods will.

CHORUS: There is one last expedient—

OEDIPUS: Tell me what it is.
  Though it seem slight, you must not hold it back.

CHORUS: A lord clairvoyant to the lord Apollo,
  As we all know, is the skilled Teiresias.
  One might learn much about this from him, Oedipus.

OEDIPUS: I am not wasting time:
  Creon spoke of this, and I have sent for him—
  Twice, in fact; it is strange that he is not here.

CHORUS: The other matter—that old report—seems useless.

OEDIPUS: Tell me. I am interested in all reports.

CHORUS: The King was said to have been killed by highwaymen.

OEDIPUS: I know. But we have no witnesses to that.

CHORUS: If the killer can feel a particle of dread,
    Your curse will bring him out of hiding!

OEDIPUS: No.
    The man who dared that act will fear no curse.
        [*Enter the blind seer* TEIRESIAS, *led by a* PAGE.]

CHORUS: But there is one man who may detect the criminal.
    This is Teiresias, this is the holy prophet
    In whom, alone of all men, truth was born.

OEDIPUS: Teiresias: seer: student of mysteries,
    Of all that's taught and all that no man tells,
    Secrets of Heaven and secrets of the earth:
    Blind though you are, you know the city lies
    Sick with plague; and from this plague, my lord,
    We find that you alone can guard or save us.

    Possibly you did not hear the messengers?
    Apollo, when we sent to him,
    Sent us back word that this great pestilence
    Would lift, but only if we established clearly
    The identity of those who murdered Laïos.
    They must be killed or exiled.
                    Can you use
    Birdflight or any art of divination
    To purify yourself, and Thebes, and me
    From this contagion? We are in your hands.
    There is no fairer duty
    Than that of helping others in distress.

TEIRESIAS: How dreadful knowledge of the truth can be
    When there's no help in truth! I knew this well,
    But did not act on it: else I should not have come.

OEDIPUS: What is troubling you? Why are your eyes so cold?

TEIRESIAS: Let me go home. Bear your own fate, and I'll
    Bear mine. It is better so: trust what I say.

20 *Sophocles*

OEDIPUS: What you say is ungracious and unhelpful
 To your native country. Do not refuse to speak.

TEIRESIAS: When it comes to speech, your own is neither temperate
 Nor opportune. I wish to be more prudent.

OEDIPUS: In God's name, we all beg you—

TEIRESIAS: You are all ignorant.
 No; I will never tell you what I know.
 Now it is my misery; then, it would be yours.

OEDIPUS: What! You do know something, and will not tell us?
 You would betray us all and wreck the State?

TEIRESIAS: I do not intend to torture myself, or you.
 Why persist in asking? You will not persuade me.

OEDIPUS: What a wicked old man you are! You'd try a stone's
 Patience! Out with it! Have you no feeling at all?

TEIRESIAS: You call me unfeeling. If you could only see
 The nature of your own feelings . . .

OEDIPUS: Why,
 Who would not feel as I do? Who could endure
 Your arrogance toward the city?

TEIRESIAS: What does it matter!
 Whether I speak or not, it is bound to come.

OEDIPUS: Then, if "it" is bound to come, you are bound to tell me.

TEIRESIAS: No, I will not go on. Rage as you please.

OEDIPUS: Rage? Why not!
                         And I'll tell you what I think:
 You planned it, you had it done, you all but
 Killed him with your own hands: if you had eyes,
 I'd say the crime was yours, and yours alone.

TEIRESIAS: So? I charge you, then,
 Abide by the proclamation you have made:
 From this day forth
 Never speak again to these men or to me;
 You yourself are the pollution of this country.

OEDIPUS: You dare say that! Can you possibly think you have
 Some way of going free, after such insolence?

TEIRESIAS: I have gone free. It is the truth sustains me.

OEDIPUS: Who taught you shamelessness? It was not your craft.

TEIRESIAS: You did. You made me speak. I did not want to.

OEDIPUS: Speak what? Let me hear it again more clearly.

TEIRESIAS: Was it not clear before? Are you tempting me?

OEDIPUS: I did not understand it. Say it again.

TEIRESIAS: I say that you are the murderer whom you seek.

OEDIPUS: Now twice you have spat out infamy. You'll pay for it!

TEIRESIAS: Would you care for more? Do you wish to be really angry?

OEDIPUS: Say what you will. Whatever you say is worthless.

TEIRESIAS: I say that you live in hideous love with her
 Who is nearest you in blood. You are blind to evil.

OEDIPUS: It seems you can go on mouthing like this for ever.

TEIRESIAS: I can, if there is power in truth.

OEDIPUS: There is:
 But not for you, not for you,
 You sightless, witless, senseless, mad old man!

TEIRESIAS: You are the madman. There is no one here
 Who will not curse you soon, as you curse me.

OEDIPUS: You child of endless night! You can not hurt me
 Or any other man who sees the sun.

TEIRESIAS: True: it is not from me your fate will come.
 That lies within Apollo's competence,
 As it is his concern.

OEDIPUS: Tell me:
 Are you speaking for Creon, or for yourself?

TEIRESIAS: Creon is no threat. You weave your own doom.

OEDIPUS: Wealth, power, craft of statesmanship!
 Kingly position, everywhere admired!
 What savage envy is stored up against these,
 If Creon, whom I trusted, Creon my friend,
 For this great office which the city once

Put in my hands unsought—if for this power
Creon desires in secret to destroy me!
He has bought this decrepit fortune-teller, this
Collector of dirty pennies, this prophet fraud—
Why, he is no more clairvoyant than I am!
                                    Tell us:
Has your mystic mummery ever approached the truth?
When that hellcat the Sphinx was performing here,
What help were you to these people?
Her magic was not for the first man who came along:
It demanded a real exorcist. Your birds—
What good were they? or the gods, for the matter of that?
But I came by,
Oedipus, the simple man, who knows nothing—
I thought it out for myself, no birds helped me!
And this is the man you think you can destroy,
That you may be close to Creon when he's king!
Well, you and your friend Creon, it seems to me,
Will suffer most. If you were not an old man,
You would have paid already for your plot.

CHORUS: We can not see that his words or yours
    Have been spoken except in anger, Oedipus,
    And of anger we have no need. How can God's will
    Be accomplished best? That is what most concerns us.

TEIRESIAS: You are a king. But where argument's concerned
    I am your man, as much a king as you.
    I am not your servant, but Apollo's.
    I have no need of Creon to speak for me.

    Listen to me. You mock my blindness, do you?
    But I say that you, with both your eyes, are blind:
    You can not see the wretchedness of your life,
    Nor in whose house you live, no, nor with whom.
    Who are your father and mother? Can you tell me?
    You do not even know the blind wrongs
    That you have done them, on earth and in the world below.
    But the double lash of your parents' curse will whip you
    Out of this land some day, with only night
    Upon your precious eyes.
    Your cries then—where will they not be heard?
    What fastness of Kithairon will not echo them?

And that bridal-descant of yours—you'll know it then,
The song they sang when you came here to Thebes
And found your misguided berthing.
All this, and more, that you can not guess at now,
Will bring you to yourself among your children.
Be angry, then. Curse Creon. Curse my words.
I tell you, no man that walks upon the earth
Shall be rooted out more horribly than you.

OEDIPUS: Am I to bear this from him?—Damnation
Take you! Out of this place! Out of my sight!

TEIRESIAS: I would not have come at all if you had not asked me.

OEDIPUS: Could I have told that you'd talk nonsense, that
You'd come here to make a fool of yourself, and of me?

TEIRESIAS: A fool? Your parents thought me sane enough.

OEDIPUS: My parents again!—Wait: who were my parents?

TEIRESIAS: This day will give you a father, and break your heart.

OEDIPUS: Your infantile riddles! Your damned abracadabra!

TEIRESIAS: You were a great man once at solving riddles.

OEDIPUS: Mock me with that if you like; you will find it true.

TEIRESIAS: It was true enough. It brought about your ruin.

OEDIPUS: But if it saved this town?

            [To the PAGE.]
TEIRESIAS: Boy, give me your hand.

OEDIPUS: Yes, boy; lead him away.
                        —While you are here
We can do nothing. Go; leave us in peace.

TEIRESIAS: I will go when I have said what I have to say.
How can you hurt me? And I tell you again:
The man you have been looking for all this time,
The damned man, the murderer of Laïos,
That man is in Thebes. To your mind he is foreign-born,
But it will soon be shown that he is a Theban,
A revelation that will fail to please.
                        A blind man,
Who has his eyes now; a penniless man, who is rich now;

And he will go tapping the strange earth with his staff.
To the children with whom he lives now he will be
Brother and father—the very same; to her
Who bore him, son and husband—the very same
Who came to his father's bed, wet with his father's blood.

Enough. Go think that over.
If later you find error in what I have said,
You may say that I have no skill in prophecy.

[*Exit* TEIRESIAS, *led by his* PAGE. OEDIPUS *goes into the palace.*]

Ode I

CHORUS: The Delphic stone of prophecies [STROPHE 1.]
Remembers ancient regicide
And a still bloody hand.
That killer's hour of flight has come.
He must be stronger than riderless
Coursers of untiring wind,
For the son of Zeus armed with his father's thunder
Leaps in lightning after him;
And the Furies follow him, the sad Furies.

Holy Parnassos' peak of snow [ANTISTROPHE 1.]
Flashes and blinds that secret man,
That all shall hunt him down:
Though he may roam the forest shade
Like a bull gone wild from pasture
To rage through glooms of stone.
Doom comes down on him; flight will not avail him;
For the world's heart calls him desolate,
And the immortal Furies follow, for ever follow.

But now a wilder thing is heard [STROPHE 2.]
From the old man skilled at hearing Fate in the wingbeat of a bird.
Bewildered as a blown bird, my soul hovers and can not find
Foothold in this debate, or any reason or rest of mind.
But no man ever brought—none can bring
Proof of strife between Thebes' royal house,
Labdakos' line, and the son of Polybos;

And never until now has any man brought word
Of Laïos' dark death staining Oedipus the King.

Divine Zeus and Apollo hold   [ANTISTROPHE 2.]
Perfect intelligence alone of all tales ever told;
And well though this diviner works, he works in his own night;
No man can judge that rough unknown or trust in second sight,
For wisdom changes hands among the wise.
Shall I believe my great lord criminal
At a raging word that a blind old man let fall?
I saw him, when the carrion woman faced him of old,
Prove his heroic mind! These evil words are lies.

SCENE II

CREON: Men of Thebes:
   I am told that heavy accusations
   Have been brought against me by King Oedipus.

   I am not the kind of man to bear this tamely.

   If in these present difficulties
   He holds me accountable for any harm to him
   Through anything I have said or done—why, then,
   I do not value life in this dishonor.
   It is not as though this rumor touched upon
   Some private indiscretion. The matter is grave.
   The fact is that I am being called disloyal
   To the State, to my fellow citizens, to my friends.

CHORUS: He may have spoken in anger, not from his mind.

CREON: But did you not hear him say I was the one
   Who seduced the old prophet into lying?

CHORUS: The thing was said; I do not know how seriously.

CREON: But you were watching him! Were his eyes steady?
   Did he look like a man in his right mind?

CHORUS: I do not know.
   I can not judge the behavior of great men.
   But here is the King himself.
         [Enter OEDIPUS.]

OEDIPUS: So you dared come back.
Why? How brazen of you to come to my house,
You murderer!

                 Do you think I do not know
That you plotted to kill me, plotted to steal my throne?
Tell me, in God's name: am I coward, a fool,
That you should dream you could accomplish this?
A fool who could not see your slippery game?
A coward, not to fight back when I saw it?
You are the fool, Creon, are you not? hoping
Without support or friends to get a throne?
Thrones may be won or bought: you could do neither.

CREON: Now listen to me. You have talked; let me talk, too.
You can not judge unless you know the facts.

OEDIPUS: You speak well: there is one fact; but I find it hard
To learn from the deadliest enemy I have.

CREON: That above all I must dispute with you.

OEDIPUS: That above all I will not hear you deny.

CREON: If you think there is anything good in being stubborn
Against all reason, then I say you are wrong.

OEDIPUS: If you think a man can sin against his own kind
And not be punished for it, I say you are mad.

CREON: I agree. But tell me: what have I done to you?

OEDIPUS: You advised me to send for that wizard, did you not?

CREON: I did. I should do it again.

OEDIPUS: Very well. Now tell me:
How long has it been since Laïos—

CREON: What of Laïos?

OEDIPUS: Since he vanished in that onset by the road?

CREON: It was long ago, a long time.

OEDIPUS: And this prophet,
Was he practicing here then?

CREON: He was; and with honor, as now.

OEDIPUS: Did he speak of me at that time?

CREON: He never did;
At least, not when I was present.

OEDIPUS: But . . . the enquiry?
I suppose you held one?

CREON: We did, but we learned nothing.

OEDIPUS: Why did the prophet not speak against me then?

CREON: I do not know; and I am the kind of man
Who holds his tongue when he has no facts to go on.

OEDIPUS: There's one fact that you know, and you could tell it.

CREON: What fact is that? If I know it, you shall have it.

OEDIPUS: If he were not involved with you, he could not say
That it was I who murdered Laïos.

CREON: If he says that, you are the one that knows it!—
But now it is my turn to question you.

OEDIPUS: Put your questions. I am no murderer.

CREON: First, then: You married my sister?

OEDIPUS: I married your sister.

CREON: And you rule the kingdom equally with her?

OEDIPUS: Everything that she wants she has from me.

CREON: And I am the third, equal to both of you?

OEDIPUS: That is why I call you a bad friend.

CREON: No. Reason it out, as I have done.
Think of this first: Would any sane man prefer
Power, with all a king's anxieties,
To that same power and the grace of sleep?
Certainly not I.
I have never longed for the king's power—only his rights.
Would any wise man differ from me in this?
As matters stand, I have my way in everything
With your consent, and no responsibilities.
If I were king, I should be a slave to policy.
How could I desire a scepter more

Than what is now mine—untroubled influence?
No, I have not gone mad; I need no honors,
Except those with the perquisites I have now.
I am welcome everywhere; every man salutes me,
And those who want your favor seek my ear,
Since I know how to manage what they ask.
Should I exchange this ease for that anxiety?
Besides, no sober mind is treasonable.
I hate anarchy
And never would deal with any man who likes it.

Test what I have said. Go to the priestess
At Delphi, ask if I quoted her correctly.
And as for this other thing: if I am found
Guilty of treason with Teiresias,
Then sentence me to death! You have my word
It is a sentence I should cast my vote for—
But not without evidence!
                 You do wrong
When you take good men for bad, bad men for good.
A true friend thrown aside—why, life itself
Is not more precious!
                 In time you will know this well:
For time, and time alone, will show the just man,
Though scoundrels are discovered in a day.

CHORUS: This is well said, and a prudent man would ponder it.
    Judgments too quickly formed are dangerous.

OEDIPUS: But is he not quick in his duplicity?
    And shall I not be quick to parry him?
    Would you have me stand still, hold my peace, and let
    This man win everything, through my inaction?

CREON: And you want—what is it, then? To banish me?

OEDIPUS: No, not exile. It is your death I want,
    So that all the world may see what treason means.

CREON: You will persist, then? You will not believe me?

OEDIPUS: How can I believe you?

CREON: Then you are a fool.

OEDIPUS: To save myself?

CREON: In justice, think of me.

OEDIPUS: You are evil incarnate.

CREON: But suppose that you are wrong?

OEDIPUS: Still I must rule.

CREON: But not if you rule badly.

OEDIPUS: O city, city!

CREON: It is my city, too!

CHORUS: Now, my lords, be still. I see the Queen,
Iocastê, coming from her palace chambers;
And it is time she came, for the sake of you both.
This dreadful quarrel can be resolved through her.
        [*Enter* IOCASTÊ.]

IOCASTÊ: Poor foolish men, what wicked din is this?
With Thebes sick to death, is it not shameful
That you should rake some private quarrel up?
        [*To* OEDIPUS.]
Come into the house.
                —And you, Creon, go now:
Let us have no more of this tumult over nothing.

CREON: Nothing? No, sister: what your husband plans for me
Is one of two great evils: exile or death.

OEDIPUS: He is right.
                Why, woman I have caught him squarely
Plotting against my life.

CREON: No! Let me die
Accurst if ever I have wished you harm!

IOCASTÊ: Ah, believe it, Oedipus!
In the name of the gods, respect this oath of his
For my sake, for the sake of these people here!

CHORUS: Open your mind to her, my lord. Be ruled by her, I beg you!
                                        [STROPHE 1.]

OEDIPUS: What would you have me do?

CHORUS: Respect Creon's word. He has never spoken like a fool,
And now he has sworn an oath.

OEDIPUS: You know what you ask?

CHORUS: I do.

OEDIPUS: Speak on, then.

CHORUS: A friend so sworn should not be baited so,
In blind malice, and without final proof.

OEDIPUS: You are aware, I hope, that what you say
Means death for me, or exile at the least.

CHORUS: No, I swear by Helios, first in Heaven!   [STROPHE 2.]
May I die friendless and accurst,
The worst of deaths, if ever I meant that!
It is the withering fields
That hurt my sick heart:
Must we bear all these ills,
And now your bad blood as well?

OEDIPUS: Then let him go. And let me die, if I must,
Or be driven by him in shame from the land of Thebes.
It is your unhappiness, and not his talk,
That touches me.
As for him—
Wherever he is, I will hate him as long as I live.

CREON: Ugly in yielding, as you were ugly in rage!
Natures like yours chiefly torment themselves.

OEDIPUS: Can you not go? Can you not leave me?

CREON: I can.
You do not know me; but the city knows me,
And in its eyes I am just, if not in yours.
[Exit CREON.]

CHORUS: Lady Iocastê, did you not ask the King to go to his chambers?
[ANTISTROPHE 1.]

IOCASTÊ: First tell me what has happened.

CHORUS: There was suspicion without evidence: yet it rankled
As even false charges will.

IOCASTÊ: On both sides?

CHORUS: On both.

IOCASTÊ: But what was said?

CHORUS: Oh let it rest, let it be done with!
    Have we not suffered enough?

OEDIPUS: You see to what your decency has brought you:
    You have made difficulties where my heart saw none.

CHORUS: Oedipus, it is not once only I have told you—

[ANTISTROPHE 2.]

        You must know I should count myself unwise
    To the point of madness, should I now forsake you—
            You, under whose hand,
                In the storm of another time,
            Our dear land sailed out free.
                But now stand fast at the helm!

IOCASTÊ: In God's name, Oedipus, inform your wife as well:
    Why are you so set in this hard anger?

OEDIPUS: I will tell you, for none of these men deserves
    My confidence as you do. It is Creon's work,
    His treachery, his plotting against me.

IOCASTÊ: Go on, if you can make this clear to me.

OEDIPUS: He charges me with the murder of Laïos.

IOCASTÊ: Has he some knowledge? Or does he speak from hearsay?

OEDIPUS: He would not commit himself to such a charge,
    But he has brought in that damnable soothsayer
    To tell his story.

IOCASTÊ: Set your mind at rest.
    If it is a question of soothsayers, I tell you
    That you will find no man whose craft gives knowledge
    Of the unknowable.

                    Here is my proof:

An oracle was reported to Laïos once
(I will not say from Phoibos himself, but from
His appointed ministers, at any rate)
That his doom would be death at the hands of his own son—
His son, born of his flesh and of mine!
Now, you remember the story: Laïos was killed
By marauding strangers where three highways meet;

But his child had not been three days in this world
Before the King had pierced the baby's ankles
And had him left to die on a lonely mountain.

Thus, Apollo never caused that child
To kill his father, and it was not Laïos' fate
To die at the hands of his son, as he had feared.
This is what prophets and prophecies are worth!
Have no dread of them.
                                   It is God himself
Who can show us what he wills, in his own way.

OEDIPUS: How strange a shadowy memory crossed my mind,
    Just now while you were speaking; it chilled my heart.

IOCASTÊ: What do you mean? What memory do you speak of?

OEDIPUS: If I understand you, Laïos was killed
    At a place where three roads meet.

IOCASTÊ: So it was said;
    We have no later story.

OEDIPUS: Where did it happen?

IOCASTÊ: Phokis, it is called: at a place where the Theban Way
    Divides into the roads toward Delphi and Daulia.

OEDIPUS: When?

IOCASTÊ: We had the news not long before you came
    And proved the right to your succession here.

OEDIPUS: Ah, what net has God been weaving for me?

IOCASTÊ: Oedipus! Why does this trouble you?

OEDIPUS: Do not ask me yet.
    First, tell me how Laïos looked, and tell me
    How old he was.

IOCASTÊ: He was tall, his hair just touched
    With white; his form was not unlike your own.

OEDIPUS: I think that I myself may be accurst
    By my own ignorant edict.

IOCASTÊ: You speak strangely.
    It makes me tremble to look at you, my King.

OEDIPUS: I am not sure that the blind man can not see.
But I should know better if you were to tell me—

IOCASTÊ: Anything—though I dread to hear you ask it.

OEDIPUS: Was the King lightly escorted, or did he ride
With a large company, as a ruler should?

IOCASTÊ: There were five men with him in all: one was a herald;
And a single chariot, which he was driving.

OEDIPUS: Alas, that makes it plain enough!
                                        But who—
Who told you how it happened?

IOCASTÊ: A household servant,
The only one to escape.

OEDIPUS: And is he still
A servant of ours?

IOCASTÊ: No; for when he came back at last
And found you enthroned in the place of the dead king,
He came to me, touched my hand with his, and begged
That I would send him away to the frontier district
Where only the shepherds go—
As far away from the city as I could send him.
I granted his prayer; for although the man was a slave,
He had earned more than this favor at my hands.

OEDIPUS: Can he be called back quickly?

IOCASTÊ: Easily.
But why?

OEDIPUS: I have taken too much upon myself
Without enquiry; therefore I wish to consult him.

IOCASTÊ: Then he shall come.
                                But am I not one also
To whom you might confide these fears of yours?

OEDIPUS: That is your right; it will not be denied you,
Now least of all; for I have reached a pitch
Of wild foreboding. Is there anyone
To whom I should sooner speak?

Polybos of Corinth is my father.
My mother is a Dorian: Meropê.
I grew up chief among the men of Corinth
Until a strange thing happened—
Not worth my passion, it may be, but strange.

At a feast, a drunken man maundering in his cups
Cries out that I am not my father's son!

I contained myself that night, though I felt anger
And a sinking heart. The next day I visited
My father and mother, and questioned them. They stormed,
Calling it all the slanderous rant of a fool;
And this relieved me. Yet the suspicion
Remained always aching in my mind;
I knew there was talk; I could not rest;
And finally, saying nothing to my parents,
I went to the shrine at Delphi.

The god dismissed my question without reply;
He spoke of other things.
                              Some were clear,
Full of wretchedness, dreadful, unbearable:
As, that I should lie with my own mother, breed
Children from whom all men would turn their eyes;
And that I should be my father's murderer.

I heard all this, and fled. And from that day
Corinth to me was only in the stars
Descending in that quartet of the sky,
As I wandered farther and farther on my way
To a land where I should never see the evil
Sung by the oracle. And I came to this country
Where, so you say, King Laïos was killed.

I will tell you all that happened there, my lady.

There were three highways
Coming together at a place I passed;
And there a herald came towards me, and a chariot
Drawn by horses, with a man such as you describe
Seated in it. The groom leading the horses
Forced me off the road at his lord's command;
But as this charioteer lurched over towards me
I struck him in my rage. The old man saw me

And brought his double goad down upon my head
As I came abreast.

            He was paid back, and more!
Swinging my club in this right hand I knocked him
Out of his car, and he rolled on the ground.

                            I killed him.

I killed them all.
Now if that stranger and Laïos were—kin,
Where is a man more miserable than I?
More hated by the gods? Citizen and alien alike
Must never shelter me or speak to me—
I must be shunned by all.

                 And I myself
Pronounced this malediction upon myself!

Think of it: I have touched you with these hands,
These hands that killed your husband. What defilement!

Am I all evil, then? It must be so,
Since I must flee from Thebes, yet never again
See my own countrymen, my own country,
For fear of joining my mother in marriage
And killing Polybos, my father.

                      Ah,
If I was created so, born to this fate,
Who could deny the savagery of God?

O holy majesty of heavenly powers!
May I never see that day! Never!
Rather let me vanish from the race of men
Than know the abomination destined me!

CHORUS: We too, my lord, have felt dismay at this.
    But there is hope: you have yet to hear the shepherd.

OEDIPUS: Indeed, I fear no other hope is left me.

IOCASTÊ: What do you hope from him when he comes?

OEDIPUS: This much:
    If his account of the murder tallies with yours,
    Then I am cleared.

IOCASTÊ: What was it that I said
    Of such importance?

OEDIPUS: Why, "marauders," you said,
Killed the King, according to this man's story.
If he maintains that still, if there were several,
Clearly the guilt is not mine: I was alone
But if he says one man, singlehanded, did it,
Then the evidence all points to me.

IOCASTÊ: You may be sure that he said there were several;
And can he call back that story now? He can not.
The whole city heard it as plainly as I.
But suppose he alters some detail of it:
He can not ever show that Laïos' death
Fulfilled the oracle: for Apollo said
My child was doomed to kill him; and my child—
Poor baby!—it was my child that died first.
No. From now on, where oracles are concerned,
I would not waste a second thought on any.

OEDIPUS: You may be right.
                              But come: let someone go
For the shepherd at once. This matter must be settled.

IOCASTÊ: I will send for him.
I would not wish to cross you in anything,
And surely not in this.—Let us go in.
        [*Exeunt into the palace.*]

❧ *Ode II*

CHORUS: Let me be reverent in the ways of right,   [STROPHE 1.]
Lowly the paths I journey on;
Let all my words and actions keep
The laws of the pure universe
From highest Heaven handed down.
For Heaven is their bright nurse,
Those generations of the realms of light;
Ah, never of mortal kind were they begot,
Nor are they slaves of memory, lost in sleep:
Their Father is greater than Time, and ages not.

The tyrant is a child of Pride   [ANTISTROPHE 1.]
Who drinks from his great sickening cup

Recklessness and vanity,
Until from his high crest headlong
He plummets to the dust of hope.
That strong man is not strong.
But let no fair ambition be denied;
May God protect the wrestler for the State
In government, in comely policy,
Who will fear God, and on His ordinance wait.

Haughtiness and the high hand of disdain   [STROPHE 2.]
Tempt and outrage God's holy law;
And any mortal who dares hold
No immortal Power in awe
Will be caught up in a net of pain:
The price for which his levity is sold.
Let each man take due earnings, then,
And keep his hands from holy things,
And from blasphemy stand apart—
Else the crackling blast of heaven
Blows on his head, and on his desperate heart;
Though fools will honor impious men,
In their cities no tragic poet sings.

Shall we lose faith in Delphi's obscurities,   [ANTISTROPHE 2.]
We who have heard the world's core
Discredited, and the sacred wood
Of Zeus at Elis praised no more?
The deeds and the strange prophecies
Must make a pattern yet to be understood.
Zeus, if indeed you are lord of all,
Throned in light over night and day,
Mirror this in your endless mind:
Our masters call the oracle
Words on the wind, and the Delphic vision blind!
Their hearts no longer know Apollo,
And reverence for the gods has died away.

SCENE III

[Enter IOCASTÊ.]

IOCASTÊ: Princes of Thebes, it has occurred to me
    To visit the altars of the gods, bearing
    These branches as a suppliant, and this incense.

Our King is not himself: his noble soul
Is overwrought with fantasies of dread,
Else he would consider
The new prophecies in the light of the old.
He will listen to any voice that speaks disaster,
And my advice goes for nothing.

     [*She approaches the altar, R.*]

                    To you, then, Apollo,
Lycean lord, since you are nearest, I turn in prayer.
Receive these offerings, and grant us deliverance
From defilement. Our hearts are heavy with fear
When we see our leader distracted, as helpless sailors
Are terrified by the confusion of their helmsman.

     [*Enter* MESSENGER.]

MESSENGER: Friends, no doubt you can direct me:
  Where shall I find the house of Oedipus,
  Or, better still, where is the King himself?

CHORUS: It is this very place, stranger; he is inside.
  This is his wife and mother of his children.

MESSENGER: I wish her happiness in a happy house,
  Blest in all the fulfillment of her marriage.

IOCASTÊ: I wish as much for you: your courtesy
  Deserves a like good fortune. But now, tell me:
  Why have you come? What have you to say to us?

MESSENGER: Good news, my lady, for your house and your husband.

IOCASTÊ: What news? Who sent you here?

MESSENGER: I am from Corinth.
  The news I bring ought to mean joy for you,
  Though it may be you will find some grief in it.

IOCASTÊ: What is it? How can it touch us in both ways?

MESSENGER: The people of Corinth, they say,
  Intend to call Oedipus to be their king.

IOCASTÊ: But old Polybos—is he not reigning still?

MESSENGER: No. Death holds him in his sepulchre.

IOCASTÊ: What are you saying? Polybos is dead?

MESSENGER: If I am not telling the truth, may I die myself.

[To a MAIDSERVANT.]

IOCASTÊ: Go in, go quickly; tell this to your master.
O riddlers of God's will, where are you now!
This was the man whom Oedipus, long ago,
Feared so, fled so, in dread of destroying him—
But it was another fate by which he died.

[Enter OEDIPUS, CHORUS.]

OEDIPUS: Dearest Iocastê, why have you sent for me?

IOCASTÊ: Listen to what this man says, and then tell me
What has become of the solemn prophecies.

OEDIPUS: Who is this man? What is his news for me?

IOCASTÊ: He has come from Corinth to announce your father's death!

OEDIPUS: Is it true, stranger? Tell me in your own words.

MESSENGER: I can not say it more clearly: the King is dead.

OEDIPUS: Was it by treason? Or by an attack of illness?

MESSENGER: A little thing brings old men to their rest.

OEDIPUS: It was sickness, then?

MESSENGER: Yes, and his many years.

OEDIPUS: Ah!
Why should a man respect the Pythian hearth, or
Give heed to the birds that jangle above his head?
They prophesied that I should kill Polybos,
Kill my own father; but he is dead and buried,
And I am here—I never touched him, never,
Unless he died of grief for my departure,
And thus, in a sense, through me. No. Polybos
Has packed the oracles off with him underground.
They are empty words.

IOCASTÊ: Had I not told you so?

OEDIPUS: You had; it was my faint heart that betrayed me.

IOCASTÊ: From now on never think of those things again.

OEDIPUS: And yet—must I not fear my mother's bed?

IOCASTÊ: Why should anyone in this world be afraid,
  Since Fate rules us and nothing can be foreseen?
  A man should live only for the present day.
  Have no more fear of sleeping with your mother:
  How many men, in dreams, have lain with their mothers!
  No reasonable man is troubled by such things.

OEDIPUS: That is true; only—
  If only my mother were not still alive!
  But she is alive. I can not help my dread.

IOCASTÊ: Yet this news of your father's death is wonderful.

OEDIPUS: Wonderful. But I fear the living woman.

MESSENGER: Tell me, who is this woman that you fear?

OEDIPUS: It is Meropê, man; the wife of King Polybos.

MESSENGER: Meropê? Why should you be afraid of her?

OEDIPUS: An oracle of the gods, a dreadful saying.

MESSENGER: Can you tell me about it or are you sworn to silence?

OEDIPUS: I can tell you, and I will.
  Apollo said through his prophet that I was the man
  Who should marry his own mother, shed his father's blood
  With his own hands. And so, for all these years
  I have kept clear of Corinth, and no harm has come—
  Though it would have been sweet to see my parents again.

MESSENGER: And is this the fear that drove you out of Corinth?

OEDIPUS: Would you have me kill my father?

MESSENGER: As for that
  You must be reassured by the news I gave you.

OEDIPUS: If you could reassure me, I would reward you.

MESSENGER: I had that in mind, I will confess: I thought
  I could count on you when you returned to Corinth.

OEDIPUS: No: I will never go near my parents again.

MESSENGER: Ah, son, you still do not know what you are doing—

OEDIPUS: What do you mean? In the name of God tell me!

MESSENGER: —If these are your reasons for not going home.

OEDIPUS: I tell you, I fear the oracle may come true.

MESSENGER: And guilt may come upon you through your parents?

OEDIPUS: That is the dread that is always in my heart.

MESSENGER: Can you not see that all your fears are groundless?

OEDIPUS: How can you say that? They are my parents, surely?

MESSENGER: Polybos was not your father.

OEDIPUS: Not my father?

MESSENGER: No more your father than the man speaking to you.

OEDIPUS: But you are nothing to me!

MESSENGER: Neither was he.

OEDIPUS: Then why did he call me son?

MESSENGER: I will tell you:
  Long ago he had you from my hands, as a gift.

OEDIPUS: Then how could he love me so, if I was not his?

MESSENGER: He had no children, and his heart turned to you.

OEDIPUS: What of you? Did you buy me? Did you find me by chance?

MESSENGER: I came upon you in the crooked pass of Kithairon.

OEDIPUS: And what were you doing there?

MESSENGER: Tending my flocks.

OEDIPUS: A wandering shepherd?

MESSENGER: But your savior, son, that day.

OEDIPUS: From what did you save me?

MESSENGER: Your ankles should tell you that.

OEDIPUS: Ah, stranger, why do you speak of that childhood pain?

MESSENGER: I cut the bonds that tied your ankles together.

OEDIPUS: I have had the mark as long as I can remember.

MESSENGER: That was why you were given the name you bear.

OEDIPUS: God! Was it my father or my mother who did it?
Tell me!

MESSENGER: I do not know. The man who gave you to me
Can tell you better than I.

OEDIPUS: It was not you that found me, but another?

MESSENGER: It was another shepherd gave you to me.

OEDIPUS: Who was he? Can you tell me who he was?

MESSENGER: I think he was said to be one of Laïos' people.

OEDIPUS: You mean the Laïos who was king here years ago?

MESSENGER: Yes; King Laïos; and the man was one of his herdsmen.

OEDIPUS: Is he still alive? Can I see him?

MESSENGER: These men here
Know best about such things.

OEDIPUS: Does anyone here
Know this shepherd that he is talking about?
Have you seen him in the fields, or in the town?
If you have, tell me. It is time things were made plain.

CHORUS: I think the man he means is that same shepherd
You have already asked to see. Iocastê perhaps
Could tell you something.

OEDIPUS: Do you know anything
About him, Lady? Is he the man we have summoned?
Is that the man this shepherd means?

IOCASTÊ: Why think of him?
Forget this herdsman. Forget it all.
This talk is a waste of time.

OEDIPUS: How can you say that,
When the clues to my true birth are in my hands?

IOCASTÊ: For God's love, let us have no more questioning!
Is your life nothing to you?
My own is pain enough for me to bear.

OEDIPUS: You need not worry. Suppose my mother a slave,
And born of slaves: no baseness can touch you.

IOCASTÊ: Listen to me, I beg you: do not do this thing!

OEDIPUS: I will not listen; the truth must be made known.

IOCASTÊ: Everything that I say is for your own good!

OEDIPUS: My own good
Snaps my patience, then; I want none of it.

IOCASTÊ: You are fatally wrong! May you never learn who you are!

OEDIPUS: Go, one of you, and bring the shepherd here.
Let us leave this woman to brag of her royal name.

IOCASTÊ: Ah, miserable!
That is the only word I have for you now.
That is the only word I can ever have.
      [*Exit into the palace.*]

CHORUS: Why has she left us, Oedipus? Why has she gone
In such a passion of sorrow? I fear this silence:
Something dreadful may come of it.

OEDIPUS: Let it come!
However base my birth, I must know about it.
The Queen, like a woman, is perhaps ashamed
To think of my low origin. But I
Am a child of Luck; I cannot be dishonored.
Luck is my mother; the passing months, my brothers,
Have seen me rich and poor.
                If this is so,
How could I wish that I were someone else?
How could I not be glad to know my birth?

🌼 *Ode III*

CHORUS: If ever the coming time were known   [STROPHE.]
To my heart's pondering,
Kithairon, now by Heaven I see the torches
At the festival of the next full moon,
And see the dance, and hear the choir sing
A grace to your gentle shade:
Mountain where Oedipus was found,

O mountain guard of a noble race!
May the god who heals us lend his aid,
And let that glory come to pass
For our king's cradling-ground. [ANTISTROPHE.]

Of the nymphs that flower beyond the years,
Who bore you, royal child,
To Pan of the hills or the timberline Apollo,
Cold in delight were the upland clears,
Or Hermês for whom Kyllenê's heights are piled?
Or flushed as evening cloud,
Great Dionysos, roamer of mountains,
He—was it he who found you there,
And caught you up in his own proud
Arms from the sweet god-ravisher
Who laughed by the Muses' fountains?

SCENE IV

OEDIPUS: Sirs: though I do not know the man,
    I think I see him coming, this shepherd we want:
    He is old, like our friend here, and the men
    Bringing him seem to be servants of my house.
    But you can tell, if you have ever seen him.
        [Enter SHEPHERD escorted by servants.]

CHORUS: I know him, he was Laïos' man. You can trust him.

OEDIPUS: Tell me first, you from Corinth: is this the shepherd
    We were discussing?

MESSENGER: This is the very man.

        [To SHEPHERD.]
OEDIPUS: Come here. No, look at me. You must answer
    Everything I ask.—You belonged to Laïos?

SHEPHERD: Yes: born his slave, brought up in his house.

OEDIPUS: Tell me: what kind of work did you do for him?

SHEPHERD: I was a shepherd of his, most of my life.

OEDIPUS: Where mainly did you go for pasturage?

SHEPHERD: Sometimes Kithairon, sometimes the hills near-by.

OEDIPUS: Do you remember ever seeing this man out there?

SHEPHERD: What would he be doing there? This man?

OEDIPUS: This man standing here. Have you ever seen him before?

SHEPHERD: No. At least, not to my recollection.

MESSENGER: And that is not strange, my lord. But I'll refresh
His memory: he must remember when we two
Spent three whole seasons together, March to September,
On Kithairon or thereabouts. He had two flocks;
I had one. Each autumn I'd drive mine home
And he would go back with his to Laïos' sheepfold.—
Is this not true, just as I have described it?

SHEPHERD: True, yes; but it was all so long ago.

MESSENGER: Well, then: do you remember, back in those days,
That you gave me a baby boy to bring up as my own?

SHEPHERD: What if I did? What are you trying to say?

MESSENGER: King Oedipus was once that little child.

SHEPHERD: Damn you, hold your tongue!

OEDIPUS: No more of that!
It is your tongue needs watching, not this man's.

SHEPHERD: My King, my Master, what is it I have done wrong?

OEDIPUS: You have not answered his question about the boy.

SHEPHERD: He does not know. . . . He is only making trouble. . . .

OEDIPUS: Come, speak plainly, or it will go hard with you.

SHEPHERD: In God's name, do not torture an old man!

OEDIPUS: Come here, one of you; bind his arms behind him.

SHEPHERD: Unhappy King! What more do you wish to learn?

OEDIPUS: Did you give this man the child he speaks of?

SHEPHERD: I did.
And I would to God I had died that very day.

OEDIPUS: You will die now unless you speak the truth.

SHEPHERD: Yet if I speak the truth, I am worse than dead.

OEDIPUS: Very well; since you insist upon delaying—

SHEPHERD: No! I have told you already that I gave him the boy.

OEDIPUS: Where did you get him? From your house? From somewhere else?

SHEPHERD: Not from mine, no. A man gave him to me.

OEDIPUS: Is that man here? Do you know whose slave he was?

SHEPHERD: For God's love, my King, do not ask me any more!

OEDIPUS: You are a dead man if I have to ask you again.

SHEPHERD: Then . . . Then the child was from the palace of Laïos.

OEDIPUS: A slave child? or a child of his own line?

SHEPHERD: Ah, I am on the brink of dreadful speech!

OEDIPUS: And I of dreadful hearing. Yet I must hear.

SHEPHERD: If you must be told, then . . .
> They said it was Laïos' child;
But it is your wife who can tell you about that.

OEDIPUS: My wife!—Did she give it to you?

SHEPHERD: My lord, she did.

OEDIPUS: Do you know why?

SHEPHERD: I was told to get rid of it.

OEDIPUS: An unspeakable mother!

SHEPHERD: There had been prophecies . . .

OEDIPUS: Tell me.

SHEPHERD: It was said that the boy would kill his own father.

OEDIPUS: Then why did you give him over to this old man?

SHEPHERD: I pitied the baby, my King,
And I thought that this man would take him far away
To his own country.
> He saved him—but for what a fate!
For if you are what this man says you are,
No man living is more wretched than Oedipus.

OEDIPUS: Ah God!
　　It was true!
　　　　　　　All the prophecies!
　　　　　　　　　　　　—Now,
O Light, may I look on you for the last time!
I, Oedipus,
Oedipus, damned in his birth, in his marriage damned,
Damned in the blood he shed with his own hand!
　　　[*He rushes into the palace.*]

🏵 *Ode IV*

CHORUS: Alas for the seed of men.　　　　　　　　　　[STROPHE 1.]

What measure shall I give these generations
That breathe on the void and are void
And exist and do not exist?

Who bears more weight of joy
Than mass of sunlight shifting in images,
Or who shall make his thoughts stay on
That down time drifts away?

Your spendor is all fallen.

O naked brow of wrath and tears,
O change of Oedipus!
I who saw your days call no man blest—
Your great days like ghósts góne.

That mind was a strong bow.　　　　　　　　　[ANTISTROPHE 1.]

Deep, how deep you drew it then, hard archer,
At a dim fearful range,
And brought dear glory down!

You overcame the stranger—
The virgin with her hooking lion claws—
And though death sang, stood like a tower
To make pale Thebes take heart.

Fortress against our sorrow!

48　　*Sophocles*

Divine king, giver of laws,
Majestic Oedipus!
No prince in Thebes had ever such renown,
No prince won such grace of power.

And now of all men ever known   [STROPHE 2.]
Most pitiful is this man's story:
His fortunes are most changed, his state
Fallen to a low slave's
Ground under bitter fate.

O Oedipus, most royal one!
The great door that expelled you to the light
Gave at night—ah, gave night to your glory:
As to the father, to the fathering son.

All understood too late.

How could that queen whom Laïos won,
The garden that he harrowed at his height,
Be silent when that act was done?

But all eyes fail before time's eye,   [ANTISTROPHE 2.]
All actions come to justice there.
Though never willed, though far down the deep past,
Your bed, your dread sirings,
Are brought to book at last.

Child by Laïos doomed to die,
Then doomed to lose that fortunate little death,
Would God you never took breath in this air
That with my wailing lips I take to cry:

For I weep the world's outcast.

Blind I was, and can not tell why;
Asleep, for you had given ease of breath;
A fool, while the false years went by.

Éxodos

[*Enter, from the palace,* SECOND MESSENGER.]

SECOND MESSENGER: Elders of Thebes, most honored in this land,
　　What horrors are yours to see and hear, what weight
　　Of sorrow to be endured, if, true to your birth,
　　You venerate the line of Labdakos!
　　I think neither Istros nor Phasis, those great rivers,
　　Could purify this place of the corruption
　　It shelters now, or soon must bring to light—
　　Evil not done unconsciously, but willed.

　　The greatest griefs are those we cause ourselves.

CHORUS: Surely, friend, we have grief enough already;
　　What new sorrow do you mean?

SECOND MESSENGER: The Queen is dead.

CHORUS: Iocastê? Dead? But at whose hand?

SECOND MESSENGER: Her own.
　　The full horror of what happened you cannot know,
　　For you did not see it; but I, who did, will tell you
　　As clearly as I can how she met her death.

　　When she had left us,
　　In passionate silence, passing through the court,
　　She ran to her apartment in the house,
　　Her hair clutched by the fingers of both hands.
　　She closed the doors behind her; then, by that bed
　　Where long ago the fatal son was conceived—
　　That son who should bring about his father's death—
　　We heard her call upon Laïos, dead so many years,
　　And heard her wail for the double fruit of her marriage,
　　A husband by her husband, children by her child.
　　Exactly how she died I do not know:
　　For Oedipus burst in moaning and would not let us
　　Keep vigil to the end: it was by him
　　As he stormed about the room that our eyes were caught.

From one to another of us he went, begging a sword,
Cursing the wife who was not his wife, the mother
Whose womb had carried his own children and himself.
I do not know: it was none of us aided him,
But surely one of the gods was in control!
For with a dreadful cry
He hurled his weight, as though wrenched out of himself,
At the twin doors: the bolts gave, and he rushed in.
And there we saw her hanging, her body swaying
From the cruel cord she had noosed about her neck.
A great sob broke from him, heartbreaking to hear,
As he loosed the rope and lowered her to the ground.

I would blot out from my mind what happened next!
For the King ripped from her gown the golden brooches
That were her ornament, and raised them, and plunged them down
Straight into his own eyeballs, crying, "No more,
No more shall you look on the misery about me,
The horrors of my own doing! Too long you have known
The faces of those whom I should never have seen,
Too long been blind to those for whom I was searching!
From this hour, go in darkness!" And as he spoke,
He struck at his eyes—not once, but many times;
And the blood spattered his beard,
Bursting from his ruined sockets like red hail.

So from the unhappiness of two this evil has sprung,
A curse on the man and woman alike. The old
Happiness of the house of Labdakos
Was happiness enough: where is it today?
It is all wailing and ruin, disgrace, death—all
The misery of mankind that has a name—
And it is wholly and for ever theirs.

CHORUS: Is he in agony still? Is there no rest for him?

SECOND MESSENGER: He is calling for someone to lead him to the gates
So that all the children of Kadmos may look upon
His father's murderer, his mother's—no,
I can not say it!
           And then he will leave Thebes,
Self-exiled, in order that the curse
Which he himself pronounced may depart from the house.
He is weak, and there is none to lead him,

So terrible is his suffering.
                              But you will see:
Look, the doors are opening; in a moment
You will see a thing that would crush a heart of stone.
            [*The central door is opened;* OEDIPUS, *blinded, is led in.*]

CHORUS: Dreadful indeed for men to see
　　Never have my own eyes
　　Looked on a sight so full of fear.

　　Oedipus!
　　What madness came upon you, what daemon
　　Leaped on your life with heavier
　　Punishment than a mortal man can bear?
　　No; I can not even
　　Look at you, poor ruined one.
　　And I would speak, question, ponder,
　　If I were able. No.
　　You make me shudder.

OEDIPUS: God.　　　　God.
　　Is there a sorrow greater?
　　Where shall I find harbor in this world?
　　My voice is hurled far on a dark wind.
　　What has God done to me?

CHORUS: Too terrible to think of, or to see.

OEDIPUS: O cloud of night,   [STROPHE 1.]
　　Never to be turned away: night coming on,
　　I can not tell how: night like a shroud!

　　My fair winds brought me here.
　　　　　　　　　　O God. Again
　　The pain of the spikes where I had sight,
　　The flooding pain
　　Of memory, never to be gouged out.

CHORUS: This is not strange.
　　You suffer it all twice over, remorse in pain,
　　Pain in remorse.

OEDIPUS: Ah dear friend   [ANTISTROPHE 1.]
　　Are you faithful even yet, you alone?
　　Are you still standing near me, will you stay here,

Patient, to care for the blind?
                                        The blind man!
Yet even blind I know who it is attends me,
By the voice's tone—
Though my new darkness hide the comforter.

CHORUS: Oh fearful act!
  What god was it drove you to rake black
  Night across your eyes?

OEDIPUS: Apollo. Apollo. Dear   [STROPHE 2.]
  Children, the god was Apollo.
  He brought my sick, sick fate upon me.
  But the blinding hand was my own!
  How could I bear to see
  When all my sight was horror everywhere?

CHORUS: Everywhere; that is true.

OEDIPUS: And now what is left?
  Images? Love? A greeting even,
  Sweet to the senses? Is there anything?
  Ah, no, friends: lead me away.
  Lead me away from Thebes.
                              Lead the great wreck
  And hell of Oedipus, whom the gods hate.

CHORUS: Your fate is clear, you are not blind to that.
  Would God you had never found it out!

OEDIPUS: Death take the man who unbound   [ANTISTROPHE 2.]
  My feet on that hillside
  And delivered me from death to life! What life?
  If only I had died,
  This weight of monstrous doom
  Could not have dragged me and my darlings down.

CHORUS: I would have wished the same.

OEDIPUS: Oh never to have come here
  With my father's blood upon me! Never
  To have been the man they call his mother's husband!
  Oh accurst! Oh child of evil,
  To have entered that wretched bed—
                                the selfsame one!
  More primal than sin itself, this fell to me.

CHORUS: I do not know how I can answer you.
  You were better dead than alive and blind.

OEDIPUS: Do not counsel me any more. This punishment
  That I have laid upon myself is just.
  If I had eyes,
  I do not know how I could bear the sight
  Of my father, when I came to the house of Death,
  Or my mother: for I have sinned against them both
  So vilely that I could not make my peace
  By strangling my own life.
                          Or do you think my children,
  Born as they were born, would be sweet to my eyes?
  Ah never, never! Nor this town with its high walls,
  Nor the holy images of the gods.
                          For I,
  Thrice miserable!—Oedipus, noblest of all the line
  Of Kadmos, have condemned myself to enjoy
  These things no more, by my own malediction
  Expelling that man whom the gods declared
  To be a defilement in the house of Laïos.
  After exposing the rankness of my own guilt,
  How could I look men frankly in the eyes?
  No, I swear it,
  If I could have stifled my hearing at its source,
  I would have done it and made all this body
  A tight cell of misery, blank to light and sound:
  So I should have been safe in a dark agony
  Beyond all recollection.
                          Ah Kithairon!
  Why did you shelter me? When I was cast upon you,
  Why did I not die? Then I should never
  Have shown the world my execrable birth.

  Ah Polybos! Corinth, city that I believed
  The ancient seat of my ancestors: how fair
  I seemed, your child! And all the while this evil
  Was cancerous within me!
                          For I am sick
  In my daily life, sick in my origin.

  O three roads, dark ravine, woodland and way
  Where three roads met: you, drinking my father's blood,

My own blood, spilled by my own hand: can you remember
The unspeakable things I did there, and the things
I went on from there to do?
                              O marriage, marriage!
The act that engendered me, and again the act
Performed by the son in the same bed—
                              Ah, the net
Of incest, mingling fathers, brothers, sons,
With brides, wives, mothers: the last evil
That can be known by men: no tongue can say
How evil!
          No. For the love of God, conceal me
Somewhere far from Thebes; or kill me; or hurl me
Into the sea, away from men's eyes for ever.

Come, lead me. You need not fear to touch me.
Of all men, I alone can bear this guilt.
        [*Enter* CREON.]

CHORUS: We are not the ones to decide; but Creon here
    May fitly judge of what you ask. He only
    Is left to protect the city in your place.

OEDIPUS: Alas, how can I speak to him? What right have I
    To beg his courtesy whom I have deeply wronged?

CREON: I have not come to mock you, Oedipus.
    Or to reproach you, either.
        [*To* ATTENDANTS.]
                              —You, standing there:
    If you have lost all respect for man's dignity,
    At least respect the flame of Lord Helios:
    Do not allow this pollution to show itself
    Openly here, an affront to the earth
    And Heaven's rain and the light of day. No, take him
    Into the house as quickly as you can.
    For it is proper
    That only the close kindred see his grief.

OEDIPUS: I pray you in God's name, since your courtesy
    Ignores my dark expectation, visiting
    With mercy this man of all men most execrable:
    Give me what I ask—for your good, not for mine.

CREON: And what is it that you would have me do?

OEDIPUS: Drive me out of this country as quickly as may be
　To a place where no human voice can ever greet me.

CREON: I should have done that before now—only,
　God's will had not be wholly revealed to me.

OEDIPUS: But his command is plain: the parricide
　Must be destroyed. I am that evil man.

CREON: —That is the sense of it, yes; but as things are,
　We had best discover clearly what is to be done.

OEDIPUS: You would learn more about a man like me?

CREON: You are ready now to listen to the god.

OEDIPUS: I will listen. But it is to you
　That I must turn for help. I beg you, hear me.

　The woman in there—
　Give her whatever funeral you think proper:
　She is your sister.
　　　　　　—But let me go, Creon!
　Let me purge my father's Thebes of the pollution
　Of my living here, and go out to the wild hills,
　To Kithairon, that has won such fame with me,
　The tomb my mother and father appointed for me,
　And let me die there, as they willed I should.
　And yet I know
　Death will not ever come to me through sickness
　Or in any natural way: I have been preserved
　For some unthinkable fate. But let that be.

　As for my sons, you need not care for them.
　They are men, they will find some way to live.
　But my poor daughters, who have shared my table,
　Who never before have been parted from their father—
　Take care of them, Creon; do this for me.
　And will you let me touch them with my hands
　A last time, and let us weep together?
　Be kind, my lord,
　Great prince, be kind!
　　　　　　　Could I but touch them,
　They would be mine again, as when I had my eyes.
　　　　[Enter ANTIGONE and ISMENE, attended.]
　Ah, God!

Is it my dearest children I hear weeping?
Has Creon pitied me and sent my daughters?

CREON: Yes, Oedipus: I knew that they were dear to you
In the old days, and know you must love them still.

OEDIPUS: May God bless you for this—and be a friendlier
Guardian to you than he has been to me!

Children, where are you?
Come quickly to my hands: they are your brother's—
Hands that have brought your father's once clear eyes
To this way of seeing—
                              Ah dearest ones,
I had neither sight nor knowledge then, your father
By the woman who was the source of his own life!
And I weep for you—having no strength to see you—,
I weep for you when I think of the bitterness
That men will visit upon you all your lives.
What homes, what festivals can you attend
Without being forced to depart again in tears?
And when you come to marriageable age,
Where is the man, my daughters, who would dare
Risk the bane that lies on all my children?
Is there any evil wanting? Your father killed
His father; sowed the womb of her who bore him;
Engendered you at the fount of his own existence!

That is what they will say of you.
                              Then, whom
Can you ever marry? There are no bridegrooms for you,
And your lives must wither away in sterile dreaming.

O Creon, son of Menoikeus!
You are the only father my daughters have,
Since we, their parents, are both of us gone for ever.
They are your own blood: you will not let them
Fall into beggary and loneliness;
You will keep them from the miseries that are mine!
Take pity on them; see, they are only children,
Friendless except for you. Promise me this,
Great Prince, and give me your hand in token of it.
                    [CREON *clasps his right hand.*]

Children:
I could say much, if you could understand me,
But as it is, I have only this prayer for you:
Live where you can, be as happy as you can—
Happier, please God, than God has made your father!

CREON: Enough. You have wept enough. Now go within.

OEDIPUS: I must; but it is hard.

CREON: Time eases all things.

OEDIPUS: But you must promise—

CREON: Say what you desire.

OEDIPUS: Send me from Thebes!

CREON: God grant that I may!

OEDIPUS: But since God hates me . . .

CREON: No, he will grant your wish.

OEDIPUS: You promise?

CREON: I can not speak beyond my knowledge.

OEDIPUS: Then lead me in.

CREON: Come now, and leave your children.

OEDIPUS: No! Do not take them from me!

CREON: Think no longer
That you are in command here, but rather think
How when you were, you served your own destruction.
[Exeunt into the house all but the CHORUS; the CHORAGOS
chants directly to the audience.]

CHORUS: Men of Thebes: look upon Oedipus.
This is the king who solved the famous riddle
And towered up, most powerful of men.
No mortal eyes but looked on him with envy,
Yet in the end ruin swept over him.

Let every man in mankind's frailty
Consider his last day; and let none
Presume on his good fortune until he find
Life, at his death, a memory without pain.

❦ *William Shakespeare*

William Shakespeare (1564–1616) is the supreme playwright of the Renaissance. His achievement is staggering. He perfected the forms of tragedy, comedy, and the history play. "Soul of the age!" So Ben Jonson called him in his dedicatory poem on the occasion of the first folio edition of Shakespeare's works (1623). He was born in Stratford-on-Avon, the son of a well-to-do tradesman who began having financial difficulties about the time William was fourteen. His first child, Susanna, was born some six months after a marriage license was issued on November 28, 1582 to him and Anne Hathaway, eight years his senior. His only other children, the twins Hamnet and Judith, were baptized on February 2, 1585. In the early 1590's he left for London.

There is little evidence of his middle-class origin in his work. His tough-minded tragic sense has no relation to the conventional ortho-doxies of the new middle-class; and his festive comic sense has no relation to the often joyless pieties of that class. He was indebted to his predecessors, particularly Marlowe, who made blank verse a supple instrument of the spoken word, and who provided examples—however imperfect—of the large-dimensioned tragic hero of the Renaissance. But Shakespeare realized what others could only aim at. *Hamlet* (1600), *Othello* (1604), *King Lear* (1605), *Macbeth* (1605), and *Antony and Cleopatra* (1606) are classics of the tragic form. Of his earlier tragedies *Romeo and Juliet* (1594) and *Julius Caesar* (1599) are also notable; of his later tragedies, *Coriolanus* (1607). All dates are approximate. *King Lear* is possibly the supreme Shakespearean tragedy, certainly the most shattering. It speaks directly to our own apocalyptic sense. The barren heath with four strange figures is an image of our time as well as Shakespeare's; it was quite possibly the inspiration for the equally barren setting of *Waiting for Godot*. For a further discussion of *Lear* in the context of the form of tragedy, see the introduction to tragedy.

READINGS:

Bonheim, Helmut, ed., *The King Lear Perplex*. Belmont, Cal.: Wads-worth Publishing Company, 1960.

BRADLEY, A. C., *Shakespearean Tragedy* (1904). New York: Meridian Books, 1955.

DANBY, JOHN F., *Shakespeare's Doctrine of Nature: A Study of King Lear*. London: Faber and Faber, 1949.

DEAN, LEONARD, ed., *Shakespeare: Modern Essays in Criticism*. New York: Oxford University Press, 1947.

GRANVILLE-BARKER, H., *Prefaces to Shakespeare*. Vol. 1. Princeton, N.J.: Princeton University Press, 1947.

HEILMAN, ROBERT B., *This Great Stage*. Baton Rouge: Louisiana State University Press, 1948.

KNIGHT, G. WILSON, *The Wheel of Fire*. London: Oxford University Press, 1930.

SPENCER, THEODORE, *Shakespeare and the Nature of Man*. New York: The Macmillan Company, 1942.

WEISINGER, HERBERT, *Tragedy and the Paradox of the Fortunate Fall*. East Lansing, Michigan: Michigan State College Press, 1953.

WILSON, HAROLD S., *On the Design of Shakespearean Tragedy*. Toronto: University of Toronto Press, 1957.

🔱 *King Lear*

D RAMATIS P ERSONAE

L EAR, *King of Britain*
K ING OF F RANCE
D UKE OF B URGUNDY
D UKE OF C ORNWALL
D UKE OF A LBANY
E ARL OF K ENT
E ARL OF G LOUCESTER
E DGAR, *son to Gloucester*
E DMUND, *bastard son to Glouces-*
ter
C URAN, *a courtier*
O LD M AN, *tenant to Gloucester*
D OCTOR
F OOL

O SWALD, *steward to Goneril*
A C APTAIN *employed by Edmund*
G ENTLEMAN attendant on Cor-
delia
H ERALD
S ERVANTS *to Cornwall*
G ONERIL ⎫
R EGAN ⎬ *daughters to Lear*
C ORDELIA ⎭
K NIGHTS *of Lear's train,* CAP-
TAINS, MESSENGERS, SOLDIERS,
and ATTENDANTS
S CENE—*Britain.*

🜂 *Act I*

SCENE 1. K ING L EAR'S *palace.*

[*Enter* KENT, GLOUCESTER, *and* EDMUND.]

KENT: I thought the King had more affected[1] the Duke of Albany than Cornwall.

GLO.: It did always seem so to us. But now, in the division of the kingdom, it appears not which of the Dukes he values most, for equalities are so weighed that curiosity in neither can make choice of either's moiety.[2]

KENT: Is not this your son, my lord?

Act I, Sc. i: As the opening words of this scene show, Lear has already decided on the division of the kingdom. There remains only the public and ceremonious announcement of his abdication. 1. more affected: had more affection for. 2. equalities . . . moiety: for their shares are so equal that a close examination (*curiosity*) cannot decide which share (*moiety*) is to be preferred.

GLO.: His breeding, sir, hath been at my charge. I have so often blushed to acknowledge him that now I am brazed[3] to it.

KENT: I cannot conceive[4] you.

GLO.: Sir, this young fellow's mother could. Whereupon she grew round-wombed, and had indeed, sir, a son for her cradle ere she had a husband for her bed. Do you smell a fault?

KENT: I cannot wish the fault undone, the issue[5] of it being so proper.[6]

GLO.: But I have, sir, a son by order of law, some year elder than this, who yet is no dearer in my account. Though this knave came something saucily into the world before he was sent for, yet was his mother fair, there was good sport at his making, and the whoreson[7] must be acknowledged. Do you know this noble gentleman, Edmund?

EDM.: No, my lord.

GLO.: My Lord of Kent. Remember him hereafter as my honorable friend.

EDM.: My services to your lordship.

KENT: I must love you, and sue to know you better.

EDM.: Sir, I shall study deserving.[8]

GLO.: He hath been out nine years, and away he shall again. The King is coming.

[*Sennet.*[9] *Enter one bearing a coronet,*[10] KING LEAR, CORN-WALL, ALBANY, GONERIL, REGAN, CORDELIA, *and* ATTENDANTS.]

LEAR: Attend[11] the lords of France and Burgundy, Gloucester.

GLO.: I shall, my liege.

[*Exeunt* GLOUCESTER *and* EDMUND.]

LEAR: Meantime we shall express our darker purpose.[12]
Give me the map there. Know that we have divided
In three our kingdom. And 'tis our fast intent
To shake all cares and business from our age,
Conferring them on younger strengths while we
Unburdened crawl toward death. Our son[13] of Cornwall,
And you, our no less loving son of Albany,
We have this hour a constant will[14] to publish
Our daughters' several[15] dowers, that future strife

---

3. brazed: become brazen; lit., brass-plated. 4. conceive: understand. 5. issue: result; i.e., child. 6. proper: handsome. 7. whoreson: rogue; lit., son of a whore. 8. I . . . deserving: I shall do my best to deserve your favor. 9. s.d., Sennet: trumpet call used to announce the approach of a procession. 10. coronet: a small crown worn by those of lesser rank than King. 11. Attend: wait on. 12. we . . . purpose: we will explain what we have hitherto kept dark. Lear, speaking officially as King, uses the royal "we." 13. son: son-in-law. 14. constant will: firm intention. 15. several: separate.

May be prevented[16] now. The Princes, France and Burgundy,
Great rivals in our youngest daughter's love,
Long in our Court have made their amorous sojourn,
And here are to be answered. Tell me, my daughters,
Since now we will divest us both of rule,
Interest of territory, cares of state,
Which of you shall we say doth love us most?
That we our largest bounty may extend
Where nature doth with merit challenge.[17] Goneril,
Our eldest-born, speak first.

GON.: Sir, I love you more than words can wield[18] the matter,
Dearer than eyesight, space, and liberty,
Beyond what can be valued, rich or rare,
No less than life, with grace, health, beauty, honor,
As much as child e'er loved or father found—
A love that makes breath poor and speech unable—
Beyond all manner of so much[19] I love you.

COR. [*Aside*]: What shall Cordelia do? Love, and be silent.

LEAR: Of all these bounds, even from this line to this,
With shadowy forests and with champaigns riched,[20]
With plenteous rivers and wide-skirted meads,[21]
We make thee lady. To thine and Albany's issue
Be this perpetual. What says our second daughter,
Our dearest Regan, wife to Cornwall? Speak.

REG.: I am made of that self metal[22] as my sister,
And prize me at her worth.[23] In my true heart
I find she names my very deed of love,
Only she comes too short. That I profess
Myself an enemy to all other joys
Which the most precious square of sense possesses,[24]
And find I am alone felicitate[25]
In your dear Highness' love.

COR. [*Aside*]: Then poor Cordelia!
And yet not so, since I am sure my love's
More ponderous than my tongue.[26]

---

16. prevented: forestalled. 17. Where . . . challenge: where natural affection and desert have an equal claim on my bounty. 18. wield: declare. 19. Beyond . . . much: i.e., beyond all these things. 20. champaigns riched: enriched with fertile fields. 21. wide-skirted meads: extensive pasture lands. 22. self metal: same material. 23. prize . . . worth: value me at the same price. 24. most . . . possesses: feeling in the highest degree possesses. square: the carpenter's rule; i.e., measurement. 25. felicitate: made happy. 26. love's . . . tongue: love is heavier than my words.

LEAR: To thee and thine hereditary ever
   Remain this ample third of our fair kingdom,
   No less in space, validity[27] and pleasure
   Than that conferred on Goneril. Now, our joy,
   Although the last, not least, to whose young love
   The vines of France and milk of Burgundy
   Strive to be interested,[28] what can you say to draw
   A third more opulent than your sisters? Speak.
COR.: Nothing, my lord.[29]
LEAR: Nothing!
COR.: Nothing.
LEAR: Nothing will come of nothing.[30] Speak again.
COR.: Unhappy that I am, I cannot heave
   My heart into my mouth. I love your Majesty
   According to my bond,[31] nor more nor less.
LEAR: How, how, Cordelia! Mend your speech a little,
   Lest it may mar your fortunes.
COR.: Good my lord,
   You have begot me, bred me, loved me. I
   Return those duties back as are right fit,
   Obey you, love you, and most honor you.
   Why have my sisters husbands if they say
   They love you all? Haply,[32] when I shall wed,
   That lord whose hand must take my plight[33] shall carry
   Half my love with him, half my care and duty.
   Sure, I shall never marry like my sisters,
   To love my father all.
LEAR: But goes thy heart with this?
COR.: Aye, good my lord.
LEAR: So young, and so untender?
COR.: So young, my lord, and true.
LEAR: Let it be so. Thy truth then be thy dower.
   For, by the sacred radiance of the sun,
   The mysteries of Hecate,[34] and the night,
   By all the operation of the orbs[35]
   From whom we do exist and cease to be,
   Here I disclaim[36] all my paternal care,

---

27. validity: value. 28. interested: have a share in. 29. Nothing, my lord: See
Intro. *Lear*, p. 1138a. 30. Nothing . . . nothing: the old maxim *Ex nihilo
nihil fit*. 31. bond: i.e., the tie of natural affection and duty which binds
daughter to father. 32. Haply: it may happen. 33. plight: promise made at
betrothal. 34. Hecate: goddess of witchcraft. Cf. *Macb.* II.i.52; III.ii.41–43.
35. orbs: stars. 36. disclaim: renounce.

Propinquity,[37] and property of blood,[38]
And as a stranger to my heart and me
Hold thee from this forever. The barbarous Scythian,[39]
Or he that makes his generation messes
To gorge his appetite[40] shall to my bosom
Be as well neighbored, pitied, and relieved[41]
As thou my sometime daughter.

KENT: Good my liege—

LEAR: Peace, Kent!
Come not between the dragon[42] and his wrath.
I loved her most, and thought to set my rest[43]
On her kind nursery.[44] Hence, and avoid[45] my sight!
So be my grave my peace, as here I give
Her father's heart from her! Call France. Who stirs?
Call Burgundy. Cornwall and Albany,
With my two daughters' dowers digest[46] this third.
Let pride, which she calls plainness,[47] marry her.
I do invest you jointly with my power,
Pre-eminence,[48] and all the large effects
That troop with majesty.[49] Ourself, by monthly course,[50]
With reservation of a hundred knights
By you to be sustained, shall our abode
Make with you by due turns. Only we still retain
The name and all the additions[51] to a king.
The sway, revenue, execution of the rest,
Belovèd Sons, be yours, which to confirm,
This coronet[52] part betwixt you.

KENT: Royal Lear,
Whom I have ever honored as my King,
Loved as my father, as my master followed,
As my great patron thought on in my prayers—

LEAR: The bow is bent and drawn, make from the shaft.[53]

37. Propinquity: relationship. 38. property of blood: claim which you have as being of my blood. 39. Scythian: inhabitant of South Russia, regarded as the worst kind of savage. 40. Or . . . appetite: or he that feeds gluttonously on his own children. 41. relieved: helped in distress. 42. dragon: the Dragon of Britain was Lear's heraldic device and also a symbol of his ferocity. 43. set . . . my rest: lit., to risk all—a term in the card game called primero. Lear uses it with the double meaning of "find rest." 44. nursery: care. 45. avoid: depart from. 46. digest: absorb. 47. plainness: honest plain speech. 48. Pre-eminence: authority. 49. large . . . majesty: the outward show of power that goes with rule. 50. course: turn. 51. additions: titles of honor. 52. coronet: i.e., the coronet which was to have been the symbol of Cordelia's kingdom. 53. shaft: arrow.

KENT: Let it fall rather, though the fork[54] invade
  The region of my heart. Be Kent unmannerly
  When Lear is mad. What wouldst thou do, old man?[55]
  Think'st thou that duty shall have dread to speak
  When power to flattery bows? To plainness honor's bound
  When majesty stoops to folly.[56] Reverse thy doom,[57]
  And in thy best consideration check
  This hideous rashness. Answer my life my judgment,
  Thy youngest daughter does not love thee least,
  Nor are those empty-hearted whose low sound
  Reverbs[58] no hollowness.
LEAR: Kent, on thy life, no more.
KENT: My life I never held but as a pawn[59]
  To wage against thy enemies, nor fear to lose it,
  Thy safety being the motive.
LEAR: Out of my sight!
KENT: See better, Lear, and let me still remain
  The true blank[60] of thine eye.
LEAR: Now, by Apollo—
KENT: Now, by Apollo, King.
  Thou swear'st thy gods in vain.
LEAR: O vassal![61] Miscreant![62]
        [*Laying his hand on his sword.*]
ALB. & CORN.: Dear sir, forbear.
KENT: Do.
  Kill thy physician, and the fee bestow
  Upon the foul disease. Revoke thy doom,
  Or whilst I can vent clamor[63] from my throat
  I'll tell thee thou dost evil.
LEAR: Hear me, recreant![64]
  On thy allegiance,[65] hear me!

---

54. fork: point of a forked arrow. See Pl. 22a.   55. old man: Kent, who is as
quick-tempered as Lear, has lost control of his tongue. The phrase to a still ruling king is grossly insulting.   56. Think'st . . . folly: This is one of many passages in *Lear* where the abstract is strikingly and effectively used for the person.
It means: "Do you think that a man who keeps his sense of duty will be afraid
to speak when he sees a king yielding to his flatterers? An honorable man is
forced to speak plainly when a king becomes a fool."   57. doom: sentence.
58. Reverbs: re-echoes.   59. pawn: a pledge to be sacrificed.   60. blank:
aim; i.e., something which you look at. The blank is the center of the target.
61. vassal: wretch.   62. Miscreant: lit., misbeliever.   63. vent clamor: utter
a cry.   64. recreant: traitor.   65. On . . . allegiance: The most solemn form
of command that can be laid upon a subject, for to disobey is to commit high
treason.

Since thou hast sought to make us break our vow,
Which we durst never yet, and with strained[66] pride
To come between our sentence and our power[67]—
Which nor our nature nor our place can bear,
Our potency made good[68]—take thy reward.
Five days we do allot thee, for provision[69]
To shield thee from diseases of the world,
And on the sixth to turn thy hated back
Upon our kingdom. If on the tenth day following
Thy banished trunk[70] be found in our dominions,
The moment is thy death. Away! By Jupiter,
This shall not be revoked.

KENT: Fare[71] thee well, King. Sith[72] thus thou wilt appear,
Freedom lives hence, and banishment is here.
[To CORDELIA] The gods to their dear shelter take thee, maid,
That justly think'st and hast most rightly said!
[To REGAN and GONERIL] And your large[73] speeches may your deeds
    approve,[74]
That good effects[75] may spring from words of love.
Thus Kent, O Princes, bids you all adieu.
He'll shape his old course in a country new. [Exit.]
    [Flourish.[76] Re-enter GLOUCESTER, with FRANCE, BURGUNDY,
    and ATTENDANTS.]

GLO.: Here's France and Burgundy, my noble lord.

LEAR: My lord of Burgundy,
We first address toward you, who with this King
Hath rivaled for our daughter. What, in the least,
Will you require[77] in present[78] dower with her,
Or cease your quest of love?

BUR.: Most royal Majesty,
I crave no more than what your Highness offered,
Nor will you tender[79] less.

LEAR: Right noble Burgundy,
When she was dear[80] to us, we did hold her so,

---

66. strained: excessive. 67. To . . . power: to interpose yourself between my decree and my royal will; i.e., to make me revoke an order. 68. Our . . . good: my power being now asserted. 69. for provision: for making your preparations. 70. trunk: body. 71. Fare . . . new: The rhyme in this passage and elsewhere in the play is used for the particular purpose of stiffening the speech and giving it a special prophetic or moral significance; cf. III.vi.109–20. 72. Sith: since. 73. large: fine-sounding. 74. approve: i.e., be shown in deeds. 75. effects: results. 76. s.d., Flourish: trumpet fanfare. 77. Require: request. 78. present: immediate. 79. tender: offer. 80. dear: in the double sense of "beloved" and "valuable."

But now her price is fall'n. Sir, there she stands.
If aught within that little seeming substance,[81]
Or all of it, with our displeasure pieced[82]
And nothing more, may fitly like[83] your Grace,
She's there, and she is yours.

BUR.: I know no answer.

LEAR: Will you, with those infirmities she owes,[84]
Unfriended, new-adopted to our hate,
Dowered with our curse and strangered with our oath,[85]
Take her, or leave her?

BUR.: Pardon me, royal sir,
Election makes not up on such conditions.[86]

LEAR: Then leave her, sir. For, by the power that made me,
I tell you all her wealth. [To FRANCE] For you, great King,
I would not from your love make such a stray,[87]
To match you where I hate. Therefore beseech you
To avert your liking[88] a more worthier way
Than on a wretch whom Nature[89] is ashamed
Almost to acknowledge hers.

FRANCE: This is most strange,
That she that even but now was your best object,
The argument[90] of your praise, balm of your age,
Most best, most dearest, should in this trice of time
Commit a thing so monstrous, to dismantle[91]
So many folds of favor. Sure, her offense
Must be of such unnatural degree
That monsters it,[92] or your forevouched[93] affection
Fall'n into taint.[94] Which to believe of her
Must be a faith that reason without miracle
Could never plant in me.[95]

COR.: I yet beseech your Majesty—
If for I want that glib and oily art,
To speak and purpose not,[96] since what I well intend

81. little . . . substance: creature that seems so small. Part of Lear's anger with Cordelia is that so small a body seems to hold so proud a heart.   82. pieced: added to it.   83. fitly like: suitably please.   84. owes: possesses.   85. strangered . . . oath: made a stranger to me by my oath.   86. Election . . . conditions: i.e., one does not choose one's wife on such conditions.   87. from . . . stray: remove myself so far from showing love to you.   88. avert . . . liking: turn your affection.   89. Nature: See Lear Intro. p. 1139b.   90. argument: topic.   91. dismantle: lit., take off (as a cloak).   92. monsters it: makes it a monster.   93. forevouched: previously declared.   94. Fall'n . . . taint: become bad.   95. Which . . . me: that is so contrary to reason that only a miracle could make me believe it.   96. and . . . not: and not mean it.

I'll do 't before I speak—that you make known
It is no vicious blot,[97] murder, or foulness,
No unchaste action or dishonored step,
That hath deprived me of your grace and favor,
But even for want of that for which I am richer,
A still-soliciting[98] eye, and such a tongue
As I am glad I have not, though not to have it
Hath lost me in[99] your liking.

LEAR: Better thou
Hadst not been born than not to have pleased me better.

FRANCE: Is it but this? A tardiness in nature[100]
Which often leaves the history unspoke
That it intends to do? My Lord of Burgundy,
What say you to the lady? Love's not love
When it is mingled with regards that stand
Aloof from the entire point.[101] Will you have her?
She is herself a dowry.

BUR.: Royal Lear,
Give but that portion which yourself proposed,
And here I take Cordelia by the hand,
Duchess of Burgundy.

LEAR: Nothing. I have sworn, I am firm.

BUR.: I am sorry then you have so lost a father
That you must lose a husband.

COR.: Peace be with Burgundy!
Since that respects of fortune[102] are his love,
I shall not be his wife.

FRANCE: Fairest Cordelia, that art most rich being poor,
Most choice forsaken, and most loved despised,
Thee and thy virtues here I seize upon,
Be it lawful I take up what's cast away.
Gods, gods! 'Tis strange that from their cold'st neglect
My love should kindle to inflamed respect.[103]
Thy dowerless daughter, King, thrown to my chance,
Is Queen of us, of ours, and our fair France.
Not all the dukes of waterish[104] Burgundy

---

97. vicious blot: vicious act which blots my honor. 98. still-soliciting: always begging favors. 99. lost me in: deprived me of. 100. tardiness in nature: natural slowness. 101. When . . . point: when it is mixed with other motives (the amount of the dowry) which have nothing to do with the thing itself (love). 102. respects of fortune: considerations of my dowry. 103. inflamed respect: warmer affection. 104. waterish: with the double meaning of "with many rivers" and "feeble."

Can buy this unprized precious maid of me.
Bid them farewell, Cordelia, though unkind.
Thou losest here, a better where to find.
LEAR: Thou hast her, France. Let her be thine, for we
Have no such daughter, nor shall ever see
That face of hers again. Therefore be gone
Without our grace, our love, our benison.[105]
Come, noble Burgundy.

> [*Flourish. Exeunt all but* FRANCE, GONERIL, REGAN, *and* CORDELIA.]

FRANCE: Bid farewell to your sisters.
COR.: The jewels of our father,[106] with washed[107] eyes
Cordelia leaves you. I know you what you are,
And, like a sister, am most loath to call
Your faults as they are named. Use well our father.
To your professèd[108] bosoms I commit him.
But yet, alas, stood I with his grace,[109]
I would prefer[110] him to a better place.
So farewell to you both.
REG.: Prescribe not us our duties.
GON.: Let your study
Be to content your lord, who hath received you
At Fortune's alms.[111] You have obedience scanted,[112]
And well are worth the want that you have wanted.[113]
COR.: Time shall unfold what plaited[114] cunning hides.
Who cover faults, at last shame them derides.
Well may you prosper!
FRANCE: Come, my fair Cordelia.

> [*Exeunt* FRANCE *and* CORDELIA.]

GON.: Sister,[115] it is not a little I have to say of what most nearly appertains to us both. I think our father will hence tonight.
REG.: That's most certain, and with you, next month with us.
GON.: You see how full of changes his age is, the observation we have made of it hath not been little. He always loved our sister most, and

---

105. benison: blessing. 106. The . . . father: i.e., creatures whom my father values so highly. 107. washed: weeping, but also made clearsighted by tears. 108. professed: which profess such love. 109. within . . . grace: in his favor. 110. prefer: promote. 111. At . . . alms: as an act of charity from Fortune. 112. scanted: neglected. 113. And . . . wanted: and well deserve the same lack of love which you have shown. 114. plaited: pleated, enfolded. Cf. ll. 220–21. 115. Sister . . . heat: The abrupt change from rhyme to prose marks the change from the emotion of the previous episodes to the cynical frankness of the two sisters.

with what poor judgment he hath now cast her off appears too grossly.

REG.: 'Tis the infirmity of his age. Yet he hath ever but slenderly known himself.

GON.: The best and soundest of his time hath been but rash. Then must we look to receive from his age not alone the imperfections of long-ingrafted condition,[116] but therewithal the unruly waywardness that infirm and choleric years bring with them.

REG.: Such unconstant starts[117] are we like to have from him as this of Kent's banishment.

GON.: There is further compliment[118] of leave-taking between France and him. Pray you, let's hit[119] together. If our father carry authority with such dispositions[120] as he bears, this last surrender of his will but offend us.

REG.: We shall further think on 't.

GON.: We must do something, and i' the heat.[121]

    [Exeunt.]

SCENE 2.   *The* EARL OF GLOUCESTER'S *castle.*

    [Enter EDMUND, *with a letter.]*

EDM.: Thou, Nature,[1] art my goddess, to thy law
My services are bound. Wherefore should I
Stand in the plague of custom, and permit
The curiosity of nations to deprive me,
For that I am some twelve or fourteen moonshines
Lag of a brother?[2] Why bastard? Wherefore base?
When my dimensions are as well compact,[3]
My mind as generous[4] and my shape as true,
As honest madam's issue? Why brand they us
With base? With baseness? Bastardy? Base, base?
Who in the lusty stealth of nature take
More composition and fierce quality[5]

---

116. long-ingrafted condition: temper which has long been part of his nature.
117. unconstant starts: sudden outbursts. 118. compliment: formality. 119. hit: agree. 120. dispositions: frame of mind. 121. i' the heat: while the iron is hot.

Sc. ii: 1. Thou, Nature: Edmund, the "natural" son of his father, appeals to Nature, whose doctrine is every man ruthlessly for himself. 2. Wherefore . . . brother: Why should I allow myself to be plagued by custom and nice distinctions (curiosity) which deprive me of my natural rights, because I am a year younger (lag: lagging behind) than my legitimate brother? 3. compact: put together, framed. 4. generous: noble. 5. more . . . quality: more fiber and ferocity.

Than doth, within a dull, stale, tired bed,
Go to the creating a whole tribe of fops[6]
Got[7] 'tween asleep and wake? Well then,
Legitimate Edgar, I must have your land.
Our father's love is to the bastard Edmund
As to the legitimate—fine word, "legitimate"!
Well, my legitimate, if this letter speed[8]
And my invention[9] thrive, Edmund the base
Shall top the legitimate. I grow, I prosper.
Now, gods, stand up for bastards!
      [*Enter* GLOUCESTER.]

GLO.: Kent banished thus! And France in choler parted!
And the King gone tonight! Subscribed[10] his power!
Confined to exhibition![11] All this done
Upon the gad![12] Edmund, how now! What news?

EDM.: So please your lordship, none.
      [*Putting up the letter.*]

GLO.: Why so earnestly seek you to put up that letter?

EDM.: I know no news, my lord.

GLO.: What paper were you reading?

EDM.: Nothing, my lord.[13]

GLO.: No? What needed then that terrible dispatch[14] of it into your pocket? The quality of nothing hath not such need to hide itself. Let's see. Come, if it be nothing, I shall not need spectacles.

EDM.: I beseech you, sir, pardon me. It is a letter from my brother that I have not all o'erread, and for so much as I have perused, I find it not fit for your o'erlooking.[15]

GLO.: Give me the letter, sir.

EDM.: I shall offend, either to detain or give it. The contents, as in part I understand them, are to blame.

GLO.: Let's see, let's see.

EDM.: I hope, for my brother's justification, he wrote this but as an essay[16] or taste of my virtue.

GLO. [*Reads.*]: "This policy and reverence of age[17] makes the world bitter to the best of our times,[18] keeps our fortunes from us till our

---

6. fops: fools. 7. Got: begotten. 8. speed: prosper. 9. invention: plan. 10. Subscribed: signed away. 11. Confined to exhibition: reduced to a pension. 12. gad: prick of a goad; i.e., the spur of the moment. 13. Nothing, my lord: Gloucester's tragedy also begins with the word "nothing." See I.i.89. 14. terrible dispatch: i.e., hasty thrusting. 15. o'erlooking: reading. 16. essay: trial. 17. policy . . . age: this custom of respecting old men. 18. best times: i.e., when we are still young.

oldness cannot relish them. I begin to find an idle and fond[19] bondage in the oppression of aged tyranny, who sways not as it hath power, but as it is suffered.[20] Come to me, that of this I may speak more. If our father would sleep till I waked him, you should enjoy half his revenue forever, and live the beloved of your brother, EDGAR." Hum! Conspiracy!—"Sleep till I waked him, you should enjoy half his revenue!"—My son Edgar! Had he a hand to write this? A heart and brain to breed it in? When came this to you? Who brought it?

EDM.: It was not brought me, my lord, there's the cunning of it. I found it thrown in at the casement[21] of my closet.[22]

GLO.: You know the character[23] to be your brother's?

EDM.: If the matter were good, my lord, I durst swear it were his, but in respect of that, I would fain think it were not.

GLO.: It is his.

EDM.: It is his hand, my lord, but I hope his heart is not in the contents.

GLO.: Hath he never heretofore sounded you in this business?

EDM.: Never, my lord. But I have heard him oft maintain it to be fit that, sons at perfect age and fathers declining, the father should be as ward to the son, and the son manage his revenue.

GLO.: Oh, villain, villain! His very opinion in the letter! Abhorred villain! Unnatural, detested, brutish villain! Worse than brutish! Go, sirrah, seek him—aye, apprehend him. Abominable villain! Where is he?

EDM.: I do not well know, my lord. If it shall please you to suspend your indignation against my brother till you can derive from him better testimony of his intent, you should run a certain course.[24] Where, if you violently proceed against him, mistaking his purpose, it would make a great gap[25] in your own honor and shake in pieces the heart of his obedience.[26] I dare pawn down my life for him that he hath wrote this to feel[27] my affection to your honor and to no further pretense of danger.

GLO.: You think so?

EDM.: If your honor judge it meet, I will place you where you shall hear us confer of this, and by an auricular assurance[28] have your satisfaction, and that without any further delay than this very evening.

GLO.: He cannot be such a monster—

---

19. fond: foolish. 20. suffered: allowed. 21. casement: window. 22. closet: room. 23. character: handwriting. 24. certain course: i.e., know where you are going. 25. gap: hole. 26. shake . . . obedience: cause him no longer to obey you loyally. 27. feel: test. 28. auricular assurance: proof heard with your own ears.

EDM.: Nor is not, sure.

GLO.: —to his father, that so tenderly and entirely loves him. Heaven and earth! Edmund, seek him out, wind me into him,[29] I pray you. Frame the business after your own wisdom. I would unstate myself, to be in a due resolution.[30]

EDM.: I will seek him, sir, presently,[31] convey[32] the business as I shall find means, and acquaint you withal.

GLO.: These late eclipses[33] in the sun and moon portend no good to us. Though the wisdom of nature[34] can reason[35] it thus and thus, yet nature finds itself scourged by the sequent[36] effects. Love cools, friendship falls off, brothers divide. In cities, mutinies; in countries, discord; in palaces, treason; and the bond cracked 'twixt son and father. This villain of mine comes under the prediction, there's son against father. The King falls from bias of nature,[37] there's father against child. We have seen the best of our time. Machinations, hollowness, treachery, and all ruinous disorders follow us disquietly to our graves. Find out this villain, Edmund, it shall lose thee nothing. Do it carefully. And the noble and true-hearted Kent banished! His offense, honesty! 'Tis strange.

[Exit.]

EDM.: This is the excellent foppery[38] of the world, that when we are sick in fortune—often the surfeit[39] of our own behavior—we make guilty of our disasters the sun, the moon, and the stars, as if we were villains by necessity, fools by heavenly compulsion; knaves, thieves, and treachers by spherical predominance;[40] drunkards, liars, and adulterers by an enforced obedience of planetary influence;[41] and all that we are evil in, by a divine thrusting on—an admirable evasion of whoremaster[42] man, to lay his goatish disposition to the charge of a star![43] My father compounded with my mother under the dragon's tail, and my nativity[44] was under Ursa Major,[45] so that it follows I am rough and lecherous. Tut, I should have been that I am had the

---

29. wind . . . him: worm your way into his confidence for me.   30. I . . . resolution: I would lose my earldom to learn the truth. This is one of many touches of bitter irony in this tragedy, for it is not until he has "unstated himself" that Gloucester does indeed learn the truth about his two sons.   31. presently: at once.   32. convey: manage.   33. These . . . eclipses: See Intro. *Lear*, p. 1136a and App. 2.   34. wisdom of nature: i.e., a rational explanation.   35. reason: explain.   36. sequent: subsequent.   37. bias of nature: natural inclination. See App. 13.   38. foppery: folly.   39. surfeit: lit., eating to excess and its results.   40. treachers . . . predominance: traitors because the stars so decreed when we were born.   41. enforced . . . influence: because we were forced to be so in obeying the influence of the stars.   42. whoremaster: lecherous.   43. to . . . star: to say that some star caused him to have the morals of a goat.   44. nativity: moment of birth.   45. Ursa Major: the Great Bear.

maidenliest star in the firmament twinkled on my bastardizing. Edgar—[*Enter* EDGAR.] And pat he comes like the catastrophe[46] of the old comedy. My cue is villainous melancholy, with a sigh like Tom o' Bedlam.[47] Oh, these eclipses do portend these divisions! Fa, sol, la, mi.[48]

EDG.: How now, Brother Edmund! What serious contemplation are you in?

EDM.: I am thinking, Brother, of a prediction I read this other day, what should follow these eclipses.

EDG.: Do you busy yourself about that?

EDM.: I promise you the effects he writes of succeed[49] unhappily, as of unnaturalness between the child and the parent; death, dearth, dissolutions of ancient amities;[50] divisions in state, menaces and maledictions against King and nobles; needless diffidences,[51] banishment of friends, dissipation of cohorts,[52] nuptial breaches, and I know not what.

EDG.: How long have you been a sectary astronomical?[53]

EDM.: Come, come, when saw you my father last?

EDG.: Why, the night gone by.

EDM.: Spake you with him?

EDG.: Aye, two hours together.

EDM.: Parted you in good terms? Found you no displeasure in him by word or countenance?

EDG.: None at all.

EDM.: Bethink yourself wherein you may have offended him. And at my entreaty forbear his presence till some little time hath qualified[54] the heat of his displeasure, which at this instant so rageth in him that with the mischief of your person it would scarcely allay.[55]

EDG.: Some villain hath done me wrong.

EDM.: That's my fear. I pray you have a continent forbearance[56] till the speed of his rage goes slower, and, as I say, retire with me to my lodging, from whence I will fitly bring you to hear my lord speak. Pray ye, go, there's my key. If you do stir abroad, go armed.

---

46. catastrophe: the final episode. 47. my . . . Bedlam: I must now pretend to be a melancholic and sigh like a lunatic beggar. Tom o' Bedlam was a lunatic discharged from Bedlam (Bethlehem Hospital for lunatics). See II.iii.14. 48. Fa . . . mi: Edmund hums to himself. 49. succeed: follow. 50. amities: friendships. 51. diffidences: distrusts. 52. dissipation of cohorts: breaking-up of established friendships (lit., of troops of soldiers). 53. sectary astronomical: a follower of the sect of astrologers. 54. qualified: lessened. 55. with . . . allay: it would scarcely be lessened even if he did you some bodily injury. 56. continent forbearance: self-control which will keep you from any rash action.

EDG.: Armed, Brother!

EDM.: Brother, I advise you to the best—go armed. I am no honest man if there be any good meaning toward you. I have told you what I have seen and heard, but faintly, nothing like the image and horror of it. Pray you, away.

EDG.: Shall I hear from you anon?

EDM.: I do serve you in this business.

    [*Exit* EDGAR.]

    A credulous father, and a brother noble,
    Whose nature is so far from doing harms
    That he suspects none, on whose foolish honesty
    My practices[57] ride easy. I see the business.
    Let me, if not by birth, have lands by wit.
    All with me's meet[58] that I can fashion fit.[59]

        [*Exit.*]

SCENE 3.   *The* DUKE OF ALBANY's *palace.*

    [*Enter* GONERIL *and* OSWALD, *her steward.*]

GON.: Did my father strike my gentleman for chiding of his fool?[1]

OSW.: Yes, madam.

GON.: By day and night he wrongs me. Every hour
    He flashes into one gross crime or other
    That sets us all at odds. I'll not endure it.
    His knights grow riotous, and himself upbraids us
    On every trifle. When he returns from hunting,
    I will not speak with him. Say I am sick.
    If you come slack of former services,[2]
    You shall do well, the fault of it I'll answer.

OSW.: He's coming, madam, I hear him.

    [*Horns within.*]

GON.: Put on what weary negligence you please,
    You and your fellows, I'd have it come to question.[3]
    If he distaste it, let him to our sister,
    Whose mind and mine, I know, in that are one,
    Not to be overruled. Idle old man,
    That still would manage those authorities

---

57. practices: plots. 58. meet: suitable. 59. fashion fit: make fit my purposes.

Sc. iii: 1. fool: professional jester. See Pl. 12j, 13c. 2. come . . . services: do not wait on him as efficiently as you used to. 3. to question: or in modern slang, to a showdown.

That he hath given away! Now, by my life,
Old fools are babes again, and must be used
With checks as flatteries when they are seen abused.[4]
Remember what I tell you.

OSW.: Very well, madam.

GON.: And let his knights have colder looks among you.
What grows of it, no matter, advise your fellows so.
I would breed from hence occasions,[5] and I shall,
That I may speak. I'll write straight to my sister
To hold my very course. Prepare for dinner.

    [*Exeunt.*]

SCENE 4. *A hall in the same.*

    [*Enter* KENT, *disguised.*]

KENT: If but as well I other accents borrow
That can my speech defuse,[1] my good intent
May carry through itself to that full issue
For which I razed[2] my likeness. Now, banished Kent,
If thou canst serve where thou dost stand condemned,
So may it come, thy master whom thou lovest
Shall find thee full of labors.

    [*Horns within.*[3] *Enter* LEAR, KNIGHTS, *and* ATTENDANTS.]

LEAR: Let me not stay a jot for dinner. Go get it ready. [*Exit an* AT-
TENDANT.] How now! What are thou?

KENT: A man, sir.

LEAR: What dost thou profess?[4] What wouldst thou with us?

KENT: I do profess to be no less than I seem—to serve him truly that
will put me in trust, to love him that is honest, to converse with him
that is wise and says little, to fear judgment,[5] to fight when I cannot
choose, and to eat no fish.[6]

LEAR: What art thou?

KENT: A very honest-hearted fellow, and as poor as the King.

LEAR: If thou be as poor for a subject as he is for a king, thou art poor
enough. What wouldst thou?

---

4. Old . . . abused: old men must be treated like babies, and scolded, not flattered, when they are naughty.   5. breed . . . occasions: find excuses for taking
action.

Sc. iv: 1. defuse: make indistinct, disguise.   2. razed: lit., shaved off, disguised.
3. s.d., within: off stage.   4. What . . . profess: what is your profession?
5. judgment: The Day of Judgment; i.e., I have a conscience.   6. eat no fish:
I don't observe fast days, and am therefore no Catholic.

KENT: Service.

LEAR: Who wouldst thou serve?

KENT: You.

LEAR: Dost thou know me, fellow?

KENT: No, sir, but you have that in your countenance[7] which I would fain call master.

LEAR: What's that?

KENT: Authority.

LEAR: What services canst thou do?

KENT: I can keep honest counsel, ride, run, mar a curious tale in telling it,[8] and deliver a plain message bluntly. That which ordinary men are fit for, I am qualified in, and the best of me is diligence.

LEAR: How old art thou?

KENT: Not so young, sir, to love a woman for singing, nor so old to dote on her for anything. I have years on my back forty-eight.

LEAR: Follow me, thou shalt serve me. If I like thee no worse after dinner, I will not part from thee yet. Dinner, ho, dinner! Where's my knave? My fool? Go you, and call my fool hither. [*Exit an* AT-TENDANT. *Enter* OSWALD.] You, you, sirrah, where's my daughter?

OSW.: So please you—
                    [*Exit.*]

LEAR: What says the fellow there? Call the clotpoll[9] back. [*Exit a* KNIGHT.] Where's my fool, ho? I think the world's asleep. [*Re-enter* KNIGHT.] How now! Where's that mongrel?

KNIGHT. He says, my lord, your daughter is not well.

LEAR: Why came not the slave back to me when I called him?

KNIGHT: Sir, he answered me, in the roundest[10] manner, he would not.

LEAR: He would not!

KNIGHT: My lord, I know not what the matter is, but, to my judgment, your Highness is not entertained[11] with that ceremonious affection[12] as you were wont. There's a great abatement of kindness appears as well in the general dependents[13] as in the Duke himself also and your daughter.

LEAR: Ha! Sayest thou so?

7. countenance: bearing. 8. mar . . . it: I'm not one to delight in overelaborate (curious) phrases when telling my tale; i.e., he will have none of the fantastic talk of the typical courtier—such as Shakespeare mocks in the character of Osric (see *Haml*, V.ii.81–201). Kent himself mimics this fashion later (II.ii.111–14). 9. clotpoll: clodpole, blockhead. 10. roundest: plainest. 11. entertained: treated. 12. ceremonious affection: affection which shows itself in ceremony. Manners even between children and parents were very formal. Neglect of courtesies to the King shows deliberate disrespect. 13. dependents: servants of the house.

KNIGHT: I beseech you pardon me, my lord, if I be mistaken, for my duty cannot be silent when I think your Highness wronged.

LEAR: Thou but rememberest[14] me of mine own conception. I have perceived a most faint neglect[15] of late, which I have rather blamed as mine own jealous curiosity[16] than as a very pretense[17] and purpose of unkindness. I will look further into 't. But where's my fool? I have not seen him this two days.

KNIGHT: Since my young lady's going into France, sir, the fool hath much pined away.

LEAR: No more of that, I have noted it well. Go you, and tell my daughter I would speak with her. [*Exit an* ATTENDANT.] Go you, call hither my fool. [*Exit an* ATTENDANT. *Re-enter* OSWALD.] Oh, you sir, you, come you hither, sir. Who am I, sir?

OSW.: My lady's father.

LEAR: My lady's father! My lord's knave. You whoreson dog! You slave! You cur!

OSW.: I am none of these, my lord, I beseech your pardon.

LEAR: Do you bandy[18] looks with me, you rascal?

[*Striking him.*]

OSW.: I'll not be struck, my lord.

KENT: Nor tripped neither, you base football player.

[*Tripping up his heels.*]

LEAR: I thank thee, fellow. Thou servest me, and I'll love thee.

KENT: Come, sir, arise, away! I'll teach you differences.[19] Away, away! If you will measure your lubber's length again, tarry. But away! Go to, have you wisdom? So.

[*Pushes* OSWALD *out.*]

LEAR: Now, my friendly knave, I thank thee. There's earnest[20] of thy service.

[*Giving* KENT *money.*]

[*Enter* FOOL.]

FOOL: Let me hire him too. Here's my coxcomb.[21]

[*Offering* KENT *his cap.*]

LEAR: How now, my pretty knave! How dost thou?

FOOL: Sirrah, you were best take my coxcomb.

KENT: Why, fool?

---

14. rememberest: remind. 15. faint neglect: i.e., the "weary negligence" commanded by Goneril (I.iii.12). 16. jealous curiosity: excessive suspicion. 17. pretense: deliberate intention. 18. bandy: lit., hit the ball to and fro as in tennis. 19. differences of rank. 20. earnest: money given on account of services to be rendered. Lear thus formally engages Kent as his servant. 21. coxcomb: the cap shaped like a cock's comb (crest) worn by the professional fool.

FOOL: Why, for taking one's part that's out of favor. Nay, an thou canst not smile as the wind sits,[22] thou'lt catch cold shortly. There, take my coxcomb. Why, this fellow hath banished two on 's daughters, and done the third a blessing against his will. If thou follow him, thou must needs wear my coxcomb. How now, Nuncle![23] Would I had two coxcombs and two daughters!

LEAR: Why, my boy?

FOOL: If I gave them all my living, I'd keep my coxcombs myself. There's mine, beg another of thy daughters.

LEAR: Take heed, sirrah, the whip.[24]

FOOL: Truth's a dog must to kennel. He must be whipped out, when Lady the brach[25] may stand by the fire and stink.

LEAR: A pestilent gall to me![26]

FOOL: Sirrah, I'll teach thee a speech.

LEAR: Do.

FOOL: Mark it, Nuncle:

> "Have more than thou showest,
> Speak less than thou knowest,
> Lend less than thou owest,[27]
> Ride more than thou goest,[28]
> Learn more than thou trowest,[29]
> Set less than thou throwest.[30]
> Leave thy drink and thy whore,
> And keep in-a-door,
> And thou shalt have more
> Than two tens to a score."[31]

KENT: This is nothing, fool.

FOOL: Then 'tis like the breath of an unfeed lawyer. You gave me nothing for 't. Can you make no use of nothing, Nuncle?

LEAR: Why, no, boy, nothing can be made out of nothing.[32]

FOOL: [To KENT] Prithee tell him so much the rent of his land comes to. He will not believe a fool.

LEAR: A bitter fool!

---

22. an . . . sits: i.e., if you can't curry favor with those in power.   23. Nuncle: Uncle.   24. the whip: The fool's profession was precarious, and in real life too smart a joke brought its painful reward. In March 1605 Stone, a professional fool, was whipped for commenting on the diplomatic mission about to sail for Spain that "there went sixty fools into Spain, besides my Lord Admiral and his two sons."   25. Lady . . . brach: Lady the pet bitch.   26. A . . . me: this pestilent fool rubs me on a sore spot.   27. owest: possess.   28. goest: walk.   29. trowest: know.   30. Set . . . throwest: don't bet a larger stake than you can afford to lose.   31. And . . . score: and then your money will increase.   32. nothing . . . nothing: Lear unconsciously repeats himself. See I.i.92.

FOOL: Dost thou know the difference, my boy, between a bitter fool and a sweet fool?

LEAR: No, lad, teach me.

FOOL:
> "That lord that counseled thee
> To give away thy land,
> Come place him here by me,
> Do thou for him stand.
> The sweet and bitter fool
> Will presently appear—
> The one in motley[33] here,
> The other found out there."

LEAR: Dost thou call me fool, boy?

FOOL: All thy titles thou hast given away. That thou wast born with.

KENT: This is not altogether fool, my lord.

FOOL: No, faith, lords and great men will not let me.[34] If I had a monopoly[35] out, they would have part on 't. And ladies, too, they will not let me have all the fool to myself, they'll be snatching. Give me an egg, Nuncle, and I'll give thee two crowns.

LEAR: What two crowns shall they be?

FOOL: Why, after I have cut the egg in the middle and eat up the meat, the two crowns of the egg. When thou clovest thy crown i' the middle and gavest away both parts, thou borest thine ass on thy back o'er the dirt.[36] Thou hadst little wit in thy bald crown when thou gavest thy golden one away. If I speak like myself[37] in this, let him be whipped that first finds it so. [*Singing*]
> "Fools had ne'er less wit in a year,
> For wise men are grown foppish,
> And know not how their wits to wear,
> Their manners are so apish."[38]

LEAR: When were you wont to be so full of songs, sirrah?

FOOL: I have used it, Nuncle, ever since thou madest thy daughters thy mother. For when thou gavest them the rod and puttest down thine own breeches, [*Singing*]
> "Then they for sudden joy did weep,
> And I for sorrow sung,

---

33. motley: the particolored uniform worn by a fool. 34. will . . . me: i.e., keep all my folly to myself. 35. monopoly: a royal patent giving the holders the sole right to deal in some commodity. The granting of such monopolies to courtiers was one of the crying scandals of the time. 36. thine . . . dirt: an old tale of the typical simple-minded countryman. 37. like myself: i.e., like a fool. 38. Fools . . . apish: there's no job left for fools nowadays, because the wise men are so like them. apish: like apes, who always imitate.

> That such a king should play bopeep,
>   And go the fools among."

Prithee, Nuncle, keep a schoolmaster that can teach thy fool to lie. I would fain learn to lie.

LEAR: An[39] you lie, sirrah, we'll have you whipped.

FOOL: I marvel what kin thou and thy daughters are. They'll have me whipped for speaking true, thou'lt have me whipped for lying, and sometimes I am whipped for holding my peace. I had rather be any kind o' thing than a fool. And yet I would not be thee, Nuncle. Thou hast pared thy wit o' both sides and left nothing i' the middle. Here comes one o' the parings.

> [Enter GONERIL.]

LEAR: How now, Daughter! What makes that frontlet[40] on? Methinks you are too much of late i' the frown.

FOOL: Thou wast a pretty fellow when thou hadst no need to care for her frowning. Now thou art an O without a figure.[41] I am better than thou art now. I am a fool, thou art nothing. [To GONERIL] Yes, forsooth, I will hold my tongue, so your face bids me, though you say nothing.

> "Mum, mum.
>   He that keeps nor crust nor crumb,[42]
>   Weary of all, shall want some."

[Pointing to LEAR] That's a shealed peascod.[43]

GON.: Not only, sir, this your all-licensed[44] fool,
But other of your insolent retinue
Do hourly carp[45] and quarrel, breaking forth
In rank and not to be endurèd riots. Sir,
I had thought, by making this well known unto you,
To have found a safe redress, but now grow fearful
By what yourself too late have spoke and done
That you protect this course and put it on[46]
By your allowance.[47] Which if you should, the fault
Would not 'scape censure, nor the redresses sleep,
Which, in the tender of a wholesome weal,
Might in their working do you that offense
Which else were shame, that then necessity
Will call discreet proceeding.[48]

---

39. An: if. 40. frontlet: frown; lit., a band worn on the forehead. 41. an . . . figure: a cipher. 42. crumb: inside of the loaf. 43. shealed peascod: a shelled peapod. 44. all-licensed: allowed to take all liberties. 45. carp: find fault. 46. put it on: encourage it. 47. allowance: approval. 48. Which . . . proceeding: if you continue to be a nuisance I shall be forced to keep my

FOOL For, you know, Nuncle,
"The hedge sparrow fed the cuckoo[49] so long
That it had it head bit off by it young."
So out went the candle, and we were left darkling.[50]
LEAR: Are you our daughter?
GON.: Come, sir,
I would you would make use of that good wisdom
Whereof I know you are fraught,[51] and put away
These dispositions[52] that of late transform you
From what you rightly are.
FOOL: May not an ass know when the cart draws the horse? Whoop,
Jug! I love thee.[53]
LEAR: Doth any here know me? This is not Lear.
Doth Lear walk thus? Speak thus? Where are his eyes?
Either his notion[54] weakens, his discernings
Are lethargied[55]—— Ha! Waking? 'Tis not so.
Who is it that can tell me who I am?
FOOL: Lear's shadow.
LEAR: I would learn that, for, by the marks of sovereignty,[56] knowledge,
and reason, I should be false persuaded I had daughters.
FOOL: Which they will make an obedient father.
LEAR: Your name, fair gentlewoman?
GON.: This admiration,[57] sir, is much o' the savor
Of[58] other your new pranks. I do beseech you
To understand my purposes aright.
As you are old and reverend, you should be wise.
Here do you keep a hundred knights and squires,
Men so disordered,[59] so deboshed[60] and bold,
That this our Court, infected with their manners,
Shows like a riotous inn. Epicurism[61] and lust
Make it more like a tavern or a brothel
Than a graced[62] palace. The same itself doth speak
For instant remedy. Be then desired

---

state peaceful by taking measures which will annoy you and would at other
times be shameful toward a father, but would be justified as mere discretion.
49. cuckoo: for the habit of the cuckoo see App. 11. 50. darkling: in the dark.
51. fraught: stored, endowed. 52. dispositions: moods. 53. Whoop . . .
thee: one of the meaningless cries made by the fool to distract attention. 54.
notion: understanding. 55. lethargied: paralyzed. 56. marks of sovereignty:
the outward signs which show that I am King. 57. admiration: pretended
astonishment. 58. much . . . Of: tastes much the same as. 59. disordered:
disorderly. 60. deboshed: debauched. 61. Epicurism: self-indulgence, riotous living. 62. graced: gracious.

By her that else will take the thing she begs
A little to disquantity your train,[63]
And the remainder that shall still depend,[64]
To be such men as may besort[65] your age,
Which know themselves and you.

LEAR: Darkness and devils!
Saddle my horses, call my train together.
Degenerate bastard! I'll not trouble thee.
Yet have I left a daughter.

GON.: You strike my people, and your disordered rabble
Make servants of their betters.
[Enter ALBANY.]

LEAR: Woe, that too late repents.—[To ALBANY] Oh, sir, are you come?
Is it your will? Speak, sir. Prepare my horses.
Ingratitude, thou marble-hearted fiend,
More hideous when thou show'st thee in a child
Than the sea monster!

ALB.: Pray, sir, be patient.

LEAR: [To GONERIL] Detested kite![66] Thou liest.
My train are men of choice and rarest parts,[67]
That all particulars of duty know,
And in the most exact regard support
The worships of their name.[68] O most small fault,
How ugly didst thou in Cordelia show!
That, like an engine, wrenched my frame of nature
From the fixed place,[69] drew from my heart all love
And added to the gall.[70] O Lear, Lear, Lear!
Beat at this gate, that let thy folly in
[Striking his head]
And thy dear judgment out![71] Go, go, my people.

ALB. My lord, I am guiltless, as I am ignorant
Of what hath moved you.

LEAR: It may be so, my lord.
Hear, Nature, hear,[72] dear goddess, hear!
Suspend thy purpose if thou didst intend

---

63. disquantity . . . train: diminish the number of your followers. 64. depend: be your dependents. 65. besort: be suitable for. 66. kite: the lowest of the birds of prey, an eater of offal. 67. parts: accomplishments. 68. in . . . name: and in every minute detail uphold their honorable names. 69. like . . . place: like a little instrument (e.g., a lever) dislodged my firm nature. 70. gall: bitterness. 71. Beat . . . out: the first signs of madness in Lear. 72. Hear . . . hear: In making this terrible curse, Lear also calls on Nature, but as goddess of natural affection. Cf. I.ii.1–22.

To make this creature fruitful.
Into her womb convey sterility.
Dry up in her the organs of increase,[73]
And from her derogate[74] body never spring
A babe to honor her! If she must teem,[75]
Create her child of spleen,[76] that it may live
And be a thwart disnatured[77] torment to her.
Let it stamp wrinkles in her brow of youth,
With cadent[78] tears fret[79] channels in her cheeks,
Turn all her mother's pains and benefits
To laughter and contempt, that she may feel
How sharper than a serpent's tooth it is
To have a thankless child! Away, away!
        [Exit.]
ALB.: Now, gods that we adore, whereof comes this?
GON.: Never afflict yourself to know the cause,
    But let his disposition have that scope
    That dotage gives it.
        [Re-enter LEAR.]
LEAR: What, fifty of my followers at a clap![80]
    Within a fortnight![81]
ALB.: What's the matter, sir?
LEAR: I'll tell thee. [To GONERIL] Life and death! I am ashamed
    That thou hast power to shake my manhood[82] thus,
    That these hot tears, which break from me perforce,
    Should make thee worth them. Blasts and frogs upon thee!
    The untented woundings[83] of a father's curse
    Pierce every sense about thee! Old fond[84] eyes,
    Beweep this cause again, I'll pluck ye out
    And cast you with the waters that you lose
    To temper[85] clay. Yea, is it come to this?
    Let it be so. Yet have I left a daughter
    Who I am sure is kind and comfortable.[86]

---

73. increase: childbearing. 74. derogate: debased. 75. teem: conceive. 76. spleen: malice. 77. thwart disnatured: perverse and unnatural. 78. cadent: falling. 79. fret: wear away. 80. at a clap: at one blow. 81. What . . . fortnight: As Lear goes out he learns that Goneril has herself already begun to take steps "a little to disquantity his train" by ordering that fifty of them shall depart within a fortnight. To a man who regards his own dignity so highly, this fresh blow is devastating. 82. shake my manhood: i.e., with sobs. 83. untented woundings: raw wounds. A tent was a small roll of lint used to clean out a wound before it was bound up. 84. fond: foolish. 85. temper: mix. 86. comfortable: full of comfort.

When she shall hear this of thee, with her nails
She'll flay thy wolvish visage. Thou shalt find
That I'll resume the shape which thou dost think
I have cast off forever. Thou shalt, I warrant thee.
[*Exeunt* LEAR, KENT, *and* ATTENDANTS.]
GON.: Do you mark that, my lord?
ALB.: I[87] cannot be so partial, Goneril,
To the great love I bear you—
GON.: Pray you, content. What, Oswald, ho!
[*To the* FOOL] You, sir, more knave than fool, after your master.
FOOL: Nuncle Lear, Nuncle Lear, tarry, take the fool with thee.[88]
"A fox, when one has caught her,
And such a daughter,
Should be sure to the slaughter,
If my cap would buy a halter.
So the fool follows after."
[*Exit.*]
GON.: This man hath had good counsel. A hundred knights!
'Tis politic[89] and safe to let him keep
At point[90] a hundred knights. Yes, that on every dream,
Each buzz,[91] each fancy, each complaint, dislike,
He may enguard his dotage with their powers
And hold our lives in mercy. Oswald, I say!
ALB.: Well, you may fear too far.
GON.: Safer than trust too far.
Let me still take away the harms I fear,
Not fear still to be taken.[92] I know his heart.
What he hath uttered I have writ my sister.
If she sustain him and his hundred knights
When I have showed the unfitness—
[*Re-enter* OSWALD.] How now, Oswald!
What, have you writ that letter to my sister?
OSW.: Yes, madam.
GON.: Take you some company, and away to horse.
Inform her full of my particular fear,
And thereto add such reasons of your own
As may compact it more.[93] Get you gone,

---

87. I . . . you: i.e., although my love makes me partial to you, yet I must protest.
88. take . . . thee: i.e., take your fool and your own folly. 89. politic: good
policy. 90. At point: fully armed. 91. buzz: rumor. 92. Let . . . taken:
let me always remove what I fear will harm me rather than live in perpetual
fear. 93. compact it more: make my argument more convincing.

And hasten your return. [*Exit* OSWALD.] No, no, my lord,
This milky gentleness and course[94] of yours
Though I condemn not, yet, under pardon,
You are much more attasked[95] for want of wisdom
Than praised for harmful mildness.[96]

ALB.: How far your eyes may pierce I cannot tell.
    Striving to better, oft we mar what's well.

GON.: Nay, then—

ALB.: Well, well, the event.[97]
      [*Exeunt.*]

SCENE 5.   *Court before the same.*

      [*Enter* LEAR, KENT, *and* FOOL.]

LEAR: Go you before to Gloucester with these letters. Acquaint my
daughter no further with anything you know than comes from her
demand out of the letter. If your diligence be not speedy, I shall
be there afore you.

KENT: I will not sleep, my lord, till I have delivered your letter.
      [*Exit.*]

FOOL: If a man's brains were in 's heels, were 't not in danger of kibes?[1]

LEAR: Aye, boy.

FOOL: Then I prithee be merry. Thy wit shall ne'er go slipshod.[2]

LEAR: Ha, ha, ha!

FOOL: Shalt see thy other daughter will use thee kindly,[3] for though
she's as like this as a crab's[4] like an apple, yet I can tell what I can tell.

LEAR: Why, what canst thou tell, my boy?

FOOL: She will taste as like this as a crab does to a crab. Thou canst tell
why one's nose stands i' the middle on 's face?

LEAR: No.

FOOL: Why, to keep one's eyes of either side 's nose, that what a man
cannot smell out he may spy into.

LEAR: I did her wrong—

FOOL: Canst tell how an oyster makes his shell?

LEAR: No.

FOOL: Nor I neither, but I can tell why a snail has a house.

---

94. milky . . . course: this milksop behavior. 95. attasked: blamed. 96. harmful mildness: a mildness which may prove harmful. 97. the event: i.e., we
must see what will happen.

Sc. v: 1. kibes: chilblains. 2. Thy . . . slipshod: i.e., you don't need slippers, for
you have no brains to be protected from chilblains. 3. kindly: after her kind;
i.e., nature. 4. crab: crab apple.

LEAR: Why?

FOOL: Why, to put 's head in, not to give it away to his daughters and leave his horns without a case.

LEAR: I will forget my nature.—So kind a father!—Be my horses ready?

FOOL: Thy asses are gone about 'em. The reason why the seven stars are no more than seven is a pretty reason.

LEAR: Because they are not eight?

FOOL: Yes, indeed. Thou wouldst make a good fool.

LEAR: To take 't again perforce![5] Monster ingratitude!

FOOL: If thou wert my fool, Nuncle, I'd have thee beaten for being old before thy time.

LEAR: How's that?

FOOL: Thou shouldst not have been old till thou hadst been wise.

LEAR: Oh, let me not be mad, not mad, sweet Heaven!
Keep me in temper.[6] I would not be mad!
[Enter GENTLEMAN.] How now! Art the horses ready?

GENT.: Ready, my lord.

LEAR: Come, boy.

FOOL: She that's a maid now and laughs at my departure
Shall not be a maid long, unless things be cut shorter.
[Exeunt.]

🎭 Act II

SCENE 1.   *The* EARL OF GLOUCESTER's *castle.*

[Enter EDMUND and CURAN, meeting.]

EDM.: Save thee,[1] Curan.

CUR.: And you, sir. I have been with your father, and given him notice that the Duke of Cornwall and Regan his Duchess will be here with him this night.

EDM.: How comes that?

CUR.: Nay, I know not. You have heard of the news abroad—I mean the whispered ones, for they are yet but ear-kissing[2] arguments?

EDM.: Not I. Pray you what are they?

---

5. To . . . perforce: I will take back my kingdom by force.   6. temper: sanity.

Act II, Sc. i: 1. Save thee: God save thee.   2. ear-kissing: whispered close in the ear.

CUR.: Have you heard of no likely wars toward 'twixt the Dukes of
  Cornwall and Albany?
EDM.: Not a word.
CUR.: You may do, then, in time. Fare you well, sir.
  [*Exit.*]
EDM.: The Duke be here tonight? The better! Best!
  This weaves itself perforce into my business.
  My father hath set guard to take my brother,
  And I have one thing, of a queasy question,[3]
  Which I must act. Briefness and fortune, work!
  Brother, a word, descend.[4] Brother, I say!
  [*Enter* EGAR.] My father watches. O sir, fly this place.
  Intelligence[5] is given where you are hid.
  You have now the good advantage of the night.
  Have you not spoken 'gainst the Duke of Cornwall?
  He's coming hither, now, i' the night, i' the haste,
  And Regan with him. Have you nothing said
  Upon his party 'gainst the Duke of Albany?
  Advise yourself.
EDG.: I am sure on 't, not a word.
EDM.: I hear my father coming. Pardon me,
  In cunning[6] I must draw my sword upon you.
  Draw. Seem to defend yourself. Now quit you well.[7]
  Yield. Come before my father. Light, ho, here!
  Fly, Brother. Torches, torches! So farewell.
    [*Exit* EDGAR.]
  Some blood drawn on me would beget opinion[8]
    [*Wounds his arm.*]
  Of my more fierce endeavor. I have seen drunkards
  Do more than this in sport. Father, Father!
  Stop, stop! No help?
    [*Enter* GLOUCESTER *and* SERVANTS *with torches.*]
GLO.: Now, Edmund, where's the villain?
EDM.: Here stood he in the dark, his sharp sword out,
  Mumbling[9] of wicked charms, conjuring the moon[10]
  To stand 's auspicious[11] mistress.

---

3. queasy question: which needs delicate handling; queasy means on the point of
  vomiting. 4. descend: i.e., from the chamber where he has been hiding.
  5. Intelligence: information. 6. In cunning: as a pretense. 7. quit . . . well:
  defend yourself well. Here they clash their swords together. 8. beget opinion:
  give the impression. 9. Mumbling . . . mistress: This is the kind of story
  which would especially appeal to Gloucester. Cf. I.ii.112. 10. conjuring . . .
  moon: calling on Hecate, goddess of witchcraft. 11. suspicious: favorable.

GLO.: But where is he?

EDM.: Look, sir, I bleed.

GLO.: Where is the villain, Edmund?

EDM.: Fled this way, sir. When by no means he could—

GLO.: Pursue him, ho!—Go after.

    [Exeunt some SERVANTS.]

  "By no means" what?

EDM.: Persuade me to the murder of your lordship,
But that I told him the revenging gods
'Gainst parricides did all their thunders bend,
Spoke with how manifold and strong a bond
The child was bound to the father. Sir, in fine,[12]
Seeing how loathly opposite I stood[13]
To his unnatural purpose, in fell[14] motion
With his preparèd[15] sword he charges home
My unprovided[16] body, lanced mine arm.
But when he saw my best alarumed spirits[17]
Bold in the quarrel's right, roused to the encounter,
Or whether gasted[18] by the noise I made,
Full suddenly he fled.

GLO.: Let him fly far.
Not in this land shall he remain uncaught,
And found—dispatch.[19] The noble Duke my master,
My worthy arch and patron,[20] comes tonight.
By his authority I will proclaim it,
That he which finds him shall deserve our thanks,
Bringing the murderous caitiff[21] to the stake.[22]
He that conceals him, death.

EDM.: When I dissuaded him from his intent
And found him pight[23] to do it, with curst[24] speech
I threatened to discover him. He replied,
"Thou unpossessing bastard! Dost thou think,
If I would stand against thee, could the reposal
Of any trust, virtue, or worth in thee
Make thy words faithed?[25] No. What I should deny—
As this I would, aye, though thou didst produce

---

12. in fine: in short. 13. how . . . stood; with what loathing I opposed. 14. fell: fearful. 15. prepared: drawn. 16. unprovided: unguarded. 17. my . . . spirits: my stoutest spirits called out by the alarm. 18. gasted: terrified. 19. And . . . dispatch: and when he's found, kill him. 20. arch . . . patron: chief support and protector. 21. caitiff: wretch; lit., captive. 22. to . . . stake: i.e., place of execution. 23. pight: determined. 24. curst: bitter. 25. faithed: believed.

My very character[26]—I'd turn it all[27]
To thy suggestion,[28] plot, and damnèd practice.[29]
And thou must make[30] a dullard of the world
If they not thought the profits of my death
Were very pregnant and potential spurs[31]
To make thee seek it."

GLO.: Strong and fastened[32] villain!
Would he deny his letter? I never got[33] him.

[*Tucket[34] within*]

Hark, the Duke's trumpets! I know not why he comes.
All ports I'll bar,[35] the villain shall not 'scape,
The Duke must grant me that. Besides, his picture
I will send far and near, that all the kingdom
May have due note of him, and of my land,
Loyal and natural[36] boy, I'll work the means
To make thee capable.[37]

[*Enter* CORNWALL, REGAN, *and* ATTENDANTS.]

CORN.: How now, my noble friend! Since I came hither,
Which I can call but now, I have heard strange news.
REG.: If it be true, all vengeance comes too short
Which can pursue the offender. How dost, my lord?
GLO.: Oh, madam, my old heart is cracked, is cracked!
REG.: What, did my father's godson seek your life?
He whom my father named? Your Edgar?
GLO.: Oh, lady, lady, shame would have it hid!
REG.: Was he not companion with the riotous knights
That tend upon my father?
GLO.: I know not, madam. 'Tis too bad, too bad.
EDM.: Yes, madam, he was of that consort.[38]
REG.: No marvel then, though he were ill affected.[39]
'Tis they have put him on[40] the old man's death,
To have the waste and spoil of his revènues.
I have this present evening from my sister

---

26. character: handwriting. Cf. I.ii.66. 27. turn it all: make it appear to be.
28. suggestion: idea. 29. practice: plot. 30. make . . . it: you would have
to make people dull indeed before they would disbelieve that your chief motive
was to benefit by my death. 31. pregnant . . . spurs: obvious and powerful
encouragements. 32. fastened: confirmed. 33. got: begot. 34. s.d., Tucket:
trumpet call. 35. ports . . . bar: I'll have the seaports watched to prevent his
escape. 36. natural: i.e., one who has the proper feelings of son to father.
Gloucester does not as yet realize what "nature" means to Edmund. See I.ii.1.
37. capable: i.e., legitimate; lit., capable of succeeding as my heir. 38. consort: party. 39. though . . . affected: if he had traitorous thoughts. 40. put
. . . on: persuaded him to cause.

Been well informed of them, and with such cautions
That if they come to sojourn at my house,
I'll not be there.

CORN.: Nor I, assure thee, Regan.
Edmund, I hear that you have shown your father
A childlike office.[41]

EDM.: 'Twas my duty, sir.

GLO.: He did bewray[42] his practice, and received
This hurt you see, striving to apprehend him.

CORN.: Is he pursued?

GLO.: Aye, my good lord.

CORN.: If he be taken, he shall never more
Be feared of doing[43] harm. Make your own purpose,
How in my strength you please.[44] For you, Edmund,
Whose virtue and obedience doth this instant
So much commend itself, you shall be ours.
Natures of such deep trust we shall much need.
You we first seize on.

EDM.: I shall serve you, sir,
Truly, however else.

GLO.: For him I thank your Grace.

CORN.: You know not why we came to visit you—

REG.: Thus out of season, threading dark-eyed night.[45]
Occasions, noble Gloucester, of some poise,[46]
Wherein we must have use of your advice.
Our father he hath writ, so hath our sister,
Of differences, which I least thought it fit
To answer from[47] our home. The several messengers
From hence attend dispatch.[48] Our good old friend,
Lay comforts to your bosom, and bestow
Your needful counsel to our business,
Which craves the instant use.[49]

GLO.: I serve you, madam.
Your Graces are right welcome.

      [*Flourish. Exeunt.*]

41. childlike office: filial service. 42. bewray: reveal. 43. of doing: because he might do. 44. Make . . . please: use my authority for any action you care to take. 45. threading . . . night: making our way through the darkness. 46. poise: weight. 47. from: away from. 48. attend dispatch: are waiting to be sent back. 49. craves . . . use: requires immediate action.

SCENE 2. *Before* GLOUCESTER's *castle*.

[*Enter* KENT *and* OSWALD, *severally.*[1]]

OSW.: Good dawning to thee, friend. Art of this house?

KENT: Aye.

OSW.: Where may we set our horses?

KENT: I' the mire.

OSW.: Prithee, if thou lovest me, tell me.

KENT: I love thee not.

OSW.: Why, then I care not for thee.

KENT: If I had thee in Lipsbury pinfold,[2] I would make thee care for me.

OSW.: Why dost thou use me thus? I know thee not.

KENT: Fellow, I know thee.

OSW.: What dost thou know me for?

KENT: A[3] knave, a rascal, an eater of broken meats; a base, proud, shallow, beggarly, three-suited, hundred-pound, filthy, worsted-stocking knave; a lily-livered, action-taking knave; a whoreson, glass-gazing, superserviceable, finical rogue; one-trunk-inheriting slave; one that wouldst be a bawd in way of good service, and art nothing but the composition of a knave, beggar, coward, pander, and the son and heir of a mongrel bitch—one whom I will beat into clamorous whining if thou deniest the least syllable of thy addition.

OSW.: Why, what a monstrous fellow art thou, thus to rail on one that is neither known of thee nor knows thee!

KENT: What a brazen-faced varlet art thou, to deny thou knowest me! It is two days ago since I tripped up thy heels and beat thee before the King? Draw, you rogue. For though it be night, yet the moon

---

Sc. ii: 1. s.d., severally: by different entrances.   2. Lipsbury pinfold: This phrase has not been convincingly explained. A pinfold is a village pound, a small enclosure in which strayed beasts are kept until reclaimed by their owners; a pinfold was a good place for a fight whence neither side could escape.   3. A . . . addition: Kent here sums up the characteristics of the more unpleasant kind of gentleman servingman of whom Oswald is a fair specimen (see App. 14). broken meats: remains of food sent down from the high table. three-suited: allowed three suits a year. hundred-pound: i.e., the extent of his wealth. worsted-stocking: no gentleman, or he would have worn silk. lily-livered: cowardly. action-taking knave: one who goes to law instead of risking a fight. glass-gazing: always looking at himself in a mirror. superserviceable: too eager to do what his master wishes. finical: finicky. one-trunk-inheriting: whose whole inheritance from his father will go into one trunk. bawd . . . service: ready to serve his master's lusts if it will please him. composition: mixture. pander: pimp. addition: lit., title of honor added to a man's name.

shines. I'll make a sop o' the moonshine of you.[4] Draw, you whoreson cullionly[5] barber-monger,[6] draw.

    [*Drawing his sword.*]

osw.: Away! I have nothing to do with thee.

kent: Draw, you rascal. You come with letters against the King, and take vanity the puppet's part[7] against the royalty of her father. Draw, you rogue, or I'll so carbonado[8] your shanks. Draw, you rascal, come your ways.

osw.: Help, ho! Murder! Help!

kent: Strike, you slave. Stand, rogue, stand, you neat slave, strike.

    [*Beating him.*]

osw.: Help, ho! Murder! Murder!

    [*Enter* edmund, *with his rapier drawn,* cornwall, regan, gloucester, *and* servants.]

edm.: How now! What's the matter?

    [*Parting them.*]

kent: With you, goodman boy,[9] an you please. Come, I'll flesh you,[10] come on, young master.

glo.: Weapons! Arms! What's the matter here?

corn.: Keep peace, upon your lives.

He dies that strikes again. What is the matter?

reg.: The messengers from our sister and the King.

corn.: What is your difference?[11] Speak.

osw.: I am scarce in breath, my lord.

kent: No marvel, you have so bestirred your valor. You cowardly rascal, Nature disclaims in thee. A tailor made thee.[12]

corn.: Thou art a strange fellow—a tailor make a man?

kent: Aye, a tailor, sir. A stonecutter or a painter could not have made him so ill, though he had been but two hours at the trade.

corn.: Speak yet, how grew your quarrel?

osw.: This ancient ruffian, sir, whose life I have spared at suit of his gray beard—

---

4. sop . . . you: Not satisfactorily explained, but obviously something unpleasant; probably Kent means no more than "I'll make a wet mess of you." 5. cullionly: base. 6. barber-monger: a man always in the barber's shop. Elizabethan gentlemen frequented the beauty parlor as much as our modern ladies do. 7. vanity . . . part: Vanity appeared as an evil character in the old Morality plays of the early sixteenth century, which still survived in a degenerate form in puppet shows exhibited at fairs. 8. carbonado: lit., a steak slashed for cooking, so "slice." 9. goodman boy: my young man. Edmund is still a young man, but it was an insult to call him boy. Cf. *R & J*, I.v.79–80; *Cor*, V.vi.101–13. 10. flesh you: give your first fight. Cf. *I Hen IV*, V.iv.133–34. 11. difference: disagreement. 12. Nature . . . thee: Nature refuses to own you, you are nothing but clothes—from the English proverb "The tailor makes the man."

KENT.: Thou whoreson zed! Thou unnecessary letter![13] My lord, if you
will give me leave, I will tread this unbolted[14] villain into mortar, and
daub the walls of a jakes[15] with him. Spare my gray beard, you wagtail?[16]

CORN.: Peace, sirrah!
You beastly knave, know you no reverence?[17]

KENT: Yes, sir, but anger hath a privilege.[18]

CORN.: Why art thou angry?

KENT: That such a slave as this should wear a sword,
Who wears no honesty. Such smiling rogues as these,
Like rats, oft bite the holy cords a-twain
Which are too intrinse to unloose;[19] smooth[20] every passion
That in the natures of their lords rebel;
Bring oil to fire, snow to their colder moods;
Renege, affirm,[21] and turn their halcyon[22] beaks
With every gale and vary of their masters,
Knowing naught, like dogs, but following.
A plague upon your epileptic visage!
Smile you my speeches, as I were a fool?
Goose,[23] if I had you upon Sarum[24] plain,
I'd drive ye cackling home to Camelot.[25]

CORN.: What, art thou mad, old fellow?

GLO.: How fell you out? Say that.

KENT: No contraries hold more antipathy
Than I and such a knave.

CORN.: Why dost thou call him knave? What is his fault?

KENT: His countenance likes me not.[26]

CORN.: No more perchance does mine, nor his, nor hers.

KENT: Sir, 'tis my occupation to be plain.
I have seen better faces in my time
Than stands on any shoulder that I see

13. zed . . . letter: because z does not exist in Latin and is not necessary in the
English alphabet, since s can usually take its place. 14. unbolted: unsifted,
coarse. 15. jakes: privy. 16. wagtail: a small bird which wags its tail up and
down as it struts. 17. know . . . reverence: i.e., do you have the impertinence to raise your voice in the presence of your betters? 18. anger . . .
privilege: something must be allowed to a man who has lost temper. 19. bite
. . . unloose: i.e., cause the bonds of holy matrimony to be broken by serving
the lusts of their employers. 20. smooth: help to gratify. 21. Renege, affirm:
deny or agree; i.e., a perfect "yes man." 22. halcyon: kingfisher. A kingfisher hung up by the neck was supposed to turn its bill into the prevailing
wind. 23. Goose . . . Camelot: These lines cannot be explained. 24.
Sarum: Salisbury Plain, in the south of England. 25. Camelot: the home of
King Arthur and the knights of his Round Table. 26. His . . . not: I don't
like his face.

Before me at this instant.

CORN.: This[27] is some fellow
Who, having been praised for bluntness, doth affect
A saucy roughness,[28] and constrains the garb
Quite from his nature.[29] He cannot flatter, he—
An honest mind and plain—he must speak truth!
An they will take it, so. If not, he's plain.
These kind of knaves I know, which in this plainness
Harbor more craft and more corrupter ends
Than twenty silly ducking observants
That stretch their duties nicely.[30]

KENT: Sir,[31] in good faith, in sincere verity,
Under the allowance of your great aspéct,
Whose influence, like the wreath of radiant fire
On flickering Phoebus'[32] front—

CORN.: What mean'st by this?

KENT: To go out of my dialect, which you discommend so much. I
know, sir, I am no flatterer. He that beguiled you in a plain accent
was a plain knave, which, for my part, I will not be, though I should
win your displeasure to entreat me to 't.[33]

CORN.: What was the offense you gave him?

OSW.: I never gave him any.
It pleased the King his master very late
To strike at me, upon his misconstruction,[34]
When he, conjunct,[35] and flattering his displeasure,
Tripped me behind; being down, insulted, railed,
And put upon him such a deal of man
That worthied him,[36] got praises of the King
For him attempting[37] who was self-subdued,[38]
And in the fleshment[39] of this dread exploit
Drew on me here again.

KENT: None of these rogues and cowards
But Ajax is their fool.[40]

---

27. This . . . nicely: See App. 4. 28. saucy roughness: impudent rudeness.
29. constrains . . . nature: affects a manner which is quite unnatural. 30. silly
. . . nicely: silly servants who are always bowing to their masters as they strain
to carry out their orders. 31. Sir . . . front: Kent now changes his tone from
the honest blunt man to the affected courtier. See I.iv.34. 32. Phoebus: the
sun god. 33. He . . . to't: the man who posed as blunt and honest and deceived you was simply a knave. I shall never be a knave, even if you ask me and
are angry because I refuse. 34. upon . . . misconstruction: because he deliberately misinterpreted my words. 35. conjunct: i.e., joining with the King.
36. worthied him: got him favor. 37. attempting: attacking. 38. self-subdued: made no resistance. 39. fleshment: excitement. 40. None . . . fool:

CORN.: Fetch forth the stocks!

    You stubborn[41] ancient knave, you reverend[42] braggart,

    We'll teach you—

KENT: Sir, I am too old to learn.

    Call not your stocks for me. I serve the King,

    On whose employment I was sent to you.

    You shall do small respect, show too bold malice

    Against the grace and person of my master,

    Stocking his messenger.[43]

CORN.: Fetch forth the stocks! As I have life and honor,

    There shall he sit till noon!

REG.: Till noon! Till night, my lord, and all night too.

KENT: Why, madam, if I were your father's dog,

    You should not use me so.

REG.: Sir, being his knave, I will.

CORN.: This is a fellow of the selfsame color

    Our sister speaks of. Come, bring away[44] the stocks!

       [*Stocks brought out.*]

GLO.: Let me beseech your Grace not to do so.

    His fault is much, and the good King his master

    Will check[45] him for 't. Your purposed low correction[46]

    Is such as basest and contemned'st[47] wretches

    For pilferings and most common trespasses

    Are punished with. The King must take it ill

    That he, so slightly valued in his messenger,

    Should have him thus restrained.

CORN.: I'll answer that.

REG.: My sister may receive it much more worse

    To have her gentleman abused, assaulted,

    For following her affairs. Put in his legs.

       [KENT *is put in the stocks.*]

This cryptic but devastating remark rouses Cornwall to fury, for he realizes from Kent's insolent tone, manner, and gesture that by "Ajax" he is himself intended. Ajax was the ridiculous braggart of the Greek army whom Shakespeare had already dramatized in *Tr & Cr.* The name Ajax had further unsavory significances for the original audience, for "Ajax" was a common synonym for a jakes—a very evil-smelling place. Kent thus implies "All these knaves and cowards are fooling this stinking braggart." See App. 4.   41. stubborn: rude. 42. reverend: old.   43. You . . . messenger: As the King's representative, Kent is entitled to respectful treatment; to put him in the stocks is to offer an intolerable insult to the King. See ll. 147–54 below and II.iv.22–24.   44. bring away: fetch out.   45. check: rebuke, punish.   46. purposed . . . correction: the degrading punishment which you propose.   47. contemned'st: most despised.

Come, my good lord, away.
[*Exeunt all but* GLOUCESTER *and* KENT.]
GLO.: I am sorry for thee, friend. 'Tis the Duke's pleasure,
Whose disposition all the world well knows
Will not be rubbed[48] nor stopped. I'll entreat for thee.
KENT: Pray do not, sir. I have watched and traveled hard,
Some time I shall sleep out, the rest I'll whistle.
A good man's fortune may grow out at heels.[49]
Give you good morrow![50]
GLO.: The Duke's to blame in this, 'twill be ill-taken.
[*Exit.*]
KENT: Good King, that must approve the common saw,[51]
Thou out of Heaven's benediction comest
To the warm sun![52]
Approach, thou beacon to this underglobe,[53]
That by thy comfortable beams I may
Peruse this letter! Nothing almost sees miracles
But misery.[54] I know 'tis from Cordelia,
Who hath most fortunately been informed
Of my obscurèd course,[55] and shall find time
From this enormous state,[56] seeking to give
Losses their remedies. All weary and o'erwatched,
Take vantage, heavy eyes, not to behold
This shameful lodging.
Fortune, good night. Smile once more, turn thy wheel!
[*Sleeps.*]

SCENE 3.   A wood.

[*Enter* EDGAR.]
EDG.: I heard myself proclaimed,[1]
And by the happy[2] hollow of a tree
Escaped the hunt. No port is free, no place,
That guard and most unusual vigilance

---

48. rubbed: turned aside, a metaphor from the game of bowls.   49. A . . . heels:
even a good man may suffer a shabby fate.   50. Give . . . morrow: a good
morning to you.   51. approve . . . saw: stress the truth of the common
proverb.   52. Thou . . . sun: you are coming out of the shade into the heat.
53. beacon . . . underglobe: the rising sun.   54. Nothing . . misery: only
those who are wretched appreciate miracles.   55. obscured course: i.e., my actions in disguise.   56. this . . . state: these wicked times.

Sc. iii: 1. proclaimed: See II.i.82–85.   2. happy: lucky.

Does not attend my taking.[3] Whiles I may 'scape
I will preserve myself, and am bethought[4]
To take the basest and most poorest shape
That ever penury in contempt of man
Brought near to beast.[5] My face I'll grime with filth,
Blanket[6] my loins, elf[7] all my hair in knots,
And with presented nakedness[8] outface
The winds and persecutions of the sky.
The country gives me proof and precedent[9]
Of Bedlam beggars,[10] who with roaring voices
Strike in their numbed and mortified[11] bare arms
Pins, wooden pricks, nails, sprigs of rosemary,
And with this horrible object, from low[12] farms,
Poor pelting[13] villages, sheepcotes and mills,
Sometime with lunatic bans,[14] sometime with prayers,
Enforce their charity. Poor Turlygod! Poor Tom![15]
That's something yet. Edgar I nothing am.[16]

    [*Exit.*]

SCENE 4. *Before* GLOUCESTER's *castle.* KENT *in the stocks.*

    [*Enter* LEAR, FOOL, *and* GENTLEMAN.]
LEAR: 'Tis strange that they should so depart from home
  And not send back my messenger.
GENT.: As I learned,
  The night before there was no purpose[1] in them
  Of this remove.
KENT: Hail to thee, noble master!
LEAR: Ha!
  Makest thou this shame thy pastime?[2]

---

3. attend my taking: watch to take me. 4. am bethought: have decided. 5.
penury . . . beast: poverty, to show that man is a contemptible creature, reduced to the level of a beast. 6. Blanket: cover with only a blanket. 7. elf:
mat. Matted hair was believed to be caused by elves. Cf. *R & J*, I.iv.88–91.
8. with . . . nakedness: bold in my nakedness. 9. proof . . . precedent: examples. 10. Bedlam beggars: lunatics discharged from Bedlam (or Bethlehem) Hospital, the London madhouse. These sturdy beggars were the terror
of the countryside. See I.ii.148. 11. mortified: numbed. 12. low: humble.
13. pelting: paltry. 14. bans: curses. 15. Poor . . . Tom: Edgar rehearses
the names which a bedlam calls himself. 16. That's . . . am: there's still a
chance for me; as Edgar I am a dead man.

Sc. iv: 1. purpose: intention. 2. Makest . . . pastime: are you sitting there for
amusement?

KENT: No, my lord.

FOOL: Ha, ha! He wears cruel[3] garters. Horses are tied by the heads, dogs and bears by the neck, monkeys by the loins, and men by the legs. When a man's overlusty at legs,[4] then he wears wooden netherstocks.[5]

LEAR: What's he that hath so much thy place mistook
To set thee here?

KENT: It is both he and she,
Your son and daughter.

LEAR: No.

KENT: Yes.

LEAR: No, I say.

KENT: I say yea.

LEAR: No, no, they would not.

KENT: Yes, they have.

LEAR: By Jupiter, I swear no.

KENT: By Juno, I swear aye.

LEAR: They durst not do 't,
They could not, would not do 't. 'Tis worse than murder
To do upon respect[6] such violent outrage.
Resolve[7] me with all modest haste which way
Thou mightest deserve, or they impose, this usage,
Coming from us.[8]

KENT: My lord, when at their home
I did commend your Highness' letters to them,
Ere I was risen from the place that showed
My duty kneeling, came there a reeking post,[9]
Stewed in his haste, half-breathless, panting forth
From Goneril his mistress salutations,
Delivered letters, spite of intermission,[10]
Which presently[11] they read. On whose contents
They summoned up their meiny,[12] straight took horse,
Commanded me to follow and attend
The leisure of their answer, gave me cold looks.
And meeting here the other messenger,
Whose welcome, I perceived, had poisoned mine—

---

3. cruel: with a pun on "crewel"—worsted. 4. overlusty at legs: i.e., a vagabond. 5. netherstocks: stockings. 6. upon respect: the respect due to me, their King and father. 7. Resolve: inform. 8. Coming . . . us: Lear uses the royal "we"—"from us, the King." 9. reeking post: sweating messenger. 10. spite of intermission: in spite of the delay in reading my letter (which should have come first). 11. presently: immediately. 12. meiny: followers.

Being the very fellow that of late
Displayed so saucily[13] against your Highness—
Having more than wit about me, drew.
He raised the house with loud and coward cries.
Your son and daughter found this trespass worth[14]
The shame which here it suffers.

FOOL: Winter's not gone yet[15] if the wild geese fly that way.

> "Fathers that wear rags
> Do make their children blind,
> But fathers that bear bags[16]
> Shall see their children kind.
> Fortune, that arrant whore,
> Ne'er turns the key[17] to the poor."

But for all this, thou shalt have as many dolors[18] for thy daughters as thou canst tell[19] in a year.

LEAR: Oh,[20] how this mother swells up toward my heart!
Hysterica passio, down, thou climbing sorrow,
Thy element's[21] below! Where is this daughter?

KENT: With the Earl, sir, here within.

LEAR: Follow me not, stay here.

[*Exit.*]

GENT.: Made you no more offense but what you speak of?

KENT: None.
How chance the King comes with so small a train?

FOOL: An thou hadst been set i' the stocks for that question, thou hadst well deserved it.

KENT: Why, fool?

FOOL: We'll[22] set thee to school to an ant, to teach thee there's no laboring i' the winter. All that follow their noses[23] are led by their eyes but blind men, and there's not a nose among twenty but can smell him that's stinking. Let go thy hold when a great wheel runs down a hill, lest it break thy neck with following it, but the great one that goes up the hill, let him draw thee after. When a wise man

---

13. Displayed so saucily: behaved so insolently. 14. worth: deserving. 15. Winter's . . . yet: there's more trouble to come. 16. bear bags: have money. 17. turns . . . key: opens the door. 18. dolors: with a pun on "dollars." 19. tell: count. 20. Oh . . . below: The *mother*, called also *hysterica passio*, was an overwhelming feeling of physical distress and suffocation. Lear's mental suffering is now beginning to cause a physical breakdown. This sensation, and the violent throbbing of his heart until finally it ceases, can be traced in Lear's speeches. See ll. 122, 138, 200–01; III.iv.14. 21. element: natural place. 22. We'll . . . it: The fool is so much amused at Kent's discomfiture that he strings off a series of wise sayings to show his own clearer understanding of Lear's state. 23. follow . . . noses: go straight ahead.

gives thee better counsel, give me mine again. I would have none
but knaves follow it, since a fool gives it.

"That sir which serves and seeks for gain,
   And follows but for form,[24]
Will pack[25] when it begins to rain,
   And leave thee in the storm.
"But I will tarry, the fool will stay,
   And let the wise man fly.
The knave turns fool that runs away,
   The fool no knave, perdy."[26]

KENT: Where learned you this, fool?

FOOL: Not i' the stocks, fool.

[Re-enter LEAR, with GLOUCESTER.]

LEAR: Deny to speak with me? They are sick? They are weary?
   They have traveled all the night? Mere fetches,[27]
   The images[28] of revolt and flying off.
   Fetch me a better answer.

GLO.: My dear lord,
   You know the fiery quality[29] of the Duke,
   How unremovable and fixed he is
   In his own course.

LEAR: Vengeance! Plague! Death! Confusion!
   Fiery? What quality? Why, Gloucester, Gloucester,
   I'd speak with the Duke of Cornwall and his wife.

GLO.: Well, my good lord, I have informed them so.

LEAR: Informed them! Dost thou understand me, man?

GLO.: Aye, my good lord.

LEAR: The King would speak with Cornwall, the dear father
   Would with his daughter speak, commands her service.
   Are they informed of this? My breath and blood!
   "Fiery"? "The fiery Duke"? Tell the hot Duke that—
   No, but not yet. Maybe he is not well.
   Infirmity doth still neglect all office
   Whereto our health is bound.[30] We are not ourselves
   When nature being oppressed commands the mind
   To suffer with the body. I'll forbear,
   And am fall'n out with my more headier will,[31]
   To take the indisposed and sickly fit

24. but . . . form: merely for show. 25. pack: clear out. 26. perdy: by God.
27. fetches: excuses. 28. images: exact likenesses. 29. quality: nature. 30.
Infirmity . . . bound: when a man is sick, he neglects his proper duty. 31. am
. . . will: regret my hastiness.

For the sound man. [*Looking on* KENT] Death on my state! Wherefore

Should he sit here? This act persuades me

That this remotion[32] of the Duke and her

Is practice[33] only. Give me my servant forth.[34]

Go tell the Duke and 's wife I'd speak with them,

Now, presently. Bid them come forth and hear me,

Or at their chamber door I'll beat the drum

Till it cry sleep to death.[35]

GLO.: I would have all well betwixt you.

      [*Exit.*]

LEAR: Oh, me, my heart, my rising heart! But down![36]

FOOL: Cry to it, Nuncle, as the cockney[37] did to the eels when she put
'em i' the paste alive. She knapped[38] 'em o' the coxcombs with a
stick, and cried "Down, wantons, down!" 'Twas her brother that, in
pure kindness to his horse, buttered his hay.

      [*Re-enter* GLOUCESTER, *with* CORNWALL, REGAN, *and* SERVANTS.]

LEAR: Good morrow to you both.

CORN.: Hail to your Grace!

      [KENT *is set at liberty.*]

REG.: I am glad to see your Highness.

LEAR: Regan, I think you are, I know what reason

I have to think so. If thou shouldst not be glad,

I would divorce me from thy mother's tomb,

Sepúlchring an adultress.[39] [*To* KENT] Oh, are you free?

Some other time for that. Belovèd Regan,

Thy sister's naught.[40] O Regan, she hath tied

Sharp-toothed unkindness, like a vulture, here.

      [*Points to his heart.*]

I can scarce speak to thee, thou'lt not believe

With how depraved a quality—O Regan!

REG.: I pray you, sir, take patience. I have hope

You less know how to value her desert

Than she to scant her duty.

LEAR: Say, how is that?

REG.: I cannot think my sister in the least

Would fail her obligation. If, sir, perchance

32. remotion: removal. 33. practice: pretense. 34. Give . . . forth: release my
servant at once. 35. cry . . . death: kill sleep by its noise. 36. Oh . . .
down: See ll. 56–58. 37. cockney: Londoner. 38. knapped: cracked. 39.
divorce . . . adultress: i.e., I would suspect that your dead mother had been
false to me. 40. naught: wicked.

She have restrained the riots of your followers,
'Tis on such ground and to such wholesome end
As clears her from all blame.

LEAR: My curses on her!

REG.: Oh, sir, you are old,
Nature in you stands on the very verge
Of her confine.[41] You should be ruled and led
By some discretion that discerns your state
Better than you yourself. Therefore I pray you
That to our sister you do make return.
Say you have wronged her, sir.

LEAR: Ask her forgiveness?
Do you but mark how this becomes the house.[42]—
[*Kneeling*] "Dear daughter, I confess that I am old,
Age is unnecessary. On my knees I beg
That you'll vouchsafe me raiment, bed, and food."

REG.: Good sir, no more, these are unsightly tricks.
Return you to my sister.

LEAR [*Rising*]: Never, Regan.
She hath abated me of half my train,
Looked black upon me, struck me with her tongue,
Most serpentlike, upon the very heart.
All the stored vengeances of Heaven fall
On her ingrateful top![43] Strike her young bones,
You taking airs, with lameness.

CORN.: Fie, sir, fie!

LEAR: You nimble lightnings, dart your blinding flames
Into her scornful eyes. Infect her beauty,
You fen-sucked fogs,[44] drawn by the powerful sun
To fall[45] and blast her pride.

REG.: Oh, the blest gods! So will you wish on me
When the rash mood is on.

LEAR: No, Regan, thou shalt never have my curse.
Thy tender-hefted[46] nature shall not give
Thee o'er to harshness. Her eyes are fierce, but thine
Do comfort and not burn. 'Tis not in thee
To grudge my pleasures, to cut off my train,
To bandy hasty words, to scant my sizes,[47]

---

41. confine: boundary, edge. 42. becomes . . . house: i.e., suits my dignity.
43. top: head. 44. fen-sucked fogs: Cf. I.iv.321. 45. fall: fall upon. 46.
tender-hefted: gently framed. 47. scant my sizes: reduce my allowances.

And in conclusion to oppose the bolt[48]
Against my coming in. Thou better know'st
The offices of nature, bond of childhood,
Effects of courtesy, dues of gratitude.
Thy half o' the kingdom hast thou not forgot,
Wherein I thee endowed.

REG.: Good sir, to the purpose.[49]

LEAR: Who put my man i' the stocks?
[*Tucket within.*]

CORN.: What trumpet's that?

REG.: I know 't, my sister's. This approves[50] her letter,
That she would soon be here.
[*Enter* OSWALD.] Is your lady come?

LEAR: This is a slave whose easy-borrowed pride
Dwells in the fickle grace of her he follows.[51]
Out varlet, from my sight!
Out, varlet,[52] from my sight!

CORN.: What means your Grace?

LEAR: Who stocked my servant? Regan, I have good hope
Thou didst not know on 't. Who comes here?
[*Enter* GONERIL.] O Heavens,
If you do love old men, if your sweet sway
Allow[53] obedience, if yourselves are old,
Make it your cause. Send down, and take my part!
[*To* GONERIL.] Art not ashamed to look upon this beard?
O Regan, wilt thou take her by the hand?

GON.: Why not by the hand, sir? How have I offended?
All's not offense that indiscretion finds
And dotage terms so.[54]

LEAR: O sides, you are too tough,
Will you yet hold?[55] How came my man i' the stocks?

CORN.: I set him there, sir. But his own disorders
Deserved much less advancement.[56]

LEAR: You! Did you?

REG.: I pray you, Father, being weak, seem so.[57]
If till the expiration of your month

48. oppose . . . bolt: bar the door. 49. Good . . . purpose: and in good time to; or, please talk sense. 50. approves: confirms. 51. whose . . . follows: who soon puts on airs because his fickle mistress favors him. 52. varlet: knave. 53. Allow: approve of. 54. that . . . so: because a silly old man says so. See I.i.149–51,n. 55. O . . . hold: See II.iv.56–58,n, above. 56. advancement: promotion. 57. seem so: i.e, behave suitably

You will return and sojourn with my sister,
Dismissing half your train, come then to me.
I am now from home and out of that provision
Which shall be needful for your entertainment.[58]
LEAR: Return to her, and fifty men dismissed?
No, rather I abjure[59] all roofs, and choose
To wage against the enmity o' the air,
To be a comrade with the wolf and owl—
Necessity's sharp pinch! Return with her?
Why, the hot-blooded France, that dowerless took
Our youngest-born—I could as well be brought
To knee his throne and, squirelike,[60] pension beg
To keep base life afoot. Return with her?
Persuade me rather to be slave and sumpter[61]
To this detested groom. [*Pointing at* OSWALD.]
GON.: At your choice, sir.
LEAR: I prithee, Daughter, do not make me mad.
I will not trouble thee, my child. Farewell.
We'll no more meet, no more see one another.
But yet thou art my flesh, my blood, my daughter,
Or rather a disease that's in my flesh
Which I must needs call mine. Thou art a boil,
A plague sore, an embossed carbuncle,[62]
In my corrupted blood. But I'll not chide thee.
Let shame come when it will, I do not call it.
I do not bid the thunderbearer[63] shoot,
Nor tell tales of thee to high-judging Jove.
Mend when thou canst, be better at thy leisure.
I can be patient, I can stay with Regan,
I and my hundred knights.
REG.: Not altogether so.
I looked not for you yet, nor am provided
For your fit welcome. Give ear, sir, to my sister,
For those that mingle reason with your passion
Must be content to think you old,[64] and so—
But she knows what she does.
LEAR: Is this well spoken?

58. entertainment: maintenance. 59. abjure: refuse with an oath. 60. squire-like: like a servant. 61. sumpter: pack horse, beast of burden. 68. embossed carbuncle: swollen boil. 63. thunderbearer: Jupiter. 64. those . . . old: those who consider your passion with reason realize that you are old—and should be wise.

REG.: I dare avouch[65] it, sir. What, fifty followers?
   Is it not well? What should you need of more?
   Yea, or so many, sith[66] that both charge and danger[67]
   Speak 'gainst so great a number? How in one house
   Should many people under two commands
   Hold amity? 'Tis hard, almost impossible.
GON.: Why might not you, my lord, receive attendance
   From those that she calls servants or from mine?
REG.: Why not, my lord? If then they chanced to slack[68] you,
   We could control them. If you will come to me,
   For now I spy a danger, I entreat you
   To bring but five and twenty. To no more
   Will I give place or notice.
LEAR: I gave you all—
REG.: And in good time you gave it.
LEAR: Made you my guardians, my depositaries,[69]
   But kept a reservation[70] to be followed
   With such a number. What, must I come to you
   With five and twenty, Regan? Said you so?
REG.: And speak 't again, my lord, no more with me.
LEAR: Those wicked creatures yet do look well-favored,[71]
   When others are more wicked. Not being the worst
   Stands in some rank of praise.[72] [To GONERIL] I'll go with thee.
   Thy fifty yet doth double five and twenty,
   And thou art twice her love.
GON.: Hear me, my lord.
   What need you five and twenty, ten, or five,
   To follow in a house where twice so many
   Have a command to tend you?
REG.: What need one?
LEAR: Oh,[73] reason not the need. Our basest beggars
   Are in the poorest thing superfluous.[74]
   Allow not nature more than nature needs,
   Man's life's as cheap as beast's. Thou art a lady.
   If only to go warm were gorgeous,

---

65. avouch: guarantee. 66. sith: since. 67. charge . . . danger: expense and
   risk of maintaining. 68. slack: neglect. 69. depositaries: trustees. 70. reservation: condition. See I.i.134–41. 71. well-favored: handsome. 72. Not
   . . . praise: i.e., since Goneril is not so bad as Regan, that is one thing in her
   favor. 73. Oh . . . need: the needs of a beggar are very different from the
   needs of a king—but above all Lear needs not dignity but patience. 74. Our
   . . . superfluous: even the few possessions of a beggar are not absolutely necessary.

Why, nature needs not what thou gorgeous wear'st,
Which scarcely keeps thee warm. But for true need—
You Heavens, give me that patience, patience I need!
You see me here, you gods, a poor old man,
As full of grief as age, wretched in both.
If it be you that stirs these daughters' hearts
Against their father, fool me not so much
To bear it tamely.[75] Touch me with noble anger,
And let not women's weapons, water drops,
Stain my man's cheeks! No, you unnatural hags,
I will have such revenges on you both
That all the world shall—I will do such things—
What they are, yet I know not, but they shall be
The terrors of the earth. You think I'll weep.
No, I'll not weep.[76]
I have full cause of[77] weeping, but this heart
Shall break into a hundred thousand flaws[78]
Or ere I'll weep. O fool, I shall go mad!
   [*Exeunt* LEAR, GLOUCESTER, KENT, *and* FOOL.]
CORN.: Let us withdraw, 'twill be a storm.
   [*Storm and tempest.*]
REG.: This house is little. The old man and his people
   Cannot be well bestowed.
GON.: 'Tis his own blame. Hath put himself from rest,
   And must needs taste his folly.
REG.: For his particular,[79] I'll receive him gladly,
   But not one follower.
GON.: So am I purposed.
   Where is my Lord of Gloucester?
CORN.: Followed the old man forth. He is returned.
   [*Re-enter* GLOUCESTER.]
GLO.: The King is in high rage.
CORN.: Whither is he going?
GLO.: He calls to horse, but will I know not whither.
CORN.: 'Tis best to give him way, he leads himself.
GON.: My lord, entreat him by no means to stay.
GLO.: Alack, the night comes on, and the bleak winds
   Do sorely ruffle. For many miles about
   There's scarce a bush.

---

75. fool . . . tamely: do not degrade me so much that I just tamely endure it.
76. No . . . weep: See *Lear* Intro. p. 1138b.   77. of: for.   78. flaws: broken
pieces.   79. his particular: himself personally.

REG.: Oh, sir, to willful men
The injuries that they themselves procure
Must be their schoolmasters. Shut up your doors.
He is attended with a desperate train,
And what they may incense[80] him to, being apt[81]
To have his ear abused,[82] wisdom bids fear.
CORN.: Shut up your doors, my lord, 'tis a wild night.
My Regan counsels well. Come out o' the storm.
[Exeunt.]

🎕 Act III

SCENE 1. A heath.

[Storm still.[1] Enter KENT and a GENTLEMAN, meeting.]
KENT: Who's there, besides foul weather?
GENT.: One minded like the weather, most unquietly.
KENT: I know you. Where's the King?
GENT.: Contending with the fretful elements.
Bids the wind blow the earth into the sea,
Or swell the curlèd waters 'bove the main,[2]
That things might change or cease; tears his white hair,
Which the impetuous blasts, with eyeless[3] rage,
Catch in their fury, and make nothing of;
Strives in his little world of man[4] to outscorn
The to-and-fro-conflicting wind and rain.
This night, wherein the cub-drawn bear[5] would couch,[6]
The lion and the belly-pinchèd[7] wolf
Keep their fur dry, unbonneted[8] he runs,
And bids what will take all.
KENT: But who is with him?
GENT.: None but the fool, who labors to outjest
His heart-struck injuries.

80. incense: incite. 81. apt: ready. 82. abused: deceived.

Act III, Sc. i: 1. s.d., still: continuing. 2. main: mainland. 3. eyeless: blind.
4. little . . . man: It was a common Elizabethan idea, sometimes elaborately
worked out, that individual man was a little world (microcosm) and repro-
duced in himself the universe (macrocosm). 5. cub-drawn bear: she-bear
sucked dry, and therefore hungry. 6. couch: take shelter. 7. belly-pinchèd:
ravenous. 8. unbonneted: without a hat.

KENT: Sir, I do know you,
    And dare, upon the warrant of my note,[9]
    Commend a dear[10] thing to you. There is division,
    Although as yet the face of it be covered
    With mutual cunning, 'twixt Albany and Cornwall,
    Who have—as who have not that their great stars
    Throned and set high?[11]—servants, who seem no less,
    Which are to France the spies and speculations[12]
    Intelligent of our state[13]—what hath been seen,
    Either in snuffs and packings[14] of the Dukes,
    Or the hard rein which both of them have borne
    Against the old kind King, or something deeper,
    Whereof perchance these are but furnishings[15]—
    But true it is, from France there comes a power[16]
    Into this scattered kingdom, who already,
    Wise in our negligence, have secret feet
    In some of our best ports and are at point[17]
    To show their open banner. Now to you.
    If on my credit[18] you dare build so far
    To make your speed to Dover, you shall find
    Some that will thank you, making just report
    Of how unnatural and bemadding sorrow
    The King hath cause to plain.[19]
    I am a gentleman of blood[20] and breeding,
    And from some knowledge and assurance[21] offer
    This office[22] to you.
GENT.: I will talk further with you.
KENT: No, do not.
    For confirmation that I am much more
    Than my outwall,[23] open this purse and take
    What it contains. If you shall see Cordelia—
    As fear not but you shall—show her this ring,
    And she will tell you who your fellow[24] is
    That yet you do not know. Fie on this storm!
    I will go seek the King.

9. upon . . . note: guaranteed by my observation of you. 10. dear: precious.
11. that . . . high: whom Fate has set in a great position. 12. speculations:
informers. 13. Intelligent . . . state: report on the state of our affairs. 14.
snuffs . . . packings: resentment and plotting against each other. 15. furnish-
ings: excuses. The sentence is not finished. 16. power: army. 17. at point:
on the point of, about to. 18. credit: trustworthiness. 19. plain: complain.
20. blood: noble family. 21. knowledge . . . assurance: sure knowledge.
22. office: undertaking. 23. outwall: outside. 24. fellow: companion.

GENT.: Give me your hand.

Have you no more to say?

KENT: Few words, but, to effect, more than all yet—
That when we have found the King—in which your pain[25]
That way, I'll this—he that first lights on him
Holloa the other.

　　[*Exeunt severally.*]

SCENE 2.　*Another part of the heath. Storm still.*

　　[*Enter* LEAR *and* FOOL.]

LEAR: Blow, winds, and crack your cheeks! Rage! Blow!
You cataracts and hurricanoes,[1] spout
Till you have drenched our steeples, drowned the cocks![2]
You sulphurous and thought-executing[3] fires,
Vaunt-couriers[4] to oak-cleaving thunderbolts,
Singe my white head! And thou, all-shaking thunder,
Smite flat the thick rotundity o' the world!
Crack nature's molds,[5] all germens[6] spill at once
That make ingrateful man!

FOOL: O Nuncle, Court holy water[7] in a dry house is better than this rain water out o' door. Good Nuncle, in, and ask thy daughters' blessing. Here's a night pities neither wise man nor fool.

LEAR: Rumble thy bellyful! Spit, fire! Spout, rain!
Nor rain, wind, thunder, fire, are my daughters.
I tax[8] not you, you elements, with unkindness.
I never gave you kingdom, called you children,
You owe me no subscription.[9] Then let fall
Your horrible pleasure. Here I stand, your slave,
A poor, infirm, weak, and despised old man.
But yet I call you servile ministers[10]
That have with two pernicious daughters joined
Your high-engendered battles[11] 'gainst a head
So old and white as this. Oh, oh! 'Tis foul!

FOOL: He that has a house to put 's head in has a good headpiece.

---

25. pain: labor.

Sc. ii: 1. hurricanoes: waterspouts.　2. cocks: weathercocks on top of the steeples. 3. thought-executing: killing as quick as thought.　4. Vaunt-couriers: fore-runners.　5. nature's molds: the molds in which men are made.　6. germens: seeds of life.　7. Court . . . water: flattery of great ones.　8. tax: accuse. 9. subscription: submission.　10. servile ministers: servants who slavishly obey your masters.　11. high-engendered battles: armies begotten on high.

"The[12] codpiece[13] that will house
    Before the head has any,
The head and he shall louse
    So beggars marry many.
The man that makes his toe
    What he his heart should make
Shall of a corn cry woe,
    And turn his sleep to wake."

For there was never yet fair woman but she made mouths in a glass.[14]

LEAR: No, I will be the pattern of all patience,
I will say nothing.

    [*Enter* KENT.]

KENT: Who's there?

FOOL: Marry,[15] here's grace and a codpiece—that's a wise man and a fool.

KENT: Alas, sir, are you here? Things that love night
Love not such nights as these. The wrathful skies
Gallow[16] the very wanderers of the dark
And make them keep their caves. Since I was man,
Such sheets of fire, such bursts of horrid thunder,
Such groans of roaring wind and rain, I never
Remember to have heard. Man's nature cannot carry[17]
The affliction nor the fear.

LEAR: Let the great gods,
That keep this dreadful pother[18] o'er our heads,
Find out their enemies now. Tremble, thou wretch,
That hast within thee undivulgèd crimes
Unwhipped of justice. Hide thee, thou bloody hand,
Thou perjured, and thou simular man of virtue[19]
That art incestuous. Caitiff, to pieces shake,
That under covert and convenient seeming[20]
Hast practiced on man's life. Close pent-up guilts,
Rive your concealing continents[21] and cry

---

12. The . . . wake: the man who goes wenching before he has a roof over his head will become a lousy beggar. The man who is kinder to his toe than to his heart will be kept awake by his corns—i.e., Lear has been kinder to his feet (his daughters) than to his heart (himself). The Fool's remarks, especially when cryptic and indecent, are not easy to paraphrase. 13. codpiece: lit., the opening in the hose. See Pl. 8c and comment on p. 93b. 14. made . . . glass: made faces in a mirror. 15. Marry: Mary, by the Virgin. 16. Gallow: terrify. 17. carry: endure. 18. pother: turmoil. 19. simular . . . virtue: a man who pretends to be virtuous. 20. under . . . seeming: under a false appearance of propriety. 21. Rive . . . continents: split open that which covers and conceals you.

These dreadful summoners grace.[22] I am a man
More sinned against than sinning.

KENT: Alack, bareheaded!
Gracious my lord, hard by here is a hovel.
Some friendship will it lend you 'gainst the tempest.
Repose you there while I to this hard house—
More harder than the stones whereof 'tis raised,
Which even but now, demanding after you,
Denied me to come in—return, and force
Their scanted courtesy.

LEAR: My wits begin to turn.
Come on, my boy. How dost, my boy? Art cold?
I am cold myself. Where is this straw, my fellow?
The art of our necessities is strange,
That can make vile things precious.[23] Come, your hovel.
Poor fool and knave, I have one part in my heart
That's sorry yet for thee.

FOOL [*Singing*]:
            "He[24] that has and a little tiny wit—
                With hey, ho, the wind and the rain—
                Must make content with his fortunes fit,[25]
                For the rain it raineth every day."

LEAR: True, my good boy. Come, bring us to this hovel.
            [*Exeunt* LEAR *and* KENT.]

FOOL: This is a brave night to cool a courtesan.
    I'll speak a prophecy[26] ere I go:
            "When priests are more in word than matter,
                When brewers mar their malt with water,
                When nobles are their tailors' tutors,[27]
                No heretics burned, but wenches' suitors,
                When every case in law is right,
                No squire in debt, nor no poor knight,

22. cry . . . grace: ask for mercy from these dreadful summoners. The summoner
was the officer of the ecclesiastical court who summoned a man to appear to
answer a charge of immorality. See Gen. Intro. p. 26a. 23. art . . . precious:
our needs are like the art of the alchemist (who was forever experimenting to
try to transmute base metal into gold). See App. 21. 24. He . . . day: another stanza of the song which the Fool in *Twelfth Night* sings at the end of
the play. 25. Must . . . fit: i.e., must be content with a fortune as slim as
his wit. 26. prophecy . . . feet: The fool gives a list of common events,
pretending that they are never likely to happen. The prophecy is a parody of
riddling prophecies popular at this time which were attributed to Merlin, the
old magician of King Arthur's Court. 27. nobles . . . tutors: Young noble-
men and gallants were very particular about the fashion and cut of their clothes.

When slanders do not live in tongues,
Nor cutpurses come not to throngs,
When usurers tell their gold i' the field,
And bawds and whores do churches build—
Then shall the realm of Albion[28]
Come to great confusion.
Then comes the time, who lives to see 't,
That going shall be used with feet."[29]
This prophecy Merlin shall make, for I live before his time.[30]
[Exit.]

SCENE 3. GLOUCESTER's castle.

[Enter GLOUCESTER and EDMUND.]

GLO.: Alack, alack, Edmund, I like not this unnatural dealing. When I
desired their leave that I might pity him,[1] they took from me the
use of mine own house, charged me, on pain of their perpetual displeasure, neither to speak of him, entreat for him, nor any way
sustain[2] him.

EDM.: Most savage and unnatural!

GLO.: Go to, say you nothing. There's a division betwixt the Dukes,
and a worse matter than that. I have received a letter this night, 'tis
dangerous to be spoken.—I have locked the letter in my closet. These
injuries the King now bears will be revenged home.[3] There is part of
a power already footed.[4] We must incline to the King. I will seek
him and privily[5] relieve him. Go you, and maintain talk with the
Duke, that my charity be not of him perceived. If he ask for me, I
am ill and gone to bed. Though I die for it, as no less is threatened
me, the King my old master must be relieved. There is some strange
thing toward, Edmund. Pray you be careful.
[Exit.]

EDM.: This courtesy, forbid thee,[6] shall the Duke
Instantly know, and of that letter too.
This seems a fair deserving,[7] and must draw me

---

28. Albion: England. 29. going . . . feet: feet will be used for walking. 30.
This . . . time: A piece of mock pedantry, for—according to Holinshed's
Chronicles—King Lear died some generations before King Arthur.

Sc. iii: 1. him: Lear. 2. sustain: relieve. 3. home: to the utmost. 4. footed:
landed. 5. privily: secretly. 6. forbid thee: forbidden to thee. 7. This
. . . deserving: i.e., by betraying my father, I shall deserve much of (be rewarded by) the Duke.

That which my father loses, no less than all.
The younger rises when the old doth fall.
    [*Exit.*]

SCENE 4.   *The heath. Before a hovel.*

    [*Enter* LEAR, KENT, *and* FOOL.]
KENT: Here is the place, my lord. Good my lord, enter.
    The tyranny[1] of the open night's too rough
    For nature to endure.
        [*Storm still.*]
LEAR: Let me alone.
KENT: Good my lord, enter here.
LEAR: Wilt break my heart?
KENT: I had rather break mine own. Good my lord, enter.
LEAR: Thou think'st 'tis much that this contentious[2] storm
    Invades us to the skin. So 'tis to thee,
    But where the greater malady is fixed[3]
    The lesser is scarce felt. Thou'dst shun a bear,
    But if thy flight lay toward the raging sea
    Thou'dst meet the bear i' the mouth. When the mind's free[4]
    The body's delicate. The tempest in my mind
    Doth from my senses take all feeling else
    Save what beats there.[5] Filial ingratitude!
    Is it not as this mouth should tear this hand
    For lifting food to 't? But I will punish home.
    No, I will weep no more. In such a night
    To shut me out! Pour on, I will endure.
    In such a night as this! O Regan, Goneril!
    Your old kind father, whose frank heart gave all—
    Oh, that way madness lies, let me shun that,
    No more of that.
KENT: Good my lord, enter here.
LEAR: Prithee, go in theyself, seek thine own ease.
    This tempest will not give me leave to ponder
    On things would hurt me more. But I'll go in.
    [*To the* FOOL] In, boy, go first. You houseless poverty[6]—

Sc. iv: 1. tyranny: cruelty. 2. contentious: striving against us. 3. the . . .
fixed: i.e., in the mind. 4. free: i.e, from cares 5. what . . . there: i.e.,
the mental anguish which is increased by the thumping of Lear's overtaxed
heart. 6. houseless poverty: poor homeless people.

Nay, get thee in. I'll pray, and then I'll sleep.
[FOOL *goes in.*]
Poor naked wretches, wheresoe'er you are,
That bide[7] the pelting of this pitiless storm,
How shall your houseless heads and unfed sides,
Your looped and windowed[8] raggedness, defend you
From seasons such as these? Oh, I have ta'en
Too little care of this! Take physic, pomp.[9]
Expose thyself to feel what wretches feel,
That thou mayst shake the superflux[10] to them
And show the Heavens more just.

EDG. [*Within*]: Fathom and half, fathom and half! Poor Tom!
[*The* FOOL *runs out from the hovel.*]

FOOL: Come not in here, Nuncle, here's a spirit.
Help me, help me!

KENT: Give me thy hand. Who's there?

FOOL: A spirit, a spirit. He says his name's Poor Tom.

KENT: What art thou that dost grumble there i' the straw?
Come forth.
[*Enter* EDGAR *disguised as a madman.*]

EDG.: Away! The foul fiend follows me!
"Through the sharp hawthorn blows the cold wind."
Hum! Go to thy cold bed and warm thee.

LEAR: Hast thou given all to thy two daughters?
And art thou come to this?[11]

EDG.: Who gives anything to Poor Tom? Whom the foul fiend hath led
through fire and through flame, through ford and whirlpool, o'er
bog and quagmire, that hath laid knives under his pillow and halters
in his pew,[12] set ratsbane[13] by his porridge, made him proud of heart
to ride on a bay trotting horse over four-inched[14] bridges, to course[15]
his own shadow for a traitor. Bless thy five wits![16] Tom's a-cold. Oh,
do de, do de, do de. Bless thee from whirlwinds, star-blasting,[17] and
taking![18] Do Poor Tom some charity, whom the foul fiend vexes.

---

7. bide: endure.   8. looped . . . windowed: full of holes and gaps.   9. Take
. . . pomp: i.e., cure yourselves, you great men.   10. superflux: superfluity,
what you do not need.   11. Hast . . . this: At the sight of the supposed
lunatic Lear goes quite mad. Such utter destitution, he says, can only have been
caused by daughters as unkind as his own.   12. pew: seat.   13. ratsbane: rat
poison.   14. four-inched: i.e., narrow.   15. course: hunt after.   16. five wits:
i.e., common wit, imagination, fantasy, estimation, and memory.   17. star-
blasting: evil caused by a planet.   18. taking: malignant influence of fairies. Cf.
Haml, I.i. 163.

There could I have him now, and there, and there again, and there.[19]

[*Storm still.*]

LEAR: What, have his daughters brought him to this pass?
Couldst thou save nothing? Didst thou give them all?

FOOL: Nay, he reserved a blanket,[20] else we had been all shamed.

LEAR: Now, all the plagues that the pendulous [21] air
Hang fated o'er men's faults light on thy daughters!

KENT: He hath no daughters, sir.

LEAR: Death, traitor! Nothing could have subdued nature
To such a lowness but his unkind daughters.
Is it the fashion that discarded fathers
Should have thus little mercy on their flesh?
Judicious punishment! 'Twas this flesh begot
Those pelican[22] daughters.

EDG.:   "Pillicock sat on Pillicock Hill.
            Halloo, halloo, loo, loo!"[23]

FOOL: This cold night will turn us all to fools and madmen.

EDG.: Take heed o' the foul fiend. Obey thy parents, keep thy word justly, swear not, commit not with man's sworn spouse, set not thy sweet heart on proud array. Tom's a-cold.

LEAR: What hast thou been?

EDG.: A servingman,[24] proud in heart and mind, that curled my hair, wore gloves in my cap, served the lust of my mistress's heart and did the act of darkness with her, swore as many oaths as I spake words and broke them in the sweet face of Heaven. One that slept in the contriving of lust and waked to do it. Wine loved I deeply, dice dearly, and in woman outparamoured[25] the Turk.[26] False of heart, light of ear, bloody of hand, hog in sloth,[27] fox in stealth, wolf in greediness, dog in madness, lion in prey. Let not the creaking of shoes nor the rustling of silks betray thy poor heart to woman. Keep thy foot out of brothels, thy hand out of plackets,[28] thy pen from lenders' books,[29] and defy the foul fiend.

---

19. There . . . there: Poor Tom is chasing his own vermin.   20. blanket: i.e., his only covering. See II.iii.10.   21. pendulous: overhanging.   22. pelican: The pelican was the pattern of devoted motherhood because it fed its young its own blood; but when the young grew strong, they turned on their parents. 23. Pillicock . . . loo: an old rhyme.   24. A servingman . . . prey: This is another description of the gentleman servingman. See II.ii.15–26.   25. outparamoured: had more mistresses than.   26. the Turk: the Turkish Emperor. 27. hog in sloth: See *Lear* Intro. p. 1139a.   28. plackets: openings in a petticoat.   29. pen . . . books: The debtor often acknowledged the debt by signing in the lender's account book. There are many such acknowledgments in Henslowe's *Diary* (see Gen. Intro. p. 65a).

"Still through the hawthorn blows the cold wind.
Says suum, mun, ha, no, nonny.
Dolphin my boy, my boy, sessa! Let him trot by."
[Storm still.]

LEAR: Why, thou wert better in thy grave than to answer with thy un-covered body this extremity of the skies. Is man no more than this? Consider him well. Thou[30] owest the worm no silk, the beast no hide, the sheep no wool, the cat no perfume.[31] Ha! Here's three on 's are sophisticated. Thou art the thing itself. Unaccommodated man is no more but such a poor, bare, forked animal as thou art. Off, off, you lendings![32] Come, unbutton here.
[Tearing off his clothes.]

FOOL: Prithee, Nuncle, be contented, 'tis a naughty night to swim in. Now a little fire in a wild field were like an old lecher's heart, a small spark, all the rest on 's body cold. Look, here comes a walking fire.
[Enter GLOUCESTER, with a torch.]

EDG.: This is the foul fiend Flibbertigibbet. He begins at curfew[33] and walks till the first cock, he gives the web and the pin,[34] squints the eye and makes the harelip, mildews the white wheat and hurts the poor creature of earth.
"Saint[35] Withold footed thrice the 'old,[36]
He met the nightmare[37] and her ninefold.[38]
Bid her alight,
And her troth plight,
And aroint thee, witch, aroint[39] thee!"

KENT: How fares your Grace?

LEAR: What's he?

KENT: Who's there? What is 't you seek?

GLO.: What are you there? Your names?

EDG.: Poor Tom, that eats the swimming frog, the toad, the tadpole,

---

30. Thou . . . here: There is usually an underlying sense in Lear's ravings. The bedlam, he says, has not borrowed silk from the silkworm, or furs from the beast, or wool from the sheep to cover himself. Kent, the Fool, and he himself are therefore sophisticated—adulterated, wearing coverings not their own. Natural man, unaccommodated (i.e., not provided with such conveniences), is just a naked animal. Lear will therefore strip himself naked and cease to be artificial.   31. cat . . . perfume: a perfume taken from the civet cat, which has glands that function in the same manner as the skunk's.   32. lendings: things borrowed.   33. curfew: sounded at 9 P.M.   34. web . . . pin: eye diseases, cataract.   35. Saint . . . thee: a charm to keep horses from suffering from nightmare.   36. 'old: wold, uncultivated downland.   37. nightmare: nightmare was believed to be caused by a fiend.   38. ninefold: nine young.   39. aroint: be gone.

the wall newt, and the water; that in the fury of his heart, when the
foul fiend rages, eats cow dung for sallets,[40] swallows the old rat and
the ditch dog,[41] drinks the green mantle of the standing pool; who
is whipped from tithing to tithing,[42] and stock-punished, and imprisoned; who hath had three suits[43] to his back, six shirts to his body,
horse to ride, and weapon to wear.

"But mice and rats and such smaller deer
Have been Tom's food for seven long year."

Beware my follower. Peace, Smulkin,[44] peace, thou fiend!

GLO.: What, hath your Grace no better company?

EDG.: The Prince of Darkness is a gentleman.
Modo he's called, and Mahu.

GLO.: Our flesh and blood is grown so vile, my lord,
That it doth hate what gets[45] it.

EDG.: Poor Tom's a-cold.

GLO.: Go in with me. My duty cannot suffer
To obey in all your daughters' hard commands.
Though their injunction be to bar my doors
And let this tyrannous night take hold upon you,
Yet have I ventured to come seek you out
And bring you where both fire and food is ready.

LEAR: First let me talk with this philosopher.
What is the cause of thunder?[46]

KENT: Good my lord, take his offer, go into the house.

LEAR: I'll talk a word with this same learnèd Theban.[47]
What is your study?[48]

EDG.: How to prevent the fiend and to kill vermin.

LEAR: Let me ask you one word in private.

KENT: Impórtune him once more to go, my lord.
His wits begin to unsettle.

GLO.: Canst thou blame him?
[Storm still.]
His daughters seek his death. Ah, that good Kent!
He said it would be thus, poor banished man!
Thou say'st the King grows mad. I'll tell thee, friend,
I am almost mad myself. I had a son,

---

40. sallets: salads.   41. ditch dog: dog drowned in a ditch.   42. tithing: district,
parish.   43. three suits: See II.ii.16.   44. Smulkin . . . Mahu: familiar spirits.
See *Lear* Intro. p. 1136b.   45. gets: begets.   46. cause of thunder: This was
much disputed by philosophers of the time.   47. Theban: i.e., Greek philosopher.   48. study: particular interest, or in modern academic jargon, "special field."

Now outlawed from my blood. He sought my life
But lately, very late. I loved him, friend,
No father his son dearer. Truth to tell thee,
The grief hath crazed my wits. What a night's this!
I do beseech your Grace—

LEAR: Oh, cry you mercy, sir.
Noble philosopher, your company.

EDG.: Tom's a-cold.

GLO.: In, fellow, there, into the hovel. Keep thee warm.

LEAR: Come, let's in all.

KENT: This way, my lord.

LEAR: With him,
I will keep still with my philosopher.

KENT: Good my lord, soothe him, let him take the fellow.

GLO.: Take him you on.

KENT: Sirrah, come on, go along with us.

LEAR: Come, good Athenian.[49]

GLO.: No words, no words. Hush.

EDG.: "Child[50] Rowland to the dark tower came.
His word was still 'Fie, foh, and fum,
I smell the blood of a British man.' "
[*Exeunt.*]

SCENE 5. GLOUCESTER's *castle.*

[*Enter* CORNWALL *and* EDMUND.]

CORN.: I will have my revenge ere I depart his house.

EDM.: How, my lord, I may be censured,[1] that nature[2] thus gives way
to loyalty, something fears me to think of.

CORN.: I now perceive it was not altogether your brother's evil disposition made him seek his death, but a provoking merit, set a-work by
a reprovable badness in himself.[3]

EDM.: How malicious is my fortune, that I must repent to be just![4]

---

49. Athenian: like "Theban," l. 162.   50. Child . . . man: jumbled snatches of
old ballads. *Child* in old ballads is used of young warriors who have not yet
been knighted.

Sc. v: 1. censured: judged.   2. nature: i.e., natural affection toward my father
yielding to loyalty to my Duke. For Edmund's real sentiments on nature see
I.ii.1–2.   3. but . . . himself: i.e., but a good quality in Edgar that provoked
him to commit murder because of the reprehensible badness in Gloucester.
4. repent . . . just: be sorry because I have acted rightly (in betraying my
father).

This is the letter he spoke of, which approves[5] him an intelligent party[6] to the advantages of France. Oh heavens, that this treason were not, or not I the detector!

CORN.: Go with me to the Duchess.

EDM.: If the matter of this paper be certain, you have mighty business in hand.

CORN.: True or false, it hath made thee Earl of Gloucester. Seek out where thy father is, that he may be ready for our apprehension.[7]

EDM. [Aside]: If I find him comforting the King, it will stuff his suspicion more fully.—I will persever[8] in my course of loyalty, though the conflict be sore between that and my blood.

CORN.: I will lay trust upon thee, and thou shalt find a dearer father in my love.

    [Exeunt.]

SCENE 6.[1]   A chamber in a farmhouse adjoining the castle.

    [Enter GLOUCESTER, LEAR, KENT, FOOL, and EDGAR.]

GLO.: Here is better than the open air, take it thankfully. I will piece out the comfort with what addition I can. I will not be long from you.

KENT: All the power of his wits has given way to his impatience.[2] The gods reward your kindness!

    [Exit GLOUCESTER.]

EDG.: Fraterretto[3] calls me, and tells me Nero[4] is an angler in the lake of darkness. Pray, innocent,[5] and beware the foul fiend.

FOOL: Prithee, Nuncle, tell me whether a madman be a gentleman or a yeoman.[6]

LEAR: A king, a king!

FOOL: No, he's a yeoman that has a gentleman to his son, for he's a mad yeoman that sees his son a gentleman before him.[7]

---

5. approves: proves. 6. intelligent party: spy, one with secret information. 7. apprehension: arrest. 8. persever: persevere.

Sc. vi: 1. In this scene Lear is completely mad, the Fool is half-witted, and Edgar is pretending to be a lunatic. 2. impatience: suffering. 3. Fraterretto: another fiend's name from Harsnett's book. See Lear Intro, p. 1136a. 4. Nero: the debauched Roman Emperor who fiddled while Rome burned. 5. innocent: fool. 6. whether . . . yeoman: The fool is much interested in the social status of a madman and proceeds to discuss the problem. yeoman: farmer, a notoriously wealthy class at this time. 7. No . . . him: Many yeomen farmers who had become wealthy by profiteering from the wars and dearths sent their sons to London to learn to become gentlemen, as fifty years ago Chicago meat packers sent their sons to Harvard and their daughters to England, to be presented at Court. This social change was much commented on, and is illustrated in Jonson's comedy Every Man out of His Humour.

LEAR: To have a thousand with red burning spits[8]
Come hissing in upon 'em—
EDG.: The foul fiend bites my back.
FOOL: He's mad that trusts in the tameness of a wolf, a horse's health, a boy's love, or a whore's oath.
LEAR: It shall be done, I will arraign them straight.[9]
[*To* EDGAR] Come, sit thou here, most learned justicer.[10]
[*To the* FOOL] Thou, sapient[11] sir, sit here. Now, you she-foxes!
EDG.: Look where he stands and glares! Wantest thou eyes at trial,[12] madam?
"Come o'er the bourn, Bessy, to me."
FOOL: "Her boat hath a leak,
And she must not speak
Why she dares not come over to thee."
EDG.: The foul fiend haunts poor Tom in the voice of a nightingale. Hopdance[13] cries in Tom's belly for two white herring. Croak not,[14] black angel, I have no food for thee.
KENT: How do you, sir? Stand you not so amazed.[15]
Will you lie down and rest upon the cushions?
LEAR: I'll see their trial first. Bring in the evidence.
[*To* EDGAR] Thou robèd man of justice,[16] take thy place.
[*To the* FOOL] And thou, his yokefellow of equity,[17]
Bench[18] by his side. [*To* KENT] You are o' the commission,[19]
Sit you too.
EDG.: Let us deal justly.
"Sleepest or wakest thou, jolly shepherd?
Thy sheep be in the corn,
And for one blast of thy minikin[20] mouth,
Thy sheep shall take no harm."
Purr! The cat is gray.
LEAR: Arraign her first. 'Tis Goneril. I here take my oath before this honorable assembly, she kicked the poor King her father.

8. spits: thin iron rods thrust through meat on which the meat was turned before the fire in roasting; very useful weapons in emergency. 9. straight: straightway. 10. justicer: judge. 11. sapient: wise. 12. Wantest . . . trial: can you not see who is at your trial (i.e., this fiend)? But Edgar is deliberately talking madly. 13. Hopdance: another name from Harsnett. 14. Croak not: don't rumble in my empty belly. The correct Elizabethan word for this embarrassing manifestation is "wamble." 15. amazed: astonished—a strong word. 16. robed . . . justice: another glance at Edgar's blanket. 17. yokefellow of equity: partner in the law. 18. Bench: sit on the judge's bench. 19. commission: Persons of high rank or those accused of extraordinary crimes were not tried before the ordinary courts, but by a commission specially appointed. 20. minikin: dainty.

FOOL: Come hither, mistress. Is your name Goneril?

LEAR: She cannot deny it.

FOOL: Cry you mercy,[21] I took you for a joint stool.[22]

LEAR: And here's another, whose warped[23] looks proclaim
What store[24] her heart is made on. Stop her there!
Arms, arms, sword, fire! Corruption[25] in the place!
False justicer, why hast thou let her 'scape?

EDG.: Bless thy five wits!

KENT: Oh, pity! Sir, where is the patience now,
That you so oft have boasted to retain?

EDG. [Aside]: My tears begin to take his part so much
They'll mar my counterfeiting.[26]

LEAR: The little dogs and all,
Tray, Blanch, and Sweetheart, see, they bark at me.

EDG.: Tom will throw his head at them. Avaunt, you curs!
   Be thy mouth or black or white,
   Tooth that poisons if it bite,
   Mastiff, greyhound, mongrel grim,
   Hound or spaniel, brach[27] or lym,[28]
   Or bobtail tike or trundletail,[29]
   Tom will make them weep and wail.
   For, with throwing thus my head,
   Dogs leap the hatch, and all are fled.
Do de, de, de. Sessa! Come, march to wakes[30] and fairs and market towns. Poor Tom, thy horn[31] is dry.

LEAR: Then let them anatomize[32] Regan, see what breeds about her heart. Is there any cause in nature that makes these hard hearts? [To EDGAR] You, sir, I entertain[33] for one of my hundred, only I do not like the fashion of your garments. You will say they are Persian attire,[34] but let them be changed.

KENT: Now, good my lord, lie here and rest awhile.

LEAR: Make no noise, make no noise. Draw the curtains. So, so, so.[35]

---

21. Cry . . . mercy: I beg your pardon. 22. joint stool: wooden stool of joiner's work. See Pl. 17a. 23. warped: malignant. 24. store: material. 25. Corruption: bribery. 26. My . . . counterfeiting: i.e, I am so sorry for the King that I can hardly keep up this pretense. 27. brach: bitch. 28. lym: bloodhound. 29. trundletail: curly tail. 30. wakes: merrymakings. 31. horn: a horn bottle carried by beggars in which they stored the drink given by the charitable. 32. anatomize: dissect. 33. entertain: engage. 34. Persian attire: i.e., of a magnificent and foreign fashion. There had been considerable interest in Persia for some years, especially after the return of some of the followers of Sir Anthony Shirley from his famous expedition. See T Night Intro. p. 845a. 35. So . . . so: In dialogue "so, so" usually indicates action. Here Lear imagines the bed curtains being drawn.

We'll go to supper i' the morning. So, so, so.

FOOL: And I'll go to bed at noon.[36]

[*Re-enter* GLOUCESTER.]

GLO.: Come hither, friend. Where is the King my master?

KENT: Here, sir, but trouble him not. His wits are gone.

GLO.: Good friend, I prithee take him in thy arms.

I have o'erheard a plot of death upon him.

There is a litter[37] ready, lay him in 't,

And drive toward Dover, friend, where thou shalt meet

Both welcome and protection. Take up thy master.

If thou shouldst dally[38] half an hour, his life,

With thine and all that offer to defend him,

Stand in assurèd loss. Take up, take up,

And follow me, that will to some provision

Give thee quick conduct.

KENT: Oppressèd nature sleeps.

This rest might yet have balmed[39] thy broken sinews,

Which, if convenience will not allow,

Stand in hard cure.[40] [*To the* FOOL] Come, help to bear thy master.

Thou must not stay behind.

GLO.: Come, come, away.

[*Exeunt all but* EDGAR.]

EDG.: When we our betters see bearing our woes,

We scarcely think our miseries our foes.

Who alone suffers suffers most i' the mind,

Leaving free things and happy shows behind,

But then the mind much sufferance doth o'erskip

When grief hath mates, and bearing fellowship.[41]

How light and portable my pain seems now

When that which makes me bend makes the King bow,

He childed as I fathered! Tom, away!

Mark the high noises,[42] and thyself[43] bewray

When false opinion, whose wrong thought defiles thee,

---

36. And . . . noon: i.e., if it's suppertime in the morning, it will be bedtime at noon. The food disappears after this scene. 37. litter: a form of bed or stretcher enclosed by curtains used for carrying the sick or the wealthy. 38. dally: hesitate. 39. balmed: soothed. 40. stand . . . cure; will hardly be cured. 41. When . . . fellowship: when we see better men than ourselves suffering as we do, our sufferings seem slight. The man who suffers endures most in his mind because he contrasts his present misery with his happy past; but when he has companions in misery (*bearing fellowship*), his mind suffers less. 42. high noises: i.e., the "hue and cry" of the pursuers. See Gen. Intro. p. 28a. 43. thyself . . . thee: do not reveal yourself until the belief in your guilt is proved wrong and you are called back.

In thy just proof repeals[44] and reconciles thee.
What will hap more tonight, safe 'scape the King!
Lurk,[45] lurk.
      [*Exit.*]

SCENE 7.   GLOUCESTER'S *castle.*

      [*Enter* CORNWALL, REGAN, GONERIL, EDMUND, *and* SERVANTS.]
CORN.: Post speedily to my lord your husband.[1] Show him this letter.
   The army of France is landed. Seek out the traitor Gloucester.
      [*Exeunt some of the* SERVANTS.]
REG.: Hang him instantly.
GON.: Pluck out his eyes.
CORN.: Leave him to my displeasure. Edmund, keep you our sister
   company. The revenges we are bound to take upon your traitorous
   father are not fit for your beholding. Advise the Duke, where you are
   going, to a most festinate[2] preparation. We are bound to the like.
   Our posts[3] shall be swift and intelligent[4] betwixt us. Farewell, dear
   Sister. Farewell, my Lord of Gloucester.[5]
      [*Enter* OSWALD.] How now! Where's the King?
OSW.: My Lord of Gloucester[6] hath conveyed him hence.
   Some five or six and thirty of his knights,
   Hot questrists[7] after him, met him at gate,
   Who, with some other of the lords dependents,[8]
   Are gone with him toward Dover, where they boast
   To have well-armèd friends.
CORN.: Get horses for your mistress.
GON.: Farewell, sweet lord, and Sister.
CORN.: Edmund, farewell.
      [*Exeunt* GONERIL, EDMUND, *and* OSWALD.]
   Go seek the traitor Gloucester.
   Pinion him like a thief, bring him before us.
      [*Exeunt other* SERVANTS.]
   Though well we may not pass[9] upon his life
   Without the form of justice, yet our power

---

44. repeals: calls back from banishment.   45. Lurk: lie hid.

Sc. vii: 1. Post . . . husband: These words are addressed to Goneril. Post: ride
   fast.   2. festinate: hasty.   3. posts: messengers. See App. 17.   4. intelligent: full of information.   5. Lord of Gloucester: i.e., Edmund, who has
   been promoted for his treachery.   6. Lord of Gloucester: i.e., the old Earl.
   7. questrists: seekers.   8. lords dependents: lords of his party.   9. pass: pass
   judgment on.

Shall do a courtesy to our wrath,[10] which men
May blame but not control. Who's there? The traitor?

[*Enter* GLOUCESTER, *brought in by two or three.*]

REG.: Ungrateful fox! 'Tis he.

CORN.: Bind fast his corky[11] arms.

GLO.: What mean your Graces? Good my friends, consider
You are my guests. Do me no foul play, friends.

CORN.: Bind him, I say.

[SERVANTS *bind him.*]

REG.: Hard, hard. O filthy traitor!

GLO.: Unmerciful lady as you are, I'm none.

CORN.: To this chair bind him. Villain, thou shalt find—

[REGAN *plucks his beard.*]

GLO.: By the kind gods, 'tis most ignobly done
To pluck me by the beard.[12]

REG.: So white, and such a traitor!

GLO.: Naughty lady,
Those hairs which thou dost ravish[13] from my chin
Will quicken[14] and accuse thee. I am your host.
With robbers' hands my hospitable favors[15]
You should not ruffle thus. What will you do?

CORN.: Come, sir, what letters had you late from France?

REG.: Be simple answerer, for we know the truth.

CORN.: And what confederacy[16] have you with the traitors
Late footed in the kingdom?

REG.: To whose hands have you sent the lunatic King?
Speak.

GLO.: I have a letter guessingly set down,
Which came from one that's of a neutral heart,
And not from one opposed.

CORN.: Cunning.

REG.: And false.

CORN.: Where hast thou sent the King?

GLO.: To Dover.

REG.: Wherefore to Dover? Wast thou not charged at peril[17]—

CORN.: Wherefore to Dover? Let him first answer that.

GLO.: I am tied to the stake, and I must stand the course.[18]

---

10. yet . . . wrath: yet because we are all-powerful we will give way to our wrath.
11. corky: dry and withered.   12. pluck . . . beard: the greatest indignity that
could be offered.   13. ravish: seize.   14. quicken: come to life.   15. hospitable favors: the face of your host.   16. confederacy: alliance, understanding.
17. At peril: under penalty.   18. I . . . course: like a bear in the bear pit I
must endure the onslaught. See App. 5.

REG.: Wherefore to Dover, sir?

GLO.: Because I would not see thy cruel nails
Pluck out his poor old eyes, nor thy fierce sister
In his anointed[19] flesh stick boarish fangs.
The sea, with such a storm as his bare head
In hell-black night endured, would have buoyed up,[20]
And quenched the stellèd fires.[21]
Yet, poor old heart, he holp[22] the heavens to rain.
If wolves had at thy gate howled that stern time,
Thou shouldst have said, "Good porter, turn the key,"[23]
All cruels else subscribed.[24] But I shall see
The wingèd vengeance overtake such children.

CORN.: See 't shalt thou never. Fellows, hold the chair.
Upon these eyes of thine I'll set my foot.

GLO.: He that will think to live till he be old,
Give me some help! Oh, cruel! Oh, you gods!

[GLOUCESTER's eye is put out.]

REG.: One side will mock another, the other too.

CORN.: If you see vengeance—

1. SERV.: Hold your hand, my lord.
I have served you ever since I was a child,
But better service have I never done you
Than now to bid you hold.

REG.: How now, you dog!

1. SERV.: If you did wear a beard upon your chin,
I'd shake it on this quarrel. What do you mean?

CORN.: My villain!

[They draw and fight. CORNWALL is wounded.]

1. SERV.: Nay, then, come on, and take the chance of anger.

REG.: Give me thy sword. A peasant stand up thus!

[Takes a sword and runs at him behind.]

1. SERV.: Oh, I am slain! My lord, you have one eye left
To see some mischief on him. Oh!

[Dies.]

CORN.: Lest it see more, prevent it. Out, vile jelly!
Where is thy luster now?

[Puts out GLOUCESTER's other eye.]

GLO.: All dark and comfortless. Where's my son Edmund?

---

19. anointed: i.e., anointed as a king, and therefore holy. 20. buoyed up:
swelled up. 21. stelled fires: the light of the stars. 22. holp: helped. 23.
turn . . . key: open the gate. 24. All . . . subscribed: all other cruel things
were on his side.

Edmund, enkindle all the sparks[25] of nature,
To quit[26] this horrid act.
REG.: Out, treacherous villain!
Thou call'st on him that hates thee. It was he
That made the overture[27] of thy treasons to us,
Who is too good to pity thee.
GLO.: Oh, my follies! Then Edgar was abused.
Kind gods, forgive me that, and prosper him!
REG.: Go thrust him out at gates, and let him smell
His way to Dover.
　　　　　[Exit one with GLOUCESTER.]
How is 't, my lord? How look you?
CORN.: I have received a hurt. Follow me, lady.
Turn out that eyeless villain. Throw this slave
Upon the dunghill. Regan, I bleed apace.[28]
Untimely comes this hurt. Give me your arm.
　　　　　[Exit CORNWALL, led by REGAN.]
2. SERV.: I'll never care what wickedness I do
If this man comes to good.
3. SERV.: If she live long,
And in the end meet the old course of death,[29]
Women will all turn monsters.
2. SERV.: Let's follow the old Earl, and get the bedlam[30]
To lead him where he would. His roguish madness
Allows itself to anything.
3. SERV.: Go thou. I'll fetch some flax and whites of eggs
To apply to his bleeding face. Now, Heaven help him!
　　　　　[Exeunt severally.]

---

25. enkindle . . . sparks: i.e., blow into flame your natural love. 26. quit: requite. 27. overture: revelation. 28. apace: quickly, profusely. 29 old . . .
death: natural death in old age. 30. bedlam: i.e., Poor Tom. See I.ii.148;
II.iii.14.

❦ Act IV

SCENE 1. *The heath.*

[*Enter* EDGAR.]

EDG.: Yet better thus, and known to be contemned,[1]
  Than still[2] contemned and flattered. To[3] be worst,
  The lowest and most dejected thing of fortune,
  Stands still in esperance, lives not in fear.
  The lamentable change is from the best,
  The worst returns to laughter. Welcome then,
  Thou unsubstantial air that I embrace!
  The wretch that thou hast blown unto the worst
  Owes nothing to thy blasts.—But who comes here?
    [*Enter* GLOUCESTER, *led by an* OLD MAN.]
  My father, poorly led?[4] World, world, O world!
  But that thy strange mutations make us hate thee,
  Life would not yield to age.

OLD MAN: Oh, my good lord, I have been your tenant, and your father's
  tenant, these fourscore years.

GLO.: Away, get thee away. Good friend, be gone.
  Thy comforts can do me no good at all,
  Thee they may hurt.

OLD MAN: Alack, sir, you cannot see your way.

GLO.: I have no way and therefore want no eyes.
  I stumbled when I saw. Full oft 'tis seen,
  Our means secure us, and our mere defects
  Prove our commodities.[5] Ah, dear Son Edgar,
  The food[6] of thy abusèd father's wrath,
  Might I but live to see thee in my touch,
  I'd say I had eyes again!

Act IV, Sc. i: 1. contemned: despised; i.e., as a beggar. 2. still: always. 3. To
. . . age: when a man has reached the lowest state of misfortune, he has hope
(esperance) for the better, and no fear for the worse. The change to be lamented
is when the best things turn to bad; the worst can only change to joy. After
this poor consolation that nothing worse can happen to him, Edgar sees his
blinded father and continues (1. 10): One would not trouble to live to old
age except to spite the world. 4. poorly led: led by one poor old man—and
not accompanied by the usual party of servants. 5. Our . . . commodities:
when we are well off we grow careless, and then our misfortunes prove blessings. 6. food: object.

OLD MAN: How now! Who's there?

EDG.: [*Aside*] Oh gods! Who is 't can say "I am at the worst"?
　I am worse than e'er I was.

OLD MAN: 'Tis poor mad Tom.

EDG.: [*Aside*] And worse I may be yet. The worst is not
　So long as we can say "This is the worst."[7]

OLD MAN: Fellow, where goest?

GLO.: Is it a beggarman?

OLD MAN: Madman and beggar too.

GLO.: He has some reason, else he could not beg.
　I' the last night's storm I such a fellow saw,
　Which made me think a man a worm. My son
　Came then into my mind, and yet my mind
　Was then scarce friends with him. I have heard more since.
　As flies to wanton boys are we to the gods,
　They kill us for their sport.

EDG.: [*Aside*] How should this be?
　Bad is the trade that must play fool to sorrow,
　Angering itself and others.[8] Bless thee, master!

GLO.: Is that the naked fellow?

OLD MAN: Aye, my lord.

GLO.: Then, prithee get thee gone. If for my sake
　Thou wilt o'ertake us hence a mile or twain
　I' the way toward Dover, do it for ancient love,
　And bring some covering for this naked soul,
　Who I'll entreat to lead me.

OLD MAN: Alack, sir, he is mad.

GLO.: 'Tis the times' plague[9] when madmen lead the blind.
　Do as I bid thee, or rather do thy pleasure.
　Above the rest, be gone.

OLD MAN: I'll bring him the best 'parel[10] that I have,
　Come on 't what will.
　　　　[*Exit.*]

GLO.: Sirrah, naked fellow—

EDG.: Poor Tom's a-cold [*Aside*] I cannot daub[11] it further.

GLO.: Come hither, fellow.

EDG.: [*Aside*] And yet I must.—Bless thy sweet eyes, they bleed.

---

7. The . . . worst: so long as a man is alive, he may yet reach a lower depth of misery.　8. Bad . . . others: this business of pretending to be mad and fooling a man in such distress as Gloucester is now hateful.　9. times' plague: a sign of these diseased times.　10. 'parel: apparel.　11. daub: plaster it over, pretend.

GLO.: Know'st thou the way to Dover?

EDG.: Both stile and gate, horseway and footpath. Poor Tom hath been scared out of his good wits. Bless thee, good man's son from the foul fiend! Five fiends have been in Poor Tom at once—of lust, as Obidicut; Hobbididence, prince of dumbness; Mahu, of stealing; Modo, of murder; Flibbertigibbet,[12] of mopping and mowing,[13] who since possesses chambermaids and waiting-women. So, bless thee, master!

GLO.: Here, take this purse, thou whom the Heavens' plagues
Have humbled to all strokes.[14] That I am wretched
Makes thee the happier. Heavens, deal so still!
Let the superfluous and lust-dieted man,
That slaves your ordinance, that will not see
Because he doth not feel, feel your power quickly.[15]
So distribution should undo excess[16]
And each man have enough. Dost thou know Dover?

EDG.: Aye, master.

GLO.: There is a cliff whose high and bending[17] head
Looks fearfully in the confinèd deep.
Bring me but to the very brim of it,
And I'll repair the misery thou dost bear
With something rich about me. From that place
I shall no leading need.

EDG.: Give me thy arm.
Poor Tom shall lead thee.
[Exeunt.]

SCENE 2. *Before the* DUKE OF ALBANY's *palace.*

[*Enter* GONERIL *and* EDMUND.]

GON.: Welcome, my lord. I marvel our mild husband
Not met us on the way.
[*Enter* OSWALD.] Now, where's your master?

OSW.: Madam, within, but never man so changed.

12. Obidicut . . . Flibbertigibbet: these names also come from Harsnett. See *Lear* Intro. p. 1136b. 13. mopping . . . mowing: making faces and grimaces. Cf. *Temp,* IV.i.47. 14. humbled . . strokes: made so humble that you can endure anything. 15. Heavens . . . quickly: you gods, deal with others as you have dealt with me; let the man who has too much and pampers his own lusts, who regards your commands as contemptuously as he regards his slaves, that will not understand until he is hurt, feel your power quickly. This passage echoes Lear's words (III.iv.33–36). 16. So . . . excess: then the man with too much would distribute his excessive wealth. 17. bending: overhanging.

I told him of the army that was landed.
He smiled at it. I told him you were coming.
His answer was "The worse." Of Gloucester's treachery
And of the loyal service of his son
When I informed him, then he called me sot
And told me I had turned the wrong side out.
What most he should dislike seems pleasant to him,
What like, offensive.
GON.: [To EDMUND] Then shall you go no further.
It is the cowish[1] terror of his spirit,
That dares not undertake.[2] He'll not feel wrongs
Which tie[3] him to an answer. Our wishes on the way
May prove effects.[4] Back, Edmund, to my brother.
Hasten his musters[5] and conduct his powers.[6]
I[7] must change arms at home and give the distaff[8]
Into my husband's hands. This trusty servant
Shall pass between us. Ere long you are like to hear,
If you dare venture in your own behalf,
A mistress's[9] command. Wear this. Spare speech.
    [Giving a favor.]
Decline your head. This kiss, if it durst speak,
Would stretch thy spirits up into the air.
Conceive,[10] and fare thee well.
EDM.: Yours in the ranks of death.
GON.: My most dear Gloucester! [Exit EDMUND.]
Oh, the difference of man and man!
To thee a woman's services are due,
My fool[11] usurps my body.
OSW.: Madam, here comes my lord. [Exit.]
    [Enter ALBANY.]
GON.: I have been worth the whistle.[12]
ALB.: O Goneril!
You are not worth the dust which the rude wind

Sc. ii: 1. cowish: cowardly. 2. undertake: show initiative, venture. 3. tie: force.
4. Our . . . effects: our hopes (of love) as we rode together may be fulfilled.
5. musters: troops which have been collected. 6. powers: forces. 7. I . . .
hands: I must become the soldier and leave my husband to do the spinning.
8. distaff: stick used in spinning, essentially the work of the housewife. 9.
mistress's: in the double sense of lady and lover. Edmund, having disposed of
his brother and father, now looks higher; he will through Goneril become possessed of her half of the kingdom of Lear. 10. Conceive: use your imagination. 11. My fool: i.e., my husband is no more than a fool to me. 12.
worth . . . whistle: There is a proverb " 'Tis a poor dog that is not worth the
whistle." Goneril means: I was once worth being regarded as your dog.

Blows in your face. I fear your disposition.
That[13] nature which contemns it origin
Cannot be bordered certain in itself.
She that herself will sliver[14] and disbranch
From her material sap,[15] perforce must wither
And come to deadly use.

GON.: No more, the text is foolish.[16]

ALB.: Wisdom and goodness to the vile seem vile.
Filths savor but themselves.[17] What have you done?
Tigers, not daughters, what have you performed?
A father, and a gracious agèd man
Whose reverence even the head-lugged bear[18] would lick,
Most barbarous, most degenerate, have you madded!
Could my good brother[19] suffer you to do it?
A man, a prince, by him so benefited!
If that the Heavens do not their visible spirits[20]
Send quickly down to tame these vile offenses,
It will come.
Humanity must perforce prey on itself,
Like monsters of the deep.[21]

GON.: Milk-livered[22] man!
That bear'st a cheek for blows, a head for wrongs,
Who hast not in thy brows an eye discerning
Thine honor from thy suffering;[23] that not know'st
Fools do those villians pity who are punished
Ere they have done their mischief.[24] Where's thy drum?
France spreads his banners in our noiseless land,
With plumèd helm thy state begins to threat,
Whiles thou, a moral[25] fool, sit'st still and criest
"Alack, why does he so?"

---

13. That . . . use: that creature which despises its father (origin) cannot be kept within bounds; she that cuts herself off from her family tree will perish and like a dead branch come to the burning. 14. sliver: slice off. 15. material sap: that sap which is part of herself. 16. text is foolish: i.e., this is a silly sermon. 17. Filths . . . themselves: the filthy like the taste only of filth. 18. head-lugged bear: a bear with its head torn off by the hounds. See App. 5. 19. good brother: Cornwall. 20. visible spirits: avenging spirits in visible form. 21. Humanity . . . deep: A thought more than once expressed by Shakespeare—that when natural law is broken, men will degenerate into beasts and prey on each other. Cf. Tr & Cr, I.iii.101–24; Gen. Intro. p. 7b–8a. 22. Milk-livered: cowardly; the liver was regarded as the seat of courage. 23. Who . . . suffering: who cannot see when the insults which you endure are dishonorable to you. 24. Fools . . . mischief: only a fool pities a villain when he is punished to prevent his committing a crime. 25. moral: moralizing.

ALB.: See thyself, devil!
Proper deformity[26] seems not in the fiend
So horrid as in woman.
GON.: O vain fool!
ALB.: Thou changèd and self-covered[27] thing, for shame,
Bemonster not thy feature.[28] Were 't my fitness
To let these hands obey my blood,[29]
They are apt enough to dislocate and tear
Thy flesh and bones. Howe'er[30] thou art a fiend,
A woman's shape doth shield thee.
GON.: Marry, your manhood![31] Mew![32]
[Enter a MESSENGER.]
ALB.: What news?
MESS.: O my good lord, the Duke of Cornwall's dead,
Slain by his servant, going to put out
The other eye of Gloucester.
ALB.: Gloucester's eyes!
MESS.: A servant that he bred, thrilled with remorse,[33]
Opposed against the act, bending his sword
To his great master, who thereat enraged
Flew on him and amongst them felled him dead,
But not without that harmful stroke which since
Hath plucked him after.
ALB.: This shows you are above,
You justicers, that these our nether crimes[34]
So speedily can venge. But, oh, poor Gloucester!
Lost he his other eye?
MESS.: Both, both my lord.
This letter, madam, craves a speedy answer.
'Tis from your sister.
GON.: [Aside] One way I like this well,
But being widow, and my Gloucester[35] with her,
May all the building in my fancy pluck[36]
Upon my hateful life. Another way,

---

26. Proper deformity: deformity natural to a fiend. 27. self-covered: hiding your
true self (i.e., devil) under the guise of a woman. 28. Bemonster . . . feature: do not change your shape into a fiend. 29. blood: anger. 30. Howe'er:
although. 31. Marry . . . manhood: you're a fine specimen of a man! 32.
Mew: a catcall. 33. thrilled . . . remorse: trembling with pity. 34. nether
crimes: crimes committed on earth below. 35. my Gloucester: i.e., Edmund.
36. May . . . pluck: may pull down my castle in the air (i.e., her desire to
marry Edmund).

The news is not so tart.—I'll read, and answer.
   [*Exit.*]
ALB.: Where was his son when they did take his eyes?
MESS.: Come with my lady hither.
ALB.: He is not here.
MESS.: No, my good lord, I met him back again.[37]
ALB.: Knows he the wickedness?
MESS.: Aye, my good lord, 'twas he informed against him,
   And quit the house on purpose, that their punishment
   Might have the freer course.
ALB.: Gloucester, I live
   To thank thee for the love thou show'dst the King,
   And to revenge thine eyes. Come hither, friend.
   Tell me what more thou know'st.
   [*Exeunt.*]

SCENE 3.   *The French camp near Dover.*

   [*Enter* KENT *and a* GENTLEMAN.]
KENT: Why the King of France is so suddenly gone back know you
   the reason?
GENT.: Something he left imperfect in the state which since his coming-
   forth is thought of, which imports to the kingdom so much fear and
   danger that his personal return was most required and necessary.
KENT: Who hath he left behind him general?
GENT.: The Marshal of France, Monsieur La Far.
KENT: Did your letters pierce the Queen to any demonstration of grief?
GENT.: Aye, sir. She took them, read them in my presence,
   And now and then an ample tear trilled down
   Her delicate cheek. It seemed she was a queen
   Over her passion,[1] who most rebel-like
   Sought to be king o'er her.
KENT: Oh, then it moved her.
GENT.: Not to a rage. Patience and Sorrow strove
   Who should express her goodliest.[2] You have seen
   Sunshine and rain at once. Her smiles and tears
   Were like a better way.[3] Those happy smilets[4]

---

37. met . . . again: met him as he was on his way back.

Sc. iii: 1. passion: emotion.   2. express . . . goodliest: make her seem more
   beautiful.   3. like . . . way: even more lovely.   4. smilets: little smiles.

That played on her ripe lip seemed not to know
What guests were in her eyes, which parted thence
As pearls from diamonds dropped. In brief,
Sorrow would be a rarity most beloved
If all could so become it.[5]

KENT: Made she no verbal question?

GENT.: Faith, once or twice she heaved the name of "Father"
Pantingly forth, as if it pressed her heart,
Cried "Sisters! Sisters! Shame of ladies! Sisters!
Kent! Father! Sister! What, i' the storm? i' the night?
Let pity not be believed!" There she shook
The holy water from her heavenly eyes,
And clamor-moistened.[6] Then away she started
To deal with grief alone.

KENT: It is the stars,
The stars above us, govern our conditions,
Else one self[7] mate and mate could not beget
Such different issues.[8] You spoke not with her since?

GENT.: No.

KENT: Was this before the King returned?

GENT.: No, since.

KENT.: Well, sir, the poor distressèd Lear's i' the town,
Who sometime in his better tune remembers
What we are come about, and by no means
Will yield to see his daughter.

GENT.: Why, good sir?

KENT: A sovereign[9] shame so elbows[10] him. His own unkindness
That stripped her from his benediction, turned her
To foreign casualties,[11] gave her dear rights
To his doghearted daughters. These things sting
His mind so venomously at burning shame
Detains him from Cordelia.

GENT.: Alack, poor gentleman!

KENT: Of Albany's and Cornwall's powers you heard not?

GENT.: 'Tis so, they are afoot.

KENT: Well, sir, I'll bring you to our master Lear,
And leave you to attend him. Some dear cause[12]

---

5. Sorrow . . . it: if everyone looked so beautiful in sorrow, it would be a quality much sought after.   6. clamor-moistened: wet her cries of grief with tears.
7. self: same.   8. issues: children.   9. sovereign: overpowering.   10. elbows: plucks him by the elbow, reminding him of the past.   11. casualties: chances, accidents.   12. dear cause: important reason.

Will in concealment wray me up awhile.
When I am known aright, you shall not grieve
Lending[13] me this acquaintance. I pray you, go
Along with me.
      [*Exeunt.*]

SCENE 4.   *The same. A tent.*

      [*Enter, with drum and colors,*[1] CORDELIA, DOCTOR, *and* SOLDIERS.]
COR.: Alack, 'tis he. Why, he was met even now
  As mad as the vexed sea, singing aloud,
  Crowned with rank fumiter and furrow weeds,
  With burdocks, hemlock, nettles, cuckoo flowers,
  Darnel,[2] and all the idle weeds that grow
  In our sustaining[3] corn. A century[4] send forth.
  Search every acre in the high-grown[5] field,
  And bring him to our eye. [*Exit an* OFFICER.] What can man's wisdom
  In the restoring his bereavèd sense?
  He that helps him take all my outward worth.[6]
DOCT.: There is means, madam.
  Our foster nurse[7] of nature is repose,
  The which he lacks. That to provoke in him
  Are many simples operative,[8] whose power
  Will close the eye of anguish.
COR.: All blest secrets,
  All you unpublished virtues[9] of the earth,
  Spring with my tears! Be aidant and remediate[10]
  In the good man's distress! Seek, seek for him,
  Lest his ungoverned rage dissolve the life
  That wants the means to lead it.[11]
      [*Enter a* MESSENGER.]
MESS.: News, madam.
  The British powers are marching hitherward.
COR.: 'Tis known before, our preparation stands

13. Lending: bestowing on.

Sc. iv: 1. s.d., drum . . . colors: a drummer and a soldier carrying a flag. 2.
  fumiter . . . Darnel: These are all English wild flowers and weeds. 3. sustaining: which maintains life. 4. century: company of a hundred soldiers. 5.
  high-grown: The season is therefore late summer. 6. outward worth: visible
  wealth. 7. foster nurse: the nurse who feeds. 8. simples operative: effica-
  cious herbs. 9. unpublished virtues: secret remedies. 10. aidant . . . remediate: helpful and remedial. 11. wants . . . it: that has no sense to guide it.

In expectation of them.[12] O dear Father,
It is thy business that I go about,
Therefore great France
My mourning and important[13] tears hath pitied.
No blown[14] ambition doth our arms incite,
But love, dear love, and our aged father's right.
Soon may I hear and see him!
    [*Exeunt.*]

SCENE 5.   GLOUCESTER's *castle.*

    [*Enter* REGAN *and* OSWALD.]
REG.: But are my brother's powers set forth?
OSW.: Aye, madam.
REG.: Himself in person there?
OSW.: Madam, with much ado.
  Your sister is the better soldier.
REG.: Lord Edmund spake not with your lord at home?
OSW.: No, madam.
REG.: What might import my sister's letter to him?
OSW.: I know not, lady.
REG.: Faith, he is posted[1] hence on serious matter.
  It was great ignorance, Gloucester's eyes being out,
  To let him live. Where he arrives he moves
  All hearts against us. Edmund, I think, is gone,
  In pity of his misery, to dispatch
  His nighted[2] life, moreover to descry
  The strength o' the enemy.
OSW.: I must needs after him, madam, with my letter.
REG.: Our troops set forth tomorrow. Stay with us,
  The ways are dangerous.
OSW.: I may not, madam.
  My lady charged my duty[3] in this business.
REG.: Why should she write to Edmund? Might not you
  Transport her purposes by word? Belike,
  Something—I know not what—I'll love thee much,
  Let me unseal the letter.

---

12. our . . . them: our army is ready to meet them.   13. important: importunate, pleading.   14. blown: puffed up.

Sc. v: 1. is posted: has ridden fast.   2. nighted: blinded.   3. charged my duty: entrusted it to me as a solemn duty.

osw.: Madam, I had rather—

REG.: I know your lady does not love her husband,
    I am sure of that. And at her late being here
    She gave strange œillades[4] and most speaking looks
    To noble Edmund. I know you are of her bosom.[5]

osw.: I, madam?

REG.: I speak in understanding. You are, I know 't.
    Therefore I do advise you, take this note.[6]
    My lord is dead, Edmund and I have talked,
    And more convenient is he for my hand
    Than for your lady's. You may gather more.
    If you do find him, pray you give him this,
    And when your mistress hears thus much from you,
    I pray desire her call her wisdom to her.
    So, fare you well.
    If you do chance to hear of that blind traitor,
    Preferment[7] falls on him that cuts him off.

osw.: Would I could meet him, madam! I should show
    What party I do follow.

REG.: Fare thee well.
    [Exeunt.]

SCENE 6.   *Fields near Dover.*

[*Enter* GLOUCESTER, *and* EDGAR *dressed like a peasant.*]

GLO.: When shall we come to the top of that same hill?

EDG.: You do climb up it now. Look how we labor.

GLO.: Methinks the ground is even.

EDG.: Horrible steep.
    Hark, do you hear the sea?

GLO.: No, truly.

EDG.: Why then your other senses grow imperfect
    By your eyes' anguish.

GLO.: So may it be, indeed.
    Methinks thy voice is altered, and thou speak'st
    In better phrase and matter than thou didst.

EDG.: You're much deceived. In nothing am I changed
    But in my garments.

GLO.: Methinks you're better-spoken.

---

4. œillades: loving looks.   5. of . . . bosom: in her confidence.   6. take . . .
    note: observe this.   7. Preferment: promotion.

EDG.: Come on, sir, here's the place. Stand still. How[1] fearful
And dizzy 'tis to cast one's eyes so low!
The crows and choughs[2] that wing the midway air
Show scarce so gross as beetles. Halfway down
Hangs one that gathers samphire,[3] dreadful trade!
Methinks he seems no bigger than his head.
The fishermen that walk upon the beach
Appear like mice, and yond tall anchoring bark[4]
Diminished to her cock[5]—her cock, a buoy
Almost too small for sight. The murmuring surge
That on the unnumbered idle pebbles chafes
Cannot be heard so high. I'll look no more,
Lest my brain turn and the deficient sight
Topple down headlong.[6]
GLO.: Set me where you stand.
EDG.: Give me your hand. You are now within a foot
Of the extreme verge. For all beneath the moon
Would I not leap upright.
GLO.: Let go my hand.
Here, friend, 's another purse, in it a jewel
Well worth a poor man's taking. Fairies and gods[7]
Prosper it with thee! Go thou further off.
Bid me farewell, and let me hear thee going.
EDG.: Now fare you well, good sir.
GLO.: With all my heart.
EDG.: Why I do trifle thus with his despair
Is done to cure it.[8]
GLO.: [Kneeling] O you mighty gods!
This world I do renounce, and in your sights
Shake patiently my great affliction off.
If[9] I could bear it longer and not fall

Sc. vi: 1. How . . . headlong: This vivid description of the cliffs of Dover seems
to have been written from direct observation. The King's Players visited Dover
in September 1606. 2. choughs: jackdaws. 3. samphire: a strongly per-
fumed plant which grows on the chalk cliffs of Dover. 4. bark: ship. 5.
cock: cockboat, the small ship's boat, usually towed behind. 6. deficient . . .
headlong: my sight failing, cause me to topple headlong. 7. Fairies . . .
gods: As this tale is pre-Christian, it is natural for the characters to call on the
gods of the "elder world." 8. Why . . . it: Edgar's purpose is to persuade his
blinded father to go on living by the thought that he has been miraculously preserved after falling from a great height. When Gloucester begins to recover
from the shock, Edgar has dropped his pretense of being a bedlam and speaks
in a natural (but still disguised) voice. 9. If . . . out: if I could endure my
misery longer without quarreling with the wish of Heaven, I would wait for the
rest of my hateful life to burn itself out.

To quarrel with your great opposeless wills,
My snuff[10] and loathèd part of nature should
Burn itself out. If Edgar live, oh, bless him!
Now, fellow, fare thee well. [*He falls forward.[11]*]

EDG.: Gone, sir. Farewell.
And yet I know not how conceit[12] may rob
The treasury of life when life itself
Yields to the theft.[13] Had he been where he thought,
By this had thought been past. Alive or dead?
Ho, you sir! Friend! Hear you, sir! Speak!
Thus might he pass[14] indeed. Yet he revives.
What are you, sir?

GLO.: Away, and let me die.

EDG.: Hadst thou been ought but gossamer,[15] feathers, air,
So many fathom down precipitating,
Thou'dst shivered like an egg. But thou dost breathe,
Hast heavy substance, bleed'st not, speak'st, art sound.
Ten masts at each[16] make not the altitude
Which thou hast perpendicularly fell.
Thy life's a miracle. Speak yet again.

GLO.: But have I fall'n, or no?

EDG.: From the dread summit of this chalky bourn.[17]
Look up a-height, the shrill-gorged[18] lark so far
Cannot be seen or heard. Do but look up.

GLO.: Alack, I have no eyes.
Is wretchedness deprived that benefit,
To end itself by death? 'Twas yet some comfort
When misery could beguile[19] the tyrant's rage
And frustrate his proud will.

EDG.: Give me your arm.
Up, so. How is 't? Feel you your legs? You stand.

GLO.: Too well, too well.

---

10. snuff: lit., smoking end of a burnt out candle. 11. s.d., falls forward. To be effective this episode needs an actor who is not afraid of hurting himself, for unless Gloucester's fall is heavy it is quite unconvincing. After his fall, he lies stunned for a few moments. 12. conceit: imagination. 13. Yields . . . theft: i.e., is willing to die. 14. pass: pass away, die. 15. gossamer: the parachute-like web made by a species of small spider by which it floats through the air. 16. Ten . . . each: ten masts, one on top of the other. 17. bourn: boundary. 18. shrill-gorged: shrill-throated. The lark is a small brown bird which flies to a great height and there remains fluttering a singing and shrill but beautiful song. 19. beguile: cheat (by death).

EDG.: This is above all strangeness.
Upon the crown o' the cliff, what thing was that
Which parted from you?
GLO.: A poor unfortunate beggar.
EDG.: As I stood here below, methought his eyes
Were two full moons, he had a thousand noses,
Horns whelked[20] and waved like the enridgèd[21] sea.
It was some fiend, therefore, thou happy father,
Think that the clearest[22] gods, who make them honors
Of men's impossibilities,[23] have preserved thee.
GLO.: I do remember now. Henceforth I'll bear
Affliction till it do cry out itself
"Enough, enough," and die. That think you speak of,
I took it for a man. Often 'twould say
"The fiend, the fiend." He led me to that place.
EDG.: Bear free[24] and patient thoughts. But who comes here?
    [*Enter* LEAR, *fantastically dressed with wild flowers.*]
The safer sense will n'er accommodate
His master thus.[25]
LEAR: No,[26] they cannot touch me for coining, I am the King himself.
EDG.: O thou side-piercing sight!
LEAR: Nature's above art[27] in that respect. There's your press money.
That fellow handles his bow like a crowkeeper,[28] draw me a clothier's
yard.[29] Look, look, a mouse! Peace, peace, this piece of toasted cheese
will do 't. There's my gauntlet,[30] I'll prove it on a[31] giant. Bring up
the brown bills.[32] Oh, well-flown, bird! I' the clout,[33] i' the clout.
Hewgh![34] Give the word.[35]

---

20. whelked: with spiral twists. 21. enridged: wavy. 22. clearest: most glorious.
23. who . . . impossibilities: who cause themselves to be honored by performing miracles impossible to men. 24. free: innocent. 25. The . . . thus:
a man in his right senses would never adorn himself. Edgar with unconscious
irony repeats Lear's "accommodated." See III.iv.110. 26. No . . . word:
Lear's madness has a sort of logical coherence. He begins by saying that he cannot be charged with coining, because it was his right as king to issue the coin,
a natural right. From coin his mind goes to the use of coin as press money for
soldiers (money given to a conscripted recruit as token that he has been engaged), thence to the recruits at archery practice. Then his mind is distracted
by a mouse, but comes back to his quarrel with his sons-in-law. He will throw
down his gauntlet as a challenge to single combat against any odds. He comes
back to the archery range, and a good shot right in the bull's-eye. 27. Nature's
. . . art: See App. 18. 28. crowkeeper: a man hired to scare away crows
from the crop. 29. clothier's yard: The expert archer drew his arrow back a
full yard to the ear. 30. gauntlet: glove, token of challenge. 31. prove . . .
a: i.e., fight even a. 32. brown bills: i.e., the infantry. See Pl. 21c. brown:
varnished to keep from rusting. 33. clout: the canvas target. 34. Hewgh:
imitation of the whizz of the arrow. 35. word: password.

EDG.: Sweet marjoram.[36]

LEAR: Pass.

GLO.: I know that voice.

LEAR: Ha! Goneril, with a white beard! They flattered me like a dog, and told me I had white hairs in my beard ere the black ones were there. To say "aye" and "no" to everything that I said! "Aye" and "no" too was no good divinity.[37] When the rain came to wet me once and the wind to make me chatter, when the thunder would not peace at my bidding, there I found 'em, there I smelt 'em out. Go to, they are not men o' their words. They told me I was everything. 'Tis a lie, I am not ague-proof.

GLO.: The trick[38] of that voice I do well remember.
Is 't not the King?

LEAR: Aye, every inch a king.
When I do stare, see how the subject quakes.
I pardon that man's life. What was thy cause?
Adultery?
Thou shalt not die. Die for adultery! No.
The wren goes to 't, and the small gilded fly
Does lecher in my sight.
Let copulation thrive, for Gloucester's bastard son
Was kinder to his father than my daughters
Got 'tween the lawful sheets.
To 't, luxury,[39] pell-mell! For I lack soldiers.
Behold yond simpering dame,
Whose face between her forks[40] presages snow,
That minces virtue[41] and does shake the head
To hear of pleasure's name.
The fitchew,[42] nor the soilèd[43] horse, goes to 't
With a more riotous appetite.
Down from the waist they are Centaurs,[44]
Though women all above.
But to[45] the girdle do the gods inherit,
Beneath is all the fiends'.
There's Hell, there's darkness, there's the sulphurous pit,
Burning, scalding, stench, consumption, fie, fie, fie!
Pah, pah! Give me an ounce of civet,[46] good apothecary, to sweeten

---

36. marjoram: a savory herb.   37. no . . . divinity: i.e., false doctrine.   38. trick: peculiar note.   39. luxury: lust.   40. forks: legs.   41. minces virtue: walks with great air of virtue.   42. fitchew: polecat, a creature demonstratively over-sexed.   43. soiled: fed on spring grass.   44. Centaurs: creatures half man and half stallion.   45. But to: only down to.   46. civet: perfume. See III.iv.108–09,n.

my imagination. There's money for thee.

GLO.: Oh, let me kiss that hand!

LEAR.: Let me wipe it first, it smells of mortality.

GLO.: O ruined piece of nature! This great world
Shall so wear out to naught.[47] Dost thou know me?

LEAR: I remember thine eyes well enough. Dost thou squiny[48] at me?
No, do thy worst, blind Cupid,[49] I'll not love. Read thou this challenge, mark but the penning on 't.

GLO.: Were all the letters suns, I could not see one.

EDG.: I would not take this from report. It is,
And my heart breaks at it.

LEAR: Read.

GLO.: What, with the case of eyes?

LEAR: Oh ho, you are there with me?[50] No eyes in your head, nor no
money in your purse? Your eyes are in a heavy case, your purse in a
light. Yet you see how this world goes.

GLO.: I see it feelingly.

LEAR: What, art mad? A man may see how this world goes with no
eyes. Look with thine ears. See how yond Justice rails upon yond
simple thief. Hard, in thine ear. Change places and, handy-dandy[51]
which is the Justice, which is the thief? Thou hast seen a farmer's
dog bark at a beggar?

GLO.: Aye, sir.

LEAR: And the creature run from the cur? There thou mightst behold
the great image of authority.[52]

A dog's obeyed in office.

Thou rascal beadle,[53] hold thy bloody hand!

Why dost thou lash that whore? Strip thine own back.

Thou hotly lust'st to use her in that kind[54]

For which thou whip'st her. The usurer hangs the cozener.[55]

Through tattered clothes small vices do appear,

Robes and furred gowns hide all. Plate sin with gold

And the strong lance of justice hurtless breaks.

Arm it in rags, a pigmy's straw does pierce it.

None does offend, none, I say, none, I'll able[56] 'em.

Take that of me, my friend, who have the power

47. O . . . naught: O ruined masterpiece of nature, the universe likewise will
come to nothing. 48. squiny: look sideways, like a prostitute. 49. blind
Cupid: the usual sign hung over a brothel. 50. are . . . me; do you agree
with me? 51. handy-dandy: the nursery game of "Handy-pandy, sugar candy,
which hand will you have?" 52. image of authority: figure showing the true
meaning of authority. 53. beadle: parish officer. 54. kind: manner. 55.
usurer . . . cozener: the swindler hangs the crook. 56. able: give power to.

To seal the accuser's lips. Get thee glass eyes[57]
And, like a scurvy[58] politician, seem
To see the things thou dost not.
Now, now, now, now. Pull off my boots. Harder, harder. So.
EDG.: Oh, matter and impertinency[59] mixed!
Reason in madness!
LEAR: If thou wilt weep my fortunes, take my eyes.
I know thee well enough. Thy name is Gloucester.
Thou must be patient, we came crying hither.
Thou know'st the first time that we smell the air,
We wawl and cry. I will preach to thee. Mark.
GLO.: Alack, alack the day!
LEAR: When we are born, we cry that we are come
To this great stage of fools. This 's a good block.[60]
It were a delicate stratagem to shoe
A troop of horse with felt. I'll put 't in proof,[61]
And when I have stol'n upon these sons-in-law,
Then, kill, kill, kill, kill, kill, kill!

[*Enter a* GENTLEMAN, *with* ATTENDANTS.]

GENT.: Oh, here he is. Lay hand upon him. Sir,
Your most dear daughter—
LEAR: No rescue? What, a prisoner? I am even
The natural fool of Fortune.[62] Use me well,
You shall have ransom.[63] Let me have a surgeon,
I am cut to the brains.
GENT.: You shall have anything.
LEAR: No seconds?[64] All myself?
Why, this would make a man a man of salt,[65]
To use his eyes for garden waterpots,
Aye, and laying autumn's dust.
GENT.: Good sir—
LEAR: I will die bravely, like a smug bridegroom.[66] What!
I will be jovial. Come, come, I am a king,
My masters, know you that.

57. glass eyes: spectacles. 58. scurvy: lit., with skin disease, "lousy." 59. matter
. . . impertinency: sense and nonsense. 60. block: hat; lit., the block on
which a felt hat is molded. From hat Lear's mind turns to *felt*. 61. put . . .
proof: try it out. 62. natural . . . Fortune: born to be fooled by Fortune.
63. ransom: Prisoners of good family could buy their freedom from their
captors. Cf. *Hen V*, IV.iii.79–125. 64. No seconds: no one to help me.
65. man of salt: because tears are salt. 66. like . . . bridegroom: It was said
of Lord Grey to Wilton, who was led out as if to be executed on December 9,
1603, that he "had such gaiety and cheer in his countenance that he seemed a
dapper young bridegroom."

GENT.: You are a royal one, and we obey you.

LEAR: Then there's life in 't. Nay, an you get it, you shall get it by running. Sa, sa, sa, sa.[67]

[Exit running. ATTENDANTS follow.]

GENT.: A sight most pitiful in the meanest wretch,
Past speaking of in a king! Thou hast one daughter
Who redeems nature from the general curse
Which twain have brought her to.[68]

EDG.: Hail, gentle sir.

GENT.: Sir, speed you. What's your will?

EDG.: Do you hear aught, sir, of a battle toward?[69]

GENT.: Most sure and vulgar.[70] Everyone hears that
Which can distinguish sound.

EDG.: But, by your favor,
How near's the other army?

GENT.: Near and on speedy foot, the main descry
Stands on the hourly thought.[71]

EDG.: I thank you, sir. That's all.

GENT.: Though that the Queen on special cause is here,
Her army is moved on.

EDG.: I thank you sir.

[Exit GENTLEMAN.]

GLO.: You ever-gentle gods, take my breath from me.
Let not my worser spirit tempt me again
To die before you please!

EDG.: Well pray you, Father.

GLO.: Now, good sir, what are you?

EDG.: A most poor man, made tame to fortune's blows,
Who, by the art[72] of known and feeling sorrows,
Am pregnant to[73] good pity. Give me your hand.
I'll lead you to some biding.[74]

GLO.: Hearty thanks.
The bounty and the benison[75] of Heaven
To boot, and boot![76]

[Enter OSWALD.]

OSW.: A proclaimed[77] prize! Most happy!

---

67. Sa . . . sa: a cry used sometimes in sudden action. 68. Who . . . to: See *Lear* Intro. p. 1139b. 69. toward: at hand. 70. vulgar: common, in everyone's mouth. 71. the . . . thought: the main body is expected to come into sight at any time now. 72. art: long experience. 73. pregnant to: able to conceive. 74. biding: resting-place. 75. benison: blessing. 76. To . . . boot: in the highest degree. 77. proclaimed: Cf. IV.v.37–8.

That eyeless head of thine was first framed flesh
To raise my fortunes. Thou old unhappy traitor,
Briefly thyself remember.[78] The sword is out
That must destroy thee.

GLO.: Now let thy friendly hand
Put strength enough to 't.

[EDGAR *interposes*.]

OSW.: Wherefore, bold peasant,
Darest thou support a published[79] traitor? Hence,
Lest that the infection of his fortune take
Like hold on thee! Let go his arm.

EDG.: Chill[80] not let go, zir, without vurther 'casion.[81]

OSW.: Let go, slave, or thou diest!

EDG.: Good gentleman, go your gait,[82] and let poor volk pass. An chud[83] ho' been zwaggered out of my life, 'twould not ha' been zo long as 'tis by a vort-night. Nay, come not near th' old man, keep out, che vor ye,[84] or I'se try whether your costard[85] or my ballow[86] be the harder. Chill be plain with you.

OSW.: Out, dunghill!

[*They fight*.]

EDG.: Chill pick your teeth, zir. Come, no matter vor your foins.[87]

[OSWALD *falls*.]

OSW.: Slave, thou hast slain me. Villain, take my purse.
If ever thou wilt thrive, bury my body,
And give the letters which thou find'st about me
To Edmund Earl of Gloucester. Seek him out
Upon the British party. Oh, untimely death!
Death!

[*Dies*.]

EDG.: I know thee well—a serviceable[88] villain,
As duteous to the vices of thy mistress
As badness would desire.

GLO.: What, is he dead?

EDG.: Sit you down, Father, rest you.
Let's see these pockets. The letters that he speaks of
May be my friends. He's dead. I am only sorry
He had no other deathsman. Let us see.

---

78. thyself remember: prepare for death—by confessing your sins. 79. published: publicly proclaimed. 80. Chill . . . you: Edgar speaks stage rustic dialect. 81. Chill: I'll. vurther 'casion: further occasion, reason. 82. go . . . gait: go your own way. 83. chud: should. 84. che . . . ye: I warn yer. 85. costard: head; lit., apple. 86. ballow: budgel. 87. foins: thrusts. 88. serviceable: diligent.

Leave, gentle wax,[89] and, manners, blame us not.
To know our enemies' minds, we'd rip their hearts,
Their papers is more lawful. [*Reads.*]
"Let our reciprocal vows be remembered. You have many oppor-
tunities to cut him off. If your will want not,[90] time and place will be
fruitfully offered. There is nothing done if he return the conqueror.
Then am I the prisoner, and his bed my jail, from the loathed
warmth whereof deliver me, and supply the place for your labor.
"Your—wife, so I would say—affectionate servant,

GONERIL."

Oh, undistinguished space[91] of woman's will!
A plot upon her virtuous husband's life,
And the exchange my brother! Here, in the sands,
Thee I'll rake up,[92] the post unsanctified[93]
Of murderous lechers, and in the mature time
With this ungracious paper strike the sight
Of the death-practiced[94] Duke. For him 'tis well
That of thy death and business I can tell.
GLO.: The King is mad. How[95] stiff[96] is my vile sense,[97]
That I stand up, and have ingenious[98] feeling
Of my huge sorrows! Better I were distract.[99]
So should my thoughts be severed from my griefs,
And woes by wrong imaginations lose
The knowledge of themselves.
      [*Drum afar off.*]
EDG.: Give me your hand.
Far off methinks I hear the beaten drum.
Come, Father, I'll bestow you with a friend.
      [*Exeunt.*]

SCENE 7.   *A tent in the French camp.* LEAR *on a bed asleep, soft
      music playing,* GENTLEMAN, *and others attending.*

      [*Enter* CORDELIA, KENT, *and* DOCTOR.]
COR.: O thou good Kent, how shall I live and work,
To match thy goodness? My life will be too short,
And every measure fail me.

89. Leave . . . wax: Here he breaks the seal. See App. 6. 90. will . . . not:
desire is not lacking. *Will* mean both willingness and lust. 91. undistinguished
space: limitless, extending beyond the range of sight. 92. rake up: hide in the
dust. 93. post unsanctified: unholy messenger. 94. death-practiced: whose
death is plotted. 95. How . . . sorrows: i.e., if only I could go mad and
forget my sorrows. 96. stiff: strong. 97. sense: sanity. 98. ingenious: sensitive. 99. distract: mad.

KENT: To be acknowledged, madam, is o'erpaid.
  All my reports go with the modest truth,
  Nor more nor clipped, but so.[1]
COR.: Be better suited.[2]
  These weeds[3] are memories of those worser hours.
  I prithee put them off.
KENT: Pardon me, dear madam,
  Yet to be known shortens my made intent.[4]
  My boon[5] I make it that you know me not
  Till time and I think meet.
COR.: Then be 't so, my good lord.
        [*To the* DOCTOR.]
  How does the King?
DOCT.: Madam, sleeps still.
COR.: O you kind gods,
  Cure this great breach in his abusèd nature!
  The unturned and jarring senses, oh, wind up[6]
  Of this child-changèd[7] father!
DOCT.: So please your Majesty
  That we may wake the King. He hath slept long.
COR.: Be governed by your knowledge, and proceed
  I' the sway[8] of your own will. Is he arrayed?
GENT.: Aye, madam. In the heaviness of his sleep
  We put fresh garments on him.
DOCT.: Be by, good madam, when we do awake him.
  I doubt not of his temperance.[9]
COR.: Very well.
DOCT.: Please you, draw near. Louder the music there!
COR.: O my dear Father! Restoration hang
  Thy medicine on my lips, and let this kiss
  Repair those violent harms that my two sisters
  Have in thy reverence made!
KENT: Kind and dear Princess!
COR.: Had you not been their father, these white flakes
  Had challenged pity of them. Was this a face
  To be opposed against the warring winds?

Sc. vii: 1. Nor . . . so: neither exaggerated nor curtailed, but exact. 2. suited: garbed. 3. weeds: garments; i.e., his livery as Lear's servant. 4. Yet . . . intent: my plan will be frustrated if I am revealed now. 5. boon: request for a favor. 6. wind up: i.e., as the loose string of a musical instrument is tightened. 7. child-changed: transformed by the treatment of his children. 8. sway: direction. 9. temperance: sanity.

To stand against the deep dread-bolted thunder?
In the most terrible and nimble stroke
Of quick, cross lightning?[10] To watch—poor perdu![11]
With this thin helm? Mine enemy's dog,
Though he had bit me, should have stood that night
Against my fire, and wast thou fain, poor Father,
To hovel thee with swine and rogues forlorn
In short and musty straw? Alack, alack!
'Tis wonder that thy life and wits at once
Had not concluded all. He wakes. Speak to him.

DOCT.: Madam, do you, 'tis fittest.

COR.: How does my royal lord? How fares your Majesty?

LEAR: You do me wrong to take me out o' the grave.
Thou art a soul in bliss,[12] but I am bound
Upon a wheel of fire that mine own tears
Do scald like molten lead.

COR.: Sir, do you know me?

LEAR: You are a spirit, I know. When did you die?

COR.: Still, still far wide!

DOCT.: He's scarce awake. Let him alone awhile.

LEAR: Where have I been? Where am I? Fair daylight?
I am mightily abused. I should e'en die with pity
To see another thus. I know not what to say.
I will not swear these are my hands. Let's see,
I feel this pin prick. Would I were assured
Of my condition!

COR.: Oh, look upon me, sir,
And hold your hands in benediction o'er me.
No, sir, you must not kneel.

LEAR: Pray do not mock me.
I am a very foolish fond old man,
Fourscore and upward, not an hour more nor less,
And, to deal plainly,
I fear I am not in my perfect mind.
Methinks I should know you and know this man,
Yet I am dobtful, for I am mainly ignorant
What place this is, and all the skill I have
Remembers not these garments, nor I know not
Where I did lodge last night. Do not laugh at me,

---

10. cross lightning: forked lightning. 11. perdu: sentry in an exposed position.
12. bliss: Heaven.

For, as I am a man, I think this lady
To be my child Cordelia.
COR.: And so I am, I am.
LEAR: Be your tears wet? Yes, faith. I pray weep not.
If you have poison for me, I will drink it.
I know you do not love me, for your sisters
Have, as I do remember, done me wrong.
You have some cause, they have not.
COR.: No cause, no cause.
LEAR: Am I in France?
KENT: In your own kingdom, sir.
LEAR: Do not abuse me.
DOCT.: Be comforted, good madam. The great rage,
You see, is killed in him. And yet it is danger
To make him even o'er[13] the time he has lost.
Desire him to go in, trouble him no more
Till further settling.
COR.: Will 't please your Highness walk?
LEAR: You must bear with me.
Pray you now, forget and forgive. I am old and foolish.
[*Exeunt all but* KENT *and* GENTLEMAN.]
GENT.: Hold it true, sir, that the Duke of Cornwall was so slain?
KENT: Most certain, sir.
GENT.: Who is conductor of his people?
KENT: As 'tis said, the bastard son of Gloucester.
GENT.: They say Edgar, his banished son, is with the Earl of Kent in
Germany.
KENT: Report is changeable.[14] 'Tis time to look about. The powers of
the kingdom approach apace.
GENT.: The arbiterment[15] is like to be bloody. Fare you well, sir.
[*Exit.*]
KENT: My point and period[16] will be throughly[17] wrought,
Or well or ill, as this day's battle's fought.
[*Exit.*]

---

13. even o'er: go over.   14. Report . . . changeable: rumors are not reliable.   15.
arbiterment: decision.   16. point . . . period: lit., full stop; the end of my
chapter.   17. throughly: thoroughly.

🏵 *Act V*

SCENE 1.   *The British camp near Dover.*

[*Enter, with drum and colors,* EDMUND, REGAN, GENTLEMEN, *and* SOLDIERS.]

EDM.: Know[1] of the Duke if his last purpose hold,
   Or whether since he is advised by aught
   To change the course. He's full of alteration
   And self-reproving. Bring his constant[2] pleasure.
      [*To a* GENTLEMAN, *who goes out.*]
REG.: Our sister's man is certainly miscarried.
EDM.: 'Tis to be doubted,[3] madam.
REG.: Now, sweet lord,
   You know the goodness I intend upon you.
   Tell me, but truly, but then speak the truth,
   Do you not love my sister?
EDM.: In honored love.
REG.: But have you never found my brother's way
   To the forfended[4] place?
EDM.: That thought abuses[5] you.
REG.: I am doubtful that you have been conjunct
   And bosomed with her, as far as we call hers.[6]
EDM.: No, by mine honor, madam.
REG.: I never shall endure her. Dear my lord,
   Be not familiar with her.
EDM.: Fear me not.—
   She and the Duke her husband!
      [*Enter, with drum and colors,* ALBANY, GONERIL, *and* SOLDIERS.]
GON.: [*Aside*] I had rather lose the battle than that sister
   Should loosen him and me.
ALB.: Our very loving sister, well bemet.
   Sir, this I hear: The King is come to his daughter,
   With others whom the rigor of our state[7]
   Forced to cry out.[8] Where I could not be honest,

Act V, Sc i: 1. Know: learn.   2. constant: firm; i.e., final decision.   3. doubted: feared.   4. forfended: forbidden.   5. abuses: wrongs; i.e., you should not have such a thought.   6. I . . . hers: I am afraid that you have been united in intimacy with her in every way.   7. rigor . . . state: our harsh government. 8. cry out: protest.

I never yet was valiant. For this business,
It toucheth us, as France invades our land,
Not bolds the King, with others, whom I fear
Most just and heavy causes make oppose.⁹
EDM.: Sir, you speak nobly.
REG.: Why is this reasoned?¹⁰
GON.: Combine together 'gainst the enemy,
For these domestic and particular broils
Are not the question here.
ALB.: Let's then determine
With the ancient of war¹¹ on our proceedings.
EDM.: I shall attend you presently at your tent.
REG.: Sister, you'll go with us?
GON.: No.
REG.: 'Tis most convenient. Pray you go with us.
GON.: [Aside] Oh ho, I know the riddle¹²—I will go.
[As they are going out, enter EDGAR disguised.]
EDG.: If e'er your Grace had speech with man so poor,
Hear me one word.
ALB.: I'll overtake you. Speak.
[Exeunt all but ALBANY and EDGAR.]
EDG.: Before you fight the battle, ope this letter.
If you have victory, let the trumpet sound
For him that brought it. Wretched though I seem,
I can produce a champion that will prove
What is avouchèd¹³ there. If you miscarry,
Your business of the world hath so an end,
And machination ceases. Fortune loved you!
ALB.: Stay till I have read the letter.
EDG.: I was forbid it.
When time shall serve, let but the herald cry
And I'll appear again.
ALB.: Why, fare thee well. I will o'erlook¹⁴ thy paper.
[Exit EDGAR.]
[Re-enter EDMUND.]
EDM.: The enemy's in view. Draw up your powers.

9. For . . . oppose: this business concerns us particularly, not because France is encouraging Lear and others who rightly oppose us, but because he is invading our country. 10. reasoned: argued. 11. ancient of war: experienced commanders. 12. Oh . . . riddle: i.e., you are afraid to leave me alone with Edmund. 13. avouched: declared. 14. o'erlook: read.

Here is the guess[15] of their true strength and forces
By diligent discovery, but your haste
  Is now urged on you.
ALB.: We will greet the time.[16]
      [Exit.]
EDM.: To[17] both these sisters have I sworn my love,
  Each jealous of the other, as the stung
  Are of the adder. Which of them shall I take?
  Both? One? Or neither? Neither can be enjoyed
  If both remain alive. To take the widow
  Exasperates, makes mad her sister Goneril,
  And hardly shall I carry out my side,[18]
  Her husband being alive. Now then we'll use
  His countenance[19] for the battle, which being done,
  Let her who would be rid of him devise
  His speedy take-off. As for the mercy
  Which he intends to Lear and to Cordelia,
  The battle done, and they within our power,
  Shall never see his pardon, for my state
  Stands on me to defend, not to debate.[20]
      [Exit.]

SCENE 2.   *A field between the two camps.*

    [*Alarum within. Enter, with drum and colors,* LEAR, CORDELIA,
    and SOLDIERS, *over the stage; and exeunt. Enter* EDGAR *and*
    GLOUCESTER.]
EDG.: Here, Father, take the shadow of this tree
  For your good host. Pray that the right may thrive.
  If ever I return to you again,
  I'll bring you comfort.
GLO.: Grace go with you, sir!
      [*Exit* EDGAR.]
      [*Alarum and retreat within. Re-enter* EDGAR.]
EDG.: Away, old man. Give me thy hand, away!

15. guess: estimate: 16. greet . . . time: i.e., go to meet our enemy. 17. To
. . . debate: Edmund has now reached the crisis in his fortunes. Both sisters
are in love with him, he can have either. Or he can aim higher and, with Lear
and Cordelia out of the way, achieve the whole kingdom for himself. 18. my
side: i.e., of the bargain. 19. countenance: authority. 20. for . . . debate:
my fortune is now in such a state that I must act, not argue.

King Lear hath lost, he and his daughter ta'en.[1]
Give me thy hand, come on.
GLO.: No farther, sir. A man may rot even here.
EDG.: What, in ill thoughts again? Men[2] must endure
   Their going hence, even as their coming hither.
   Ripeness[3] is all. Come on.
GLO.: And that's true too.
      [*Exeunt.*]

SCENE 3.   *The British camp near Dover.*

      [*Enter, in conquest, with drum and colors,* EDMUND, LEAR *and*
         CORDELIA, *as prisoners,* CAPTAIN, SOLDIERS, *etc.*]
EDM.: Some officers take them away. Good guard,
   Until their greater pleasures[1] first be known
   That are to censure them.
COR.: We are not the first
   Who with best meaning have incurred the worst.
   For thee, oppressèd King, am I cast down.
   Myself could else outfrown false fortune's frown.[2]
   Shall we not see these daughters and these sisters?
LEAR: No, no, no, no! Come, let's away to prison.
   We two alone will sing like birds i' the cage.
   When thu dost ask me blessing, I'll kneel down
   And ask of thee forgiveness. So we'll live,
   And pray, and sing, and tell old tales, and laugh
   At gilded butterflies,[3] and hear poor rogues
   Talk of Court news. And we'll talk with them too,
   Who loses and who wins, who's in, who's out,
   And take upon 's the mystery of things[4]
   As if we were God's spies. And we'll wear out,
   In a walled prison, packs of sects of great ones
   That ebb and flow by the moon.[5]
EDM.: Take them away.
LEAR: Upon such sacrifices, my Cordelia,

Sc. ii: 1. ta'en: taken.   2. Men . . . all: Shakespeare had already impressed this
   stoical view of life in *Haml*, V.ii.231.   3. Ripeness: perfect readiness.

Sc. iii: 1. their . . . pleasures: the will of my superiors.   2. We . . . frown: See
   I.i.183–90,n.   3. gilded butterflies: i.e., Court folk.   4. take . . . things: pretend to understand deep secrets.   5. packs . . . moon: parties at Court whose
   fortunes change monthly.

The gods themselves throw incense. Have I caught thee?
He that parts us shall bring a brand[6] from Heaven,
And fire us[7] hence like foxes. Wipe thine eyes.
The goodyears[8] shall devour them, flesh and fell,[9]
Ere they shall make us weep. We'll see 'em starve first.
Come.

> [*Exeunt* LEAR *and* CORDELIA, *guarded.*]

EDM.: Come hither, Captain, hark.
Take thou this note. Go follow them to prison.
One step I have advanced thee. If thou dost
As this instructs thee, thou dost make thy way
To noble fortunes. Know thou this, that men
Art as the time is.[10] To be tender-minded
Does not become a sword.[11] Thy great employment
Will not bear question.[12] Either say thou'lt do 't,
Or thrive by other means.

CAPT.: I'll do 't, my lord.

EDM.: About it, and write happy[13] when thou hast done.
Mark, I say, instantly, and carry it so
As I have set it down.

CAPT.: I cannot draw a cart, nor eat dried oats.
If it be man's work, I'll do 't.

> [*Exit.*]
>
> [*Flourish. Enter* ALBANY, GONERIL, REGAN, *another* CAPTAIN,
> *and* SOLDIERS.]

ALB.: Sir, you have shown today your valiant strain,[14]
And fortune led you well. You have the captives
That were the opposites[15] of this day's strife,
We do require them of you, so to use them
As we shall find their merits and our safety
May equally determine.

EDM.: Sir, I thought it fit
To send the old and miserable King
To some retention and appointed guard,[16]
Whose age has charms in it, whose title more,

---

6. a brand: fire.   7. fire us: drive us out by fire.   8. goodyears: The phrase "what the goodyear" meant "what the deuce"; hence "goodyear" means something vaguely evil. Lear is talking baby talk—"The bogeymen shall have them."
9. fell: skin.   10.   men . . . is: i.e., in brutal times men must be brutes.
11. sword: soldier.   12. Thy . . . question: the duty now laid on you is too important and brutal to be argued about.   13. happy: fortunate.   14. strain: blood, courage.   15. opposites: opponents.   16. retention . . . guard: where he can be kept and properly guarded.

To pluck the common bosom[17] on his side
And turn our impressed lances[18] in our eyes
Which do command them. With him I sent the Queen,
My reason all the same, and they are ready
Tomorrow or at further space to appear
Where you shall hold your session.[19] At this time
We sweat and bleed. The friend hath lost his friend,
And the best quarrels, in the heat, are cursed
By those that feel their sharpness.[20]
The question of Cordelia and her father
Requires a fitter place.

ALB.: Sir, by your patience,
I hold you but a subject[21] of this war,
Not as a brother.

REG.: That's as we list to grace him.
Methinks our pleasure might have been demanded
Ere you had spoke so far. He had our powers,
Bore the commission of my place and person,[22]
The which immediacy may well stand up
And call itself your brother.[23]

GON.: Not so hot.
In his own grace he doth exalt himself
More than in your addition.[24]

REG.: In my rights,
By me invested, he compeers[25] the best.

GON.: That were the most, if he should husband you.

REG.: Jesters do oft prove prophets.

GON.: Holloa, holloa!
That eye that told you so looked but a-squint.

REG.: Lady, I am not well, else I should answer
From a full-flowing stomach.[26] General,
Take thou my soldiers, prisoners, patrimony,
Dispose of them, of me, the walls are thine.[27]

---

17. common bosom: the sympathies of our soldiers. 18. impressed lances: the soldiers we have conscripted. 19. session: trial. 20. And . . . sharpness: i.e., with the battle hardly over we are in no condition to judge this matter calmly. 21. subject: i.e., not one who gives orders. 22. commission . . . person: commission appointing him commander as my deputy. 23. The . . . brother: since he is my general, he is fit to be considered your equal. 24. your addition: the title which you have given him. See I.i.138. 25. compeers: equals. 26. full-flowing stomach: in full wrath. 27. walls . . . thine: i.e., you have won the outer defenses.

Witness the world that I create thee here
My lord and master.

GON.: Mean you to enjoy him?

ALB.: The let-alone[28] lies not in your goodwill.

EDM.: Nor in thine, lord.

ALB.: Half-blooded fellow, yes.

REG.: [*To* EDMUND] Let the drum strike, and prove my title thine.

ALB.: Stay yet, hear reason. Edmund, I arrest thee
On capital treason,[29] and in thine attaint[30]
This gilded serpent. [*Pointing to* GONERIL] For your claim, fair Sister,
I bar it in the interest of my wife.
'Tis she is subcontracted[31] to this lord,
And I, her husband, contradict your bans.[32]
If you will marry, make your loves to me.
My lady is bespoke.[33]

GON.: An interlude![34]

ALB.: Thou art armed, Gloucester. Let the trumpet sound.
If none appear to prove upon thy person
Thy heinous,[35] manifest, and many treasons,
There is my pledge. [*Throwing down a glove*] I'll prove it on thy heart
Ere I taste bread, thou art in nothing less
Than I have here proclaimed thee.

REG.: Sick, oh, sick!

GON.: [*Aside*] If not, I'll ne'er trust medicine.[36]

EDM.: [*Throwing down a glove*] There's my exchange. What in the
world he is
That names me traitor, villainlike he lies.[37]
Call by thy trumpet. He that dares approach,
On him, on you—who not?—I will maintain
My truth and honor firmly.

ALB.: A herald, ho!

EDM.: A herald, ho, a herald!

ALB.: Trust to thy single[38] virtue, for thy soldiers,
All levied in my name, have in my name
Took their discharge.

---

28. let-alone: power to prevent. 29. capital treason: treason deserving death.
30. and . . . attaint: and accused with you (*attaint*: impeachment). 31. subcontracted: already betrothed. 32. bans: notice of intention to marry, read
out in church for three Sundays previous to the marriage. 33. bespoke: already reserved. 34. An interlude: i.e., this is mere play-acting. 35. heinous:
odious. 36. medicine: poison. 37. villainlike . . . lies: he lies like a villain.
This is the lie direct, whch was a direct challenge to mortal combat. Cf. *AYLI*,
V.iv.69–108. 38. single: solitary, unaided.

REG.: My sickness grows upon me.

ALB.: She is not well. Convey her to my tent.

[*Exit* REGAN, *led.*]

[*Enter a* HERALD.] Come hither, herald.—Let the trumpet sound.—

And read out this.

CAPT.: Sound, trumpet!

[*A trumpet sounds.*]

HER.: [*Reads.*] "If any man of quality or degree[39] within the lists[40] of the army will maintain upon Edmund, supposed Earl of Gloucester, that he is a manifold traitor, let him appear by the third sound of the trumpet. He is bold in his defense."

EDM.: Sound!

[*First trumpet.*]

HER.: Again!

[*Second trumpet.*]

Again!

[*Third trumpet.*]

[*Trumpet answers within.*]

[*Enter* EDGAR *at the third sound, armed, with a trumpet before him.*]

ALB.: Ask him his purposes, why he appears

Upon this call o' the trumpet.[41]

HER.: What are you?

Your name, your quality? And why you answer

This present summons?

EDG.: Know my name is lost,

By treason's tooth bare-gnawn and canker-bit.[42]

Yet am I noble as the adversary

I come to cope.[43]

ALB.: Which is that adversary?

EDG.: What's he that speaks for Edmund, Earl of Gloucester?

EDM.: Himself. What say'st thou to him?

EDG.: Draw thy sword,

That if my speech offend a noble heart,

Thy arm may do thee justice. Here is mine.

Behold, it is the privilege of mine honors,

---

39. quality or degree: rank or high position.   40. lists: roll call, roster.   41. Ask
... trumpet: The combat follows the normal procedure of chivalry. Cf. *Rich II*,
I.iii. Edgar is wearing full armor, his face concealed by his closed helmet. See
Pl. 8a.   42. canker-bit: corrupted by maggots.   43. cope: meet, encounter.

My oath, and my profession.[44] I protest,
Mauger[45] thy strength, youth, place, and eminence,
Despite thy victor sword and fire-new[46] fortune,
Thy valor and thy heart, thou art a traitor,
False to thy gods, thy brother, and thy father,
Conspirant[47] 'gainst this high illustrious Prince,
And from the extremest upward of thy head
To the descent and dust below thy foot
A most toad-spotted[48] traitor. Say thou "No,"
This sword, this arm, and my best spirits are bent
To prove upon thy heart, whereto I speak,
Thou liest.
EDM.: In wisdom I should ask thy name,
But since thy outside look so fair and warlike
And that thy tongue some say of breeding[49] breathes,
What safe and nicely[50] I might well delay
By rule of knighthood I disdain and spurn.
Back do I toss these treasons to thy head,
With the hell-hated lie o'erwhelm thy heart,
Which for they yet glance by and scarcely bruise,
This sword of mine shall give them instant way
Where they shall rest forever. Trumpets, speak!
        [*Alarums. They fight.* EDMUND *falls.*]
ALB.: Save him, save him!
GON.: This is practice,[51] Gloucester.
By the law of arms thou wast not bound to answer
An unknown opposite. Thou art not vanquished,
But cozened[52] and beguiled.
ALB.: Shut your mouth, dame,
Or with this paper[53] shall I stop it. Hold, sir,
Thou worse than any name, read thine own evil.
No tearing, lady. I perceive you know it.
GON.: Say if I do, the laws are mine, not thine.
Who can arraign me for 't?
ALB.: Most monstrous!
Know'st thou this paper?

44. profession: i.e., as a knight. 45. Mauger: in spite of. 46. fire-new: brand-new—like a new coin. 47. Conspirant: conspiring. 48. toad-spotted: i.e., venomous as a toad. Cf. *AYLI*, II.i.13. 49. say of breeding: accent of a gentleman. 50. nicely: i.e., if I stood on niceties of procedure. 51. practice: treachery. 52. cozened: cheated. 53. this paper: her love letter to Edmund, which Edgar had taken from Oswald's corpse. See IV.vi.267–76.

GON.: Ask me not what I know.
　　　[*Exit.*]
ALB.: Go after her. She's desperate, govern[54] her.
EDM.: What you have charged me with, that have I done,
　　And more, much more. The time will bring it out.
　　'Tis past, and so am I. But what art thou
　　That hast this fortune on me? If thou 'rt noble,
　　I do forgive thee.
EDG.: Let's exchange charity.
　　I am no less in blood than thou art, Edmund.
　　If more, the more thou hast wronged me.
　　My name is Edgar, and thy father's son.
　　The gods are just, and of our pleasant vices
　　Make instruments to plague us.[55]
　　The dark and vicious place where thee he got[56]
　　Cost him his eyes.
EDM.: Thou hast spoken right, 'tis true.
　　The wheel is come full circle,[57] I am here.
ALB.: Methought thy very gait did prophesy
　　A royal nobleness. I must embrace thee.
　　Let sorrow split my heart if ever I
　　Did hate thee or thy father!
EDG.: Worthy Prince, I know 't.
ALB.: Where have you hid yourself?
　　How have you known the miseries of your father?
EDG.: By nursing them, my lord. List a brief tale,
　　And when 'tis told, oh, that my heart would burst!
　　The bloody proclamation to escape[58]
　　That followed me so near—Oh, our lives' sweetness!
　　That we the pain of death would hourly die
　　Rather than die at once![59]—tought me to shift
　　Into a madman's rags, to assume a semblance
　　That very dogs disdained. And in this habit
　　Met I my father with his bleeding rings,
　　Their precious stones new-lost, became his guide,
　　Led him, begged for him, saved him from despair,

---

54. govern: control. 55. of . . . us: This is the answer to Gloucester's light-
hearted words at the opening of the play—"Do you smell a fault?" (I.i.16).
56. got: begot. 57. The . . . circle: i.e., I end as I began—an outcast of
fortune. 58. The . . . escape: in order to escape after the proclamation for
my arrest See II.iii.1. 59. Oh . . . once: life is so sweet to us that we will
endure the pains of death hourly if only we can live.

Never—oh, fault!—revealed myself unto him
Until some half-hour past, when I was armed.
Not sure, though hoping, of this good success,
I asked his blessing, and from first to last
Told him my pilgrimage. But his flawed heart—
Alack, too weak the conflict to support!—
'Twixt two extremes of passion, joy and grief,
Burst smilingly.[60]

EDM.: This speech of yours hath moved me,
And shall perchance do good. But speak you on.
You look as you had something more to say.

ALB.: If there be more, more woeful, hold it in,
For I am almost ready to dissolve,
Hearing of this.

EDG.: This would have seemed a period[61]
To such as love not sorrow, but another,
To amplify too much, would make much more,
And top extremity.[62]
Whilst I was big in clamor,[63] came there in a man
Who, having seen me in my worst estate,
Shunned my abhorred society. But then, finding
Who 'twas that so endured, with his strong arms
He fastened on my neck, and bellowed out
As he'd burst heaven, threw him on my father,
Told the most piteous tale of Lear and him
That ever ear received. Which in recounting
His grief grew puissant,[64] and the strings of life[65]
Began to crack. Twice then the trumpets sounded,
And there I left him tranced.[66]

ALB.: But who was this?

EDG.: Kent, sir, the banished Kent, who in disguise
Followed his enemy King,[67] and did him service
Improper for a slave.

[Enter a GENTLEMAN, with a bloody knife.]

GENT.: Help, help, oh, help!

EDG.: What kind of help?

60. But . . . smilingly: In the performance the significance of Edgar's speech can
easily be missed. Gloucester has died from excessive emotion (passion), and
Kent is near his end. 61. period: end. 62. top extremity: exceed the extreme limit of what could be endured. 63. clamor: grief. 64. puissant:
powerful, overwhelming. 65. strings of life: heartstrings. 66. tranced: in a
faint. 67. enemy King: the King who had declared him an enemy.

ALB.: Speak, man.

EDG.: What means this bloody knife?

GENT.: 'Tis hot, it smokes.

It came even from the heart of—oh, she's dead!

ALB.: Who dead? Speak, man.

GENT.: Your lady, sir, your lady. And her sister

By her is poisoned. She hath confessed it.

EDM.: I was contracted[68] to them both. All three

Now marry in an instant.

EDG.: Here comes Kent.

ALB.: Produce the bodies, be they alive or dear.

    [Exit GENTLEMAN.*]*

This judgment of the Heavens, that makes us tremble,

Touches us not with pity.

    [Enter KENT.*]* Oh, is this he?

The time will not allow the compliment

Which very manners urges.

KENT: I am come

To bid my King and master aye good night.

Is he not here?

ALB.: Great thing of us forgot!

Speak, Edmund, where's the King? And where's Cordelia?

See's thou this object, Kent?

    [The bodies of GONERIL *and* REGAN *are brought in.]*

KENT: Alack, why thus?

EDM.: Yet Edmund was beloved.[69]

The one the other poisoned for my sake,

And after slew herself.

ALB.: Even so. Cover their faces.

EDM.: I pant for life. Some good I mean to do,

Despite of mine own nature. Quickly send—

Be brief in it—to the castle, for my writ

Is on the life of Lear and on Cordelia.

Nay, sent in time.

ALB.: Run, run, oh, run!

EDG.: To who, my lord? Who hath the office? Send

Thy token of reprieve.[70]

EDM.: Well thought on. Take my sword.

Give it the Captain.

---

68. contracted: betrothed. 69. Yet . . . beloved: The bastard's last grim triumph—two women died for his love. 70. token of reprieve: sign that they are reprieved.

ALB.: Haste thee, for thy life.

    [Exit EDGAR.]

EDM.: He hath commission from thy wife and me
  To hang Cordelia in the prison and
  To lay the blame upon her own despair,
  That she fordid[71] herself.

ALB.: The gods defend her! Bear him hence awhile.

    [EDMUND *is borne off.*]

    [*Re-enter* LEAR, *with* CORDELIA *dead in his arms,* EDGAR, CAP-
    TAIN, *and others following.*]

LEAR: Howl, howl, howl, howl! Oh, you are men of stones.
  Had I your tongues and eyes, I'd use them so
  That heaven's vault should crack. She's gone forever!
  I know when one is dead and when one lives.
  She's dead as earth. Lend me a looking-glass
  If that her breath will mist or stain the stone,[72]
  Why, then she lives.

KENT: Is this the promised end?[73]

EDG.: Or image of that horror?

ALB.: Fall and cease.[74]

LEAR: This feather stirs, she lives. If it be so,
  It is a chance which does redeem all sorrows
  That ever I have felt.

KENT: [*Kneeling*] Oh, my good master!

LEAR: Prithee, away.

EDG.: 'Tis noble Kent, your friend.

LEAR: A plague upon you, murderers, traitors all!
  I might have saved her. Now she's gone forever!
  Cordelia, Cordelia! Stay a little. Ha!
  What is 't thou say'st? Her voice was ever soft,
  Gentle and low, an excellent thing in woman.
  I killed the slave that was a-hanging thee.

CAPT.: 'Tis true, my lords, he did.

LEAR: Did I not, fellow?
  I have seen the day with my good biting falchion[75]
  I would have made them skip. I am old now,
  And these same crosses[76] spoil me. Who are you?
  Mine eyes are not o' the best, I'll tell you straight.

---

71. fordid: destroyed. 72. stone: glass. 73. the . . . end: i.e., Doomsday. 74. Fall . . . cease: i.e., let Doomsday come and the world end. 75. falchion: curved sword. 76. crosses: troubles.

KENT: If fortune brag of two she loved and hated,
  One of them we behold.
LEAR: This is a dull sight. Are you not Kent?
KENT: The same,
  Your servant Kent. Where is your servant Caius?
LEAR: He's a good fellow, I can tell you that.
  He'll strike, and quickly too. He's dead and rotten.
KENT: No, my good lord, I am the very man[77]—
LEAR: I'll see that straight.
KENT: That from your first of difference[78] and decay
  Have followed your sad steps.
LEAR: You are welcome hither.
KENT: Nor no man else. All's cheerless, dark, and deadly.
  Your eldest daughters have fordone themselves,
  And desperately are dead.
LEAR: Aye, so I think.
ALB.: He knows not what he says, and vain is it
  That we present us to him.
EDG.: Very bootless.[79]
        [*Enter a* CAPTAIN.]
CAPT.: Edmund is dead, my lord.
ALB.: That's but a trifle here.
  You lords and noble friends, know our intent.
  What comfort to this great decay[80] may come
  Shall be applied. For us, we will resign,
  During the life of this old Majesty,
  To him our absolute power.
        [*To* EDGAR *and* KENT] You, to your rights,
  With boot,[81] and such addition as your honors
  Have more than merited. All friends shall taste
  The wages of their virtue, and all foes
  The cup of their deservings. Oh, see, see![82]
LEAR: And my poor fool[83] is hanged! No, no, no life!
  Why should a dog, a horse, a rat, have life
  And thou no breath at all? Thou'lt come no more,
  Never, never, never, never, never!
  Pray you undo this button.[84] Thank you, sir.

---

77. Your . . . man: This is the first and only mention of a Caius, which was apparently the name assumed by Kent in his disguise.   78. difference: changed state.   79. bootless: useless.   80. decay: i.e., Lear.   81. boot: advantage.   82. Oh . . . see: There is a sudden change in Lear.   83. fool: Cordelia; *fool* is often used as a term of affection.   84. Pray . . . button: For the last time Lear is oppressed by the violent beating of his heart before it is stilled forever.

Do you see this? Look on her, look, her lips,
Look there, look there!
            [*Dies.*]
EDG.: He faints. My lord, my lord!
KENT: Break, heart, I prithee break!
EDG.: Look up, my lord.
KENT: Vex not his ghost. Oh, let him pass! He hates him
    That would upon the rack[85] of this tough world
    Stretch him out longer.
EDG.: He is gone indeed.
KENT: The wonder is he hath endured so long.
    He but usurped his life.
ALB.: Bear them form thence. Our present business
    Is general woe. [*To* KENT *and* EDGAR] Friends of my soul, you twain
    Rule in this realm and the gored state sustain.
KENT: I have a journey, sir, shortly to go.
    My master calls me,[86] I must not say no.
ALB.: The weight of this sad time we must obey,
    Speak what we feel, not what we ought to say.
    The oldest hath borne most. We that are young
    Shall never see so much, nor live so long.
            [*Exeunt, with a dead march.*]

85. rack: See App. 10.   86. calls me: i.e., to follow him into the darkness.

🎭 Introduction to Traditional Comedy

In turning from tragedy to comedy, we must consider the comic view of life and its expression through the comic form or pattern. Against the background of the discussion of tragedy, we want to ask, what are the elements of traditional comic drama? Though we cannot cover the wide range of commentary on the subject, we can suggest some of the essential features of traditional comedy, reminding the reader that these views are inevitably partial and necessarily limited to a summary approach.

Comedy is most simply defined as a work that ends happily. It is therefore affirmative and optimistic. Yet the comic view is also realistic, supporting reason and common sense against the foolish and extreme. Since comedy laughs at the person who deviates from a social standard or norm, it has been traditionally conservative, flourishing during periods of stability, in cultures whose values were clearly defined. In classical Greece and Rome, during the Renaissance, the Restoration and eighteenth century, fairly stable societies expressed their faith in the social sanity of man through the comic form.

Though the division of classical comedy into three types—Old, Middle, and New—conforms roughly to the stages of development in Greek comic drama, this kind of cataloguing is misleading, since we have only the plays of Aristophanes (445–385 B.C.) as examples of Old and Middle Comedy, and the fragments of Menander (343–291 B.C.) to illustrate Greek New Comedy. Fortunately, we have other specimens of Greek New Comedy in the Roman plays of Plautus (254–184 B.C.) and Terence (195–159 B.C.), which are mainly adaptations from Menander and other Greek dramatists. And though Greek New Comedy evolved from the last plays of Aristophanes, it developed its own form and subject matter. Instead of the freer form of Old Comedy, with its mixture of political satire, lyric poetry and bawdy humor, New Comedy established a definite plot sequence and stylized subject matter, with its treatment of everyday life, its use of stock characters—the braggart soldier, the clever servant, the tyrannical father and playboy son—and its recurrent formula of the trials and triumphs of young love. In New Comedy, we find a young man in love with a young girl; but the father, known as the *senex* (old man) or "blocking character," will not let them marry. The opposition may be due to a conflict between the tyrannical father and playboy son, or to class distinction—the girl might be a slave. To complicate the plot, playwrights often added another pair of lovers and another blocking father. In Terence's *The Phormio* (161 B.C.), for example, the young men are cousins, opposed by father and uncle. One couple is secretly married and the boy must win approval from his domineering father; his cousin is in love with a slave girl and must raise money to obtain her freedom. The married girl turns out to be the abandoned daughter of the young man's uncle. We can see in this device of the abandoned child, with its recognition scene, the influence of tragic drama, and later of romance literature, on comedy. At the end, lovers and parents are reconciled, usually with the aid of a clever servant, the "parasite" of classical comedy.

New Comedy, then, with its romantic complication and resolution, its celebration of human ingenuity, of love and life, established a pattern or formula that has persisted from ancient times to the present. In this classic situation, the father tries to prevent society from perpetuating itself through the convention of marriage. The young man's struggle against the older generation may be interpreted as a triumph of spring and youth over winter and old age, recalling the primitive, mythic basis of comedy. In Aristotle's *Poetics*, the origins of comedy are linked to the phallic ceremonies that were part of the spring fertility rites associated with the worship of Dionysus. (The word comedy apparently comes from *komos*, or the "revel" that was part of the Dionysian festival.) Tragedy and comedy, then, can be traced to a similar source in ancient Greece: the celebration of the death in winter of the old god, the old year; and the rebirth in spring of the new god, the new year. Originating in the spring fertility rites, comedy reflects man's constant effort to drive out winter, darkness, and death; it celebrates life, the coming of spring and the new year, all embodied in the sexual element. But comedy also celebrates the social group. Its usual ending, in marriage, reconciles the life force, sex, to society. Nature and society are thus the primary elements of comedy. Nature is represented by the young lovers; society is represented by the comic spirit which laughs at those blocking forces, like the older generation, which would prevent the lovers from coming together. The young lovers are the force for life, or spring; the older generation is the force for death, or winter. The lovers join with the comic spirit in routing the blocking forces. But the potentially anarchic force of sex is controlled by the convention of marriage. Thus sex is made to work as a conservative element, the means for perpetuating the established order. In this way, the usually hostile forces of nature and society are reconciled.

At this point we might consider the question of the protagonist or hero in the context of comedy. A hero is usually a superior being associated with epic and tragic forms, while the young lovers in comedy represent the norm. Shakespeare's romantic heroines, such as Rosalind, Viola, and Beatrice, are witty, complex characters who play active roles in their respective comedies; but the fact that it is the heroine who is clever or realistic in love is in itself an anti-heroic, comic judgment on romantic love. Tragedy tends to isolate and focus on the tragic hero, so that we identify him with the tragic pattern. But comedy is ultimately concerned with society, or the going social order, and is only partly committed to the romantic triumph of the young. Indeed, we tend to smile indulgently at the so-called comic hero or protagonist, who is not really a hero, and often a little absurd. While the idea of love may be at the center of a tragedy like Romeo and Juliet, it is usually treated obliquely in comedy. The same theme, of course, may be used for tragic or comic purposes, but where tragedy pursues life to its inevitable conclusion, comedy returns us to the world, subordinating the idea of love to the larger perspective or framework of society.

A more interesting comparison might be made between the tragic hero and the blocking character, or comic figure, as we shall call him. Both are cured of their pride or flaw, one tragically, the other comically. Comic detachment, laughter, and ridicule are all part of the symbolic process of purging and curing the comic figure. But in plays such as *Twelfth Night* and *The Misanthrope*, we shall see that the cure requires an expulsion that strikes a discord in the classically harmonious ending. The usual fate of the comic character is only temporary exile or discomfort, while that of the tragic character is inevitable suffering or death. Tragedy moves in a linear fashion to its fated end, while comedy seems to progress in an episodic or circular manner, until its fortuitous, happy ending.

Having considered some of the formal elements of traditional comedy, we can now look at examples of the comic form in the work of Shakespeare and Molière. While both follow the classical tradition of New Comedy, Shakespeare tends to play with the theme of love itself, while Molière stresses the realistic, satiric tendency of New

Comedy. Shakespearean comedy is more inclusive, making fun of foolish lovers (like the Duke in *Twelfth Night*) who sentimentalize love, and ridiculing the traditional comic figures who obstruct nature and the life of society. Where his contemporary, Ben Jonson, attacks the corruption and folly of his age, Shakespeare creates a freer, more fanciful world of romance. Classical and native traditions of romance, folklore, and the pastoral provided Shakespeare with his unreal situations and remote settings: the shipwrecks, disguises, misunderstandings, and recognition scenes; the fairyland of *A Midsummer Night's Dream*, the Forest of Arden in *As You Like It*, Illyria in *Twelfth Night*. And yet, though Shakespeare's imagination plays with a romantic world, he sees it from the perspective of comic realism. He gives his characters poetic license, but they must all answer finally to the laws of nature and social reality.

In *As You Like It* there is a retreat to nature, from a corrupt court to the idyllic Forest of Arden. This is a return to a more innocent state, but the innocence is only apparent. Even in the Forest there is a realistic, comic critique of the various pastoral and romantic poses: real rustics play at romantic love and romantic lovers play at the pastoral life. The melancholy Jaques, himself a comic figure, stands outside the idealized romantic world. Touchstone, the fool, is in the pastoral group, but, in motley, a realist (his name suggests a critical standard) who satirizes the lovers and escapist courtiers. At the end, there is the usual comic resolution of marriage and a realistic return to the court—except for Jaques, the comic malcontent, who rejects the world.

In *Twelfth Night*, there is no retreat to a forest or garden, but the characters still play at idyllic love. Orsino, Duke of Illyria, is seemingly in love with the proud Countess Olivia, although she remains cold and indifferent to his wooing and would rather mourn her dead brother for seven years, cloistered from the world. Both attitudes are satirized. The Duke's passion is really romantic excess; he is not in love with Olivia but with the language and postures of love; and Olivia is just as unnatural in her vow of chastity and excessive grief. When the heroine, Viola, enters the play by the romantic means of a shipwreck, she becomes (disguised as a boy) the Duke's envoy to Olivia. In contrast to Olivia, Viola behaves more naturally in similar circumstances. When she lands in Illyria, she thinks her brother has been lost and grieves, but she also remembers that the Duke is a "bachelor." To complicate matters, Viola is secretly in love with the Duke, and when she pleads his case to Olivia, the proud, chaste Countess falls immediately in love with the disguised Viola. The lovers, then, must pass through temporary confusion and pain before they learn the realistic basis of love. But it is comic pain and the play ends happily amid the familiar untangling and reconciling of lovers. Viola will marry the Duke; while her brother Sebastian is conveniently washed ashore to become the husband of Olivia.

In the sub-plot of *Twelfth Night* Sir Toby Belch, Olivia's uncle, is a lesser Falstaff who defends his natural vices against the unnatural virtue of Olivia's steward, the ambitious puritan, Malvolio. Sir Toby's group of revelers represent the amoral, festive world of comedy, while Malvolio stands for a restrictive, middle-class morality. Olivia accuses Malvolio of being "sick of self-love." In the comic sense, she and the Duke, as we have seen, suffer from the same disease, though their self-indulgence is more easily cured by the sanative power of real love. But Malvolio's disease is different, more complex and not so easily cured, even by the comic weapons of ridicule and laughter. His self-love—comic *hubris* or pride—is antisocial. He is ambitious and wants to rise out of his class. In an age when the social order was considered part of a fixed scheme, he wishes to move out of his element, but becomes instead a social victim and comic scapegoat. Sir Toby and his followers play a trick on Malvolio—tricks are appropriate in the comic world—to cure him of his pride and ambition. When Fabian, a servant and fellow-conspirator, explains the joke to Olivia at the end, he remarks that it is cause for laughter rather than revenge. In other words, *Twelfth Night* is a comedy and not some dark drama. But Malvolio's last words indicate that he takes the matter more seriously, placing him outside the typical harmony of the comic ending: "I'll be revenged on the whole pack of you."

Comedy involves as many characters as possible in its final reconciliation, and Shakespeare's romantic comedy reveals his great capacity for indulging and accepting human folly. Even his so-called villains are left unpunished in the context of the play (Don John in *Much Ado About Nothing*) or are suddenly converted (Duke Frederick in *As You Like It*, and the unfaithful Proteus in *Two Gentlemen From Verona*). The outsiders, Jaques and especially Malvolio, seem to belong more properly to Ben Jonson's comedy of "humors." Jonson's "humors" are based on the old physiological belief in four bodily fluids—blood, phlegm, yellow and black bile or choler—which supposedly determined one's mental disposition. In this view, a phlegmatic person would have an over-abundance of phlegm; while the predominance of black bile or choler would account for the melancholy "humor" of Jaques. As a character related to the New Comedy types described earlier, the "humor" is an eccentric or obsessive figure—the miser, the hypochondriac, the misanthrope—who acts contrary to the norms of reason and society. One can see, then, that the blocking character, comic figure, or "humor" are interchangeable terms in comedy.

Molière's plays, such as *The Miser, The Imaginary Invalid, Tartuffe,* and *The Misanthrope,* follow the classical Jonsonian pattern, focusing on a "humor" or comic figure whose ruling passion perverts the individual and social norm. Molière's comedies are Jonsonian in form, but generally Shakespearean in spirit—genial and indulgent in their treatment of the "humorous" character. In *Tartuffe* and *The Misanthrope,* however, Molière is closer to the Jonsonian satiric temper. Like Malvolio, Tartuffe, the religious hypocrite, is a "humor" who stands outside or apart from the social norm, even at the end of the play.

Alceste, in *The Misanthrope,* is another comic figure in conflict with the rational, social norm. His obsession, his misanthropy, is antisocial. But where Malvolio or Tartuffe are clearly outsiders, Alceste is part of the social group. Actually, he is both inside society and outside of it; he seems to be the comic protagonist and a comic figure or "humor" at the same time. It is this ambiguity in *The Misanthrope* that has produced such a range of commentary on the play. While some readers see Alceste as a classic comic figure, others feel that he is a serious protagonist and that the comedy itself is too serious, too dark, to be a real comedy. The ambiguity is in the play and *The Misanthrope* is richer for it; but we should remember that for Molière's audience Alceste was a comic figure. After all, he is funny, even ridiculous in his speech and actions. His demands for absolute honesty, for truth, conflict with the normal compromises of society. His opening tirade against Philinte is less a plea for sincere friendship than a protest against Philinte's having other friends. Similarly, his demand that Célimène see only him reveals an egotistical desire to be distinguished above all others. It is not that Alceste is completely wrong about man and society; but, as with Molière's Tartuffe, we see that the moralist is really out of place in comedy. Malvolio disrupts the festive, carnival world; Tartuffe, a corrupt or inverted moralist, and the moral Alceste disturb the reasonable norm. Philinte (Molière's spokesman or *raisonneur*) tries to cure, or at least temper Alceste's misanthropy, and goes on to define the reasonable, indulgent morality of traditional comedy.

> Come, let's forget the follies of the times
> And pardon mankind for its petty crimes;
> Let's have an end of rantings and of railings,
> And show some leniency toward human failings.

This world requires a pliant rectitude;
Too stern a virtue makes one stiff and rude;
Good sense views all extremes with detestation,
And bids us to be noble in moderation.   (Act I, Scene I)

In tragedy it is the immoral person—Claudius, Edmund, Iago—who disturbs the natural order; in comedy it is the moralist. The hero in tragedy properly makes the highest moral demands. But a raging moralist is sadly out of place in a comedy of manners.

At the end, Alceste's proposed exile is linked to his demand that Célimène go with him. When she refuses to abandon society, Alceste's reply is comic because we see that his misanthropy is mere vanity. "Must you have me, and all the world beside?" Molière provides a comic contrast between Alceste's "tragic" manner and his petty matter. Alceste's tragic posture is funny because it is so far above Célimène's drawing-room society and its point of view. But in the world of comedy society prevails. Philinte and Eliante, the reasonable, honest lovers, are rewarded. Alceste is rejected. Molière does leave room, however, for a possible reconciliation when Philinte says to Eliante that they must try to change Alceste's mind, to persuade the misanthrope to accept the world as it is—the world of comedy.

English Restoration comedy reflects the tradition of Jonson's comedy of "humors" and the French comedy of manners. Its subject is the familiar one of love, but in place of the affirmation of love, as in Shakespearean comedy, we have a cynical commentary on sex and marriage. This represents the reaction of court society against the Puritanism of the previous decades, as well as the influence of the French theatre. A product of the court and an intellectual élite, Restoration comedy is characterized by a relentless play of wit that served for dialogue and a bewildering round of intrigue that served for plot. It was a comedy of elegant manners and casual morals which satirized society without seriously disturbing its accepted values; so Wycherley's *The Country Wife* and Farquhar's *The Beaux Stratagem*. Congreve's *The Way of the World*, the classic of the Restoration stage, has another dimension. Though using the conventions of wit and intrigue, it attempts a critical renewal of society by posing once again the idea of married love.

The middle class was not happy with the stylized, aristocratic Restoration stage, nor with its morality, and by the beginning of the eighteenth century a reaction had set in, as we see from the title of Jeremy Collier's tract, *A Short View of The Immorality and Profaneness of the English Stage* (1698). A new kind of comedy, *sentimental* comedy, began to flourish; typical is *The Conscious Lovers*, by Richard Steele, its most famous exemplar. It was pious, highly moral, and sentimental; all this in contrast to the largely amoral tough-mindedness of the traditional comic spirit. Its weaknesses were brilliantly outlined by Oliver Goldsmith in his *Essay on the Theatre* (1772). He observed that in sentimental comedy

> the virtues of private life are exhibited, rather than the vices exposed; and the distresses rather than the faults of mankind make our interest in the piece. . . . In these plays almost all the characters are good, and exceedingly generous; they are lavish enough of their *tin* money on the stage; and though they want humor, have abundance of sentiment and feeling. If they happen to have faults or foibles, the spectator is taught, not only to pardon, but to applaud them, in consideration of the goodness of their hearts; so that folly, instead of being ridiculed, is commended, and the comedy aims at touching our passions without the power of being truly pathetic.

These plays were turned out according to formula, much like our own commercial drama on the stage and in the movies.

> It is only sufficient [Goldsmith explains] to raise the characters a little; to deck out the hero with a riband, or give the heroine a title; then to put an insipid dialogue, without character or humor, into their mouths, give them mighty good hearts, very fine clothes, furnish a new set of scenes, make a pathetic scene or two, with a sprinkling of tender melancholy conversation through the whole, and there is no doubt but all the ladies will cry and all the gentlemen applaud.

Goldsmith's *She Stoops to Conquer* and Sheridan's *School for Scandal* resisted the sentimentality of the period by satirizing it. They retained the wit of Restoration comedy, but their tone was more benign.

We have seen that comedy flourished in a society with a reasonably fixed order, a coherent standard of values, and a rational relation between the individual and that society. We noted that traditional comedy was able to identify nature with society; through the convention of marriage sex was turned into a conservative force, perpetuating the established order. Molière insisted on the social function of comedy. From the perspective of reason and good sense, comedy should aim, he declares, at correcting man's vices, or what we would now call follies. And as late as the nineteenth century, when the traditional structure was already being undermined (as in the comedies of Shaw and Wilde), George Meredith could still make a case for comedy as the ultimate civilizer, the guardian of our "social intelligence."

Since comedy is so closely tied to society, its form and function may change as social conditions change. What is reasonable or natural may only be an expression of a particular historical perspective or social milieu. From the nineteenth century on, with the Romantic emphasis on the value of emotions and individual freedom in a restrictive society, we can see a new "vitalist" theory of comedy beginning to conflict with the older conservative view. Traditional comedy was able to reconcile nature and society, the individual and the established order. But the Romantic or modern view, identifying virtue with freedom, idealizes the comic hero's triumph over the established order. As society begins to lose its coherent standard of values, and a dominant upper class yields to the middle class, the writer finds it increasingly difficult to establish a social perspective from which he can ridicule the comic offender. There are hints of this comic ambivalence, of a satire on the established order as well as on the "humorous" figure, in Shakespeare's *Henry IV*, *The Misanthrope*, and Congreve's *The Way of the World*; but it is in the late Victorian comedies of Wilde and Shaw that we begin to see the dissolution of the social structure of traditional comedy.

Though there are still critics who believe in the social function of modern comedy, others have abandoned the traditional view for an approach to comedy as a release of vital energies. In Santayana's concern for the comic mask or carnival mood; in Susan Langer's theory of a comic "vital rhythm"; in the psychoanalytic interest in the subconscious forces of freedom and expression, we find a new emphasis on the individual, primitive, even antisocial aspects of comedy. Comedy for these critics is no longer a social corrective but a restorer of natural freedom and flexibility in a society that has grown increasingly mechanical, rigid, repressive.

Traditional comedy depends on a rational relation between man and society. Neo-classical theories supported the traditional view of nature as a function of reason and good sense. But the emphasis on innate, anti-rational energies points to a new direction for comedy in the modern world. As the Victorian prophets predicted, middle-class values have gradually gained control in a democratic society. The comic writer finds himself an outsider in this social order, in a middle-class world where the norm is no longer vitalizing but conventional or dead. He no longer defends the status-quo against the comic figure, but is on the side of a new comic hero whose freedom and vitality are natural virtues now threatened by a restrictive, unnatural society.

Society itself acquires the qualities of the comic figure, the "humor" or scapegoat who must be ridiculed and, if possible, cured. In other words, the traditional comic relation has been reversed; the hero is now a critic of society and sometimes even outside of it. But this brings us to modern drama, in which the traditional view of comedy and the comic form are no longer viable. It will be seen, in the discussion of modern drama, that comic and tragic elements tend to merge under these conditions and evolve as a new form.

READINGS:

BERGSON, HENRI, "Laughter" (1900), in Comedy, ed. Wylie Sypher. New York: Doubleday Anchor, 1956.

COOK ALBERT, The Dark Voyage and The Golden Mean. Cambridge, Mass.: Harvard Press, 1949.

FELHEIM, MARVIN, ed. Comedy, Plays, Theory, Practice. New York: Harcourt, Brace & World, 1962.

FRYE, NORTHROP, Anatomy of Criticism. Princeton: Princeton University Press, 1957.

LAUTER, PAUL, ed. Theories of Comedy. New York: Doubleday Anchor, 1964.

MEREDITH, GEORGE, "An Essay on Comedy" (1897), in Comedy, ed. Wylie Sypher. New York: Doubleday, 1956.

NORWOOD, GILBERT, Greek Comedy. London: Methuen & Co., 1931.

POTTS, L. J., Comedy. London: Hutchinson's University Library, 1949.

WIMSATT, W. K. and BROOKS, CLEANTH, Literary Criticism: a Short History. New York: Alfred Knopf, 1957.

For further titles, see readings after headnotes on Shakespeare (Twelfth Night) and Molière.

◈ William Shakespeare

Socrates' curious statement at the end of the *Symposium*, that the "true artist in tragedy" is the "artist in comedy also" seems to apply less to any Greek dramatist than to William Shakespeare (1564–1616). *King Lear* is of course one of the masterpieces of Shakespeare's tragic vision. *Twelfth Night* is an equally great expression of his comic view of life.

Twelfth Night is the last and, for most critics, the best of his so-called "romantic" comedies, beginning with *Love's Labor's Lost* (1592) and *Two Gentlemen of Verona* (1594) and moving through *A Midsummer Night's Dream* (1596) to the great comic trio apparently written in rapid succession: *Much Ado About Nothing* (1599), *As You Like It* (1600), and *Twelfth Night* (1601). All dates are approximate. Shakespeare's romantic comedy combines elements from both classical New Comedy and romance literature. In *Twelfth Night*, we find the farcical confusion of his early *Comedy of Errors* (1592), —based on Plautus' *The Twin Menaechmi*, 200 B.C.— along with the romantic atmosphere of *Two Gentlemen of Verona*. On one level we have the romantic situation, involving Orsino, Olivia, Viola and Sebastian; and in the sub-plot we find the farce, the trickery and revelry of Sir Toby, Sir Andrew, Maria and Feste. (Malvolio belongs to both levels in the plot but he is the real outsider in this festive comedy.) The two patterns interweave as the romantic lovers find their real selves and a realistic approach to love beneath the disguise and the delusion of mistaken identity. Sir Toby's festive world finds release through "misrule" until the comic ending restores order to the revelers as well as realism to the lovers.

Twelfth Night (January 6th), celebrating the visit of the wise men to the infant Jesus, was a festive Elizabethan holiday, a time of merriment and licensed or temporary "misrule." Like Falstaff, Sir Toby is apparently a "lord of misrule"; and Feste, the clown, seems to be the presiding spirit of *Twelfth Night*. (It would be interesting to compare the Fool's role in a tragedy such as *Lear* with the role of Feste in a comedy such as *Twelfth Night*.) Only Malvolio is the real outsider, the antagonist in this comedy; he is the comic figure who restricts the festive, free world of *Twelfth Night*, and he becomes, therefore, the victim or comic scapegoat, imprisoned in the dark world of his narrow, anti-comic spirit. For a biographical note on Shakespeare, see the introduction to *King Lear;* and for a fuller discussion of *Twelfth Night* in the context of the comic form, see the introduction to comedy.

READINGS :

BARBER, C. L., *Shakespeare's Festive Comedy.* Princeton: Princeton University Press, 1959.

CHARLTON, H. B., *Shakesperian Comedy.* New York: Macmillan, 1938.

DRAPER, JOHN W., *The Twelfth Night of Shakespeare's Audience.* Stanford: Stanford University Press, 1950.

FRYE, NORTHROP, "The Argument of Shakespeare's Comedy," in Leonard Dean, ed. *Shakespeare: Modern Essays in Criticism.* New York: Oxford University Press, 1957.

GORDON, GEORGE, *Shakespearian Comedy.* Oxford: Oxford University Press, 1944.

HOLZKNECHT, KARL, *The Backgrounds of Shakespeare's Plays.* New York: American Book Co., 1950.

PARROTT, THOMAS MARC, *Shakesperean Comedy.* New York: Oxford University Press, 1949.

SUMMERS, JOSEPH, "The Masks of Twelfth Night," in *Comedy,* ed. Marvin Felheim. New York: Harcourt, Brace, 1962.

❧ Twelfth Night

DRAMATIS PERSONAE

ORSINO, Duke of Illyria
SEBASTIAN, brother to Viola
ANTONIO, a sea captain, friend to
   Sebastian
A SEA CAPTAIN, friend to Viola
VALENTINE⎱ gentlemen attending
CURIO   ⎰ on the Duke
SIR TOBY BELCH, uncle to Olivia
SIR ANDREW AGUECHEEK
MALVOLIO, steward to Olivia

FABIAN   ⎱ servants to
FESTE, a clown ⎰ Olivia
OLIVIA
VIOLA
MARIA, Olivia's woman

LORDS, PRIESTS, SAILORS, OFFI-
   CERS, MUSICIANS, and other
   ATTENDANTS

SCENE—A city in Illyria, and the
   seacoast near it.

❧ Act I

SCENE 1. An apartment in the DUKE'S palace.

[Enter DUKE, CURIO, and other LORDS; MUSICIANS attending.]
DUKE: If music be the food of love, play on.
   Give me excess of it, that, surfeiting,[1]
   The appetite may sicken, and so die.
   That strain again! It had a dying fall.[2]
   Oh, it came o'er my ear like the sweet sound
   That breathes upon a bank of violets,
   Stealing and giving odor! Enough, no more.
   'Tis not so sweet now as it was before.
   O spirit of love, how quick and fresh art thou!

Act I, Sc. i: 1. surfeiting: being overfull. 2. dying fall: cadence which falls away.

That, notwithstanding thy capacity
Receiveth as the sea, naught enters there,
Of what validity and pitch soe'er,
But falls into abatement and low price,
Even in a minute![3] So full of shapes is fancy
That it alone is high fantastical.[4]

CUR.: Will you go hunt, my lord?

DUKE: What, Curio?

CUR.: The hart.

DUKE: Why, so I do, the noblest that I have.
Oh, when mine eyes did see Olivia first,
Methought she purged the air of pestilence![5]
That instant was I turned into a hart,
And my desires, like fell[6] and cruel hounds,
E'er since pursue me.
          [Enter VALENTINE.] How now! What news from her?

VAL.: So please my lord, I might not be admitted,
But from her handmaid do return this answer:
The element[7] itself, till seven years' heat,[8]
Shall not behold her face at ample view;[9]
But, like a cloistress,[10] she will veilèd walk
And water once a day her chamber round
With eye-offending brine—all this to season[11]
A brother's dead love, which would keep fresh
And lasting in her sad remembrance.

DUKE: Oh, she that hath a heart of that fine frame
To pay this debt of love but to a brother,
How will she love when the rich golden shaft[12]
Hath killed the flock of all affections[13] else
That live in her; when liver, brain, and heart,[14]
These sovereign thrones, are all supplied, and filled
Her sweet perfections with one self king![15]

---

3. capacity . . . minute: i.e., though the spirit of love is as wide and deep as the sea, yet whatever falls into it, no matter how valuable and lofty, becomes worthless in a moment. pitch: lit., the soaring flight of a hawk. 4. So . . . fantastical: love (fancy) is so full of imagination (shapes) that above all others (alone) it is overflowing with fantasies (high fantastical). 5. purged . . . pestilence: The plague was believed by many to be caused by foul air. 6. fell: fierce. 7. element: sky. 8. seven . . . heat: till seven years have passed. 9. ample view: fully. 10. cloistress: nun in a cloister. 11. season: keep fresh. 12. golden shaft: Cupid has two arrows; the golden causes love, the leaden dislike. 13. affections: desires. 14. liver . . . heart: These parts were believed to be the seat of the passions, intelligence, and affection. 15. self king: sole object of adoration.

Away before me to sweet beds of flowers.
Love thoughts lie rich when canopied with bowers.
    [Exeunt.]

SCENE 2.   *The seacoast.*

       [Enter VIOLA, *a* CAPTAIN, *and* SAILORS.]
VIO.: What country, friends, is this?
CAP.: This is Illyria,[1] lady.
VIO.: And what should I do in Illyria?
    My brother he is in Elysium.[2]
    Perchance he is not drowned. What think you, sailors?
CAP.: It is perchance that you yourself were saved.
VIO.: Oh, my poor brother! And so perchance may he be.
CAP.: True, madam. And to comfort you with chance,
    Assure yourself, after our ship did split,
    When you and those poor number saved with you
    Hung on our driving[3] boat, I saw your brother,
    Most provident in peril, bind himself,
    Courage and hope both teaching him the practice,
    To a strong mast that lived upon the sea;
    Where, like Arion[4] on the dolphin's back,
    I saw him hold acquaintance with the waves
    So long as I could see.
VIO.: For saying so, there's gold.
    Mine own escape unfoldeth to my hope,
    Whereto thy speech serves for authority,
    The like of him.[5] Know'st thou this country?
CAP.: Aye, madam, well, for I was bred and born
    Not three hours' travel from this very place.
VIO.: Who governs here?
CAP.: A noble Duke, in nature as in name.
VIO.: What is his name?
CAP.: Orsino.

Sc. ii: 1. Illyria: actually on the east coast of the Adriatic sea, but Shakespeare has in fact chosen a picturesque name for an imaginary kingdom. 2. Elysium: Paradise. 3. driving: driven before the wind. 4. Arion: for the F1 reading "Orion." Arion was a singer. He was captured by pirates who were about to kill him. He asked to be allowed to sing for the last time. Then he jumped into the sea, where a dolphin, charmed by his song, carried him safe to land. 5. Mine . . . him: i.e., my escape and your speech give me hope that he is still alive.

VIO.: Orsino! I have heard my father name him.
He was a bachelor then.
CAP.: And so is now, or was so very late.
For but a month ago I went from hence,
And then 'twas fresh in murmur—as, you know,
What great ones do the less will prattle of—
That he did seek the love of fair Olivia.
VIO.: What's she?
CAP.: A virtuous maid, the daughter of a Count
That died some twelvemonth since, then leaving her
In the protection of his son, her brother,
Who shortly also died. For whose dear love,
They say, she hath abjured the company
And sight of men.
VIO.: Oh, that I served that lady,
And might not be delivered to the world
Till I had made mine own occasion mellow,
What my estate is![6]
CAP.: That were hard to compass,
Because she will admit no kind of suit,
No, not the Duke's.
VIO.: There is a fair behavior in thee, Captain.
And though that Nature with a beauteous wall
Doth oft close in pollution, yet of thee
I will believe thou hast a mind that suits
With this thy fair and outward character.[7]
I prithee, and I'll pay thee bounteously,
Conceal me what I am, and be my aid
For such disguise as haply shall become
The form of my intent. I'll serve this Duke.
Thou shalt present me as a eunuch[8] to him.
It may be worth thy pains, for I can sing,[9]
And speak to him in many sorts of music,
That will allow me very worth his service.[10]
What else may hap to time I will commit,
Only shape thou thy silence to my wit.

---

6. mine . . . is: i.e., until the time is ripe for me to reveal my own affairs. 7. character: face—an outward indication of the nature within. 8. eunuch: boy singer. 9. I . . . sing: The part of Viola was originally written for a boy with a good voice, but later small alterations were made and the songs were given to the Clown. 10. allow . . . service: approve me as worth employing.

CAP.: Be you his eunuch, and your mute I'll be.
When my tongue blabs, then let mine eyes not see.
VIO.: I thank thee. Lead me on.
    [*Exeunt.*]

SCENE 3. OLIVIA's *house.*

    [*Enter* SIR TOBY BELCH *and* MARIA.]

SIR TO.: What a plague means my niece, to take the death of her brother thus? I am sure care's an enemy to life.

MAR.: By my troth, Sir Toby, you must come in earlier o' nights. Your cousin, my lady, takes great exceptions to your ill hours.

SIR TO.: Why, let her except, before excepted.[1]

MAR.: Aye, but you must confine yourself within the modest limits of order.

SIR TO.: Confine! I'll confine myself no finer than I am. These clothes are good enough to drink in, and so be these boots too. An[2] they be not, let them hang themselves in their own straps.

MAR.: That quaffing and drinking will undo you. I heard my lady talk of it yesterday, and of a foolish knight that you brought in one night here to be her wooer.

SIR TO.: Who, Sir Andrew Aguecheek?

MAR.: Aye, he.

SIR TO.: He's as tall[3] a man as any 's in Illyria.

MAR.: What's that to the purpose?

SIR TO.: Why, he has three thousand ducats a year.

MAR.: Aye, but he'll have but a year in all these ducats. He's a very fool and a prodigal.

SIR TO.: Fie that you'll say so! He plays o' the viol de gamboys,[4] and speaks three or four languages word for word without book, and hath all the good gifts of nature.

MAR.: He hath indeed, almost natural,[5] for besides that he's a fool, he's a great quarreler. And but that he hath the gift of a coward to allay the gust[6] he hath in quarreling, 'tis thought among the prudent he would quickly have the gift of a grave.

Sc. iii: 1. except . . . excepted: Toby caps Maria's "exception" with a common legal phrase *exceptis excipiendis* (with the exceptions already excepted). 2. An: if. 3. tall: Andrew is tall and thin, but Toby implies that he is also "tall" in the common meaning of "brave." 4. viol de gamboys: bass viol, viola da gamba, so called because it was held between the legs. See Pl. 18a. 5. natural: with a pun on "natural," meaning born fool. 6. allay . . . gust: water down the taste.

SIR TO.: By this hand, they are scoundrels and substractors[7] that say so of him. Who are they?

MAR.: They that add, moreover, he's drunk nightly in your company.

SIR TO.: With drinking healths to my niece. I'll drink to her as long as there is a passage in my throat and drink in Illyria. He's a coward and a coystrill[8] that will not drink to my niece till his brains turn o' the toe like a parish top.[9] What, wench! *Castiliano vulgo;*[10] for here comes Sir Andrew Agueface.

[*Enter* SIR ANDREW AGUECHEEK.]

SIR AND.: Sir Toby Belch! How now, Sir Toby Belch!

SIR TO.: Sweet Sir Andrew!

SIR AND.: Bless you, fair shrew.

MAR.: And you too, sir.

SIR TO.: Accost, Sir Andrew, accost.[11]

SIR AND.: What's that?

SIR TO.: My niece's chambermaid.

SIR AND.: Good Mistress Accost, I desire better acquaintance.

MAR.: My name is Mary, sir.

SIR AND.: Good Mistress Mary Accost—

SIR TO.: You mistake, knight. "Accost" is front her, board her, woo her, assail her.

SIR AND.: By my troth, I would not undertake her in this company. Is that the meaning of "accost"?

MAR.: Fare you well, gentlemen.

SIR TO.: An thou let part so, Sir Andrew, would thou mightst never draw sword again.

SIR AND.: An you part so, mistress, I would I might never draw sword again. Fair lady, do you think you have fools in hand?

MAR.: Sir, I have not you by the hand.

SIR AND.: Marry,[12] but you shall have, and here's my hand.

MAR.: Now, sir, "thought is free." I pray you, bring your hand to the buttery bar[13] and let it drink.

SIR AND.: Wherefore, sweetheart? What's your metaphor?

MAR.: It's dry,[14] sir.

---

7. substractors: detractors. 8. coystrill: knave. 9. parish top: a large spinning top used by villagers on frosty days when it was too cold to work. 10. Castiliano vulgo: i.e., keep a straight face; lit., a Castilian face. The origin of the phrase is disputed. 11. accost: introduce yourself. 12. Marry: Mary, by the Virgin. 13. buttery bar: ledge on the half-door of the buttery on which tankards were rested. "Bar" is still used in this sense in "cocktail bar." The phrase "bring your hand to the buttery bar" is an invitation to a flirtation which Andrew is too simple to understand. 14. dry: A dry hand denoted lack of generosity and desire.

SIR AND.: Why, I think so. I am not such an ass but I can keep my hand dry. But what's your jest?

MAR.: A dry jest, sir.

SIR AND.: Are you full of them?

MAR.: Aye, sir, I have them at my fingers' ends. Marry, now I let go your hand, I am barren.

    [*Exit.*]

SIR TO.: O knight, thou lackest a cup of canary.[15] When did I see thee so put down?

SIR AND.: Never in your life, I think, unless you see canary put me down. Methinks sometimes I have no more wit than a Christian or an ordinary man has. But I am a great eater of beef[16] and I believe that does harm to my wit.

SIR TO.: No question.

SIR AND.: An I thought that, I'd forswear it. I'll ride home tomorrow, Sir Toby.

SIR TO.: *Pourquoi,*[17] my dear knight?

SIR AND.: What is "*pourquoi*"? Do or not do? I would I had bestowed that time in the tongues that I have in fencing, dancing and bear-baiting. Oh, had I but followed the arts!

SIR TO.: Then hadst thou had an excellent head of hair.

SIR AND.: Why, would that have mended my hair?

SIR TO.: Past question, for thou seest it will not curl by nature.[18]

SIR AND.: But it becomes me well enough, does 't not?

SIR TO.: Excellent. It hangs like flax on a distaff,[19] and I hope to see a housewife take thee between her legs and spin it off.[20]

SIR AND.: Faith, I'll home tomorrow, Sir Toby. Your niece will not be seen, or if she be, it's four to one she'll none of me. The Count himself here hard by woos her.

SIR TO.: She'll none o' the Count. She'll not match above her degree,[21] neither in estate, years, nor wit. I have heard her swear 't. Tut, there's life in 't, man.

SIR AND.: I'll stay a month longer. I am a fellow o' the strangest mind i' the world. I delight in masques and revels[22] sometimes altogether.

SIR TO.: Art thou good at these kickshawses,[23] knight?

---

15. canary: wine from the Canary Isles. 16. eater of beef: Diet was believed to have considerable influence on bodily and mental health. 17. Pourquoi: why. 18. curl by nature: emendation for the F1 reading "cool my nature." 19. distaff: used in spinning. 20. spin it off: cause you to lose your hair as a result of venereal disease. 21. degree: rank. 22. masques . . . revels: Courtly entertainments. See Gen. Intro. p. 32a. 23. kickshawses: trifles.

SIR AND.: As any man in Illyria, whatsoever he be, under the degree of
my betters. And yet I will not compare with an old man.[24]

SIR TO.: What is thy excellence in a galliard,[25] knight?

SIR AND.: Faith, I can cut a caper.[26]

SIR TO.: And I can cut the mutton[27] to 't.

SIR AND.: And I think I have the backtrick[28] simply as strong as any man
in Illyria.

SIR TO.: Wherefore are these things hid? Wherefore have these gifts a
curtain before 'em? Are they like to take dust, like Mistress Mall's
picture?[29] Why dost thou not go to church in a galliard and come
home in a coranto?[30] My very walk should be a jig,[31] I would not so
much as make water but in a sinkapace.[32] What dost thou mean? Is
it a world to hide virtues in? I did think, by the excellent constitution of thy leg, it was formed under the star of a galliard.

SIR AND.: Aye, 'tis strong, and it does indifferent well in a flame-colored
stock. Shall we set about some revels?

SIR TO.: What shall we do else? Were we not born under Taurus?[33]

SIR AND.: Taurus! That's sides and heart.

SIR TO.: No, sir, it is legs and thighs. Let me see thee caper. Ha! higher.
Ha, ha! excellent!

[Exeunt.]

SCENE 4. *The* DUKE's *palace.*

[*Enter* VALENTINE, *and* VIOLA *in man's attire.*]

VAL.: If the Duke continue these favors toward you, Cesario, you are
like to be much advanced. He hath known you but three days, and
already you are no stranger.

VIO.: You either fear his humor[1] or my negligence, that you call in
question the continuance of his love. Is he inconstant, sir, in his
favors?

---

24. old man: expert. 25. galliard: a quick, lively dance. See App. 24. 26. caper:
jump into the air. 27. cut . . . mutton: Mutton was often served with caper
sauce. 28. backtrick: a movement in dancing. 29. Mistress . . . picture: a
topical allusion now lost. Mall or Moll was a common nickname for a prostitute. This Mall may have been the notorious Mall Newberry. See T Night
Intro. p. 846a. 30. coranto: a running dance. 31. jig: a lively dance. 32.
sinkapace: "cinque pace," a dance of five steps. 33. born . . . Taurus: The
common penny almanac of the time printed the figure of a naked man surrounded by the signs of the zodiac with lines pointing to the parts of the
body governed by each. Both Andrew and Toby are wrong, as Taurus governed the neck and throat.

Sc. iv: 1. humor: whim, inclination. See App. 3.

VAL.: No, believe me.

VIO.: I thank you. Here comes the Count.

[*Enter* DUKE, CURIO, *and* ATTENDANTS.]

DUKE: Who saw Cesario, ho?

VIO.: On your attendance, my lord. Here.

DUKE: Stand you a while aloof. Cesario,
Thou know'st no less but all. I have unclasped
To thee the book even of my secret soul.
Therefore, good youth, address thy gait unto her.
Be not denied access, stand at her doors,
And tell them there thy fixèd foot shall grow
Till thou have audience.

VIO.: Sure, my noble lord,
If she be so abandoned to her sorrow
As it is spoke, she never will admit me.

DUKE: Be clamorous and leap all civil bounds[2]
Rather than make unprofited return.

VIO.: Say I do speak with her, my lord, what then?

DUKE: Oh, then unfold the passion of my love,
Surprise her with discourse of my dear faith.
It shall become thee well to act my woes.
She will attend it better in thy youth
Than in a nuncio's[3] of more grave aspéct.[4]

VIO.: I think not so, my lord.

DUKE: Dear lad, believe it,
For they shall yet belie thy happy years
That say thou art a man. Diana's lip
Is not more smooth and rubious;[5] thy small pipe[6]
Is as the maiden's organ, shrill and sound,
And all is semblative[7] a woman's part.
I know thy constellation is right apt[8]
For this affair. Some four or five attend him,
All, if you will; for I myself am best
When least in company. Prosper well in this,
And thou shalt live as freely as thy lord,
To call his fortunes thine.

---

2. civil bounds: restraints of good manners. 3. nuncio: messenger. 4. grave aspect: sober countenance. 5. rubious: ruby-red. 6. small pipe: little throat. 7. semblative: resembling. 8. constellation . . . apt: you are born under a lucky star.

VIO.: I'll do my best
   To woo your lady. [*Aside*] Yet, a barful[9] strife!
   Whoe'er I woo, myself would be his wife.
      [*Exeunt.*]

SCENE 5.   OLIVIA's *house.*

      [*Enter* MARIA *and* CLOWN.]
MAR.: Nay, either tell me where thou hast been, or I will not open my
   lips so wide as a bristle may enter in way of thy excuse. My lady will
   hang thee for thy absence.
CLO.: Let her hang me. He that is well hanged in this world needs to
   fear no colors.[1]
MAR.: Make that good.[2]
CLO.: He shall see none to fear.
MAR.: A good lenten[3] answer. I can tell thee where that saying was
   born, of "I fear no colors."
CLO.: Where, good Mistress Mary?
MAR.: In the wars, and that may you be bold to say in your foolery.
CLO.: Well, God give them wisdom that have it, and those that are
   fools, let them use their talents.
MAR.: Yet you will be hanged for being so long absent—or to be turned
   away, is not that as good as a hanging to you?
CLO.: Many a good hanging prevents a bad marriage, and for turning
   away, let summer bear it out.[4]
MAR.: You are resolute, then?
CLO.: Not so, neither, but I am resolved on two points.[5]
MAR.: That if one break, the other will hold, or if both break, your
   gaskins[6] fall.
CLO.: Apt, in good faith, very apt. Well, go thy way. If Sir Toby would
   leave drinking, thou wert as witty a piece of Eve's flesh[7] as any in
   Illyria.
MAR.: Peace, you rogue, no more o' that. Here comes my lady. Make
   your excuse wisely, you were best.

---

9. barful: full of bars, impediments.

Sc. v: 1. fear no colors: proverbial phrase meaning "I dare anyone." Since "collar,"
"color," and "choler" were pronounced alike, puns on these words were endless.   2. Make . . . good: prove it.   3. lenten: fasting, lean.   4. let . . . out:
have the upper hand; i.e., if I have to go, I hope it's good weather.   5. points:
laces used to attach the hose to the doublet.   6. gaskins: breeches.   7. Eve's
flesh: erring woman—the first hint that there is something between Toby and
Maria.

CLO.: Wit, an 't be thy will, put me into good fooling! Those wits that think they have thee do very oft prove fools, and I that am sure I lack thee may pass for a wise man. For what says Quinapalus?[8] "Better a witty fool than a foolish wit."

[*Enter* LADY OLIVIA *with* MALVOLIO.] God bless thee, lady!

OLI.: Take the fool away.

CLO.: Do you not hear, fellows? Take away the lady.

OLI.: Go to, you're a dry fool, I'll no more of you. Besides, you grow dishonest.

CLO.: Two faults,[9] madonna, that drink and good counsel will amend. For give the dry fool drink, then is the fool not dry. Bid the dishonest man mend himself; if he mend, he is no longer dishonest; if he cannot, let the botcher[10] mend him. Anything that's mended is but patched. Virtue that transgresses is but patched with sin, and sin that amends is but patched with virtue. If that this simple syllogism[11] will serve, so. If it will not, what remedy? As there is no true cuckold[12] but calamity, so beauty's a flower. The lady bade take away the fool, therefore I say again, take her away.

OLI.: Sir, I bade them take away you.

CLO.: Misprision[13] in the highest degree! Lady, *cucullus non facit monachum*.[14] That's as much to say as I wear not motley[15] in my brain. Good madonna, give me leave to prove you a fool.

OLI.: Can you do it?

CLO.: Dexteriously, good madonna.

OLI.: Make your proof.

CLO.: I must catechize you for it, madonna. Good my mouse[16] of virtue, answer me.

OLI.: Well, sir, for want of other idleness, I'll bide your proof.

CLO.: Good madonna, why mournest thou?

OLI.: Good fool, for my brother's death.

CLO.: I think his soul is in Hell, madonna.

OLI.: I know his soul is in Heaven, fool.

CLO.: The more fool, madonna, to mourn for your brother's soul being in Heaven. Take away the fool, gentlemen.

---

8. Quinapalus: a character invented by Rabelais. The clown specializes in mock learning. 9. Two faults: The fool is in disgrace and to cajole Olivia into good humor rattles out mock learned nonsense. 10. botcher: an unskilled mender of old garments. 11. syllogism: learned argument. 12. cuckold: husband deceived by his wife. 13. Misprision: error. 14. cucullus . . . monachum: a cowl does not make a monk. 15. motley: the fool's particolored costume. See Pl. 12f, 13c. 16. mouse: a term of endearment, like "duck."

OLI.: What think you of this fool, Malvolio? Doth he not mend?

MAL.: Yes, and shall do till the pangs of death shake him. Infirmity, that decays the wise, doth ever make the better fool.

CLO.: God send you, sir, a speedy infirmity, for the better increasing your folly! Sir Toby will be sworn that I am no fox, but he will not pass his word for twopence that you are no fool.

OLI.: How say you to that, Malvolio?

MAL.: I marvel your ladyship takes delight in such a barren rascal.[17] I saw him put down the other day with an ordinary fool that has no more brain than a stone. Look you now, he's out of his guard already. Unless you laugh and minister occasion[18] to him, he is gagged. I protest, I take these wise men that crow so at these set kind of fools no better than the fools' zanies.[19]

OLI.: Oh, you are sick of self-love, Malvolio, and taste with a distempered appetite. To be generous, guiltless, and of free[20] disposition is to take those things for bird bolts[21] that you deem cannon bullets. There is no slander in an allowed[22] fool, though he do nothing but rail; nor no railing in a known discreet man, though he do nothing but reprove.

CLO.: Now Mercury[23] endue thee with leasing,[24] for thou speakest well of fools!

[Re-enter MARIA.]

MAR.: Madam, there is at the gate a young gentleman much desires to speak with you.

OLI.: From the Count Orsino, is it?

MAR.: I know not, madam. 'Tis a fair young man, and well attended.

OLI.: Who of my people hold him in delay?

MAR.: Sir Toby, madam, your kinsman.

OLI.: Fetch him off, I pray you. He speaks nothing but madman, fie on him! [Exit MARIA.] Go you, Malvolio. If it be a suit from the Count, I am sick, or not at home—what you will, to dismiss it. [Exit MALVOLIO.] Now you see, sir, how your fooling grows old, and people dislike it.

CLO.: Thou hast spoke for us, madonna, as if thy eldest son should be

---

17. barren rascal: By this remark Malvolio rouses the malice of the fool, and so ultimately brings about his own downfall. 18. minister occasion: i.e., give him a lead. 19. zanies: stooges; the zany was the clown's assistant who tried to copy his tricks. 20. free: innocent. 21. bird bolts: short, blunt headed arrows used in a crossbow for killing small birds. See Pl. 22a. 22. allowed: licensed. 23. Mercury: the god of thieves and rascals. 24. endue . . . leasing: endow you with lying.

a fool, whose skull Jove cram with brains! for—here he comes[25]—one of thy kin has a most weak pia mater.[26]

[*Enter* SIR TOBY.]

OLI.: By mine honor, half-drunk. What is he at the gate, Cousin?

SIR TO.: A gentleman.

OLI.: A gentleman! What gentleman?

SIR TO.: 'Tis a gentleman here—a plague o' these pickle-herring![27] How now, sot!

CLO.: Good Sir Toby!

OLI.: Cousin, Cousin, how have you come so early by this lethargy?[28]

SIR TO.: Lechery! I defy lechery. There's one at the gate.

OLI.: Aye, marry, what is he?

SIR TO.: Let him be the Devil an he will, I care not. Give me faith, say I. Well, it's all one.

[*Exit.*]

OLI.: What's a drunken man like, fool?

CLO.: Like a drowned man, a fool, and a madman. One draught above heat makes him a fool, the second mads him, and a third drowns him.

OLI.: Go thou and seek the crowner,[29] and let him sit o' my coz,[30] for he's in the third degree of drink, he's drowned. Go look after him.

CLO.: He is but mad yet, madonna, and the fool shall look to the madman.

[*Exit.*]

[*Re-enter* MALVOLIO.]

MAL.: Madam, yond young fellow swears he will speak with you. I told him you were sick; he takes on him to understand so much, and therefore comes to speak with you. I told him you were asleep; he seems to have a foreknowledge of that too, and therefore comes to speak with you. What is to be said to him, lady? He's fortified against any denial.

OLI.: Tell him he shall not speak with me.

MAL.: Has been told so, and he says he'll stand at your door like a sheriff's post,[31] and be the supporter[32] to a bench, but he'll speak with you.

---

25. here he comes: i.e., Toby. This is the usual phrase to draw attention to a character entering at the back of the stage. See Gen. Intro. p. 56b.   26. pia mater: brain.   27. pickle-herring: very salt and indigestible, and so causing thirst and wind.   28. lethargy: lack of sense.   29. crowner: coroner, whose function is to hold an inquest on the bodies of those who die unnaturally.   30. coz: cousin—used for any near relation.   31. sheriff's post: painted post set up before the house of the sheriff as a sign of office.   32. supporter: support.

OLI.: What kind o' man is he?

MAL.: Why, of mankind.

OLI.: What manner of man?

MAL.: Of very ill manner. He'll speak with you, will you or no.

OLI.: Of what personage and years is he?

MAL.: Not yet old enough for a man, nor young enough for a boy, as a squash[33] is before 'tis a peascod, or a codling when 'tis almost an apple. 'Tis with him in standing water,[34] between boy and man. He is very well-favored[35] and he speaks very shrewishly.[36] One would think his mother's milk were scarce out of him.

OLI.: Let him approach. Call in my gentlewoman.

MAL.: Gentlewoman, my lady calls.

    [Exit.]

    [Re-enter MARIA.*]*

OLI.: Give me my veil. Come, throw it o'er my face. We'll once more hear Orsino's embassy.

    [Enter VIOLA *and* ATTENDANTS.*]*

VIO.: The honorable lady of the house, which is she?

OLI.: Speak to me, I shall answer for her. Your will?

VIO.: Most radiant, exquisite, and unmatchable beauty, I pray you tell me if this be the lady of the house, for I never saw her. I would be loath to cast away my speech, for besides that it is excellently well penned, I have taken great pains to con[37] it. Good beauties, let me sustain no scorn. I am very comptible,[38] even to the least sinister[39] usage.

OLI.: Whence came you, sir?

VIO.: I can say little more than I have studied, and that question's out of my part. Good gentle one, give me modest assurance if you be the lady of the house, that I may proceed in my speech.

OLI.: Are you a comedian?[40]

VIO.: No, my profound heart. And yet, by the very fangs of malice I swear, I am not that I play.[41] Are you the lady of the house?

OLI.: If I do not usurp myself, I am.

VIO.: Most certain, if you are she, you do usurp yourself; for what is yours to bestow is not yours to reserve. But this is from my commission.[42] I will on with my speech in your praise, and then show you the heart of my message.

33. squash: unripe peapod.   34. standing water: the moment at the change of the tide when the water neither ebbs nor flows.   35. well-favored: good-looking.   36. shrewishly: like a shrew, shrill.   37. con: learn by heart.   38. comptible: susceptible.   39. sinister: left-handed, unkind.   40. comedian: actor.   41. that I play: i.e., the part I act, that of a man.   42. from my commission: not included in my instructions.

OLI.: Come to what is important in 't. I forgive you the praise.

VIO.: Alas, I took great pains to study it, and 'tis poetical.

OLI.: It is the more like to be feigned. I pray you keep it in. I heard you were saucy at my gates, and allowed your approach rather to wonder[43] at you than to hear you. If you be not mad, be gone. If you have reason, be brief. 'Tis not that time of moon[44] with me to make one in so skipping[45] a dialogue.

MAR.: Will you hoist sail, sir? Here lies your way.

VIO.: No, good swabber,[46] I am to hull[47] here a little longer. Some mollification for your giant,[48] sweet lady. Tell me your mind. I am a messenger.

OLI.: Sure, you have some hideous matter to deliver when the courtesy of it is so fearful.[49] Speak your office.

VIO.: It alone concerns your ear. I bring no overture[50] of war, no taxation of[51] homage. I hold the olive in my hand, my words are as full of peace as matter.

OLI.: Yet you began rudely. What are you? What would you?

VIO.: The rudeness that hath appeared in me have I learned from my entertainment. What I am, and what I would, are as secret as maidenhead—to your ears, divinity; to any other's, profanation.

OLI.: Give us the place alone. We will hear this divinity.[52] [*Exeunt* MARIA *and* ATTENDANTS.] Now, sir, what is your text?

VIO.: Most sweet lady—

OLI.: A comfortable doctrine, and much may be said of it. Where lies your text?

VIO.: In Orsino's bosom.

OLI.: In his bosom! In what chapter of his bosom?

VIO.: To answer by the method,[53] in the first of his heart.

OLI.: Oh, I have read it. It is heresy. Have you no more to say?

VIO.: Good madam, let me see your face.

OLI.: Have you any commission from your lord to negotiate with my face? You are now out of your text. But we will draw the curtain

43. allowed . . . wonder: I allowed you to come in so that I might look at you—not to listen to your prepared speeches. 44. time of moon: lucky end of the month. 45. skipping: frivolous. 46. swabber: one who swabs the decks. Viola retorts to Maria's "hoist sail" with a series of nautical metaphors. 47. hull: lie at anchor. 48. mollification . . . giant: Viola apologizes to Olivia for the interruption—"I had to pacify your little lady." Maria's smallness is emphasized. See Gen. Intro. pp. 59b–60a. 49. courtesy . . . fearful: you must have some dreadful message to deliver if it need such elaborate introduction. 50. overture: declaration. 51. taxation of: demand for. 52. divinity: Olivia takes up Viola's *divinity*, and the two follow up the metaphor in their conversation. 53. To . . . method: to keep up the metaphor.

and show you the picture. Look you, sir, [*Unveiling*] such a one I
was this present[54]—is 't not well done?

OLI.: Excellently done, if God did all.

OLI.: 'Tis in grain,[55] sir, 'twill endure wind and weather.

VIO.: 'Tis beauty truly blent,[56] whose red and white
Nature's own sweet and cunning hand laid on.
Lady, you are the cruel'st she alive
If you will lead these graces to the grave
And leave the world no copy.[57]

OLI.: Oh, sir, I will not be so hardhearted, I will give out divers sched-
ules of my beauty. It shall be inventoried, and every particle and
utensil labeled to my will—as, item, two lips, indifferent red; item,
two gray eyes, with lids to them; item, one neck, one chin, and so
forth. Were you sent hither to praise me?

VIO.: I see what you are, you are too proud;
But if you were the Devil, you are fair.
My lord and master loves you. Oh, such love
Could be but recompensed, though you were crowned
The nonpareil[58] of beauty!

OLI.: How does he love me?

VIO.: With adorations, fertile tears,
With groans that thunder love, with sighs of fire.

OLI.: Your lord does know my mind. I cannot love him.
Yet I suppose him virtuous, know him noble,
Of great estate, of fresh and stainless youth;
In voices well divulged,[59] free, learned, and valiant;
And in dimension[60] and the shape of nature
A gracious person. But yet I cannot love him.
He might have took his answer long ago.

VIO.: If I did love you in my master's flame,
With such a suffering, such a deadly life,
In your denial I would find no sense.
I would not understand it.

OLI.: Why, what would you?

VIO.: Make me a willow cabin[61] at your gate,
And call upon my soul within the house;

54. such . . . present: This is the F1 reading, and has been much emended. The
general meaning is "This is what I really am." 55. in grain: i.e., the colors
are fast, they will not wash out. 56. blent: blended. 57. leave . . . copy:
die without children to carry on the pattern. Cf. Sonnets 1–17. 58. nonpareil: without an equal. 59. voices . . . divulged: spoken well of. 60. dimension: bodily form. 61. willow cabin: an arbor of willow—the unhappy
lover's tree.

Write loyal cantons[62] of contemnèd[63] love
And sing them loud even in the dead of night;
Halloo your name to the reverberate hills,
And make the babbling gossip of the air
Cry out "Olivia!" Oh, you should not rest
Between the elements of air and earth,
But you should pity me!

OLI.: You might do much.
What is your parentage?

VIO.: Above my fortunes, yet my state is well.
I am a gentleman.

OLI.: Get you to your lord.
I cannot love him. Let him send no more,
Unless, perchance, you come to me again
To tell me how he takes it. Fare you well.
I thank you for your pains. Spend this for me.

VIO.: I am no fee'd post,[64] lady, keep your purse.
My master, not myself, lacks recompense.
Love make his heart of flint that you shall love;
And let your fervor, like my master's, be
Placed in contempt! Farewell, fair cruelty.
        [Exit.]

OLI.: "What is your parentage?"
"Above my fortunes, yet my state is well.
I am a gentleman." I'll be sworn thou art.
Thy tongue, thy face, thy limbs, actions, and spirit,
Do give thee fivefold blazon.[65] Not too fast, Soft, soft!
Unless the master were the man. How now!
Even so quickly may one catch the plague?
Methinks I feel this youth's perfections
With an invisible and subtle stealth
To creep in at mine eyes. Well, let it be.
What ho, Malvolio!
        [Re-enter MALVOLIO.]

MAL.: Here, madam, at your service.

OLI.: Run after that same peevish messenger,
The County's[66] man. He left this ring behind him,
Would I or not. Tell him I'll none of it.
Desire him not to flatter with his lord,

---

62. cantons: songs. 63. contemned: despised. 64. fee'd post: paid messenger.
  65. blazon: coat of arms denoting a gentleman. 66. County: Count.

Nor hold him up with hopes. I am not for him.
If that the youth will come this way tomorrow,
I'll give him reasons for 't. Hie thee,[67] Malvolio.
MAL.: Madam, I will.
    [Exit.]
OLI.: I do I know not what, and fear to find
Mine eye too great a flatterer for my mind.
Fate, show thy force, ourselves we do not owe.[68]
What is decreed must be, and be this so.
    [Exit.]

❀ Act II

SCENE 1. *The seacoast.*

    [*Enter* ANTONIO *and* SEBASTIAN.]
ANT.: Will you stay no longer? Nor will you not that I go with you?
SEB.: By your patience, no. My stars shine darkly over me. The malignancy[1] of my fate might perhaps distemper[2] yours, therefore I shall crave of you your leave that I may bear my evils alone. It were a bad recompense for your love to lay any of them on you.
ANT.: Let me yet know of you whither you are bound.
SEB.: No, sooth, sir. My determinate voyage is mere extravagancy.[3] But I perceive in you so excellent a touch of modesty that you will not extort from me what I am willing to keep in; therefore it charges me in manners the rather to express myself.[4] You must know of me then, Antonio, my name is Sebastian, which I called Roderigo.[5] My father was that Sebastian of Messaline[6] whom I know you have heard of. He left behind him myself and a sister, both born in an hour. If the Heavens had been pleased, would we had so ended! But you, sir, altered that, for some hour before you took me from the breach[7] of the sea was my sister drowned.
ANT.: Alas the day!

---

67. Hie thee: hasten. 68. owe: own.

Act II, Sc. i: 1. malignancy: evil disposition. See App. 1. 2. distemper: disturb.
  3. determinate . . . extravagancy: the journey I have determined is mere wandering. There is a touch of affectation in Sebastian's language. 4. it . . . myself: good manners demand that I tell you who I am. 5. I . . . Roderigo: hitherto I have pretended that my name was Roderigo. 6. Messaline: Messina in Sicily. 7. breach: where the waves break.

SEB.: A lady, sir, though it was said she much resembled me, was yet of many accounted beautiful. But though I could not with such estimable wonder[8] overfar believe that, yet thus far I will boldly publish[9] her—she bore a mind that envy could not but call fair. She is drowned already, sir, with salt water, though I seem to drown her remembrance again with more.

ANT.: Pardon me, sir, your bad entertainment.[10]

SEB.: O good Antonio, forgive me your trouble.

ANT.: If you will not murder me for my love, let me be your servant.

SEB.: If you will not undo what you have done—that is, kill him whom you have recovered—desire it not. Fare ye well at once. My bosom is full of kindness,[11] and I am yet so near the manners of my mother that upon the least occasion more mine eyes will tell tales of me. I am bound to the Count Orsino's Court. Farewell.

    [Exit.]

ANT.: The gentleness of all the gods go with thee!
I have many enemies in Orsino's Court,
Else would I very shortly see thee there.
But, come what may, I do adore thee so
That danger shall seem sport, and I will go.

    [Exit.]

SCENE 2. A street.

    [Enter VIOLA, MALVOLIO following.]

MAL.: Were not you even now with the Countess Olivia?

VIO.: Even now, sir. On a moderate pace I have since arrived but hither.

MAL.: She returns this ring to you, sir. You might have saved me my pains, to have taken it away yourself. She adds, moreover, that you should put your lord into a desperate assurance[1] she will none of him. And one thing more, that you be never so hardy to come again in his affairs, unless it be to report your lord's taking of this. Receive it so.

VIO.: She took the ring of me. I'll none of it.

MAL.: Come, sir, you peevishly threw it to her; and her will is, it should be so returned. If it be worth stooping for, there it lies in your eye. If not, be it his that finds it.

    [Exit.]

---

8. estimable wonder: admiring judgment. 9. publish: proclaim. 10. your . . . entertainment: looking after you so badly. 11. kindness: tender feeling.

Sc. ii: 1. desperate assurance: certainty that there is no hope.

VIO.: I left no ring with her. What means this lady?
Fortune forbid my outside have not charmed her!
She made good view of me;[2] indeed, so much
That sure methought her eyes had lost her tongue,
For she did speak in starts distractedly.
She loves me, sure, the cunning of her passion
Invites me in this churlish messenger.
None of my lord's ring! Why, he sent her none.
I am the man. If it be so, as 'tis,
Poor lady, she were better love a dream.
Disguise, I see thou art a wickedness,
Wherein the pregnant[3] enemy does much.
How easy is it for the proper-false[4]
In women's waxen hearts to set their forms!
Alas, our frailty is the cause, not we!
For such as we are made of, such we be.
How will this fadge?[5] My master loves her dearly;
And I, poor monster, fond as much on him,
And she, mistaken, seems to dote on me.
What will become of this? As I am man,
My state is desperate for my master's love;
As I am woman—now alas the day!—
What thriftless[6] sighs shall poor Olivia breathe!
O Time, thou must untangle this, not I!
It is too hard a knot for me to untie!
        [*Exit.*]

SCENE 3. OLIVIA's *house.*

[*Enter* SIR TOBY *and* SIR ANDREW.]

SIR TO.: Approch, Sir Andrew. Not to be abed after midnight is to be
up betimes; and "*diluculo surgere*,"[1] thou know'st—

SIR AND.: Nay, by my troth,[2] I know not. But I know to be up late is
to be up late.

SIR TO.: A false conclusion. I hate it as an unfilled can.[3] To be up after
midnight, and to go to bed then, is early, so that to go to bed after

2. made . . . me: took a good look at me. 3. pregnant: resourceful. 4. proper-
false: men who are handsome but deceitful. 5. fadge: turn out. 6. thriftless: useless.

Sc. iii: 1. diluculo surgere: early to rise—a tag from the schoolboy's Latin gram-
mar. 2. troth: truth. 3. can: pot.

midnight is to go to bed betimes. Does not our life consist of the four elements?[4]

SIR AND.: Faith, so they say, but I think it rather consists of eating and drinking.

SIR TO.: Thou 'rt a scholar. Let us therefore eat and drink. Marian, I say, a stoup[5] of wine!

[*Enter* CLOWN.]

SIR AND.: Here comes the fool, i' faith.

CLO.: How now, my hearts! Did you never see the picture of "we three"?[6]

SIR TO.: Welcome, ass. Now let's have a catch.[7]

SIR AND.: By my troth, the fool has an excellent breast.[8] I had rather than forty shillings I had such a leg, and so sweet a breath to sing, as the fool has. In sooth, thou wast in very gracious fooling last night, when thou spokest of Pigrogromitus, of the Vaspians passing the equinoctial of Queubus.[9] 'Twas very good, i' faith. I sent thee six-pence for thy leman.[10] Hadst it?

CLO.: I did impeticos thy gratillity,[11] for Malvolio's nose is no whip-stock. My lady has a white hand, and the Myrmidons are no bottle-ale houses.

SIR AND.: Excellent! Why, this is the best fooling, when all is done. Now, a song.

SIR TO.: Come on, there is sixpence for you—let's have a song.

SIR AND.: There's a testril[12] of me too. If one knight give a—

CLO.: Would you have a love song, or a song of good life?

SIR TO.: A love song, a love song.

SIR AND.: Aye, aye. I care not for good life.

CLO.: [*Sings.*]
　　　O mistress mine, where are you roaming?
　　　Oh, stay and hear, your truelove's coming,
　　　　　That can sing both high and low.
　　　Trip no further, pretty sweeting,
　　　Journeys end in lovers meeting,
　　　　　Every wise man's son doth know.

SIR AND.: Excellent good, i' faith.

---

4. four elements: See App. 3.　5. stoup: large drinking pot. See Pl. 20e and g.
6. we three: a picture of two asses, the spectator being the third.　7. catch: rowdy song, where each singer in turn catches up the song a few words after the others.　8. breast: voice.　9. Pigrogromitus . . . Queubus: more mock learned foolery.　10. leman: sweetheart.　11. impeticos . . . gratillity: pocket your tip. The rest of the fool's profundity is unexplained; but as both knights are growing more and more fuddled, it is not important.　12. testril: coin worth sixpence.

SIR TO.: Good, good.

CLO.: [*Sings.*]

> What is love? 'Tis not hereafter,
> Present mirth hath present laughter,
>   What's to come is still unsure.
> In delay there lies no plenty,
> Then come kiss me, sweet and twenty,[13]
>   Youth's a stuff will not endure.

SIR AND.: A mellifluous[14] voice, as I am a true knight.

SIR TO.: A contagious breath.

SIR AND.: Very sweet and contagious, i' faith.

SIR TO.: To hear by the nose, it is dulcet in contagion.[15] But shall we make the welkin[16] dance indeed? Shall we rouse the night owl in a catch[17] that will draw three souls out of one weaver?[18] Shall we do that?

SIR AND.: On you love me, let's do 't. I am dog at a catch.

CLO.: By 'r lady, sir, and some dogs will catch well.

SIR AND.: Most certain. Let our catch be "Thou knave."

CLO.: "Hold thy peace, thou knave," knight? I shall be constrained in 't to call thee knave, knight.

SIR AND.: 'Tis not the first time I have constrained one to call me knave. Begin, fool. It begins "Hold thy peace."

CLO.: I shall never begin if I hold my peace.

SIR AND.: Good, i' faith. Come, begin.

[*Catch sung.*]

[*Enter* MARIA.]

MAR.: What a caterwauling do you keep here! If my lady have not called up her steward Malvolio and bid him turn you out of doors, never trust me.

SIR TO.: My lady's a Cataian,[19] we are politicians,[20] Malvolio's a Peg-a-Ramsey,[21] and "Three merry men be we." Am not I consanguineous?[22] Am I not of her blood? Tillyvally.[23] Lady! [*Sings.*] "There dwelt a man in Babylon, lady, lady!"

CLO.: Beshrew me,[24] the knight's in admirable fooling.

---

13. sweet . . . twenty: gay girl. 14. mellifluous: honey-sweet. 15. dulcet in contagion: sweetly catching. 16. welkin: sky. 17. catch: See l. 18,n. The words of the catch which they sing at l. 75 are "Hold thy peace, thou knave." 18. three . . . weaver: Weavers, mostly Puritan refugees from the Netherlands, were noted psalm singers. It will need a powerful song to draw out three souls. 19. Cataian: Chinaman. 20. politicians: deep ones. 21. Peg-a-Ramsey: It is not known who this lady was or why Malvolio resembled her. 22. consanguineous: related by blood. Toby's mind has now strayed to Olivia. 23. Tillyvally: "hoity-toity."   24. Beshrew me: lit., ill luck take me.

SIR AND.: Aye, he does well enough if he be disposed, and so do I too. He does it with a better grace, but I do it more natural.

SIR TO. [*Sings*]: "Oh, the twelfth day of December"—

MAR.: For the love o' God, peace!

[*Enter* MALVOLIO.]

MAL.: My masters, are you mad? Or what are you? Have you no wit, manners, nor honesty, but to gabble like tinkers at this time of night? Do ye make an alehouse of my lady's house, that ye squeak out your coziers[25] catches without any mitigation or remorse of voice? Is there no respect of place, persons, nor time in you?

SIR TO.: We did keep time, sir, in our catches. Sneck up![26]

MAL.: Sir Toby, I must be round[27] with you. My lady bade me tell you that though she harbors you as her kinsman, she's nothing allied to your disorders. If you can separate yourself and your misdemeanors, you are welcome to the house. If not, an it would please you to take leave of her, she is very willing to bid you farewell.

SIR TO.: "Farewell,[28] dear heart, since I must needs be gone."

MAR.: Nay, good Sir Toby.

CLO.: "His eyes do show his days are almost done."

MAL.: Is't even so?

SIR TO.: "But I will never die."

CLO.: Sir Toby, there you lie.

MAL.: This is much credit to you.

SIR TO.: "Shall I bid him go?"

CLO.: "What an if you do?"

SIR TO.: "Shall I bid him go, and spare not?"

CLO.: "Oh, no, no, no, no, you dare not."

SIR TO.: Out o' tune, sir. Ye lie. Art any more than a steward? Dost thou think because thou art virtuous, there shall be no more cakes and ale?

CLO.: Yes, by Saint Anne, and ginger shall be hot i' the mouth too.

SIR TO.: Thou 'rt i' the right. Go, sir, rub your chain[29] with crumbs.[30] A stoup of wine, Maria!

MAL.: Mistress Mary, if you prized my lady's favor at anything more than contempt, you would not give means for this uncivil rule.[31] She shall know of it, by this hand.

[*Exit.*]

25. coziers: cobblers. 26. Sneck up: be hanged. 27. round: direct. 28. Farewell . . . not: Toby and the Clown here indulge in an impromptu duet. 29. chain: i.e., of office as a steward. 30. with crumbs: used for polishing silver. 31. uncivil rule: disorderly conduct.

MAR.: Go shake your ears.

SIR AND.: 'Twere as good a deed as to drink when a man's a-hungry, to challenge him the field, and then to break promise with him and make a fool of him.

SIR TO.: Do 't, knight. I'll write thee a challenge, or I'll deliver thy indignation to him by word of mouth.

MAR.: Sweet Sir Toby, be patient for tonight. Since the youth of the Count's was today with my lady, she is much out of quiet. For Monsieur Malvolio, let me alone with him. If I do not gull him into a nayword,[32] and make him a common recreation,[33] do not think I have wit enough to lie straight in my bed. I know I can do it.

SIR TO.: Possess us, possess us. Tell us something of him.

MAR.: Marry, sir, sometimes he is a kind of Puritan.

SIR AND.: Oh, if I thought that, I'd beat him like a dog!

SIR TO.: What, for being a Puritan? Thy exquisite reason, dear knight?

SIR AND.: I have no exquisite reason for 't, but I have reason good enough.

MAR.: The devil a Puritan that he is, or anything constantly, but a timepleaser;[34] an affectioned[35] ass, that cons state[36] without book and utters it by great swarths—the best persuaded of himself, so crammed, as he thinks, with excellencies, that it is his grounds of faith that all that look on him love him. And on that vice in him will my revenge find notable cause to work.

SIR TO.: What wilt thou do?

MAR.: I will drop in his way some obscure epistles of love, wherein, by the color of his beard, the shape of his leg, the manner of his gait, the expressure of his eye, forehead, and complexion, he shall find himself most feelingly[37] personated. I can write very like my lady your niece. On a forgotten matter we can hardly make distinction of our hands.

SIR TO.: Excellent! I smell a device.

SIR AND.: I have 't in my nose too.

SIR TO.: He shall think, by the letters that thou wilt drop, that they come from my niece, and that she's in love with him.

MAR.: My purpose is indeed a horse of that color.

SIR AND.: And your horse now would make him an ass.

MAR.: Ass, I doubt not.

SIR AND.: Oh, 'twill be admirable!

---

32. nayword: byword.   33. common recreation: general laughingstock.   34. time-pleaser: one who suits his behavior to his own advantage.   35. affectioned: affected.   36. cons state: learns courtly behavior by heart.   37. feelingly: exactly.

MAR.: Sport royal, I warrant you. I know my physic will work with him. I will plant you two, and let the fool make a third, where he shall find the letter. Observe his construction of it. For this night, to bed, and dream on the event. Farewell.

    [*Exit.*]

SIR TO.: Good night, Penthesilea.[38]

SIR AND.: Before me, she's a good wench.

SIR TO.: She's a beagle,[39] true-bred, and one that adores me. What o' that?

SIR AND.: I was adored once too.

SIR TO.: Let's to bed, knight. Thou hadst need send for more money.

SIR AND.: If I cannot recover[40] your niece, I am a foul way out.[41]

SIR TO.: Send for money, knight. If thou hast her not i' the end, call me cut.[42]

SIR AND.: If I do not, never trust me, take it how you will.

SIR TO.: Come, come, I'll go burn some sack.[43] 'Tis too late to go to bed now. Come, knight, come, knight.

    [*Exeunt.*]

SCENE 4. *The* DUKE's *palace.*

    [*Enter* DUKE, VIOLA, CURIO, *and others.*]

DUKE: Give me some music. Now, good morrow, friends.
  Now, good Cesario, but that piece of song,[1]
  That old and antique song we heard last night.
  Methought it did relieve my passion much,
  More than light airs and recollected terms[2]
  Of these most brisk and giddy-pacèd[3] times.
  Come, but one verse.

CUR.: He is not here, so please your lordship, that should sing it.

DUKE: Who was it?

CUR.: Feste, the jester, my lord, a fool that the Lady Olivia's father took much delight in. He is about the house.

---

38. Penthesilea: Queen of the Amazons, a large, muscular lady—an ironical description of the little gentlewoman. 39. beagle: a small hound. 40. recover: win. 41. foul . . . out: have wasted a lot of money. 42. cut: gelded. 43. burn . . . sack: warm some sack. Sack (Falstaff's favorite drink; see *II Hen IV*, IV.iii.103–35) was a Spanish wine. It was sometimes sweetened and drunk warm.

Sc. iv: 1. piece of song: another indication that Viola was originally intended to be the singer. See I.ii.57,n. 2. recollected terms: artificial phrases. 3. giddy-paced: frivolous.

DUKE: Seek him out, and play the tune the while.

[*Exit* CURIO. *Music plays.*]

Come hither, boy. If ever thou shalt love,
In the sweet pangs of it remember me;
For such as I am all truelovers are,
Unstaid and skittish in all motions else
Save in the constant image of the creature
That is beloved. How dost thou like this tune?

VIO.: It gives a very echo to the seat
Where Love is throned.

DUKE: Thou dost speak masterly.
My life upon 't, young though thou art, thine eye
Hath stayed upon some favor[4] that it loves.
Hath it not, boy?

VIO.: A little, by your favor.

DUKE: What kind of woman is 't?

VIO.: Of your complexion.

DUKE: She is not worth thee, then. What years, i' faith?

VIO.: About your years, my lord.

DUKE: Too old, by Heaven. Let still[5] the woman take
An elder than herself, so wears she to him,
So sways she level in her husband's heart.
For, boy, however we do praise ourselves,
Our fancies are more giddy and unfirm,
More longing, wavering, sooner lost and worn,
Than women's are.

VIO.: I think it well, my lord.

DUKE: Then let thy love be younger than thyself,
Or thy affection cannot hold the bent.[6]
For women are as roses, whose fair flower
Being once displayed, doth fall that very hour.

VIO.: And so they are. Alas, that they are so—
To die, even when they to perfection grow!

[*Re-enter* CURIO *and* CLOWN.]

DUKE: Oh, fellow, come, the song we had last night.
Mark it, Cesario, it is old and plain.
The spinsters and the knitters in the sun
And the free maids that weave their thread with bones[7]

---

4. favor: face. Viola (l. 26) in the safety of disguise takes up the word "by your favor," which Orsino interprets as "by your leave." 5. still: always. 6. hold . . . bent: keep the tension; the image is of a strong bow. 7. weave . . . bones: i.e., make lace with bone bobbins.

Do use to chant it. It is silly sooth,[8]
And dallies with the innocence of love,
  Like the old age.
CLO.: Are you ready, sir?
DUKE: Aye, prithee sing.
CLO.: [Sings.]

> Come away, come away, death,
>   And in sad cypress[9] let me be laid.
> Fly away, fly away, breath,
>   I am slain by a fair cruel maid.
> My shroud[10] of white, stuck all with yew,
>   Oh, prepare it!
> My part of death, no one so true
>   Did share it!
> Not a flower, not a flower sweet,
>   On my black coffin let there be strown.
> Not a friend, not a friend greet
>   My poor corpse, where my bones shall be thrown.
> A thousand thousand sighs to save,
>   Lay me, oh, where
> Sad truelover never find my grave,
>   To weep there!

DUKE: There's for thy pains.
CLO.: No pains, sir. I take pleasure in singing, sir.
DUKE: I'll pay thy pleasure then.
CLO.: Truly, sir, and pleasure will be paid, one time or another.
DUKE: Give me now leave to leave thee.
CLO.: Now, the melancholy god protect thee, and the tailor make thy doublet[11] of changeable[12] taffeta, for thy mind is a very opal. I would have men of such constancy[13] put to sea, that their business might be everything and their intent everywhere; for that's it that always makes a good voyage of nothing. Farewell.
  [Exit.]
DUKE: Let all the rest give place.
  [CURIO and ATTENDANTS retire.]
Once more, Cesario,
Get thee to yond same sovereign cruelty.
Tell her my love, more noble than the world,

---

8. silly sooth: simple truth. 9. cypress: coffin of cypress wood. 10. shroud: See App. 16. 11. doublet: jacket. See Pl. 8b and comment on p. 93a. 12. changeable: changing its color as the light falls. 13. such constancy: The fool is ironical, for Orsino hitherto has been "to one thing constant never."

Prizes not quantity of dirty lands.
The parts[14] that fortune hath bestowed upon her,
Tell her I hold as giddily as fortune.[15]
But 'tis that miracle and queen of gems
That nature pranks[16] her in attracts my soul.

VIO.: But if she cannot love you, sir?

DUKE: I cannot be so answered.

VIO.: Sooth, but you must.
Say that some lady, as perhaps there is,
Hath for your love as great a pang of heart
As you have for Olivia. You cannot love her,
You tell her so. Must she not then be answered?

DUKE: There is no woman's sides
Can bide the beating of so strong a passion
As love doth give my heart, no woman's heart
So big to hold so much. They lack retention.
Alas, their love may be called appetite—
No motion of the liver,[17] but the palate—
That suffer surfeit, cloyment, and revolt;
But mine is all as hungry as the sea,
And can digest as much. Make no compare
Between that love a woman can bear me
And that I owe Olivia.

VIO.: Aye, but I know—

DUKE: What dost thou know?

VIO.: Too well what love women to men may owe.
In faith, they are as true of heart as we.
My father had a daughter loved a man,
As it might be, perhaps, were I a woman,
I should your lordship.

DUKE: And what's her history?

VIO.: A blank, my lord. She never told her love,
But let concealment, like a worm i' the bud,
Feed on her damask[18] cheek. She pined in thought,
And with a green and yellow melancholy
She sat like Patience on a monument,[19]
Smiling with grief, Was not this love indeed?
We men may say more, swear more, but indeed

14. parts: wealth. 15. giddily as fortune: i.e., I am not interested in her wealth.
16. pranks: adorns. 17. liver: true passion, as in I.i.37. 18. damask: color
of the damask rose, pink and white. 19. Patience . . . monument: a statue
of Patience.

Our shows are more than will,[20] for still we prove
Much in our vows, but little in our love.
DUKE: But died thy sister of her love, my boy?
VIO.: I am all the daughters of my father's house,
And all the brothers too. And yet I know not.
Sir, shall I to this lady?
DUKE: Aye, that's the theme.
To her in haste. Give her this jewel. Say
My love can give no place, bide no denay.[21]
[Exeunt.]

SCENE 5.   OLIVIA's garden.

[Enter SIR TOBY, SIR ANDREW, and FABIAN.]
SIR TO.: Come thy ways, Signior Fabian.
FAB.: Nay, I'll come. If I lose a scruple[1] of this sport, let me be boiled
to death with melancholy.
SIR TO.: Wouldst thou not be glad to have the niggardly rascally sheep-
biter[2] come by some notable shame?
FAB.: I would exult, man. You know he brought me out o' favor with
my lady about a bearbaiting[3] here.
SIR TO.: To anger him we'll have the bear again, and we will fool him
black and blue. Shall we not, Sir Andrew?
SIR AND.: An we do not, it is pity of our lives.
SIR TO.: Here comes the little villain.
[Enter MARIA.]
How now, my metal of India![4]
MAR.: Get ye all three into the box tree.[5] Malvolio's coming down
this walk. He has been yonder i' the sun practicing behavior to his
own shadow this half-hour. Observe him, for the love of mockery,
for I know this letter will make a contemplative idiot[6] of him. Close,
in the name of jesting! Lie thou there, [Throws down a letter] for
here comes the trout that must be caught with tickling.[7]
[Exit.]
[Enter MALVOLIO.]

20. Our . . . will: our outward appearances are greater than our feelings.   21.
denay: denial.

Sc. v: 1. scruple: minute part.   2. sheepbiter: sheepstealer.   3. bearbaiting: a
popular sport, detested by the Puritans. See App. 5.   4. metal of India: fine
gold.   5. box tree: an evergreen shrub much used by Elizabethan gardeners
for ornamental hedges.   6. contemplative idiot: pompous ass.   7. caught . . .
tickling: a poacher's method of catching trout with the bare hand.

MAL.: 'Tis but fortune, all is fortune. Mario once told me she did affect me.[8] And I have heard herself come thus near, that, should she fancy, it should be one of my complexion. Besides, she uses me with a more exalted respect than anyone else that follows her. What should I think on 't?

SIR TO.: Here's an overweening rougue!

FAB.: Oh, peace! Contemplation makes a rare turkeycock of him. How he jets under his advance plumes![9]

SIR AND.: 'Slight,[10] I could so beat the rogue!

SIR TO.: Peace, I say.

MAL.: To be Count Malvolio!

SIR TO.: Ah, rogue!

SIR AND.: Pistol him, pistol him.

SIR TO.: Peace, peace!

MAL.: There is example for 't. The lady of the Strachy[11] married the yeoman of the wardrobe.[12]

SIR AND.: Fie on him, Jezebel![13]

FAB.: Oh, peace! Now he's deeply in. Look how imagination blows him.

MAL.: Having been three months married to her, sitting in my state[14]

SIR TO.: Oh, for a stonebow,[15] to hit him in the eye!

MAL.: Calling my officers above me, in my branched[16] velvet gown, having come from a day bed,[17] where I have left Olivia sleeping—

SIR TO.: Fire and brimstone!

FAB.: Oh, peace, peace!

MAL.: And then to have the humor of state.[18] And after a demure travel of regard,[19] telling them I know my place as I would they should do theirs, to ask for my kinsman Toby—

SIR TO.: Bolts and shackles!

FAB.: Oh, peace, peace, peace! Now, now.

MAL.: Seven of my people, with an obedient start, make out for him. I frown the while, and perchance wind up my watch, or play with my —some rich jewel.[20] Toby approaches, curtsies there to me—

SIR TO.: Shall this fellow live?

8. she . . . me: Olivia liked me.   9. jets . . . plumes: struts with his tail feathers up.   10. 'Slight: by God's light.   11. lady . . . Strachy: She has not been identified.   12. yeoman . . . wardrobe: in a great household each department was under the control of a yeoman, or upper servant, and a "gentleman." See App. 14.   13. Jezebel: Andrew's knowledge of the Bible is weak, but at least he does know that Jezebel was a shameless person.   14. state: chair of state. 15. stonebow: crossbow for shooting stones. See Pl. 22c.   16. branched: embroidered with a pattern of leaves and branches. See Pl. 8b.   17. day bed: couch.   18. humor of state: dignified manner of some statesman.   19. demure . . . regard: glancing gravely from one to the other.   20. my—some rich jewel: Malvolio inadvertently touches his steward's chain.

FAB.: Though our silence be drawn from us with cars,[21] yet peace.

MAL.: I extend my hand to him thus, quenching my familiar smile with an austere regard of control[22]—

SIR TO.: And does not Toby take you a blow o' the lips then?

MAL.: Saying, "Cousin Toby, my fortunes having cast me on your niece, give me this prerogative[23] of speech—"

SIR TO.: What, what?

MAL.: "You must amend your drunkenness."

SIR TO.: Out, scab!

FAB.: Nay, patience, or we break the sinews of our plot.

MAL.: "Besides, you waste the treasure of your time with a foolish knight—"

SIR AND.: That's me, I warrant you.

MAL.: "One Sir Andrew—"

SIR AND.: I knew 'twas I, for many do call me fool.

MAL.: What employment have we here?
[Taking up the letter.]

FAB.: Now is the woodcock[24] near the gin.[25]

SIR TO.: Oh, peace! And the spirit of humors[26] intimate reading aloud to him!

MAL.: By my life, this is my lady's hand. These be her very C's, her U's, and her T's; and thus makes she her great P's. It is, in contempt of question[27] her hand.

SIR AND.: Her C's, her U's and her T's. Why that?

MAL. [Reads.]: "To the unknown beloved, this, and my good wishes:—"
Her very phrases! By your leave, wax.[28] Soft, and the impressure her Lucrece,[29] with which she uses to seal. 'Tis my lady. To whom should this be?

FAB.: This wins, him, liver and all.

MAL. [Reads.]: "Jove knows I love.
　　　But who?
　　Lips, do not move.
　　No man must know."
"No man must know." What follows? The numbers[30] altered! "No man must know." If this should be thee, Malvilio?

SIR TO.: Marry, hang thee, brock![31]

---

21. drawn . . . cars: though we should be torn to pieces by chariots and wild horses. 22. austere . . . control: severe look of authority. 23. prerogative: privilege. 24. woodcock: regarded as a very simple bird. 25. gin: trap. 26. spirit of humors: i.e., of mockery, as in a comedy of humors. See Gen. Intro. p. 42a and App. 3. 27. contempt of question: without any doubt. 28. wax: See App. 6. 29. her Lucrece: the head of Lucrece, the device on her seal. 30. numbers: meter. 31. brock: badger.

MAL. [*Reads.*]:

> "I may command where I adore,
> But silence, like a Lucrece knife,[32]
> With bloodless stroke my heart doth gore.
> M, O, A, I, doth sway my life."

FAB.: A fustian[33] riddle!

SIR TO.: Excellent wench, say I.

MAL.: "M, O, A, I, doth sway my life." Nay, but first, let me see, let me see, let me see.

FAB.: What dish o' poison has she dressed him!

SIR TO.: And with what wing the staniel[34] checks at it!

MAL.: "I may command where I adore." Why, she may command me. I serve her, she is my lady. Why, this is evident to any formal capacity,[35] there is no obstruction in this. And the end—what should that alphabetical position portend? If I could make that resemble something in me—Softly! M, O, A, I—

SIR TO.: Oh, aye, make up that. He is now at a cold scent.

FAB.: Sowter[36] will cry upon 't for all this, though it be as rank as a fox.[37]

MAL.: M—Malvolio. M—why, that begins my name.

FAB.: Did not I say he would work it out? The cur is excellent at faults.[38]

MAL.: M—but then there is no consonancy[39] in the sequel, that suffers under probation.[40] A should follow, but O does.

FAB.: And O shall end, I hope.

SIR TO.: Aye, or I'll cudgel him and make him cry O!

MAL.: And then I comes behind.

FAB.: Aye, an you had any eye behind you, you might see more detraction at your heels than fortunes before you.

MAL.: M, O, A, I. This simulation[41] is not as the former. And yet, to crush[42] this a little, it would bow to me,[43] for every one of these letters are in my name. Soft! Here follows prose.

[*Reads.*]

> "If this fall into thy hand, revolve.[44] In my stars[45] I am above thee;

---

32. Lucrece knife: the knife with which Lucrece killed herself. 33. fustian: coarse cloth, so "common." 34. staniel: kestrel, an inferior kind of hawk. See App. 26. 35. formal capacity: normal intelligence. 36. Sowter: lit., cobbler, nickname for a clumsy hound. 37. cry . . . fox: he'll make a great cry, and follow it up, for the scent is as strong as a fox's. 38. excellent at faults: will follow the scent, however bad. fault: a break in a scent. 39. consonancy: consistency. 40. suffers . . . probation: fails when tested. 41. simulation: disguised meaning. 42. crush: force. 43. bow . . . me: incline my way. 44. revolve: ponder. 45. stars: fate.

but be not afraid of greatness. Some are born great, some achieve greatness, and some have greatness thrust upon 'em. Thy Fates open their hands. Let thy blood and spirit embrace them, and to inure thyself to what thou art like to be, cast thy humble slough[46] and appear fresh. Be opposite with a kinsman, surly with servants, let thy tongue tang[47] arguments of state, put thyself into the trick of singularity.[48] She thus advises thee that sighs for thee. Remember who commended thy yellow stockings, and wished to see thee ever crossgartered.[49] I say, remember. Go to, thou art made, if thou desirest to be so. If not, let me see thee a steward still, the fellow of servants, and not worthy to touch Fortune's fingers. Farewell. She that would alter services with thee,

"The Fortunate-Unhappy"

Daylight and champain[50] discovers not more. This is open. I will be proud, I will read politic authors,[51] I will baffle[52] Sir Toby, I will wash off gross acquaintance, I will be point-device[53] the very man. I do not now fool myself, to let imagination jade me,[54] for every reason excites to this, that my lady loves me. She did commend my yellow stockings of late, she did praise my leg being cross-gartered; and in this she manifests herself to my love, and with a kind of injunction drives me to these habits of her liking. I thank my stars I am happy. I will be strange,[55] stout,[56] in yellow stockings, and crossgartered, even with the switfness of putting on. Jove and my stars be praised! Here is yet a postscript.
    [Reads.]
"Thou canst not choose but know who I am. If thou entertainest my love, let it appear in thy smiling. Thy smiles become thee well, therefore in my presence still smile, dear my sweet, I prithee."
Jove, I thank thee. I will smile, I will do everything that thou wilt have me.
    [Exit.]
FAB.: I will not give my part of this sport for a pension of thousands to be paid from the Sophy.[57]
SIR TO.: I could marry this wench for this device—
SIR AND.: So could I too.
SIR TO.: And ask no other dowry with her but such another jest.

46. slough: snakeskin. 47. tang: resound. 48. trick of singularity: unusual behavior. 49. cross-gartered: See Pl. 8c and comment on p. 93b. 50. champain: open country. 51. politic authors: books on statecraft. 52. baffle: bring into disgrace. See *Rich II*, I.i.170,n. 53. point-device: exactly. 54. jade me: play me a dirty trick. 55. strange: distant. 56. stout: haughty. 57. Sophy: Shah of Persia. See *T Night* Intro. p. 845a.

SIR AND.: Nor I neither.

FAB.: Here comes my noble gull-catcher.[58]

[*Re-enter* MARIA.]

SIR TO.: Wilt thou set thy foot o' my neck?

SIR AND.: Or o' mine either?

SIR TO.: Shall I play my freedom at trey-trip,[59] and become thy bond-slave?

SIR AND.: I' faith, or I either?

SIR TO.: Why, thou hast put him in such a dream that when the image of it leaves him he must run mad.

MAR.: Nay, but say true. Does it work upon him?

SIR TO.: Like aqua vitae[60] with a midwife.

MAR.: If you will then see the fruits of the sport, mark his first approach before my lady. He will come to her in yellow stockings, and 'tis a color she abhors, and cross-gartered, a fashion she detests. And he will smile upon her, which will now be so unsuitable to her disposition, being addicted to a melancholy as she is, that it cannot but turn him into a notable contempt. If you will see it, follow me.

SIR TO.: To the gates of Tartar, thou most excellent devil of wit!

SIR AND.: I'll make one too.

[*Exeunt.*]

❦ Act III

SCENE 1. OLIVIA's *garden.*

[*Enter* VIOLA, *and* CLOWN *with a tabor.*[1]]

VIO.: Save thee, friend, and thy music. Dost thou live by thy tabor?

CLO.: No, sir, I live by the church.

VIO.: Art thou a churchman?[2]

CLO.: No such matter, sir. I do live by the church, for I do live at my house, and my house doth stand by[3] the church.

VIO.: So thou mayst say the King lies by a beggar, if a beggar dwell near him, or the church stands by thy tabor, if thy tabor stand by the church.

---

58. gull-catcher: fool-catcher. 59. trey-trip: game played with cards and dice. 60. aqua vitae: spirits especially favored by old women such as Juliet's Nurse. See *R & J*, IV.v.16.

Act III, Sc. i: 1. s.d., tabor: small drum. See Pl. 13d. 2. churchman: cleric. 3. by: near.

CLO.: You have said, sir. To see this age! A sentence is but a cheveril[4] glove to a good wit. How quickly the wrong side may be turned outward!

VIO.: Nay, that's certain. They that dally[5] nicely with words may quickly make them wanton.

CLO.: I would, therefore, my sister had had no name, sir.

VIO.: Why, man?

CLO.: Why, sir, her name's a word, and to dally with that word might make my sister wanton. But indeed words are very rascals since bonds disgraced them.[6]

VIO.: Thy reason, man?

CLO.: Troth, sir, I can yield you none without words, and words are grown so false I am loath to prove reason with them.

VIO.: I warrant thou art a merry fellow and carest for nothing.

CLO.: Not so, sir. I do care for something, but in my conscience, sir, I do not care for you. If that be to care for nothing, sir, I would it would make you invisible.

VIO.: Art not thou the Lady Olivia's fool?

CLO.: No indeed, sir. The Lady Olivia has no folly. She will keep no fool, sir, till she be married, and fools are as like husbands as pilchards[7] are to herrings—the husband's the bigger. I am indeed not her fool, but her corrupter of words.

VIO.: I saw thee late at the Count Orsino's.

CLO.: Foolery, sir, does walk about the orb like the sun. It shines everywhere. I would be sorry, sir, but the fool should be as oft with your master as with my mistress. I think I saw your wisdom there.

VIO.: Nay, an thou pass upon[8] me. I'll no more with thee. Hold, there's expenses for thee.

CLO.: Now Jove, in his next commodity[9] of hair, send thee a beard!

VIO.: By my troth, I'll tell thee, I am almost sick for one—[Aside] though I would not have it grow on my chin. Is thy lady within?

CLO.: Would not a pair of these[10] have bred, sir?

VIO.: Yes, being kept together and put to use.

CLO.: I would play Lord Pandarus[11] of Phrygia,[12] sir, to bring a Cressida to this Troilus.

VIO.: I understand you, sir. 'Tis well begged.

4. cheveril: kidskin. 5. dally: play. 6. sister . . . them: See *T Night* Intro. p. 845b. 7. pilchard: a smaller variety of herring. 8. pass upon: make a thrust at. 9. commodity: consignment. 10. pair of these: i.e., wouldn't you like to give me another coin? 11. Pandarus: the go-between in the love affair of Cressida and Troilus. See *Tr & Cr.* 12. Phrygia: the district of Asia Minor in which Troy stood.

CLO.: The matter, I hope, is not great, sir, begging but a beggar.[13] Cressida was a beggar. My lady is within, sir. I will construe to them whence you come, who you are and what you would are out of my welkin—I might say "element,"[14] but the word is overworn.

[Exit.]

VIO.: This fellow[15] is wise enough to play the fool,
And to do that well craves[16] a kind of wit.
He must observe their mood on whom he jests,
The quality of persons, and the time,
And, like the haggard,[17] check at[18] every feather
That comes before his eye. This is a practice
As full of labor as a wise man's art.
For folly that he wisely shows is fit,
But wise men, folly-fall'n, quite taint their wit.

[Enter SIR TOBY, and SIR ANDREW.]

SIR TO.: Save[19] you, gentleman.

VIO.: And you, sir.

SIR AND.: *Dieu vous garde, monsieur.*

VIO.: *Et vous aussi. Votre serviteur.*

SIR AND.: I hope, sir, you are, and I am yours.

SIR TO.: Will you encounter[20] the house? My niece is desirous you should enter, if your trade be to her.

VIO.: I am bound to your niece, sir. I mean she is the list[21] of my voyage.

SIR TO.: Taste your legs, sir, put them to motion.

VIO.: My legs do better understand me, sir, than I understand what you mean by bidding me taste my legs.

SIR TO.: I mean to go, sir, to enter.

VIO.: I will answer you with gait and entrance. But we are prevented.[22]

[Enter OLIVIA and MARIA.]

Most excellent accomplished lady, the heavens rain odors on you!

SIR AND.: That youth's a rare courtier. "Rain odors," well.

VIO.: My matter hath no voice, lady, but to your own most pregnant[23] and vouchsafed[24] ear.

---

13. The . . . beggar: the Clown is himself an incorrigible beggar. See V.i.31–42. 14. welkin . . . element: both words mean sky. *Element* is still overworn by writers of textbooks who cannot avoid the "supernatural element," the "pastoral element," etc. 15. This fellow: See *T Night* Intro. p. 845a–b. 16. craves: calls for. 17. haggard: wild hawk. As this line seems to contradict the preceding, some editors emend "And" to "But." 18. check at: go after. 19. Save: God save. 20. encounter: lit., go to meet. Toby addresses this young courtier with the extravagant terms fashionable at the time. 21. list: boundary, objective. 22. prevented: forestalled. 23. pregnant: receptive. 24. vouchsafed: condescending.

SIR AND.: "Odors," "pregnant," and "vouchsafed." I'l get 'em all three all ready.

OLI: Let the garden door be shut, and leave me to my hearing. [*Exeunt* SIR TOBY, SIR ANDREW, *and* MARIA.] Give me your hand, sir.

VIO.: My duty, madam, and most humble service.

OLI.: What is your name?

VIO.: Cesario is your servant's name, fair Princess.

OLI.: My servant, sir! 'Twas never merry world
Since lowly feigning was called compliment.
You're servant to the Count Orsino, youth.

VIO.: And he is yours, and his must needs be yours.
Your servant's servant is your servant, madam.

OLI.: For him, I think not on him. For his thoughts,
Would they were blanks rather than filled with me!

VIO.: Madam, I come to whet your gentle thoughts
On his behalf.

OLI.: Oh, by your leave, I pray you,
I bade you never speak again of him.
But would you undertake another suit,
I had rather hear you to solicit that
Than music from the spheres.[25]

VIO.: Dear lady—

OLI.: Give me leave, beseech you. I did send,
After the last enchantment you did here,
A ring in chase of you. So did I abuse[26]
Myself, my servant, and, I fear me, you.
Under your hard construction[27] must I sit,
To force that on you, in a shameful cunning,
Which you knew none of yours. What might you think?
Have you not set mine honor at the stake
And baited it with all the unmuzzled thoughts[28]
That tyrannous heart can think? To one of your receiving[29]
Enough is shown. A cypress,[30] not a bosom,
Hides my heart. So let me hear you speak.

VIO.: I pity you.

OLI.: That's a degree to love.

VIO.: No, not a grize,[31] for 'tis a vulgar proof[32]
That very oft we pity enemies.

---

25. music . . . spheres: See App. 1, and M of Ven, V.i.60. 26. abuse: wrong.
27. construction: interpretation, judgment. 28. at . . . thoughts: An image from bearbaiting. See App. 5. 29. receiving: understanding. 30. cypress: a sheer material. 31. grize: step. 32. vulgar proof: common experience.

OLI.: Why, then, methinks 'tis time to smile again.
O world, how apt the poor are to be proud!
If one should be a prey, how much the better
To fall before the lion than the wolf!
     [*Clock strikes.*]
The clock upbraids me with the waste of time.
Be not afraid, good youth, I will not have you.
And yet, when wit and youth is come to harvest,
Your wife is like to reap a proper man.
There lies your way, due west.
VIO.: Then westward ho![33]
  Grace and good disposition attend your ladyship!
  You'll nothing, madam, to my lord by me?
OLI.: Stay.
  I prithee tell me what thou think'st of me.
VIO.: That you do think you are not what you are.
OLI.: If I think so, I think the same of you.
VIO.: Then think you right. I am not what I am.
OLI.: I would you were as I would have you be!
VIO.: Would it be better, madam, than I am?
  I wish it might, for now I am your fool.
OLI.: Oh, what a deal of scorn looks beautiful
In the contempt and anger of his lip!
A murderous guilt shows not itself more soon
Than love that would seem hid. Love's night is noon.
Cesario, by the roses of the spring,
By maidhood, honor, truth, and everything,
I love thee so, that, mauger[34] all thy pride,
Nor wit nor reason can my passion hide.
Do not extort thy reasons from this clause,
For that I woo, thou therefore hast no cause,
But rather reason thus with reason fetter,
Love sought is good, but given unsought is better.[35]
VIO.: By innocence I swear, and by my youth,
I have one heart, one bosom, and one truth,
And that no woman has; nor never none
Shall mistress be of it, save I alone.

33. westward ho: the Thames waterman's cry. See Gen. Intro. p. 16b. 34. mauger: in spite of. 35. Do . . . better: i.e, do not argue to yourself that because I (the woman) am the wooer, you should therefore have no reason to return my love; rather rebut that argument by this—it is good for a man to ask for a woman's love, but better still to receive it without asking.

And so adieu, good madam. Nevermore
Will I my master's tears to you deplore.
OLI.: Yet come again, for thou perhaps mayst move
That heart which now abhors to like his love.
　　　[*Exeunt.*]

SCENE 2.　OLIVIA'S *house.*

　　　[*Enter* SIR TOBY, SIR ANDREW, *and* FABIAN.]
SIR AND.: No, faith, I'll not stay a jot longer.
SIR TO.: Thy reason, dear venom,[1] give thy reason.
FAB.: You must needs yield your reason, Sir Andrew.
SIR AND.: Marry, I saw your niece do more favors to the Count's
　　servingman[2] than ever she bestowed upon me. I saw 't i' the orchard.
SIR TO.: Did she see thee the while, old boy? Tell me that.
SIR AND.: As plain as I see you now.
FAB.: This was a great argument of love in her toward you.
SIR AND.: 'Slight, will you make an ass o' me?
FAB.: I will prove it legitimate, sir, upon the oaths of judgment and
　　reason.
SIR TO.: And they have been grand jurymen[3] since before Noah was a
　　sailor.
FAB.: She did show favor to the youth in your sight only to exasperate
　　you, to awake your dormouse valor, to put fire in your heart and
　　brimstone in your liver. You should then have accosted her, and
　　with some excellent jests, fire-new from the mint,[4] you should have
　　banged the youth into dumbness. This was looked for at your hand,
　　and this was balked. The double gilt[5] of this opportunity you let
　　time wash off, and you are now sailed into the north of my lady's
　　opinion, where you will hang like an icicle on a Dutchman's beard
　　unless you do redeem it by some laudable attempt either of valor or
　　policy.
SIR AND.: An 't be any way, it must be with valor, for policy I hate.
　　I had as lief be a Brownist[6] as a politician.
SIR TO.: Why then, build me thy fortunes upon the basis of valor.
　　Challenge me the Count's youth to fight with him. Hurt him in

Sc. ii: 1. venom: poison, because Andrew is full of hate.　2. servingman: attendant.　3. grand juryman: The grand jury was chosen from the most respectable citizens. Fabian means "Judgment and Reason have been a most
highly respected pair since the Flood."　4. fire-new . . . mint: i.e., as bright
as new pennies.　5. double gilt: The best gold plate was twice dipped. Fabian
amuses himself and Toby by puzzling Andrew with this metaphorical talk.　6.
Brownist: The Brownists were one of the most extreme sects of Puritans.

eleven places. My niece shall take note of it, and assure thyself there is no love broker[7] in the world can more prevail in man's commendation with woman than report of valor.

FAB.: There is no way but this, Sir Andrew.

SIR AND.: Will either of you bear me a challenge to him?

SIR TO.: Go, write it in a martial hand. Be curst[8] and brief. It is no matter how witty, so it be eloquent and full of invention.[9] Taunt him with the license of ink. If thou thou'st[10] him some thrice, it shall not be amiss. And as many lies as will lie in thy sheet of paper, although the sheet were big enough for the bed of Ware[11] in England, set 'em down. Go, about it. Let there be gall[12] enough in thy ink, though thou write with a goose pen,[13] no matter. About it.

SIR AND.: Where shall I find you?

SIR TO.: We'll call thee at the cubiculo.[14] Go.

[Exit SIR ANDREW.]

FAB.: This is a dear manikin to you, Sir Toby.

SIR TO.: I have been dear to him, lad, some two thousand strong, or so.[15]

FAB.: We shall have a rare letter from him. But you'll not deliver 't?

SIR TO.: Never trust me, then, and by all means stir on the youth to an answer. I think oxen and wainropes[16] cannot hale them together. For Andrew, if he were opened and you find so much blood in his liver as will clog the foot of a flea, I'll eat the rest of the anatomy.

FAB.: And his opposite, the youth, bears in his visage no great presage of cruelty.

[Enter MARIA.]

SIR TO.: Look where the youngest wren of nine[17] comes.

MAR.: If you desire the spleen, and will laugh yourself into stitches, follow me. Yond gull Malvolio is turned heathen, a very renegado,[18] for there is no Christian that means to be saved by believing rightly can ever believe such impossible passages of grossness. He's in yellow stockings.

---

7. love broker: go-between in making a marriage, an important office when marriages were arranged. 8. curst: vicious. 9. invention: wit. 10. thou thou'st: to call a stranger "thou" was a considerable insult, as it implied that he was an inferior. 11. bed of Ware: a famous bed, made after the pattern of the bed illustrated in Pl. 17b. It could hold 7 couples at a time. It is now in the Victoria and Albert Museum in London. 12. gall: "oak apple," produced in the branches of an oak by a parasite, and used for making ink. Toby puns on "gall," meaning bitterness. 13. goose pen: the pen used at this time was made of a goose quill. 14. cubiculo: bedchamber. 15. I . . . so: I've cost him some 2,000 ducats. 16. wainropes: cart ropes. 17. youngest . . . nine: the youngest of the brood, sometimes called the "rickling," is often smaller than the rest. The wren is the smallest of English birds. 18. renegado: Christian turned heathen.

SIR TO.: And cross-gartered?

MAR.: Most villainously, like a pedant that keeps a school i' the church. I have dogged him like his murderer. He does obey every point of the letter that I dropped to betray him. He does smile his face into more lines than is in the new map[19] with the augmentation of the Indies. You have not seen such a thing as 'tis. I can hardly forbear hurling things at him. I know my lady will strike him. If she do, he'll smile and take 't for a great favor.

SIR TO.: Come, bring us, bring us where he is.

[Exeunt.]

SCENE 3.   *A street.*

[*Enter* SEBASTIAN *and* ANTONIO.]

SEB.: I would not by my will have troubled you,
But since you make your pleasure of your pains,
I will no further chide you.

ANT.: I could not stay behind you. My desire,
More sharp than filèd steel, did spur me forth;
And not all love to see you, though so much
As might have drawn one to a longer voyage,
But jealousy what might befall your travel,
Being skill-less in these parts, which to a stranger,
Unguided and unfriended, often prove
Rough and unhospitable. My willing love,
The rather by these arguments of fear,
Set forth in your pursuit.

SEB.: My kind Antonio,
I can no other answer make but thanks,
And thanks, and everoft[1] good turns
Are shuffled off with such uncurrent[2] pay.
But were my worth as is my conscience firm,
You should find better dealing. What's to do?
Shall we go see the reliques[3] of this town?

ANT.: Tomorrow, sir. Best first go see your lodging.

SEB.: I am not weary, and 'tis long to night.
I pray you, let us satisfy our eyes

---

19. new map: See *T Night* Intro. p. 845a, and Pl. 1a.

Sc. iii: 1. and . . . oft: Two words have apparently been omitted in this line. Some editors read "ever *thanks, and* oft." 2. uncurrent: worthless. 3. reliques: antiquities.

With the memorials and the things of fame
That do renown this city.

ANT.: Would you'd pardon me.
I do not without danger walk these streets.
Once, in a sea fight, 'gainst the Count his galleys
I did some service, of such note indeed
That were I ta'en here it would scarce be answered.

SEB.: Belike you slew great number of his people.

ANT.: The offense is not of such a bloody nature,
Albeit the quality[4] of the time and quarrel
Might well have given us bloody argument.
It might have since been answered in repaying
What we took from them, which, for traffic's sake,[5]
Most of our city did. Only myself stood out,
For which, if I be lapsèd[6] in this place,
I shall pay dear.

SEB.: Do not then walk too open.

ANT.: It doth not fit me. Hold, sir, here's my purse.
In the south suburbs, at the Elephant,[7]
Is best to lodge. I wil bespeak our diet[8]
While you beguile the time and feed your knowledge
With viewing of the town. There shall you have me.

SEB.: Why I your purse?

ANT.: Haply[9] your eye shall light upon some toy[10]
You have desire to purchase, and your store,
I think, is not for idle markets,[11] sir.

SEB.: I'll be your purse bearer and leave you
For an hour.

ANT.: To the Elephant.

SEB.: I do remember.
        [*Exeunt.*]

---

4. quality: nature. 5. traffic's sake: for the sake of business. 6. lapsed: taken.
7. Elephant: There was a famous London Inn of this name on the south side
of the Thames; it is now known as the Elephant and Castle. 8. bespeak:
. . . diet: order our dinner. 9. Haply: perchance. 10. toy: trifle. 11. idle
markets: unnecessary purchases.

SCENE 4. OLIVIA's *garden*.

[*Enter* OLIVIA *and* MARIA.]

OLI.: I have sent after him. He says he'll come.
How shall I feast him? What bestow of him?[1]
For youth is bought more oft than begged or borrowed.
I speak too loud.
Where is Malvolio? He is sad and civil,[2]
And suits well for a servant with my fortunes.
Where is Malvolio?

MAR.: He's coming, madam, but in very strange manner. He is sure possessed,[3] madam.

OLI.: Why, what's the matter? Does he rave?

MAR.: No, madam, he does nothing but smile. Your ladyship were best to have some guard about you if he come, for sure the man is tainted in 's wits.

OLI.: Go call him hither. [*Exit* MARIA.] I am as mad as he,
If sad and merry madness equal be.

[*Re-enter* MARIA, *with* MALVOLIO.] How now, Malvolio!

MAL.: Sweet lady, ho, ho.

OLI.: Smilest thou?
I sent for thee upon a sad occasion.

MAL.: Sad, lady? I could be sad. This does make some obstruction in the blood, this cross-gartering, but what of that? If it please the eye of one, it is with me as the very true sonnet is, "Please one, and please all."[4]

OLI.: Why, how dost thou, man? What is the matter with thee?

MAL.: Not black in my mind, though yellow in my legs. It did come to his hands, and commands shall be executed. I think we do know the sweet Roman hand.[5]

OLI.: Wilt thou go to bed, Malvolio?

MAL.: To bed! Aye, sweetheart, and I'll come to thee.

OLI.: God comfort thee! Why dost thou smile so and kiss thy hand so oft?

MAR.: How do you, Malvolio?

Sc. iv: 1. of him: on him. 2. civil: sober, serious. 3. possessed: i.e., with an evil spirit. See *T Night* Intro. p. 847a–b. 4. Please . . . all: The ditty is not a sonnet but a ballad, called "The crow sits upon the wall, Please one and please all." It was not at all the kind of song suitable for Malvolio. 5. Roman hand: The Italian handwriting (from which modern handwriting and *italic* type derives) was coming into fashion among aristocratic writers, and superseding the old English "Court" or "secretary" hand.

MAL.: At your request! Yes, nightingales answer daws.[6]
MAR.: Why appear you with this ridiculous boldness before my lady?
MAL.: "Be not afraid of greatness." 'Twas well writ.
OLI.: What meanest thou by that, Malvolio?
MAL.: "Some are born great—"
OLI.: Ha!
MAL.: "Some achieve greatness—"
OLI.: What sayest thou?
MAL.: "And some have greatness thrust upon them."
OLI.: Heaven restore thee!
MAL.: "Remember who commended thy yellow stockings."
OLI.: Thy yellow stockings!
MAL.: "And wished to see thee cross-gartered."
OLI.: Cross-gartered!
MAL.: "Go to, thou art made, if thou desirest to be so."
OLI.: Am I made?
MAL.: "If not, let me see thee a servant still."
OLI.: Why, this is very midsummer madness.

    [Enter SERVANT.*]*

SERV.: Madam, the young gentleman of the Count Orsino's is returned.
    I could hardly entreat him back. He attends your ladyship's pleasure.
OLI.: I'll come to him. *[Exit* SERVANT.*]* Good Maria, let this fellow be
    looked to. Where's my cousin Toby? Let some of my people have
    a special care of him. I would not have him miscarry[7] for the half of
    my dowry.

    [Exeunt OLIVIA *and* MARIA.*]*

MAL.: Oh, ho! Do you come near me now? No worse man than Sir
    Toby to look to me! This concurs directly with the letter. She sends
    him on purpose, that I may appear stubborn to him, for she incites
    me to that in the letter. "Cast thy humble slough," says she. "Be
    opposite with a kinsman, surly with servants, let thy tongue tang
    with arguments of state, put thyself into the trick of singularity"—
    and consequently sets down the manner how, as a sad face, a reverend
    carriage, a slow tongue, in the habit of some sir of note,[8] and so forth.
    I have limed[9] her, but it is Jove's doing, and Jove make me thankful!
    And when she went away now, "Let this fellow be looked to."
    Fellow! Not Malvolio, nor after my degree, but fellow.[10] Why,

---

6. nightingales . . . daws: songbirds answer jackdaws.　7. miscarry: come to harm.
  8. air of note: great man.　9. limed: caught, as with birdlime.　10. fellow:
the word has a double meaning. The fellow of a college or learned society is a
man of dignity; the word is also used of an inferior.

everything adheres together, that no dram of a scruple,[11] no scruple of a scruple, no obstacle, no incredulous or unsafe circumstance— What can be said? Nothing that can be can come between me and the full prospect of my hopes. Well, Jove, not I, is the doer of this, and he is to be thanked.

[Re-enter MARIA, with SIR TOBY and FABIAN.]

SIR TO.: Which way is he, in the name of sanctity? If all the devils of Hell be drawn in little,[12] and Legion himself[13] possessed him, yet I'll speak to him.

FAB.: Here he is, here he is. How is 't with you, sir? How is 't with you, man?

MAL.: Go off, I discard you. Let me enjoy my private. Go off.

MAR.: Lo, how hollow the fiend speaks within him! Did not I tell you? Sir Toby, my lady prays you to have a care of him.

MAL.: Ah, ha! Does she so?

SIR TO.: Go to, go to; peace, peace. We must deal gently with him. Let me alone. How do you, Malvolio? How is 't with you? What, man! defy the Devil. Consider, he's an enemy to mankind.

MAL.: Do you know what you say?

MAR.: La you, an you speak ill of the Devil, how he takes it at heart! Pray God he be not bewitched!

FAB.: Carry his water[14] to the wise woman.

MAR.: Marry, and it shall be done tomorrow morning, if I live. My lady would not lose him for more than I'll say.

MAL.: How now, mistress!

MAR.: Oh Lord!

SIR TO.: Prithee, hold thy peace, this is not the way. Do you not see you move him? Let me alone with him.

FAB.: No way but gentleness—gently, gently. The fiend is rough, and will not be roughly used.

SIR TO.: Why, how now, my bawcock![15] How dost thou, chuck?[16]

MAL.: Sir!

11. dram . . . scruple: minutest part. 12. in little: into a small space. 13. Legion himself: the name given to the devils cast out of the man from the tombs (Mark 5:1–19). Toby pretends that Malvolio is possessed and treats him accordingly. Witches (who could be of either sex) were often accused of causing possession. See *T Night* Intro. p. 847a–b. 14. his water: diagnosis of diseases by inspection of the urine was practiced by qualified doctors as well as by quacks. Cf. the gloomy report on Falstaff's health (*II Hen IV*, I.ii.1–6). 15. bawcock: fine fellow. Toby humors Malvolio by talking baby talk to him. 16. chuck: chick.

SIR TO.: Aye, biddy,[17] come with me. What, man! 'Tis not for gravity to play at cherry pit[18] with Satan. Hang him, foul collier![19]

MAR.: Get him to say his prayers, good Sir Toby, get him to pray.

MAL.: My prayers, minx!

MAR.: No, I warrant you, he will not hear of godliness.[20]

MAL.: Go, hang yourselves all! You are idle shallow things. I am not of your element. You shall know more hereafter.

    [*Exit.*]

SIR TO.: Is 't possible?

FAB.: If this were played upon a stage now, I could condemn it as an improbable fiction.

SIR TO.: His very genius[21] hath taken the infection[22] of the device,[23] man.

MAR.: Nay, pursue him now, lest the device take air and taint.[24]

FAB.: Why, we shall make him mad indeed.

MAR.: The house will be the quieter.

SIR TO.: Come, we'll have him in a dark room and bound. My niece is already in the belief that he's mad. We may carry it thus, for our pleasure and his penance, till our very pastime, tired out of breath, prompt us to have mercy on him, at which time we will bring the device to the bar[25] and crown thee for a finder of madmen. But see, but see.

    [*Enter* SIR ANDREW.]

FAB.: More matter for a May morning.[26]

SIR AND.: Here's the challenge, read it. I warrant there's vinegar and pepper in 't.

FAB.: Is 't so saucy?

SIR AND.: Aye, is 't, I warrant him. Do but read.

SIR TO.: Give me. [*Reads.*] "Youth, whatsoever thou art, thou art but a scurvy fellow."

FAB.: Good, and valiant.

SIR TO. [*Reads.*]: "Wonder not, nor admire[27] not in thy mind, why I do call thee so, for I will show thee no reason for 't."

FAB.: A good note. That keeps you from the blow of the law.

SIR TO. [*Reads.*]: "Thou comest to the Lady Olivia, and in my sight she

17. biddy: child's name for a chick.   18. cherry pit: a game of throwing cherry stones into a hole.   19. foul collier: The Devil is a collier (coalman) because he is black.   20. will . . . godliness: One of the tests usually applied to a witch was to ask him to say the Lord's Prayer. If he could not, or would not, it was a most suspicious sign of guilt.   21. genius: guardian angel.   22. taken . . . infection: caught the plague.   23. device: plan.   24. take . . . taint: be spoiled and go bad.   25. device . . . bar: bring to public trial.   26. May morning: Mayday was a general holiday.   27. admire: be amazed.

uses thee kindly; but thou liest in thy throat.[28] That is not the matter I challenge thee for."

FAB.: Very brief, and to exceeding good sense—less.

SIR TO. [Reads.]: "I will waylay thee going home, where if it be thy chance to kill me—"

FAB.: Good.

SIR TO. [Reads.]: "Thou killest me like a rogue and a villain."

FAB.: Still you keep o' the windy side[29] of the law. Good.

SIR TO. [Reads.]: "Fare thee well, and God have mercy upon one of our souls! He may have mercy upon mine, but my hope is better, and so look to thyself. Thy friend, as thou usest him, and thy sworn enemy,
ANDREW AGUECHEEK."

If this letter move him not, his legs cannot. I'll give 't him.

MAR.: You may have very fit occasion for 't. He is now in some commerce with my lady, and will by and by depart.

SIR TO.: Go, Sir Andrew. Scout me for him at the corner of the orchard like a bumbaily.[30] So soon as ever thou seest him, draw, and, as thou drawest, swear horrible; for it comes to pass oft that a terrible oath, with a swaggering accent sharply twanged off, gives manhood more approbation than ever proof itself would have earned him. Away!

SIR AND.: Nay, let me alone for swearing.[31]
[Exit.]

SIR TO.: Now will not I deliver his letter, for the behavior of the young gentleman gives him out to be of good capacity and breeding. His employment between his lord and my niece confirms no less. Therefore this letter, being so excellently ignorant, will breed no terror in the youth. He will find it comes from a clodpole.[32] But, sir, I will deliver his challenge by word of mouth, set upon Aguecheek a notable report of valor, and drive the gentleman, as I know his youth will aptly receive it, into a most hideous opinion of his rage, skill, fury, and impetuosity. This will so fright them both that they will kill one another by the look, like cockatrices.[33]
[Re-enter OLIVIA, with VIOLA.]

FAB.: Here he comes with your niece. Give them way till he take leave, and presently after him.

SIR TO.: I will meditate the while upon some horrid message for a challenge.
[Exeunt SIR TOBY, FABIAN, and MARIA.]

28. liest . . . throat: This was the bitterest insult possible.   29. windy side: safe side.   30. bumbaily: sheriff's officer who made arrests for debt.   31. let . . . swearing: i.e., I'm an expert at swearing.   32. clodpole: blockhead.   33. cockatrice: a fabulous serpent, able to kill by its mere look. See *Rich III*, I.ii.151,n.

OLI.: I have said too much unto a heart of stone,
   And laid mine honor too unchary[34] out.
   There's something in me that reproves my fault,
   But such a headstrong potent fault it is
   That it but mocks reproof.
VIO.: With the same 'havior that your passion bears
   Goes on my master's grief.
OLI.: Here, wear this jewel for me, 'tis my picture.
   Refuse it not, it hath no tongue to vex you.
   And I beseech you come again tomorrow.
   What shall you ask of me that I'll deny,
   That honor saved may upon asking give?
VIO.: Nothing but this—your true love for my master.
OLI.: How with mine honor may I give him that
   Which I have given to you?
VIO.: I will acquit[35] you.
OLI.: Well, come again tomorrow. Fare thee well.
   A fiend like thee might bear my soul to Hell.
      [Exit.]
      [Re-enter SIR TOBY and FABIAN.]
SIR TO.: Gentleman, God save thee.
VIO.: And you, sir.
SIR TO.: That defense thou hast, betake thee to 't. Of what nature the
   wrongs are thou hast done him, I know not, but thy interceptor, full
   of despite,[36] bloody as the hunter, attends thee at the orchard end.
   Dismount thy tuck,[37] be yare[38] in thy preparation, for thy assailant
   is quick, skillful, and deadly.
VIO.: You mistake, sir. I am sure no man hath any quarrel to me.
   My remembrance is very free and clear from any image of offense
   done to any man.
SIR TO.: You'll find it otherwise, I assure you. Therefore, if you hold
   your life at any price, betake you to your guard; for your opposite
   hath in him what youth, strength, skill, and wrath can furnish man
   withal.
VIO.: I pray you, sir, what is he?
SIR TO.: He is knight, dubbed[39] with unhatched[40] rapier and on carpet
   consideration,[41] but he is a devil in private brawl. Souls and bodies
   hath he divorced three, and his incensement at this moment is so

---

34. unchary: heedlessly.   35. acquit: release from a payment.   36. despite: spite.
   37. tuck: sword.   38. yare: handy.   39. dubbed: knighted.   40. unhatched:
   unhacked, not dented by use in battle.   41. carpet consideration: kneeling
   on a carpet, and not on the battlefield.

implacable that satisfaction can be none but by pangs of death and sepulcher. Hob, nob,[42] is his word, give 't or take 't.

VIO.: I will return again into the house and desire some conduct of the lady. I am no fighter. I have heard of some kind of men that put quarrels purposely on others, to taste their valor. Belike this is a man of that quirk.[43]

SIR TO.: Sir, no, his indignation derives itself out of a very competent[44] injury. Therefore get you on and give him his desire. Back you shall not to the house, unless you undertake that with me which with as much safety you might answer him. Therefore on, or strip your sword stark-naked, for meddle you must, that's certain, or forswear[45] to wear iron about you.

VIO.: This is as uncivil as strange. I beseech you, do me this courteous office, as to know of the knight what my offense to him is. It is something of my negligence, nothing of my purpose.

SIR TO.: I will do so. Signior Fabian, stay you by this gentleman till my return.

    [*Exit.*]

VIO.: Pray you, sir, do you know of this matter?

FAB.: I know the knight is incensed against you, even to a mortal arbitrament,[46] but nothing of the circumstance more.

VIO.: I beseech you, what manner of man is he?

FAB.: Nothing of that wonderful promise, to read him by his form, as you are like to find him in the proof of his valor. He is, indeed, sir, the most skillful, bloody, and fatal opposite that you could possibly have found in any part of Illyria. Will you walk toward him? I will make your peace with him if I can.

VIO.: I shall be much bound to you for 't. I am one that had rather go with sir priest[47] than sir knight. I care not who knows so much of my mettle.

    [*Re-enter* SIR TOBY, *with* SIR ANDREW.]

SIR TO.: Why, man, he's a very devil. I have not seen such a firago.[48] I had a pass with him, rapier, scabbard, and all, and he gives me the stuck-in[49] with such a mortal motion that it is inevitable; and on the answer, he pays you as surely as your feet hit the ground they step on. They say he has been fencer to the Sophy.

---

42. Hob, nob: hit or miss.　43. quirk: whim.　44. competent: considerable. 45. forswear: swear not to.　46. mortal arbitrament: decision by deadly combat.　47. sir priest: a Bachelor of Arts was termed "Dominus" (= Sir); in the class lists at Cambridge University the B.A.'s are still noted as "Ds." As most priests were graduates, they were called "Sir."　48. firago: for virago, a mannish woman.　49. stuck-in: thrust.

SIR AND.: Pox on 't, I'll not meddle with him.

SIR TO.: Aye, but he will not now be pacified. Fabian can scarce hold him yonder.

SIR AND.: Plague on 't, an I thought he had been valiant and so cunning in fence, I'd have seen him damned ere I'd have challenged him. Let him let the matter slip, and I'll give him my horse, gray Capilet.

SIR TO.: I'll make the motion. Stand here, make a good show on 't. This shall end without the perdition of souls. [Aside] Marry, I'll ride your horse as well as I ride you.

[Re-enter FABIAN and VIOLA.]

[To FABIAN] I have his horse to take up the quarrel.

I have persuaded him the youth's a devil.

FAB.: He is as horribly conceited[50] of him, and pants and looks pale, as if a bear were at his heels.

SIR TO. [To VIOLA]: There's no remedy, sir, he will fight with you for 's oath sake. Marry, he hath better bethought him of his quarrel, and he finds that now scarce to be worth talking of. Therefore draw, for the supportance of his vow. He protests he will not hurt you.

VIO.: [Aside] Pray God defend me! A little thing would make me tell them how much I lack of a man.

FAB.: Give ground, if you see him furious.

SIR TO.: Come, Sir Andrew, there's no remedy. The gentleman will, for his honor's sake, have one bout with you. He cannot by the duello[51] avoid it. But he has promised me, as he is a gentleman and a soldier, he will not hurt you. Come on—to 't.

SIR AND.: Pray God he keep his oath!

VIO.: I do assure you 'tis against my will.

[They draw.]

[Enter ANTONIO.]

ANT.: Put up your sword. If this young gentleman
Have done offense, I take the fault on me.
If you offend him, I for him defy you.

SIR TO.: You, sir! Why, what are you?

ANT.: One, sir, that for his love dares yet do more
Than you have heard him brag to you he will.

SIR TO.: Nay, if you be an undertaker,[52] I am for you.

[They draw.]

[Enter OFFICERS.]

FAB.: O good Sir Toby, hold! Here comes the officers.

---

50. as . . . conceited: has as horrible ideas of. 51. duello: the rules of duelling, a matter of great importance to a man of honor. 52. undertaker: meddler.

SIR TO.: I'll be with you anon.

VIO.: Pray, sir, put your sword up, if you please.

SIR AND.: Marry will I, sir, and, for that I promised you, I'll be as good as my word. He will bear you easily and reins well.

1. OFF.: This is the man. Do thy office.

2. OFF.: Antonio, I arrest thee at the suit of Count Orsino.

ANT.: You do mistake me, sir.

1. OFF.: No, sir, no jot. I know your favor[53] well,
Though now you have no sea cap on your head.
Take him away. He knows I know him well.

ANT.: I must obey. [*To viola*] This comes with seeking you.
But there's no remedy, I shall answer it.
What will you do, now my necessity
Makes me to ask you for my purse? It grieves me
Much more for what I cannot do for you
Than what befalls myself. You stand amazed,
But be of comfort.

2. OFF.: Come, sir, away.

ANT.: I must entreat of you some of that money.

VIO.: What money, sir?
For the fair kindness you have showed me here,
And, part, being prompted by your present trouble,
Out of my lean and low ability[54]
I'll lend you something. My having is not much;
I'll make division of my present[55] with you.
Hold, there's half my coffer.[56]

ANT.: Will you deny me now?
Is 't possible that my deserts to you
Can lack persuasion? Do not tempt my misery,
Lest that it make me so unsound a man
As to upbraid you with those kindnesses
That I have done for you.

VIO.: I know of none,
Nor know I you by voice or any feature.
I hate ingratitude more in a man
Than lying vainness, babbling drunkenness,
Or any taint of vice whose strong corruption
Inhabits our frail blood.

ANT.: Oh, Heavens themselves!

---

53. favor: face. 54. low ability: small means. 55. my present: what I have at present. 56. coffer: purse, lit., chest.

2. OFF.: Come, sir, I pray you, go.

ANT.: Let me speak a little. This youth that you see here
    I snatched one half out of the jaws of death,
    Relieved him with such sanctity of love,
    And to his image, which methought did promise
    Most venerable worth, did I devotion.

1. OFF.: What's that to us? The time goes by—away!

ANT.: But oh, how vile an idol proves this god!
    Thou hast, Sebastian, done good feature shame.
    In nature there's no blemish but the mind;
    None can be called deformed but the unkind.
    Virtue is beauty, but the beauteous evil
    Are empty trunks, o'erflourished by the Devil.[57]

1. OFF.: The man grows mad. Away with him! Come, come sir.

ANT.: Lead me on.
             [Exit with OFFICERS.]

VIO.: Methinks his words do from such passion fly
    That he believes himself. So do not I.
    Prove true, imagination,[58] oh, prove true,
    That I, dear brother, be now ta'en for you!

SIR TO.: Come hither, knight, come hither, Fabian. We'll whisper o'er
    a couplet or two of most sage saws.[59]

VIO.: He named Sebastian. I my brother know
    Yet living in my glass, even such and so
    In favor was my brother, and he went
    Still in this fashion, color, ornament,
    For him I imitate. Oh, if it prove,
    Tempests are kind and salt waves fresh in love![60]
             [Exit.]

SIR TO.: A very dishonest paltry boy, and more a coward than a hare.
    His dishonesty appears in leaving his friend here in necessity and
    denying him, and for his cowardship, ask Fabian.

FAB.: A coward, a most devout coward, religious in it.

SIR AND.: 'Slid,[61] I'll after him again and beat him.

SIR TO.: Do. Cuff him soundly, but never draw thy sword.

SIR AND.: An I do not—
             [Exit.]

57. empty . . . Devil: over-elaborately carved chests which have nothing inside.
See Pl. 17c. 58. Prove . . . imagination: Viola has never given up hope. Now
she realizes from Antonio's words that Sebastian is not only alive but near.
59. saws: wise sayings. 60. salt . . . love: i.e., the sea has been kind, with a
play of words on "salt" and "fresh" = good, unsalted, and recent. 61. 'Slid:
by God's eyelid.

FAB.: Come, let's see the event.

SIR TO.: I dare lay any money 'twill be nothing yet.

[*Exeunt.*]

❦ *Act IV*

SCENE 1. *Before* OLIVIA'S *house.*

[*Enter* SEBASTIAN *and* CLOWN.]

CLO.: Will you make me believe that I am not sent for you?

SEB.: Go to, go to, thou art a foolish fellow. Let me be clear of thee.

CLO.: Well held out, i' faith! No, I do not know you; nor I am not sent to you by my lady, to bid you come speak with her; nor your name is not Master Cesario; nor this is not my nose neither. Nothing that is so is so.

SEB.: I prithee, vent[1] thy folly somewhere else. Thou know'st not me.

CLO.: Vent my folly! He has heard that word of some great man and now applies it to a fool. Vent my folly! I am afraid this great lubber, the world, will prove a cockney.[2] I prithee now, ungird thy strangeness and tell me what I shall vent to my lady. Shall I vent to her that thou art coming?

SEB.: I prithee, foolish Greek,[3] depart from me. There's money for thee. If you tarry longer, I shall give worse payment.

CLO.: By my troth, thou hast an open hand. These wise men that give fools money get themselves a good report—after fourteen years' purchase.[4]

[*Enter* SIR ANDREW, SIR TOBY, *and* FABIAN.]

SIR AND.: Now, sir, have I met you again? There's for you.

SEB.: Why, there's for thee, and there, and there. Are all the people mad?

SIR TO.: Hold, sir, or I'll throw your dagger o'er the house.

CLO.: This will I tell my lady straight. I would not be in some of your coats for twopence.

[*Exit.*]

Act IV, Sc. i: 1. vent: utter. 2. lubber . . . cockney: a much-disputed passage. The fool when posing as a philosopher is not always very clear. As it stands, the passage means "this great clumsy world will turn out to be a spoiled child (cockney)." 3. foolish Greek: foolish jester. The Greeks were considered empty-headed and merry folk. 4. fourteen . . . purchase: the value of land was reckoned to be twelve times the annual rent, so this is a high rate.

SIR TO.: Come on, sir, hold.

SIR AND.: Nay, let him alone. I'll go another way to work with him. I'll have an action of battery against him, if there be any law in Illyria. Though I struck him first, yet it's no matter for that.

SEB.: Let go thy hand.

SIR TO.: Come, sir, I will not let you go. Come, my young soldier, put up your iron. You are well fleshed.[5] Come on.

SEB.: I will be free from thee. What wouldst thou now?
If thou darest tempt me further, draw thy sword.

SIR TO.: What, what? Nay, then I must have an ounce or two of this malapert[6] blood from you.

[*Enter* OLIVIA.]

OLI.: Hold, Toby. On thy life, I charge thee, hold!

SIR TO.: Madam!

OLI.: Will it be ever thus? Ungracious wretch,
Fit for the mountains and the barbarous caves,
Where manners ne'er were preached! Out of my sight!
Be not offended, dear Cesario.
Rudesby,[7] be gone!

[*Exeunt* SIR TOBY, SIR ANDREW, *and* FABIAN.]

I prithee, gentle friend,
Let thy fair wisdom, not thy passion, sway
In this uncivil and unjust extent[8]
Against thy peace. Go with me to my house,
And hear thou there how many fruitless pranks
This ruffian hath botched[9] up, that thou thereby
Mayst smile at this. Thou shalt not choose but go.
Do not deny. Beshrew his soul for me,
He started one poor heart of mine in thee.

SEB.: What relish is in this? How runs the stream?
Or I am mad, or else this is a dream.
Let fancy still my sense in Lethe[10] steep.
If it be thus to dream, still let me sleep!

OLI.: Nay, come, I prithee. Would thou'dst be ruled by me!

SEB.: Madam, I will.

OLI.: Oh, say so, and so be!

[*Exeunt.*]

---

5. well fleshed: lit., you have shown courage in your first action; i.e., you've had enough fighting for the present. Cf. *I Hen IV*, V.iv.133. 6. malapert: saucy. 7. Rudesby: ruffian. 8. extent: attack. 9. botched: patched. 10. Lethe: the river of forgetfulness in the underworld.

SCENE 2. OLIVIA'S *house.*

[*Enter* MARIA *and* CLOWN.]

MAR.: Nay, I prithee put on this gown and this beard. Make him believe thou art Sir Topas[1] the curate. Do it quickly. I'll call Sir Toby
the whilst.

[*Exit.*]

CLO.: Well, I'll put it on, and I will dissemble[2] myself in 't, and I would
I were the first that ever dissembled in such a gown. I am not tall
enough to become the function well, nor lean enough to be thought
a good student, but to be said an honest man and a good housekeeper goes as fairly as to say a careful man and a great scholar. The
competitors[3] enter.

[*Enter* SIR TOBY *and* MARIA.]

SIR TO.: Jove bless thee, Master Parson.

CLO.: *Bonos dies,* Sir Toby. For, as the old hermit of Prague, that never
saw pen and ink, very wittily said to a niece of King Gorboduc,[4]
"That that is is," so I, being Master Parson, am Master Parson; for
what is "that" but "that," and "is" but "is"?

SIR TO.: To him, Sir Topas.

CLO.: What ho,[5] I say! Peace in this prison!

SIR TO.: The knave counterfeits well—a good knave.

MAL. [*Within*]: Who calls there?

CLO.: Sir Topas the curate, who comes to visit Malvolio the lunatic.

MAL.: Sir Topas, Sir Topas, good Sir Topas, go to my lady.

CLO.: Out, hyperbolical[6] fiend! How vexest thou this man! Talkest thou
nothing but of ladies?

SIR TO.: Well said, Master Parson.

MAL.: Sir Topas, never was man thus wronged. Good Sir Topas, do not
think I am mad. They have laid me here in hideous darkness.

CLO.: Fie, thou dishonest Satan! I call thee by the most modest terms,
for I am one of those gentle ones that will use the Devil himself with
courtesy. Sayest thou that house is dark?

MAL.: As Hell, Sir Topas.

CLO.: Why, it hath bay windows transparent as barricadoes,[7] and the

---

Sc. ii: 1. Sir Topas: See III.iv.298,n.   2. dissemble: disguise.   3. competitors:
conspirators.   4. King Gorboduc: one of the legendary kings invented by
early chroniclers to fill the gaps in English history before records began; but
the Clown as usual introduces the name to give an air of learning to his nonsense.   5. What ho: Here the fool assumes a ministerial voice.   6. hyperbolical: extravagant.   7. barricadoes: barricades.

clerestories[8] toward the south-north are as lustrous as ebony—and yet complainest thou of obstruction?

MAL.: I am not mad, Sir Topas. I say to you, this house is dark.

CLO.: Madman, thou errest. I say, there is no darkness but ignorance, in which thou art more puzzled than the Egyptians in their fog.[9]

MAL.: I say, this house is as dark as ignorance, though ignorance were as dark as Hell. And I say there was never man thus abused. I am no more mad than you are. Make the trial of it in any constant question.[10]

CLO.: What is the opinion of Pythagoras[11] concerning wild fowl?

MAL.: That the soul of our grandam might haply inhabit a bird.

CLO.: What thinkest thou of his opinion?

MAL.: I think nobly of the soul, and no way approve his opinion.

CLO.: Fare thee well. Remain thou still in darkness. Thou shalt hold the opinion of Pythagoras ere I will allow of thy wits, and fear to kill a woodcock[12] lest thou dispossess the soul of thy grandam. Fare thee well.

MAL.: Sir Topas, Sir Topas!

SIR TO.: My most exquisite Sir Topas!

CLO.: Nay, I am for all waters.[13]

MAR.: Thou mightst have done this without thy beard and gown. He sees thee not.

SIR TO.: To him in thine own voice, and bring me word how thou findest him. I would we were well rid of this knavery. If he may be conveniently delivered, I would he were, for I am now so far in offense with my niece that I cannot pursue with any safety this sport to the upshot.[14] Come by and by to my chamber.

[*Exeunt* SIR TOBY *and* MARIA.]

CLO. [*Sings.*]

Hey, Robin, jolly Robin,
Tell me how thy lady does.

MAL.: Fool—

CLO.: "My lady is unkind, perdy."[15]

MAL.: Fool—

CLO.: "Alas, why is she so?"

---

8. clerestories: the upper part of the inner wall of a church above the arches, containing a row of windows.   9. fog: darkness; i.e., the ninth of the plagues of Egypt. See Exodus 10:21–23.   10. constant question: coherent argument. 11. Pythagoras: Pythagoras held that the human soul after death could pass into a beast or a bird.   12. woodcock: regarded as a foolish bird.   13. for . . . waters: i.e., can turn my hand to anything.   14. upshot: conclusion. 15. perdy: by God.

MAL.: Fool, I say—

CLO.: "She loves another—" Who calls, ha?

MAL.: Good fool, as ever thou wilt deserve well at my hand, help me to a candle, and pen, ink, and paper. As I am a gentleman, I will live to be thankful to thee for 't.

CLO.: Master Malvolio!

MAL.: Aye, good fool.

CLO.: Alas, sir, how fell you besides your five wits?[16]

MAL.: Fool, there was never man so notoriously abused. I am as well in my wits, fool, as thou art.

CLO.: But as well? Then you are mad indeed, if you be no better in your wits than a fool.

MAL.: They have here propertied[17] me, keep me in darkness, send ministers to me, asses, and do all they can to face me out of my wits.

CLO.: Advise you what you say. The minister is here. Malvolio, Malvolio, thy wits the Heavens restore! Endeavor thyself to sleep, and leave thy vain bibble-babble.

MAL.: Sir Topas—

CLO.: Maintain no words[18] with him, good fellow. Who, I, sir? Not I, sir. God be wi' you, good Sir Topas. Marry, amen. I will, sir, I will.

MAL.: Fool, fool, fool, I say—

CLO.: Alas, sir, be patient. What say you, sir? I am shent[19] for speaking to you.

MAL.: Good fool, help me to some light and some paper. I tell thee I am as well in my wits as any man in Illyria.

CLO.: Welladay[20] that you were, sir!

MAL.: By this hand, I am. Good fool, some ink, paper, and light; and convey that I will set down to my lady. It shall advantage thee more than ever the bearing of letter did.

CLO.: I will help you to 't. But tell me true, are you not mad indeed? Or do you but counterfeit?

MAL.: Believe me, I am not, I tell thee true.

CLO.: Nay, I'll ne'er believe a madman till I see his brains. I will fetch you light and paper and ink.

MAL.: Fool, I'll requite it in the highest degree. I prithee be gone.

---

16. five wits: i.e., full possession of your senses. The five were common wit, imagination, fantasy, estimation, and memory. 17. propertied: treated like a property; i.e., "thrust me into the attic." 18. Maintain no words: Here the fool resumes his assumed voice as he keeps up a dialogue with himself as Sir Topas addressing the Clown. 19. shent: rebuked. 20. Welladay: alas.

CLO. [*Sings.*]

> I am gone, sir,
>> And anon, sir,
> I'll be with you again,
>> In a trice,
>> Like to the old vice,
> Your need to sustain,
> Who, with dagger of lath,[21]
> In his rage and his wrath,
>> Cries, ah, ha! to the Devil.
> Like a mad lad,
> Pare thy nails, dad.
>> Adieu, Goodman Devil.

[*Exit.*]

SCENE 3. OLIVIA's *garden.*

[*Enter* SEBASTIAN.]

SEB.: This is the air, that is the glorious sun,
  This pearl she gave me, I do feel 't and see 't.
And though 'tis wonder that enwraps me thus,
Yet 'tis not madness. Where's Antonio, then?
I could not find him at the Elephant.
Yet there he was, and there I found this credit,[1]
That he did range[2] the town to seek me out.
His counsel now might do me golden service.
For though my soul disputes well with my sense,
That this may be some error, but no madness,
Yet doth this accident and flood of fortune
So far exceed all instance,[3] all discourse,
That I am ready to distrust mine eyes
And wrangle with my reason, that persuades me
To any other trust but that I am mad,
Or else the lady's mad—yet, if 'twere so,
She could not sway her house, command her followers,
Take and give back affairs and their dispatch

---

21. vice . . . lath: the clown's part in the old Morality plays. He was armed with
a wooden dagger (*dagger of lath*), with which he attacked the Devil and tried
to cut his nails.

Sc. iii: 1. credit: report. 2. range: traverse. 3. exceed . . . instance: go beyond anything recorded.

With such a smooth, discreet, and stable bearing
As I perceive she does. There's something in 't
That is deceivable.[4] But here the lady comes.
    [*Enter* OLIVIA *and* PRIEST.]
OLI.: Blame not this haste of mine. If you mean well,
  Now go with me and with this holy man
  Into the chantry[5] by. There, before him,
  And underneath that consecrated roof,
  Plight[6] me the full assurance of your faith,
  That my most jealous and too doubtful soul
  May live at peace. He shall conceal it
  While you are willing it shall come to note,
  What time we will our celebration keep
  According to my birth. What do you say?
SEB.: I'll follow this good man, and go with you,
  And, having sworn truth, ever will be true.
OLI.: Then lead the way, good Father, and Heavens so shine,
  That they may fairly note this act of mine!
    [*Exeunt.*]

🏵 *Act V*

SCENE 1. *Before* OLIVIA's *house.*

    [*Enter* CLOWN *and* FABIAN.]
FAB.: Now, as thou lovest me, let me see his letter.
CLO.: Good Master Fabian, grant me another request.
FAB.: Anything.
CLO.: Do not desire to see this letter.
FAB.: This is to give a dog,[1] and in recompense desire my dog again.
    [*Enter* DUKE, VIOLA, CURIO, *and* LORDS.]
DUKE: Belong you to the Lady Olivia, friends?

---

4. deceivable: deceptive. 5. chantry: chapel. 6. Plight: promise. Olivia is proposing not full marriage but formal betrothal, which will legally bind Sebastian. See Gen. Intro. p. 20a.

Act V, Sc. i: 1. give a dog: This was a contemporary anecdote recorded in Manningham's diary: "Dr. Bullein, the Queen's kinsman, had a dog which he doted on, so much that the Queen understanding of it requested he would grant her one desire, and he should have whatsoever he should ask. She demanded his dog; he gave it, and, 'Now, Madam,' quoth he, 'you promised to give me my desire.' 'I will,' quoth she. 'Then I pray you give me my dog again.'"

CLO.: Aye, sir, we are some of her trappings.[2]

DUKE: I know thee well. How dost thou, my good fellow?

CLO.: Truly, sir, the better for my foes and the worse for my friends.

DUKE: Just the contrary—the better for thy friends.

CLO.: No, sir, the worse.

DUKE: How can that be?

CLO.: Marry, sir, they praise me and make an ass of me. Now my foes tell me plainly I am an ass, so that by my foes, sir, I profit in the knowledge of myself, and by my friends I am abused. So that, conclusions to be as kisses,[3] if your four negatives make your two affirmatives, why then, the worse for my friends, and the better for my foes.

DUKE: Why, this is excellent.

CLO.: By my troth, sir, no, though it please you to be one of my friends.

DUKE: Thou shalt not be the worse for me. There's gold.

CLO.: But that it would be double-dealing,[4] sir, I would you could make it another.

DUKE: Oh, you give me ill counsel.

CLO.: Put your grace in your pocket,[5] sir, for this once, and let your flesh and blood obey it.

DUKE: Well, I will be so much a sinner, to be a double-dealer. There's another.

CLO.: Primo, secundo, tertio, is a good play, and the old saying is, the third pays for all. The triplex, sir, is a good tripping measure, or the bells of Saint Bennet,[6] sir, may put you in mind—one, two, three.

DUKE: You can fool no more money out of me at this throw. If you will let your lady know I am here to speak with her, and bring her along with you, it may awake my bounty further.

CLO.: Marry, sir, lullaby to your bounty till I come again. I go, sir, but I would not have you to think that my desire of having is the sin of covetousness. But, as you say, sir, let your bounty take a nap. I will awake it anon.

    [Exit.]

VIO.: Here comes the man, sir, that did rescue me.

    [Enter ANTONIO *and* OFFICERS.]

DUKE: That face of his I do remember well,

Yet when I saw it last it was besmeared

As black as Vulcan[7] in the smoke of war.

---

2. trappings: ornamental accessories. 3. conclusions . . . kisses: as a kiss stops all lovers' arguments. 4. double-dealing: The Clown is trying to extract another coin from the Duke. 5. Put . . . pocket: forget your respectability. 6. Saint Bennet: St. Benedict, a London church. 7. Vulcan: the blacksmith god.

A bawbling[8] vessel was he captain of,
For shallow draught and bulk unprizable,[9]
  With which such scathful grapple[10] did he make
With the most noble bottom[11] of our fleet
That very envy and the tongue of loss
Cried fame and honor on him. What's the matter?
1. OFF.: Orsino, this is that Antonio
That took the *Phoenix* and her fraught[12] from Candy,[13]
And this is he that did the *Tiger* board,
When your young nephew Titus lost his leg.
Here in the streets, desperate[14] of shame and state,[15]
In private brabble[16] did we apprehend him.
VIO.: He did me kindness, sir, drew on my side,
  But in conclusion put strange speech upon me.
I know not what 'twas but distraction.[17]
DUKE: Notable pirate! Thou salt-water thief!
  What foolish boldness brought thee to their mercies
Whom thou, in terms so bloody and so dear,
  Hast made thine enemies?
ANT.: Orsino, noble sir,
Be pleased that I shake off these names you give me.
Antonio never yet was thief or pirate,
Though I confess, on base and ground enough,
Orsino's enemy. A witchcraft drew me hither.
That most ingrateful boy there by your side
From the rude sea's enraged and foamy mouth
Did I redeem—a wreck past hope he was.
His life I gave him and did thereto add
My love, without retention or restraint,
All his in dedication. For his sake
Did I expose myself, pure for his love,
Into the danger of this adverse[18] town,
Drew to defend him when he was beset,
Where being apprehended, his false cunning,
Not meaning to partake with me in danger,
Taught him to face me out of his acquaintance,
And grew a twenty years' removèd thing

---

8. bawbling: trifling. 9. unprizable: not worth taking as a prize. 10. scathful grapple: destructive attack. 11. bottom: vessel. 12. fraught: cargo. 13. Candy: Crete. 14. desperate: utterly regardless. 15. state: civil behavior. 16. brabble: brawl. 17. distraction: madness. 18. adverse: hostile.

While one would wink—denied me mine own purse,
Which I had recommended to his use
Not half an hour before.

VIO.: How can this be?

DUKE: When came he to this town?

ANT.: Today, my lord, and for three months before,
No interim, not a minute's vacancy,
Both day and night did we keep company.

[*Enter* OLIVIA *and* ATTENDANTS.]

DUKE: Here comes the Countess. Now Heaven walk on earth.
But for thee, fellow—fellow, thy words are madness.
Three months this youth hath tended upon me.
But more of that anon. Take him aside.

OLI.: What would my lord, but that he may not have,
Wherein Olivia may seem serviceable?
Cesario, you do not keep promise with me.

VIO.: Madam!

DUKE: Gracious Olivia—

OLI.: What do you say, Cesario? Good my lord—

VIO.: My lord would speak, my duty hushes me.

OLI.: If it be aught to the old tune, my lord,
It is as fat[19] and fulsome[20] to mine ear
As howling after music.

DUKE: Still so cruel?

OLI.: Still so constant, lord.

DUKE: What, to perverseness? You uncivil lady,
To whose ingrate[21] and unauspicious altars
My soul the faithful'st offerings hath breathed out
That e'er devotion tendered! What shall I do?

OLI.: Even what it please my lord that shall become him.

DUKE: Why should I not, had I the heart to do it,
Like to the Egyptian thief[22] at point of death,
Kill what I love?—A savage jealousy
That sometime savors nobly. But hear me this.
Since you to nonregardance cast my faith,
And that I partly know the instrument
That screws[23] me from my true place in your favor,

---

19. fat: gross. 20. fulsome: nauseous. 21. integrate: ungrateful. 22. Egyptian theft: Thyamis, an Egyptian robber, captured Chariclea and shut her in a cave. Being attacked by other robbers, he rushed into the cave intending to slay her rather than that she should fall into other hands. 23. instrument . . . screws: a jack that forces.

Live you the marble-breasted tyrant still.
But this your minion,[24] whom I know you love,
And whom, by Heaven I swear, I tender dearly,
Him will I tear out of that cruel eye,
Where he sits crownèd in his master's spite.[25]
Come, boy, with me. My thoughts are ripe in mischief.
I'll sacrifice the lamb that I do love,
To spite a raven's heart within a dove.

VIO.: And I, most jocund, apt, and willingly,
To do you rest, a thousand deaths would die.

OLI.: Where goes Cesario?

VIO.: After him I love
More than I love these eyes, more than my life,
More, by all mores, than e'er I shall love wife.
If I do feign, you witnesses above
Punish my life for tainting of my love!

OLI.: Aye me, detested! How am I beguiled!

VIO.: Who does beguile you? Who does do you wrong?

OLI.: Hast thou forgot thyself? Is it so long?
Call forth the holy Father.

DUKE: Come, away!

OLI.: Whither, my lord? Cesario, husband, stay.

DUKE: Husband!

OLI.: Aye, husband. Can he that deny?

DUKE: Her husband, sirrah!

VIO.: No, my lord, not I.

OLI.: Alas, it is the baseness of thy fear
That makes thee strangle thy propriety.[26]
Fear not, Cesario. Take thy fortunes up.
Be that thou know'st thou art, and then thou art
As great as that thou fear'st.
                    [Enter PRIEST.]
Oh, welcome, Father!
Father, I charge thee, by thy reverence,
Here to unfold, though lately we intended
To keep in darkness what occasion now
Reveals before 'tis ripe, what thou dost know
Hath newly passed between this youth and me.

PRIEST: A contract of eternal bond of love,

24. minion: darling. 25. in . . . spite: to the vexation of his master. 26.
  strangle . . . propriety: lit., choke your proper self; i.e., behave like a coward.

Confirmed by mutual joinder of your hands,
Attested by the holy close of lips,
Strengthened by interchangement of your rings.
And all the ceremony of this compáct[27]
Sealed in my function, by my testimony.
Since when, my watch hath told me, toward my grave
I have traveled but two hours.
DUKE: O thou dissembling cub! What wilt thou be
When time hath sowed a grizzle on thy case?[28]
Or will not else thy craft so quickly grow
That thine own trip shall be thine overthrow?[29]
Farewell, and take her, but direct thy feet
Where thou and I henceforth may never meet.
VIO.: My lord, I do protest—
OLI.: Oh, do not swear!
Hold little faith, though thou hast too much fear.
　　　[*Enter* SIR ANDREW.]
SIR AND.: For the love of God, a surgeon! Send one presently[30] to Sir
Toby.
OLI.: What's the matter?
SIR AND.: He has broke my head across and has given Sir Toby a bloody
coxcomb[31] too. For the love of God, your help! I had rather than
forty pound I were at home.
OLI.: Who has done this, Sir Andrew?
SIR AND.: The Count's gentleman, one Cesario. We took him for a
coward, but he's the very Devil incardinate.[32]
DUKE: My gentleman, Cesario?
SIR AND.: 'Od's lifelings,[33] here he is! You broke my head for nothing,
and that that I did, I was set on to do 't by Sir Toby.
VIO.: Why do you speak to me? I never hurt you.
You drew your sword upon me without cause,
But I bespake you fair, and hurt you not.
SIR AND.: If a bloody coxcomb be a hurt, you have hurt me. I think you
set nothing by a bloody coxcomb. [*Enter* SIR TOBY *and* CLOWN.] Here
comes Sir Toby halting.[34] You shall hear more. But if he had not
been in drink, he would have tickled you othergates[35] than he did.
DUKE: How now, gentleman! How is 't with you?

27. compact: agreement.　28. hath . . . case: has brought you gray hairs.　29.
thine . . . overthrow; your tricky will overthrow you.　30. presently: immediately.　31. bloody coxcomb: broken head.　32. incardinate: incarnate.
33. 'Od's lifelings: by God's little life.　34. halting: limping.　35. othergates:
otherwise.

SIR TO.: That's all one. Has hurt me, and there's the end on 't. Sot, didst see Dick surgeon, sot?

CLO.: Oh, he's drunk, Sir Toby, an hour agone. His eyes were set at eight i' the morning.[36]

SIR TO.: Then he's a rogue, and a passy measures pavin.[37] I hate a drunken rogue.

OLI.: Away with him! Who hath made this havoc with them?

SIR AND.: I'll help you, Sir Toby, because we'll be dressed together.

SIR TO.: Will you help? An asshead and a coxcomb and a knave, a thin-faced knave, a gull!

OLI.: Get him to bed, and let his hurt be looked to.

[*Exeunt* CLOWN, FABIAN, SIR TOBY, *and* SIR ANDREW.]
[*Enter* SEBASTIAN.]

SEB.: I am sorry, madam, I have hurt your kinsman,
But had it been the brother of my blood,
I must have done no less with wit and safety.
You throw a strange regard[38] upon me, and by that
I do perceive it hath offended you.
Pardon me, sweet one, even for the vows
We made each other but so late ago.

DUKE: One face, one voice, one habit, and two persons,
A natural perspective,[39] that is and is not!

SEB.: Antonio, O my dear Antonio!
How have the hours racked and tortured me
Since I have lost thee!

ANT.: Sebastian are you?

SEB.: Fear'st thou that, Antonio?

ANT.: How have you made division of yourself?
An apple, cleft in two, is not more twin
Than these two creatures. Which is Sebastian?

OLI.: Most wonderful!

SEB.: Do I stand there? I never had a brother,
Nor can there be that deity in my nature,
Of here and everywhere.[40] I had a sister,
Whom the blind waves and surges have devoured.

---

36. Set . . . morning: dimmed by drink (set) since eight in the morning. 37. passy . . . pavin: The folio reads "passy measures panyn" (misprint for "pauyn"). Toby is very drunk. The fool's words "set at eight" stir in his fuddled head the memory that there were eight strains in the "passa measures pavan," a slow, stately dance. See App. 24. 38. regard: look. 39. perspective: a picture which shows one image when seen in front and another when viewed from an angle. See *Rich II*, II.ii.18–20. 40. Nor . . . everywhere: I cannot be a god to be in two places at once.

Of charity, what kin are you to me?
What countryman? What name? What parentage?
vio.: Of Messaline. Sebastian was my father.
Such a Sebastian was my brother too,
So went he suited[41] to his watery tomb.
If spirits can assume both form and suit,
You come to fright us.
seb.: A spirit I am indeed,
But am in that dimension grossly clad[42]
Which from the womb I did participate.
Were you a woman, as the rest goes even,
I should my tears let fall upon your cheek,
And say "Thrice welcome, drownèd Viola!"
vio.: My father had a mole upon his brow.
seb.: And so had mine.
vio.: And died that day when Viola from her birth
Had numbered thirteen years.
seb.: Oh, that recórd is lively in my soul!
He finishèd indeed his mortal act
That day that made my sister thirteeen years.
vio.: If nothing lets[43] to make us happy both
But this my masculine usurped attire,
Do not embrace me till each circumstance
Of place, time, fortune, do cohere and jump[44]
That I am Viola. Which to confirm,
I'll bring you to a captain in this town,
Where lie my maiden weeds,[45] by whose gentle help
I was preserved to serve this noble Count.
All the occurrence of my fortune since
Hath been between this lady and this lord.
seb. [To olivia]: So comes it, lady, you have been mistook.
But nature to her bias[46] drew in that.
You would have been contracted to a maid,
Nor are you therein, by my life, deceived,
You are betrothed both to a maid and man.
duke: Be not amazed. Right noble is his blood.
If this be so, as yet the glass[47] seems true,

---

41. suited: clothed. 42. in . . . clad: enclosed in bodily form. 43. lets: hinders.
44. jump: agree. 45. weeds: garments. 46. bias: natural inclination. 47.
glass: reflection.

I shall have share in this most happy wreck.
>   [*To* VIOLA] Boy, thou hast said to me a thousand times
>   Thou never shouldst love woman like to me.
VIO.: And all those sayings will I overswear,
>   And all those swearings keep as true in soul
>   As doth that orbèd continent the fire[48]
>   That severs day from night.
DUKE: Give me thy hand,
>   And let me see thee in thy woman's weeds.
VIO.: The captain that did bring me first on shore
>   Hath my maid's garments. He upon some action
>   Is now in durance,[49] at Malvolio's suit,
>   A gentleman, and follower of my lady's.
OLI.: He shall enlarge him. Fetch Malvolio hither.
>   And yet, alas, now I remember me,
>   They say, poor gentleman, he's much distract.
>   [*Re-enter* CLOWN *with a letter, and* FABIAN.]
>   A most extracting frenzy[50] of mine own
>   From my remembrance clearly banished his.
>   How does he, sirrah?
CLO.: Truly, madam, he holds Belzebub at the stave's end[51] as well as a man in his case may do. Has here writ a letter to you. I should have given 't you today morning, but as a madman's epistles are no gospels, so it skills[52] not much when they are delivered.
OLI.: Open 't, and read it.
CLO.: Look then to be well edified when the fool delivers[53] the madman. [*Reads.*] "By the Lord, madam"—
OLI.: How now! Art thou mad?
CLO.: No, madam, I do but read madness. An your ladyship will have it as it ought to be, you must allow Vox.[54]
OLI.: Prithee, read i' thy right wits.
CLO.: So I do, madonna, but to read his right wits is to read thus. Therefore perpend,[55] my Princess, and give ear.
OLI. [*To* FABIAN]: Read it you, sirrah.
FAB. [*Reads.*]: "By the Lord, madam, you wrong me, and the world shall know it. Though you have put me into darkness and given your

---

48. orbed . . . fire: the sun. 49. durance: confinement. 50. frenzy: madness. 51. holds . . . end: he keeps the fiend at bay; i.e., he is putting up a fight against Belzebub, who possesses him. 52. skills: makes little difference. 53. delivers: utters the words of. 54. allow Vox: the proper tone of voice. 55. perpend: consider.

drunken cousin rule over me, yet have I the benefit of my senses as
well as your ladyship. I have your own letter that induced me to the
semblance I put on, with the which I doubt not but to do myself
much right, or you much shame. Think of me as you please. I leave
my duty a little unthought-of,[56] and speak out of my injury.

"The madly used Malvolio"

OLI.: Did he write this?

CLO.: Aye, madam.

DUKE: This savors not much of distraction.

OLI.: See him delivered, Fabian. Bring him hither.

> [*Exit* FABIAN.]

My lord, so please you, these things further thought on,
To think me as well a sister as a wife,
One day shall crown the alliance on 't, so please you,
Here at my house and at my proper[57] cost.

DUKE: Madam, I am most apt to embrace your offer.

> [*To* VIOLA] Your master quits[58] you, and for your service done him,
So much against the mettle[59] of your sex,
So far beneath your soft and tender breeding,
And since you called me master for so long,
Here is my hand. You shall from this time be
Your master's mistress.

OLI.: A sister! You are she.

> [*Re-enter* FABIAN, *with* MALVOLIO.]

DUKE: Is this the madman?

OLI.: Aye, my lord, this same.

How now, Malvolio!

MAL.: Madman, you have done me wrong,
Notorious wrong.

OLI.: Have I, Malvolio? No.

MAL.: Lady, you have. Pray you peruse that letter.
You must not now deny it is your hand.
Write from[60] it, if you can, in hand or phrase,
Or say 'tis not your seal, not your invention.
You can say none of this. Well, grant it then
And tell me, in the modesty of honor,
Why you have given me such clear lights of favor,
Bade me come smiling and cross-gartered to you,
To put on yellow stockings and to frown

---

56. duty . . . unthought-of: i.e., I do not write with the formal phrases that a
steward should use to his mistress.   57. proper: own.   58. quits: releases.
59. mettle: material, nature.   60. Write from: deny.

Upon Sir Toby and the lighter people.
And, acting this in an obedient hope,
Why have you suffered me to be imprisoned,
Kept in a dark house, visited by the priest,
And made the most notorious geck[61] and gull
That e'er invention played on? Tell me why.

OLI.: Alas, Malvolio, this is not my writing,
Though, I confess, much like the character.[62]
But out of question 'tis Maria's hand.
And now I do bethink me it was she
First told me thou wast mad, then camest in smiling.
And in such forms which here were presupposed
Upon thee in the letter. Prithee, be content.
This practice[63] hath most shrewdly passed upon thee,
But when we know the grounds and authors of it,
Thou shalt be both the plaintiff and the judge
Of thine own cause.

FAB.: Good madam, hear me speak,
And let no quarrel nor no brawl to come
Taint the condition[64] of this present hour,
Which I have wondered at. In hope it shall not,
Most freely I confess, myself and Toby
Set this device against Malvolio here,
Upon some stubborn and uncourteous parts
We had conceived[65] against him. Maria writ
The letter at Sir Toby's great importance,[66]
In recompense whereof he hath married her.
How with a sportful malice it was followed
May rather pluck on laughter than revenge,
If that the injuries be justly weighed
That have on both sides passed.

OLI.: Alas, poor fool, how have they baffled[67] thee!

CLO.: Why, "some are born great, some achieve greatness, and some have greatness thrown upon them." I was one, sir, in this interlude; one Sir Topas, sir. But that's all one. "By the Lord, fool, I am not mad." But do you remember? "Madam, why laugh you at such a barren rascal? An you smile not, he's gagged." And thus the whirligig of time brings in his revenges.[68]

---

61. geck: fool.   62. character: handwriting.   63. practice: plot.   64. Taint . . . condition: spoil the harmony.   65. conceived: perceived.   66. importance: importunity, insistence.   67. baffled: disgrace.   68. brings . . . revenges: i.e., now I have my own back. See I.v.88.

MAL.: I'll be revenged on the whole pack of you.
    [*Exit.*]
OLI.: He hath been most notoriously abused.
DUKE: Pursue him, and entreat him to a peace.
  He hath not told us of the captain yet.
  When that is known, and golden time convents,[69]
  A solemn combination shall be made
  Of our dear souls. Meantime, sweet sister,
  We will not part from hence. Cesario, come—
  For so you shall be, while you are a man,
  But when in other habits you are seen,
  Orsino's mistress and his fancy's Queen.
    [*Exeunt all, except* CLOWN.]
CLO. [*Sings.*]:

    When that I was and a little tiny boy,
      With hey, ho, the wind and the rain,
    A foolish thing was but a toy,
      For the rain it raineth every day.

    But when I came to man's estate,
      With hey, ho, the wind and the rain,
    'Gainst knaves and thieves men shut their gate,
      For the rain it raineth every day.

    But when I came, alas! to wive,
      With hey, ho, the wind and the rain,
    By swaggering could I never thrive,
      For the rain it raineth every day.

    But when I came unto my beds,[70]
      With hey, ho, the wind and the rain,
    With tosspots[71] still had drunken heads,
      For the rain it raineth every day.

    A great while ago the world begun,
      With hey, ho, the wind and the rain,
    But that's all one, our play is done,
      And we'll strive to please you every day.
    [*Exit.*]

---

69. golden . . . convents: happy time summons.　70. unto my beds: a difficult phrase, meaning probably "when I came to the end of my life."　71. tosspots: drunkards.

🔆 Molière

Jean Baptiste Poquelin (1622–1673), known to us as Molière, was the son of a prosperous upholsterer and decorator attached to the King's court. Molière received a good education and worked for a time in his father's business, but soon abandoned the bourgeois world for the stage. He assumed the name of Molière at this time, but we do not know its source. After failing in Paris, Molière toured the provinces with his troupe (1645–1658) as an actor-manager, getting his real education in life and the theatre, adapting other works and writing short pieces in preparation for his own career as a playwright. Returning to Paris in 1658, Molière established the Palais Royal theatre, under the patronage of King Louis XIV. Success soon followed as Molière began to produce the great comedies for which he is famous, *The School for Wives* (1664, 1667), *The Misanthrope* (1666), *The Miser* (1668), *The Would-Be Gentleman* (1670), *The Imaginary Invalid* (1673), and many more. Though his public fame was assured, Molière was plagued by private misfortunes, chronic illness and an unhappy marriage to an actress much younger than himself and supposedly unfaithful. At a performance of his last play, *The Imaginary Invalid*, Molière began to hemorrhage on stage during the final scene, but managed to finish, dying a few hours later at his home.

Where Shakespeare creates a "romantic" comedy, Molière follows the realistic, satiric pattern of classical New Comedy. Molière's plays focus on a "humor" or comic figure whose ruling passion perverts the individual or social norm. Molière's comedy is concerned with correcting the comic figure's foolish behavior or freeing him from his unreasonable obsession or monomania. The liberating laughter is usually genial and indulgent, through in *Tartuffe* and *The Misanthrope* there is a more stringent satiric temper and, for some critics, darker overtones.

Alceste, in *The Misanthrope*, is one of Molière's comic figures in conflict with a reasonable norm. Though he is part of the dominant social group, he is antagonistic to its worldly values. Alceste is caught between his confirmed misanthropy and his inability to come to terms with society. He seems to be both protagonist and comic figure. It is not that Alceste is completely wrong about man, but that the "tragic" posturing of the moralist is out of place in comedy. As Malvolio disrupted the festive world of *Twelfth Night*, so Alceste disturbs the reasonable norm, the going social order of *The Misanthrope*. Alceste is also a comic figure because Molière contrasts his "tragic" manner with Célimène's trivial world of polished manners and petty morality. Yet it is the comic world, society, that must triumph over the unyielding moralist. Philinte, Molière's spokesman (*raisonneur*) tries to counter Alceste's misanthropy with the comic argument for an Aristotelian mean of rational behavior. At the end, though, Alceste rejects and is rejected by society. Unlike the usual comic figure, he remains unreconciled, outside the social circle; though Philinte and Eliante suggest the possibility of changing Alceste's mind about man and society. For a fuller discussion of Molière and *The Misanthrope* in the context of the comic form, see the introduction to comedy.

READINGS:

FERNANDEZ, RAMON, *Molière: The Man Seen Through the Plays*. New York: Hill and Wang, 1958.

GOSSMAN, LIONEL, *Men and Masks: A Study of Molière*. Baltimore: Johns Hopkins, 1963.

GUICHARNAULD, JACQUES, ed., *Molière: A Collection of Critical Essays*. Englewood Cliffs, New Jersey: Prentice-Hall, 1964.

HUBERT, J. D., *Molière and the Comedy of Intellect*. Berkeley: University of California, 1962.

MOORE, W. G., *Molière: A New Criticism*. Oxford: Oxford University Press, 1949.

TURNELL, MARTIN, *The Classical Moment*. New York: New Directions, 1948.

❧ The Misanthrope

Molière

CHARACTERS

ALCESTE, *in love with Célimène*
PHILINTE, *Alceste's friend*
ORONTE, *in love with Célimène*
CÉLIMÈNE, *Alceste's beloved*
ÉLIANTE, *Célimène's cousin*
ARSINOÉ, *a friend of Célimène's*

ACASTE ⎱ Marquesses
CLITANDRE ⎰
BASQUE, *Célimène's servant*
A GUARD *of the Marshalsea*
DUBOIS, *Alceste's valet*

The Scene throughout is in Célimène's house at Paris.

❧ Act I

SCENE 1. [PHILINTE, ALCESTE]

PHILINTE: Now, what's got into you?
ALCESTE [*seated*]: Kindly leave me alone.
PHILINTE: Come, come, what is it? This lugubrious tone . . .
ALCESTE: Leave me, I said; you spoil my solitude.
PHILINTE: Oh, listen to me, now, and don't be rude.
ALCESTE: I choose to be rude, Sir, and to be hard of hearing.
PHILINTE: These ugly moods of yours are not endearing;
    Friends though we are, I really must insist . . .
ALCESTE [*abruptly rising*]: Friends? Friends, you say? Well, cross me
      off your list.
    I've been your friend till now, as you well know;
    But after what I saw a moment ago

The *Misanthrope* by Molière, translated by Richard Wilbur, copyright © 1954, 1955 by Richard Wilbur. Reprinted by permission of Harcourt, Brace & World, Inc.

I tell you flatly that our ways must part.
I wish no place in a dishonest heart.
PHILINTE: Why, what have I done, Alceste? Is this quite just?
ALCESTE: My God, you ought to die of self-disgust.
I call your conduct inexcusable, Sir,
And every man of honor will concur.
I see you almost hug a man to death,
Exclaim for joy until you're out of breath,
And supplement these loving demonstrations
With endless offers, vows, and protestations;
Then when I ask you "Who was that?" I find
That you can barely bring his name to mind!
Once the man's back is turned, you cease to love him,
And speak with absolute indifference of him!
By God, I say it's base and scandalous
To falsify the heart's affections thus;
If I caught myself behaving in such a way,
I'd hang myself for shame, without delay.
PHILINTE: It hardly seems a hanging matter to me;
I hope that you will take it graciously
If I extend myself a slight reprieve,
And live a little longer, by your leave.
ALCESTE: How dare you joke about a crime so grave?
PHILINTE: What crime? How else are people to behave?
ALCESTE: I'd have them be sincere, and never part
With any word that isn't from the heart.
PHILINTE: When someone greets us with a show of pleasure,
It's but polite to give him equal measure,
Return his love the best that we know how,
And trade him offer for offer, vow for vow.
ALCESTE: No, no, this formula you'd have me follow,
However fashionable, is false and hollow,
And I despise the frenzied operations
Of all these barterers of protestations,
These lavishers of meaningless embraces,
These utterers of obliging commonplaces,
Who court and flatter everyone on earth
And praise the fool no less than the man of worth.
Should you rejoice that someone fondles you,
Offers his love and service, swears to be true,
And fills your ears with praises of your name,
When to the first damned fob he'll say the same?

No, no: no self-respecting heart would dream
Of prizing so promiscuous an esteem;
However high the praise, there's nothing worse
Than sharing honors with the universe.
Esteem is founded on comparison:
To honor all men is to honor none.
Since you embrace this indiscriminate vice,
Your friendship comes at far too cheap a price;
I spurn the easy tribute of a heart
Which will not set the worthy man apart:
I chose, Sir, to be chosen; and in fine,
The friend of mankind is no friend of mine.

PHILINTE: But in polite society, custom decrees
That we show certain outward courtesies. . . .

ALCESTE: Ah, no! we should condemn with all our force
Such false and artificial intercourse.
Let men behave like men; let them display
Their inmost hearts in everything they say;
Let the heart speak, and let our sentiments
Not mask themselves in silly compliments.

PHILINTE: In certain cases it would be uncouth
And most absurd to speak the naked truth;
With all respect for your exalted notions,
It's often best to veil one's true emotions.
Wouldn't the social fabric come undone
If we were wholly frank with everyone?
Suppose you met with someone you couldn't bear;
Would you inform him of it then and there?

ALCESTE: Yes.

PHILINTE: Then you'd tell old Emilie it's pathetic
The way she daubs her features with cosmetic
And plays the gay coquette at sixty-four?

ALCESTE: I would.

PHILINTE: And you'd call Dorilas a bore,
And tell him every ear at court is lame
From hearing him brag about his noble name?

ALCESTE: Precisely.

PHILINTE: Ah, you're joking.

ALCESTE: Au contraire:
In this regard there's none I'd choose to spare.
All are corrupt; there's nothing to be seen
In court or town but aggravates my spleen.

I fall into deep gloom and melancholy
When I survey the scene of human folly,
Finding on every hand base flattery,
Injustice, fraud, self-interest, treachery. . . .
Ah, it's too much; mankind has grown so base,
I mean to break with the whole human race.
PHILINTE: This philosophic rage is a bit extreme;
You've no idea how comical you seem;
Indeed, we're like those brothers in the play
Called *School for Husbands*, one of whom was prey . . .
ALCESTE: Enough, now! None of your stupid similes.
PHILINTE: Then let's have no more tirades, if you please.
The world won't change, whatever you say or do;
And since plain speaking means so much to you,
I'll tell you plainly that by being frank
You've earned the reputation of a crank,
And that you're thought ridiculous when you rage
And rant against the manners of the age.
ALCESTE: So much the better; just what I wish to hear.
No news could be more grateful to my ear.
All men are so detestable in my eyes,
I should be sorry if they thought me wise.
PHILINTE: Your hatred's very sweeping, is it not?
ALCESTE: Quite right: I hate the whole degraded lot.
PHILINTE: Must all poor human creatures be embraced,
Without distinction, by your vast distaste?
Even in these bad times, there are surely a few . . .
ALCESTE: No, I include all men in one dim view:
Some men I hate for being rogues; the others
I hate because they treat the rogues like brothers,
And, lacking a virtuous scorn for what is vile,
Receive the villain with a complaisant smile.
Notice how tolerant people choose to be
Toward that bold rascal who's at law with me.
His social polish can't conceal his nature;
One sees at once that he's a treacherous creature;
No one could possibly be taken in
By those soft speeches and that sugary grin.
The whole world knows the shady means by which
The low-brow's grown so powerful and rich,
And risen to a rank so bright and high
That virtue can but blush, and merit sigh.

Whenever his name comes up in conversation,
None will defend his wretched reputation;
Call him knave, liar, scoundrel, and all the rest,
Each head will nod, and no one will protest.
And yet his smirk is seen in every house,
He's greeted everywhere with smiles and bows,
And when there's any honor that can be got
By pulling strings, he'll get it, like as not.
By God! It chills my heart to see the ways
Men come to terms with evil nowadays;
Sometimes, I swear, I'm moved to flee and find
Some desert land unfouled by humankind.

PHILINTE: Come, let's forget the follies of the times
And pardon mankind for its petty crimes;
Let's have an end of rantings and of railings,
And show some leniency toward human failings.
This world requires a pliant rectitude;
Too stern a virtue makes one stiff and rude;
Good sense views all extremes with detestation,
And bids us to be noble in moderation.
The rigid virtues of the ancient days
Are not for us; they jar with all our ways
And ask of us too lofty a perfection.
Wise men accept their times without objection,
And there's no greater folly, if you ask me,
Than trying to reform society.
Like you, I see each day a hundred and one
Unhandsome deeds that might be better done,
But still, for all the faults that meet my view,
I'm never known to storm and rave like you.
I take men as they are, or let them be,
And teach my soul to bear their frailty;
And whether in court or town, whatever the scene,
My phlegm's as philosophic as your spleen.

ALCESTE: This phlegm which you so eloquently commend,
Does nothing ever rile it up, my friend?
Suppose some man you trust should treacherously
Conspire to rob you of your property,
And do his best to wreck your reputation?
Wouldn't you feel a certain indignation?

PHILINTE: Why, no. These faults of which you so complain
Are part of human nature, I maintain,

And it's no more a matter for disgust
That men are knavish, selfish and unjust,
Than that the vulture dines upon the dead,
And wolves are furious, and apes ill-bred.
ALCESTE: Shall I see myself betrayed, robbed, torn to bits,
And not . . . Oh, let's be still and rest our wits.
Enough of reasoning, now. I've had my fill.
PHILINTE: Indeed, you would do well, Sir, to be still.
Rage less at your opponent, and give some thought
To how you'll win this lawsuit that he's brought.
ALCESTE: I assure you I'll do nothing of the sort.
PHILINTE: Then who will plead your case before the court?
ALCESTE: Reason and right and justice will plead for me.
PHILINTE: Oh, Lord. What judges do you plan to see?
ALCESTE: Why, none. The justice of my cause is clear.
PHILINTE: Of course, man; but there's politics to fear. . . .
ALCESTE: No, I refuse to lift a hand. That's flat.
I'm either right, or wrong.
PHILINTE: Don't count on that.
ALCESTE: No, I'll do nothing.
PHILINTE: Your enemy's influence
Is great, you know . . .
ALCESTE: That makes no difference.
PHILINTE: It will; you'll see.
ALCESTE: Must honor bow to guile?
If so, I shall be proud to lose the trial.
PHILINTE: Oh, really . . .
ALCESTE: I'll discover by this case
Whether or not men are sufficiently base
And impudent and villainous and perverse
To do me wrong before the universe.
PHILINTE: What a man!
ALCESTE: Oh, I could wish, whatever the cost,
Just for the beauty of it, that my trial were lost.
PHILINTE: If people heard you talking so, Alceste,
They'd split their sides. Your name would be a jest.
ALCESTE: So much the worse for jesters.
PHILINTE: May I enquire
Whether this rectitude you so admire,
And these hard virtues you're enamored of
Are qualities of the lady whom you love?
It much surprises me that you, who seem

To view mankind with furious disesteem,
Have yet found something to enchant your eyes
Amidst a species which you so despise.
And what is more amazing, I'm afraid,
Is the most curious choice your heart has made.
The honest Éliante is fond of you,
Arsinoé, the prude, admires you too;
And yet your spirit's been perversely led
To choose the flighty Célimène instead,
Whose brittle malice and coquettish ways
So typify the manners of our days.
How is it that the traits you most abhor
Are bearable in this lady you adore?
Are you so blind with love that you can't find them?
Or do you contrive, in her case, not to mind them?

ALCESTE: My love for that young widow's not the kind
   That can't perceive defects; no, I'm not blind.
   I see her faults, despite my ardent love,
   And all I see I fervently reprove.
   And yet I'm weak; for all her falsity,
   That woman knows the art of pleasing me,
   And though I never cease complaining of her,
   I swear I cannot manage not to love her.
   Her charm outweighs her faults; I can but aim
   To cleanse her spirit in my love's pure flame.

PHILINTE: That's no small task; I wish you all success.
   You think then that she loves you?

ALCESTE: Heavens, yes!
   I wouldn't love her did she not love me.

PHILINTE: Well, if her taste for you is plain to see,
   Why do these rivals cause you such despair?

ALCESTE: True love, Sir, is possessive, and cannot bear
   To share with all the world. I'm here today
   To tell her she must send that mob away.

PHILINTE: If I were you, and had your choice to make,
   Éliante, her cousin, would be the one I'd take;
   That honest heart, which cares for you alone,
   Would harmonize far better with your own.

ALCESTE: True, true: each day my reason tells me so;
   But reason doesn't rule in love, you know.

PHILINTE: I fear some bitter sorrow is in store;
   This love . . .

SCENE 2. [ORONTE, ALCESTE, PHILINTE]

ORONTE [to ALCESTE]: The servants told me at the door
  That Éliante and Célimène were out,
  But when I heard, dear Sir, that you were about,
  I came to say, without exaggeration,
  That I hold you in the vastest admiration,
  And that it's always been my dearest desire
  To be the friend of one I so admire.
  I hope to see my love of merit requited,
  And you and I in friendship's bond united.
  I'm sure you won't refuse—if I may be frank—
  A friend of my devotedness—and rank.

> [During this speech of ORONTE'S, ALCESTE is abstracted, and
> seems unaware that he is being spoken to. He only breaks off
> his reverie when ORONTE says:]

  It was for you, if you please, that my words were intended.
ALCESTE: For me, Sir?
ORONTE: Yes, for you. You're not offended?
ALCESTE: By no means. But this much surprises me. . . .
  The honor comes most unexpectedly. . . .
ORONTE: My high regard should not astonish you,
  The whole world feels the same. It is your due.
ALCESTE: Sir . . .
ORONTE: Why, in all the State there isn't one
  Can match your merits; they shine, Sir, like the sun.
ALCESTE: Sir . . .
ORONTE: You are higher in my estimation
  Than all that's most illustrious in the nation.
ALCESTE: Sir . . .
ORONTE: If I lie, may heaven strike me dead!
  To show you that I mean what I have said,
  Permit me, Sir, to embrace you most sincerely,
  And swear that I will prize our friendship dearly.
  Give me your hand. And now, Sir, if you choose,
  We'll make our vows.
ALCESTE: Sir . . .
ORONTE: What! You refuse?
ALCESTE: Sir, it's a very great honor you extend:
  But friendship is a sacred thing, my friend;
  It would be profanation to bestow
  The name of friend on one you hardly know.

All parts are better played when well-rehearsed;
Let's put off friendship, and get acquainted first.
We may discover it would be unwise
To try to make our natures harmonize.
ORONTE: By heaven! You're sagacious to the core;
This speech has made me admire you even more.
Let time, then, bring us closer day by day;
Meanwhile, I shall be yours in every way.
If, for example, there should be anything
You wish at court, I'll mention it to the King.
I have his ear, of course; it's quite well known
That I am much in favor with the throne.
In short, I am your servant. And now, dear friend,
Since you have such fine judgment, I intend
To please you, if I can, with a small sonnet
I wrote not long ago. Please comment on it,
And tell me whether I ought to publish it.
ALCESTE: You must excuse me, Sir; I'm hardly fit
To judge such matters.
ORONTE: Why not?
ALCESTE: I am, I fear,
Inclined to be unfashionably sincere.
ORONTE: Just what I ask; I'd take no satisfaction
In anything but your sincere reaction.
I beg you not to dream of being kind.
ALCESTE: Since you desire it, Sir, I'll speak my mind.
ORONTE: *Sonnet*. It's a sonnet. . . . *Hope* . . . The poem's addressed
To a lady who wakened hopes within my breast.
Hope . . . this is not the pompous sort of thing,
Just modest little verses, with a tender ring.
ALCESTE: Well, we shall see.
ORONTE: *Hope* . . . I'm anxious to hear
Whether the style seems properly smooth and clear,
And whether the choice of words is good or bad.
ALCESTE: We'll see, we'll see.
ORONTE: Perhaps I ought to add
That it took me only a quarter-hour to write it.
ALCESTE: The time's irrelevant, Sir: kindly recite it.
ORONTE [reading]:
> *Hope comforts us awhile, 'tis true,*
> *Lulling our cares with careless laughter,*

And yet such joy is full of rue,
My Phyllis, if nothing follows after.

PHILINTE: I'm charmed by this already; the style's delightful.

ALCESTE [*sotto voce, to* PHILINTE]: How can you say that? Why, the
  thing is frightful.

ORONTE: *Your fair face smiled on me awhile,*
  But was it kindness so to enchant me?
  'Twould have been fairer not to smile,
  If hope was all you meant to grant me.

PHILINTE: What a clever thought! How handsomely you phrase it!

ALCESTE [*sotto voce, to* PHILINTE]: You know the thing is trash.
  How dare you praise it?

ORONTE: *If it's to be my passion's fate*
  Thus everlastingly to wait,
  Then death will come to set me free:
  For death is fairer than the fair;
  Phyllis, to hope is to despair
  When one must hope eternally.

PHILINTE: The close is exquisite—full of feeling and grace.

ALCESTE [*sotto voce, aside*]: Oh, blast the close; you'd better close
  your face
Before you send your lying soul to hell.

PHILINTE: I can't remember a poem I've liked so well.

ALCESTE [*sotto voice, aside*]: Good Lord!

ORONTE [*to* PHILINTE]: I fear you're flattering me a bit.

PHILINTE: Oh, no!

ALCESTE [*sotto voce, aside*]: What else d'you call it, you hypocrite?

ORONTE [*to* ALCESTE]: But you, Sir, keep your promise now: don't
  shrink
From telling me sincerely what you think.

ALCESTE: Sir, these are delicate matters; we all desire
To be told that we've the true poetic fire.
But once, to one whose name I shall not mention,
I said, regarding some verse of his invention,
That gentlemen should rigorously control
That itch to write which often afflicts the soul;
That one should curb the heady inclination
To publicize one's little avocation;
And that in showing off one's works of art
One often plays a very clownish part.

ORONTE: Are you suggesting in a devious way
That I ought not . . .

ALCESTE: Oh, that I do not say.
   Further, I told him that no fault is worse
   Than that of writing frigid, lifeless verse,
   And that the merest whisper of such a shame
   Suffices to destroy a man's good name.
ORONTE: D'you mean to say my sonnet's dull and trite?
ALCESTE: I don't say that. But I went on to cite
   Numerous cases of once-respected men
   Who came to grief by taking up the pen.
ORONTE: And am I like them? Do I write so poorly?
ALCESTE: I don't say that. But I told this person, "Surely
   You're under no necessity to compose;
   Why you should wish to publish, heaven knows.
   There's no excuse for printing tedious rot
   Unless one writes for bread, as you do not.
   Resist temptation, then, I beg of you;
   Conceal your pastimes from the public view;
   And don't give up, on any provocation,
   Your present high and courtly reputation,
   To purchase at a greedy printer's shop
   The name of silly author and scribbling fop."
   These were the points I tried to make him see.
ORONTE: I sense that they are also aimed at me;
   But now—about my sonnet—I'd like to be told . . .
ALCESTE: Frankly, that sonnet should be pigeonholed.
   You've chosen the worst models to imitate.
   The style's unnatural. Let me illustrate:
         For example, Your fair face smiled on me awhile,
         Followed by, 'Twould have been fairer not to smile!
      Or this: such joy is full of rue;
      Or this: For death is fairer than the fair;
      Or, Phyllis, to hope is to despair
         When one must hope eternally!
   This artificial style, that's all the fashion,
   Has neither taste, nor honesty, nor passion;
   It's nothing but a sort of wordy play,
   And nature never spoke in such a way.
   What, in this shallow age, is not debased?
   Our fathers, though less refined, had better taste;
   I'd barter all that men admire today
   For one old love song I shall try to say:

> If the King had given me for my own
>   Paris, his citadel,
> And I for that must leave alone
>   Her whom I love so well,
>   I'd say then to the Crown,
>   Take back your glittering town;
> My darling is more fair, I swear,
>   My darling is more fair.

The rhyme's not rich, the style is rough and old,
But don't you see that it's the purest gold
Beside the tinsel nonsense now preferred,
And that there's passion in its every word?

> If the King had given me for my own
>   Paris, his citadel,
> And I for that must leave alone
>   Her whom I love so well,
>   I'd say then to the Crown,
>   Take back your glittering town;
> My darling is more fair, I swear,
>   My darling is more fair.

There speaks a loving heart. [To PHILINTE.] You're laughing, eh?
Laugh on, my precious wit. Whatever you say,
I hold that song's worth all the bibelots
The people hail today with ah's and oh's.

ORONTE: And I maintain my sonnet's very good.

ALCESTE: It's not at all surprising that you should.
You have your reasons; permit me to have mine
For thinking that you cannot write a line.

ORONTE: Others have praised my sonnet to the skies.

ALCESTE: I lack their art of telling pleasant lies.

ORONTE: You seem to think you've got no end of wit.

ALCESTE: To praise your verse, I'd need still more of it.

ORONTE: I'm not in need of your approval, Sir.

ALCESTE: That's good; you couldn't have it if you were.

ORONTE: Come now, I'll lend you the subject of my sonnet;
I'd like to see you try to improve upon it.

ALCESTE: I might, by chance, write something just as shoddy;
But then I wouldn't show it to everybody.

ORONTE: You're most opinionated and conceited.

ALCESTE: Go find your flatterers, and be better treated.

ORONTE: Look here, my little fellow, pray watch your tone.

ALCESTE: My great big fellow, you'd better watch your own.

PHILINTE [*stepping between them*]: Oh, please, please, gentlemen!
　This will never do.
ORONTE: The fault is mine, and I leave the field to you.
　I am your servant, Sir, in every way.
ALCESTE: And I, Sir, am your most abject valet.

SCENE 3.　[PHILINTE, ALCESTE]

PHILINTE: Well, as you see, sincerity in excess
　Can get you into a very pretty mess;
　Oronte was hungry for appreciation. . . .
ALCESTE: Don't speak to me.
PHILINTE: What?
ALCESTE: No more conversation.
PHILINTE: Really, now . . .
ALCESTE: Leave me alone.
PHILINTE: If I . . .
ALCESTE: Out of my sight!
PHILINTE: But what . . .
ALCESTE: I won't listen.
PHILINTE: But . . .
ALCESTE: Silence!
PHILINTE: Now, is it polite . . .
ALCESTE: By heaven, I've had enough. Don't follow me.
PHILINTE: Ah, you're just joking. I'll keep you company.

🍀 *Act II*

SCENE 1.　[ALCESTE, CÉLIMÈNE]

ALCESTE: Shall I speak plainly, Madam? I confess
　Your conduct gives me infinite distress,
　And my resentment's grown to hot to smother.
　Soon, I foresee, we'll break with one another.
　If I said otherwise, I should deceive you;
　Sooner or later, I shall be forced to leave you,
　And if I swore that we shall never part,
　I should misread the omens of my heart.
CÉLIMÈNE: You kindly saw me home, it would appear,
　So as to pour invectives in my ear.

ALCESTE: I've no desire to quarrel. But I deplore
　　Your inability to shut the door
　　On all these suitors who beset you so.
　　There's what annoys me, if you care to know.
CÉLIMÈNE: Is it my fault that all these men pursue me?
　　Am I to blame if they're attracted to me?
　　And when they gently beg an audience,
　　Ought I to take a stick and drive them hence?
ALCESTE: Madam, there's no necessity for a stick;
　　A less responsive heart would do the trick.
　　Of your attractiveness I don't complain;
　　But those your charms attract, you then detain
　　By a most melting and receptive manner,
　　And so enlist their hearts beneath your banner.
　　It's the agreeable hopes which you excite
　　That keep these lovers round you day and night;
　　Were they less liberally smiled upon,
　　That sighing troop would very soon be gone.
　　But tell me, Madam, why it is that lately
　　This man Clitandre interests you so greatly?
　　Because of what high merits do you deem
　　Him worthy of the honor of your esteem?
　　Is it that your admiring glances linger
　　On the splendidly long nail of his little finger?
　　Or do you share the general deep respect
　　For the blond wig he chooses to affect?
　　Are you in love with his embroidered hose?
　　Do you adore his ribbons and his bows?
　　Or is it that this paragon bewitches
　　Your tasteful eye with his vast German breeches?
　　Perhaps his giggle, or his falsetto voice,
　　Makes him the latest gallant of your choice?
CÉLIMÈNE: You're much mistaken to resent him so.
　　Why I put up with him you surely know:
　　My lawsuit's very shortly to be tried,
　　And I must have his influence on my side.
ALCESTE: Then lose your lawsuit, Madam, or let it drop;
　　Don't torture me by humoring such a fop.
CÉLIMÈNE: You're jealous of the whole world, Sir.
ALCESTE: That's true,
　　Since the whole world is well-received by you.

CÉLIMÈNE: That my good nature is so unconfined
   Should serve to pacify your jealous mind;
   Were I to smile on one, and scorn the rest,
   Then you might have some cause to be distressed.
ALCESTE: Well, if I mustn't be jealous, tell me, then,
   Just how I'm better treated than other men.
CÉLIMÈNE: You know you have my love. Will that not do?
ALCESTE: What proof have I that what you say is true?
CÉLIMÈNE: I would expect, Sir, that my having said it
   Might give the statement a sufficient credit.
ALCESTE: But how can I be sure that you don't tell
   The selfsame thing to other men as well?
CÉLIMÈNE: What a gallant speech! How flattering to me!
   What a sweet creature you make me out to be!
   Well then, to save you from the pangs of doubt,
   All that I've said I hereby cancel out;
   Now, none but yourself shall make a monkey of you:
   Are you content?
ALCESTE: Why, why am I doomed to love you?
   I swear that I shall bless the blissful hour
   When this poor heart's no longer in your power!
   I make no secret of it: I've done my best
   To exorcise this passion from my breast;
   But thus far all in vain; it will not go;
   It's for my sins that I must love you so.
CÉLIMÈNE: Your love for me is matchless, Sir; that's clear.
ALCESTE: Indeed, in all the world it has no peer;
   Words can't describe the nature of my passion,
   And no man ever loved in such a fashion.
CÉLIMÈNE: Yes, it's a brand-new fashion, I agree:
   You show your love by castigating me,
   And all your speeches are enraged and rude.
   I've never been so furiously wooed.
ALCESTE: Yet you could calm that fury, if you chose.
   Come, shall we bring our quarrels to a close?
   Let's speak with open hearts, then, and begin . . .

SCENE 2. [CÉLIMÈNE, ALCESTE, BASQUE]

CÉLIMÈNE: What is it?
BASQUE: Acaste is here.
CÉLIMÈNE: Well, send him in.

SCENE 3. [CÉLIMÈNE, ALCESTE]

ALCESTE: What! Shall we never be alone at all?
  You're always ready to receive a call,
  And you can't bear, for ten ticks of the clock,
  Not to keep open house for all who knock.
CÉLIMÈNE: I couldn't refuse him: he'd be most put out.
ALCESTE: Surely that's not worth worrying about.
CÉLIMÈNE: Acaste would never forgive me if he guessed
  That I consider him a dreadful pest.
ALCESTE: If he's a pest, why bother with him then?
CÉLIMÈNE: Heavens! One can't antagonize such men;
  Why, they're the chartered gossips of the court,
  And have a say in things of every sort.
  One must receive them, and be full of charm;
  They're no great help, but they can do you harm,
  And though your influence be ever so great,
  They're hardly the best people to alienate.
ALCESTE: I see, dear lady, that you could make a case
  For putting up with the whole human race;
  These friendships that you calculate so nicely . . .

SCENE 4. [ALCESTE, CÉLIMÈNE, BASQUE]

BASQUE: Madam, Clitandre is here as well.
ALCESTE: Precisely.
CÉLIMÈNE: Where are you going?
ALCESTE: Elsewhere.
CÉLIMÈNE: Stay.
ALCESTE: No, no.
CÉLIMÈNE: Stay, Sir.
ALCESTE: I can't.
CÉLIMÈNE: I wish it.
ALCESTE: No, I must go.
  I beg you, Madam, not to press the matter;
  You know I have no taste for idle chatter.
CÉLIMÈNE: Stay: I command you.
ALCESTE: No, I cannot stay.
CÉLIMÈNE: Very well; you have my leave to go away.

SCENE 5. [ÉLIANTE, PHILINTE, ACASTE, CLITANDRE, ALCESTE,
CÉLIMÈNE, BASQUE]

ÉLIANTE [to CÉLIMÈNE]: The Marquesses have kindly come to call.
  Were they announced?
CÉLIMÈNE: Yes. Basque, bring chairs for all.
      [BASQUE provides the chairs, and exits.]
      [to ALCESTE.] You haven't gone?
ALCESTE: No; and I shan't depart
  Till you decide who's foremost in your heart.
CÉLIMÈNE: Oh, hush.
ALCESTE: It's time to choose; take them, or me.
CÉLIMÈNE: You're mad.
ALCESTE: I'm not, as you shall shortly see.
CÉLIMÈNE: Oh?
ALCESTE: You'll decide.
CÉLIMÈNE: You're joking now, dear friend.
ALCESTE: No, no; you'll choose; my patience is at an end.
CLITANDRE: Madam, I come from court, where poor Cléonte
  Behaved like a perfect fool, as is his wont.
  Has he no friend to counsel him, I wonder,
  And teach him less unerringly to blunder?
CÉLIMÈNE: It's true, the man's a most accomplished dunce;
  His gauche behavior charms the eye at once;
  And every time one sees him, on my word,
  His manner's grown a trifle more absurd.
ACASTE: Speaking of dunces, I've just now conversed
  With old Damon, who's one of the very worst;
  I stood a lifetime in the broiling sun
  Before his dreary monologue was done.
CÉLIMÈNE: Oh, he's a wondrous talker, and has the power
  To tell you nothing hour after hour:
  If, by mistake, he ever came to the point,
  The shock would put his jawbone out of joint.
ÉLIANTE [to PHILINTE]: The conversation takes its usual turn,
  And all our dear friends' ears will shortly burn.
CLITANDRE: Timante's a character, Madam.
CÉLIMÈNE: Isn't he, though?
  A man of mystery from top to toe,
  Who moves about in a romantic mist
  On secret missions which do not exist.

His talk is full of eyebrows and grimaces;
How tired one gets of his momentous faces;
He's always whispering something confidential
Which turns out to be quite inconsequential;
Nothing's too slight for him to mystify;
He even whispers when he says "good-by."

ACASTE: Tell us about Géralde.

CÉLIMÈNE: That tiresome ass.
He mixes only with the titled class,
And fawns on dukes and princes, and is bored
With anyone who's not at least a lord.
The man's obsessed with rank, and his discourses
Are all of hounds and carriages and horses;
He uses Christian names with all the great,
And the word Milord, with him, is out of date.

CLITANDRE: He's very taken with Bélise, I hear.

CÉLIMÈNE: She is the dreariest company, poor dear.
Whenever she comes to call, I grope about
To find some topic which will draw her out,
But, owing to her dry and faint replies,
The conversation wilts, and droops, and dies.
In vain one hopes to animate her face
By mentioning the ultimate commonplace;
But sun or shower, even hail or frost
Are matters she can instantly exhaust.
Meanwhile her visit, painful though it is,
Drags on and on through mute eternities,
And though you ask the time, and yawn, and yawn,
She sits there like a stone and won't be gone.

ACASTE: Now for Adraste.

CÉLIMÈNE: Oh, that conceited elf
Has a gigantic passion for himself;
He rails against the court, and cannot bear it
That none will recognize his hidden merit;
All honors given to others give offense
To his imaginary excellence.

CLITANDRE: What about young Cléon? His house, they say,
Is full of the best society, night and day.

CÉLIMÈNE: His cook has made him popular, not he:
It's Cléon's table that people come to see.

ÉLIANTE: He gives a splendid dinner, you must admit.

CÉLIMÈNE: But must he serve himself along with it?
   For my taste, he's a most insipid dish
   Whose presence sours the wine and spoils the fish.
PHILINTE: Damis, his uncle, is admired no end.
   What's your opinion, Madam?
CÉLIMÈNE: Why, he's my friend.
PHILINTE: He seems a decent fellow, and rather clever.
CÉLIMÈNE: He works too hard at cleverness, however.
   I hate to see him sweat and struggle so
   To fill his conversation with bons mots.
   Since he's decided to become a wit
   His taste's so pure that nothing pleases it;
   He scolds at all the latest books and plays,
   Thinking that wit must never stoop to praise,
   That finding fault's a sign of intellect,
   That all appreciation is abject,
   And that by damning everything in sight
   One shows oneself in a distinguished light.
   He's scornful even of our conversations:
   Their trivial nature sorely tries his patience;
   He folds his arms, and stands above the battle,
   And listens sadly to our childish prattle.
ACASTE: Wonderful, Madam! You've hit him off precisely.
CLITANDRE: No one can sketch a character so nicely.
ALCESTE: How bravely, Sirs, you cut and thrust at all
   These absent fools, till one by one they fall:
   But let one come in sight, and you'll at once
   Embrace the man you lately called a dunce,
   Telling him in a tone sincere and fervent
   How proud you are to be his humble servant.
CLITANDRE: Why pick on us? Madame's been speaking, Sir,
   And you should quarrel, if you must, with her.
ALCESTE: No, no, by God, the fault is yours, because
   You lead her on with laughter and applause,
   And make her think that she's the more delightful
   The more her talk is scandalous and spiteful.
   Oh, she would stoop to malice far, far less
   If no such claque approved her cleverness.
   It's flatterers like you whose foolish praise
   Nourishes all the vices of these days.
PHILINTE: But why protest when someone ridicules
   Those you'd condemn, yourself, as knaves or fools?

CÉLIMÈNE: Why, Sir? Because he loves to make a fuss.
  You don't expect him to agree with us,
  When there's an opportunity to express
  His heaven-sent spirit of contrariness?
  What other people think, he can't abide;
  Whatever they say, he's on the other side;
  He lives in deadly terror of agreeing;
  'Twould make him seem an ordinary being.
  Indeed, he's so in love with contradiction,
  He'll turn against his most profound conviction
  And with a furious eloquence deplore it,
  If only someone else is speaking for it.
ALCESTE: Go on, dear lady, mock me as you please;
  You have your audience in ecstasies.
PHILINTE: But what she says is true: you have a way
  Of bridling at whatever people say;
  Whether they praise or blame, your angry spirit
  Is equally unsatisfied to hear it.
ALCESTE: Men, Sir, are always wrong, and that's the reason
  That righteous anger's never out of season;
  All that I hear in all their conversation
  Is flattering praise or reckless condemnation.
CÉLIMÈNE: But . . .
ALCESTE: No, no, Madam, I am forced to state
  That you have pleasures which I deprecate,
  And that these others, here, are much to blame
  For nourishing the faults which are your shame.
CLITANDRE: I shan't defend myself, Sir; but I vow
  I'd thought this lady faultless until now.
ACASTE: I see her charms and graces, which are many;
  But as for faults, I've never noticed any.
ALCESTE: I see them, Sir; and rather than ignore them,
  I strenuously criticize her for them.
  The more one loves, the more one should object
  To every blemish, every least defect.
  Were I this lady, I would soon get rid
  Of lovers who approved of all I did,
  And by their slack indulgence and applause
  Endorsed my follies and excused my flaws.
CÉLIMÈNE: If all hearts beat according to your measure,
  The dawn of love would be the end of pleasure;

And love would find its perfect consummation
In ecstasies of rage and reprobation.
ÉLIANTE: Love, as a rule, affects men otherwise,
And lovers rarely love to criticize.
They see their lady as a charming blur,
And find all things commendable in her.
If she has any blemish, fault, or shame,
They will redeem it by a pleasing name.
The pale-faced lady's lily-white, perforce;
The swarthy one's a sweet brunette, of course;
The spindly lady has a slender grace;
The fat one has a most majestic pace;
The plain one, with her dress in disarray,
They classify as *beauté négligée*;
The hulking one's a goddess in their eyes,
The dwarf, a concentrate of Paradise;
The haughty lady has a noble mind;
The mean one's witty, and the dull one's kind;
The chatterbox has liveliness and verve,
The mute one has a virtuous reserve.
So lovers manage, in their passion's cause,
To love their ladies even for their flaws.
ALCESTE: But I still say . . .
CÉLIMÈNE: I think it would be nice
To stroll around the gallery once or twice.
What! You're not going, Sirs?
CLITANDRE AND ACASTE: No, Madam, no.
ALCESTE: You seem to be in terror lest they go.
Do what you will, Sirs; leave, or linger on,
But I shan't go till after you are gone.
ACESTE: I'm free to linger, unless I should perceive
Madame is tired, and wishes me to leave.
CLITANDRE: And as for me, I needn't go today
Until the hour of the King's *coucher*.
CÉLIMÈNE [to ALCESTE]: You're joking surely?
ALCESTE: Not in the least; we'll see
Whether you'd rather part with them, or me.

SCENE 6. [ALCESTE, CÉLIMÈNE, ÉLIANTE, ACASTE, PHILINTE,
CLITANDRE, BASQUE]

BASQUE [to ALCESTE]: Sir, there's a fellow here who bids me state
That he must see you, and that it can't wait.

ALCESTE: Tell him that I have no such pressing affairs.

BASQUE: It's a long tailcoat that this fellow wears,
With gold all over.

CÉLIMÈNE [to ALCESTE]: You'd best go down and see.
Or—have him enter.

SCENE 7.   [ALCESTE, CÉLIMÈNE, ÉLIANTE, ACASTE, PHILINTE,
CLITANDRE, GUARD]

ALCESTE [confronting the GUARD]: Well, what do you want with me?
Come in, Sir.

GUARD: I've a word, Sir, for your ear.

ALCESTE: Speak it aloud, Sir; I shall strive to hear.

GUARD: The Marshals have instructed me to say
You must report to them without delay.

ALCESTE: Who? Me, Sir?

GUARD: Yes, Sir; you.

ALCESTE: But what do they want?

PHILINTE [to ALCESTE]: To scotch your silly quarrel with Oronte.

CÉLIMÈNE [to PHILINTE]: What quarrel?

PHILINTE: Oronte and he have fallen out
Over some verse he spoke his mind about;
The Marshals wish to arbitrate the matter.

ALCESTE: Never shall I equivocate or flatter!

PHILINTE: You'd best obey their summons; come, let's go.

ALCESTE: How can they mend our quarrel, I'd like to know?
Am I to make a cowardly retraction,
And praise those jingles to his satisfaction?
I'll not recant; I've judged that sonnet rightly.
It's bad.

PHILINTE: But you might say so more politely. . . .

ALCESTE: I'll not back down; his verses make me sick.

PHILINTE: If only you could be more politic!
But come, let's go.

ALCESTE: I'll go, but I won't unsay
A single word.

PHILINTE: Well, let's be on our way.

ALCESTE: Till I am ordered by my lord the King
To praise that poem, I shall say the thing
Is scandalous, by God, and that the poet
Ought to be hanged for having the nerve to show it.

[*To* CLITANDRE *and* ACASTE, *who are laughing.*]

By heaven, Sirs, I really didn't know
That I was being humorous.
CÉLIMÈNE: Go, Sir, go;
Settle your business.
ALCESTE: I shall, and when I'm through,
I shall return to settle things with you.

❧ *Act III*

SCENE 1. [CLITANDRE, ACASTE]

CLITANDRE: Dear Marquess, how contented you appear;
All things delight you, nothing mars your cheer.
Can you, in perfect honesty, declare
That you've a right to be so debonair?
ACASTE: By Jove, when I survey myself, I find
No cause whatever for distress of mind.
I'm young and rich; I can in modesty
Lay claim to an exalted pedigree;
And owing to my name and my condition
I shall not want for honors and position.
Then as to courage, that most precious trait,
I seem to have it, as was proved of late
Upon the field of honor, where my bearing,
They say, was very cool and rather daring.
I've wit, of course; and taste in such perfection
That I can judge without the least reflection,
And at the theater, which is my delight,
Can make or break a play on opening night,
And lead the crowd in hisses or bravos,
And generally be known as one who knows.
I'm clever, handsome, gracefully polite;
My waîst is small, my teeth are strong and white;
As for my dress, the world's astonished eyes
Assure me that I bear away the prize.
I find myself in favor everywhere,
Honored by men, and worshiped by the fair;
And since these things are so, it seems to me
I'm justified in my complacency.

CLITANDRE: Well, if so many ladies hold you dear,
Why do you press a hopeless courtship here?
ACASTE: Hopeless, you say? I'm not the sort of fool
That likes his ladies difficult and cool.
Men who are awkward, shy, and peasantish
May pine for heartless beauties, if they wish,
Grovel before them, bear their cruelties,
Woo them with tears and sighs and bended knees,
And hope by dogged faithfulness to gain
What their poor merits never could obtain.
For men like me, however, it makes no sense
To love on trust, and foot the whole expense.
Whatever any lady's merits be,
I think, thank God, that I'm as choice as she;
That if my heart is kind enough to burn
For her, she owes me something in return;
And that in any proper love affair
The partners must invest an equal share.
CLITANDRE: You think, then, that our hostess favors you?
ACASTE: I've reason to believe that that is true.
CLITANDRE: How did you come to such a mad conclusion?
You're blind, dear fellow. This is sheer delusion.
ACASTE: All right, then: I'm deluded and I'm blind.
CLITANDRE: Whatever put the notion in your mind?
ACASTE: Delusion.
CLITANDRE: What persuades you that you're right?
ACASTE: I'm blind.
CLITANDRE: But have you any proofs to cite?
ACASTE: I tell you I'm deluded.
CLITANDRE: Have you, then,
Received some secret pledge from Célimène?
ACASTE: Oh, no: she scorns me.
CLITANDRE: Tell me the truth, I beg.
ACASTE: She just can't bear me.
CLITANDRE: Ah, don't pull my leg.
Tell me what hope she's given you, I pray.
ACASTE: I'm hopeless, and it's you who win the day.
She hates me thoroughly, and I'm so vexed
I mean to hang myself on Tuesday next.
CLITANDRE: Dear Marquess, let us have an armistice
And make a treaty. What do you say to this?
If ever one of us can plainly prove

That Célimène encourages his love,
The other must abandon hope, and yield,
And leave him in possession of the field.
ACASTE: Now, there's a bargain that appeals to me;
With all my heart, dear Marquess, I agree.
But hush.

SCENE 2. [CÉLIMÈNE, ACASTE, CLITANDRE]

CÉLIMÈNE: Still here?
CLITANDRE: 'Twas love that stayed our feet.
CÉLIMÈNE: I think I heard a carriage in the street.
Whose is it? D'you know?

SCENE 3. [CÉLIMÈNE, ACASTE, CLITANDRE, BASQUE]

BASQUE: Arsinoé is here,
Madame.
CÉLIMÈNE: Arsinoé, you say? Oh, dear.
BASQUE: Éliante is entertaining her below.
CÉLIMÈNE: What brings the creature here, I'd like to know?
ACASTE: They say she's dreadfully prudish, but in fact
I think her piety . . .
CÉLIMÈNE: It's all an act.
At heart she's worldly, and her poor success
In snaring men explains her prudishness.
It breaks her heart to see the beaux and gallants
Engrossed by other women's charms and talents,
And so she's always in a jealous rage
Against the faulty standards of the age.
She lets the world believe that she's a prude
To justify her loveless solitude,
And strives to put a brand of moral shame
On all the graces that she cannot claim.
But still she'd love a lover; and Alceste
Appears to be the one she'd love the best.
His visits here are poison to her pride;
She seems to think I've lured him from her side;
And everywhere, at court or in the town,
The spiteful, envious woman runs me down.
In short, she's just as stupid as can be,
Vicious and arrogant in the last degree,
And . . .

SCENE 4. [ARSINOÉ, CÉLIMÈNE, CLITANDRE, ACASTE]

CÉLIMÈNE: Ah! What happy chance has brought you here?
　I've thought about you ever so much, my dear.
ARSINOÉ: I've come to tell you something you should know.
CÉLIMÈNE: How good of you to think of doing so!

　　[CLITANDRE and ACASTE go out, laughing.]

SCENE 5. [ARSINOÉ, CÉLIMÈNE]

ARSINOÉ: It's just as well those gentlemen didn't tarry.
CÉLIMÈNE: Shall we sit down?
ARSINOÉ: That won't be necessary.
　Madam, the flame of friendship ought to burn
　Brightest in matters of the most concern,
　And as there's nothing which concerns us more
　Than honor, I have hastened to your door
　To bring you, as your friend, some information
　About the status of your reputation.
　I visited, last night, some virtuous folk,
　And, quite by chance, it was of you they spoke;
　There was, I fear, no tendency to praise
　Your light behavior and your dashing ways.
　The quantity of gentlemen you see
　And your by now notorious coquetry
　Were both so vehemently criticized
　By everyone, that I was much surprised.
　Of course, I needn't tell you where I stood;
　I came to your defense as best I could,
　Assured them you were harmless, and declared
　Your soul was absolutely unimpaired.
　But there are some things, you must realize,
　One can't excuse, however hard one tries,
　And I was forced at last into conceding
　That your behavior, Madam, is misleading,
　That it makes a bad impression, giving rise
　To ugly gossip and obscene surmise,
　And that if you were more *overtly* good,
　You wouldn't be so much misunderstood.
　Not that I think you've been unchaste—no! no!
　The saints preserve me from a thought so low!

But mere good conscience never did suffice:
One must avoid the outward show of vice.
Madam, you're too intelligent, I'm sure,
To think my motives anything but pure
In offering you this counsel—which I do
Out of a zealous interest in you.

CÉLIMÈNE: Madam, I haven't taken you amiss;
I'm very much obliged to you for this;
And I'll at once discharge the obligation
By telling you about your reputation.
You've been so friendly as to let me know
What certain people say of me, and so
I mean to follow your benign example
By offering you a somewhat similar sample.
The other day, I went to an affair
And found some most distinguished people there
Discussing piety, both false and true.
The conversation soon came round to you.
Alas! Your prudery and bustling zeal
Appeared to have a very slight appeal.
Your affectation of a grave demeanor,
Your endless talk of virtue and of honor,
The aptitude of your suspicious mind
For finding sin where there is none to find,
Your towering self-esteem, that pitying face
With which you contemplate the human race,
Your sermonizings and your sharp aspersions
On people's pure and innocent diversions—
All these were mentioned, Madam, and, in fact,
Were roundly and concertedly attacked.
"What good," they said, "are all these outward shows,
When everything belies her pious pose?
She prays incessantly; but then, they say,
She beats her maids and cheats them of their pay;
She shows her zeal in every holy place,
But still she's vain enough to paint her face;
She holds that naked statues are immoral,
But with a naked man she'd have no quarrel."
Of course, I said to everybody there
That they were being viciously unfair;
But still they were disposed to criticize you,
And all agreed that someone should advise you

To leave the morals of the world alone,
And worry rather more about your own.
They felt that one's self-knowledge should be great
Before one thinks of setting others straight;
That one should learn the art of living well
Before one threatens other men with hell,
And that the Church is best equipped, no doubt,
To guide our souls and root our vices out.
Madam, you're too intelligent, I'm sure,
To think my motives anything but pure
In offering you this counsel—which I do
Out of a zealous interest in you.

ARSINOÉ: I dared not hope for gratitude, but I
    Did not expect so acid a reply;
    I judge, since you've been so extremely tart,
    That my good counsel pierced you to the heart.

CÉLIMÈNE: Far from it, Madam. Indeed, it seems to me
    We ought to trade advice more frequently.
    One's vision of oneself is so defective
    That it would be an excellent corrective.
    If you are willing, Madam, let's arrange
    Shortly to have another frank exchange
    In which we'll tell each other, entre nous,
    What you've heard tell of me, and I of you.

ARSINOÉ: Oh, people never censure you, my dear;
    It's me they criticize. Or so I hear.

CÉLIMÈNE: Madam, I think we either blame or praise
    According to our taste and length of days.
    There is a time of life for coquetry,
    And there's a season, too, for prudery.
    When all one's charms are gone, it is, I'm sure,
    Good strategy to be devout and pure:
    It makes one seem a little less forsaken.
    Some day, perhaps, I'll take the road you've taken:
    Time brings all things. But I have time aplenty,
    And see no cause to be a prude at twenty.

ARSINOÉ: You give your age in such a gloating tone
    That one would think I was an ancient crone;
    We're not so far apart, in sober truth,
    That you can mock me with a boast of youth!
    Madam, you baffle me. I wish I knew
    What moves you to provoke me as you do.

CÉLIMÈNE: For my part, Madam, I should like to know
   Why you abuse me everywhere you go.
   Is it my fault, dear lady, that your hand
   Is not, alas, in very great demand?
   If men admire me, if they pay me court
   And daily make me offers of the sort
   You'd dearly love to have them make to you,
   How can I help it? What would you have me do?
   If what you want is lovers, please feel free
   To take as many as you can from me.
ARSINOÉ: Oh, come. D'you think the world is losing sleep
   Over that flock of lovers which you keep,
   Or that we find it difficult to guess
   What price you pay for their devotedness?
   Surely you don't expect us to suppose
   Mere merit could attract so many beaux?
   It's not your virtue that they're dazzled by;
   Nor is it virtuous love for which they sigh.
   You're fooling no one, Madam; the world's not blind;
   There's many a lady heaven has designed
   To call men's noblest, tenderest feelings out,
   Who has no lovers dogging her about;
   From which it's plain that lovers nowadays
   Must be acquired in bold and shameless ways,
   And only pay one court for such reward
   As modesty and virtue can't afford.
   Then don't be quite so puffed up, if you please,
   About your tawdry little victories;
   Try, if you can, to be a shade less vain,
   And treat the world with somewhat less disdain.
   If one were envious of your amours,
   One soon could have a following like yours;
   Lovers are no great trouble to collect
   If one prefers them to one's self-respect.
CÉLIMÈNE: Collect them then, my dear; I'd love to see
   You demonstrate that charming theory;
   Who knows, you might . . .
ARSINOÉ: Now, Madam, that will do;
   It's time to end this trying interview.
   My coach is late in coming to your door,
   Or I'd have taken leave of you before.
CÉLIMÈNE: Oh, please don't feel that you must rush away;

I'd be delighted, Madam, if you'd stay.
However, lest my conversation bore you,
Let me provide some better company for you;
This gentleman, who comes most apropos,
Will please you more than I could do, I know.

SCENE 6. [ALCESTE, CÉLIMÈNE, ARSINOÉ]

CÉLIMÈNE: Alceste, I have a little note to write
Which simply must go out before tonight;
Please entertain Madame; I'm sure that she
Will overlook my incivility.

SCENE 7. [ALCESTE, ARSINOÉ]

ARSINOÉ: Well, Sir, our hostess graciously contrives
For us to chat until my coach arrives;
And I shall be forever in her debt
For granting me this little tête-à-tête.
We women very rightly give our hearts
To men of noble character and parts,
And your especial merits, dear Alceste,
Have roused the deepest sympathy in my breast.
Oh, how I wish they had sufficient sense
At court, to recognize your excellence!
They wrong you greatly, Sir. How it must hurt you
Never to be rewarded for your virtue!
ALCESTE: Why, Madam, what cause have I to feel aggrieved?
What great and brilliant thing have I achieved?
What service have I rendered to the King
That I should look to him for anything?
ARSINOÉ: Not everyone who's honored by the State
Has done great services. A man must wait
Till time and fortune offer him the chance.
Your merit, Sir, is obvious at a glance,
And . . .
ALCESTE: Ah, forget my merit; I am not neglected.
The court, I think, can hardly be expected
To mine men's souls for merit, and unearth
Our hidden virtues and our secret worth.
ARSINOÉ: Some virtues, though, are far too bright to hide;
Yours are acknowledged, Sir, on every side.

Indeed, I've heard you warmly praised of late
By persons of considerable weight.
ALCESTE: This fawning age has praise for everyone,
   And all distinctions, Madam, are undone.
   All things have equal honor nowadays,
   And no one should be gratified by praise.
   To be admired, one only need exist,
   And every lackey's on the honors list.
ARSINOÉ: I only wish, Sir, that you had your eye
   On some position at court, however high;
   You'd only have to hint at such a notion
   For me to set the proper wheels in motion;
   I've certain friendships I'd be glad to use
   To get you any office you might choose.
ALCESTE: Madam, I fear that any such ambition
   Is wholly foreign to my disposition.
   The soul God gave me isn't of the sort
   That prospers in the weather of a court.
   It's all too obvious that I don't possess
   The virtues necessary for success.
   My one great talent is for speaking plain;
   I've never learned to flatter or to feign;
   And anyone so stupidly sincere
   Had best not seek a courtier's career.
   Outside the court, I know, one must dispense
   With honors, privilege, and influence;
   But still one gains the right, foregoing these,
   Not to be tortured by the wish to please.
   One needn't live in dread of snubs and slights,
   Nor praise the verse that every idiot writes,
   Nor humor silly Marquesses, nor bestow
   Politic sighs on Madam So-and-So.
ARSINOÉ: Forget the court, then; let the matter rest.
   But I've another cause to be distressed
   About your present situation, Sir.
   It's to your love affair that I refer.
   She whom you love, and who pretends to love you,
   Is, I regret to say, unworthy of you.
ALCESTE: Why, Madam? Can you seriously intend
   To make so grave a charge against your friend?
ARSINOÉ: Alas, I must. I've stood aside too long
   And let that lady do you grievous wrong;

But now my debt to conscience shall be paid:
I tell you that your love has been betrayed.
ALCESTE: I thank you, Madam; you're extremely kind.
Such words are soothing to a lover's mind.
ARSINOÉ: Yes, though she *is* my friend, I say again
You're very much too good for Célimène.
She's wantonly misled you from the start.
ALCESTE: You may be right; who knows another's heart?
But ask yourself if it's the part of charity
To shake my soul with doubts of her sincerity.
ARSINOÉ: Well, if you'd rather be a dupe than doubt her,
That's your affair. I'll say no more about her.
ALCESTE: Madam, you know that doubt and vague suspicion
Are painful to a man in my position;
It's most unkind to worry me this way
Unless you've some real proof of what you say.
ARSINOÉ: Sir, say no more: all doubts shall be removed,
And all that I've been saying shall be proved.
You've only to escort me home, and there
We'll look into the heart of this affair.
I've ocular evidence which will persuade you
Beyond a doubt, that Célimène's betrayed you.
Then, if you're saddened by that revelation,
Perhaps I can provide some consolation.

🜚 *Act IV*

SCENE 1.   [ÉLIANTE, PHILINTE]

PHILINTE: Madam, he acted like a stubborn child;
I thought they never would be reconciled;
In vain we reasoned, threatened, and appealed;
He stood his ground and simply would not yield.
The Marshals, I feel sure, have never heard
An argument so splendidly absurd.
"No, gentlemen," said he, "I'll not retract.
His verse is bad: extremely bad, in fact.
Surely it does the man no harm to know it.
Does it disgrace him, not to be a poet?
A gentleman may be respected still,

Whether he writes a sonnet well or ill.
That I dislike his verse should not offend him;
In all that touches honor, I commend him;
He's noble, brave, and virtuous—but I fear
He can't in truth be called a sonneteer.
I'll gladly praise his wardrobe; I'll endorse
His dancing, or the way he sits a horse;
But, gentlemen, I cannot praise his rhyme.
In fact, it ought to be a capital crime
For anyone so sadly unendowed
To write a sonnet, and read the thing aloud."
At length he fell into a gentler mood
And, striking a concessive attitude,
He paid Oronte the following courtesies:
"Sir, I regret that I'm so hard to please,
And I'm profoundly sorry that your lyric
Failed to provoke me to a panegyric."
After these curious words, the two embraced,
And then the hearing was adjourned—in haste.

ÉLIANTE: His conduct has been very singular lately;
　　Still, I confess that I respect him greatly.
　　The honesty in which he takes such pride
　　Has—to my mind—its noble, heroic side.
　　In this false age, such candor seems outrageous;
　　But I could wish that it were more contagious.

PHILINTE: What most intrigues me in our friend Alceste
　　Is the grand passion that rages in his breast.
　　The sullen humors he's compounded of
　　Should not, I think, dispose his heart to love;
　　But since they do, it puzzles me still more
　　That he should choose your cousin to adore.

ÉLIANTE: It does, indeed, belie the theory
　　That love is born of gentle sympathy,
　　And that the tender passion must be based
　　On sweet accords of temper and of taste.

PHILINTE: Does she return his love, do you suppose?

ÉLIANTE: Ah, that's a difficult question, Sir. Who knows?
　　How we can judge the truth of her devotion?
　　Her heart's a stranger to its own emotion.
　　Sometimes it thinks it loves, when no love's there;
　　At other times it loves quite unaware.

PHILINTE: I rather think Alceste is in for more
 Distress and sorrow than he's bargained for;
 Were he of my mind, Madam, his affection
 Would turn in quite a different direction,
 And we would see him more responsive to
 The kind regard which he receives from you.
ÉLIANTE: Sir, I believe in frankness, and I'm inclined,
 In matters of the heart, to speak my mind.
 I don't oppose his love for her; indeed,
 I hope with all my heart that he'll succeed,
 And were it in my power, I'd rejoice
 In giving him the lady of his choice.
 But if, as happens frequently enough
 In love affairs, he meets with a rebuff—
 If Célimène should grant some rival's suit—
 I'd gladly play the role of substitute;
 Nor would his tender speeches please me less
 Because they'd once been made without success.
PHILINTE: Well, Madam, as for me, I don't oppose
 Your hopes in this affair; and heaven knows
 That in my conversations with the man
 I plead your cause as often as I can.
 But if those two should marry, and so remove
 All chance that he will offer you his love,
 Then I'll declare my own, and hope to see
 Your gracious favor pass from him to me.
 In short, should you be cheated of Alceste,
 I'd be most happy to be second best.
ÉLIANTE: Philinte, you're teasing.
PHILINTE: Ah, Madam, never fear;
 No words of mine were ever so sincere,
 And I shall live in fretful expectation
 Till I can make a fuller declaration.

SCENE 2. [ALCESTE, ÉLIANTE, PHILINTE]

ALCESTE: Avenge me, Madam! I must have satisfaction,
 Or this great wrong will drive me to distraction!
ÉLIANTE: Why, what's the matter? What's upset you so?
ALCESTE: Madam, I've had a mortal, mortal blow.
 If Chaos repossessed the universe,
 I swear I'd not be shaken any worse.

I'm ruined. . . . I can say no more. . . . My soul . . .

ÉLIANTE: Do try, Sir, to regain your self-control.

ALCESTE: Just heaven! Why were so much beauty and grace
    Bestowed on one so vicious and so base?

ÉLIANTE: Once more, Sir, tell us. . . .

ALCESTE: My world has gone to wrack;
    I'm—I'm betrayed; she's stabbed me in the back:
    Yes, Célimène (who would have thought it of her?)
    Is false to me, and has another lover.

ÉLIANTE: Are you quite certain? Can you prove these things?

PHILINTE: Lovers are prey to wild imaginings
    And jealous fancies. No doubt there's some mistake. . . .

ALCESTE: Mind your own business, Sir, for heaven's sake.

    [*To* ÉLIANTE.]

Madam, I have the proof that you demand
Here in my pocket, penned by her own hand.
Yes, all the shameful evidence one could want
Lies in this letter written to Oronte—
Oronte! whom I felt sure she couldn't love,
And hardly bothered to be jealous of.

PHILINTE: Still, in a letter, appearances may deceive;
    This may not be so bad as you believe.

ALCESTE: Once more I beg you, Sir, to let me be;
    Tend to your own affairs; leave mine to me.

ÉLIANTE: Compose yourself; this anguish that you feel . . .

ALCESTE: Is something, Madam, you alone can heal.
    My outraged heart, beside itself with grief,
    Appeals to you for comfort and relief.
    Avenge me on your cousin, whose unjust
    And faithless nature has deceived my trust;
    Avenge a crime your pure soul must detest.

ÉLIANTE: But how, Sir?

ALCESTE: Madam, this heart within my breast
    Is yours; pray take it; redeem my heart from her,
    And so avenge me on my torturer.
    Let her be punished by the fond emotion,
    The ardent love, the bottomless devotion,
    The faithful worship which this heart of mine
    Will offer up to yours as to a shrine.

ÉLIANTE: You have my sympathy, Sir, in all you suffer;
    Nor do I scorn the noble heart you offer;

But I suspect you'll soon be mollified,
And this desire for vengeance will subside.
When some belovèd hand has done us wrong
We thirst for retribution—but not for long;
However dark the deed that she's committed,
A lovely culprit's very soon acquitted.
Nothing's so stormy as an injured lover,
And yet no storm so quickly passes over.
ALCESTE: No, Madam, no—this is no lovers' spat;
   I'll not forgive her; it's gone too far for that;
   My mind's made up; I'll kill myself before
   I waste my hopes upon her any more.
   Ah, here she is. My wrath intensifies.
   I shall confront her with her tricks and lies,
   And crush her utterly, and bring you then
   A heart no longer slave to Célimène.

SCENE 3. [CÉLIMÈNE, ALCESTE]

ALCESTE [aside]: Sweet heaven, help me to control my passion.
CÉLIMÈNE [aside]: Oh, Lord.
      [To ALCESTE.]
Why stand there staring in that fashion?
And what d'you mean by those dramatic sighs,
And that malignant glitter in your eyes?
ALCESTE: I mean that sins which cause the blood to freeze
   Look innocent beside your treacheries;
   That nothing Hell's or Heaven's wrath could do
   Ever produced so bad a thing as you.
CÉLIMÈNE: Your compliments were always sweet and pretty.
ALCESTE: Madam, it's not the moment to be witty.
   No, blush and hang your head; you've ample reason,
   Since I've the fullest evidence of your treason.
   Ah, this is what my sad heart prophesied;
   Now all my anxious fears are verified;
   My dark suspicion and my gloomy doubt
   Divined the truth, and now the truth is out.
   For all your trickery, I was not deceived;
   It was my bitter stars that I believed.
   But don't imagine that you'll go scot-free;
   You shan't misuse me with impunity.
   I know that love's irrational and blind;

I know the heart's not subject to the mind,
And can't be reasoned into beating faster;
I know each soul is free to choose its master;
Therefore had you but spoken from the heart,
Rejecting my attentions from the start,
I'd have no grievance, or at any rate
I could complain of nothing but my fate.
Ah, but so falsely to encourage me—
That was a treason and a treachery
For which you cannot suffer too severely,
And you shall pay for that behavior dearly.
Yes, now I have no pity, not a shred;
My temper's out of hand; I've lost my head;
Shocked by the knowledge of your double-dealings,
My reason can't restrain my savage feelings;
A righteous wrath deprives me of my senses,
And I won't answer for the consequences.

CÉLIMÈNE: What does this outburst mean? Will you please explain?
Have you, by any chance, gone quite insane?

ALCESTE: Yes, yes, I went insane the day I fell
A victim to your black and fatal spell,
Thinking to meet with some sincerity
Among the treacherous charms that beckoned me.

CÉLIMÈNE: Pooh. Of what treachery can you complain?

ALCESTE: How sly you are, how cleverly you feign!
But you'll not victimize me any more.
Look: here's a document you've seen before.
This evidence, which I acquired today,
Leaves you, I think, without a thing to say.

CÉLIMÈNE: Is this what sent you into such a fit?

ALCESTE: You should be blushing at the sight of it.

CÉLIMÈNE: Ought I to blush? I truly don't see why.

ALCESTE: Ah, now you're being bold as well as sly;
Since there's no signature, perhaps you'll claim . . .

CÉLIMÈNE: I wrote it, whether or not it bears my name.

ALCESTE: And you can view with equanimity
This proof of your disloyalty to me!

CÉLIMÈNE: Oh, don't be so outrageous and extreme.

ALCESTE: You take this matter lightly, it would seem.
Was it no wrong to me, no shame to you,
That you should send Oronte this billet-doux?

CÉLIMÈNE: Oronte! Who said it was for him?

ALCESTE: Why, those
  Who brought me this example of your prose.
  But what's the difference? If you wrote the letter
  To someone else, it pleases me no better.
  My grievance and your guilt remain the same.
CÉLIMÈNE: But need you rage, and need I blush for shame,
  If this was written to a *woman* friend?
ALCESTE: Ah! Most ingenious. I'm impressed no end;
  And after that incredible evasion
  Your guilt is clear. I need no more persuasion.
  How dare you try so clumsy a deception?
  D'you think I'm wholly wanting in perception?
  Come, come, let's see how brazenly you'll try
  To bolster up so palpable a lie:
  Kindly construe this ardent closing section
  As nothing more than sisterly affection!
  Here, let me read it. Tell me, if you dare to,
  That this is for a woman . . .
CÉLIMÈNE: I don't care to.
  What right have you to badger and berate me,
  And so highhandedly interrogate me?
ALCESTE: Now, don't be angry; all I ask of you
  Is that you justify a phrase or two . . .
CÉLIMÈNE: No, I shall not. I utterly refuse,
  And you may take those phrases as you choose.
ALCESTE: Just show me how this letter could be meant
  For a woman's eyes, and I shall be content.
CÉLIMÈNE: No, no, it's for Oronte; you're perfectly right.
  I welcome his attentions with delight,
  I prize his character and his intellect,
  And everything is just as you suspect.
  Come, do your worst now; give your rage free rein;
  But kindly cease to bicker and complain.
ALCESTE [*aside*]: Good God! Could anything be more inhuman?
  Was ever a heart so mangled by a woman?
  When I complain of how she has betrayed me,
  She bridles, and commences to upbraid me,
  She tries my tortured patience to the limit;
  She won't deny her guilt; she glories in it!
  And yet my heart's too faint and cowardly
  To break these chains of passion, and be free,

To scorn her as it should, and rise above
This unrewarded, mad, and bitter love.

[*To* CÉLIMÈNE.]

Ah, traitress, in how confident a fashion
You take advantage of my helpless passion,
And use my weakness for your faithless charms
To make me once again throw down my arms!
But do at least deny this black transgression;
Take back that mocking and perverse confession;
Defend this letter and your innocence,
And I, poor fool, will aid in your defense.
Pretend, pretend, that you are just and true,
And I shall make myself believe in you.
CÉLIMÈNE: Oh, stop it. Don't be such a jealous dunce,
Or I shall leave off loving you at once.
Just why should I *pretend*? What could impel me
To stoop so low as that? And kindly tell me
Why, if I loved another, I shouldn't merely
Inform you of it, simply and sincerely!
I've told you where you stand, and that admission
Should altogether clear me of suspicion;
After so generous a guarantee,
What right have you to harbor doubts of me?
Since women are (from natural reticence)
Reluctant to declare their sentiments,
And since the honor of our sex requires
That we conceal our amorous desires,
Ought any man for whom such laws are broken
To question what the oracle has spoken?
Should he not rather feel an obligation
To trust that most obliging declaration?
Enough, now. Your suspicions quite disgust me;
Why should I love a man who doesn't trust me?
I cannot understand why I continue,
Fool that I am, to take an interest in you.
I ought to choose a man less prone to doubt,
And give you something to be vexed about.
ALCESTE: Ah, what a poor enchanted fool I am;
These gentle words, no doubt, were all a sham;
But destiny requires me to entrust
My happiness to you, and so I must.

I'll love you to the bitter end, and see
How false and treacherous you dare to be.
CÉLIMÈNE: No, you don't really love me as you ought.
ALCESTE: I love you more than can be said or thought;
    Indeed, I wish you were in such distress
    That I might show my deep devotedness.
    Yes, I could wish that you were wretchedly poor,
    Unloved, uncherished, utterly obscure;
    That fate had set you down upon the earth
    Without possessions, rank, or gentle birth;
    Then, by the offer of my heart, I might
    Repair the great injustice of your plight;
    I'd raise you from the dust, and proudly prove
    The purity and vastness of my love.
CÉLIMÈNE: This is a strange benevolence indeed!
    God grant that I may never be in need. . . .
    Ah, here's Monsieur Dubois, in quaint disguise.

SCENE 4. [CÉLIMÈNE, ALCESTE, DUBOIS]

ALCESTE: Well, why this costume? Why those frightened eyes?
    What ails you?
DUBOIS: Well, Sir, things are most mysterious.
ALCESTE: What do you mean?
DUBOIS: I fear they're very serious.
ALCESTE: What?
DUBOIS: Shall I speak more loudly?
ALCESTE: Yes; speak out.
DUBOIS: Isn't there someone here, Sir?
ALCESTE: Speak, you lout!
    Stop wasting time.
DUBOIS: Sir, we must slip away.
ALCESTE: How's that?
DUBOIS: We must decamp without delay.
ALCESTE: Explain yourself.
DUBOIS: I tell you we must fly.
ALCESTE: What for?
DUBOIS: We mustn't pause to say good-by.
ALCESTE: Now what d'you mean by all of this, you clown?
DUBOIS: I mean, Sir, that we've got to leave this town.
ALCESTE: I'll tear you limb from limb and joint from joint
    If you don't come more quickly to the point.

DUBOIS: Well, Sir, today a man in a black suit,
   Who wore a black and ugly scowl to boot,
   Left us a document scrawled in such a hand
   As even Satan couldn't understand.
   It bears upon your lawsuit, I don't doubt;
   But all hell's devils couldn't make it out.
ALCESTE: Well, well, go on. What then? I fail to see
   How this event obliges us to flee.
DUBOIS: Well, Sir: an hour later, hardly more,
   A gentleman who's often called before
   Came looking for you in an anxious way.
   Not finding you, he asked me to convey
   (Knowing I could be trusted with the same)
   The following message. . . . Now, what was his name?
ALCESTE: Forget his name, you idiot. What did he say?
DUBOIS: Well, it was one of your friends, Sir, anyway.
   He warned you to begone, and he suggested
   That if you stay, you may well be arrested.
ALCESTE: What? Nothing more specific? Think, man, think!
DUBOIS: No, Sir. He had me bring him pen and ink,
   And dashed you off a letter which, I'm sure,
   Will render things distinctly less obscure.
ALCESTE: Well—let me have it!
CÉLIMÈNE: What *is* this all about?
ALCESTE: God knows; but I have hopes of finding out.
   How long am I to wait, you blitherer?
DUBOIS [*after a protracted search for the letter*]: I must have left it on
      your table, Sir.
ALCESTE: I ought to . . .
CÉLIMÈNE: No, no, keep your self-control;
   Go find out what's behind his rigmarole.
ALCESTE: It seems that fate, no matter what I do,
   Has sworn that I may not converse with you;
   But, Madam, pray permit your faithful lover
   To try once more before the day is over.

✿ *Act V*

SCENE 1.   [ALCESTE, PHILINTE]

ALCESTE: No, it's too much. My mind's made up, I tell you.
PHILINTE: Why should this blow, however hard, compel you . . .
ALCESTE: No, no, don't waste your breath in argument;
    Nothing you say will alter my intent;
    This age is vile, and I've made up my mind
    To have no further commerce with mankind.
    Did not truth, honor, decency, and the laws
    Oppose my enemy and approve my cause?
    My claims were justified in all men's sight;
    I put my trust in equity and right;
    Yet, to my horror and the world's disgrace,
    Justice is mocked, and I have lost my case!
    A scoundrel whose dishonesty is notorious
    Emerges from another lie victorious!
    Honor and right condone his brazen fraud,
    While rectitude and decency applaud!
    Before his smirking face, the truth stands charmed,
    And virtue conquered, and the law disarmed!
    His crime is sanctioned by a court decree!
    And not content with what he's done to me,
    The dog now seeks to ruin me by stating
    That I composed a book now circulating,
    A book so wholly criminal and vicious
    That even to speak its title is seditious!
    Meanwhile Oronte, my rival, lends his credit
    To the same libelous tale, and helps to spread it!
    Oronte! a man of honor and of rank,
    With whom I've been entirely fair and frank;
    Who sought me out and forced me, willy-nilly,
    To judge some verse I found extremely silly;
    And who, because I properly refused
    To flatter him, or see the truth abused,
    Abets my enemy in a rotten slander!
    There's the reward of honesty and candor!
    The man will hate me to the end of time
    For failing to commend his wretched rhyme!
    And not this man alone, but all humanity

Do what they do from interest and vanity;
They prate of honor, truth, and righteousness,
But lie, betray, and swindle nonetheless.
Come then: man's villainy is too much to bear;
Let's leave this jungle and this jackal's lair.
Yes! treacherous and savage race of men,
You shall not look upon my face again.

PHILINTE: Oh, don't rush into exile prematurely;
Things aren't as dreadful as you make them, surely.
It's rather obvious, since you're still at large,
That people don't believe your enemy's charge.
Indeed, his tale's so patently untrue
That it may do more harm to him than you.

ALCESTE: Nothing could do that scoundrel any harm:
His frank corruption is his greatest charm,
And, far from hurting him, a further shame
Would only serve to magnify his name.

PHILINTE: In any case, his bald prevarication
Has done no injury to your reputation,
And you may feel secure in that regard.
As for your lawsuit, it should not be hard
To have the case reopened, and contest
This judgment . . .

ALCESTE: No, no, let the verdict rest.
Whatever cruel penalty it may bring,
I wouldn't have it changed for anything.
It shows the times' injustice with such clarity
That I shall pass it down to our posterity
As a great proof and signal demonstration
Of the black wickedness of this generation.
It may cost twenty thousand francs; but I
Shall pay their twenty thousand, and gain thereby
The right to storm and rage at human evil,
And send the race of mankind to the devil.

PHILINTE: Listen to me. . . .

ALCESTE: Why? What can you possibly say?
Don't argue, Sir; your labor's thrown away.
Do you propose to offer lame excuses
For men's behavior and the times' abuses?

PHILINTE: No, all you say I'll readily concede:
This is a low, conniving age indeed;
Nothing but trickery prospers nowadays,

And people ought to mend their shabby ways.
Yes, man's a beastly creature; but must we then
Abandon the society of men?
Here in the world, each human frailty
Provides occasion for philosophy,
And that is virtue's noblest exercise;
If honesty shone forth from all men's eyes,
If every heart were frank and kind and just,
What could our virtues do but gather dust
(Since their employment is to help us bear
The villainies of men without despair)?
A heart well-armed with virtue can endure. . . .
ALCESTE: Sir, you're a matchless reasoner, to be sure;
Your words are fine and full of cogency;
But don't waste time and eloquence on me.
My reason bids me go, for my own good.
My tongue won't lie and flatter as it should;
God knows what frankness it might next commit,
And what I'd suffer on account of it.
Pray let me wait for Célimène's return
In peace and quiet. I shall shortly learn,
By her response to what I have in view,
Whether her love for me is feigned or true.
PHILINTE: Till then, let's visit Éliante upstairs.
ALCESTE: No, I am too weighed down with somber cares.
Go to her, do; and leave me with my gloom
Here in the darkened corner of this room.
PHILINTE: Why, that's no sort of company, my friend;
I'll see if Éliante will not descend.

SCENE 2.   [CÉLIMÈNE, ORONTE, ALCESTE]

ORONTE: Yes, Madam, if you wish me to remain
Your true and ardent lover, you must deign
To give me some more positive assurance.
All this suspense is quite beyond endurance.
If your heart shares the sweet desires of mine,
Show me as much by some convincing sign;
And here's the sign I urgently suggest:
That you no longer tolerate Alceste,
But sacrifice him to my love, and sever
All your relations with the man forever.

CÉLIMÈNE: Why do you suddenly dislike him so?
  You praised him to the skies not long ago.
ORONTE: Madam, that's not the point. I'm here to find
  Which way your tender feelings are inclined.
  Choose, if you please, between Alceste and me,
  And I shall stay or go accordingly.
ALCESTE [*emerging from the corner*]: Yes, Madam, choose; this gentle-
    man's demand
  Is wholly just, and I support his stand.
  I too am true and ardent; I too am here
  To ask you that you make your feelings clear.
  No more delays, now; no equivocation;
  The time has come to make your declaration.
ORONTE: Sir, I've no wish in any way to be
  An obstacle to your felicity.
ALCESTE: Sir, I've no wish to share her heart with you;
  That may sound jealous, but at least it's true.
ORONTE: If, weighing us, she leans in your direction . . .
ALCESTE: If she regards you with the least affection . . .
ORONTE: I swear I'll yield her to you there and then.
ALCESTE: I swear I'll never see her face again.
ORONTE: Now, Madam, tell us what we've come to hear.
ALCESTE: Madam, speak openly and have no fear.
ORONTE: Just say which one is to remain your lover.
ALCESTE: Just name one name, and it will all be over.
ORONTE: What! Is it possible that you're undecided?
ALCESTE: What! Can your feelings possibly be divided?
CÉLIMÈNE: Enough: this inquisition's gone too far:
  How utterly unreasonable you are!
  Not that I couldn't make the choice with ease;
  My heart has no conflicting sympathies;
  I know full well which one of you I favor,
  And you'd not see me hesitate or waver.
  But how can you expect me to reveal
  So cruelly and bluntly what I feel?
  I think it altogether too unpleasant
  To choose between two men when both are present;
  One's heart has means more subtle and more kind
  Of letting its affections be divined,
  Nor need one be uncharitably plain
  To let a lover know he loves in vain.

ORONTE: No, no, speak plainly; I for one can stand it.
  I beg you to be frank.
ALCESTE: And I demand it.
  The simple truth is what I wish to know,
  And there's no need for softening the blow.
  You've made an art of pleasing everyone,
  But now your days of coquetry are done:
  You have no choice now, Madam, but to choose,
  For I'll know what to think if you refuse;
  I'll take your silence for a clear admission
  That I'm entitled to my worst suspicion.
ORONTE: I thank you for this ultimatum, Sir,
  And I may say I heartily concur.
CÉLIMÈNE: Really, this foolishness is very wearing:
  Must you be so unjust and overbearing?
  Haven't I told you why I must demur?
  Ah, here's Éliante; I'll put the case to her.

SCENE 3. [ÉLIANTE, PHILINTE, CÉLIMÈNE, ORONTE, ALCESTE]

CÉLIMÈNE: Cousin, I'm being persecuted here
  By these two persons, who, it would appear,
  Will not be satisfied till I confess
  Which one I love the more, and which the less,
  And tell the latter to his face that he
  Is henceforth banished from my company.
  Tell me, has ever such a thing been done?
ÉLIANTE: You'd best not turn to me; I'm not the one
  To back you in a matter of this kind:
  I'm all for those who frankly speak their mind.
ORONTE: Madam, you'll search in vain for a defender.
ALCESTE: You're beaten, Madam, and may as well surrender.
ORONTE: Speak, speak, you must; and end this awful strain.
ALCESTE: Or don't, and your position will be plain.
ORONTE: A single word will close this painful scene.
ALCESTE: But if you're silent, I'll know what you mean.

SCENE 4. [ARSINOÉ, CÉLIMÈNE, ÉLIANTE, ALCESTE, PHILINTE, ACASTE, CLITANDRE, ORONTE]

ACASTE [to CÉLIMÈNE]: Madam, with all due deference, we two
  Have come to pick a little bone with you.

CLITANDRE [*to* ORONTE *and* ALCESTE]: I'm glad you're present, Sirs; as
  you'll soon learn,
Our business here is also your concern.
ARSINOÉ [*to* CÉLIMÈNE]: Madam, I visit you so soon again
Only because of these two gentlemen,
Who came to me indignant and aggrieved
About a crime too base to be believed.
Knowing your virtue, having such confidence in it,
I couldn't think you guilty for a minute,
In spite of all their telling evidence;
And, rising above our little difference,
I've hastened here in friendship's name to see
You clear yourself of this great calumny.
ACASTE: Yes, Madam, let us see with what composure
You'll manage to respond to this disclosure.
You lately sent Clitandre this tender note.
CLITANDRE: And this one, for Acaste, you also wrote.
ACASTE [*to* ORONTE *and* ALCESTE]: You'll recognize this writing, Sirs, I
  think;
The lady is so free with pen and ink
That you must know it all too well, I fear.
But listen: this is something you should hear.

"How absurd you are to condemn my lightheartedness in society,
and to accuse me of being happiest in the company of others. Nothing could be more unjust; and if you do not come to me instantly
and beg pardon for saying such a thing, I shall never forgive you as
long as I live. Our big bumbling friend the Viscount . . ."

What a shame that he's not here.

"Our big bumbling friend the Viscount, whose name stands first
in your complaint, is hardly a man to my taste; and ever since the
day I watched him spend three-quarters of an hour spitting into a
well, so as to make circles in the water, I have been unable to think
highly of him. As for the little Marquess . . ."

In all modesty, gentlemen, that is I.

"As for the little Marquess, who sat squeezing my hand for such
a long while yesterday, I find him in all respects the most trifling
creature alive; and the only things of value about him are his cape
and his sword. As for the man with the green ribbons . . ."

[*To* ALCESTE.] It's your turn now, Sir.

"As for the man with the green ribbons, he amuses me now and then with his bluntness and his bearish ill-humor; but there are many times indeed when I think him the greatest bore in the world. And as for the sonneteer . . ."

[*To* ORONTE.] Here's your helping.

"And as for the sonneteer, who has taken it into his head to be witty, and insists on being an author in the teeth of opinion, I simply cannot be bothered to listen to him, and his prose wearies me quite as much as his poetry. Be assured that I am not always so well-entertained as you suppose; that I long for your company, more than I dare to say, at all these entertainments to which people drag me; and that the presence of those one loves is the true and perfect seasoning to all one's pleasures."

CLITANDRE: And now for me.

"Clitandre, whom you mention, and who so pesters me with his saccharine speeches, is the last man on earth for whom I could feel any affection. He is quite mad to suppose that I love him, and so are you, to doubt that you are loved. Do come to your senses; exchange your suppositions for his; and visit me as often as possible, to help me bear the annoyance of his unwelcome attentions."

It's a sweet character that these letters show,
And what to call it, Madam, you well know.
Enough. We're off to make the world acquainted
With this sublime self-portrait that you've painted.
ACASTE: Madam, I'll make you no farewell oration;
No, you're not worthy of my indignation.
Far choicer hearts than yours, as you'll discover,
Would like this little Marquess for a lover.

SCENE 5. [CÉLIMÈNTE, ÉLIANTE, ARSINOÉ, ALCESTE, ORONTE, PHILINTE]

ORONTE: So! After all those loving letters you wrote,
You turn on me like this, and cut my throat!
And your dissembling, faithless heart, I find,
Has pledged itself by turns to all mankind!
How blind I've been! But now I clearly see;
I thank you, Madam, for enlightening me.
My heart is mine once more, and I'm content;
The loss of it shall be your punishment.

[*To* ALCESTE.]

Sir, she is yours; I'll seek no more to stand
Between your wishes and this lady's hand.

SCENE 6. [CÉLIMÈNE, ÉLIANTE, ARSINOÉ, ALCESTE, PHILINTE]

ARSINOÉ [*to* CÉLIMÈNE]: Madam, I'm forced to speak. I'm far too stirred
    To keep my counsel, after what I've heard.
    I'm shocked and staggered by your want of morals.
    It's not my way to mix in others' quarrels;
    But really, when this fine and noble spirit,
    This man of honor and surpassing merit,
    Laid down the offering of his heart before you,
    How *could* you . . .
ALCESTE: Madam, permit me, I implore you,
    To represent myself in this debate.
    Don't bother, please, to be my advocate.
    My heart, in any case, could not afford
    To give your services their due reward;
    And if I chose, for consolation's sake,
    Some other lady, 'twould not be you I'd take.
ARSINOÉ: What makes you think you could, Sir? And how dare you
    Imply that I've been trying to ensnare you?
    If you can for a moment entertain
    Such flattering fancies, you're extremely vain.
    I'm not so interested as you suppose
    In Célimène's discarded gigolos.
    Get rid of that absurd illusion, do.
    Women like me are not for such as you.
    Stay with this creature, to whom you're so attached;
    I've never seen two people better matched.

SCENE 7. [CÉLIMÈNE, ÉLIANTE, ALCESTE, PHILINTE]

ALCESTE [*to* CÉLIMÈNE]: Well, I've been still throughout this exposé,
    Till everyone but me has said his say.
    Come, have I shown sufficient self-restraint?
    And may I now . . .
CÉLIMÈNE: Yes, make your just complaint.
    Reproach me freely, call me what you will;
    You've every right to say I've used you ill.
    I've wronged you, I confess it; and in my shame

The Misanthrope   **299**

I'll make no effort to escape the blame.
The anger of those others I could despise;
My guilt toward you I sadly recognize.
Your wrath is wholly justified, I fear;
I know how culpable I must appear,
I know all things bespeak my treachery,
And that, in short, you've grounds for hating me.
Do so; I give you leave.
ALCESTE: Ah, traitress—how,
How should I cease to love you, even now?
Though mind and will were passionately bent
On hating you, my heart would not consent.

[To ÉLIANTE and PHILINTE.]

Be witness to my madness, both of you;
See what infatuation drives one to;
But wait; my folly's only just begun,
And I shall prove to you before I'm done
How strange the human heart is, and how far
From rational we sorry creatures are.

[To CÉLIMÈNE.]

Woman, I'm willing to forget your shame,
And clothe your treacheries in a sweeter name;
I'll call them youthful errors, instead of crimes,
And lay the blame on these corrupting times.
My one condition is that you agree
To share my chosen fate, and fly with me
To that wild, trackless, solitary place
In which I shall forget the human race.
Only by such a course can you atone
For those atrocious letters; by that alone
Can you remove my present horror of you,
And make it possible for me to love you.
CÉLIMÈNE: What! I renounce the world at my young age,
And die of boredom in some hermitage?
ALCESTE: Ah, if you really loved me as you ought,
You wouldn't give the world a moment's thought;
Must you have me, and all the world beside?
CÉLIMÈNE: Alas, at twenty one is terrified
Of solitude. I fear I lack the force
And depth of soul to take so stern a course.

300 *Molière*

But if my hand in marriage will content you,
Why, there's a plan which I might well consent to,
And . . .
ALCESTE: No, I detest you now. I could excuse
Everything else, but since you thus refuse
To love me wholly, as a wife should do,
And see the world in me, as I in you,
Go! I reject your hand, and disenthrall
My heart from your enchantments, once for all.

SCENE 8. [ÉLIANTE, ALCESTE, PHILINTE]

ALCESTE [to ÉLIANTE]: Madam, your virtuous beauty has no peer;
Of all this world, you only are sincere;
I've long esteemed you highly, as you know;
Permit me ever to esteem you so,
And if I do not now request your hand,
Forgive me, Madam, and try to understand.
I feel unworthy of it; I sense that fate
Does not intend me for the married state,
That I should do you wrong by offering you
My shattered heart's unhappy residue,
And that in short . . .
ÉLIANTE: Your argument's well taken:
Nor need you fear that I shall feel forsaken.
Were I to offer him this hand of mine,
Your friend Philinte, I think, would not decline.
PHILINTE: Ah, Madam, that's my heart's most cherished goal,
For which I'd gladly give my life and soul.
ALCESTE [to ÉLIANTE and PHILINTE]: May you be true to all you now
        profess,
And so deserve unending happiness.
Meanwhile, betrayed and wronged in everything,
I'll flee this bitter world where vice is king,
And seek some spot unpeopled and apart
Where I'll be free to have an honest heart.
PHILINTE: Come, Madam, let's do everything we can
To change the mind of this unhappy man.

⚜ *Introduction to*

Modern Drama

I

A discussion of modern drama may properly begin with a few words on the cultural situation out of which it comes. We live in a time when nothing is certain. The traditional structures—philosophical, religious, political, and social—which have heretofore given shape and meaning to our lives seem to have broken down. We see little or no connection between these structures and the life we actually live. We recognize them now as ideal creations of the human spirit, wonderful as such, but nonetheless merely creations, the inventions of men. These structures once gave meaning and coherence to life; their loss has led to a sense of meaninglessness, incoherence, disintegration. We are not sure now who we are, what we are doing, what the point of it all is.

It is out of this sense of the contemporary situation that we can begin to understand modern drama; and we can begin by asking, first, why comedy and tragedy no longer seem valid in their pure form. Traditionally, these forms assumed that there was a coherent, meaningful order: in the community for comedy, and in the universe for tragedy. As we saw in the introduction to comedy, the function of comedy was to celebrate and perpetuate the established social order. It defended this order against malcontents who would undermine it: Malvolio, in *Twelfth Night*, Jaques in *As You Like It*, Alceste in *The Misanthrope*. It perpetuated the social order through marriage. In this way the anarchic spirit of sex was given an orderly, conservative, social direction.

The old comic spirit, we see, flourished in a time reasonably sure of its values, in coherent communities like those of Elizabethan England or the France of Louis XIV, communities shaped by meaningful ceremonies, rituals, manners, and values. Now much of comedy is ceremonial. But contemporary society is collective rather than communal, routine rather than genuinely ceremonial. The person has become a replaceable unit on the assembly line or in the organization. He has a mechanical function rather than a human life. A collective has its ceremonies and rituals, but they are without meaningful personal content. They are merely exploited, converted into the rhetoric of public occasions. They are no longer authentic, part of the natural rhythms of the community year; they are staged, managed. We cannot take these managed ceremonies seriously. And so modern comedy, which reflects society, is often a spoof of society. Thus in *Arms and the Man* Shaw uses the facade of the traditional comedy of manners to expose the ways of society; and he uses the trappings of the romantic theatre to make fun of it. Social forms and values have now become objects of comic criticism; for example, the state, the class structure, middle class values, the family, the idea of love. The comic hero has become a rebel against the status quo rather than its representative.

If the traditional comic form is not easily applicable today, the same can be said of the tragic form. As we saw in the introduction, tragedy assumes a transcendent, ideal, universal order, generally presided over by the gods. The tragic action is precipitated by the breakdown of this order. But now, when God is "dead," when the notion of a universal design, religious or secular, is difficult to believe in—at such a time the tragic sense is unlikely. The tragic abyss was populated by heroes in the old style, figures like Oedipus, Othello, and Lear, more than life-size, who filled the abyss with their tragic howls as they suffered the collapse of a world. Now we have a void, not a universal design; this is the overriding theme of modern drama. The void is populated by tramps, buffoons, or half-buried, grotesque blondes with parasols, likely to giggle rather than howl, wriggle rather than struggle. They have no values they are clear about, and so hardly know how to react, what to do, what choices to make. They are anti-heroic, often more comic than tragic. All this does not mean that there are not occasional plays in the spirit of traditional tragedy, like *Ghosts* or *Death of a Salesman*. But these instances are not representative. They do not express the peculiarly modern spirit, that ambiguity and uncertainty which prevents an unqualified tragic response.

The modern spirit is likely to be found in those plays which are shaped by what we may call the *mixed* mode. Here the situation is ambiguous, relative, problematic. The anti-hero does not have and thus cannot make those clear-cut choices available to Oedipus and Lear. Things are generally unresolved, and we remain in a state of tension, our emotions blocked, unrelieved. Thus we do not experience the catharsis of traditional tragedy, the purification which comes with the hero's discovery of the absolute character of his tragic condition, and his consequent transcendence of it. In the modern theatre the playwright often deliberately kills the possibility of catharsis. Pirandello rejects romantic passion (see his Preface) and Brecht did everything he could to leave his audience tense, frustrated emotionally (see the headnote on Brecht for a fuller account of this). In modern drama the hero—more accurately anti-hero or un-hero—finds it difficult to sustain a tragic mood. The solemn slips into the ridiculous, the tragic into farce. The modern mixed mode might be said to combine the vertical plunge of tragedy with the horizontal movement of comedy. Burlesque is now an authentic mode, parody a way of being serious. *Waiting for Godot* is subtitled a tragicomedy, Ionesco's *The Chairs* a tragic farce, and Pirandello's largely tragic *Six Characters* a comedy in the making. *The Wild Duck* is really a comical tragedy; and *The Cherry Orchard* may be seen as either tragedy, or as Chekhov himself understood it, a comedy. This mixture of the tragic and the comic is not new. It goes back at least to Euripides' *Alcestis*. It defines the relationship between the tragic trilogy and the satyr play in Greek drama, and it is beautifully realized in *Henry the Fourth, Part One*. But in these older plays the tragic and the comic were presented separately; their function was to comment on each other, providing a comic or tragic counterpoint. In our time the comic and the tragic are irresistibly bound to each other; they express each other; they are the discordant elements of one single, total response. This fusion is present with some frequency in *Hamlet* and *King Lear*, but it is not the defining factor. It accounts, though, for part of their appeal to a modern audience.

II

The theatre of the last hundred years is highly varied. No designations are altogether satisfactory; any are sure to do injustice to particular writers. Categories are a necessary evil here; the content of a play is the thing. Eric Bentley divides the plays of this period into two kinds, *realistic* and *anti-realistic*. But the latter term might be taken to imply that such plays are merely, or primarily, a reaction against realism; that is, that they are largely negative in their inspiration. On the contrary, they make their own positive statement of reality, but not in the conventionally realistic manner. It should be further understood that they often drew upon the familiar, the everyday; but through exaggeration, caricature and fragmentation they transformed it, made us see it differently, non-realistically. Instead of *anti-realistic*, then, we prefer the term *non-realistic*. This is a loose term at best, meant to include such different kinds of theatre as the symbolist plays of Yeats and Maeterlinck, Strindberg's dream and chamber plays, Brecht's epic theatre, Pirandello's theatre of the grotesque, the doctrinal drama of Eliot and Fry, and the theatre of the absurd of Beckett, Ionesco, Genet, Pinter, and others.

Realistic drama was a salutary reaction to the romantic boulevard plays of the mid-nineteenth century. Zola and others attacked the boulevard play on many grounds. He argued that it was inconsistent, dishonest, and superficial in its characters and situations; that it used formulas and contrived plots; that it exploited the emotions with cheap tricks to extract tears or laughter; that its characters spoke only one language, the clever language of the Parisian drawing room which was superficial and fatiguing rather than enlivening; and that it was at the same time marked by the blown-up language of declamation, majestic speech, and noble sentiments. What was wanted was a fidelity to life as it was "really" lived. This led to the presentation of everyday people of the middle and lower classes, and a change in setting from the elegant drawing rooms of the upper bourgeoisie and aristocracy to prosaic parlors and kitchens.

The middle class was the primary object of criticism, unlike the lower class, which was generally sentimentalized, though not, certainly, in *Ghosts*. This difference in treatment reflected contemporary liberal political attitudes. The middle class was criticized for its materialism, its concern with social status, its sentimentalization of the home and the family, its mediocrity, its general complacency; and worst of all, perhaps, its inability to commit itself with passion to anything but money. Historically, Ibsen is generally regarded as the most significant figure in realistic drama, and Zola the most influential spokesman for its naturalist subdivision. Ibsen's *A Doll's House* (1879) and the much superior *Ghosts* (1881) and *The Wild Duck* (1884) are landmarks. Strindberg was influenced by both Ibsen and Zola in his early and middle periods. *The Father* (1887), *Miss Julie* (1888), and *Creditors* (1890) are great examples of naturalism. Later, both Ibsen and, more radically, Strindberg broke in varying degrees with the realistic theatre. As a matter of fact, Ibsen had already experimented in non-realistic drama with *Peer Gynt* (1867), a tragicomic masterpiece.

The realists might be said to have developed their own kind of romanticism, the romance of the real. They sometimes sentimentalized poverty and made a virtue of mediocrity, of the common man. But at their best they were critical, sometimes humorously, as in Shaw and O'Casey; sometimes pessimistically. This pessimism particularly characterized that militant off-shoot of realism known as naturalism, a movement which included figures like Zola, the early Strindberg, and Gorky. Some naturalists seemed to go out of their way to offend gentility in the interest of what they believed to be the harsh, squalid truth—much of Tennessee Williams is a latter-day instance. In general, they argued that the person was subject to the laws of heredity and environment, and they followed the apparent logic of this argument with the harsh conclusion that he had no free will. Such an attitude reflected the scientific spirit of the day. It revealed a naive faith in scientific laws, and a passive submission to them. It was really unscientific, for we cannot verify so-called laws of human nature as we presumably can those of non-human nature.

Non-realistic drama developed in good measure out of a sense of the limitations of the realistic theatre, but also out of a dissatisfaction with realism in general as a way of getting at reality. It was felt that realism was limited by its preoccupation with the social surface, and by its empiricism, common sense, and rationalism. It overestimated reason and objectivity. This was the case even in plays which were complex psychologically, as were those of Strindberg. The psychology was still rationalistic; it explained motives. Realism did not account, in a word, for the irrational, the unexplainable. This included the strange world of the unconscious revealed by psychoanalysis, the source not only of aberrations but also of the reality in dreams, fairy tales, and myths. This reality had its own language, that of symbols, and its own forms, those of archetypes and archetypal patterns. Anthropologists and students of language had already argued for the universal character of symbols and myths. In *The Golden Bough*, Sir James Frazer has shown the prevalence of the archetype of the dying and resurrected god. The pattern of death and rebirth is a central theme of modern literature, religious and secular, central to Strindberg, Eliot, Joyce, Mann, Lawrence, Beckett, Yeats, Genet, and others. These archetypes, and the myths that embodied them, pointed up the underlying significance of the surface of life, as in the use of myth in the plays of O'Neill, Gide, Anouilh, Giraudoux, Sartre, Eliot, and others. In these instances the mythic subsurface secured its credibility through a realistic, that is familiar, surface. Further, as Eliot remarked, the "mythical method" was a way "of controlling, of ordering, of giving shape and a significance to the immense panorama of futility and anarchy which is contemporary history." It gave permanence to the transitory, a universal meaning to the local.

As the student will see, *Six Characters* is a kind of dramatic manifesto rejecting realism (and the romanticism of the emotions as well, as Pirandello points out in his preface), and announcing a new non-realistic drama. Of course, by this time (1921) the modern non-realistic drama had had a fairly long history, going back at least to Alfred Jarry's *Ubu Roi* (1896). Strindberg made his own declaration in his note to *A Dream Play* (1902). He remarks that "Anything can happen; everything is possible and probable. Time and space do not exist on a slight groundwork of reality, imagination spins and weaves new patterns made up of memories, experiences, unfettered fancies, absurdities and improvisations." This is a classic statement of non-realistic drama, especially that kind known as *expressionism*, a term invented *after* Strindberg. His note pointed to the direction expressionistic drama would take, the writer's *subjective* world, in which reality is fluid, shifting, unstable. Language of course falls short of this intention, but the intention is nonetheless there. In this drama the familiar is often seen through caricature, farce, fantasy, cartoon, and the like. This means a radical change in the *form* of the drama, which we shall treat further on. Some expressionists dealt largely with public, political subjects, as in Capek's *R.U.R.*, Kaiser's *Gas*, Rice's *Adding Machine*, and Toller's *Man and the Masses*. As Toller put it, they wanted to influence the environment, give it "a juster, a brighter face." Their aim was abstract, curiously Platonic; to re-create the environment "in its very essence." The social expressionists turned from the banal data of realism to capture its essence. The epic theatre of Bertolt Brecht (*Mother Courage* in this volume) was in some measure influenced by them. The form was generally fragmentary and episodic, the images grotesque, exaggerated; all this unlike realistic, dialectically conceived political dramas such as Ibsen's *The Enemy of the People* and Sartre's *Dirty Hands*.

One final point may be noted. Both realistic and non-realistic drama are critical of the values of middle class society. But the realists remain civilized; like Shaw, they continue to accept the idea of society; they criticize society within its framework. Non-realists like Beckett reject the idea of society; they consider civilization to be bankrupt. Social expressionists like Brecht, however, are politically, thus socially oriented; they merely want to substitute one kind of society (generally Marxist) for another. In this sense, Beckett is clearly more radical than the politically radical Brecht.

The opposing views of the realistic and non-realistic drama make for a difference in content, which means a difference in form. It is this we want now to consider. We should be aware, of course, that neither kind of drama is likely to be found in a pure form. Brecht's expressionistic epic theatre is strongly realistic, and Chekhov's realism anticipates the interiority and grotesquerie of non-realism. For pedagogical purposes, however, we will talk about the two kinds of drama as if they do exist in a pure form.

III

We may begin with the question of plot. In the last half of the nineteenth century popular drama took the form of the well-made play, a term coined by the French playwright Scribe, its most famous practitioner. In the well-made play cause leads to effect, conflicts have their resolutions, a logical structure builds up to a strong climax at the end of each act. The structure satisfies our need for order and clarity; and the resolution satisfies our need for catharsis. It has what we may call a *linear* development. Such a view of plot structure assumes a logic in the order of things. It reflects the rationalism of the bourgeois epoch, present in contemporary science, morality, economics, and politics. This rationalistic bias is evident in the frequent use of what we may call the dialectical mode. Question and answer, or point and counterpoint follow each other as in the dialectic of a Platonic dialogue. The early masters of this drama of ideas, as it is sometimes called, are Ibsen and Shaw, and their works in the present collection are examples. This kind of drama is a strong force in the modern theatre, as the plays of Sartre, Giraudoux, Anouilh, Osborne, and Miller attest. Shaw was its most articulate spokesman; he argued that it was superior even to Elizabethan drama because of its utilitarian value.

Ibsen appropriated the linear form from Scribe and his most famous successor, Sardou, but he gave it a more realistic substance. He did away with cleverly manipulated puppet characters (though not in *A Doll's House*), romantic intrigues, contrived plots, forced resolutions, and those other features we noted in connection with Zola's objections to boulevard drama. Yet even in the hands of a master the form has distinct limitations. The stress on the developing line of the plot tends to minimize the particular moment; the moment is subordinate to the development. And since the action builds up to a climax, the *discovery* of the true situation, there is a temptation to overdo the climax; they are often sensational, melodramatic, as in *A Doll's House* and *Ghosts*. This is the case even with *The Wild Duck*, where Ibsen had begun to break away from the linear play. Understated endings are more credible in the modern view; they are in keeping with our ironic, anti-heroic temper.

Many writers felt that the well-made play, resting on the assumption that existence is rational and orderly, did not correspond to the modern sense of things. They argued that we are no longer sure who we are, that at extreme moments we tend to doubt our very existence. Existence seemed to be a sequence of discrete, unrelated events, without form or meaning. With such a sense of things the self-contained, neatly resolved work of art did not seem valid. As we saw in our remarks on expressionism, a form whose structure was fragmented, made up of random, seemingly disconnected episodes seemed to be more appropriate. And so modern playwrights tend to avoid plots with resounding climaxes, powerful discoveries. They tend towards an action or non-action with a fairly even tenor, as in *The Cherry Orchard* and *Happy Days*. There is a development, of course; changes do take place, but these are not so obvious: for example, the harsher images in the second act of *Happy Days*. All this is anti-Aristotelian. We can see why Aristotle did not prefer the random, episodic structure. It does not suit tragedy; but it does suit comedy and the mixed mode of modern tragicomedy very well.

The *episodic* form, as we shall call it, has come to be characteristic of a good deal of modern theatre. In the episodic play each moment receives a maximum concentration; it is there in its own right, not subordinate to the line of development. Ideally, the total complex of meaning is thus continuously present. Such a play is shaped by the internal, organic relation of characters, ideas, motifs, and symbols rather than by the largely external, mechanical linkage of scenes. This external linkage rests on clock time, the basis of the rationalized structures and processes of industry and business, and, of course, the society which depends on them. The very word *episodic* suggests an attitude contrary to the synchronized business world. In the episodic play time is durational, flowing, the time of memory, of reflection, as in *The Cherry Orchard* and *Happy Days*. This kind of time is appropriate to the existential preoccupations of much of the non-realistic theatre.

IV

Let us turn now to another element of the drama, that of character. The general breakdown of traditional structures has led to a corresponding breakdown in the individual's sense of himself. Our philosophy, our religion, our politics, our society—all these seem less certain, less clearly *there* than they were a hundred years ago. Since it is these things which define a person, a clear definition now lacks credibility, is in fact often a comic subject, as in Ionesco. We have become problematic. We are vague about ourselves. We do not know who we are. We are strangers to ourselves in a world from which we have become estranged. Often, then, we do not find familiar, recognizable characters and situations in modern plays. This remark must, of course, be qualified. In *The Wild Duck, Arms and the Man,* and *The Cherry Orchard* the figures are clearly recognizable for they are conceived within the framework of a familiar society. But as we move further into the modern period, the tendency is for characters to become odd, difficult to feel at home with, as in *Six Characters;* or fairly improbable, as in *Happy Days.*

Our difficulties are multiplied by the fact that characters are sometimes generalized, conceived abstractly. This is literally the case in *Six Characters* (Father, Mother), *Mother Courage* (Protestant Chaplain, Cook) and other modern plays. But even where characters have particular names, they seem to be abstractions to some extent. Explanations for this are various; none are altogether satisfactory; and not all pertain to every writer. One factor, certainly, is the breakdown of those traditional structures we noted a moment ago. In middle class drama like that of Ibsen the interest was in the particular person, in his particular problems, and this within the framework of society. Now our interest is more in the total situation, in the largest questions: what is the meaning of life, what are we here for at all? The shift in concern is from the social to the metaphysical, or more popularly, the existential. This makes for characters whose concerns are general, and who therefore represent everyone. They can be likened to Everyman in the medieval morality play, *Everyman.* This was an allegory of the central concern of the Middle Ages—perhaps our age too—that of redemption, set in the total situation of the Middle Ages. It may be helpful to see some modern plays as quasi-redemptive. The search is now for meaning rather than redemption; or, we might say, the redemption is in the meaning and the search for it. Both medieval, pre-bourgeois drama and modern post-bourgeois drama stem from the same center of interest, the general human situation rather than the concerns of a particular class. And this general concern gives rise to generalized characters.

Other factors contributing to the generalization of character include forces like science, technology, political ideology, governmental and other bureaucracies, economic organization, and the conformist tendencies in society. For example, science approaches man abstractly, as something to be formulated and classified. Or, again, governmental bureaucracies, military and industrial organizations also see the individual abstractly, and treat him as a faceless unit; or, in Toller's phrase, "dreadful puppets dimly aware of the compelling fate that governs them." The individual cooperates in this tendency to facelessness by conforming to the pressures of the organization, society, national ideologies and the like. And this is compounded by the conventions which regulate our lives, a sequence of mechanical habits, habits of speech as well as action—which to some degree reduce us to automata.

This tendency towards abstraction in character corresponds to the tendency towards farce in modern drama. Soren Kierkegaard, the nineteenth century Danish existentialist, pointed out that "characters in the farce are all sketched on the abstract scale of 'the general.' Situation, action, and dialogue are all on this scale." He speaks also of "the roominess of its abstraction," a remark which suggests the free-wheeling mood of plays like those of Pirandello, Brecht, and Ionesco. It suggests as well the lack of social and esthetic guidelines, codes or decorum in the modern drama. Everything seems to be absurd, and so farce becomes the appropriate mode.

We might sum up our discussion of character and plot in a formula which may be helpful if used with circumspection. We may say that as we move further into the modern period we see a tendency toward characterless characters in plotless plots.

V

The abstract, generalized nature of the non-realistic theatre required its own peculiar setting, about which a word is in order. The solidity implicit in the three-walled, three-dimensional theatre was clearly inappropriate. Equally so was the faithful, objective reproduction of actuality, usually the parlor or kitchen, as an adequate representation of reality. Now the setting in the realistic theatre was, of course, meaningful; the middle-class drawing room reflected the material and cultural values and tastes of that class. In a loose sense, the setting might also be called symbolic. There is a radical difference, however, in the symbolism of the non-realistic theatre. Put simply, the world here is re-created in symbolic terms. Examples would include the fantasy world of Six Characters and the scorched, bare plain of Happy Days. The stage was the abstract, symbolic equivalent of the human situation.

VI

Our new sense of our existence calls for new means of expressing it. Language, of course, is the primary means, and this too has changed. The idioms of the nineteenth century are no longer appropriate. The often inflated style of that period fitted its heroic gestures and its romanticism; and its didacticism and sententiousness was appropriate to the certainties of the rising middle class. But now the gestures, moods, and certainties seem invalid, and the styles are parodied—for example, as with Hialmar Ekdal and Gregers Werle in *The Wild Duck*, and Lyubov, Petya, Gaev and others in *The Cherry Orchard*. This parody points to the emptiness of past forms: language, manners, the style of life; and the emptiness of the ideas those forms expressed.

The old idiom was conventional, wornout, dead. If the playwright could not use the old rhetoric, he could at least abuse it—in fact, he had to to clear the way. The task of the playwright, like that of the poet and novelist, was to renew the language. Our prevailing idiom in the drama is now homely and conversational; though it may at times have a lyric counterpoint. Metaphor is scarce, as though even this honored figure is pretentious, too literary. The sustained speech is more or less suspect; it implies an unwarranted confidence in logical argument. In *Happy Days*, Winnie frequently uses only phrases, as though distrusting the implications of logic, order, and wholeness in the sentence. But this does not mean that the modern idiom is flat and lifeless. In the hands of Beckett and others, homely language and simple syntax are heightened through stylization. This is realized through a style which becomes rigorous by way of an exaggerated simplicity; through a supple alternation of this simplicity with more formal language; through refrains and other devices of repetition; all of which give to prose the rigor of the best modern verse. From his simple base the playwright makes forays into the older, more elaborate rhetorical forms. But these forays are usually parodistic, not innocently rhetorical.

The modern playwright has a relatively limited rhetoric to work with; he uses the more expansive rhetoric of the past with guile. This limitation points to the fact that his hero is generally underprivileged. By this we mean that he is deprived of the wealth of the traditional hero: a universe shaped by Divine purpose, blessed with a sense of order generally conceived in the figure of the great chain of being: above, the angelic hierarchy; and below, the ecclesiastical, political, social and natural hierarchies. The traditional hero had a magnificent conception of himself, and he could call freely on a fitting rhetoric when the occasion demanded it. Sometimes it was high-powered, sometimes low-powered. Together they made for an imposing means of expression.

An unself-conscious, high-powered rhetoric—though undercut in various ways—fitted tragic figures who were kings and princes, or noble figures like Othello. It was one of the means of enlarging the hero, contributing to a general magnificence which made his transcendence credible to us. It is otherwise with the modern hero, more accurately an un-hero or anti-hero. He is deprived of a meaningful universe and society, and an unself-conscious rhetoric. This last deprivation points to the fact that he is further underprivileged since emotion is now suspect, likely to degenerate into mere words, as in Chekhov. We are too conscious to have unrestrained emotions; they are too readily qualified by all kinds of reservations, as with the Father in *Six Characters*. Still, his example indicates that we can nonetheless be passionate, if only to curse our excessive consciousness. The modern hero transcends his situation—if at all—through his consciousness, his awareness of it. This consciousness is attractive at its best, endowed with a marvelous humor and, at the same time, an intensity of feeling and a range of speculation which does honor to the seriousness with which the playwrights take the modern situation.

From all that has been said it is easy to see why our playwrights are so eccentric, seemingly perverse. But these qualities are merely modest reflections of the general perversion of human values in the last several decades. Our playwrights have merely made us aware of our situation; they have not created it. But we could ask for no better affirmation of the human spirit (to use the old rhetoric) than their incredibly fertile inventiveness. They have transformed the drama—and us too—with wit, humor, irony, and savage indignation. And—not the least—their new forms have given us new pleasures.

READINGS:

ARTAUD, ANTONIN, *The Theater and Its Double* (1938), tr. by M. C. Richards. New York: Grove Press, 1958.

BENTLEY, ERIC, *The Playwright as Thinker* (1946). New York: Meridian Books, 1955.

BRUSTEIN, ROBERT, *The Theatre of Revolt*. Boston: Little, Brown, 1964.

ESSLIN, MARTIN, *The Theatre of the Absurd*. New York: Doubleday Anchor, 1961.

GASSNER, JOHN, *Form and Idea in Modern Theatre*. New York: The Dryden Press, 1956.

GROSSVOGEL, DAVID I., *The Self-Conscious Stage in Modern French Drama*. New York: Columbia University Press, 1958.

———, *Four Playwrights and a Postscript*. Ithaca, New York: Cornell University Press, 1962.

GUICHARNAUD, JACQUES, *Modern French Theatre*. New Haven: Yale University Press, 1961.

KRUTCH, J. W., *Modernism in Modern Drama* (1953). Cornell: Cornell University Press, 1966.

McCARTHY, MARY, *Sights and Spectacles*. New York: Farrar, Straus & Cudahy, 1956.

Playwrights on Playwriting, ed. by Toby Cole. New York: Hill and Wang, Inc., 1961.

WELLWARTH, GEORGE, *The Theater of Protest and Paradox*. New York: New York University Press, 1964.

WILLIAMS, RAYMOND, *Drama from Ibsen to Eliot*. London: Chatto & Windus, 1954.

YOUNG, STARK, *Immortal Shadows*. New York: Scribners, 1948.

🎋 *Henrik Ibsen*

Henrik Ibsen (1828–1906) is best known for establishing the realistic drama at a time when the shallow, well-made boulevard plays of Sardou dominated the theatre. He set his plays in realistic, middle-class parlors; yet *A Doll's House* (1879) retained a number of the contrivances as well as the melodramatic pathos of the well-made play; and even the classic *Ghosts* (1881) relied upon sensational curtains. Ibsen dramatized the moral and social pretensions of the middle class. Sometimes he championed idealism, at other times—as in *The Wild Duck*—he exposed it, often hilariously. His early years no doubt influenced the work of this period. He was born in a merchant family in Skien, in southern Norway, but his father went bankrupt when Henrik was eight. At eighteen he was the father of an illegitimate child. By the 1840's he was writing plays, and from 1851 to 1862 he directed theatres in Bergen and Christiana. Constrained by small town, middle class ways, Ibsen left Norway in 1864 with his wife and child after the failure of his country to support Denmark against Prussia. He did not return until 1891.

Ibsen's range was enormous. Before his realistic period he wrote several verse plays, among them *Brand* (1866): powerful, tightly constructed, dealing with the conflict between our obligations to God and man; and *Peer Gynt* (1867): episodic, epic in structure, a brilliant, funny and moving criticism of the romantic self. Ibsen became increasingly symbolic in his later work; *The Wild Duck* (1884) marks the transition from his realistic period, though he does return to realism in *Hedda Gabler* (1890). Some of the major, symbolic works of his later years include *Rosmersholm* (1886), *The Master Builder* (1892), *John Gabriel Borkman* (1896), and his last play, *When We Dead Awaken* (1899).

READINGS:

BRADBROOK, M. C., *Ibsen, The Norwegian*. London: Chatto and Windus, 1948.

DOWNS, BRIAN W., *A Study of Six Plays by Ibsen*. Cambridge: Cambridge University Press, 1950.

McFarlane, James W., *Ibsen and the Temper of Norwegian Literature*. London: Oxford University Press, 1960.

Northam, John, *Ibsen's Dramatic Method*. London: Faber and Faber, 1953.

Tennant, P., *Ibsen's Dramatic Technique*. Cambridge: Bowes and Bowes, 1948.

Shaw, G. B., *The Quintessence of Ibsenism* (1891). New York: Hill and Wang, Inc., 1957.

Valency, M., *The Flower and the Castle*. New York: Macmillan Company, 1963.

Weigand, H. J., *The Modern Ibsen* (1925). New York: E. P. Dutton and Company, 1960.

⚜ The Wild Duck

Henrik Ibsen

Translated by Frances E. Archer

CHARACTERS

WERLE, a merchant, manufac-
turer, etc.
GREGERS WERLE, his son
OLD EKDAL
HIALMAR EKDAL, his son, a pho-
tographer
GINA EKDAL, Hialmar's wife
HEDVIG, their daughter, a girl of
fourteen
MRS. SÖRBY, Werle's housekeeper
RELLING, a doctor

MOLVIK, student of theology
GRÅBERG, Werle's bookkeeper
PETTERSEN, Werle's servant
SIX OTHER GENTLEMEN, guests at
Werle's dinner-party
SEVERAL HIRED WAITERS
JENSEN, a hired waiter
FLABBY GENTLEMAN
THIN-HAIRED GENTLEMAN
SHORT-SIGHTED GENTLEMAN

The first act passes in WERLE'S house, the remaining acts at HIALMAR
EKDAL'S.

⚜ Act I

SCENE—At WERLE'S house. A richly and comfortably furnished
study; bookcases and upholstered furniture; a writing-table, with
papers and documents, in the centre of the room; lighted lamps with
green shades, giving a subdued light. At the back, open folding-doors
with curtains drawn back. Within is seen a large and handsome room,
brilliantly lighted with lamps and branching candlesticks. In front, on
the right (in the study), a small baize door leads into WERLE'S office.
On the left, in front, a fireplace with a glowing coal fire, and farther
back a double door leading into the dining-room.

WERLE'S servant, PETTERSEN, in livery, and JENSEN, the hired waiter,
in black, are putting the study in order. In the large room, two or three

other hired waiters are moving about, arranging things and lighting more candles. From the dining-room, the hum of conversation and laughter of many voices are heard; a glass is tapped with a knife; silence follows, and a toast is proposed; shouts of "Bravo!" and then again a buzz of conversation.

PETTERSEN [*lights a lamp on the chimney-place and places a shade over it*]: Listen to them, Jensen! Now the old man's on his legs holding a long palaver about Mrs. Sörby.

JENSEN [*pushing forward an armchair*]: Is it true, what folks say, that they're—very good friends, eh?

PETTERSEN: Lord knows.

JENSEN: I've heard tell as he's been a lively customer in his day.

PETTERSEN: May be.

JENSEN: And he's giving this spread in honor of his son, they say.

PETTERSEN: Yes. His son came home yesterday.

JENSEN: This is the first time I ever heard as Mr. Werle had a son.

PETTERSEN: Oh, yes, he has a son, right enough. But he's a fixture, as you might say, up at the Höidal works. He's never once come to town all the years I've been in service here.

A WAITER [*in the doorway of the other room*]: Pettersen, here's an old fellow wanting——

PETTERSEN [*mutters*]: The devil—who's this now?

[OLD EKDAL *appears from the right, in the inner room. He is dressed in a threadbare overcoat with a high collar; he wears woollen mittens and carries in his hand a stick and a fur cap. Under his arm, a brown paper parcel. Dirty red-brown wig and small grey moustache.*]

PETTERSEN [*goes toward him*]: Good Lord—what do you want here?

EKDAL [*in the doorway*]: Must get into the office, Pettersen.

PETTERSEN: The office was closed an hour ago, and—

EKDAL: So they told me at the front door. But Gråberg's in there still. Let me slip in this way, Pettersen; there's a good fellow. [*points towards the baize door*] It's not the first time I've come this way.

PETTERSEN: Well, you may pass. [*opens the door*] But mind you go out again the proper way, for we've got company.

EKDAL: I know, I know—h'm! Thanks, Pettersen, good old friend! Thanks! [*mutters softly*] Ass!

[*He goes into the office;* PETTERSEN *shuts the door after him.*]

JENSEN: Is he one of the office people?

PETTERSEN: No he's only an outside hand that does odd jobs of copying. But he's been a tip-topper in his day, has old Ekdal.

JENSEN: You can see he's been through a lot.

PETTERSEN: Yes; he was an army officer, you know.

JENSEN: You don't say so?

PETTERSEN: No mistake about it. But then he went into the timber trade or something of the sort. They say he once played Mr. Werle a very nasty trick. They were partners in the Höidal works at the time. Oh, I know old Ekdal well, I do. Many a nip of bitters and bottle of ale we two have drunk at Madame Eriksen's.

JENSEN: He don't look as if he'd much to stand treat with.

PETTERSEN: Why, bless you, Jensen, it's me that stands treat. I always think there's no harm in being a bit civil to folks that have seen better days.

JENSEN: Did he go bankrupt, then?

PETTERSEN: Worse than that. He went to prison.

JENSEN: To prison!

PETTERSEN: Or perhaps it was the Penitentiary.[1] [listens] Sh! They're leaving the table.

> [The dining-room door is thrown open from within by a couple of waiters. MRS. SÖRBY comes out conversing with two GENTLEMEN. Gradually the whole company follows, amongst them WERLE. Last come HIALMAR EKDAL and GREGERS WERLE.]

MRS. SÖRBY [in passing, to the servant]: Tell them to serve the coffee in the music-room, Pettersen.

PETTERSEN: Very well, Madam.

> [She goes with the two GENTLEMEN into the inner room and thence out to the right. PETTERSEN and JENSEN go out the same way.]

FLABBY GENTLEMAN [to THIN-HAIRED GENTLEMAN]: Whew! What a dinner!—It was no joke to do it justice!

THIN-HAIRED GENTLEMAN: Oh, with a little good-will one can get through a lot in three hours.

FLABBY GENTLEMAN: Yes, but afterwards, afterwards, my dear Chamberlain![2]

THIRD GENTLEMAN: I hear the coffee and maraschino are to be served in the music-room.

FLABBY GENTLEMAN: Bravo! Then perhaps Mrs. Sörby will play us something.

---

1. "Penitentiary" implies a less severe sentence than "prison." Like any good gossip, Pettersen opens with the shocker and backtracks toward the truth.   2. "Chamberlain" was the nonhereditary honorary title conferred by the King upon men of wealth and position. [Translator's note.]

THIN-HAIRED GENTLEMAN [*in a low voice*]: I hope Mrs. Sörby mayn't play us a tune we don't like, one of these days!

FLABBY GENTLEMAN: Oh, no, not she! Bertha will never turn against her old friends.

[*They laugh and pass into the inner room.*]

WERLE [*in a low voice, dejectedly*]: I don't think anybody noticed it, Gregers.

GREGERS [*looks at him*]: Noticed what?

WERLE: Did you not notice it either?

GREGERS: What do you mean?

WERLE: We were thirteen at table.

GREGERS: Indeed? Were there thirteen of us?

WERLE [*glances towards* HIALMAR EKDAL]: Our usual party is twelve. [*to the others*] This way, gentlemen!

[WERLE *and the others, all except* HIALMAR *and* GREGERS, *go out by the back, to the right.*]

HIALMAR [*who has overheard the conversation*]: You ought not to have invited me, Gregers.

GREGERS: What! Not ask my best and only friend to a party supposed to be in my honor——?

HIALMAR: But I don't think your father likes it. You see I am quite outside his circle.

GREGERS: So I hear. But I wanted to see you and have a talk with you, and I certainly shan't be staying long.—Ah, we two old schoolfellows have drifted far apart from each other. It must be sixteen or seventeen years since we met.

HIALMAR: Is it so long?

GREGERS: It is indeed. Well, how goes it with you? You look well. You have put on flesh and grown almost stout.

HIALMAR: Well, "stout" is scarcely the word; but I daresay I look a little more of a man than I used to.

GREGERS: Yes, you do; your outer man is in first-rate condition.

HIALMAR [*in a tone of gloom*]: Ah, but the inner man! That is a very different matter, I can tell you! Of course you know of the terrible catastrophe that has befallen me and mine since last we met.

GREGERS [*more softly*]: How are things going with your father now?

HIALMAR: Don't let us talk of it, old fellow. Of course my poor unhappy father lives with me. He hasn't another soul in the world to care for him. But you can understand that this is a miserable subject for me.—Tell me, rather, how you have been getting on up at the works.

GREGERS: I have had a delightfully lonely time of it—plenty of leisure to think and think about things. Come over here; we may as well make ourselves comfortable.

[*He seats himself in an armchair by the fire and draws* HIALMAR *down into another alongside of it.*]

HIALMAR [*sentimentally*]: After all, Gregers, I thank you for inviting me to your father's table, for I take it as a sign that you have got over your feeling against me.

GREGERS [*surprised*]: How could you imagine I had any feeling against you?

HIALMAR: You had at first, you know.

GREGERS: How at first?

HIALMAR: After the great misfortune. It was natural enough that you should. Your father was within an ace of being drawn into that— well, that terrible business.

GREGERS: Why should that give me any feeling against you? Who can have put that into your head?

HIALMAR: I know it did, Gregers; your father told me so himself.

GREGERS [*starts*]: My father! Oh, indeed. H'm.—Was that why you never let me hear from you?—not a single word.

HIALMAR: Yes.

GREGERS: Not even when you made up your mind to become a photographer?

HIALMAR: Your father said I had better not write to you at all, about anything.

GREGERS [*looking straight before him*]: Well, well, perhaps he was right.—But tell me now, Hialmar: are you pretty well satisfied with your present position?

HIALMAR [*with a little sigh*]: Oh, yes, I am; I have really no cause to complain. At first, as you may guess, I felt it a little strange. It was such a totally new state of things for me. But of course my whole circumstances were totally changed. Father's utter, irretrievable ruin, —the shame and disgrace of it, Gregers——

GREGERS [*affected*]: Yes, yes; I understand.

HIALMAR: I couldn't think of remaining at college; there wasn't a shilling to spare; on the contrary, there were debts—mainly to your father, I believe——

GREGERS: H'm——

HIALMAR: In short, I thought it best to break, once for all, with my old surroundings and associations. It was your father that specially urged me to it; and since he interested himself so much in me——

GREGERS: My father did?

HIALMAR: Yes, you surely knew that, didn't you? Where do you suppose I found the money to learn photography, and to furnish a studio and make a start? All that cost a pretty penny, I can tell you.

GREGERS: And my father provided the money?

HIALMAR: Yes, my dear fellow, didn't you know? I understood him to say he had written to you about it.

GREGERS: Not a word about his part in the business. He must have forgotten it. Our correspondence has always been purely a business one. So it was my father that——!

HIALMAR: Yes, certainly. He didn't wish it to be generally known; but he was. And of course it was he, too, that put me in a position to marry. Don't you—don't you know about that either?

GREGERS: No, I haven't heard a word of it. [shakes him by the arm] But, my dear Hialmar, I can't tell you what pleasure all this gives me—pleasure, and self-reproach. I have perhaps done my father injustice after all—in some things. This proves that he has a heart. It shows a sort of compunction——

HIALMAR: Compunction——?

GREGERS: Yes, yes—whatever you like to call it. Oh, I can't tell you how glad I am to hear this of father.—So you are a married man, Hialmar! That is further than I shall ever get. Well, I hope you are happy in your married life?

HIALMAR: Yes, thoroughly happy. She is as good and capable a wife as any man could wish for. And she is by no means without culture.

GREGERS [rather surprised]: No, of course not.

HIALMAR: You see, life is itself an education. Her daily intercourse with me—— And then we know one or two rather remarkable men, who come a good deal about us. I assure you, you would hardly know Gina again.

GREGERS: Gina?

HIALMAR: Yes; had you forgotten that her name was Gina?

GREGERS: Whose name? I haven't the slightest idea——

HIALMAR: Don't you remember that she used to be in service here?

GREGERS [looks at him]: Is it Gina Hansen——?

HIALMAR: Yes, of course it is Gina Hansen.

GREGERS: ——who kept house for us during the last year of my mother's illness?

HIALMAR: Yes, exactly. But, my dear friend, I'm quite sure your father told you that I was married.

GREGERS [who has risen]: Oh, yes, he mentioned it; but not that—— [walking about the room] Stay—perhaps he did—now that I think of it. My father always writes such short letters. [half seats himself *on the arm of the chair*] Now tell me, Hialmar—this is interesting —how did you come to know Gina—your wife?

HIALMAR: The simplest thing in the world. You know Gina did not stay here long; everything was so much upset at that time, owing to your mother's illness and so forth, that Gina was not equal to it all; so she gave notice and left. That was the year before your mother died—or it may have been the same year.

GREGERS: It was the same year. I was up at the works then. But afterwards——?

HIALMAR: Well, Gina lived at home with her mother, Madame Hansen, an excellent hard-working woman, who kept a little eating-house. She had a room to let, too, a very nice comfortable room.

GREGERS: And I suppose you were lucky enough to secure it?

HIALMAR: Yes; in fact, it was your father that recommended it to me. So it was there, you see, that I really came to know Gina.

GREGERS: And then you got engaged?

HIALMAR: Yes. It doesn't take young people long to fall in love——; h'm—

GREGERS [*rises and moves about a little*]: Tell me: was it after your engagement—was it then that my father—I mean was it then that you began to take up photography?

HIALMAR: Yes, precisely. I wanted to make a start and to set up house as soon as possible; and your father and I agreed that this photography business was the readiest way. Gina thought so, too. Oh, and there was another thing in its favor, by-the-bye: it happened, luckily, that Gina had learnt to retouch.

GREGERS: That chimed in marvellously.

HIALMAR [*pleased, rises*]: Yes, didn't it? Don't you think it was a marvellous piece of luck?

GREGERS: Oh, unquestionably. My father seems to have been almost a kind of providence for you.

HIALMAR [*with emotion*]: He did not forsake his old friend's son in the hour of his need. For he has a heart, you see.

MRS. SÖRBY [*enters, arm-in-arm with* WERLE]: Nonsense, my dear Mr. Werle; you mustn't stop there any longer staring at all the lights. It's very bad for you.

WERLE [*lets go her arm and passes his hand over his eyes*]: I daresay you are right.

[PETTERSEN *and* JENSEN *carry round refreshment trays.*]

MRS. SÖRBY [*to the guests in the other room*]: This way, if you please, gentlemen. Whoever wants a glass of punch must be so good as to come in here.

FLABBY GENTLEMAN [*comes up to* MRS. SÖRBY]: Surely, it isn't possible that you have suspended our cherished right to smoke?

MRS. SÖRBY: Yes. No smoking here, in Mr. Werle's sanctum, Chamberlain.

THIN-HAIRED GENTLEMAN: When did you enact these stringent amendments to the cigar law, Mrs. Sörby?

MRS. SÖRBY: After the last dinner, Chamberlain, when certain persons permitted themselves to overstep the mark.

THIN-HAIRED GENTLEMAN: And may one never overstep the mark a little bit, Madame Bertha? Not the least little bit?

MRS. SÖRBY: Not in any respect whatsoever, Mr. Balle.

[*Most of the guests have assembled in the study; servants hand round glasses of punch.*]

WERLE [*to* HIALMAR, *who is standing beside a table*]: What are you studying so intently, Ekdal?

HIALMAR: Only an album, Mr. Werle.

THIN-HAIRED GENTLEMAN [*who is wandering about*]: Ah, photographs! They are quite in your line, of course.

FLABBY GENTLEMAN [*in an armchair*]: Haven't you brought any of your own with you?

HIALMAR: No, I haven't.

FLABBY GENTLEMAN: You ought to have; it's very good for the digestion to sit and look at pictures.

THIN-HAIRED GENTLEMAN: And it contributes to the entertainment, you know.

SHORT-SIGHTED GENTLEMAN: And all contributions are thankfully received.

MRS. SÖRBY: The Chamberlains think that when one is invited out to dinner, one ought to exert oneself a little in return, Mr. Ekdal.

FLABBY GENTLEMAN: Where one dines so well, that duty becomes a pleasure.

THIN-HAIRED GENTLEMAN: And when it's a case of the struggle for existence, you know——

MRS. SÖRBY: I quite agree with you!

[*They continue the conversation, with laughter and joking.*]

GREGERS [*softly*]: You must join in, Hialmar.

HIALMAR [*writhing*]: What am I to talk about?

FLABBY GENTLEMAN: Don't you think, Mr. Werle, that Tokay may be considered one of the more wholesome sorts of wine?

WERLE [*by the fire*]: I can answer for the Tokay you had today, at any rate; it's one of the very finest seasons. Of course you would notice that.

FLABBY GENTLEMAN: Yes, it had a remarkably delicate flavor.

HIALMAR [shyly]: Is there any difference between the seasons?

FLABBY GENTLEMAN [laughs]: Come! That's good!

WERLE [smiles]: It really doesn't pay to set fine wine before you.

THIN-HAIRED GENTLEMAN: Tokay is like photographs, Mr. Ekdal: they both need sunshine. Am I not right?

HIALMAR: Yes, light is important, no doubt.

MRS. SÖRBY: And it's exactly the same with Chamberlains—they, too, depend very much on sunshine,[3] as the saying is.

THIN-HAIRED GENTLEMAN: Oh, fie! That's a very threadbare sarcasm!

SHORT-SIGHTED GENTLEMAN: Mrs. Sörby is coming out——

FLABBY GENTLEMAN: ——and at our expense, too. [holds up his finger] reprovingly] Oh, Madame Bertha, Madame Bertha!

MRS. SÖRBY: Yes, and there's not the least doubt that the seasons differ greatly. The old vintages are the finest.

SHORT-SIGHTED GENTLEMAN: Do you reckon me among the old vintages?

MRS. SÖRBY: Oh, far from it.

THIN-HAIRED GENTLEMAN: There now! But me, dear Mrs. Sörby——?

FLABBY GENTLEMAN: Yes, and me? What vintage should you say that we belong to?

MRS. SÖRBY: Why, to the sweet vintages, gentlemen.

[She sips a glass of punch. The GENTLEMEN laugh and flirt with her.]

WERLE: Mrs. Sörby can always find a loop-hole—when she wants to. Fill your glasses, gentlemen! Pettersen, will you see to it—! Gregers, suppose we have a glass together. [GREGERS does not move.] Won't you join us, Ekdal? I found no opportunity of drinking with you at table.

[GRÅBERG, the bookkeeper, looks in at the baize door.]

GRÅBERG: Excuse me, sir, but I can't get out.

WERLE: Have you been locked in again?

GRÅBERG: Yes, and Flakstad has carried off the keys.

WERLE: Well, you can pass out this way.

GRÅBERG: But there's some one else——

WERLE: All right; come through, both of you. Don't be afraid.

[GRÅBERG and OLD EKDAL come out of the office.]

WERLE [involuntarily]: Ugh!

[The laughter and talk among the guests cease. HIALMAR

3. The "sunshine" of court favor. [Translator's note.]

starts at the sight of his father, puts down his glass and turns towards the fireplace.]

EKDAL [does not look up, but makes little bows to both sides as he passes, murmuring]: Beg pardon, come the wrong way. Door locked —door locked. Beg pardon.

[He and GRÅBERG go out by the back, to the right.]

WERLE [between his teeth]: That idiot Gråberg.

GREGERS [opened-mouthed and staring, to HIALMAR]: Why surely that wasn't——!

FLABBY GENTLEMAN: What's the matter? Who was it?

GREGERS: Oh, nobody; only the bookkeeper and some one with him.

SHORT-SIGHTED GENTLEMAN [to HIALMAR]: Did you know that man?

HIALMAR: I don't know—I didn't notice——

FLABBY GENTLEMAN: What the deuce has come over every one?

[He joins another group who are talking softly.]

MRS. SÖRBY [whispers to the servant]: Give him something to take with him;—something good, mind.

PETTERSEN [nods]: I'll see to it. [goes out]

GREGERS [softly and with emotion, to HIALMAR]: So that was really he!

HIALMAR: Yes.

GREGERS: And you could stand there and deny that you knew him!

HIALMAR [whispers vehemently]: But how could I——!

GREGERS: ——acknowledge your own father?

HIALMAR [with pain]: Oh, if you were in my place——

[The conversation amongst the guests, which has been carried on in a low tone, now swells into constrained joviality.]

THIN-HAIRED GENTLEMAN [approaching HIALMAR and GREGERS in a friendly manner]: Aha! Reviving old college memories, eh? Don't you smoke, Mr. Ekdal? May I give you a light? Oh, by-the-bye, we mustn't——

HIALMAR: No, thank you, I won't——

FLABBY GENTLEMAN: Haven't you a nice little poem you could recite to us, Mr. Ekdal? You used to recite so charmingly.

HIALMAR: I am sorry I can't remember anything.

FLABBY GENTLEMAN: Oh, that's a pity. Well, what shall we do, Balle? [Both GENTLEMEN move away and pass out into the other room.]

HIALMAR [gloomily]: Gregers—I am going! When a man has felt the crushing hand of Fate, you see—— Say good-bye to your father for me.

GREGERS: Yes, yes. Are you going straight home?

HIALMAR: Yes. Why?

GREGERS: Oh, because I may perhaps look in on you later.

HIALMAR: No, you mustn't do that. You must not come to my home. Mine is a melancholy abode, Gregers, especially after a splendid banquet like this. We can always arrange to meet somewhere in the town.

MRS. SÖRBY [who has quietly approached]: Are you going, Ekdal?

HIALMAR: Yes.

MRS. SÖRBY: Remember me to Gina.

HIALMAR: Thanks.

MRS. SÖRBY: And say I am coming up to see her one of these days.

HIALMAR: Yes, thank you. [to GREGERS] Stay here; I will slip out unobserved.

[He saunters away, then into the other room, and so out to the right.]

MRS. SÖRBY [softly to the servant, who has come back]: Well, did you give the old man something?

PETTERSEN: Yes; I sent him off with a bottle of cognac.

MRS. SÖRBY: Oh, you might have thought of something better than that.

PETTERSEN: Oh, no, Mrs. Sörby; cognac is what he likes best in the world.

FLABBY GENTLEMAN [in the doorway with a sheet of music in his hand]: Shall we play a duet, Mrs. Sörby?

MRS. SÖRBY: Yes, suppose we do.

THE GUESTS: Bravo, bravo!

[She goes with all the guests through the back room, out to the right. GREGERS remains standing by the fire. WERLE is looking for something on the writing-table and appears to wish that GREGERS would go; as GREGERS does not move, WERLE goes towards the door.]

GREGERS: Father, won't you stay a moment?

WERLE [stops]: What is it?

GREGERS: I must have a word with you.

WERLE: Can it not wait till we are alone?

GREGERS: No, it cannot; for perhaps we shall never be alone together.

WERLE [drawing nearer]: What do you mean by that?

[During what follows, the pianoforte is faintly heard from the distant music-room.]

GREGERS: How has that family been allowed to go so miserably to the wall?

WERLE: You mean the Ekdals, I suppose.

GREGERS: Yes, I mean the Ekdals. Lieutenant Ekdal was once so closely associated with you.

WERLE: Much too closely; I have felt that to my cost for many a year. It is thanks to him that I—yes I—have had a kind of slur cast upon my reputation.

GREGERS [softly]: Are you sure that he alone was to blame?

WERLE: Who else do you suppose——?

GREGERS: You and he acted together in that affair of the forests——

WERLE: But was it not Ekdal that drew the map of the tracts we had bought—that fraudulent map! It was he who felled all that timber illegally on Government ground. In fact, the whole management was in his hands. I was quite in the dark as to what Lieutenant Ekdal was doing.

GREGERS: Lieutenant Ekdal himself seems to have been very much in the dark as to what he was doing.

WERLE: That may be. But the fact remains that he was found guilty and I acquitted.

GREGERS: Yes, I know that nothing was proved against you.

WERLE: Acquittal is acquittal. Why do you rake up these old miseries that turned my hair grey before its time? Is that the sort of thing you have been brooding over up there, all these years? I can assure you, Gregers, here in the town the whole story has been forgotten long ago—so far as I am concerned.

GREGERS: But that unhappy Ekdal family——

WERLE: What would you have had me do for the people? When Ekdal came out of prison he was a broken-down being, past all help. There are people in the world who dive to the bottom the moment they get a couple of slugs in their body and never come to the surface again. You may take my word for it, Gregers, I have done all I could without positively laying myself open to all sorts of suspicion and gossip——

GREGERS: Suspicion——? Oh, I see.

WERLE: I have given Ekdal copying to do for the office, and I pay him far, far more for it than his work is worth——

GREGERS [without looking at him]: H'm; that I don't doubt.

WERLE: You laugh? Do you think I am not telling you the truth? Well, I certainly can't refer you to my books, for I never enter payments of that sort.

GREGERS [smiles coldly]: No, there are certain payments it is best to keep no account of.

WERLE [taken aback]: What do you mean by that?

GREGERS [*mustering up courage*]: Have you entered what it cost you to have Hialmar Ekdal taught photography?

WERLE: I? How "entered" it?"

GREGERS: I have learnt that it was you who paid for his training. And I have learnt, too, that it was you who enabled him to set up house so comfortably.

WERLE: Well, and yet you talk as though I had done nothing for the Ekdals! I can assure you these people have cost me enough in all conscience.

GREGERS: Have you entered any of these expenses in your books?

WERLE: Why do you ask?

GREGERS: Oh, I have my reasons. Now tell me: when you interested yourself so warmly in your old friend's son—it was just before his marriage, was it not?

WERLE: Why, deuce take it—after all these years, how can I——?

GREGERS: You wrote me a letter about that time—a business letter, of course; and in a postscript you mentioned—quite briefly—that Hialmar Ekdal had married a Miss Hansen.

WERLE: Yes, that was quite right. That was her name.

GREGERS: But you did not mention that this Miss Hansen was Gina Hansen—our former housekeeper.

WERLE [*with a forced laugh of derision*]: No; to tell the truth, it didn't occur to me that you were so particularly interested in our former housekeeper.

GREGERS: No more I was. But [*lowers his voice*] there were others in this house who were particularly interested in her.

WERLE: What do you mean by that? [*flaring up*] You are not alluding to me, I hope?

GREGERS [*softly but firmly*]: Yes, I am alluding to you.

WERLE: And you dare——! You presume to——! How can that ungrateful hound—that photographer fellow—how dare he go making such insinuations!

GREGERS: Hialmar has never breathed a word about this. I don't believe he has the faintest suspicion of such a thing.

WERLE: Then where have you got it from? Who can have put such notions in your head?

GREGERS: My poor unhappy mother told me; and that the very last time I saw her.

WERLE: Your mother! I might have known as much! You and she— you always held together. It was she who turned you against me, from the first.

GREGERS: No, it was all that she had to suffer and submit to, until she broke down and came to such a pitiful end.

WERLE: Oh, she had nothing to suffer or submit to; not more than most people, at all events. But there's no getting on with morbid, overstrained creatures—that I have learnt to my cost.—And you could go on nursing such a suspicion—burrowing into all sorts of old rumors and slanders against your own father! I must say, Gregers, I really think that at your age you might find something more useful to do.

GREGERS: Yes, it is high time.

WERLE: Then perhaps your mind would be easier than it seems to be now. What can be your object in remaining up at the works, year out and year in, drudging away like a common clerk, and not drawing a farthing more than the ordinary monthly wage? It is downright folly.

GREGERS: Ah, if I were only sure of that.

WERLE: I understand you well enough. You want to be independent; you won't be beholden to me for anything. Well, now there happens to be an opportunity for you to become independent, your own master in everything.

GREGERS: Indeed? In what way——?

WERLE: When I wrote you insisting on your coming to town at once—h'm——

GREGERS: Yes, what is it you really want of me? I have been waiting all day to know.

WERLE: I want to propose that you should enter the firm, as partner.

GREGERS: I! Join your firm? As partner?

WERLE: Yes. It would not involve our being constantly together. You could take over the business here in town, and I should move up to the works.

GREGERS: You would?

WERLE: The fact is, I am not so fit for work as I once was. I am obliged to spare my eyes, Gregers; they have begun to trouble me.

GREGERS: They have always been weak.

WERLE: Not as they are now. And, besides, circumstances might possibly make it desirable for me to live up there—for a time, at any rate.

GREGERS: That is certainly quite a new idea to me.

WERLE: Listen, Gregers: there are many things that stand between us; but we are father and son after all. We ought surely to be able to come to some sort of understanding with each other.

GREGERS: Outwardly, you mean, of course?

WERLE: Well, even that would be something. Think it over, Gregers. Don't you think it ought to be possible? Eh?

GREGERS [*looking at him coldly*]: There is something behind all this.

WERLE: How so?

GREGERS: You want to make use of me in some way.

WERLE: In such a close relationship as ours, the one can always be useful to the other.

GREGERS: Yes, so people say.

WERLE: I want very much to have you at home with me for a time. I am a lonely man, Gregers; I have always felt lonely, all my life through; but most of all now that I am getting up in years. I feel the need of some one about me——

GREGERS: You have Mrs. Sörby.

WERLE: Yes, I have her; and she has become, I may say, almost indispensable to me. She is lively and even-tempered; she brightens up the house; and that is a very great thing for me.

GREGERS: Well, then, you have everything just as you wish it.

WERLE: Yes, but I am afraid it can't last. A woman so situated may easily find herself in a false position, in the eyes of the world. For that matter it does a man no good, either.

GREGERS: Oh, when a man gives such dinners as you give, he can risk a great deal.

WERLE: Yes, but how about the woman, Gregers? I fear she won't accept the situation much longer; and even if she did—even if, out of attachment to me, she were to take her chance of gossip and scandal and all that——? Do you think, Gregers—you with your strong sense of justice——

GREGERS [*interrupts him*]: Tell me in one word: are you thinking of marrying her?

WERLE: Suppose I were thinking of it? What then?

GREGERS: That's what I say: what then?

WERLE: Should you be inflexibly opposed to it!

GREGERS: Not at all. Not by any means.

WERLE: I was not sure whether your devotion to your mother's memory——

GREGERS: I am not overstrained.

WERLE: Well, whatever you may or may not be, at all events you have lifted a great weight from my mind. I am extremely pleased that I can reckon on your concurrence in this matter.

GREGERS [*looking intently at him*]: Now I see the use you want to put me to.

WERLE: Use to put you to? What an expression!

GREGERS: Oh, don't let us be nice in our choice of words—not when we are alone together, at any rate. [*with a short laugh*] Well, well. So this is what made it absolutely essential that I should come to town in person. For the sake of Mrs. Sörby, we are to get up a pretence at family life in the house—a tableau of filial affection! That will be something new indeed.

WERLE: How dare you speak in that tone!

GREGERS: Was there ever any family life here? Never since I can remember. But now, forsooth, your plans demand something of the sort. No doubt it will have an excellent effect when it is reported that the son has hastened home, on the wings of filial piety, to the grey-haired father's wedding-feast. What will then remain of all the rumors as to the wrongs the poor dead mother had to submit to? Not a vestige. Her son annihilates them at one stroke.

WERLE: Gregers—I believe there is no one in the world you detest as you do me.

GREGERS [*softly*]: I have seen you at too close quarters.

WERLE: You have seen me with your mother's eyes. [*lowers his voice a little*] But you should remember that her eyes were—clouded now and then.

GREGERS [*quivering*]: I see what you are hinting at. But who was to blame for mother's unfortunate weakness? Why, you, and all those——! The last of them was this woman that you palmed off upon Hialmar Ekdal, when you were—— Ugh!

WERLE [*shrugs his shoulders*]: Word for word as if it were your mother speaking!

GREGERS [*without heeding*]: And there he is now, with his great, confiding, childlike mind, compassed about with all this treachery— living under the same roof with such a creature and never dreaming that what he calls his home is built upon a lie! [*comes a step nearer*] When I look back upon your past, I seem to see a battle-field with shattered lives on every hand.

WERLE: I begin to think the chasm that divides us is too wide.

GREGERS [*bowing, with self-command*]: So I have observed; and therefore I take my hat and go.

WERLE: You are going! Out of the house?

GREGERS: Yes. For at last I see my mission in life.

WERLE: What mission?

GREGERS: You would only laugh if I told you.

WERLE: A lonely man doesn't laugh so easily, Gregers.

GREGERS [*pointing towards the background*]: Look, father,—the

The Wild Duck   **333**

Chamberlains are playing blind-man's-buff with Mrs. Sörby.—Good-night and good-bye.

[*He goes out by the back to the right. Sounds of laughter and merriment from the company, who are now visible in the outer room.*]

WERLE [*muttering contemptuously after* GREGERS]: Ha——! Poor wretch—and he says he is not overstrained!

❦ Act II

SCENE—HIALMAR EKDAL's *studio, a good-sized room, evidently in the top story of the building. On the right, a sloping roof of large panes of glass, half-covered by a blue curtain. In the right-hand corner, at the back, the entrance door; farther forward, on the same side, a door leading to the sitting-room. Two doors on the opposite side, and between them an iron stove. At back, a wide double sliding-door. The studio is plainly but comfortably fitted up and furnished. Between the doors on the right, standing out a little from the wall, a sofa with a table and some chairs; on the table a lighted lamp with a shade; beside the stove an old arm-chair. Photographic instruments and apparatus of different kinds lying about the room. Against the back wall, to the left of the double door, stands a bookcase containing a few books, boxes, and bottles of chemicals, instruments, tools, and other objects. Photographs and small articles, such as camel's-hair pencils, paper, and so forth, lie on the table.*

GINA EKDAL *sits on a chair by the table, sewing.* HEDVIG *is sitting on the sofa, with her hands shading her eyes and her thumbs in her ears, reading a book.*

GINA [*glances once or twice at* HEDVIG, *as if with secret anxiety; then says*]: Hedvig!

[HEDVIG *does not hear.*]

GINA [*repeats more loudly*]: Hedvig!

HEDVIG [*takes away her hands and looks up*]: Yes, mother?

GINA: Hedvig dear, you mustn't sit reading any longer now.

HEDVIG: Oh, mother, mayn't I read a little more? Just a little bit?

GINA: No, no, you must put away your book now. Father doesn't like it; he never reads hisself in the evening.

HEDVIG [*shuts the book*]: No, father doesn't care much about reading.

GINA [*puts aside her sewing and takes up a lead pencil and a little account-book from the table*]: Can you remember how much we paid for the butter today?

HEDVIG: It was one crown sixty-five.

GINA: That's right. [*puts it down*] Its terrible what a lot of butter we get through in this house. Then there was the smoked sausage, and the cheese—let me see—[*writes*]—and the ham—[*adds up*] Yes, that makes just——

HEDVIG: And then the beer.

GINA: Yes, to be sure. [*writes*] How it do mount up! But we can't manage with no less.

HEDVIG: And then you and I didn't need anything hot for dinner, as father was out.

GINA: No; that was so much to the good. And then I took eight crowns fifty for the photographs.

HEDVIG: Really! So much as that?

GINA: Exactly eight crowns fifty.

> [*Silence.* GINA *takes up her sewing again;* HEDVIG *takes paper and pencil and begins to draw, shading her eyes with her left hand.*]

HEDVIG: Isn't it jolly to think that father is at Mr. Werle's big dinner-party?

GINA: You know he's not really Mr. Werle's guest. It was the son invited him. [*after a pause*] We have nothing to do with that Mr. Werle.

HEDVIG: I'm longing for father to come home. He promised to ask Mrs. Sörby for something nice for me.

GINA: Yes, there's plenty of good things in that house, I can tell you.

HEDVIG [*goes on drawing*]: And I believe I'm a little hungry, too.

> [OLD EKDAL, *with the paper parcel under his arm and another parcel in his coat pocket, comes in by the entrance door.*]

GINA: How late you are today, grandfather!

EKDAL: They had locked the office door. Had to wait in Gråberg's room. And then they let me through—h'm.

HEDVIG: Did you get some more copying to do, grandfather?

EKDAL: This whole packet. Just look.

GINA: That's capital.

HEDVIG: And you have another parcel in your pocket.

EKDAL: Eh? Oh, never mind, that's nothing. [*puts his stick away in a corner*] This work will keep me going a long time, Gina. [*opens one of the sliding-doors in the back wall a little*] Hush! [*peeps into the room for a moment, then pushes the door carefully to again*] Hee-

hee! They're fast asleep, all the lot of them. And she's gone into the basket herself. Hee-hee!

HEDVIG: Are you sure she isn't cold in that basket, grandfather?

EKDAL: Not a bit of it! Cold? With all that straw? [*goes towards the farther door on the left*] There are matches in here, I suppose.

GINA: The matches is on the drawers.

[EKDAL *goes into his room.*]

HEDVIG: It's nice that grandfather has got all that copying.

GINA: Yes, poor old father; it means a bit of pocket-money for him.

HEDVIG: And he won't be able to sit the whole forenoon down at that horrid Madame Eriksen's.

GINA: No more he won't.

[*Short silence.*]

HEDVIG: Do you suppose they are still at the dinner-table?

GINA: Goodness knows; as like as not.

HEDVIG: Think of all the delicious things father is having to eat! I'm certain he'll be in splendid spirits when he comes. Don't you think so, mother?

GINA: Yes; and if only we could tell him that we'd got the room let——

HEDVIG: But we don't need that this evening.

GINA: Oh, we'd be none the worst of it, I can tell you. It's no use to us as it is.

HEDVIG: I mean we don't need it this evening, for father will be in a good humor at any rate. It is best to keep the letting of the room for another time.

GINA [*looks across at her*]: You like having some good news to tell father when he comes home in the evening?

HEDVIG: Yes; for then things are pleasanter somehow.

GINA [*thinking to herself*]: Yes, yes, there's something in that.

[OLD EKDAL *comes in again and is going out by the foremost door to the left.*]

GINA [*half turning in her chair*]: Do you want something out of the kitchen, grandfather?

EKDAL: Yes, yes, I do. Don't you trouble. [*goes out*]

GINA: He's not poking away at the fire, is he? [*waits a moment*] Hedvig, go and see what he's about.

[EKDAL *comes in again with a small jug of steaming hot water.*]

HEDVIG: Have you been getting some hot water, grandfather?

EKDAL: Yes, hot water. Want it for something. Want to write, and the ink has got as thick as porridge—h'm.

GINA: But you'd best have your supper first, grandfather. It's laid in there.

EKDAL: Can't be bothered with supper, Gina. Very busy, I tell you. No one's to come to my room. No one—h'm.

[He goes into his room; GINA and HEDVIG look at each other.]

GINA [softly]: Can you imagine where he's got money from?

HEDVIG: From Gråberg, perhaps.

GINA: Not a bit of it. Gråberg always send money to me.

HEDVIG: Then he must have got a bottle on credit somewhere.

GINA: Poor grandfather, who'd give him credit?

[HIALMAR EKDAL, in an overcoat and grey felt hat, comes in from the right.]

GINA [throws down her sewing and rises]: Why, Ekdal, is that you already?

HEDVIG [at the same time, jumping up]: Fancy your coming so soon, father!

HIALMAR [taking off his hat]: Yes, most of the people were coming away.

HEDVIG: So early?

HIALMAR: Yes, it was a dinner-party, you know. [taking off his overcoat]

GINA: Let me help you.

HEDVIG: Me, too.

[They draw off his coat; GINA hangs it up on the back wall.]

HEDVIG: Were there many people there, father?

HIALMAR: Oh, no, not many. We were about twelve or fourteen at table.

GINA: And you had some talk with them all?

HIALMAR: Oh, yes, a little; but Gregers took up most of my time.

GINA: Is Gregers as ugly as ever?

HIALMAR: Well, he's not very much to look at. Hasn't the old man come home?

HEDVIG: Yes, grandfather is in his room, writing.

HIALMAR: Did he say anything?

GINA: No, what should he say?

HIALMAR: Didn't he say anything about——? I heard something about his having been with Gråberg. I'll go in and see him for a moment.

GINA: No, no, better not.

HIALMAR: Why not? Did he say he didn't want me to go in?

GINA: I don't think he wants to see nobody this evening——

HEDVIG [making signs]: H'm—h'm!

GINA [not noticing]: ——he has been in to fetch hot water——

HIALMAR: Aha! Then he's——

GINA: Yes, I suppose so.

HIALMAR: Oh, God! my poor old white-haired father!—— Well, well; there let him sit and get all the enjoyment he can.

[OLD EKDAL, *in an indoor coat and with a lighted pipe, comes from his room.*]

EKDAL: Got home? Thought it was you I heard talking.

HIALMAR: Yes, I have just come.

EKDAL: You didn't see me, did you?

HIALMAR: No, but they told me you had passed through—so I thought I would follow you.

EKDAL: H'm, good of you, Hialmar.—Who were they, all those fellows?

HIALMAR:—Oh, all sorts of people. There was Chamberlain Flor, and Chamberlain Balle, and Chamberlain Kaspersen and Chamberlain —this, that, and the other—I don't know who all——

EKDAL [*nodding*]: Hear that, Gina! Chamberlains every one of them!

GINA: Yes, I hear as they're terrible genteel in that house nowadays.

HEDVIG: Did the Chamberlains sing, father? Or did they read aloud?

HIALMAR: No, they only talked nonsense. They wanted me to recite something for them; but I knew better than that.

EKDAL: You weren't to be persuaded, eh?

GINA: Oh, you might have done it.

HIALMAR: No; one mustn't be at everybody's beck and call. [*walks about the room*] That's not my way, at any rate.

EKDAL: No, no; Hialmar's not to be had for the asking, he isn't.

HIALMAR: I don't see why *I* should bother myself to entertain people on the rare occasions when I go into society. Let the others exert themselves. These fellows go from one great dinner-table to the next and gorge and guzzle day out and day in. It's for them to bestir themselves and do something in return for all the good feeding they get.

GINA: But you didn't say that?

HIALMAR [*humming*]: Ho-ho-ho——; faith, I gave them a bit of my mind.

EKDAL: Not the Chamberlains?

HIALMAR: Oh, why not? [*lightly*] After that, we had a little discussion about Tokay.

EKDAL: Tokay! There's a fine wine for you!

HIALMAR [*comes to a standstill*]: It may be a fine wine. But of course you know the vintages differ; it all depends on how much sunshine the grapes have had.

GINA: Why, you know everything, Ekdal.

EKDAL: And did they dispute that?

HIALMAR: They tried to; but they were requested to observe that it was just the same with Chamberlains—that with them, too, different batches were of different qualities.

GINA: What things you do think of!

EKDAL: Hee-hee! So they got that in their pipes, too?

HIALMAR: Right in their teeth.

EKDAL: Do you hear that, Gina? He said it right in the very teeth of all the Chamberlains.

GINA: Fancy——! Right in their teeth!

HIALMAR: Yes, but I don't want it talked about. One doesn't speak of such things. The whole affair passed off quite amicably of course. They were nice, genial fellows; I didn't want to wound them—not I!

EKDAL: Right in their teeth, though——!

HEDVIG [caressingly]: How nice it is to see you in a dress-coat! It suits you so well, father.

HIALMAR: Yes, don't you think so? And this one really sits to perfection. It fits almost as if it had been made for me;—a little tight in the arm-holes perhaps;—help me, Hedvig. [takes off the coat] I think I'll put on my jacket. Where is my jacket, Gina?

GINA: Here it is. [brings the jacket and helps him]

HIALMAR: That's it! Don't forget to send the coat back to Molvik first thing tomorrow morning.

GINA [laying it away]: I'll be sure and see to it.

HIALMAR [stretching himself]: After all, there's a more homely feeling about this. A free-and-easy indoor costume suits my whole personality better. Don't you think so, Hedvig?

HEDVIG: Yes, father.

HIALMAR: When I loosen my necktie into a pair of flowing ends—like this—eh?

HEDVIG: Yes, that goes so well with your moustache and the sweep of your curls.

HIALMAR: I should not call them curls exactly; I should rather say locks.

HEDVIG: Yes, they are too big for curls.

HIALMAR: Locks describes them better.

HEDVIG [after a pause, twitching his jacket]: Father!

HIALMAR: Well, what is it?

HEDVIG: Oh, you know very well.

HIALMAR: No, really I don't——

HEDVIG [*half laughing, half whispering*]: Oh, yes, father; now don't tease me any longer!

HIALMAR: Why, what do you mean?

HEDVIG [*shaking him*]: Oh, what nonsense; come, where are they, father? All the good things you promised me, you know?

HIALMAR: Oh—if I haven't forgotten all about them!

HEDVIG: Now you're only teasing me, father! Oh, it's too bad of you! Where have you put them?

HIALMAR: No, I positively forgot to get anything. But wait a little! I have something else for you, Hedvig. [*goes and searches in the pockets of the coat*]

HEDVIG [*skipping and clapping her hands*]: Oh, mother, mother!

GINA: There, you see; if you only give him time——

HIALMAR [*with a paper*]: Look, here it is.

HEDVIG: That? Why, that's only a paper.

HIALMAR: That is the bill of fare, my dear; the whole bill of fare. Here you see: "Menu"—that means bill of fare.

HEDVIG: Haven't you anything else?

HIALMAR: I forgot the other things, I tell you. But you may take my word for it, these dainties are very unsatisfying. Sit down at the table and read the bill of fare, and then I'll describe to you how the dishes taste. Here you are, Hedvig.

HEDVIG [*gulping down her tears*]: Thank you. [*She seats herself, but does not read; GINA makes signs to her; HIALMAR notices it.*]

HIALMAR [*pacing up and down the room*]: It's monstrous what absurd things the father of a family is expected to think of; and if he forgets the smallest trifle, he is treated to sour faces at once. Well, well, one gets used to that, too. [*stops near the stove, by the old man's chair*] Have you peeped in there this evening, father?

EKDAL: Yes, to be sure I have. She's gone into the basket.

HIALMAR: Ah, she has gone into the basket. Then she's beginning to get used to it.

EKDAL: Yes; just as I prophesied. But you know there are still a few little things—

HIALMAR: A few improvements, yes.

EKDAL: They've got to be made, you know.

HIALMAR: Yes, let us have a talk about the improvements, father. Come, let us sit on the sofa.

EKDAL: All right. H'm—think I'll just fill my pipe first. Must clean it out, too. H'm.

[*He goes into his room.*]

GINA [*smiling to HIALMAR*]: His pipe!

HIALMAR: Oh, yes, yes, Gina; let him alone—the poor shipwrecked old man.—Yes, these improvements—we had better get them out of hand tomorrow.

GINA: You'll hardly have time tomorrow, Ekdal.

HEDVIG [interposing]: Oh, yes he will, mother!

GINA: ——for remember them prints that has to be retouched; they've sent for them time after time.

HIALMAR: There now! those prints again! I shall get them finished all right! Have any new orders come in?

GINA: No, worse luck; tomorrow I have nothing but those two sittings, you know.

HIALMAR: Nothing else? Oh, no, if people won't set about things with a will——

GINA: But what more can I do? Don't I advertise in the papers as much as we can afford?

HIALMAR: Yes, the papers, the papers; you see how much good they do. And I suppose no one has been to look at the room either?

GINA: No, not yet.

HIALMAR: That was only to be expected. If people won't keep their eyes open——. Nothing can be done without a real effort, Gina!

HEDVIG [going towards him]: Shall I fetch you the flute, father?

HIALMAR: No; no flute for me; I want no pleasures in this world. [pacing about] Yes, indeed I will work tomorrow; you shall see if I don't. You may be sure I shall work as long as my strength holds out.

GINA: But my dear, good Ekdal, I didn't mean it in that way.

HEDVIG: Father, mayn't I bring in a bottle of beer?

HIALMAR: No, certainly not. I require nothing, nothing—— [comes to a standstill] Beer? Was it beer you were talking about?

HEDVIG [cheerfully]: Yes, father; beautiful, fresh beer.

HIALMAR: Well—since you insist upon it, you may bring in a bottle.

GINA: Yes, do; and we'll be nice and cosy.

HEDVIG runs towards the kitchen door.]

HIALMAR [by the stove, stops her, looks at her, puts his arm around her neck and presses her to him]: Hedvig, Hedvig!

HEDVIG [with tears of joy]: My dear, kind father!

HIALMAR: No, don't call me that. Here have I been feasting at the rich man's table,—battening at the groaning board——! And I couldn't even——!

GINA [sitting at the table]: Oh, nonsense, nonsense, Ekdal.

HIALMAR: It's not nonsense! And yet you mustn't be too hard upon me. You know that I love you for all that.

HEDVIG [*throwing her arms round him*]: And we love you, oh, so dearly, father!

HIALMAR: And if I am unreasonable once in a while,—why then—you must remember that I am a man beset by a host of cares. There, there! [*dries his eyes*] No beer at such a moment as this. Give me the flute.

[HEDVIG *runs to the bookcase and fetches it.*]

HIALMAR: Thanks! That's right. With my flute in my hand and you two at my side—ah—!

[HEDVIG *seats herself at the table near* GINA; HIALMAR *paces backwards and forwards, pipes up vigorously and plays a Bohemian peasant dance, but in a slow plaintive tempo, and with sentimental expression.*]

HIALMAR [*breaking off the melody, holds out his left hand to* GINA *and says with emotion*]: Our roof may be poor and humble, Gina, but it is home. And with all my heart I say: here dwells my happiness.

[*He begins to play again; almost immediately after, a knocking is heard at the entrnce door.*]

GINA [*rising*]: Hush, Ekdal,—I think there's some one at the door.

HIALMAR [*laying the flute on the bookcase*]: There! Again!

[GINA *goes and opens the door.*]

GREGERS WERLE [*in the passage*]: Excuse me——

GINA [*starting back slightly*]: Oh!

GREGERS: ——does not Mr. Ekdal, the photographer, live here?

GINA: Yes, he does.

HIALMAR [*going towards the door*]: Gregers! You here after all? Well, come in then.

GREGERS [*coming in*]: I told you I would come and look you up.

HIALMAR: But this evening——? Have you left the party?

GREGERS: I have left both the party and my father's house.—Good evening, Mrs. Ekdal. I don't know whether you recognize me?

GINA: Oh, yes; it's not difficult to know young Mr. Werle again.

GREGERS: No, I am like my mother; and no doubt you remember her.

HIALMAR: Left your father's house, did you say?

GREGERS: Yes, I have gone to a hotel.

HIALMAR: Indeed. Well, since you're here, take off your coat and sit down.

GREGERS: Thanks.

[*He takes off his overcoat. He is now dressed in a plain grey suit of a countrified cut.*]

HIALMAR: Here, on the sofa. Make yourself comfortable.

[GREGERS *seats himself on the sofa;* HIALMAR *takes a chair at the table.*]

GREGERS [*looking around him*]: So these are your quarters, Hialmar—this is your home.

HIALMAR: This is the studio, as you see——

GINA: But it's the largest of our rooms, so we generally sit here.

HIALMAR: We used to live in a better place; but this flat has one great advantage; there are such capital outer rooms——

GINA: And we have a room on the other side of the passage that we can let.

GREGERS [*to* HIALMAR]: Ah—so you have lodgers, too?

HIALMAR: No, not yet. They're not so easy to find, you see; you have to keep your eyes open. [*to* HEDVIG] What about the beer, eh?

[HEDVIG *nods and goes out into the kitchen.*]

GREGERS: So that is your daughter?

HIALMAR: Yes, that is Hedvig.

GREGERS: And she is your only child?

HIALMAR: Yes, the only one. She is the joy of our lives, and—[*lowering his voice*]—at the same time our deepest sorrow, Gregers.

GREGERS: What do you mean?

HIALMAR: She is in serious danger of losing her eyesight.

GREGERS: Becoming blind?

HIALMAR: Yes. Only the first symptoms have appeared as yet, and she may not feel it much for some time. But the doctor has warned us. It is coming, inexorably.

GREGERS: What a terrible misfortune! How do you account for it?

HIALMAR [*sighs*]: Hereditary, no doubt.

GREGERS [*starting*]: Hereditary?

GINA: Ekdal's mother had weak eyes.

HIALMAR: Yes, so my father says; I can't remember her.

GREGERS: Poor child! And how does she take it?

HIALMAR: Oh, you can imagine we haven't the heart to tell her of it. She dreams of no danger. Gay and careless and chirping like a little bird, she flutters onward into a life of endless night. [*overcome*] Oh, it is cruelly hard on me, Gregers.

[HEDVIG *brings a tray with beer and glasses, which she sets upon the table.*]

HIALMAR [*stroking her hair*]: Thanks, thanks, Hedvig.

[HEDVIG *puts her arm around his neck and whispers in his ear.*]

HIALMAR: No, no bread and butter just now. [*looks up*] But perhaps you would like some, Gregers.

GREGERS [with a gesture of refusal]: No, no, thank you.

HIALMAR [still melancholy]: Well, you can bring in a little all the same. If you have a crust, that is all I want. And plenty of butter on it, mind.

[HEDVIG nods gaily and goes out into the kitchen again.]

GREGERS [who has been following her with his eyes]: She seems quite strong and healthy otherwise.

GINA: Yes. In other ways there's nothing amiss with her, thank goodness.

GREGERS: She promises to be very like you, Mrs. Ekdal. How old is she now?

GINA: Hedvig is close on fourteen; her birthday is the day after tomorrow.

GREGERS: She is pretty tall for her age, then.

GINA: Yes, she's shot up wonderful this last year.

GREGERS: It makes one realize one's own age to see these young people growing up—How long is it now since you were married?

GINA: We've been married—let me see—just on fifteen years.

GREGERS: Is it so long as that?

GINA [becomes attentive; looks at him]: Yes, it is indeed.

HIALMAR: Yes, so it is. Fifteen years all but a few months. [changing his tone] They must have been long years for you, up at the works, Gregers.

GREGERS: They seemed long while I was living them; now they are over, I hardly know how the time has gone.

[OLD EKDAL comes from his room without his pipe, but with his old-fashioned uniform cap on his head; his gait is somewhat unsteady.]

EKDAL: Come now, Hialmar, let's sit down and have a good talk about this—h'm—what was it again?

HIALMAR [going towards him]: Father, we have a visitor here—Gregers Werle.—I don't know if you remember him.

EKDAL [looking at GREGERS, who has risen]: Werle? Is that the son? What does he want with me?

HIALMAR: Nothing; it's me he has come to see.

EKDAL: Oh! Then there's nothing wrong?

HIALMAR: No, no, of course not.

EKDAL [with a large gesture]: Not that I'm afraid, you know; but——

GREGERS [goes over to him]: I bring you a greeting from your old hunting-grounds, Lieutenant Ekdal.

EKDAL: Hunting-grounds?

GREGERS: Yes, up in Höidal, about the works, you know.

EKDAL: Oh, up there. Yes, I knew all those places well in the old days.

GREGERS: You were a great sportsman then.

EKDAL: So I was, I don't deny it. You're looking at my uniform cap. I don't ask anybody's leave to wear it in the house. So long as I don't go out in the streets with it——

[HEDVIG brings a plate of bread and butter, which she puts upon the table.]

HIALMAR: Sit down, father, and have a glass of beer. Help yourself, Gregers.

[EKDAL mutters and stumbles over to the sofa. GREGERS seats himself on the chair nearest to him, HIALMAR on the other side of GREGERS. GINA sits a little way from the table, sewing; HEDVIG stands beside her father.]

GREGERS: Can you remember, Lieutenant Ekdal, how Hialmar and I used to come up and visit you in the summer and at Christmas?

EKDAL: Did you? No, no, no; I don't remember it. But sure enough I've been a tidy bit of a sportsman in my day. I've shot bears, too. I've shot nine of 'em, no less.

GREGERS [looking sympathetically at him]: And now you never get any shooting?

EKDAL: Can't just say that, sir. Get a shot now and then perhaps. Of course not in the old way. For the woods, you see—the woods, the woods——! [drinks] Are the woods fine up there now?

GREGERS: Not so fine as in your time. They have been thinned a good deal.

EKDAL: Thinned? [more softly, and as if afraid] It's dangerous work that. Bad things come of it. The woods revenge themselves.

HIALMAR [filling up his glass]: Come—a little more, father.

GREGERS: How can a man like you—such a man for the open air—live in the midst of a stuffy town, boxed within four walls?

EKDAL [laughs quietly and glances at HIALMAR]: Oh, it's not so bad here. Not at all so bad.

GREGERS: But don't you miss all the things that used to be a part of your very being—the cool sweeping breezes, the free life in the woods and on the uplands, among beasts and birds——?

EKDAL [smiling]: Hialmar, shall we let him see it?

HIALMAR [hastily and a little embarrassed]: Oh, no, no, father; not this evening.

GREGERS: What does he want to show me?

HIALMAR: Oh, it's only something—you can see it another time.

GREGERS [*continues, to the old man*]: You see I have been thinking, Lieutenant Ekdal, that you should come up with me to the works; I am sure to be going back soon. No doubt you could get some copying there, too. And here, you have nothing on earth to interest you—nothing to liven you up.

EKDAL [*stares in astonishment at him*]: Have I nothing on earth to——!

GREGERS: Of course you have Hialmar; but then he has his own family. And a man like you, who has always had such a passion for what is free and wild——

EKDAL [*thumps the table*]: Hialmar, he shall see it!

HIALMAR: Oh, do you think it's worth while, father? It's all dark.

EKDAL: Nonsense; it's moonlight. [*rises*] He shall see it, I tell you. Let me pass! Come and help me, Hialmar.

HEDVIG: Oh, yes, do, father!

HIALMAR [*rising*]: Very well then.

GREGERS [*to* GINA]: What is it?

GINA: Oh, nothing so very wonderful, after all.

[EKDAL *and* HIALMAR *have gone to the back wall and are each pushing back a side of the sliding door;* HEDVIG *helps the old man;* GREGERS *remains standing by the sofa;* GINA *sits still and sews. Through the open doorway a large, deep irregular garret is seen with odd nooks and corners; a couple of stove-pipes running through it, from rooms below. There are skylights through which clear moonbeams shine in on some parts of the great room; others lie in deep shadow.*]

EKDAL [*to* GREGERS]: You may come close up if you like.

GREGERS [*going over to them*]: Why, what is it?

EKDAL: Look for yourself. H'm.

HIALMAR [*somewhat embarrassed*]: This belongs to father, you understand.

GREGERS [*at the door, looks into the garret*]: Why, you keep poultry, Lieutenant Ekdal.

EKDAL: Should think we did keep poultry. They've gone to roost now. But you should just see our fowls by daylight, sir!

HEDVIG: And there's a——

EKDAL: Sh—sh! don't say anything about it yet.

GREGERS: And you have pigeons, too, I see.

EKDAL: Oh, yes, haven't we just got pigeons! They have their nest-boxes up there under the roof-tree; for pigeons like to roost high, you see.

HIALMAR: They aren't all common pigeons.

EKDAL: Common! Should think not indeed! We have tumblers and a pair of pouters, too. But come here! Can you see that hutch down there by the wall?

GREGERS: Yes; what do you use it for?

EKDAL: That's where the rabbits sleep, sir.

GREGERS: Dear me, so you have rabbits, too?

EKDAL: Yes, you may take my word for it, we have rabbits! He wants to know if we have rabbits, Hialmar! H'm! But now comes the thing, let me tell you! Here we have it! Move away, Hedvig. Stand here; that's right,—and now look down there.—Don't you see a basket with straw in it?

GREGERS: Yes. And I can see a fowl lying in the basket.

EKDAL: H'm—"a fowl"——

GREGERS: Isn't it a duck?

EKDAL [hurt]: Why, of course it's a duck.

HIALMAR: But what kind of duck, do you think?

HEDVIG: It's not just a common duck——

EKDAL: Sh!

GREGERS: And it's not a Muscovy duck either.

EKDAL: No, Mr.—Werle; it's not a Muscovy duck; for it's a wild duck!

GREGERS: Is it really? A wild duck?

EKDAL: Yes, that's what it is. That "fowl" as you call it—is the wild duck. It's our wild duck, sir.

HEDVIG: My wild duck. It belongs to me.

GREGERS: And can it live up here in the garret? Does it thrive?

EKDAL: Of course it has a trough of water to splash about in, you know.

HIALMAR: Fresh water every other day.

GINA [turning towards HIALMAR]: But my dear Ekdal, it's getting icy cold here.

EKDAL: H'm, we had better shut up then. It's as well not to disturb their night's rest, too. Close up, Hedvig.

[HIALMAR and HEDVIG push the garret doors together.]

EKDAL: Another time you shall see her properly. [seats himself in the armchair by the stove] Oh, they're curious things, these wild ducks, I can tell you.

GREGERS: How did you manage to catch it, Lieutenant Ekdal?

EKDAL: I didn't catch it. There's a certain man in this town whom we have to thank for it.

GREGERS [starts slightly]: That man was not my father, was he?

EKDAL: You've hit it. Your father and no one else. H'm.

HIALMAR: Strange that you should guess that, Gregers.

GREGERS: You were telling me that you owed so many things to my father; and so I thought perhaps——

GINA: But we didn't get the duck from Mr. Werle himself——

EKDAL: It's Håkon Werle we have to thank for her, all the same, Gina. [to GREGERS] He was shooting from a boat, you see, and he brought her down. But your father's sight is not very good now. H'm; she was only wounded.

GREGERS: Ah! She got a couple of slugs in her body, I suppose.

HIALMAR: Yes, two or three.

HEDVIG: She was hit under the wing, so that she couldn't fly.

GREGERS: And I suppose she dived to the bottom, eh?

EKDAL [sleepily, in a thick voice]: Of course. Always do that, wild ducks do. They shoot to the bottom as deep as they can get, sir— and bite themselves fast in the tangle and seaweed—and all the devil's own mess that grows down there. And they never come up again.

GREGERS: But your wild duck came up again, Lieutenant Ekdal.

EKDAL: He had such an amazingly clever dog, your father had. And that dog—he dived in after the duck and fetched her up again.

GREGERS [who has turned to HIALMAR]: And then she was sent to you here?

HIALMAR: Not at once; at first your father took her home. But she wouldn't thrive there; so Pettersen was told to put an end to her——

EKDAL [half asleep]: H'm—yes—Pettersen—that ass——

HIALMAR [speaking more softly]: That was how we got her, you see; for father knows Pettersen a little; and when he heard about the wild duck he got him to hand her over to us.

GREGERS: And now she thrives as well as possible in the garret there?

HIALMAR: Yes, wonderfully well. She has got fat. You see, she has lived in there so long now that she has forgotten her natural wild life; and it all depends on that.

GREGERS: You are right there, Hialmar. Be sure you never let her get a glimpse of the sky and the sea——. But I mustn't stay any longer; I think your father is asleep.

HIALMAR: Oh, as for that——

GREGERS: But, by-the-bye—you said you had a room to let—a spare room?

HIALMAR: Yes; what then? Do you know of anybody——?

GREGERS: Can I have that room?

HIALMAR: You?

GINA: Oh, no, Mr. Werle, you——

GREGERS: May I have the room? If so, I'll take possession first thing tomorrow morning.

HIALMAR: Yes, with the greatest pleasure——

GINA: But, Mr. Werle, I'm sure it's not at all the sort of room for you.

HIALMAR: Why, Gina! how can you say that?

GINA: Why, because the room's neither large enough nor light enough, and——

GREGERS: That really doesn't matter, Mrs. Ekdal.

HIALMAR: I call it quite a nice room, and not at all badly furnished, either.

GINA: But remember the pair of them underneath.

GREGERS: What pair?

GINA: Well, there's one as has been a tutor——

HIALMAR: That's Molvik—Mr. Molvik, B.A.

GINA: And then there's a doctor, by the name of Relling.

GREGERS: Relling? I know him a little; he practised for a time up in Höidal.

GINA: They're a regular rackety pair, they are. As often as not, they're out on the loose in the evenings; and then they come home at all hours, and they're not always just——

GREGERS: One soon gets used to that sort of thing. I daresay I shall be like the wild duck——

GINA: H'm; I think you ought to sleep upon it first, anyway.

GREGERS: You seem very unwilling to have me in the house, Mrs. Ekdal.

GINA: Oh, no! What makes you think that?

HIALMAR: Well, you really behave strangely about it, Gina. [to GREGERS] Then I suppose you intend to remain in the town for the present?

GREGERS [putting on his overcoat]: Yes, now I intend to remain here.

HIALMAR: And yet not at your father's? What do you propose to do, then?

GREGERS: Ah, if I only knew that, Hialmar, I shouldn't be so badly off! But when one has the misfortune to be called Gregers—! "Gregers" —and then "Werle" after it; did you ever hear anything so hideous?

HIALMAR: Oh, I don't think so at all.

GREGERS: Ugh! Bah! I feel I should like to spit upon the fellow that answers to such a name. But when a man is once for all doomed to be Gregers—Werle in this world, as I am——

HIALMAR [laughs]: Ha, ha! If you weren't Gregers Werle, what would you like to be?

GREGERS: If I should choose, I should like best to be a clever dog.

GINA: A dog!

HEDVIG [involuntarily]: Oh, no!

GREGERS: Yes, an amazingly clever dog; one that goes to the bottom after wild ducks when they dive and bite themselves fast in tangle and seaweed, down among the ooze.

HIALMAR: Upon my word now, Gregers—I don't in the least know what you're driving at.

GREGERS: Oh, well, you might not be much the wiser if you did. It's understood, then, that I move in early tomorrow morning. [to GINA] I won't give you any trouble; I do everything for myself. [to HIALMAR] We can talk about the rest tomorrow.—Goodnight, Mrs. Ekdal. [nods to HEDVIG] Goodnight.

GINA: Goodnight, Mr. Werle.

HEDVIG: Goodnight.

HIALMAR [who has lighted a candle]: Wait a moment; I must show you a light; the stairs are sure to be dark.

[GREGERS and HIALMAR go out by the passage door.]

GINA [looking straight before her, with her sewing in her lap]: Wasn't that queer-like talk about wanting to be a dog?

HEDVIG: Do you know, mother—I believe he meant something quite different by that.

GINA: Why, what should he mean?

HEDVIG: Oh, I don't know; but it seemed to me he meant something different from what he said—all the time.

GINA: Do you think so? Yes, it was sort of queer.

HIALMAR [comes back]: The lamp was still burning. [puts out the candle and sets it down] Ah, now one can get a mouthful of food at last. [begins to eat the bread and butter] Well, you see, Gina—if only you keep your eyes open——

GINA: How, keep your eyes open——?

HIALMAR: Why, haven't we at last had the luck to get the room let? And just think—to a person like Gregers—a good old friend.

GINA: Well, I don't know what to say about it.

HEDVIG: Oh, mother, you'll see; it'll be such fun!

HIALMAR: You're very strange. You were so bent upon getting the room let before; and now you don't like it.

GINA: Yes, I do, Ekdal; if it had only been to someone else—— But what do you suppose Mr. Werle will say?

HIALMAR: Old Werle? It doesn't concern him.

GINA: But surely you can see that there's something amiss between them again, or the young man wouldn't be leaving home. You know very well those two can't get on with each other.

HIALMAR: Very likely not, but——

GINA: And now Mr. Werle may fancy it's you that has egged him on——

HIALMAR: Let him fancy so, then! Mr. Werle has done a great deal for me; far be it from me to deny it. But that doesn't make me everlastingly dependent upon him.

GINA: But, my dear Ekdal, maybe grandfather'll suffer for it. He may lose the little bit of work he gets from Gråberg.

HIALMAR: I could almost say: so much the better! Is it not humiliating for a man like me to see his grey-haired father treated as a pariah? But now I believe the fulness of time is at hand. [takes a fresh piece of bread and butter] As sure as I have a mission in life, I mean to fulfil it now!

HEDVIG: Oh, yes, father, do!

GINA: Hush! Don't wake him!

HIALMAR [more softly]: I will fulfil it, I say. The day shall come when—— And that is why I say it's a good thing we have let the room; for that makes me more independent. The man who has a mission in life must be independent. [by the armchair, with emotion] Poor old white-haired father! Rely on your Hialmar. He has broad shoulders—strong shoulders, at any rate. You shall yet wake up some fine day and—— [to GINA] Do you not believe it?

GINA [rising]: Yes, of course I do; but in the meantime suppose we see about getting him to bed.

HIALMAR: Yes, come.

[They take hold of the old man carefully.]

❦ Act III

SCENE—HIALMAR EKDAL's studio. It is morning: the daylight shines through the large window in the slanting roof; the curtain is drawn back.

HIALMAR is sitting at the table, busy retouching a photograph; several others lie before him. Presently GINA, wearing her hat and cloak, enters by the passage door; she has a covered basket on her arm.

HIALMAR: Back already, Gina?

GINA: Oh, yes, one can't let the grass grow under one's feet. [*sets her basket on a chair and takes off her things.*]

HIALMAR: Did you look in at Greger's room?

GINA: Yes, that I did. It's a rare sight, I can tell you; he's made a pretty mess to start off with.

HIALMAR: How so?

GINA: He was determined to do everything for himself, he said; so he sets to work to light the stove, and what must he do but screw down the damper till the whole room is full of smoke. Ugh! There was a smell fit to——

HIALMAR: Well, really!

GINA: But that's not the worst of it; for then he thinks he'll put out the fire, and goes and empties his water-jug into the stove and so makes the whole floor one filthy puddle.

HIALMAR: How annoying!

GINA: I've got the porter's wife to clear up after him, pig that he is! But the room won't be fit to live in till the afternoon.

HIALMAR: What's he doing with himself in the meantime?

GINA: He said he was going out for a little while.

HIALMAR. I looked in upon him, too, for a moment—after you had gone.

HIALMAR: So I heard. You've asked him to lunch.

HIALMAR: Just to a little bit of early lunch, you know. It's his first day —we can hardly do less. You've got something in the house, I suppose?

GINA: I shall have to find something or other.

HIALMAR: And don't cut it too fine, for I fancy Relling and Molvik are coming up, too. I just happened to meet Relling on the stairs, you see; so I had to——

GINA: Oh, are we to have those two as well?

HIALMAR: Good Lord—couple more or less can't make any difference.

OLD EKDAL [*opens his door and looks in*]: I say, Hialmar—— [*sees GINA*] Oh!

GINA: Do you want anything, grandfather?

EKDAL: Oh, no, it doesn't matter. H'm! [*retires again*]

GINA [*takes up the basket*]: Be sure you see that he doesn't go out.

HIALMAR: All right, all right. And, Gina, a little herring-salad wouldn't be a bad idea; Relling and Molvik were out on the loose again last night.

GINA: If only they don't come before I'm ready for them——

HIALMAR: No, of course they won't; take your own time.

GINA: Very well; and meanwhile you can be working a bit.

HIALMAR: Well, I am working! I am working as hard as I can!

GINA: Then you'll have that job off your hands, you see.

[*She goes out to the kitchen with her basket.* HIALMAR *sits for a time penciling away at the photograph in an indolent and listless manner.*]

EKDAL [*peeps in, looks round the studio and says softly*]: Are you busy?

HIALMAR: Yes, I'm toiling at these wretched pictures——

EKDAL: Well, well, never mind,—since you're so busy—h'm!

[*He goes out again; the door stands open.*]

HIALMAR [*continues for some time in silence; then he lays down his brush and goes over to the door*]: Are you busy, father?

EKDAL [*in a grumbling tone, within*]: If you're busy, I'm busy, too. H'm!

HIALMAR: Oh, very well, then. [*goes to his work again*]

EKDAL [*presently, coming to the door again*]: H'm; I say, Hialmar, I'm not so very busy, you know.

HIALMAR: I thought you were writing.

EKDAL: Oh, the devil take it! can't Gråberg wait a day or two? After all, it's not a matter of life and death.

HIALMAR: No; and you're not his slave either.

EKDAL: And about that other business in there——

HIALMAR: Just what I was thinking of. Do you want to go in? Shall I open the door for you?

EKDAL: Well, it wouldn't be a bad notion.

HIALMAR [*rises*]: Then we'd have that off our hands.

EKDAL: Yes, exactly. It's got to be ready first thing tomorrow. It is tomorrow, isn't it? H'm?

HIALMAR: Yes, of course it's tomorrow.

[HIALMAR *and* EKDAL *push aside each his half of the sliding door. The morning sun is shining in through the skylights: some doves are flying about; others sit cooing, upon the perches; the hens are heard clucking now and then, further back in the garret.*]

HIALMAR: There; now you can get to work, father.

EKDAL [*goes in*]: Aren't you coming, too?

HIALMAR: Well, really, do you know——; I almost think—— [*sees* GINA *at the kitchen door*] I? No; I haven't time; I must work.—But now for our new contrivance——

[*He pulls a cord, a curtain slips down inside, the lower part consisting of a piece of old sailcloth, the upper part of a stretched fishing net. The floor of the garret is thus no longer visible.*]

HIALMAR [*goes to the table*]: So! Now, perhaps I can sit in peace for a little while.

GINA: Is he rampaging in there again?

HIALMAR: Would you rather have had him slip down to Madame Eriksen's? [*seats himself*] Do you want anything? You know you said——

GINA: I only wanted to ask if you think we can lay the table for lunch here?

HIALMAR: Yes; we have no early appointment, I suppose?

GINA: No, I expect no one today except those two sweethearts that are to be taken together.

HIALMAR: Why the deuce couldn't they be taken together another day?

GINA: Don't you know I told them to come in the afternoon, when you are having your nap?

HIALMAR: Oh, that's capital. Very well, let us have lunch here then.

GINA: All right; but there's no hurry about laying the cloth; you can have the table for a good while yet.

HIALMAR: Do you think I am not sticking at my work? I'm at it as hard as I can!

GINA: Then you'll be free later on, you know. [*goes out into the kitchen again*]

　　　[*Short pause.*]

EKDAL [*in the garret doorway, behind the net*]: Hialmar!

HIALMAR: Well?

EKDAL: Afraid we shall have to move the water-trough, after all.

HIALMAR: What else have I been saying all along?

EKDAL: H'm—h'm—h'm.

　　　[*Goes away from the door again.* HIALMAR *goes on working a little; glances toward the garret and half rises.* HEDVIG *comes in from the kitchen.*]

HIALMAR [*sits down again hurriedly*]: What do you want?

HEDVIG: I only wanted to come in beside you, father.

HIALMAR [*after a pause*]: what makes you go prying around like that? Perhaps you are told off to watch me?

HEDVIG: No, no.

HIALMAR: What is your mother doing out there?

HEDVIG: Oh, mother's in the middle of making the herring-salad. [*goes to the table*] Isn't there any little thing I could help you with, father?

HIALMAR: Oh, no. It is right that I should bear the whole burden—so long as my strength holds out. Set your mind at rest, Hedvig; if only your father keeps his health——

HEDVIG: Oh, no, father! You mustn't talk in that horrid way.

[*She wanders about a little, stops by the doorway and looks into the garret.*]

HIALMAR: Tell me, what is he doing?

HEDVIG: I think he's making a new path to the water-trough.

HIALMAR: He can never manage that by himself! And here am I doomed to sit——!

HEDVIG [*goes to him*]: Let me take the brush, father; I can do it, quite well.

HIALMAR: Oh, nonsense; you will only hurt your eyes.

HEDVIG: Not a bit. Give me the brush.

HIALMAR [*rising*]: Well, it won't take more than a minute or two.

HEDVIG: Pooh, what harm can it do then? [*takes the brush*] There! [*seats herself*] I can begin upon this one.

HIALMAR: But mind you don't hurt your eyes! Do you hear? I won't be answerable; you do it on your own responsibility—understand that.

HEDVIG [*retouching*]: Yes, yes, I understand.

HIALMAR: You are quite clever at it, Hedvig. Only a minute or two, you know.

[*He slips through by the edge of the curtain into the garret.* HEDVIG *sits at her work.* HIALMAR *and* EKDAL *are heard disputing inside.*]

HIALMAR [*appears behind the net*]: I say, Hedvig—give me those pincers that are lying on the shelf. And the chisel. [*turns away inside*] Now you shall see, father. Just let me show you first what I mean!

[HEDVIG *has fetched the required tools from the shelf and hands them to him through the net.*]

HIALMAR: Ah, thanks. I didn't come a moment too soon.

[*Goes back from the curtain again; they are heard carpentering and talking inside.* HEDVIG *stands looking in at them. A moment later there is a knock at the passage door; she does not notice it.*]

GREGERS WERLE [*bareheaded, in indoor dress, enters and stops near the door*]: H'm——!

HEDVIG [*turns and goes towards him*]: Good morning. Please come in.

GREGERS: Thank you. [*looking towards the garret*] You seem to have workpeople in the house.

HEDVIG: No, it is only father and grandfather. I'll tell them you are here.

GREGERS: No, no, don't do that; I would rather wait a little. [seats himself on the sofa]

HEDVIG: It looks so untidy here—— [begins to clear away the photographs]

GREGERS: Oh, don't take them away. Are those prints that have to be finished off?

HEDVIG: Yes, they are a few I was helping father with.

GREGERS: Please don't let me disturb you.

HEDVIG: Oh, no.

[She gathers the things to her and sits down to work; GREGERS looks at her, meanwhile, in silence.]

GREGERS: Did the wild duck sleep well last night?

HEDVIG: Yes, I think so, thanks.

GREGERS [turning towards the garret]: It looks quite different by day from what it did last night in the moonlight.

HEDVIG: Yes, it changes ever so much. It looks different in the morning and in the afternoon; and it's different on rainy days from what it is in fine weather.

GREGERS: Have you noticed that?

HEDVIG: Yes, how could I help it?

GREGERS: Are you, too, fond of being in there with the wild duck?

HEDVIG: Yes, when I can manage it——

GREGERS: But I suppose you haven't much spare time; you go to school, no doubt.

HEDVIG: No, not now; father is afraid of my hurting my eyes.

GREGERS: Oh; then he reads with you himself?

HEDVIG: Father has promised to read with me; but he has never had time yet.

GREGERS: Then is there nobody else to give you a little help?

HEDVIG: Yes, there is Mr. Molvik; but he is not always exactly— quite——

GREGERS: Sober?

HEDVIG: Yes, I suppose that's it!

GREGERS: Why, then you must have any amount of time on your hands. And in there I suppose it is a sort of world by itself?

HEDVIG: Oh, yes, quite. And there are such lots of wonderful things.

GREGERS: Indeed?

HEDVIG: Yes, there are big cupboards full of books; and a great many of the books have pictures in them.

GREGERS: Aha!

HEDVIG: And there's an old bureau with drawers and flaps, and a big clock with figures that go out and in. But the clock isn't going now.

GREGERS: So time has come to a standstill in there—in the wild duck's domain.

HEDVIG: Yes. And then there's an old paint-box and things of that sort, and all the books.

GREGERS: And you read the books, I suppose?

HEDVIG: Oh, yes, when I get the chance. Most of them are English though, and I don't understand English. But then I look at the pictures.—There is one great big book called "Harrison's History of London." It must be a hundred years old; and there are such heaps of pictures in it. At the beginning there is Death with an hour-glass and a woman. I think that is horrid. But then there are all the other pictures of churches, and castles, and streets, and great ships sailing on the sea.

GREGERS: But tell me, where did all those wonderful things come from?

HEDVIG: Oh, an old sea captain once lived here, and he brought them home with him. They used to call him "The Flying Dutchman." That was curious, because he wasn't a Dutchman at all.

GREGERS: Was he not?

HEDVIG: No. But at last he was drowned at sea, and so he left all those things behind him.

GREGERS: Tell me now—when you are sitting in there looking at the pictures, don't you wish you could travel and see the real world for yourself?

HEDVIG: Oh, no! I mean always to stay at home and help father and mother.

GREGERS: To retouch photographs?

HEDVIG: No, not only that. I should love above everything to learn to engrave pictures like those in the English books.

GREGERS: H'm. What does your father say to that?

HEDVIG: I don't think father likes it; father is strange about such things. Only think, he talks of my learning basket-making and straw-plaiting! But I don't think that would be much good.

GREGERS: Oh, no, I don't think so either.

HEDVIG: But father was right in saying that if I had learnt basket-making I could have made the new basket for the wild duck.

GREGERS: So you could; and it was you that ought to have done it, wasn't it?

HEDVIG: Yes, for it's my wild duck.

GREGERS: Of course it is.

HEDVIG: Yes, it belongs to me. But I lend it to father and grandfather as often as they please.

GREGERS: Indeed? What do they do with it?

HEDVIG: Oh, they look after it, and build places for it, and so on.

GREGERS: I see; for no doubt the wild duck is by far the most distinguished inhabitant of the garret?

HEDVIG: Yes, indeed she is; for she is a real wild fowl, you know. And then she is so much to be pitied; she has no one to care for, poor thing.

GREGERS: She has no family, as the rabbits have—

HEDVIG: No. The hens, too, many of them, were chickens together; but she has been taken right away from all her friends. And then there is so much that is strange about the wild duck. Nobody knows her, and nobody knows where she came from either.

GREGERS: And she has been down in the depths of the sea.

HEDVIG [with a quick glance at him, represses a smile and asks]: Why do you say "depths of the sea"?

GREGERS: What else should I say?

HEDVIG: You could say "the bottom of the sea."[4]

GREGERS: Oh, mayn't I just as well say the depths of the sea?

HEDVIG: Yes; but sounds so strange to me when other people speak of the depths of the sea.

GREGERS: Why so? Tell me why?

HEDVIG: No, I won't; it's so stupid.

GREGERS: Oh, no, I am sure it's not. Do tell me why you smiled.

HEDVIG: Well, this is the reason: whenever I come to realize suddenly —in a flash—what is in there, it always seems to me that the whole room and everything in it should be called "the depths of the sea."—But that is so stupid.

GREGERS: You mustn't say that.

HEDVIG: Oh, yes, for you know it is only a garret.

GREGERS: [looks fixedly at her]: Are you so sure of that?

HEDVIG [astonished]: That it's a garret?

GREGERS: Are you quite certain of it?

> [HEDVIG is silent, and looks at him open-mouthed. GINA comes in from the kitchen with the table things.]

GREGERS [rising]: I have come in upon you too early.

GINA: Oh, you must be somewhere; and we're nearly ready now, anyway. Clear the table, Hedvig.

4. Gregers here uses the old-fashioned expression "havsens bund," while Hedvig would have him use the more commonplace "havets bund" or "havbunden." [Translator's note.]

[HEDVIG *clears away her things; she and* GINA *lay the cloth during what follows.* GREGERS *seats himself in the armchair and turns over an album.*]

GREGERS: I hear you can retouch, Mrs. Ekdal.

GINA [*with a side glance*]: Yes, I can.

GREGERS: That was exceedingly lucky.

GINA: How—lucky?

GREGERS: Since Ekdal took to photography, I mean.

HEDVIG: Mother can take photographs, too.

GINA: Oh, yes; I was bound to learn that.

GREGERS: So it is really you that carry on the business, I suppose?

GINA: Yes, when Ekdal hasn't time himself——

GREGERS: He is a great deal taken up with his old father, I daresay.

GINA: Yes, and then you can't expect a man like Ekdal to do nothing but take pictures of Dick, Tom, and Harry.

GREGERS: I quite agree with you; but having once gone in for the thing——

GINA: You can surely understand, Mr. Werle, that Ekdal's not like one of your common photographers.

GREGERS: Of course not; but still——

[*A shot is fired within the garret.*]

GREGERS [*starting up*]: What's that?

GINA: Ugh! now they're firing again!

GREGERS: Have they firearms in there?

HEDVIG: They are out shooting.

GREGERS: What! [*at the door of the garret*] Are you shooting, Hialmar?

HIALMAR [*inside the net*]: Are you there? I didn't know; I was so taken up—— [*to* HEDVIG] Why did you not let us know? [*comes into the studio*]

GREGERS: Do you go shooting in the garret?

HIALMAR [*showing a double-barrelled pistol*]: Oh, only with this thing.

GINA: Yes, you and grandfather will do yourselves a mischief some day with that there pigstol.

HIALMAR [*with irritation*]: I believe I have told you that this kind of firearm is called a pistol.

GINA: Oh, that doesn't make it much better, that I can see.

GREGERS: So you have become a sportsman, too, Hialmar?

HIALMAR: Only a little rabbit-shooting now and then. Mostly to please father, you understand.

GINA: Men are strange beings; they must always have something to pervert theirselves with.

HIALMAR [*snappishly*]: Just so; we must always have something to divert ourselves with.

GINA: Yes, that's just what I say.

HIALMAR: H'm. [*to* GREGERS] You see the garret is fortunately so situated that no one can hear us shooting. [*lays the pistol on the top shelf of the bookcase*] Don't touch the pistol, Hedvig! One of the barrels is loaded; remember that.

GREGERS [*looking through the net*]: You have a fowling-piece, too, I see.

HIALMAR: That is father's old gun. It's no use now; something has gone wrong with the lock. But it's fun to have it all the same; for we can take it to pieces now and then, and clean and grease it, and screw it together again.—Of course, it's mostly father that fiddle-faddles with all that sort of thing.

HEDVIG [*beside* GREGERS]: Now you can see the wild duck properly.

GREGERS: I was just looking at her. One of her wings seems to me to droop a bit.

HEDVIG: Well, no wonder; her wing was broken, you know.

GREGERS: And she trails one foot a little. Isn't that so?

HIALMAR: Perhaps a very little bit.

HEDVIG: Yes, it was by that foot the dog took hold of her.

HIALMAR: But otherwise she hasn't the least thing the matter with her; and that is simply marvellous for a creature that has a charge of shot in her body and has been between a dog's teeth——

GREGERS [*with a glance at* HEDVIG]: ——and that has lain in the depths of the sea—so long.

HEDVIG [*smiling*]: Yes.

GINA [*laying the table*]: That blessed wild duck! What a lot of fuss you do make over her.

HIALMAR: H'm;—will lunch soon be ready?

GINA: Yes, directly. Hedvig, you must come and help me now.

[GINA *and* HEDVIG *go out into the kitchen.*]

HIALMAR [*in a low voice*]: I think you had better not stand there looking in at father; he doesn't like it. [GREGERS *moves away from the garret door.*] Besides, I may as well shut up before the others come. [*claps his hands to drive the fowls back*] Shh—shh, in with you! [*draws up the curtain and pulls the doors together*] All the contrivances are my own invention. It's really quite amusing to have things of this sort to potter with and to put to rights when they get out of order. And it's absolutely necessary, too; for Gina objects to having rabbits and fowls in the studio.

GREGERS: To be sure; and I suppose the studio is your wife's special department?

HIALMAR: As a rule, I leave the everyday details of business to her; for then I can take refuge in the parlor and give my mind to more important things.

GREGERS: What things may they be, Hialmar?

HIALMAR: I wonder you have not asked that question sooner. But perhaps you haven't heard of the invention?

GREGERS: The invention? No.

HIALMAR: Really? Have you not? Ah, no, out there in the wilds——

GREGERS: So you have invented something, have you?

HIALMAR: It is not quite completed yet; but I am working at it. You can easily imagine that when I resolved to devote myself to photography, it wasn't simply with the idea of taking likenesses of all sorts of commonplace people.

GREGERS: No; your wife was saying the same thing just now.

HIALMAR: I swore that if I consecrated my powers to this handicraft, I would so exalt it that it should become both an art and a science. And to that end I determined to make this great invention.

GREGERS: And what is the nature of the invention? What purpose does it serve?

HIALMAR: Oh, my dear fellow, you mustn't ask for details yet. It takes time, you see. And you must not think that my motive is vanity. It is not for my own sake that I am working. Oh, no; it is my life's mission that stands before me night and day.

GREGERS: What is your life's mission?

HIALMAR: Do you forget the old man with the silver hair?

GREGERS: Your poor father? Well, but what can you do for him?

HIALMAR: I can raise up his self-respect from the dead, by restoring the name of Ekdal to honor and dignity.

GREGERS: Then that is your life's mission?

HIALMAR: Yes. I will rescue the shipwrecked man. For shipwrecked he was, by the very first blast of the storm. Even while those terrible investigations were going on, he was no longer himself. That pistol there—the one we use to shoot rabbits with—has played its part in the tragedy of the house of Ekdal.

GREGERS: The pistol? Indeed?

HIALMAR: When the sentence of imprisonment was passed—he had the pistol in his hand——

GREGERS: Had he——?

HIALMAR: Yes; but he dared not use it. His courage failed him. So broken, so demoralized was he even then! Oh, can you understand it? He, a soldier; he, who had shot nine bears, and who was descended from two lieutenant-colonels—one after the other, of course. Can you understand it, Gregers?

GREGERS: Yes, I understand it well enough.

HIALMAR: I cannot. And once more the pistol played a part in the history of our house. When he had put on the grey clothes and was under lock and key—oh, that was a terrible time for me, I can tell you. I kept the blinds drawn down over both my windows. When I peeped out, I saw the sun shining as if nothing had happened. I could not understand it. I saw people going along the street, laughing and talking about indifferent things. I could not understand it. It seemed to me that the whole of existence must be at a standstill—as if under an eclipse.

GREGERS: I felt that, too, when my mother died.

HIALMAR: It was in such an hour that Hialmar Ekdal pointed the pistol at his own breast.

GREGERS: You, too, thought of——!

HIALMAR: Yes.

GREGERS: But you did not fire?

HIALMAR: No. At the decisive moment I won the victory over myself. I remained in life. But I can assure you it takes some courage to choose life under circumstances like those.

GREGERS: Well, that depends on how you look at it.

HIALMAR: Yes, indeed, it takes courage. But I am glad I was firm: for now I shall soon perfect my invention; and Dr. Relling thinks, as I do myself, that father may be allowed to wear his uniform again. I will demand that as my sole reward.

GREGERS: So that is what he meant about his uniform——?

HIALMAR: Yes, that is what he most yearns for. You can't think how my heart bleeds for him. Every time we celebrate any little family festival—Gina's and my wedding-day, or whatever it may be—in comes the old man in the lieutenant's uniform of happier days. But if he only hears a knock at the door—for he daren't show himself to strangers, you know—he hurries back to his room again as fast as his old legs can carry him. Oh, it's heart-rending for a son to see such things!

GREGERS: How long do you think it will take you to finish your invention?

HIALMAR: Come now, you mustn't expect me to enter into particulars like that. An invention is not a thing completely under one's own control. It depends largely on inspiration—on intuition—and it is almost impossible to predict when the inspiration may come.

GREGERS: But it's advancing?

HIALMAR: Yes, certainly, it is advancing. I turn it over in my mind every day; I am full of it. Every afternoon, when I have had my dinner, I shut myself up in the parlor, where I can ponder undisturbed. But I can't be goaded to it; it's not a bit of good; Relling says so, too.

GREGERS: And you don't think that all that business in the garret draws you off and distracts you too much?

HIALMAR: No, no, no; quite the contrary. You mustn't say that. I cannot be everlastingly absorbed in the same laborious train of thought. I must have something alongside of it to fill up the time of waiting. The inspiration, the intuition, you see—when it comes, it comes, and there's an end of it.

GREGERS: My dear Hialmar, I almost think you have something of the wild duck in you.

HIALMAR: Something of the wild duck? How do you mean?

GREGERS: You have dived down and bitten yourself fast in the undergrowth.

HIALMAR: Are you alluding to the well-nigh fatal shot that has broken my father's wing—and mine, too?

GREGERS: Not exactly to that. I don't say that your wing has been broken; but you have strayed into a poisonous marsh, Hialmar; an insidious disease has taken hold of you, and you have sunk down to die in the dark.

HIALMAR: I? To die in the dark? Look here, Gregers, you must really leave off talking such nonsense.

GREGERS: Don't be afraid; I shall find a way to help you up again. I, too, have a mission in life now; I found it yesterday.

HIALMAR: That's all very well; but you will please leave me out of it. I can assure you that—apart from my very natural melancholy, of course—I am as contented as any one can wish to be.

GREGERS: Your contentment is an effect of the marsh poison.

HIALMAR: Now, my dear Gregers, pray do not go on about disease and poison; I am not used to that sort of talk. In my house nobody ever speaks to me about unpleasant things.

GREGERS: Ah, that I can easily believe.

HIALMAR: It's not good for me, you see. And there are no marsh poisons here, as you express it. The poor photographer's roof is lowly, I know—and my circumstances are narrow. But I am an inventor, and I am the breadwinner of a family. That exalts me above my mean surroundings.—Ah, here comes lunch!

[GINA *and* HEDVIG *bring bottles of ale, a decanter of brandy, glasses, etc. At the same time,* RELLING *and* MOLVIK *enter from the passage; they are both without hat or overcoat.* MOLVIK *is dressed in black.*]

GINA [*placing the things upon the table*]: Ah, you two have come in the nick of time.

RELLING: Molvik got it into his head that he could smell herring-salad, and then there was no holding him.—Good morning again, Ekdal.

HIALMAR: Gregers, let me introduce you to Mr. Molvik. Doctor—— Oh, you know Relling, don't you?

GREGERS: Yes, slightly.

RELLING: Oh, Mr. Werle, junior! Yes, we two have had one or two little skirmishes up at the Höidal works. You've just moved in?

GREGERS: I moved in this morning.

RELLING: Molvik and I live right under you, so you haven't far to go for the doctor and the clergyman, if you should need anything in that line.

GREGERS: Thanks, it's not quite unlikely, for yesterday we were thirteen at table.

HIALMAR: Oh, come now, don't let us get upon unpleasant subjects again!

RELLING: You may make your mind easy, Ekdal; I'll be hanged if the finger of fate points to you.

HIALMAR: I should hope not, for the sake of my family. But let us sit down now, and eat and drink and be merry.

GREGERS: Shall we not wait for your father?

HIALMAR: No, his lunch will be taken in to him later. Come along!

[*The men seat themselves at table, and eat and drink.* GINA *and* HEDVIG *go in and out and wait upon them.*]

RELLING: Molvik was frightfully stewed yesterday, Mrs. Ekdal.

GINA: Really? Yesterday again?

RELLING: Didn't you hear him when I brought him home last night?

GINA: No, I can't say I did.

RELLING: That was a good thing, for Molvik was disgusting last night.

GINA: Is that true, Molvik?

MOLVIK: Let us draw a veil over last night's proceedings. That sort of thing is totally foreign to my better self.

RELLING [*to* GREGERS]: It comes over him like a sort of possession, and then I have to go out on the loose with him. Mr. Molvik is dæmonic, you see.

GREGERS: Dæmonic?

RELLING: Molvik is dæmonic, yes.

GREGERS: H'm.

RELLING: And dæmonic natures are not made to walk straight through the world; they must meander a little now and then.—Well, so you still stick up there at those horrible grimy works?

GREGERS: I have stuck there until now.

RELLING: And did you ever manage to collect that claim you went about presenting?

GREGERS: Claim? [understands him] Ah. I see.

HIALMAR: Have you been presenting claims, Gregers?

GREGERS: Oh, nonsense.

RELLING: Faith, but he has, though! He went around to all the cotters' cabins presenting something he called "the claim of the ideal."

GREGERS: I was young then.

RELLING: You're right; you were very young. And as for the claim of the ideal—you never got it honored while I was up there.

GREGERS: Nor since either.

RELLING: Ah, then you've learnt to knock a little discount off, I expect.

GREGERS: Never, when I have a true man to deal with.

HIALMAR: No, I should think not, indeed. A little butter, Gina.

RELLING: And a slice of bacon for Molvik.

MOLVIK: Ugh; not bacon!

[A knock at the garret door.]

HIALMAR: Open the door, Hedvig; father wants to come out.

[HEDVIG goes over and opens the door a little way; EKDAL enters with a fresh rabbit-skin; she closes the door after him.]

EKDAL: Good morning, gentlemen! Good sport today. Shot a big one.

HIALMAR: And you've gone and skinned it without waiting for me——!

EKDAL: Salted it, too. It's good tender meat, is rabbit; it's sweet; it tastes like sugar. Good appetite to you, gentlemen! [goes into his room]

MOLVIK [rising]: Excuse me——; I can't——; I must get downstairs immediately—

RELLING: Drink some soda water, man!

MOLVIK [hurrying away]: Ugh—ugh! [goes out by the passage door]

RELLING [to HIALMAR]: Let us drain a glass to the old hunter.

HIALMAR [clinks glasses with him]: To the undaunted sportsman who has looked death in the face!

RELLING: To the grey-haired—— [drinks] By-the-bye, is his hair grey or white?

HIALMAR: Something between the two, I fancy; for that matter, he has very few hairs left of any color.

RELLING: Well, well, one can get through the world with a wig. After all, you are a happy man, Ekdal; you have your noble mission to labor for——

HIALMAR: And I do labor, I can tell you.

RELLING: And then you have your excellent wife, shuffling quietly in and out in her felt slippers, and that seesaw walk of hers, and making everything cosy and comfortable about you.

HIALMAR: Yes, Gina—[nods to her]—you were a good helpmate on the path of life.

GINA: Oh, don't sit there cricketizing me.

RELLING: And your Hedvig, too, Ekdal!

HIALMAR [affected]: The child, yes! The child before everything! Hedvig, come here to me. [strokes her hair] What day is it tomorrow, eh?

HEDVIG [shaking him]: Oh, no, you're not to say anything, father.

HIALMAR: It cuts me to the heart when I think what a poor affair it will be; only a little festivity in the garret——

HEDVIG: Oh, but that's just what I like!

RELLING: Just you wait till the wonderful invention sees the light, Hedvig!

HIALMAR: Yes, indeed—then you shall see——! Hedvig, I have resolved to make your future secure. You shall live in comfort all your days. I will demand—something or other—on your behalf. That shall be the poor inventor's sole reward.

HEDVIG [whispering, with her arms round his neck]: Oh, you dear, kind father!

RELLING [to GREGERS]: Come now, don't you find it pleasant, for once in a way, to sit at a well-spread table in a happy family circle?

HIALMAR: Ah, yes, I really prize these social hours.

GREGERS: For my part, I don't thrive in marsh vapors.

RELLING: Marsh vapors?

HIALMAR: Oh, don't begin with that stuff again!

GINA: Goodness knows there's no vapors in this house, Mr. Werle; I give the place a good airing every blessed day.

GREGERS [leaves the table]: No airing you can give will drive out the taint I mean.

HIALMAR: Taint!

GINA: Yes, what do you say to that, Ekdal?

RELLING: Excuse me—may it not be you yourself that have brought the taint from those mines up there?

GREGERS: It is like you to call what I bring into this house a taint.

RELLING [goes up to him]: Look here, Mr. Werle, junior: I have a strong suspicion that you are still carrying about that "claim of the ideal," large as life, in your coat-tail pocket.

GREGERS: I carry it in my breast.

RELLING: Well, wherever you carry it, I advise you not to come dunning us with it here, so long as I am on the premises.

GREGERS: And if I do so nonetheless?

RELLING: Then you'll go head-foremost down the stairs; now I've warned you.

HIALMAR [rising]: Oh, but Relling——!

GREGERS: Yes, you may turn me out——

GINA [interposing between them]: We can't have that, Relling. But I must say, Mr. Werle, it ill becomes you to talk about vapors and taints, after all the mess you made with your stove.

[A knock at the passage door.]

HEDVIG: Mother, there's somebody knocking.

HIALMAR: There now, we're going to have a whole lot of people!

GINA: I'll go—— [goes over and opens the door, starts, and draws back] Oh—oh, dear!

[WERLE, in a fur coat, advances one step into the room.]

WERLE: Excuse me, but I think my son is staying here.

GINA [with a gulp]: Yes.

HIALMAR [approaching him]: Won't you do us the honor to——?

WERLE: Thank you, I merely wish to speak to my son.

GREGERS: What is it? Here I am.

WERLE: I want a few words with you, in your room.

GREGERS: In my room? Very well—— [about to go]

GINA: No, no, your room's not in a fit state——

WERLE: Well then, out in the passage here; I want to have a few words with you alone.

HIALMAR: You can have them here, sir. Come into the parlor, Relling.

[HIALMAR and RELLING go off to the right. GINA takes HEDVIG with her into the kitchen.]

GREGERS [after a short pause]: Well, now we are alone.

WERLE: From something you let fall last evening, and from your coming to lodge with the Ekdals, I can't help inferring that you intend to make yourself unpleasant to me in one way or another.

GREGERS: I intend to open Hialmar Ekdal's eyes. He shall see his position as it really is—that is all.

WERLE: Is that the mission in life you spoke of yesterday?

GREGERS: Yes. You have left me no other.

WERLE: Is it I, then, that have crippled your mind, Gregers?

GREGERS: You have crippled my whole life. I am not thinking of all that about mother—— But it's thanks to you that I am continually haunted and harassed by a guilty conscience.

WERLE: Indeed! It is your conscience that troubles you, is it?

GREGERS: I ought to have taken a stand against you when the trap was set for Lieutenant Ekdal. I ought to have cautioned him, for I had a misgiving as to what was in the wind.

WERLE: Yes, that was the time to have spoken.

GREGERS: I did not dare to, I was so cowed and spiritless. I was mortally afraid of you—not only then, but long afterwards.

WERLE: You have got over that fear now, it appears.

GREGERS: Yes, fortunately. The wrong done to old Ekdal, both by me and by—others, can never be undone; but Hialmar I can rescue from all the falsehood and deception that are bringing him to ruin.

WERLE: Do you think that will be doing him a kindness?

GREGERS: I have not the least doubt of it.

WERLE: You think our worthy photographer is the sort of man to appreciate such friendly offices?

GREGERS: Yes, I do.

WERLE: H'm—we shall see.

GREGERS: Besides, if I am to go on living, I must try to find some cure for my sick conscience.

WERLE: It will never be sound. Your conscience has been sickly from childhood. That is a legacy from your mother, Gregers—the only one she left you.

GREGERS [with a scornful half-smile]: Have you not yet forgiven her for the mistake you made in supposing she would bring you a fortune?

WERLE: Don't let us wander from the point.—Then you hold to your purpose of setting young Ekdal upon what you imagine to be the right scent?

GREGERS: Yes, that is my fixed resolve.

WERLE: Well, in that case I might have spared myself this visit; for, of course, it is useless to ask whether you will return home with me?

GREGERS: Quite useless.

WERLE: And I suppose you won't enter the firm either?

GREGERS: No.

WERLE: Very good. But as I am thinking of marrying again, your share in the property will fall to you at once.[5]

5. By Norwegian law, before a widower can marry again, a certain proportion of his property must be settled on his children by his former marriage. [Translator's note.]

GREGERS [quickly]: No, I do not want that.

WERLE: You don't want it?

GREGERS: No, I dare not take it, for conscience' sake.

WERLE [after a pause]: Are you going up to the works again?

GREGERS: No; I consider myself released from your service.

WERLE: But what are you going to do?

GREGERS: Only to fulfil my mission; nothing more.

WERLE: Well, but afterwards? What are you going to live upon?

GREGERS: I have laid by a little out of my salary.

WERLE: How long will that last?

GREGERS: I think it will last my time.

WERLE: What do you mean?

GREGERS: I shall answer no more questions.

WERLE: Good-bye then, Gregers.

GREGERS: Good-bye.

[WERLE goes.]

HIALMAR [peeping in]: He's gone, isn't he?

GREGERS: Yes.

[HIALMAR and RELLING enter; also GINA and HEDVIG from the kitchen.]

RELLING: That luncheon-party was a failure.

GREGERS: Put on your coat, Hialmar; I want you to come for a long walk with me.

HIALMAR: With pleasure. What was it your father wanted? Had it anything to do with me?

GREGERS: Come along. We must have a talk. I'll go and put on my overcoat. [goes out by the passage door]

GINA: You shouldn't go out with him, Ekdal.

RELLING: No, don't you do it. Stay where you are.

HIALMAR [gets his hat and overcoat]: Oh, nonsense! When a friend of my youth feels impelled to open his mind to me in private——

RELLING: But devil take it—don't you see that the fellow's mad, cracked, demented?

GINA: There, what did I tell you? His mother before him had crazy fits like that sometimes.

HIALMAR: The more need for a friend's watchful eye. [to GINA] Be sure you have dinner ready in good time. Good-bye for the present. [goes out by the passage door]

RELLING: It's a thousand pities the fellow didn't go to hell through one of the Höidal mines.

GINA: Good Lord! what makes you say that?

RELLING [muttering]: Oh, I have my own reasons.

GINA: Do you think young Werle is really mad?

RELLING: No, worse luck; he's no madder than most other people. But one disease he has certainly got in his system.

GINA: What's the matter with him?

RELLING: Well, I'll tell you, Mrs. Ekdal. He is suffering from an acute attack of integrity.

GINA: Integrity?

HEDVIG: Is that a kind of disease?

RELLING: Yes, it's a national disease; but it only appears sporadically. [nods to GINA] Thanks for your hospitality.

[He goes out by the passage door.]

GINA [moving restlessly to and fro]: Ugh, that Gregers Werle—he was always a wretched creature.

HEDVIG [standing by the table and looking searchingly at her]: I think all this is very strange.

❀ Act IV

SCENE—HIALMAR EKDAL's studio. A photograph has just been taken; a camera with the cloth over it, a pedestal, two chairs, a folding table, etc., are standing out in the room. Afternoon light; the sun is going down; a little later it begins to grow dusk.

GINA stands in the passage doorway, with a little box and a wet glass plate in her hand, and is speaking to somebody outside.

GINA: Yes, certainly. When I make a promise I keep it. The first dozen shall be ready on Monday. Good afternoon.

[Someone is heard going downstairs. GINA shuts the door, slips the plate into the box and puts it into the covered camera.]

HEDVIG [comes in from the kitchen]: Are they gone?

GINA [tidying up]: Yes, thank goodness, I've got rid of them at last.

HEDVIG: But can you imagine why father hasn't come home yet?

GINA: Are you sure he's not down in Relling's room?

HEDVIG: No, he's not; I ran down the kitchen stair just now and asked.

GINA: And his dinner standing and getting cold, too.

HEDVIG: Yes, I can't understand it. Father's always so careful to be home to dinner!

GINA: Oh, he'll be here directly, you'll see.

HEDVIG: I wish he would come; everything seems so queer today.

GINA [calls out]: There he is!

[HIALMAR EKDAL comes in at the passage door.]

HEDVIG [going to him]: Father! Oh, what a time we've been waiting for you!

GINA [glancing sidelong at him]: You've been out a long time, Ekdal.

HIALMAR [without looking at her]: Rather long, yes.

[He takes off his overcoat; GINA and HEDVIG go to help him; he motions them away.]

GINA: Perhaps you've had dinner with Werle?

HIALMAR [hanging up his coat]: No.

GINA [going towards the kitchen door]: Then I'll bring some in for you.

HIALMAR: No; let the dinner alone. I want nothing to eat.

HEDVIG [going nearer to him]: Are you not well, father?

HIALMAR: Well? Oh, yes, well enough. We have had a tiring walk, Gregers and I.

GINA: You didn't ought to have gone so far, Ekdal; you're not used to it.

HIALMAR: H'm; there's many a thing a man must get used to in this world. [wanders about the room] Has any one been here whilst I was out?

GINA: Nobody but the two sweethearts.

HIALMAR: No new orders?

GINA: No, not today.

HEDVIG: There will be some tomorrow, father; you'll see.

HIALMAR: I hope there will, for tomorrow I am going to set to work in real earnest.

HEDVIG: Tomorrow! Don't you remember what day it is tomorrow?

HIALMAR: Oh, yes, by-the-bye——. Well, the day after, then. Henceforth I mean to do everything myself; I shall take all the work into my own hands.

GINA: Why, what can be the good of that, Ekdal? It'll only make your life a burden to you. I can manage the photography all right, and you can go on working at your invention.

HEDVIG: And think of the wild duck, father,—and all the hens and rabbits and——!

HIALMAR: Don't talk to me of all that trash! From tomorrow I will never set foot in the garret again.

HEDVIG: Oh, but father, you promised that we should have a little party——

HIALMAR: H'm, true. Well, then, from the day after tomorrow. I should almost like to wring that cursed wild duck's neck!

HEDVIG [*shrieks*]: The wild duck!

GINA: Well, I never!

HEDVIG [*shaking him*]: Oh, no, father; you know it's my wild duck!

HIALMAR: That is why I don't do it. I haven't the heart to—for your sake, Hedvig. But in my inmost soul I feel that I ought to do it. I ought not to tolerate under my roof a creature that has been through those hands.

GINA: Why, good gracious, even if grandfather did get it from that poor creature, Pettersen——

HIALMAR [*wandering about*]: There are certain claims—what shall I call them?—let me say claims of the ideal—certain obligations, which a man cannot disregard without injury to his soul.

HEDVIG [*going after him*]: But think of the wild duck,—the poor wild duck!

HIALMAR [*stops*]: I tell you I will spare it—for your sake. Not a hair of its head shall be—I mean, it shall be spared. There are greater problems than that to be dealt with. But you should go out a little now, Hedvig, as usual; it is getting dusk enough for you now.

HEDVIG: No, I don't care about going out now.

HIALMAR: Yes, do; it seems to me your eyes are blinking a great deal; all these vapors in here are bad for you. The air is heavy under this roof.

HEDVIG: Very well, then, I'll run down the kitchen stair and go for a little walk. My cloak and hat?—oh, they're in my own room. Father—be sure you don't do the wild duck any harm while I'm out.

HIALMAR: Not a feather of its head shall be touched. [*draws her to him*] You and I, Hedvig—we two——! Well, go along.

[HEDVIG *nods to her parents and goes out through the kitchen.*]

HIALMAR [*walks about without looking up*]: Gina.

GINA: Yes?

HIALMAR: From tomorrow—or, say, from the day after tomorrow—I should like to keep the household account-book myself.

GINA: Do you want to keep the accounts, too, now?

HIALMAR: Yes; or to check the receipts at any rate.

GINA: Lord help us! that's soon done.

HIALMAR: One would hardly think so; at any rate, you seem to make the money go a very long way. [*stops and looks at her*] How do you manage it?

GINA: It's because me and Hedvig, we need so little.

HIALMAR: Is it the case that father is very liberally paid for the copying he does for Mr. Werle?

GINA: I don't know as he gets anything out of the way. I don't know the rates for that sort of work.

HIALMAR: Well, what does he get, about? Let me hear!

GINA: Oh, it varies; I daresay it'll come to about as much as he costs us, with a little pocket-money over.

HIALMAR: As much as he costs us! And you have never told me this before!

GINA: No, how could I tell you? It pleased you so much to think he got everything from you.

HIALMAR: And he gets it from Mr. Werle.

GINA: Oh, well, he has plenty and to spare, he has.

HIALMAR: Light the lamp for me, please!

GINA [lighting the lamp]: And, of course, we don't know as it's Mr. Werle himself; it may be Gråberg——

HIALMAR: Light the lamp for me, please!

GINA: I don't know; I only thought——

HIALMAR: H'm.

GINA: It wasn't me that got grandfather that copying. It was Bertha, when she used to come about us.

HIALMAR: It seems to me your voice is trembling.

GINA [putting the lamp-shade on]: Is it?

HIALMAR: And your hands are shaking, are they not?

GINA [firmly]: Come right out with it, Ekdal. What has he been saying about me?

HIALMAR: Is it true—can it be true that—that there was an—an understanding between you and Mr. Werle, while you were in service there?

GINA: That's not true. Not at that time. Mr. Werle did come after me, that's a fact. And his wife thought there was something in it, and then she made such a hocus-pocus and hurly-burly, and she hustled me and bustled me about so that I left her service.

HIALMAR: But afterwards, then?

GINA: Well, then I went home. And mother—well, she wasn't the woman you took her for, Ekdal; she kept on worrying and worrying at me about one thing and another—for Mr. Werle was a widower by that time.

HIALMAR: Well, and then?

GINA: I suppose you've got to know it. He gave me no peace until he'd had his way.

HIALMAR [striking his hands together]: And this is the mother of my child! How could you hide this from me?

GINA: Yes, it was wrong of me; I ought certainly to have told you long ago.

HIALMAR: You should have told me at the very first;—then I should have known the sort of woman you were.

GINA: But would you have married me all the same?

HIALMAR: How can you dream that I would?

GINA: That's just why I didn't dare tell you anything, then. For I'd come to care for you so much, you see; and I couldn't go and make myself utterly miserable——

HIALMAR [walks about]: And this is my Hedvig's mother. And to know that all I see before me—[kicks a chair]—all that I call my home—I owe to a favored predecessor! Oh, that scoundrel Werle!

GINA: Do you repent of the fourteen—the fifteen years we've lived together?

HIALMAR [placing himself in front of her]: Have you not every day, every hour, repented of the spider's-web of deceit you have spun around me? Answer me that! How could you help writhing with penitence and remorse?

GINA: Oh, my dear Ekdal, I've had all I could do to look after the house and get through the day's work——

HIALMAR: Then you never think of reviewing your past?

GINA: No; Heaven knows I'd almost forgotten those old stories.

HIALMAR: Oh, this dull, callous contentment! To me there is something revolting about it. Think of it—never so much as a twinge of remorse!

GINA: But tell me, Ekdal—what would have become of you if you hadn't had a wife like me?

HIALMAR: Like you——!

GINA: Yes; for you know I've always been a bit more practical and wide-awake than you. Of course I'm a year or two older.

HIALMAR: What would have become of me!

GINA: You'd got into all sorts of bad ways when first you met me; that you can't deny.

HIALMAR: "Bad ways" do you call them? Little do you know what a man goes through when he is in grief and despair—especially a man of my fiery temperament.

GINA: Well, well, that may be so. And I've no reason to crow over you, neither; for you turned a moral of a husband, that you did, as soon as ever you had a house and home of your own.—And now we've got everything so nice and cosy about us; and me and Hedvig was just thinking we'd soon be able to let ourselves go a bit, in the way of both food and clothes.

HIALMAR: In the swamp of deceit, yes.

GINA: I wish to goodness that detestable thing had never set his foot inside our doors!

HIALMAR: And I, too, thought my home such a pleasant one. That was a delusion. Where shall I now find the elasticity of spirit to bring my invention into the world of reality? Perhaps it will die with me; and then it will be your past, Gina, that will have killed it.

GINA [nearly crying]: You mustn't say such things, Ekdal. Me, that has only wanted to do the best I could for you, all my days!

HIALMAR: I ask you, what becomes of the breadwinner's dream? When I used to lie in there on the sofa and brood over my invention, I had a clear enough presentiment that it would sap my vitality to the last drop. I felt even then that the day when I held the patent in my hand—that day—would bring my—release. And then it was my dream that you should live on after me, the dead inventor's well-to-do widow.

GINA [drying her tears]: No, you mustn't talk like that, Ekdal. May the Lord never let me see the day I am left a widow!

HIALMAR: Oh, the whole dream has vanished. It is all over now. All over!

[GREGERS WERLE opens the passage door cautiously and looks in.]

GREGERS: May I come in?

HIALMAR: Yes, come in.

GREGERS [comes forward, his face beaming with satisfaction, and holds out both his hands to them]: Well, dear friends——! [looks from one to the other and whispers to HIALMAR] Have you not done it yet?

HIALMAR [aloud]: It is done.

GREGERS: It is?

HIALMAR: I have passed through the bitterest moments of my life.

GREGERS: But also, I trust, the most ennobling.

HIALMAR: Well, at any rate, we have got through it for the present.

GINA: God forgive you, Mr. Werle.

GREGERS [in great surprise]: But I don't understand this.

HIALMAR: What don't you understand?

GREGERS: After so great a crisis—a crisis that is to be the starting-point of an entirely new life—of a communion founded on truth, and free from all taint of deception——

HIALMAR: Yes, yes, I know; I know that quite well.

The Wild Duck   375

GREGERS: I confidently expected, when I entered the room, to find the light of transfiguration shining upon me from both husband and wife. And now I see nothing but dulness, oppression, gloom——

GINA: Oh, is that it? [takes off the lamp-shade]

GREGERS: You will not understand me, Mrs. Ekdal. Ah, well, you, I suppose, need time to——. But you, Hialmar? Surely you feel a new consecration after the great crisis.

HIALMAR: Yes, of course I do. That is—in a sort of way.

GREGERS: For surely nothing in the world can compare with the joy of forgiving one who has erred and raising her up to oneself in love.

HIALMAR: Do you think a man can so easily throw off the bitter cup I have drained?

GREGERS: No, not a common man, perhaps. But a man like you——!

HIALMAR: Good God! I know that well enough. But you must keep me up to it, Gregers. It takes time, you know.

GREGERS: You have much of the wild duck in you, Hialmar.

[RELLING has come in at the passage door.]

RELLING: Oho! is the wild duck to the fore again?

HIALMAR: Yes; Mr. Werle's wing-broken victim.

RELLING: Mr. Werle's——? So it's him you are talking about?

HIALMAR: Him and—ourselves.

RELLING [in an undertone to GREGERS]: May the devil fly away with you!

HIALMAR: What is that you are saying?

RELLING: Only uttering a heartfelt wish that this quack-salver would take himself off. If he stays here, he is quite equal to making an utter mess of life, for both of you.

GREGERS: These two will not make a mess of life, Mr. Relling. Of course I won't speak of Hialmar—him we know. But she, too, in her innermost heart, has certainly something loyal and sincere——

GINA [almost crying]: You might have let me alone for what I was, then.

RELLING [to GREGERS]: Is it rude to ask what you really want in this house?

GREGERS: To lay the foundations of a true marriage.

RELLING: So you don't think Ekdal's marriage is good enough as it is?

GREGERS: No doubt it is as good a marriage as most others, worse luck. But a true marriage it has yet to become.

HIALMAR: You have never had eyes for the claims of the ideal, Relling.

RELLING: Rubbish, my boy!—but excuse me, Mr. Werle: how many —in round numbers—how many true marriages have you seen in the course of your life?

GREGERS: Scarcely a single one.

RELLING: Nor I either.

GREGERS: But I have seen innumerable marriages of the opposite kind. And it has been my fate to see at close quarters what ruin such a marriage can work in two human souls.

HIALMAR: A man's whole moral basis may give away beneath his feet; that is the terrible part of it.

RELLING: Well, I can't say I've ever been exactly married, so I don't pretend to speak with authority. But this I know, that the child enters into the marriage problem. And you must leave the child in peace.

HIALMAR: Oh—Hedvig! my poor Hedvig!

RELLING: Yes, you must be good enough to keep Hedvig outside of all this. You two are grown-up people; you are free, in God's name, to make what mess and muddle you please of your life. But you must deal cautiously with Hedvig, I tell you; else you may do her a great injury.

HIALMAR: An injury!

RELLING: Yes, or she may do herself an injury—and perhaps others, too.

GINA: How can you know that, Relling?

HIALMAR: Her sight is in no immediate danger, is it?

RELLING: I am not talking about her sight. Hedvig is at a critical age. She may be getting all sorts of mischief into her head.

GINA: That's true—I've noticed it already! She's taken to carrying on with the fire, out in the kitchen. She calls it playing at house-on-fire. I'm often scared for fear she really sets fire to the house.

RELLING: You see; I thought as much.

GREGERS [to RELLING]: But how do you account for that?

RELLING [sullenly]: Her constitution's changing, sir.

HIALMAR: So long as the child has me——! So long as I am above ground——!

[A knock at the door.]

GINA: Hush, Ekdal; there's some one in the passage. [calls out] Come in!

[MRS. SÖRBY, in walking dress, comes in.]

MRS. SÖRBY: Good evening.

GINA [going towards her]: Is it really you, Bertha?

MRS. SÖRBY: Yes, of course it is. But I'm disturbing you, I'm afraid?

HIALMAR: No, not at all; an emissary from that house——

MRS. SÖRBY [to GINA]: To tell the truth, I hoped your men-folk would be out at this time. I just ran up to have a little chat with you, and to say good-bye.

GINA: Good-bye? Are you going away, then?

MRS. SÖRBY: Yes, tomorrow morning,—up to Höidal. Mr. Werle started this afternoon. [*lightly to* GREGERS] He asked me to say good-bye for him.

GINA: Only fancy——!

HIALMAR: So Mr. Werle has gone? And now you are going after him?

MRS. SÖRBY: Yes, what do you say to that, Ekdal?

HIALMAR: I say: beware!

GREGERS: I must explain the situation. My father and Mrs. Sörby are going to be married.

HIALMAR: Going to be married!

GINA: Oh, Bertha! So it's come to that at last!

RELLING [*his voice quivering a little*]: This is surely not true?

MRS. SÖRBY: Yes, my dear Relling, it's true enough.

RELLING: You are going to marry again?

MRS. SÖRBY: Yes, it looks like it. Werle has got a special license, and we are going to be married quite quietly, up at the works.

GREGERS: Then I must wish you all happiness, like a dutiful stepson.

MRS. SÖRBY: Thank you very much—if you mean what you say. I certainly hope it will lead to happiness, both for Werle and for me.

RELLING: You have every reason to hope that. Mr. Werle never gets drunk—so far as I know; and I don't suppose he's in the habit of thrashing his wives, like the late lamented horse-doctor.

MRS. SÖRBY: Come now, let Sörby rest in peace. He had his good points, too.

RELLING: Mr. Werle has better ones, I have no doubt.

MRS. SÖRBY: He hasn't frittered away all that was good in him, at any rate. The man who does that must take the consequences.

RELLING: I shall go out with Molvik this evening.

MRS. SÖRBY: You mustn't do that, Relling. Don't do it—for my sake.

RELLING: There's nothing else for it. [*to* HIALMAR] If you're going with us, come along.

GINA: No, thank you. Ekdal doesn't go in for that sort of dissertation.

HIALMAR [*half aloud, in vexation*]: Oh, do hold your tongue!

RELLING: Good-bye, Mrs.—Werle. [*goes out through the passage door*]

GREGERS [*to* MRS. SÖRBY]: You seem to know Dr. Relling pretty intimately.

MRS. SÖRBY: Yes, we have known each other for many years. At one time it seemed as if things might have gone further between us.

GREGERS: It was surely lucky for you that they did not.

MRS. SÖRBY: You may well say that. But I have always been wary of acting on impulse. A woman can't afford absolutely to throw herself away.

GREGERS: Are you not in the least afraid that I may let my father know about this old friendship?

MRS. SÖRBY: Why, of course, I have told him all about it myself.

GREGERS: Indeed?

MRS. SÖRBY: Your father knows every single thing that can, with any truth, be said about me. I have told him all; it was the first thing I did when I saw what was in his mind.

GREGERS: Then you have been franker than most people, I think.

MRS. SÖRBY: I have always been frank. We women find that the best policy.

HIALMAR: What do you say to that, Gina?

GINA: Oh, we're not all alike, us women aren't. Some are made one way, some another.

MRS. SÖRBY: Well, for my part, Gina, I believe it's wisest to do as I've done. And Werle has no secrets either, on his side. That's really the great bond between us, you see. Now he can talk to me as openly as a child. He has never had the chance to do that before. Fancy a man like him, full of health and vigor, passing his whole youth and the best years of his life in listening to nothing but penitential sermons! And very often the sermons had for their text the most imaginary offences—at least so I understand.

GINA: That's true enough.

GREGERS: If you ladies are going to follow up this topic, I had better withdraw.

MRS. SÖRBY: You can stay as far as that's concerned. I shan't say a word more. But I wanted you to know that I had done nothing secretly or in an underhand way. I may seem to have come in for a great piece of luck; and so I have, in a sense. But after all, I don't think I am getting any more than I am giving. I shall stand by him always, and I can tend and care for him as no one else can, now that he is getting helpless.

HIALMAR: Getting helpless?

GREGERS [to MRS. SÖRBY]: Hush, don't speak of that here.

MRS. SÖRBY: There is no disguising it any longer, however much he would like to. He is going blind.

HIALMAR [starts]: Going blind? That's strange. He, too, going blind!

GINA: Lots of people do.

MRS. SÖRBY: And you can imagine what that means to a business man.

Well, I shall try as well as I can to make my eyes take the place of his. But I mustn't stay any longer; I have heaps of things to do.— Oh, by-the-bye, Ekdal, I was to tell you that if there is anything Werle can do for you, you must just apply to Gråberg.

GREGERS: That offer I am sure Hialmar Ekdal will decline with thanks.

MRS. SÖRBY: Indeed? I don't think he used to be so——

GINA: No, Bertha, Ekdal doesn't need anything from Mr. Werle now.

HIALMAR [slowly, and with emphasis]: Will you present my compliments to your future husband and say that I intend very shortly to call upon Mr. Gråberg——

GREGERS: What! You don't really mean that?

HIALMAR: To call upon Mr. Gråberg, I say, and obtain an account of the sum I owe his principal. I will pay that debt of honor—ha ha ha! a debt of honor, let us call it! In any case, I will pay the whole with five per cent interest.

GINA: But, my dear Ekdal, God knows we haven't got the money to do it.

HIALMAR: Be good enough to tell your future husband that I am working assiduously at my invention. Please tell him that what sustains me in this laborious task is the wish to free myself from a torturing burden of debt. That is my reason for proceeding with the invention. The entire profits shall be devoted to releasing me from my pecuniary obligations to your future husband.

MRS. SÖRBY: Something has happened here.

HIALMAR: Yes, you are right.

MRS. SÖRBY: Well, good-bye. I had something else to speak to you about, Gina; but it must keep till another time. Good-bye.

[HIALMAR and GREGERS bow silently. GINA follows MRS. SÖRBY to the door.]

HIALMAR: Not beyond the threshold, Gina!

[MRS. SÖRBY goes; GINA shuts the door after her.]

HIALMAR: There now, Gregers; I have got that burden of debt off my mind.

GREGERS: You soon will, at all events.

HIALMAR: I think my attitude may be called correct.

GREGERS: You are the man I have always taken you for.

HIALMAR: In certain cases, it is impossible to disregard the claim of the ideal. Yet, as the breadwinner of a family, I cannot but writhe and groan under it. I can tell you it is no joke for a man without capital to attempt the repayment of a long-standing obligation, over which, so to speak, the dust of oblivion had gathered. But it cannot be helped: the Man in me demands his rights.

GREGERS [*laying his hand on* HIALMAR's *shoulder*]: My dear Hialmar—was it not a good thing I came?

HIALMAR: Yes.

GREGERS: Are you not glad to have had your true position made clear to you?

HIALMAR [*somewhat impatiently*]: Yes, of course I am. But there is one thing that is revolting to my sense of justice.

GREGERS: And what is that?

HIALMAR: It is that—but I don't know whether I ought to express myself so unreservedly about your father.

GREGERS: Say what you please, so far as I am concerned.

HIALMAR: Well, then, is it not exasperating to think that it is not I, but he, who will realize the true marriage?

GREGERS: How can you say such a thing?

HIALMAR: Because it is clearly the case. Isn't the marriage between your father and Mrs. Sörby founded upon complete confidence, upon entire and unreserved candor on both sides? They hide nothing from each other; they keep no secrets in the background; their relation is based, if I may put it so, on mutual confession and absolution.

GREGERS: Well, what then?

HIALMAR: Well, is not that the whole thing? Did you not yourself say this was precisely the difficulty that had to be overcome in order to found a true marriage?

GREGERS: But this is a totally different matter, Hialmar. You surely don't compare either yourself or your wife with those two——? Oh, you understand me well enough.

HIALMAR: Say what you like, there is something in all this that hurts and offends my sense of justice. It really looks as if there were no just providence to rule the world.

GINA: Oh, no, Ekdal; for God's sake don't say such things.

GREGERS: H'm; don't let us get upon those questions.

HIALMAR: And yet, after all, I cannot but recognize the guiding finger of fate. He is going blind.

GINA: Oh, you can't be sure of that.

HIALMAR: There is no doubt about it. At all events there ought not to be; for in that very fact lies the righteous retribution. He has hoodwinked a confiding fellow-creature in days gone by——

GREGERS: I fear he has hoodwinked many.

HIALMAR: And now comes inexorable, mysterious Fate and demands Werle's own eyes.

GINA: Oh, how dare you say such dreadful things! You make me quite scared.

HIALMAR: It is profitable, now and then, to plunge deep into the night side of existence.

[HEDVIG, *in her hat and cloak, comes in by the passage door. She is pleasurably excited and out of breath.*]

GINA: Are you back already?

HEDVIG: Yes, I didn't care to go any farther. It was a good thing, too; for I've just met some one at the door.

HIALMAR: It must have been that Mrs. Sörby.

HEDVIG: Yes.

HIALMAR [*walks up and down*]: I hope you have seen her for the last time.

[*Silence.* HEDVIG, *discouraged, looks first at one and then at the other, trying to divine their frame of mind.*]

HEDVIG [*approaching, coaxingly*]: Father.

HIALMAR: Well—what is it, Hedvig?

HEDVIG: Mrs. Sörby had something with her for me.

HIALMAR [*stops*]: For you?

HEDVIG: Yes. Something for tomorrow.

GINA: Bertha has always given you some little thing on your birthday.

HIALMAR: What is it?

HEDVIG: Oh, you mustn't see it now. Mother is to give it to me tomorrow morning before I'm up.

HIALMAR: What is all this hocus-pocus that I am to be in the dark about?

HEDVIG [*quickly*]: Oh, no, you may see it if you like. It's a big letter. [*takes the letter out of her cloak pocket*]

HIALMAR: A letter, too?

HEDVIG: Yes, it is only a letter. The rest will come afterwards, I suppose. But fancy—a letter! I've never had a letter before. And there's "Miss" written upon it. [*reads*] "Miss Hedvig Ekdal." Only fancy—that's me!

HIALMAR: Let me see that letter.

HEDVIG [*hands it to him*]: There it is.

HIALMAR: That is Mr. Werle's hand.

GINA: Are you sure of that, Ekdal?

HIALMAR: Look for yourself.

GINA: Oh, what do *I* know about such-like things?

HIALMAR: Hedvig, may I open the letter—and read it?

HEDVIG: Yes, of course you may, if you want to.

GINA: No, not tonight, Ekdal; it's to be kept till tomorrow.

HEDVIG [*softly*]: Oh, can't you let him read it? It's sure to be something good; and then father will be glad, and everything will be nice again.

HIALMAR: I may open it, then?

HEDVIG: Yes, do, father. I'm so anxious to know what it is.

HIALMAR: Well and good. [*opens the letter, takes out a paper, reads it through and appears bewildered*] What is this——?

GINA: What does it say?

HEDVIG: Oh, yes, father—tell us!

HIALMAR: Be quiet. [*reads it through again; he has turned pale, but says with self-control*] It is a deed of gift, Hedvig.

HEDVIG: Is it? What sort of gift am I to have?

HIALMAR: Read for yourself.

[*HEDVIG goes over and reads for a time by the lamp.*]

HIALMAR [*half-aloud, clenching his hands*]: The eyes! The eyes—and then that letter!

HEDVIG [*leaves off reading*]: Yes, but it seems to me that it's grandfather that's to have it.

HIALMAR [*takes letter from her*]: Gina—can you understand this?

GINA: I know nothing whatever about it; tell me what's the matter.

HIALMAR: Mr. Werle writes to Hedvig that her old grandfather need not trouble himself any longer with the copying, but that he can henceforth draw on the office for a hundred crowns a month——

GREGERS: Aha!

HEDVIG: A hundred crowns, mother! I read that.

GINA: What a good thing for grandfather!

HIALMAR: ——a hundred crowns a month so long as he needs it—that means, of course, so long as he lives.

GINA: Well, so he's provided for, poor dear.

HIALMAR: But there is more to come. You didn't read that, Hedvig. Afterwards this gift is to pass on to you.

HEDVIG: To me! The whole of it?

HIALMAR: He says that the same amount is assured to you for the whole of your life. Do you hear that, Gina?

GINA: Yes, I hear.

HEDVIG: Fancy—all that money for me! [*shakes him*] Father, father, aren't you glad——?

HIALMAR [*eluding her*]: Glad! [*walks about*] Oh, what vistas—what perspectives open up before me! It is Hedvig, Hedvig that he showers these benefactions upon!

GINA: Yes, because it's Hedvig's birthday——

HEDVIG: And you'll get it all the same, father! You know quite well I shall give all the money to you and mother.

HIALMAR: To mother, yes! There we have it.

GREGERS: Hialmar, this is a trap he is setting for you.

HIALMAR: Do you think it's another trap?

GREGERS: When he was here this morning he said: Hialmar Ekdal is not the man you imagine him to be.

HIALMAR: Not the man——!

GREGERS: That you shall see, he said.

HIALMAR: He meant you should see that I would let myself be bought off——!

HEDVIG: Oh, mother, what does all this mean?

GINA: Go and take off your things.

[HEDVIG goes out by the kitchen door, half-crying.]

GREGERS: Yes, Hialmar—now is the time to show who was right, he or I.

HIALMAR [slowly tears the paper across, lays both pieces on the table and says] : Here is my answer.

GREGERS: Just what I expected.

HIALMAR [goes over to GINA, who stands by the stove, and says in a low voice]: Now please make a clean breast of it. If the connection between you and him was quite over when you—came to care for me, as you call it—why did he place us in a position to marry?

GINA: I suppose he thought as he could come and go in our house.

HIALMAR: Only that? Was not he afraid of a possible contingency?

GINA: I don't know what you mean.

HIALMAR: I want to know whether—your child has the right to live under my roof.

GINA [draws herself up; her eyes flash]: You ask that?

HIALMAR: You shall answer me this one question: Does Hedvig belong to me—or——? Well?

GINA [looking at him with cold defiance]: I don't know.

HIALMAR [quivering a little]: You don't know!

GINA: How should I know? A creature like me——

HIALMAR [quietly turning away from her]: Then I have nothing more to do in this house.

GREGERS: Take care, Hialmar! Think what you are doing!

HIALMAR [puts on his overcoat]: In this case, there is nothing for a man like me to think twice about.

GREGERS: Yes, indeed, there are endless things to be considered. You three must be together if you are to attain the true frame of mind for self-sacrifice and forgiveness.

HIALMAR: I don't want to attain it. Never, never! My hat! [takes his hat] My home has fallen in ruins about me. [bursts into tears] Gregers, I have no child!

HEDVIG [who has opened the kitchen door]: What is that you're saying? [coming to him] Father, father!

GINA: There, you see!

HIALMAR: Don't come near me, Hedvig! Keep far away. I cannot bear to see you! Oh! those eyes——! Good-bye. [makes for the door]

HEDVIG [clinging close to him and screaming loudly]: No! no! Don't leave me!

GINA [cries out]: Look at the child, Ekdal! Look at the child!

HIALMAR: I will not! I cannot! I must get out—away from all this!
    [He tears himself away from HEDVIG and goes out by the passage door.]

HEDVIG [with despairing eyes]: He is going away from us, mother! He is going away from us! He will never come back again!

GINA: Don't cry, Hedvig. Father's sure to come back again.

HEDVIG [throws herself sobbing on the sofa]: No, no, he'll never come home to us any more.

GREGERS: Do you believe I meant all for the best, Mrs. Ekdal?

GINA: Yes, I daresay you did; but God forgive you, all the same.

HEDVIG [lying on the sofa]: Oh, this will kill me! What have I done to him? Mother, you must fetch him home again!

GINA: Yes, yes, yes; only be quiet, and I'll go out and look for him. [puts on her outdoor things] Perhaps he's gone in to Relling's. But you mustn't lie there and cry. Promise me!

HEDVIG [weeping convulsively]: Yes, I'll stop, I'll stop; if only father comes back!

GREGERS [to GINA, who is going]: After all, had you not better leave him to fight out his bitter fight to the end?

GINA: Oh, he can do that afterwards. First of all, we must get the child quieted. [goes out by the passage door]

HEDVIG [sits up and dries her tears]: Now you must tell me what all this means? Why doesn't father want me any more?

GREGERS: You mustn't ask that till you are a big girl—quite grownup.

HEDVIG [sobs]: But I can't go on being as miserable as this till I'm grown-up.—I think I know what it is.—Perhaps I'm not really father's child.

GREGERS [uneasily]: How could that be?

HEDVIG: Mother might have found me. And perhaps father has just got to know it; I've read of such things.

GREGERS: Well, but if it were so——

HEDVIG: I think he might be just as fond of me for all that. Yes, fonder almost. We got the wild duck in a present, you know, and I love it so dearly all the same.

GREGERS [turning the conversation]: Ah, the wild duck, by-the-bye! Let us talk about the wild duck a little, Hedvig.

HEDVIG: The poor wild duck! He doesn't want to see it any more either. Only think, he wanted to wring its neck!

GREGERS: Oh, he won't do that.

HEDVIG: No; but he said he would like to. And I think it was horrid of father to say it, for I pray for the wild duck every night and ask that it may be preserved from death and all that is evil.

GREGERS [looking at her]: Do you say your prayers every night?

HEDVIG: Yes.

GREGERS: Who taught you to do that?

HEDVIG: I myself, one time when father was very ill, and had leeches on his neck and said that death was staring him in the face.

GREGERS: Well?

HEDVIG: Then I prayed for him as I lay in bed, and since then I have always kept it up.

GREGERS: And now you pray for the wild duck, too?

HEDVIG: I thought it was best to bring in the wild duck, for she was so weakly at first.

GREGERS: Do you pray in the morning, too?

HEDVIG: No, of course not.

GREGERS: Why not in the morning as well?

HEDVIG: In the morning it's light, you know, and there's nothing in particular to be afraid of.

GREGERS: And your father was going to wring the neck of the wild duck that you love so dearly?

HEDVIG: No; he said he ought to wring its neck, but he would spare it for my sake; and that was kind of father.

GREGERS [coming a little nearer]: But suppose you were to sacrifice the wild duck of your own free will for his sake.

HEDVIG [rising]: The wild duck!

GREGERS: Suppose you were to make a free-will offering, for his sake, of the dearest treasure you have in the world!

HEDVIG: Do you think that would do any good?

GREGERS: Try it, Hedvig.

HEDVIG [softly, with flashing eyes]: Yes, I will try it.

GREGERS: Have you really the courage for it, do you think?

HEDVIG: I'll ask grandfather to shoot the wild duck for me.

GREGERS: Yes, do. But not a word to your mother about it.

HEDVIG: Why not?

GREGERS: She doesn't understand us.

HEDVIG: The wild duck! I'll try it tomorrow morning.

[GINA *comes in by the passage door.*]

HEDVIG [*going towards her*]: Did you find him, mother?

GINA: No, but I heard as he had called and taken Relling with him.

GREGERS: Are you sure of that?

GINA: Yes, the porter's wife said so. Molvik went with them, too, she said.

GREGERS: This evening, when his mind so sorely needs to wrestle in solitude——!

GINA [*takes off her things*]: Yes, men are strange creatures, so they are. The Lord only knows where Relling has dragged him to! I ran over to Madame Eriksen's, but they weren't there.

HEDVIG [*struggling to keep back her tears*]: Oh, if he should never come home any more!

GREGERS: He will come home again. I shall have news to give him tomorrow; and then you shall see how he comes home. You may rely upon that, Hedvig, and sleep in peace. Good-night!

[*He goes out by the passage door.*]

HEDVIG [*throws herself sobbing on* GINA's *neck*]: Mother, mother!

GINA [*pats her shoulder and sighs*]: Ah, yes; Relling was right, he was. That's what comes of it when crazy creatures go about presenting the claims of the—what-you-may-call-it.

❀ *Act V*

SCENE—HIALMAR EKDAL's *studio. Cold, grey morning light. Wet snow lies upon the large panes of the sloping roof-window.*

GINA *comes from the kitchen with an apron and bib on, and carrying a dusting-brush and a duster; she goes towards the sitting-room door. At the same moment* HEDVIG *comes hurriedly in from the passage.*

GINA [*stops*]: Well?

HEDVIG: Oh, mother, I almost think he's down at Relling's——

GINA: There, you see!

HEDVIG: ——because the porter's wife says she could hear that Relling had two people with him when he came home last night.

GINA: That's just what I thought.

HEDVIG: But it's no use his being there, if he won't come up to us.

GINA: I'll go down and speak to him at all events.

[OLD EKDAL, *in dressing-gown and slippers, and with a lighted pipe, appears at the door of his room.*]

EKDAL: Hialmar—— Isn't Hialmar at home?

GINA: No, he's gone out.

EKDAL: So early? And in such a tearing snowstorm? Well, well; just as he pleases; I can take my morning walk alone.

[*He slides the garret door aside;* HEDVIG *helps him; he goes in; she closes it after him.*]

HEDVIG [*in an undertone*]: Only think, mother, when poor grandfather hears that father is going to leave us.

GINA: Oh, nonsense; grandfather mustn't hear anything about it. It was a heaven's mercy he wasn't at home yesterday in all that hurly-burly.

HEDVIG: Yes, but——

[GREGERS *comes in by the passage door.*]

GREGERS: Well, have you any news of him?

GINA: They say he's down at Relling's.

GREGERS: At Relling's! Has he really been out with those creatures?

GINA: Yes, like enough.

GREGERS: When he ought to have been yearning for solitude, to collect and clear his thoughts——

GINA: Yes, you may well say so.

[RELLING *enters from the passage.*]

HEDVIG [*going to him*]: Is father in your room?

GINA [*at the same time*]: Is he there?

RELLING: Yes, to be sure he is.

HEDVIG: And you never let us know!

RELLING: Yes, I'm a brute. But in the first place I had to look after the other brute; I mean our dæmonic friend, of course; and then I fell so dead asleep that——

GINA: What does Ekdal say today?

RELLING: He says nothing whatever.

HEDVIG: Not a blessed word.

GREGERS: No, no; I can understand that very well.

GINA: But what's he doing then?

RELLING: He's lying on the sofa, snoring.

GINA: Oh, is he? Yes, Ekdal's a rare one to snore.

HEDVIG: Asleep? Can he sleep?

RELLING: Well, it certainly looks like it.

GREGERS: No wonder, after the spiritual conflict that has rent him——

GINA: And then he's never been used to gadding about out of doors at night.

HEDVIG: Perhaps it's a good thing that he's getting sleep, mother.

GINA: Of course it is; and we must take care we don't wake him up too early. Thank you, Relling. I must get the house cleaned up a bit now, and then—— Come and help me, Hedvig.

[GINA and HEDVIG go into the sitting-room.]

GREGERS [turning to RELLING]: What is your explanation of the spiritual tumult that is now going on in Hialmar Ekdal?

RELLING: Devil a bit of a spiritual tumult have I noticed in him.

GREGERS: What! Not at such a crisis, when his whole life has been placed on a new foundation——? How can you think that such an individuality as Hialmar's——?

RELLING: Oh, individuality—he! If he ever had any tendency to the abnormal development you call individuality, I can assure you it was rooted out of him while he was still in his teens.

GREGERS: That would be strange indeed,—considering the loving care with which he was brought up.

RELLING: By those two high-flown, hysterical maiden aunts, you mean?

GREGERS: Let me tell you that they were women who never forgot the claim of the ideal—but of course you will only jeer at me again.

RELLING: No, I'm in no humor for that. I know all about those ladies; for he has ladled out no end of rhetoric on the subject of his "two soul-mothers." But I don't think he has much to thank them for. Ekdal's misfortune is that in his own circle he has always been looked upon as a shining light——

GREGERS: Not without reason, surely. Look at the depth of his mind!

RELLING: I have never discovered it. That his father believed in it I don't so much wonder; the old lieutenant has been an ass all his days.

GREGERS: He has had a child-like mind all his days; that is what you cannot understand.

RELLING: Well, so be it. But then, when our dear, sweet Hialmar went to college, he at once passed for the great light of the future amongst his comrades, too! He was handsome, the rascal—red and white—a shop-girl's dream of manly beauty; and with his super-ficially emotional temperament, and his sympathetic voice and his talent for declaiming other people's verses and other people's thoughts——

GREGERS [*indignantly*]: Is it Hialmar Ekdal you are talking about in this strain?

RELLING: Yes, with your permission; I am simply giving you an inside view of the idol you are grovelling before.

GREGERS: I should hardly have thought I was quite stone blind.

RELLING: Yes, you are—or not far from it. You are a sick man, too, you see.

GREGERS: You are right there.

RELLING: Yes. Yours is a complicated case. First of all there is that plaguy integrity-fever; and then—what's worse—you are always in a delirium of hero-worship; you must always have something to adore, outside yourself.

GREGERS: Yes, I must certainly seek it outside myself.

RELLING: But you make such shocking mistakes about every new phœnix you think you have discovered. Here again you have come to a cotter's cabin with your claim of the ideal; and the people of the house are insolvent.

GREGERS: If you don't think better than that of Hialmar Ekdal, what pleasure can you find in being everlastingly with him?

RELLING: Well, you see, I'm supposed to be a sort of doctor—save the mark! I can't but give a hand to the poor sick folk who live under the same roof with me.

GREGERS: Oh, indeed! Hialmar Ekdal is sick, too, is he?

RELLING: Most people are, worse luck.

GREGERS: And what remedy are you applying in Hialmar's case?

RELLING: My usual one. I am cultivating the life-illusion[6] in him.

GREGERS: Life-illusion? I didn't catch what you said.

RELLING: Yes, I said illusion. For illusion, you know, is the stimulating principle.

GREGERS: May I ask with what illusion Hialmar is inoculated?

RELLING: No, thank you; I don't betray professional secrets to quack-salvers. You would probably go and muddle his case still more than you have already. But my method is infallible. I have applied it to Molvik as well. I have made him "dæmonic." That's the blister I have to put on his neck.

GREGERS: Is he not really dæmonic, then?

RELLING: What the devil do you mean by dæmonic? It's only a piece of gibberish I've invented to keep up a spark of life in him. But for that, the poor harmless creature would have succumbed to self-

6. "Livslögnen," literally "the life-lie." [Translator's note.]

contempt and despair many a long year ago. And then the old lieutenant! But he has hit upon his own cure, you see.

GREGERS: Lieutenant Ekdal? What of him?

RELLING: Just think of the old bear-hunter shutting himself up in that dark garret to shoot rabbits! I tell you there is not a happier sportsman in the world than that old man pottering about in there among all that rubbish. The four or five withered Christmas trees he has saved up are the same to him as the whole great fresh Höidal forest; the cock and the hens are big game-birds in the fir-tops; and the rabbits that flop about the garret floor are the bears he has to battle with—the mighty hunter of the mountains!

GREGERS: Poor unfortunate old man! Yes; he has indeed had to narrow the ideals of his youth.

RELLING: While I think of it, Mr. Werle, junior—don't use that foreign word: ideals. We have the excellent native word: lies.

GREGERS: Do you think the two things are related?

RELLING: Yes, just about as closely as typhus and putrid fever.

GREGERS: Dr. Relling, I shall not give up the struggle until I have rescued Hialmar from your clutches!

RELLING: So much the worse for him. Rob the average man of his life-illusion, and you rob him of his happiness at the same stroke. [to HEDVIG, who comes in from the sitting-room] Well, little wild-duck-mother, I'm just going down to see whether papa is still lying meditating upon that wonderful invention of his. [goes out by passage door]

GREGERS [approaches HEDVIG]: I can see by your face that you have not yet done it.

HEDVIG: What? Oh, that about the wild duck! No.

GREGERS: I suppose your courage failed when the time came.

HEDVIG: No, that wasn't it. But when I awoke this morning and remembered what we had been talking about, it seemed so strange.

GREGERS: Strange?

HEDVIG: Yes, I don't know—— Yesterday evening, at the moment, I thought there was something so delightful about it; but since I have slept and thought of it again, it somehow doesn't seem worth while.

GREGERS: Ah, I thought you could not have grown up quite unharmed in this house.

HEDVIG: I don't care about that, if only father would come up——

GREGERS: Oh, if only your eyes had been opened to that which gives life its value—if you possessed the true, joyous, fearless spirit of sacrifice, you would soon see how he would come up to you.—But I believe in you still, Hedvig.

[*He goes out by the passage door.* HEDVIG *wanders about the room for a time; she is on the point of going into the kitchen when a knock is heard at the garret door.* HEDVIG *goes over and opens it a little;* OLD EKDAL *comes out; she pushes the door to again.*]

EKDAL: H'm, it's not much fun to take one's morning walk alone.

HEDVIG: Wouldn't you like to go shooting, grandfather?

EKDAL: It's not the weather for it today. It's so dark there, you can scarcely see where you're going.

HEDVIG: Do you never want to shoot anything besides the rabbits?

EKDAL: Do you think the rabbits aren't good enough?

HEDVIG: Yes, but what about the wild duck?

EKDAL: Ho-ho! are you afraid I shall shoot your wild duck? Never in the world. Never.

HEDVIG: No, I suppose you couldn't; they say it's very difficult to shoot wild ducks.

EKDAL: Couldn't! Should rather think I could.

HEDVIG: How would you set about it, grandfather?—I don't mean with my wild duck, but with others?

EKDAL: I should take care to shoot them in the breast, you know; that's the surest place. And then you must shoot against the feathers, you see—not the way of the feathers.

HEDVIG: Do they die then, grandfather?

EKDAL: Yes, they die right enough—when you shoot properly. Well, I must go and brush up a bit. H'm—understand—h'm. [*goes into his room*]

[HEDVIG *waits a little, glances towards the sitting-room door, goes over to the book-case, stands on tip-toe, takes the double-barrelled pistol down from the shelf and looks at it.* GINA, *with brush and duster, comes from the sitting-room.* HEDVIG *hastily lays down the pistol, unobserved.*]

GINA: Don't stand raking amongst father's things, Hedvig.

HEDVIG [*goes away from the bookcase*]: I was only going to tidy up a little.

GINA: You'd better go into the kitchen and see if the coffee's keeping hot; I'll take his breakfast on a tray, when I go down to him.

[HEDVIG *goes out.* GINA *begins to sweep and clean up the studio. Presently the passage door is opened with hesitation, and* HIALMAR EKDAL *looks in. He has on his overcoat, but not his hat; he is unwashed, and his hair is dishevelled and unkempt. His eyes are dull and heavy.*]

GINA [*standing with the brush in her hand and looking at him*]: Oh, there now, Ekdal—so you've come after all!

HIALMAR [*comes in and answers in a toneless voice*]: I come—only to depart again immediately.

GINA: Yes, yes, I suppose so. But, Lord help us! what a sight you are!

HIALMAR: A sight?

GINA: And your nice winter coat, too! Well, that's done for.

HEDVIG [*at the kitchen door*]: Mother, hadn't I better——? [*sees* HIALMAR, *gives a loud scream of joy and runs to him*] Oh, father, father!

HIALMAR [*turns away and makes a gesture of repulsion*]: Away, away, away! [*to* GINA] Keep her away from me, I say!

GINA [*in a low tone*]: Go into the sitting-room, Hedvig.

[HEDVIG *does so without a word.*]

HIALMAR [*fussily pulls out the table-drawer*]: I must have my books with me. Where are my books?

GINA: Which books?

HIALMAR: My scientific books, of course; the technical magazines I require for my invention.

GINA [*searches in the bookcase*]: Is it these here paper-covered ones?

HIALMAR: Yes, of course.

GINA [*lays a heap of magazines on the table*]: Shan't I get Hedvig to cut them for you?

HIALMAR: I don't require to have them cut for me.

[*Short silence.*]

GINA: Then you're still set on leaving us, Ekdal?

HIALMAR [*rummaging amongst the books*]: Yes, that is a matter of course, I should think.

GINA: Well, well.

HIALMAR [*vehemently*]: How can I live here, to be stabbed to the heart every hour of the day?

GINA: God forgive you for thinking such vile things of me.

HIALMAR: Prove——!

GINA: I think it's you as has got to prove.

HIALMAR: After a past like yours? There are certain claims—I may almost call them claims of the ideal——

GINA: But what about grandfather? What's to become of him, poor dear?

HIALMAR: I know my duty; my helpless father will come with me. I am going out into the town to make arrangements—— H'm—[*hesitatingly*]—has any one found my hat on the stairs?

GINA: No. Have you lost your hat?

HIALMAR: Of course I had it on when I came in last night; there's no doubt about that; but I couldn't find it this morning.

GINA: Lord help us! where have you been to with those two ne'er-do-wells?

HIALMAR: Oh, don't bother me about trifles. Do you suppose I am in the mood to remember details?

GINA: If only you haven't caught cold, Ekdal—— [goes out into the kitchen]

HIALMAR [talks to himself in a low tone of irritation, while he empties the table-drawer]: You're a scoundrel, Relling!—You're a low fellow!—Ah, you shameless tempter!—I wish I could get some one to stick a knife into you!

> [He lays some old letters on one side, finds the torn document of yesterday, takes it up and looks at the pieces; puts it down hurriedly as GINA enters.]

GINA [sets a tray with coffee, etc., on the table]: Here's a drop of something hot, if you'd fancy it. And there's some bread and butter and a snack of salt meat.

HIALMAR [glancing at the tray]: Salt meat? Never under this roof! It's true I have not had a mouthful of solid food for nearly twenty-four hours; but no matter.—My memoranda! The commencement of my autobiography! What has become of my diary, and all my important papers? [opens the sitting-room door but draws back] She is there, too!

GINA: Good Lord! the child must be somewhere!

HIALMAR: Come out.

> [He makes room; HEDVIG comes, scared, into the studio.]

HIALMAR [with his hand upon the door-handle, says to GINA]: In these, the last moments I spend in my former home, I wish to be spared from interlopers——[goes into the room]

HEDVIG [with a bound towards her mother, asks softly, trembling: Does that mean me?

GINA: Stay out in the kitchen, Hedvig; or, no—you'd best go into your own room. [speaks to HIALMAR as she goes in to him] Wait a bit, Ekdal; don't rummage so in the drawers; I know where everything is.

HEDVIG [stands a moment immovable, in terror and perplexity, biting her lips to keep back the tears; then she clenches her hands convulsively and says softly]: The wild duck.

> [She steals over and takes the pistol from the shelf, opens the garret door a little way, creeps in and draws the door to after her. HIALMAR and GINA can be heard disputing in the sitting-room.]

HIALMAR [*comes in with some manuscript books and old loose papers,* *which he lays upon the table*]: That portmanteau is of no use! There are a thousand and one things I must drag with me.

GINA [*following with the portmanteau*]: Why not leave all the rest for the present and only take a shirt and a pair of woollen drawers with you?

HIALMAR: Whew!—all these exhausting preparations——! [*pulls off his overcoat and throws it upon the sofa*]

GINA: And there's the coffee getting cold.

HIALMAR: H'm. [*drinks a mouthful without thinking of it and then another*]

GINA [*dusting the backs of the chairs*]: A nice job you'll have to find such another big garret for the rabbits.

HIALMAR: What! Am I to drag all those rabbits with me, too?

GINA: You don't suppose grandfather can get on without his rabbits.

HIALMAR: He must just get used to doing without them. Have not *I* to sacrifice very much greater things than rabbits?

GINA [*dusting the bookcase*]: Shall I put the flute in the portmanteau for you?

HIALMAR: No. No flute for me. But give me the pistol!

GINA: Do you want to take the pistol with you?

HIALMAR: Yes. My loaded pistol.

GINA [*searching for it*]: It's gone. He must have taken it in with him.

HIALMAR: Is he in the garret?

GINA: Yes, of course he's in the garret.

HIALMAR: H'm—poor lonely old man.

[*He takes a piece of bread and butter, eats it, and finishes his cup of coffee.*]

GINA: If we hadn't have let that room, you could have moved in there.

HIALMAR: And continued to live under the same roof with——! Never, —never!

GINA: But couldn't you put up with the sitting-room for a day or two? You could have it all to yourself.

HIALMAR: Never within these walls!

GINA: Well, then, down with Relling and Molvik.

HIALMAR: Don't mention those wretches' names to me! The very thought of them almost takes away my appetite.—Oh, no, I must go out into the storm and the snow-drift,—go from house to house and seek shelter for my father and myself.

GINA: But you've got no hat, Ekdal! You've been and lost your hat, you know.

HIALMAR: Oh, those two brutes, those slaves of all the vices! A hat must be procured. [takes another piece of bread and butter] Some arrangements must be made. For I have no mind to throw away my life, either. [looks for something on the tray]

GINA: What are you looking for?

HIALMAR: Butter.

GINA: I'll get some at once. [goes out into the kitchen]

HIALMAR [calls after her]: Oh, it doesn't matter; dry bread is good enough for me.

GINA [brings a dish of butter]: Look here; this is fresh churned.

[She pours out another cup of coffee for him; he seats himself on the sofa, spreads more butter on the already buttered bread and eats and drinks awhile in silence.]

HIALMAR: Could I, without being subject to intrusion—intrusion of any sort—could I live in the sitting-room there for a day or two?

GINA: Yes, to be sure you could, if you only would.

HIALMAR: For I see no possibility of getting all father's things out in such a hurry.

GINA: And, besides, you've surely got to tell him first as you don't mean to live with us others no more.

HIALMAR [pushes away his coffee cup]: Yes, there is that, too; I shall have to lay bare the whole tangled story to him—— I must turn matters over; I must have breathing-time; I cannot take all these burdens on my shoulders in a single day.

GINA: No, especially in such horrible weather as it is outside.

HIALMAR [touching WERLE's letter]: I see that paper is still lying about here.

GINA: Yes, I haven't touched it.

HIALMAR: So far as I am concerned it is mere waste paper——

GINA: Well, I have certainly no notion of making any use of it.

HIALMAR: ——but we had better not let it get lost all the same;—in all the upset when I move, it might easily——

GINA: I'll take good care of it, Ekdal.

HIALMAR: The donation is in the first instance made to father, and it rests with him to accept or decline it.

GINA [sighs]: Yes, poor old father——

HIALMAR: To make quite safe—— Where shall I find some gum?

GINA [goes to the bookcase]: Here's the gum-pot.

HIALMAR: And a brush?

GINA: The brush is here, too. [brings him the things]

HIALMAR [takes a pair of scissors]: Just a strip of paper at the back——
[clips and gums] Far be it from me to lay hands upon what is not
my own—and least of all upon what belongs to a destitute old
man—and to—the other as well.—There now. Let it lie there for a
time; and when it is dry, take it away. I wish never to see that
document again. Never!

[GREGERS WERLE enters from the passage.]

GREGERS [somewhat surprised]: What,—are you sitting here, Hialmar?

HIALMAR [rises hurriedly]: I had sunk down from fatigue.

GREGERS: You have been having breakfast, I see.

HIALMAR: The body sometimes makes its claims felt, too.

GREGERS: What have you decided to do?

HIALMAR: For a man like me, there is only one course possible. I am
just putting my most important things together. But it takes time,
you know.

GINA [with a touch of impatience]: Am I to get the room ready for
you, or am I to pack your portmanteau?

HIALMAR [after a glance of annoyance at GREGERS]: Pack—and get the
room ready!

GINA [takes the portmanteau]: Very well; then I'll put in the shirt and
the other things. [goes into the sitting-room and draws the door to
after her]

GREGERS [after a short silence]: I never dreamed that this would be the
end of it. Do you really feel it a necessity to leave house and home?

HIALMAR [wanders about restlessly]: What would you have me do?—I
am not fitted to bear unhappiness, Gregers. I must feel secure and at
peace in my surroundings.

GREGERS: But can you not feel that here? Just try it. I should have
thought you had firm ground to build upon now—if only you start
afresh. And, remember, you have your invention to live for.

HIALMAR: Oh, don't talk about my invention. It's perhaps still in the
dim distance.

GREGERS: Indeed!

HIALMAR: Why, great heavens, what would you have me invent? Other
people have invented almost everything already. It becomes more
and more difficult every day——

GREGERS: And you have devoted so much labor to it.

HIALMAR: It was that blackguard Relling that urged me to it.

GREGERS: Relling?

HIALMAR: Yes, it was he that first made me realize my aptitude for
making some notable discovery in photography.

GREGERS: Aha—it was Relling!

HIALMAR: Oh, I have been so truly happy over it! Not so much for the sake of the invention itself, as because Hedvig believed in it—believed in it with a child's whole eagerness of faith.—At least, I have been fool enough to go and imagine that she believed in it.

GREGERS: Can you really think Hedvig has been false towards you?

HIALMAR: I can think anything now. It is Hedvig that stands in my way. She will blot out the sunlight from my whole life.

GREGERS: Hedvig! Is it Hedvig you are talking of? How should she blot out your sunlight?

HIALMAR [*without answering*]: How unutterably I have loved that child! How unutterably happy I have felt every time I came home to my humble room, and she flew to meet me, with her sweet little blinking eyes. Oh, confiding fool that I have been! I loved her unutterably;—and I yielded myself up to the dream, the delusion, that she loved me unutterably in return.

GREGERS: Do you call that a delusion?

HIALMAR: How should I know? I can get nothing out of Gina; and besides, she is totally blind to the ideal side of these complications. But to you I feel impelled to open my mind, Gregers. I cannot shake off this frightful doubt—perhaps Hedvig has never really and honestly loved me.

GREGERS: What would you say if she were to give you a proof of her love? [*listens*] What's that? I thought I heard the wild duck——?

HIALMAR: It's the wild duck quacking. Father's in the garret.

GREGERS: Is he? [*His face lights up with joy.*] I say, you may yet have proof that your poor misunderstood Hedvig loves you!

HIALMAR: Oh, what proof can she give me? I dare not believe in any assurance from that quarter.

GREGERS: Hedvig does not know what deceit means.

HIALMAR: Oh, Gregers, that is just what I cannot be sure of. Who knows what Gina and that Mrs. Sörby may many a time have sat here whispering and tattling about? And Hedvig usually has her ears open, I can tell you. Perhaps the deed of gift was not such a surprise to her, after all. In fact, I'm not sure but that I noticed something of the sort.

GREGERS: What spirit is this that has taken possession of you?

HIALMAR: I have had my eyes opened. Just you notice;—you'll see, the deed of gift is only a beginning. Mrs. Sörby has always been a good deal taken up with Hedvig, and now she has the power to do whatever she likes for the child. They can take her from me whenever they please.

GREGERS: Hedvig will never, never leave you.

HIALMAR: Don't be so sure of that. If only they beckon to her and throw out a golden bait——! And, oh! I have loved her so unspeakably! I would have counted it my highest happiness to take her tenderly by the hand and lead her, as one leads a timid child through a great dark empty room!—I am cruelly certain now that the poor photographer in his humble attic has never really and truly been anything to her. She has only cunningly contrived to keep on a good footing with him until the time came.

GREGERS: You don't believe that yourself, Hialmar.

HIALMAR: That is just the terrible part of it—I don't know what to believe,—I never can know it. But can you really doubt that it must be as I say? Ho-ho, you have far too much faith in the claim of the ideal, my good Gregers! If those others came, with the glamour of wealth about them, and called to the child:—"Leave him: come to us: here life awaits you——!"

GREGERS [quickly]: Well, what then?

HIALMAR: If I then asked her: Hedvig, are you willing to renounce that life for me? [laughs scornfully] No thank you! You would soon hear what answer I should get.

[A pistol shot is heard from within the garret.]

GREGERS [loudly and joyfully]: Hialmar!

HIALMAR: There now; he must needs go shooting, too.

GINA [comes in]: Oh, Ekdal, I can hear grandfather blazing away in the garret by hisself.

HIALMAR: I'll look in——

GREGERS [eagerly, with emotion]: Wait a moment! Do you know what that was?

HIALMAR: Yes, of course I know.

GREGERS: No, you don't know. But I do. That was the proof!

HIALMAR: What proof?

GREGERS: It was a child's free-will offering. She has got your father to shoot the wild duck.

HIALMAR: To shoot the wild duck!

GINA: Oh, think of that——!

HIALMAR: What was that for?

GREGERS: She wanted to sacrifice to you her most cherished possession; for then she thought you would surely come to love her again.

HIALMAR [tenderly, with emotion]: Oh, poor child!

GINA: What things she does think of!

GREGERS: She only wanted your love again, Hialmar. She could not live without it.

GINA [struggling with her tears]: There, you can see for yourself, Ekdal.

HIALMAR: Gina, where is she?

GINA [sniffs]: Poor dear, she's sitting out in the kitchen, I dare say.

HIALMAR [goes over, tears open the kitchen door and says]: Hedvig, come, come in to me! [looks around] No, she's not here.

GINA: Then she must be in her own little room.

HIALMAR [without]: No, she's not here either. [comes in] She must have gone out.

GINA: Yes, you wouldn't have her anywheres in the house.

HIALMAR: Oh, if she would only come home quickly, so that I can tell her—— Everything will come right now, Gregers; now I believe we can begin life afresh.

GREGERS [quietly]: I knew it; I knew the child would make amends.
[OLD EKDAL appears at the door of his room; he is in full uniform and is busy buckling on his sword.]

HIALMAR [astonished]: Father! Are you there?

GINA: Have you been firing in your room?

EKDAL [resentfully, approaching]: So you go shooting alone, do you, Hialmar?

HIALMAR [excited and confused]: Then it wasn't you that fired that shot in the garret?

EKDAL: Me that fired? H'm.

GREGERS [calls out to HIALMAR]: She has shot the wild duck herself!

HIALMAR: What can it mean? [hastens to the garret door, tears it aside, looks in and calls loudly] Hedvig!

GINA [runs to the door]: Good God, what's that?

HIALMAR [goes in]: She's lying on the floor!

GREGERS: Hedvig! lying on the floor? [goes in to HIALMAR]

GINA [at the same time]: Hedvig! [inside the garret] No, no, no!

EKDAL: Ho-ho! does she go shooting, too, now?
[HIALMAR, GINA, and GREGERS carry HEDVIG into the studio; in her dangling right hand she holds the pistol fast clasped in her fingers.]

HIALMAR [distracted]: The pistol has gone off. She has wounded herself. Call for help! Help!

GINA [runs into the passage and calls down]: Relling! Relling! Doctor Relling; come up as quick as you can!
[HIALMAR and GREGERS lay HEDVIG down on the sofa.]

EKDAL [quietly]: The woods avenge themselves.

HIALMAR [on his knees beside HEDVIG]: She'll soon come to now. She's coming to——; yes, yes, yes.

GINA [who has come in again]: Where has she hurt herself? I can't see anything——

    [RELLING comes hurriedly, and immediately after him MOLVIK; the latter without his waistcoat and necktie, and with his coat open.]

RELLING: What's the matter here?

GINA: They say Hedvig has shot herself.

HIALMAR: Come and help us!

RELLING: Shot herself!

    [He pushes the table aside and begins to examine her.]

HIALMAR [kneeling and looking anxiously up at him]: It can't be dangerous? Speak, Relling! She is scarcely bleeding at all. It can't be dangerous?

RELLING: How did it happen?

HIALMAR: Oh, we don't know——

GINA: She wanted to shoot the wild duck.

RELLING: The wild duck?

HIALMAR: The pistol must have gone off.

RELLING: H'm. Indeed.

EKDAL: The woods avenge themselves. But I'm not afraid, all the same.
    [goes into the garret and closes the door after him]

HIALMAR: Well, Relling,—why don't you say something?

RELLING: The ball has entered the breast.

HIALMAR: Yes, but she's coming to!

RELLING: Surely you can see that Hedvig is dead.

GINA [bursts into tears]: Oh, my child, my child——

GREGERS: [huskily]: In the depths of the sea——

HIALMAR [jumps up]: No, no, she must live! Oh, for God's sake, Relling—only a moment—only just till I can tell her how unspeakably I loved her all the time!

RELLING: The bullet has gone through her heart. Internal hemorrhage. Death must have been instantaneous.

HIALMAR: And I! I hunted her from me like an animal! And she crept terrified into the garret and died for love of me! [sobbing] I can never atone to her! I can never tell her——! [clenches his hands and cries, upwards] O thou above——! If thou be indeed! Why hast thou done this thing to me?

GINA: Hush, hush, you mustn't go on that awful way. We had no right to keep her, I suppose.

MOLVIK: The child is not dead, but sleepeth.

RELLING: Bosh.

HIALMAR [*becomes calm, goes over to the sofa, folds his arms and looks at* HEDVIG]: There she lies so stiff and still.

RELLING [*tries to loosen the pistol*]: She's holding it so tight, so tight.

GINA: No, no, Relling, don't break her fingers; let the pistol be.

HIALMAR: She shall take it with her.

GINA: Yes, let her. But the child mustn't lie here for a show. She shall go to her own room, so she shall. Help me, Ekdal.

[HIALMAR *and* GINA *take* HEDVIG *between them.*]

HIALMAR [*as they are carrying her*]: Oh, Gina, Gina, can you survive this?

GINA: We must help each other to bear it. For now at least she belongs to both of us.

MOLVIK [*stretches out his arms and mumbles*]: Blessed be the Lord; to earth thou shalt return; to earth thou shalt return——

RELLING [*whispers*]: Hold your tongue, you fool; you're drunk.

[HIALMAR *and* GINA *carry the body out through the kitchen door.* RELLING *shuts it after them.* MOLVIK *slinks out into the passage.*]

RELLING [*goes over to* GREGERS *and says*]: No one shall ever convince me that the pistol went off by accident.

GREGERS [*who has stood terrified, with convulsive twitchings*]: Who can say how the dreadful thing happened?

RELLING: The powder has burnt the body of her dress. She must have pressed the pistol right against her breast and fired.

GREGERS: Hedvig has not died in vain. Did you not see how sorrow set free what is noble in him?

RELLING: Most people are ennobled by the actual presence of death. But how long do you suppose this nobility will last in him?

GREGERS: Why should it not endure and increase throughout his life?

RELLING: Before a year is over, little Hedvig will be nothing to him but a pretty theme for declamation.

GREGERS: How dare you say that of Hialmar Ekdal?

RELLING: We will talk of this again, when the grass has first withered on her grave. Then you'll hear him spouting about "the child too early torn from her father's heart;" then you'll see him steep himself in a syrup of sentiment and self-admiration and self-pity. Just you wait!

GREGERS: If you are right and I am wrong, then life is not worth living.

RELLING: Oh, life would be quite tolerable, after all, if only we could be rid of the confounded duns that keep on pestering us, in our poverty, with the claim of the ideal.

GREGERS [looking straight before him]: In that case, I am glad that my destiny is what it is.

RELLING: May I inquire,—what is your destiny?

GREGERS [going]: To be the thirteenth at table.

RELLING: The devil it is.

❀ Comments

However, I have supposed that Hialmar will be played by Reimers. This part must definitely not be rendered with any touch of parody nor with the faintest suggestion that the actor is aware that there is anything funny about his remarks. He has a warm and sympathetic voice, as Relling says, and that should be maintained above all else. His sentimentality is genuine, his melancholy charming in its way—not a bit of affectation. Confidentially, I would like to call your attention to Kristofer Janson who, frankly, can be charming when he's talking the worst nonsense. This is a hint for the actor in question.

Gina, I think, could be acted well by Mrs. Wolf. But where can we get Hedvig? I do not know. And Mrs. Sörby? She is supposed to be attractive, witty, and not at all vulgar. Could Miss Reimers solve the problem? Or can Mrs. Gunderson? Gregers is the most difficult character in the play as far as acting is concerned.

Letter to Hans Schrøder, Rome, November 14, 1884. In Evert Sprinchorn, ed. *Ibsen: Letters and Speeches* (New York: Hill and Wang, Inc., 1964), p. 242.

After *An Enemy of the People*, Ibsen, as I have said, left the vulgar ideals for dead, and set about the exposure of those of the choicer spirits, beginning with the incorrigible idealists who had idealized his very self, and were becoming known as Ibsenites. His first move in this direction was such a tragi-comic slaughtering of sham Ibsenism that his astonished victims plaintively declared that *The Wild Duck*, as the new play was called, was a satire on his former works; whilst the pious, whom he had disappointed so severely by his interpretation of Brand, began to hope that he was coming back repentant to the fold.

Bernard Shaw, *The Quintessence of Ibsenism* (New York: Hill and Wang, Inc.), p. 97.

But perhaps for those who make a case for Ibsen's use of symbolism in his prose plays, none of the works mentioned would be a main text. Such a text would almost certainly be *The Wild Duck*. This play, written in 1884, when Ibsen was 56, is frequently singled out by his critics as his greatest work.

Ibsen speaks of *The Wild Duck* as occupying

> a place apart among my dramatic production; its method of progress is in many respects divergent from that of its predecessors.

This has never been satisfactorily explained; but it would seem that the change is that the device, the "symbol," is used at every point in the presentation. It sets the total atmosphere of the broken, frustrated people who have forgotten "their natural life," and is the embodiment of the debt which Gregers so fatally pays. It thus covers the whole of the situation and action. In this respect it resembles the orphanage of Captain Alving or the infected baths or the unseaworthy ship. But it also does more: it is a means of definition of the main characters, who are all explicitly "revealed" in its terms. And it is this preoccupation with "character-revelation" that is the really new element of the play.

Like all such plays, the humanity it depicts is of a rather special kind. The key word, used by all its critics, is "charm." This useful word (it can be alternated with "delicacy") covers the two extremes of character: the pathetic, lyrical Hedvig, a charming child; and the old caricature Ekdal, with his uniform cap and his secret drinking. There is something very conscious about this charm, an unmistakable quality of theatrical artifice. The characters laugh at each other, and we see our cue and join them. Then the laughter fades on our lips, which tremble; a cry of pathos, a glance at the attic, and we have passed to the identity of full, lovable human beings, poised between laughter and tears. The very thing, in fact, for an evening at the theatre.

This is a difficult judgment, but I think it is true that, in spite of the substantial human emotions behind the play, the actual effect is sentimental. "We are evidently intended to accept the character's sentimental interpretation of himself," Mr. Eliot wrote, of the earlier sentimental drama. In *The Wild Duck* this process is taken further: we are evidently intended to accept the sentimental self-interpretation of all the characters in the play, the whole group. And the focus of this attention is the figure of the wild duck.

The method almost succeeds; indeed it succeeds entirely for all those who are satisfied by this essentially naturalist mode of consciousness. The difficulty is that one can see how nearly Ibsen succeeded in establishing, through the figure of the wild duck, a total form, which would achieve dramatic concentration and unity. The reason for his failure, it seems to me, is that the characters, who have, "in the course of our long daily association, endeared themselves to me," take charge. The relaxation of judgment implied in Ibsen's phrase made of the figure of the wild duck, not a form, within which all the emotions of the play might be controlled and valued, but simply a pressure-point for all kinds of feeling: mature and immature, genuine and calculated, precise and vague. By its very function of uniting such varieties of feeling, it prevents that process of distinction and evaluation which a play of strong, overt emotion particularly needs. The figure, that is to say, while intended to integrate the minutely observed details of the drama, integrates only at the level of theatrical effect; its very sufficiency prevents the achievement of a more conclusive dramatic form.

Raymond Williams, *Drama From Ibsen to Eliot* (New York: Oxford Press, 1953), p. 75.

In Ibsen's career *The Wild Duck* seems to me to mark the beginning of a new and higher plateau, which extends through *Rosmersholm* and *Hedda Gabler* to *The Master Builder*. *A Doll's House* and *Ghosts*, with all their skill and wisdom and passion, did not blend so perfectly together reality, irony, pity, and poetry. But here, at moments, one may be reminded of that other master of all these qualities—Thomas Hardy. . . . Further, in *The Wild Duck* Ibsen has finally perfected that symbolism which, without growing too unreal, yet helps to cast a light of poetry and mystery across a harsh world of prose. There had been plenty of symbols in his earlier work; such as the onion and the button-moulder in *Peer Gynt*, the coffin-ship in *Pillars of Society*, the Christmas tree in *A Doll's House*, the disease in *Ghosts*. But in *The Wild Duck* the symbol, which actually gives its title to the drama, plays from first to last a far more vivid part. It becomes one of the actors. The wild duck is a real wild duck; yet, with the other creatures in that strange attic, it also symbolizes the world of pathetic fantasy in which crippled characters can live; it symbolizes too the crippled characters themselves. The symbol becomes a kind of abbreviated fable, or parable. When Henry James remarked, "Ibsen's later manner is the very prose of prose," he should have thought again.

The Wild Duck also differs, I think, from the plays before it, not only in having rounder, deeper characters and more poetry, but in its almost Russian combination of picturesque squalor and whimsicality. The Ekdal household with its livestock in the garret, its drunken doctor and parson in the room below, its general, mooning fecklessness, seems shifted from the Western, bourgeois atmosphere of *Pillars of Society*, *A Doll's House*, and *Ghosts*, far further East towards the world of Chekhov and Maxim Gorky. But though Ibsen thus gains more of the unaccountable, freakish vitality of human existence, he still remains a Western European, with a sense of measure; with him one never feels as one feels with some Russian writers in their excesses and extremes, that either one is mad oneself, or they are.

F. L. Lucas, *The Drama of Ibsen and Strindberg* (New York: The Macmillan Company, 1962). Reprinted by permission of the publisher.

🕸 *George Bernard Shaw*

Like his contemporary, Oscar Wilde, George Bernard Shaw (1856–1950) was an Irishman, born in Dublin. His formal education ended at fifteen and, after five years as an office clerk, he followed his mother to London where she gave music lessons and Shaw wrote novels and discovered socialism. Turning from novels to criticism, Shaw began a brilliant career as a reviewer of art, music, and drama. As drama critic for the *Saturday Review* he championed the cause of Ibsen and gave his own interpretation of Ibsen's drama in *The Quintessence of Ibsenism* (1891). After his apprenticeship as novelist, pamphleteer, and critic, Shaw began his long career as a playwright with *Widowers' Houses* (1892) and *Mrs. Warren's Profession* (1893). While attacking slum landlords and prostitution, these plays also reverse the expectations of an audience conditioned by the dramatic and sentimental excesses of the "well-made" play.

Though Shaw came late to the theater, his productivity was enormous. After his first early successes, *Arms and the Man* and *Candida* (1894), there followed the other plays and prefaces for which he is famous: *Caesar and Cleopatra* (1898), *Man and Superman* (1903), *Major Barbara* (1905), *The Doctor's Dilemma* (1906), *Pygmalion* (1912), *Heartbreak House* (1916), *Back to Methuselah* (1921), and *Saint Joan* (1923). In 1925 Shaw received the Nobel Prize for Literature. On November 19, 1950, at the age of 94, he died at his home in Ayot St. Lawrence.

Though *Arms and the Man* is early Shaw, one can see the dominant Shavian themes emerging in this treatment of man's operatic tendencies in love and war. In *Arms and the Man*, as in the later plays, Shaw exposes the myths men live by to fool themselves and their neighbors. Though it is the romantic illusion about war that is shattered, one illusion leads to another, so that the love of war and the war of love are not only in the same play but are part of the same sentimental attitude attacked by the realist Shaw. Where traditional comedy ridiculed the comic figure who deviated from the norm, Shaw's modern comedy has a new protagonist in Bluntschli, the realist who sees things from the playwright's perspective and turns on society itself as the subject for ridicule.

Bluntschli's entrance into the comic-opera world of Bulgaria and the Petkoffs signals the Shavian destruction of 19th-century romantic melodrama. Shaw wants to expose through laughter the idols of love and war, but his characteristic device of comic reversal goes further in *Arms and the Man* than a mere inversion of our conventional views. Raina and Sergius have their romantic illusions shattered, but Shaw goes on to show that they are actually bored by their own romantic poses and happy to escape through the realistic presence of Bluntschli and Louka. Shaw's satire on romantic idealism brings about an exchange of partners and a change in values, as our ideas on love and war, class and country, are reversed and revealed in a new realistic light. Shaw adds a typical, further twist to the basic reversal as Bluntschli is trapped by his own brilliance. Raina, like Louka, reveals a deeper, feminine quality—which Shaw later associated with the "life force"—that is fatal to Bluntschli's freedom. Ironically, he succumbs to the very reality he has produced. Yet Bluntschli has already told us that he is not actually a realist but a lifelong romantic. Shaw's final point is that the greatest romance is, after all, life itself.

READINGS:

BENTLEY, ERIC, *Bernard Shaw*. New York: New Directions, 1957.

CHESTERTON, G. K., *George Bernard Shaw* (1910). New York: Hill and Wang Dramabook, 1956.

ERVINE, ST. JOHN, *Bernard Shaw, His Life, Works, and Friends*. New York: Morrow, 1956.

KAUFMANN, R. J., Ed., *Shaw, A Collection of Critical Essays*. Englewood Cliffs, N.J.: Prentice-Hall, 1965.

KRONENBERGER, LOUIS, Ed., *George Bernard Shaw: A Critical Survey*. Cleveland: The World Publishing Co., 1953.

NETHERCOT, ARTHUR, *Men and Supermen*. Cambridge: Harvard University Press, 1954.

OHMANN, RICHARD, *Shaw: The Style and the Man*. Middletown: Wesleyan University Press, 1962.

⚜ Arms and the Man

George Bernard Shaw

A Romantic Comedy in Three Acts
Written in 1894. First Performed, London 1894.

✿ Act I

NIGHT. A lady's bedchamber in Bulgaria, in a small town near the Dragoman Pass, late in November in the year 1885. Through an open window with a little balcony a peak of the Balkans, wonderfully white and beautiful in the starlit snow, seems quite close at hand, though it is really miles away. The interior of the room is not like anything to be seen in the west of Europe. It is half rich Bulgarian, half cheap Viennese. Above the head of the bed, which stands against a little wall cutting off the left hand corner of the room, is a painted wooden shrine, blue and gold, with an ivory image of Christ, and a light hanging before it in a pierced metal ball suspended by three chains. The principal seat, placed towards the other side of the room and opposite the window, is a Turkish ottoman. The counterpane and hangings of the bed, the window curtains, the little carpet, and all the ornamental textile fabrics in the room are oriental and gorgeous: the paper on the walls is occidental and paltry. The washstand, against the wall on the side nearest the ottoman and window, consists of an enamelled iron basin with a pail beneath it in a painted metal frame, and a single towel on the rail at the side. The dressing table, between the bed and the window, is a common pine table, covered with a cloth of many colors, with an expensive toilet mirror on it. The door is on the side nearest the bed; and there is a chest of drawers between. This chest of drawers is also covered by a variegated native cloth; and on it there is a pile of paper-backed novels, a box of chocolate creams, and a miniature easel with a large photograph of an extremely handsome officer, whose lofty bearing and magnetic glance can be felt even from the portrait. The room is lighted by a candle on the chest of drawers, and another on the dressing table with a box of matches beside it.

The window is hinged doorwise and stands wide open. Outside, a pair of wooden shutters, opening outwards, also stand open. On the balcony a young lady, intensely conscious of the romantic beauty of the night, and of the fact that her own youth and beauty are part of it, is gazing at the snowy Balkans. She is in her nightgown, well covered by a long mantle of furs, worth, on a moderate estimate, about three times the furniture of her room.

Her reverie is interrupted by her mother, CATHERINE PETKOFF, a woman over forty, imperiously energetic, with magnificent black hair and eyes, who might be a very splendid specimen of the wife of a mountain farmer, but is determined to be a Viennese lady, and to that end wears a fashionable tea gown on all occasions.

CATHERINE [entering hastily, full of good news]: Raina! [She pronounces it Rah-eena, with the stress on the ee]. Raina! [She goes to the bed, expecting to find RAINA there]. Why, where—? [RAINA looks into the room]. Heavens, child! are you out in the night air instead of in your bed? Youll catch your death. Louka told me you were asleep.

RAINA [dreamily]: I sent her away. I wanted to be alone. The stars are so beautiful! What is the matter?

CATHERINE: Such news! There has been a battle.

RAINA [her eyes dilating]: Ah! [She comes eagerly to Catherine].

CATHERINE: A great battle at Slivnitza! A victory! And it was won by Sergius.

RAINA [with a cry of delight]: Ah! [They embrace rapturously] Oh, mother! [Then, with sudden anxiety] Is father safe?

CATHERINE: Of course: he sends me the news. Sergius is the hero of the hour, the idol of the regiment.

RAINA: Tell me, tell me. How was it? [Ecstatically] Oh, mother! mother! mother! [She pulls her mother down on the ottoman; and they kiss one another frantically].

CATHERINE [with surging enthusiasm]: You can't guess how splendid it is. A cavalry charge! think of that! He defied our Russian commanders—acted without orders—led a charge on his own responsibility—headed it himself—was the first man to sweep through their guns. Cant you see it, Raina: our gallant splendid Bulgarians with their swords and eyes flashing, thundering down like an avalanche and scattering the wretched Serbs and their dandified Austrian officers like chaff. And you! you kept Sergius waiting a year before you would be betrothed to him. Oh, if you have a drop of Bulgarian blood in your veins, you will worship him when he comes back.

RAINA: What will he care for my poor little worship after the acclamations of a whole army of heroes? But no matter: I am so happy! so proud! [*She rises and walks about excitedly*]. It proves that all our ideas were real after all.

CATHERINE [*indignantly*]: Our ideas real! What do you mean?

RAINA: Our ideas of what Sergius would do. Our patriotism. Our heroic ideals. I sometimes used to doubt whether they were anything but dreams. Oh, what faithless little creatures girls are! When I buckled on Sergius's sword he looked so noble: it was treason to think of disillusion or humiliation or failure. And yet—and yet— [*She sits down again suddenly*] Promise me youll never tell him.

CATHERINE: Dont ask me for promises until I know what I'm promising.

RAINA: Well, it came into my head just as he was holding me in his arms and looking into my eyes, that perhaps we only had our heroic ideas because we are so fond of reading Byron and Pushkin, and because we were so delighted with the opera that season at Bucharest. Real life is so seldom like that! indeed never, as far as I knew it then. [*Remorsefully*] Only think, mother: I doubted him: I wondered whether all his heroic qualities and his soldiership might not prove mere imagination when he went into a real battle. I had an uneasy fear that he might cut a poor figure there beside all those clever officers from the Tsar's court.

CATHERINE: A poor figure! Shame on you! The Serbs have Austrian officers who are just as clever as the Russians; but we have beaten them in every battle for all that.

RAINA [*laughing and snuggling against her mother*]: Yes: I was only a prosaic little coward. Oh, to think that it was all true! that Sergius is just as splendid and noble as he looks! that the world is really a glorious world for women who can see its glory and men who can act its romance! What happiness! what unspeakable fulfilment!

[*They are interrupted by the entry of* LOUKA, *a handsome proud girl in a pretty Bulgarian peasant's dress with double apron, so defiant that her servility to* RAINA *is almost insolent. She is afraid of* CATHERINE, *but even with her goes as far as she dares.*]

LOUKA: If you please, madam, all the windows are to be closed and the shutters made fast. They say there may be shooting in the streets. [RAINA *and* CATHERINE *rise together, alarmed*]. The Serbs are being chased right back through the pass; and they say they may run into the town. Our cavalry will be after them; and our people will be ready for them, you may be sure, now theyre running away. [*She goes out on the balcony, and pulls the outside shutters to; then steps back into the room*].

CATHERINE [*businesslike, her housekeeping instincts aroused*]: I must see that everything is made safe downstairs.

RAINA: I wish our people were not so cruel. What glory is there in killing wretched fugitives?

CATHERINE: Cruel! Do you suppose they would hesitate to kill you —or worse?

RAINA [*to* LOUKA]: Leave the shutters so that I can just close them if I hear any noise.

CATHERINE [*authoritatively, turning on her way to the door*]: Oh no, dear: you must keep them fastened. You would be sure to drop off to sleep and leave them open. Make them fast, Louka.

LOUKA: Yes, madam. [*She fastens them*].

RAINA: Don't be anxious about me. The moment I hear a shot, I shall blow out the candles and roll myself up in bed with my ears well covered.

CATHERINE: Quite the wisest thing you can do, my love. Goodnight.

RAINA: Goodnight. [*Her emotion comes back for a moment*]. Wish me joy. [*They kiss*]. This is the happiest night of my life—if only there are no fugitives.

CATHERINE: Go to bed, dear; and dont think of them. [*She goes out*].

LOUKA [*secretly, to* RAINA]: If you would like the shutters open, just give them a push like this [*she pushes them: they open: she pulls them to again*]. One of them ought to be bolted at the bottom; but the bolt's gone.

RAINA [*with dignity, reproving her*]: Thanks, Louka; but we must do what we are told. [LOUKA *makes a grimace*]. Goodnight.

LOUKA [*carelessly*]: Goodnight. [*She goes out, swaggering*].

[RAINA, *left alone, takes off her fur cloak and throws it on the ottoman. Then she goes to the chest of drawers, and adores the portrait there with feelings that are beyond all expression. She does not kiss it or press it to her breast, or shew it any mark of bodily affection; but she takes it in her hands and elevates it, like a priestess.*]

RAINA [*looking up at the picture*]: Oh, I shall never be unworthy of you any more, my soul's hero: never, never, never. [*She replaces it reverently. Then she selects a novel from the little pile of books. She turns over the leaves dreamily; finds her page; turns the book inside*] out at it; and, with a happy sigh, gets into bed and prepares to read herself to sleep. But before abandoning herself to fiction, she raises her eyes once more, thinking of the blessed reality, and murmurs] My hero! my hero!

A distant shot breaks the quiet of the night. She starts, listening; and two more shots, much nearer, follow, startling her so that she scrambles out of bed, and hastily blows out the candle on the chest of drawers. Then, putting her fingers in her ears, she runs to the dressing table, blows out the light there, and hurries back to bed in the dark, nothing being visible but the glimmer of the light in the pierced ball before the image, and the starlight seen through the slits at the top of the shutters. The firing breaks out again: there is a startling fusillade quite close at hand. Whilst it is still echoing, the shutters disappear, pulled open from without; and for an instant the rectangle of snowy starlight flashes out with the figure of a man silhouetted in black upon it. The shutters close immediately; and the room is dark again. But the silence is now broken by the sound of panting. Then there is a scratch; and the flame of a match is seen in the middle of the room.

RAINA [crouching on the bed]: Who's there? [The match is out instantly]. Who's there? Who is that?

A MAN'S VOICE [in the darkness, subduedly, but threateningly]: Sh-sh! Dont call out; or youll be shot. Be good; and no harm will happen to you. [She is heard leaving her bed, and making for the door]. Take care: it's no use trying to run away.

RAINA: But who—

THE VOICE [warning]: Remember: if you raise your voice my revolver will go off. [Commandingly]. Strike a light and let me see you. Do you hear. [Another moment of silence and darkness as she retreats to the chest of drawers. Then she lights a candle; and the mystery is at an end. He is a man of about 35, in a deplorable plight, bespattered with mud and blood and snow, his belt and the strap of his revolver-case keeping together the torn ruins of the blue tunic of a Serbian artillery officer. All that the candlelight and his unwashed unkempt condition make it possible to discern is that he is of middling stature and undistinguished appearance, with strong neck and shoulders, roundish obstinate looking head covered with short crisp bronze curls, clear quick eyes and good brows and mouth, hopelessly prosaic nose like that of a strong minded baby, trim soldierlike carriage and energetic manner, and with all his wits about him in spite of his desperate predicament: even with a sense of the humor of it, without, however, the least intention of trifling with it or throwing away a *chance. Reckoning up what he can guess about* RAINA: *her age, her social position, her character, and the extent to which she is frightened, he continues, more politely but still most determinedly*] Excuse my disturbing you; but you recognize my uniform? Serb! If I'm caught I shall be killed. [*Menacingly*] Do you understand that?

RAINA: Yes.

THE MAN: Well, I dont intend to get killed if I can help it. [*Still more formidably*] Do you understand that? [*He locks the door quickly and quietly*].

RAINA [*disdainfully*]: I suppose not. [*She draws herself up superbly, and looks him straight in the face, adding, with cutting emphasis*] Some soldiers, I know, are afraid to die.

THE MAN [*with grim goodhumor*]: All of them, dear lady, all of them, believe me. It is our duty to live as long as we can. Now, if you raise an alarm—

RAINA [*cutting him short*]: You will shoot me. How do you know that *I* am afraid to die?

THE MAN [*cunningly*]: Ah; but suppose I dont shoot you, what will happen then? A lot of your cavalry will burst into this pretty room of yours and slaughter me here like a pig; for I'll fight like a demon: they shant get me into the street to amuse themselves with: I know what they are. Are you prepared to receive that sort of company in your present undress? [RAINA, *suddenly conscious of her nightgown, instinctively shrinks, and gathers it more closely about her neck. He watches her, and adds, pitilessly*] Hardly presentable, eh? [*She turns to the ottoman. He raises his pistol instantly, and cries*] Stop! [*She stops*]. Where are you going?

RAINA [*with dignified patience*]: Only to get my cloak.

THE MAN [*passing swiftly to the ottoman and snatching the cloak*]: A good idea! I'll keep the cloak; and youll take care that nobody comes in and sees you without it. This is a better weapon than the revolver: eh? [*He throws the pistol down on the ottoman*].

RAINA [*revolted*]: It is not the weapon of a gentleman!

THE MAN: It's good enough for a man with only you to stand between him and death. [*As they look at one another for a moment,* RAINA *hardly able to believe that even a Serbian officer can be so cynically and selfishly unchivalrous, they are startled by a sharp fusillade in the street. The chill of imminent death hushes the man's voice as he adds*] Do you hear? If you are going to bring those blackguards in on me you shall receive them as you are.

Clamor and disturbance. The pursuers in the street batter at the house door, shouting Open the door! Open the door! Wake up, will you! *A man servant's voice calls to them angrily from within* This is Major Petkoff's house: you cant come in here; *but a renewal of the clamor, and a torrent of blows on the door, end with his letting a chain down with a clank, followed by a rush of heavy footsteps and a din of triumphant yells, dominated at last by the voice of* CATHERINE, *indignantly addressing an officer with* What does this mean, sir? Do you know where you are? *The noise subsides suddenly.*

LOUKA [*outside, knocking at the bedroom door*]: My lady! my lady! get up quick and open the door. If you dont they will break it down.

> [*The fugitive throws up his head with the gesture of a man who sees that it is all over with him, and drops the manner he has been assuming to intimidate* RAINA.]

THE MAN [*sincerely and kindly*]: No use, dear: I'm done for. [*Flinging the cloak to her*] Quick! wrap yourself up: theyre coming.

RAINA: Oh, thank you. [*She wraps herself up with intense relief*].

THE MAN [*between his teeth*]: Dont mention it.

RAINA [*anxiously*]: What will you do?

THE MAN [*grimly*]: The first man in will find out. Keep out of the way; and dont look. It wont last long; but it will not be nice. [*He draws his sabre and faces the door, waiting*].

RAINA [*impulsively*]: I'll help you. I'll save you.

THE MAN: You cant.

RAINA: I can. I'll hide you. [*She drags him towards the window*]. Here! behind the curtains.

THE MAN [*yielding to her*]: Theres just half a chance, if you keep your head.

RAINA [*drawing the curtain before him*]: S-sh! [*She makes for the ottoman*].

THE MAN [*putting out his head*]: Remember—

RAINA [*running back to him*]: Yes?

THE MAN: —nine soldiers out of ten are born fools.

RAINA: Oh! [*She draws the curtain angrily before him*].

THE MAN [*looking out at the other side*]: If they find me, I promise you a fight: a devil of a fight.

> [*She stamps at him. He disappears hastily. She takes off her cloak, and throws it across the foot of the bed. Then, with a sleepy, disturbed air, she opens the door.* LOUKA *enters excitedly.*]

LOUKA: One of those beasts of Serbs has been seen climbing up the waterpipe to your balcony. Our men want to search for him; and they are so wild and drunk and furious. [*She makes for the other*

side of the room to get as far from the door as possible]. My lady
says you are to dress at once, and to—[*She sees the revolver lying on
the ottoman, and stops, petrified*].

RAINA [*as if annoyed at being disturbed*]: They shall not search here.
Why have they been let in?

CATHERINE [*coming in hastily*]: Raina, darling: are you safe? Have you
seen anyone or heard anything?

RAINA: I heard the shooting. Surely the soldiers will not dare come in
here?

CATHERINE: I have found a Russian officer, thank Heaven: he knows
Sergius. [*Speaking through the door to someone outside*] Sir: will
you come in now. My daughter will receive you.

[*A young Russian officer, in Bulgarian uniform, enters, sword
in hand.*]

OFFICER [*with soft feline politeness and stiff military carriage*]: Good
evening, gracious lady. I am sorry to intrude; but there is a Serb
hiding on the balcony. Will you and the gracious lady your mother
please to withdraw whilst we search?

RAINA [*petulantly*]: Nonsense, sir: you can see that there is no one on
the balcony. [*She throws the shutters wide open and stands with her
back to the curtain where the man is hidden, pointing to the moonlit
balcony. A couple of shots are fired right under the window; and a
bullet shatters the glass opposite* RAINA, *who winks and gasps, but
stands her ground; whilst* CATHERINE *screams, and the officer, with a
cry of* Take care! *rushes to the balcony*].

THE OFFICER [*on the balcony, shouting savagely down to the street*]:
Cease firing there, you fools: do you hear? Cease firing, damn you!
[*He glares down for a moment; then turns to* RAINA, *trying to
resume his polite manner*]. Could anyone have got in without your
knowledge? Were you asleep?

RAINA: No: I have not been to bed.

THE OFFICER [*impatiently, coming back into the room*]: Your neighbors have their heads so full of runaway Serbs that they see them
everywhere. [*Politely*] Gracious lady: a thousand pardons. Good-
night. [*Military bow, which* RAINA *returns coldly. Another to*
CATHERINE, *who follows him out*].

[RAINA *closes the shutters. She turns and sees* LOUKA, *who has
been watching the scene curiously.*]

RAINA: Dont leave my mother, Louka, until the soldiers go away.

[LOUKA *glances at* RAINA, *at the ottoman, at the curtain; then
purses her lips secretively, laughs insolently, and goes out.*
RAINA, *highly offended by this demonstration, follows her to*

*the door, and shuts it behind her with a slam, locking it
violently. The man immediately steps out from behind the
curtain, sheathing his sabre, and closes the shutters. Then,
dismissing the danger from his mind in a businesslike way, he
comes affably to* RAINA.]

THE MAN: A narrow shave; but a miss is as good as a mile. Dear young
lady: your servant to the death. I wish for your sake I had joined the
Bulgarian army instead of the other one. I am not a native Serb.

RAINA [*haughtily*]: No: you are one of the Austrians who set the Serbs
on to rob us of our national liberty, and who officer their army for
them. We hate them!

THE MAN: Austrian! not I. Dont hate me, dear young lady. I am a
Swiss, fighting merely as a professional soldier. I joined the Serbs
because they came first on the road from Switzerland. Be generous:
youve beaten us hollow.

RAINA: Have I not been generous?

THE MAN: Noble! Heroic! But I'm not saved yet. This particular rush
will soon pass through; but the pursuit will go on all night by fits and
starts. I must take my chance to get off in a quiet interval. [*Pleasantly*] You dont mind my waiting just a minute or two, do you?

RAINA [*putting on her most genteel society manner*]: Oh, not at all.
Wont you sit down?

THE MAN: Thanks. [*He sits on the foot of the bed*].

[RAINA *walks with studied elegance to the ottoman and sits
down. Unfortunately she sits on the pistol, and jumps up
with a shriek. The man, all nerves, shies like a frightened
horse to the other side of the room.*]

THE MAN [*irritably*]: Dont frighten me like that. What is it?

RAINA: Your revolver! It was staring that officer in the face all the time.
What an escape!

THE MAN [*vexed at being unnecessarily terrified*]: Oh, is that all?

RAINA [*staring at him rather superciliously as she conceives a poorer
and poorer opinion of him, and feels proportionately more and more
at her ease*]: I am sorry I frightened you. [*She takes up the pistol
and hands it to him*]. Pray take it to protect yourself against me.

THE MAN [*grinning wearily at the sarcasm as he takes the pistol*]: No
use, dear young lady: theres nothing in it. It's not loaded. [*He makes
a grimace at it, and drops it disparagingly into his revolver case.*]

RAINA: Load it by all means.

THE MAN: Ive no ammunition. What use are cartridges in battle? I
always carry chocolate instead; and I finished the last cake of that
hours ago.

RAINA [*outraged in her most cherished ideals of manhood*]: Chocolate! Do you stuff your pockets with sweets—like a schoolboy—even
in the field?

THE MAN [*grinning*]: Yes: isn't it contemptible? [*Hungrily*] I wish I
had some now.

RAINA: Allow me. [*She sails away scornfully to the chest of drawers,
and returns with the box of confectionery in her hand*]. I am sorry I
have eaten them all except these. [*She offers him the box*].

THE MAN [*ravenously*]: Youre an angel! [*He gobbles the contents*].
Creams! Delicious! [*He looks anxiously to see whether there are any
more. There are none: he can only scrape the box with his fingers
and suck them. When that nourishment is exhausted he accepts the
inevitable with pathetic goodhumor, and says, with grateful emotion*] Bless you, dear lady! You can always tell an old soldier by the
inside of his holsters and cartridge boxes. The young ones carry
pistols and cartridges: the old ones, grub. Thank you. [*He hands
back the box. She snatches it contemptuously from him and throws
it away. He shies again, as if she had meant to strike him*]. Ugh!
Dont do things so suddenly, gracious lady. It's mean to revenge
yourself because I frightened you just now.

RAINA [*loftily*]: Frighten me! Do you know, sir, that though I am only
a woman, I think I am at heart as brave as you.

THE MAN: I should think so. You havnt been under fire for three days
as I have. I can stand two days without shewing it much; but no man
can stand three days: I'm as nervous as a mouse. [*He sits down on
the ottoman, and takes his head in his hands*]. Would you like to see
me cry?

RAINA [*alarmed*]: No.

THE MAN: If you would, all you have to do is to scold me just as if I
were a little boy and you my nurse. If I were in camp now, theyd
play all sorts of tricks on me.

RAINA [*a little moved*]: I'm sorry. I wont scold you. [*Touched by the
sympathy in her tone, he raises his head and looks gratefully at her:
she immediately draws back and says stiffly*] You must excuse me:
our soldiers are not like that. [*She moves away from the ottoman*].

THE MAN: Oh yes they are. There are only two sorts of soldiers: old
ones and young ones. Ive served fourteen years: half of your fellows
never smelt powder before. Why, how is if that youve just beaten us?
Sheer ignorance of the art of war, nothing else. [*Indignantly*] I
never saw anything so unprofessional.

RAINA [*ironically*]: Oh! was it unprofessional to beat you?

THE MAN: Well, come! is it professional to throw a regiment of cavalry

on a battery of machine guns, with the dead certainty that if the
guns go off not a horse or man will ever get within fifty yards of the
fire? I couldnt believe my eyes when I saw it.

RAINA [*eagerly turning to him, as all her enthusiasm and her dreams of
glory rush back on her*]: Did you see the great cavalry charge? Oh,
tell me about it. Describe it to me.

THE MAN: You never saw a cavalry charge, did you?

RAINA: How could I?

THE MAN: Ah, perhaps not. No: of course not! Well, it's a funny sight.
It's like slinging a handful of peas against a window pane: first one
comes; then two or three close behind him; and then all the rest in a
lump.

RAINA [*her eyes dilating as she raises her clasped hands ecstatically*]:
Yes, first One! the bravest of the brave!

THE MAN [*prosaically*]: Hm! you should see the poor devil pulling at
his horse.

RAINA: Why should he pull at his horse?

THE MAN [*impatient of so stupid a question*]: It's running away with
him, of course: do you suppose the fellow wants to get there before
the others and be killed? Then they all come. You can tell the young
ones by their wildness and their slashing. The old ones come
bunched up under the number one guard: they know that theyre
mere projectiles, and that it's no use trying to fight. The wounds are
mostly broken knees, from the horses cannoning together.

RAINA: Ugh! But I dont believe the first man is a coward. I know he is
a hero!

THE MAN [*goodhumoredly*]: Thats what youd have said if youd seen
the first man in the charge today.

RAINA [*breathless, forgiving him everything*]: Ah, I knew it! Tell me.
Tell me about him.

THE MAN: He did it like an operatic tenor. A regular handsome fellow,
with flashing eyes and lovely moustache, shouting his war-cry and
charging like Don Quixote at the windmills. We did laugh.

RAINA: You dared to laugh!

THE MAN: Yes; but when the sergeant ran up as white as a sheet, and
told us theyd sent us the wrong ammunition, and that we couldnt
fire a round for the next ten minutes, we laughed at the other side of
our mouths. I never felt so sick in my life; though Ive been in one or
two very tight places. And I hadnt even a revolver cartridge: only
chocolate. We'd no bayonets: nothing. Of course, they just cut us to
bits. And there was Don Quixote flourishing like a drum major,
thinking he'd done the cleverest thing ever known, whereas he ought

to be courtmartialled for it. Of all the fools ever let loose on a field of battle, that man must be the very maddest. He and his regiment simply committed suicide; only the pistol missed fire: thats all.

RAINA [deeply wounded, but steadfastly loyal to her ideals]: Indeed! Would you know him again if you saw him?

THE MAN: Shall I ever forget him!

[She again goes to the chest of drawers. He watches her with a vague hope that she may have something more for him to eat. She takes the portrait from its stand and brings it to him.]

RAINA: That is a photograph of the gentleman—the patriot and hero—to whom I am betrothed.

THE MAN [recognizing it with a shock]: I'm really very sorry. [Looking at her] Was it fair to lead me on? [He looks at the portrait again] Yes: thats Don Quixote: not a doubt of it. [He stifles a laugh].

RAINA [quickly]: Why do you laugh?

THE MAN [apologetic, but still greatly tickled]: I didn't laugh, I assure you. At least I didnt mean to. But when I think of him charging the windmills and imagining he was doing the finest thing—[He chokes with suppressed laughter].

RAINA [sternly]: Give me back the portrait, sir.

THE MAN [with sincere remorse]: Of course. Certainly. I'm really very sorry. [He hands her the picture. She deliberately kisses it and looks him straight in the face before returning to the chest of drawers to replace it. He follows her, apologizing]. Perhaps I'm quite wrong, you know: no doubt I am. Most likely he had got wind of the cartridge business somehow, and knew it was a safe job.

RAINA: That is to say, he was a pretender and a coward! You did not dare say that before.

THE MAN [with a comic gesture of despair]: It's no use, dear lady: I cant make you see it from the professional point of view. [As he turns away to get back to the ottoman, a couple of distant shots threaten renewed trouble].

RAINA [sternly, as she sees him listening to the shots]: So much the better for you!

THE MAN [turning]: How?

RAINA: You are my enemy; and you are at my mercy. What would I do if I were a professional soldier?

THE MAN: Ah, true, dear young lady: youre always right. I know how good youve been to me: to my last hour I shall remember those three chocolate creams. It was unsoldierly; but it was angelic.

RAINA [coldly]: Thank you. And now I will do a soldierly thing. You cannot stay here after what you have just said about my future husband; but I will go out on the balcony and see whether it is safe for you to climb down into the street. [She turns to the window].

THE MAN [changing countenance]: Down that waterpipe! Stop! Wait! I cant! I darent! The very thought of it makes me giddy. I came up it fast enough with death behind me. But to face it now in cold blood—! [He sinks on the ottoman]. It's no use: I give up: I'm beaten. Give the alarm. [He drops his head on his hands in the deepest dejection].

RAINA [disarmed by pity]: Come: dont be disheartened. [She stoops over him almost maternally: he shakes his head]. Oh, you are a very poor soldier: a chocolate cream soldier! Come, cheer up! it takes less courage to climb down than to face capture: remember that.

THE MAN [dreamily, lulled by her voice]: No: capture only means death; and death is sleep: oh, sleep, sleep, sleep, undisturbed sleep! Climbing down the pipe means doing something—exerting myself—thinking! Death ten times over first.

RAINA [softly and wonderingly, catching the rhythm of his weariness]: Are you as sleepy as that?

THE MAN: Ive not had two hours undisturbed sleep since I joined. I havnt closed my eyes for forty-eight hours.

RAINA [at her wit's end]: But what am I to do with you?

THE MAN [staggering up, roused by her desperation]: Of course. I must do something. [He shakes himself; pulls himself together; and speaks with rallied vigor and courage]. You see, sleep or no sleep, hunger or no hunger, tired or not tired, you can always do a thing when you know it must be done. Well, that pipe must be got down: [he hits himself on the chest] do you hear that, you chocolate cream soldier? [He turns to the window].

RAINA [anxiously]: But if you fall?

THE MAN: I shall sleep as if the stones were a feather bed. Goodbye. [He makes boldly for the window; and his hand is on the shutter when there is a terrible burst of firing in the street beneath].

RAINA [rushing to him]: Stop! [She seizes him recklessly, and pulls him quite round]. Theyll kill you.

THE MAN [coolly, but attentively]: Never mind: this sort of thing is all in my day's work. I'm bound to take my chance. [Decisively] Now do what I tell you. Put out the candles; so that they shant see the light when I open the shutters. And keep away from the window, whatever you do. If they see me theyre sure to have a shot at me.

RAINA [*clinging to him*]: Theyre sure to see you: it's bright moonlight. I'll save you. Oh, how can you be so indifferent! You want me to save you, dont you?

THE MAN: I really dont want to be troublesome. [*She shakes him in her impatience*]. I am not indifferent, dear young lady, I assure you. But how is it to be done?

RAINA: Come away from the window. [*She takes him firmly back to the middle of the room. The moment she releases him he turns mechanically towards the window again. She seizes him and turns him back, exclaiming*] Please! [*He becomes motionless, like a hypnotized rabbit, his fatigue gaining fast on him. She releases him, and addresses him patronizingly*]. Now listen. You must trust to our hospitality. You do not yet know in whose house you are. I am a Petkoff.

THE MAN: A pet what?

RAINA [*rather indignantly*]: I mean that I belong to the family of the Petkoffs, the richest and best known in our country.

THE MAN: Oh yes, of course. I beg your pardon. The Petkoffs, to be sure. How stupid of me!

RAINA: You know you never heard of them until this moment. How can you stoop to pretend!

THE MAN: Forgive me: I'm too tired to think; and the change of subject was too much for me. Dont scold me.

RAINA: I forgot. It might make you cry. [*He nods, quite seriously. She pouts and then resumes her patronizing tone*]. I must tell you that my father holds the highest command of any Bulgarian in our army. He is [*proudly*] a Major.

THE MAN [*pretending to be deeply impressed*]: A Major! Bless me! Think of that!

RAINA: You shewed great ignorance in thinking that it was necessary to climb up to the balcony because ours is the only private house that has two rows of windows. There is a flight of stairs inside to get up and down by.

THE MAN: Stairs! How grand! You live in great luxury indeed, dear young lady.

RAINA: Do you know what a library is?

THE MAN: A library? A roomful of books?

RAINA: Yes. We have one, the only one in Bulgaria.

THE MAN: Actually a real library! I should like to see that.

RAINA [*affectedly*]: I tell you these things to shew you that you are not in the house of ignorant country folk who would kill you the moment they saw your Serbian uniform, but among civilized people.

We go to Bucharest every year for the opera season; and I have spent a whole month in Vienna.

THE MAN: I saw that, dear young lady. I sat at once that you knew the world.

RAINA: Have you ever seen the opera of Ernani?

THE MAN: Is that the one with the devil in it in red velvet, and a soldiers' chorus?

RAINA [contemptuously]: No!

THE MAN [stifling a heavy sigh of weariness]: Then I dont know it.

RAINA: I thought you might have remembered the great scene where Ernani, flying from his foes just as you are tonight, takes refuge in the castle of his bitterest enemy, an old Castilian noble. The noble refuses to give him up. His guest is sacred to him.

THE MAN [quickly, waking up a little]: Have your people got that notion?

RAINA [with dignity]: My mother and I can understand that notion, as you call it. And if instead of threatening me with your pistol as you did you had simply thrown yourself as a fugitive on our hospitality, you would have been as safe as in your father's house.

THE MAN: Quite sure?

RAINA [turning her back on him in disgust]: Oh, it is useless to try to make you understand.

THE MAN: Dont be angry: you see how awkward it would be for me if there was any mistake. My father is a very hospitable man: he keeps six hotels; but I couldnt trust him as far as that. What about your father?

RAINA: He is away at Slivnitza fighting for his country. I answer for your safety. There is my hand in pledge of it. Will that reassure you? [She offers him her hand].

THE MAN [looking dubiously at his own hand]: Better not touch my hand, dear young lady. I must have a wash first.

RAINA [touched]: That is very nice of you. I see that you are a gentleman.

THE MAN [puzzled]: Eh?

RAINA: You must not think I am surprised. Bulgarians of really good standing—people in our position—wash their hands nearly every day. So you see I can appreciate your delicacy. You may take my hand. [She offers it again].

THE MAN [kissing it with his hands behind his back]: Thanks, gracious young lady: I feel safe at last. And now would you mind breaking the news to your mother? I had better not stay here secretly longer than is necessary.

RAINA: If you will be so good as to keep perfectly still whilst I am away.

THE MAN: Certainly. [*He sits down on the ottoman*].

> [RAINA *goes to the bed and wraps herself in the fur cloak. His eyes close. She goes to the door. Turning for a last look at him, she sees that he is dropping off to sleep.*]

RAINA [*at the door*]: You are not going asleep, are you? [*He murmurs inarticulately: she runs to him and shakes him*]. Do you hear? Wake up: you are falling asleep.

THE MAN: Eh? Falling aslee—? Oh no: not the least in the world: I was only thinking. It's all right: I'm wide awake.

RAINA [*severely*]: Will you please stand up while I am away. [*He rises reluctantly*]. All the time, mind.

THE MAN [*standing unsteadily*]: Certainly. Certainly: you may depend on me.

> [RAINA *looks doubtfully at him. He smiles weakly. She goes reluctantly, turning again at the door, and almost catching him in the act of yawning. She goes out.*]

THE MAN [*drowsily*]: Sleep, sleep, sleep, sleep, slee—[*The words trail off into a murmur. He wakes again with a shock on the point of falling*]. Where am I? Thats what I want to know: where am I? Must keep awake. Nothing keeps me awake except danger: remember that: [*intently*] danger, danger, danger, dan—[*trailing off again: another shock*] Wheres danger? Mus' find it. [*He starts off vaguely round the room in search of it*]. What am I looking for? Sleep—danger—dont know. [*He stumbles against the bed*]. Ah yes: now I know. All right now. I'm to go to bed, but not to sleep. Be sure not to sleep, because of danger. Not to lie down either, only sit down. [*He sits on the bed. A blissful expression comes into his face*]. Ah! [*With a happy sigh he sinks back at full length; lifts his boots into the bed with a final effort; and falls fast asleep instantly*].

> [CATHERINE *comes in, followed by* RAINA.]

RAINA [*looking at the ottoman*]: He's gone! I left him here.

CATHERINE: Here! Then he must have climbed down from the—

RAINA [*seeing him*]: Oh! [*She points*].

CATHERINE [*scandalized*]: Well! [*She strides to the bed*, RAINA *following until she is opposite her on the other side*]. He's fast asleep. The brute!

RAINA [*anxiously*]: Sh!

CATHERINE [*shaking him*]: Sir! [*Shaking him again, harder*] Sir!! [*Vehemently, shaking very hard*] Sir!!!

RAINA [catching her arm]: Dont, mamma: the poor darling is worn
out. Let him sleep.

CATHERINE [letting him go, and turning amazed to RAINA]: The poor
darling! Raina!!! [She looks sternly at her daughter].
[The man sleeps profoundly.]

🌼 Act II

THE sixth of March, 1886. In the garden of MAJOR PETKOFF's
house. It is a fine spring morning: the garden looks fresh and pretty.
Beyond the paling the tops of a couple of minarets can be seen,
shewing that there is a valley there, with the little town in it. A few
miles further the Balkan mountains rise and shut in the landscape.
Looking towards them from within the garden, the side of the house is
seen on the left, with a garden door reached by a little flight of steps.
On the right the stable yard, with its gateway, encroaches on the
garden. There are fruit bushes along the paling and house, covered
with washing spread out to dry. A path runs by the house, and rises by
two steps at the corner, where it runs out of sight. In the middle, a
small table, with two bent-wood chairs at it, is laid for breakfast with
Turkish coffee pot, cups, rolls, etc.; but the cups have been used and
the bread broken. There is a wooden garden seat against the wall on
the right.

LOUKA, smoking a cigaret, is standing between the table and the
house, turning her back wtih angry disdain on a man servant who is
lecturing her. He is a middle-aged man of cool temperament and low
but clear and keen intelligence, with the complacency of the servant
who values himself on his rank in servitude, and the imperturbability
of the accurate calculator who has no illusions. He wears a white
Bulgarian costume: jacket with embroidered border, sash, wide
knickerbockers, and decorated gaiters. His head is shaved up to the
crown, giving him a high Japanese forehead. His name is NICOLA.

NICOLA: Be warned in time, Louka: mend your manners. I know the
mistress. She is so grand that she never dreams that any servant
could dare be disrespectful to her; but if she once suspects that you
are defying her, out you go.

LOUKA: I do defy her. I will defy her. What do I care for her?

NICOLA: If you quarrel with the family, I never can marry you. It's the
same as if you quarrelled with me!

LOUKA: You take her part against me, do you?

NICOLA [*sedately*]: I shall always be dependent on the good will of the family. When I leave their service and start a shop in Sofia, their custom will be half my capital: their bad word would ruin me.

LOUKA: You have no spirit. I should like to catch them saying a word against me!

NICOLA [*pityingly*]: I should have expected more sense from you, Louka. But youre young: youre young!

LOUKA: Yes; and you like me the better for it, dont you? But I know some family secrets they wouldnt care to have told, young as I am. Let them quarrel with me if they dare!

NICOLA [*with compassionate superiority*]: Do you know what they would do if they heard you talk like that?

LOUKA: What could they do?

NICOLA: Discharge you for untruthfulness. Who would believe any stories you told after that? Who would give you another situation? Who in this house would dare be seen speaking to you ever again? How long would your father be left on his little farm? [*She impatiently throws away the end of the cigaret, and stamps on it*]. Child: you dont know the power such high people have over the like of you and me when we try to rise out of our poverty against them. [*He goes close to her and lowers his voice*]. Look at me, ten years in their service. Do you think I know no secrets? I know things about the mistress that she wouldnt have the master know for a thousand levas. I know things about him that she wouldnt let him hear the last of for six months if I blabbed them to her. I know things about Raina that would break off her match with Sergius if—

LOUKA [*turning on him quickly*]: How do you know? I never told you!

NICOLA [*opening his eyes cunningly*]: So thats your little secret, is it? I thought it might be something like that. Well, you take my advice and be respectful; and make the mistress feel that no matter what you know or dont know, she can depend on you to hold your tongue and serve the family faithfully. Thats what they like; and thats how youll make most out of them.

LOUKA [*with searching scorn*]: You have the soul of a servant, Nicola.

NICOLA [*complacently*]: Yes: thats the secret of success in service.

    [*A loud knocking with a whip handle on a wooden door is heard from the stable yard.*]

MALE VOICE OUTSIDE: Hollo! Hollo there! Nicola!

LOUKA: Master! back from the war!

NICOLA [*quickly*]: My word for it, Louka, the war's over. Off with you and get some fresh coffee. [*He runs out into the stable yard*].

426   *George Bernard Shaw*

LOUKA [as she collects the coffee pot and cups on the tray, and carries it into the house]: Youll never put the soul of a servant into me.

[MAJOR PETKOFF comes from the stable yard, followed by NICOLA. He is a cheerful, excitable, insignificant, unpolished man of about 50, naturally unambitious except as to his income and his importance in local society, but just now greatly pleased with the military rank which the war has thrust on him as a man of consequence in his town. The fever of plucky patriotism which the Serbian attack roused in all the Bulgarians has pulled him through the war; but he is obviously glad to be home again.]

PETKOFF [pointing to the table with his whip]: Breakfast out here, eh?

NICOLA: Yes, sir. The mistress and Miss Raina have just gone in.

PETKOFF [sitting down and taking a roll]: Go in and say Ive come; and get me some fresh coffee.

NICOLA: It's coming, sir. [He goes to the house door. LOUKA, with fresh coffee, a clean cup, and a brandy bottle on her tray, meets him]. Have you told the mistress?

LOUKA: Yes: she's coming.

[NICOLA goes into the house. LOUKA brings the coffee to the table.]

PETCOFF: Well: the Serbs havnt run away with you, have they?

LOUKA: No, sir.

PETKOFF: Thats right. Have you brought me some cognac?

LOUKA [putting the bottle on the table]: Here, sir.

PETKOFF: Thats right. [He pours some into his coffee].

[CATHERINE, who, having at this early hour made only a very perfunctory toilet, wears a Bulgarian apron over a once brilliant but now half worn-out dressing gown, and a colored handkerchief tied over her thick black hair, comes from the house with Turkish slippers on her bare feet, looking astonishingly handsome and stately under all the circumstances. LOUKA goes into the house.]

CATHERINE: My dear Paul: what a surprise for us! [She stoops over the back of his chair to kiss him]. Have they brought you fresh coffee?

PETKOFF: Yes: Louka's been looking after me. The war's over. The treaty was signed three days ago at Bucharest; and the decree for our army to demobilize was issued yesterday.

CATHERINE [springing erect, with flashing eyes]: Paul: have you let the Austrians force you to make peace?

PETKOFF [submissively]: My dear: they didnt consult me. What could

I do? [*She sits down and turns away from him*]. But of course we saw to it that the treaty was an honorable one. It declares peace—

CATHERINE [*outraged*]: Peace!

PETKOFF [*appeasing her*]: —but not friendly relations: remember that. They wanted to put that in; but I insisted on its being struck out. What more could I do?

CATHERINE: You could have annexed Serbia and made Prince Alexander Emperor of the Balkans. Thats what I would have done.

PETKOFF: I dont doubt it in the least, my dear. But I should have had to subdue the whole Austrian Empire first; and that would have kept me too long away from you. I missed you greatly.

CATHERINE [*relenting*]: Ah! [*She stretches her hand affectionately across the table to squeeze his*].

PETKOFF: And how have you been, my dear?

CATHERINE: Oh, my usual sore throats: thats all.

PETKOFF [*with conviction*]: That comes from washing your neck every day. Ive often told you so.

CATHERINE: Nonsense, Paul!

PETKOFF [*over his coffee and cigaret*]: I dont believe in going too far with these modern customs. All this washing cant be good for the health: it's not natural. There was an Englishman at Philippopolis who used to wet himself all over with cold water every morning when he got up. Disgusting! It all comes from the English: their climate makes them so dirty that they have to be perpetually washing themselves. Look at my father! he never had a bath in his life; and he lived to be ninety-eight, the healthiest man in Bulgaria. I dont mind a good wash once a week to keep up my position; but once a day is carrying the thing to a ridiculous extreme.

CATHERINE: You are a barbarian at heart still, Paul. I hope you behaved yourself before all those Russian officers.

PETKOFF: I did my best. I took care to let them know that we have a library.

CATHERINE: Ah; but you didnt tell them that we have an electric bell in it? I have had one put up.

PETKOFF: Whats an electric bell?

CATHERINE: You touch a button; something tinkles in the kitchen; and then Nicola comes up.

PETKOFF: Why not shout for him?

CATHERINE: Civilized people never shout for their servants. Ive learnt that while you were away.

PETKOFF: Well, I'll tell you something Ive learnt too. Civilized people dont hang out their washing to dry where visitors can see it; so youd

better have all that [*indicating the clothes on the bushes*] put
somewhere else.

CATHERINE: Oh, thats absurd, Paul: I dont believe really refined people
notice such things.

SERGIUS [*knocking at the stable gates*]: Gate, Nicola!

PETKOFF: Theres Sergius. [*Shouting*]: Hollo, Nicola!

CATHERINE: Oh, dont shout, Paul: it really isnt nice.

PETKOFF: Bosh! [*He shouts louder than before*]: Nicola!

NICOLA [*appearing at the house door*]: Yes, sir.

PETKOFF: Are you deaf? Dont you hear Major Saranoff knocking?
Bring him round this way. [*He pronounces the name with the stress
on the second syllable: Sarahnoff*].

NICOLA: Yes, major. [*He goes into the stable yard*].

PETKOFF: You must talk to him, my dear, until Raina takes him off our
hands. He bores my life out about our not promoting him. Over my
head, if you please.

CATHERINE: He certainly ought to be promoted when he marries
Raina. Besides, the country should insist on having at least one
native general.

PETKOFF: Yes; so that he could throw away whole brigades instead of
regiments. It's no use, my dear: he hasnt the slightest chance of
promotion until we're quite sure that the peace will be a lasting
one.

NICOLA [*at the gate, announcing*]: Major Sergius Saranoff! [*He goes
into the house and returns presently with a third chair, which he
places at the table. He then withdraws*].

> MAJOR SERGIUS SARANOFF, *the original of the portrait in* RAINA's
> *room, is a tall romantically handsome man, with the physical
> hardihood, the high spirit, and the susceptible imagination of an
> untamed mountaineer chieftain. But his remarkable personal dis-
> tinctions are of a characteristically civilized type. The ridges of his
> eyebrows, curving with an interrogative twist round the projections
> at the outer corners; his jealously observant eye; his nose, thin, keen,
> and apprehensive in spite of the pugnacious high bridge and large
> nostril; his assertive chin, would not be out of place in a Parisian
> salon, shewing that the clever imaginative barbarian has an acute
> critical faculty which has been thrown into intense activity by the
> arrival of western civilization in the Balkans. The result is precisely
> what the advent of nineteenth century thought first produced in
> England: to wit, Byronism. By his brooding on the perpetual failure,
> not only of others, but of himself, to live up to his ideals; by his
> consequent cynical scorn for humanity; by his jejune credulity as to*

the absolute validity of his concepts and the unworthiness of the world in disregarding them; by his wincings and mockeries under the sting of the petty disillusions which every hour spent among men brings to his sensitive observation, he has acquired the half tragic, half ironic air, the mysterious moodiness, the suggestion of a strange and terrible history that has left nothing but undying remorse, by which Childe Harold fascinated the grandmothers of his English contemporaries. It is clear that here or nowhere is RAINA's ideal hero. CATHERINE is hardly less enthusiastic about him than her daughter, and much less reserved in shewing her enthusiasm. As he enters from the stable gate, she rises effusively to greet him. PETKOFF is distinctly less disposed to make a fuss about him.

PETKOFF: Here already, Sergius! Glad to see you.

CATHERINE: My dear Sergius! [She holds out both her hands].

SERGIUS [kissing them with scrupulous gallantry]: My dear mother, if I may call you so.

PETKOFF [drily]: Mother-in-law, Sergius: mother-in-law! Sit down; and have some coffee.

SERGIUS: Thank you: none for me. [He gets away from the table with a certain distaste for PETOKFF's enjoyment of it, and posts himself with conscious dignity against the rail of the steps leading to the house].

CATHERINE: You look superb. The campaign has improved you, Sergius. Everybody here is mad about you. We were all wild with enthusiasm about that magnificent cavalry charge.

SERGIUS [with grave irony]: Madam: it was the cradle and the grave of my military reputation.

CATHERINE: How so?

SERGIUS: I won the battle the wrong way when our worthy Russian generals were losing it the right way. In short, I upset their plans, and wounded their self-esteem. Two Cossack colonels had their regiments routed on the most correct principles of scientific warfare. Two major-generals got killed strictly according to military etiquette. The two colonels are now major-generals; and I am still a simple major.

CATHERINE: You shall not remain so, Sergius. The women are on your side; and they will see that justice is done you.

SERGIUS: It is too late. I have only waited for the peace to send in my resignation.

PETKOFF [dropping his cup in his amazement]: Your resignation!

CATHERINE: Oh, you must withdraw it!

SERGIUS [with resolute measured emphasis, folding his arms]: I never withdraw.

PETKOFF [vexed]: Now who could have supposed you were going to do such a thing?

SERGIUS [with fire]: Everyone that knew me. But enough of myself and my affairs. How is Raina; and where is Raina?

RAINA [suddenly coming round the corner of the house and standing at the top of the steps in the path]: Raina is here.

[She makes a charming picture as they turn to look at her. She wears an underdress of pale green silk, draped with an overdress of thin ecru canvas embroidered with gold. She is crowned with a dainty eastern cap of gold tinsel. SERGIUS goes impulsively to meet her. Posing regally, she presents her hand: he drops chivalrously on one knee and kisses it.]

PETKOFF [aside to CATHERINE, beaming with parental pride]: Pretty, isn't it? She always appears at the right moment.

CATHERINE [impatiently]: Yes: she listens for it. It is an abominable habit.

[SERGIUS leads RAINA forward with splendid gallantry. When they arrive at the table, she turns to him with a bend of the head: he bows; and thus they separate, he coming to his place, and she going behind her father's chair.]

RAINA [stooping and kissing her father]: Dear father! Welcome home!

PETKOFF [patting her cheek]: My little pet girl. [He kisses her. She goes to the chair left by NICOLA for SERGIUS, and sits down].

CATHERINE: And so youre no longer a soldier, Sergius.

SERGIUS: I am no longer a soldier. Soldiering, my dear madam, is the coward's art of attacking mercilessly when you are strong, and keeping out of harm's way when you are weak. That is the whole secret of successful fighting. Get your enemy at a disadvantage; and never, on any account, fight him on equal terms.

PETKOFF: They wouldnt let us make a fair stand-up fight of it. However, I suppose soldiering has to be a trade like any other trade.

SERGIUS: Precisely. But I have no ambition to shine as a tradesman; so I have taken the advice of that bagman of a captain that settled the exchange of prisoners with us at Pirot, and given it up.

PETKOFF: What! that Swiss fellow? Sergius: Ive often thought of that exchange since. He over-reached us about those horses.

SERGIUS: Of course he over-reached us. His father was a hotel and livery stable keeper; and he owed his first step to his knowledge of horse-dealing. [With mock enthusiasm] Ah, he was a soldier: every inch a soldier! If only I had bought the horses for my regiment instead of foolishly leading it into danger, I should have been a field-marshal now!

CATHERINE: A Swiss? What was he doing in the Serbian army?

PETKOFF: A volunteer, of course: keen on picking up his profession. [Chuckling] We shouldnt have been able to begin fighting if these foreigners hadnt shewn us how to do it: we knew nothing about it; and neither did the Serbs. Egad, there'd have been no war without them!

RAINA: Are there many Swiss officers in the Serbian army?

PETKOFF: No. All Austrians, just as our officers were all Russians. This was the only Swiss I came across. I'll never trust a Swiss again. He humbugged us into giving him fifty ablebodied men for two hundred worn out chargers. They werent even eatable!

SERGIUS: We were two children in the hands of that consummate soldier, Major: simply two innocent little children.

RAINA: What was he like?

CATHERINE: Oh, Raina, what a silly question!

SERGIUS: He was like a commercial traveller in uniform. Bourgeois to his boots!

PETKOFF [grinning]: Sergius: tell Catherine that queer story his friend told us about how he escaped after Slivnitza. You remember. About his being hid by two women.

SERGIUS [with bitter irony]: Oh yes: quite a romance! He was serving in the very battery I so unprofessionally charged. Being a thorough soldier, he ran away like the rest of them, with our cavalry at his heels. To escape their sabres he climbed a waterpipe and made his way into the bedroom of a young Bulgarian lady. The young lady was enchanted by his persuasive commercial traveller's manners. She very modestly entertained him for an hour or so, and then called in her mother lest her conduct should appear unmaidenly. The old lady was equally fascinated; and the fugitive was sent on his way in the morning, disguised in an old coat belonging to the master of the house, who was away at the war.

RAINA [rising with marked stateliness]: Your life in the camp has made you coarse, Sergius. I did not think you would have repeated such a story before me. [She turns away coldly].

CATHERINE [also rising]: She is right, Sergius. If such women exist, we should be spared the knowledge of them.

PETKOFF: Pooh! nonsense! what does it matter?

SERGIUS [ashamed]: No, Petkoff: I was wrong. [To RAINA, with earnest humility] I beg your pardon. I have behaved abominably. Forgive me, Raina. [She bows reservedly]. And you too, madam. [CATHERINE bows graciously and sits down. He proceeds solemnly, again addressing RAINA] The glimpses I have had of the seamy side of life during the last few months have made me cynical; but I should not have brought my cynicism here: least of all into your presence, Raina. I—[Here, turning to the others, he is evidently going to begin a long speech when the MAJOR interrupts him].

PETKOFF: Stuff and nonsense, Sergius! Thats quite enough fuss about nothing: a soldier's daughter should be able to stand up without flinching to a little strong conversation. [He rises]. Come: it's time for us to get to business. We have to make up our minds how those three regiments are to get back to Philippopolis: theres no forage for them on the Sofia route. [He goes towards the house]. Come along. [SERGIUS is about to follow him when CATHERINE rises and intervenes].

CATHERINE: Oh, Paul, cant you spare Sergius for a few moments? Raina has hardly seen him yet. Perhaps I can help you to settle about the regiments.

SERGIUS [protesting]: My dear madam, impossible: you—

CATHERINE [stopping him playfully]: You stay here, my dear Sergius: theres no hurry. I have a word or two to say to Paul. [SERGIUS instantly bows and steps back]. Now, dear [taking PETKOFF's arm]: come and see the electric bell.

PETOKFF: Oh, very well, very well.

       [They go into the house together affectionately. SERGIUS, left alone with RAINA, looks anxiously at her, fearing that she is still offended. She smiles, and stretches out her arms to him.]

SERGIUS [hastening to her]: Am I forgiven?

RAINA [placing her hands on his shoulders as she looks up at him with admiration and worship]: My hero! My king!

SERGIUS: My queen! [He kisses her on the forehead].

RAINA: How I have envied you, Sergius! You have been out in the world, on the field of battle, able to prove yourself there worthy of any woman in the world; whilst I have had to sit at home inactive—dreaming—useless—doing nothing that could give me the right to call myself worthy of any man.

SERGIUS: Dearest: all my deeds have been yours. You inspired me. I have gone through the war like a knight in a tournament with his lady looking down at him!

RAINA: And you have never been absent from my thoughts for a moment. [Very solemnly] Sergius: I think we two have found the higher love. When I think of you, I feel that I could never do a base deed or think an ignoble thought.

SERGIUS: My lady and my saint! [He clasps her reverently].

RAINA [returning his embrace]: My lord and my—

SERGIUS: Sh—sh! Let me be the worshipper, dear. You little know how unworthy even the best man is of a girl's pure passion!

RAINA: I trust you. I love you. You will never disappoint me, Sergius. [LOUKA is heard singing within the house. They quickly release each other]. I cant pretend to talk indifferently before her: my heart is too full. [LOUKA comes from the house with her tray. She goes to the table, and begins to clear it, with her back turned to them]. I will get my hat; and then we can go out until lunch time. Wouldnt you like that?

SERGIUS: Be quick. If you are away five minutes, it will seem five hours. [RAINA runs to the top of the steps, and turns there to exchange looks with him and wave him a kiss with both hands. He looks after her with emotion for a moment; then turns slowly away, his face radiant with the loftiest exaltation. The movement shifts his field of vision, into the corner of which there now comes the tail of LOUKA's double apron. His attention is arrested at once. He takes a stealthy look at her, and begins to twirl his moustache mischievously, with his left hand akimbo on his hip. Finally, striking the ground with his heels in something of a cavalry swagger, he strolls over to the other side of the table, opposite her, and says] Louka: do you know what the higher love is?

LOUKA [astonished]: No, sir.

SERGIUS: Very fatiguing thing to keep up for any length of time, Louka. One feels the need of some relief after it.

LOUKA [innocently]: Perhaps you would like some coffee, sir? [She stretches her hand across the table for the coffee pot].

SERGIUS [taking her hand]: Thank you, Louka.

LOUKA [pretending to pull]: Oh, sir, you know I didnt mean that. I'm surprised at you!

SERGIUS [coming clear of the table and drawing her with him]: I am surprised at myself, Louka. What would Sergius, the hero of Slivnitza, say if he saw me now? What would Sergius, the apostle of the higher love, say if he saw me now? What would the half dozen Sergiuses who keep popping in and out of this handsome figure of mine say if they caught us here? [Letting go her hand and slipping his arm dexterously round her waist] Do you consider my figure handsome, Louka?

LOUKA: Let me go, sir. I shall be disgraced. [She struggles: he holds her inexorably]. Oh, will you let go?

SERGIUS [looking straight into her eyes]: No.

LOUKA: Then stand back where we cant be seen. Have you no common sense?

SERGIUS: Ah! thats reasonable. [*He takes her into the stableyard gateway, where they are hidden from the house*].

LOUKA [*plaintively*]: I may have been seen from the window: Miss Raina is sure to be spying about after you.

SERGIUS [*stung: letting her go*]: Take care, Louka. I may be worthless enough to betray the higher love; but do not you insult it.

LOUKA [*demurely*]: Not for the world, sir, I'm sure. May I go on with my work, please, now?

SERGIUS [*again putting his arm round her*]: You are a provoking little witch, Louka. If you were in love with me, would you spy out of windows on me?

LOUKA: Well, you see, sir, since you say you are half a dozen different gentlemen all at once, I should have a great deal to look after.

SERGIUS [*charmed*]: Witty as well as pretty. [*He tries to kiss her*].

LOUKA [*avoiding him*]: No: I dont want your kisses. Gentlefolk are all alike: you making love to me behind Miss Raina's back; and she doing the same behind yours.

SERGIUS [*recoiling a step*]: Louka!

LOUKA: It shews how little you really care.

SERGIUS [*dropping his familiarity, and speaking with freezing politeness*]: If our conversation is to continue, Louka, you will please remember that a gentleman does not discuss the conduct of the lady he is engaged to with her maid.

LOUKA: It's so hard to know what a gentleman considers right. I thought from your trying to kiss me that you had given up being so particular.

SERGIUS [*turning from her and striking his forehead as he comes back into the garden from the gateway*]: Devil! devil!

LOUKA: Ha! ha! I expect one of the six of you is very like me, sir; though I am only Miss Raina's maid. [*She goes back to her work at the table, taking no further notice of him*].

SERGIUS [*speaking to himself*]: Which of the six is the real man? thats the question that torments me. One of them is a hero, another a buffoon, another a humbug, another perhaps a bit of a blackguard. [*He pauses, and looks furtively at* LOUKA *as he adds, with deep bitterness*] And one, at least, is a coward: jealous, like all cowards. [*He goes to the table*]. Louka.

LOUKA: Yes?

SERGIUS: Who is my rival?

LOUKA: You shall never get that out of me, for love or money.

SERGIUS: Why?

LOUKA: Never mind why. Besides, you would tell that I told you; and I should lose my place.

SERGIUS [holding out his right hand in affirmation]: No! on the honor of a—[He checks himself; and his hand drops, nerveless, as he concludes sardonically]—of a man capable of behaving as I have been behaving for the last five minutes. Who is he?

LOUKA: I dont know. I never saw him. I only heard his voice through the door of her room.

SERGIUS: Damnation! How dare you?

LOUKA [retreating]: Oh, I mean no harm: youve no right to take up my words like that. The mistress knows all about it. And I tell you that if that gentleman ever comes here again, Miss Raina will marry him, whether he likes it or not. I know the difference between the sort of manner you and she put on before one another and the real manner.

[SERGIUS shivers as if she had stabbed him. Then, setting his face like iron, he strides grimly to her, and grips her above the elbows with both hands.]

SERGIUS: Now listen you to me.

LOUKA [wincing]: Not so tight: youre hurting me.

SERGIUS: That doesnt matter. You have stained my honor by making me a party to your eavesdropping. And you have betrayed your mistress.

LOUKA [writhing]: Please—

SERGIUS: That shews that you are an abominable little clod of common clay, with the soul of a servant. [He lets her go as if she were an unclean thing, and turns away, dusting his hands of her, to the bench by the wall, where he sits down with averted head, meditating gloomily].

LOUKA [whimpering angrily with her hands up her sleeves, feeling her bruised arms]: You know how to hurt with your tongue as well as with your hands. But I dont care, now Ive found out that whatever clay I'm made of, youre made of the same. As for her, she's a liar; and her fine airs are a cheat; and I'm worth six of her. [She shakes the pain off hardily; tosses her head; and sets to work to put the things on the tray].

[He looks doubtfully at her. She finishes packing the tray, and laps the cloth over the edges, so as to carry all out together. As she stoops to lift it, he rises.]

SERGIUS: Louka! [She stops and looks defiantly at him]. A gentleman has no right to hurt a woman under any circumstances. [With profound humility, uncovering his head] I beg your pardon.

LOUKA: That sort of apology may satisfy a lady. Of what use is it to a servant?

SERGIUS [*rudely crossed in his chivalry, throws it off with a bitter laugh, and says slightingly*]: Oh! you wish to be paid for the hurt? [*He puts on his shako, and takes some money from his pocket*].

LOUKA [*her eyes filling with tears in spite of herself*]: No: I want my hurt made well.

SERGIUS [*sobered by her tone*]: How?

[*She rolls up her left sleeve; clasps her arm with the thumb and fingers of her right hand; and looks down at the bruise. Then she raises her head and looks straight at him. Finally, with a superb gesture, she presents her arm to be kissed. Amazed, he looks at her; at the arm; at her again; hesitates; and then, with shuddering intensity, exclaims Never! and gets away as far as possible from her.*

Her arm drops. Without a word, and with unaffected dignity, she takes her tray, and is approaching the house when RAINA *returns, wearing a hat and jacket in the height of the Vienna fashion of the previous year, 1885.* LOUKA *makes way proudly for her, and then goes into the house.*]

RAINA: I'm ready. Whats the matter? [*Gaily*] Have you been flirting with Louka?

SERGIUS [*hastily*]: No, no. How can you think such a thing?

RAINA [*ashamed of herself*]: Forgive me, dear: it was only a jest. I am so happy to-day.

[*He goes quickly to her, and kisses her hand remorsefully.* CATHERINE *comes out and calls to them from the top of the steps.*]

CATHERINE [*coming down to them*]: I am sorry to disturb you, children; but Paul is distracted over those three regiments. He doesnt know how to send them to Philippopolis; and he objects to every suggestion of mine. You must go and help him, Sergius. He is in the library.

RAINA [*disappointed*]: But we are just going out for a walk.

SERGIUS: I shall not be long. Wait for me just five minutes. [*He runs up the steps to the door*].

RAINA [*following him to the foot of the steps and looking up at him with timid coquetry*]: I shall go round and wait in full view of the library windows. Be sure you draw father's attention to me. If you are a moment longer than five minutes, I shall go in and fetch you, regiments or no regiments.

SERGIUS [*laughing*]: Very well. [*He goes in*].

[RAINA *watches him until he is out of her sight. Then, with a perceptible relaxation of manner, she begins to pace up and down the garden in a brown study.*]

CATHERINE: Imagine their meeting that Swiss and hearing the whole story! The very first thing your father asked for was the old coat we sent him off in. A nice mess you have got us into!

RAINA [*gazing thoughtfully at the gravel as she walks*]: The little beast!

CATHERINE: Little beast! What little beast?

RAINA: To go and tell! Oh, if I had him here, I'd cram him with chocolate creams til he couldnt ever speak again!

CATHERINE: Dont talk such stuff. Tell me the truth, Raina. How long was he in your room before you came to me?

RAINA [*whisking round and recommencing her march in the opposite direction*]: Oh, I forget.

CATHERINE: You cannot forget! Did he really climb up after the soldiers were gone; or was he there when that officer searched the room?

RAINA: No. Yes: I think he must have been there then.

CATHERINE: You think! Oh, Raina! Raina! Will anything ever make you straightforward? If Sergius finds out, it will be all over between you.

RAINA [*with cool impertinence*]: Oh, I know Sergius is your pet. I sometimes wish you could marry him instead of me. You would just suit him. You would pet him, and spoil him, and mother him to perfection.

CATHERINE [*opening her eyes very widely indeed*]: Well, upon my word!

RAINA [*capriously: half to herself*]: I always feel a longing to do or say something dreadful to him—to shock his propriety—to scandalize the five senses out of him. [*To* CATHERINE, *perversely*] I dont care whether he finds out about the chocolate cream soldier or not. I half hope he may. [*She again turns and strolls flippantly away up the path to the corner of the house*].

CATHERINE: And what should I be able to say to your father, pray?

RAINA [*over her shoulder, from the top of the two steps*]: Oh, poor father! As if he could help himself! [*She turns the corner and passes out of sight*].

CATHERINE [*looking after her, her fingers itching*]: Oh, if you were only ten years younger! [LOUKA *comes from the house with a salver, which she carries hanging down by her side*]. Well?

LOUKA: Theres a gentleman just called, madam. A Serbian officer.

CATHERINE [*flaming*]: A Serb! And how dare he—[*checking herself bitterly*] Oh, I forgot. We are at peace now. I suppose we shall have them calling every day to pay their compliments. Well: if he is an officer why dont you tell your master? He is in the library with Major Saranoff. Why do you come to me?

LOUKA: But he asks for you, madam. And I dont think he knows who you are: he said the lady of the house. He gave me this little ticket for you. [*She takes a card out of her bosom; puts it on the salver; and offers it to* CATHERINE].

CATHERINE [*reading*]: "Captain Bluntschli"? Thats a German name.

LOUKA: Swiss, madam, I think.

CATHERINE [*with a bound that makes* LOUKA *jump back*]: Swiss! What is he like?

LOUKA [*timidly*]: He has a big carpet bag, madam.

CATHERINE: Oh Heavens! he's come to return the coat. Send him away: say we're not at home: ask him to leave his address and I'll write to him. Oh stop: that will never do. Wait! [*She throws herself into a chair to think it out.* LOUKA *waits*]. The master and Major Saranoff are busy in the library, arnt they?

LOUKA: Yes, madam.

CATHERINE [*decisively*]: Bring the gentleman out here at once. [*Peremptorily*] And be very polite to him. Dont delay. Here [*impatiently snatching the salver from her*]: leave that here; and go straight back to him.

LOUKA: Yes, madam [*going*].

CATHERINE: LOUKA!

LOUKA [*stopping*]: Yes, madam.

CATHERINE: Is the library door shut?

LOUKA: I think so, madam.

CATHERINE: If not, shut it as you pass through.

LOUKA: Yes, madam [*going*].

CATHERINE: Stop! [LOUKA *stops*]. He will have to go that way [*indicating the gate of the stableyard*]. Tell Nicola to bring his bag here after him. Dont forget.

LOUKA [*surprised*]: His bag?

CATHERINE: Yes: here: as soon as possible. [*Vehemently*] Be quick! [LOUKA *runs into the house.* CATHERINE *snatches her apron off and throws it behind a bush. She then takes up the salver and uses it as a mirror, with the result that the handkerchief tied round her head follows the apron. A touch to her hair and a shake to her dressing gown make her presentable*]. Oh, how? how? how can a man be such a fool! Such a moment to select! [LOUKA *appears at the door of* the house, announcing CAPTAIN BLUNTSCHLI. *She stands aside at the top of the steps to let him pass before she goes in again. He is the man of the midnight adventure in* RAINA's *room, clean, well brushed, smartly uniformed, and out of trouble, but still unmistakably the same man. The moment* LOUKA's *back is turned,* CATHERINE *swoops on him with impetuous, urgent, coaxing appeal].* Captain Bluntschli: I am very glad to see you; but you must leave this house at once. [*He raises his eyebrows*]. My husband has just returned with my future son-in-law; and they know nothing. If they did, the consequences would be terrible. You are a foreigner: you do not feel our national animosities as we do. We still hate the Serbs: the effect of the peace on my husband has been to make him feel like a lion baulked of his prey. If he discovers our secret, he will never forgive me; and my daughter's life will hardly be safe. Will you, like the chivalrous gentleman and soldier you are, leave at once before he finds you here?

BLUNTSCHLI [*disappointed, but philosophical*]: At once, gracious lady. I only came to thank you and return the coat you lent me. If you will allow me to take it out of my bag and leave it with your servant as I pass out, I need detain you no further. [*He turns to go into the house*].

CATHERINE [*catching him by the sleeve*]: Oh, you must not think of going back that way. [*Coaxing him across to the stable gates*] This is the shortest way out. Many thanks. So glad to have been of service to you. Good-bye.

BLUNTSCHLI: But my bag?

CATHERINE: It shall be sent on. You will leave me your address.

BLUNTSCHLI: True. Allow me. [*He takes out his card-case, and stops to write his address, keeping* CATHERINE *in an agony of impatience. As he hands her the card,* PETKOFF, *hatless, rushes from the house in a fluster of hospitality, followed by* SERGIUS].

PETKOFF [*as he hurries down the steps*]: My dear Captain Bluntschli—

CATHERINE: Oh Heavens! [*She sinks on the seat against the wall*].

PETKOFF [*too preoccupied to notice her as he shakes* BLUNTSCHLI's *hand heartily*]. Those stupid people of mine thought I was out here, instead of in the—haw!—library [*he cannot mention the library without betraying how proud he is of it*]. I saw you through the window. I was wondering why you didnt come in. Saranoff is with me: you remember him, dont you?

SERGIUS [*saluting humorously, and then offering his hand with great charm of manner*]: Welcome, our friend the enemy!

PETKOFF: No longer the enemy, happily. [*Rather anxiously*] I hope youve called as a friend, and not about horses or prisoners.

CATHERINE: Oh, quite as a friend, Paul. I was just asking Captain Bluntschli to stay to lunch; but he declares he must go at once.

SERGIUS [*sardonically*]: Impossible, Bluntschli. We want you here badly. We have to send on three cavalry regiments to Philippopolis; and we dont in the least know how to do it.

BLUNTSCHLI [*suddenly attentive and businesslike*]: Philippopolis? The forage is the trouble, I suppose.

PETKOFF [*eagerly*]: Yes: thats it. [*To* SERGIUS] He sees the whole thing at once.

BLUNTSCHLI: I think I can shew you how to manage that.

SERGIUS: Invaluable man! Come along! [*Towering over* BLUNTSCHLI, *he puts his hand on his shoulder and takes him to the steps,* PETKOFF *following*].

[RAINA *comes from the house as* BLUNTSCHLI *puts his foot on the first step.*]

RAINA: Oh! The chocolate cream soldier!

[BLUNTSCHLI *stands rigid.* SERGIUS, *amazed, looks at* RAINA, *then at* PETKOFF, *who looks back at him and then at his wife.*]

CATHERINE [*with commanding presence of mind*]: My dear Raina, dont you see that we have a guest here? Captain Bluntschli: one of our new Serbian friends.

[RAINA *bows:* BLUNTSCHLI *bows.*]

RAINA: How silly of me! [*She comes down into the center of the group, between* BLUNTSCHLI *and* PETKOFF]. I made a beautiful ornament this morning for the ice pudding; and that stupid Nicola has just put down a pile of plates on it and spoilt it. [*To* BLUNTSCHLI, *winningly*] I hope you didnt think that you were the chocolate cream soldier, Captain Bluntschli.

BLUNTSCHLI [*laughing*]: I assure you I did. [*Stealing a whimsical glance at her*] Your explanation was a relief.

PETKOFF [*suspiciously to* RAINA]: And since when, pray, have you taken to cooking?

CATHERINE: Oh, whilst you were away. It is her latest fancy.

PETKOFF [*testily*]: And has Nicola taken to drinking? He used to be careful enough. First he shews Captain Bluntschli out here when he knew quite well I was in the library; and then he goes downstairs and breaks Raina's chocolate soldier. He must—[*Nicola appears at the top of the steps with the bag. He descends; places it respectfully before* BLUNTSCHLI; *and waits for further orders. General amazement.* NICOLA, *unconscious of the effect he is producing, looks perfectly satisfied with himself. When* PETKOFF *recovers his power of speech, he breaks out at him with]* Are you mad, Nicola?

NICOLA *[taken aback]*: Sir?

PETKOFF: What have you brought that for?

NICOLA: My lady's orders, major. Louka told me that—

CATHERINE *[interrupting him]*: My orders! Why should I order you to bring Captain Bluntschli's luggage out here? What are you thinking of, Nicola?

NICOLA *[after a moment's bewilderment, picking up the bag as he addresses* BLUNTSCHLI *with the very perfection of servile discretion]*: I beg your pardon, captain, I am sure. *[To* CATHERINE*]* My fault, madam: I hope youll overlook it. *[He bows, and is going to the steps with the bag, when* PETKOFF *addresses him angrily]*.

PETKOFF. Youd better go and slam that bag, too, down on Miss Raina's ice pudding! *[This is too much for* NICOLA. *The bag drops from his hand almost on his master's toes, eliciting a roar of]* Begone, you butter-fingered donkey.

NICOLA *[snatching up the bag, and escaping into the house]*: Yes, major.

CATHERINE: Oh, never mind, Paul: dont be angry.

PETKOFF *[blustering]*: Scoundrel! He's got out of hand while I was away. I'll teach him. Infernal blackguard! The sack next Saturday! I'll clear out the whole establishment—*[He is stifled by the caresses of his wife and daughter, who hang round his neck, petting him]*.

CATHERINE ⎰
RAINA ⎱ { *[Together]* } Now, now, now, it mustnt be Wow, wow, wow: not on your angry. He meant no

⎰ harm. Be good to first day at home. I'll make another ice
⎨ please me, dear. Sh-sh-sh-sh!
⎱ pudding. Tch-ch-ch!

PETKOFF *[yielding]*: Oh well, never mind. Come, Bluntschli: let's have no more nonsense about going away. You know very well youre not going back to Switzerland yet. Until you do go back youll stay with us.

RAINA: Oh, do, Captain Bluntschli.

PETKOFF *[to* CATHERINE*]*: Now, Catherine: it's of you he's afraid. Press him; and he'll stay.

CATHERINE: Of course I shall be only too delighted if *[appealingly]* Captain Bluntschli really wishes to stay. He knows my wishes.

BLUNTSCHLI *[in his direst military manner]*: I am at madam's orders.

SERGIUS *[cordially]*: That settles it!

PETKOFF [*heartily*]: Of course!

RAINA: You see you must stay.

BLUNTSCHLI [*smiling*]: Well, if I must, I must.

[*Gesture of despair from* CATHERINE.]

✿ *Act III*

IN the library after lunch. *It is not much of a library. Its literary equipment consists of a single fixed shelf stocked with old paper-covered novels, broken backed, coffee stained, torn and thumbed; and a couple of little hanging shelves with a few gift books on them: the rest of the wall space being occupied by trophies of war and the chase. But it is a most comfortable sitting room. A row of three large windows shews a mountain panorama, just now seen in one of its friendliest aspects in the mellowing afternoon light. In the corner next the right hand window a square earthenware stove, a perfect tower of glistening pottery, rises nearly to the ceiling and guarantees plenty of warmth. The ottoman is like that in* RAINA's *room, and similarly placed; and the window seats are luxurious with decorated cusions. There is one object, however, hopelessly out of keeping with its surroundings. This is a small kitchen table, much the worse for wear, fitted as a writing table with an old canister full of pens, an eggcup filled with ink, and a deplorable scrap of heavily used pink blotting paper.*

At the side of this table, which stands to the left of anyone facing the window, BLUNTSCHLI *is hard at work with a couple of maps before him, writing orders. At the head of it sits* SERGIUS, *who is supposed to be also at work, but is actually gnawing the feather of a pen, and contemplating* BLUNTSCHLI's *quick, sure, businesslike progress with a mixture of envious irritation at his own incapacity and awestruck wonder at an ability which seems to him almost miraculous, though its prosaic character forbids him to esteem it. The Major is comfortably established on the ottoman, with a newspaper in his hand and the tube of his hookah within easy reach. Catherine sits at the stove, with her back to them, embroidering.* RAINA, *reclining on the divan, is gazing in a daydream out at the Balkan landscape, with a neglected novel in her lap.*

The door is on the same side as the stove, farther from the window. The button of the electric bell is at the opposite side, behind BLUNTSCHLI.

PETKOFF [*looking up from his paper to watch how they are getting on at the table*]: Are you sure I cant help you in any way, Bluntschli?

BLUNTSCHLI [*without interrupting his writing or looking up*]: Quite sure, thank you. Saranoff and I will manage it.

SERGIUS [*grimly*]: Yes: we'll manage it. He finds out what to do; draws up the orders; and I sign em. Division of labor! [BLUNTSCHLI *passes him a paper*]. Another one? Thank you. [*He plants the paper squarely before him; sets his chair carefully parallel to it; and signs with his cheek on his elbow and his protruded tongue following the movements of his pen*]. This hand is more accustomed to the sword than to the pen.

PETKOFF: It's very good of you, Bluntschli: it is indeed, to let yourself be put upon in this way. Now are you quite sure I can do nothing?

CATHERINE [*in a low warning tone*]: You can stop interrupting, Paul.

PETKOFF [*starting and looking round at her*]: Eh? Oh! Quite right, my love: quite right. [*He takes his newspaper up again, but presently lets it drop*]. Ah, you havn't been campaigning, Catherine: you dont know how pleasant it is for us to sit here, after a good lunch, with nothing to do but enjoy ourselves. Theres only one thing I want to make me thoroughly comfortable.

CATHERINE: What is that?

PETKOFF: My old coat. I'm not at home in this one: I feel as if I were on parade.

CATHERINE: My dear Paul, how absurd you are about that old coat! It must be hanging in the blue closet where you left it.

PETKOFF: My dear Catherine, I tell you Ive looked there. Am I to believe my own eyes or not? [CATHERINE *rises and crosses the room to press the button of the electric bell*]. What are you shewing off that bell for? [*She looks at him majestically and silently resumes her chair and her needlework*]. My dear: if you think the obstinacy of your sex can make a coat out of two old dressing gowns of Raina's, your waterproof, and my mackintosh, youre mistaken. Thats exactly what the blue closet contains at present.

[NICOLA *presents himself*.]

CATHERINE: Nicola: go to the blue closet and bring your master's old coat here: the braided one he wears in the house.

NICOLA: Yes, madame. [*He goes out*].

PETKOFF: Catherine.

CATHERINE: Yes, Paul?

PETKOFF: I bet you any piece of jewellery you like to order from Sofia against a week's housekeeping money that the coat isnt there.

CATHERINE: Done, Paul!

PETKOFF [excited by the prospect of a gamble]: Come: here's an opportunity for some sport. Wholl bet on it? Bluntschli: I'll give you six to one.

BLUNTSCHLI [imperturbably]: It would be robbing you, major. Madame is sure to be right. [Without looking up, he passes another batch of papers to SERGIUS].

SERGIUS [also excited]: Bravo, Switzerland! Major: I bet my best charger against an Arab mare for Raina that Nicola finds the coat in the blue closet.

PETKOFF [eagerly]: Your best char—

CATHERINE [hastily interrupting him]: Dont be foolish, Paul. An Arabian mare will cost you 50,000 levas.

RAINA [suddenly coming out of her picturesque revery]: Really, mother, if you are going to take the jewellery, I dont see why you should grudge me my Arab.

[NICOLA comes back with the coat, and brings it to PETKOFF, who can hardly believe his eyes.]

CATHERINE: Where was it, Nicola?

NICOLA: Hanging in the blue closet, madame.

PETKOFF: Well, I am d—

CATHERINE [stopping him]: Paul!

PETKOFF: I could have sworn it wasnt there. Age is beginning to tell on me. I'm getting hallucinations. [To NICOLA] Here: help me to change. Excuse me, Bluntschli. [He begins changing coats, NICOLA acting as valet]. Remember: I didnt take that bet of yours, Sergius. Youd better give Raina that Arab steed yourself, since youve roused her expectations. Eh, Raina? [He looks round at her; but she is again rapt in the landscape. With a little gush of parental affection and pride, he points her out to them, and says] She's dreaming, as usual.

SERGIUS: Assuredly she shall not be the loser.

PETKOFF: So much the better for her. I shant come off so cheaply, I expect. [The change is now complete. NICOLA goes out with the discarded coat.] . Ah, now I feel at home at last. [He sits down and takes his newspaper with a grunt of relief].

BLUNTSCHLI [to SERGIUS, handing a paper]: Thats the last order.

PETKOFF [jumping up]: What! Finished?

BLUNTSCHLI: Finished.

PETKOFF [with childlike envy]: Havnt you anything for me to sign?

BLUNTSCHLI: Not necessary. His signature will do.

PETKOFF [inflating his chest and thumping it]: Ah well, I think weve done a thundering good day's work. Can I do anything more?

BLUNTSCHLI: You had better both see the fellows that are to take these. [SERGIUS *rises*] Pack them off at once; and shew them that Ive marked on the orders the time they should hand them in by. Tell them that if they stop to drink or tell stories—if theyre five minutes late, theyll have the skin taken off their backs.

SERGIUS [*stiffening indignantly*]: I'll say so. [*He strides to the door*]. And if one of them is man enough to spit in my face for insulting him, I'll buy his discharge and give him a pension. [*He goes out*].

BLUNTSCHLI [*confidentially*]: Just see that he talks to them properly, major, will you?

PETKOFF [*officiously*]: Quite right, Bluntschli, quite right. I'll see to it. [*He goes to the door importantly, but hesitates on the threshold*]. By the bye, Catherine, you may as well come too. They'll be far more frightened of you than of me.

CATHERINE [*putting down her embroidery*]: I daresay I had better. You would only splutter at them. [*She goes out,* PETKOFF *holding the door for her and following her*].

BLUNTSCHLI: What an army! They make cannons out of cherry trees; and the officers send for their wives to keep discipline! [*He begins to fold and docket the papers*].

> [RAINA, *who has risen from the divan, marches slowly down the room with her hands clasped behind her, and looks mischievously at him*.]

RAINA: You look ever so much nicer than when we last met. [*He looks up, surprised*]. What have you done to yourself?

BLUNTSCHLI: Washed; brushed; good night's sleep and breakfast. Thats all.

RAINA: Did you get back safely that morning?

BLUNTSCHLI: Quite, thanks.

RAINA: Were they angry with you for running away from Sergius's charge?

BLUNTSCHLI [*grinning*]: No: they were glad; because theyd all just run away themselves.

RAINA [*going to the table, and leaning over it towards him*]: It must have made a lovely story for them: all that about me and my room.

BLUNTSCHLI: Capital story. But I only told it to one of them: a particular friend.

RAINA: On whose discretion you could absolutely rely?

BLUNTSCHLI: Absolutely.

RAINA: Hm! He told it all to my father and Sergius the day you exchanged the prisoners. [*She turns away and strolls carelessly across to the other side of the room*].

BLUNTSCHLI [*deeply concerned, and half incredulous*]: No! You dont mean that, do you?

RAINA [*turning, with sudden earnestness*]: I do indeed. But they dont know that it was in this house you took refuge. If Sergius knew, he would challenge you and kill you in a duel.

BLUNTSCHLI: Bless me! then dont tell him.

RAINA: Please be serious, Captain Bluntschli. Can you not realize what it is to me to deceive him? I want to be quite perfect with Sergius: no meanness, no smallness, no deceit. My relation to him is the one really beautiful and noble part of my life. I hope you can understand that.

BLUNTSCHLI [*sceptically*]: You mean that you wouldnt like him to find out that the story about the ice pudding was a—a—a—You know.

RAINA [*wincing*]: Ah, don't talk of it in that flippant way. I lied: I know it. But I did it to save your life. He would have killed you. That was the second time I ever uttered a falsehood. [BLUNTSCHLI *rises quickly and looks doubtfully and somewhat severely at her*]. Do you remember the first time?

BLUNTSCHLI: I! No. Was I present?

RAINA: Yes; and I told the officer who was searching for you that you were not present.

BLUNTSCHLI: True. I should have remembered it.

RAINA [*greatly encouraged*]: Ah, it is natural that you should forget it first. It cost you nothing: it cost me a lie! A lie!!

> [*She sits down on the ottoman, looking straight before her with her hands clasped round her knee.* BLUNTSCHLI, *quite touched, goes to the ottoman with a particularly reassuring and considerate air, and sits down beside her.*]

BLUNTSCHLI: My dear young lady, dont let this worry you. Remember: I'm a soldier. Now what are the two things that happen to a soldier so often that he comes to think nothing of them? One is hearing people tell lies [RAINA *recoils*]: the other is getting his life saved in all sorts of ways by all sorts of people.

RAINA [*rising in indignant protest*]: And so he becomes a creature incapable of faith and of gratitude.

BLUNTSCHLI [*making a wry face*]: Do you like gratitude? I dont. If pity is akin to love, gratitude is akin to the other thing.

RAINA: Gratitude! [*Turning on him*] If you are incapable of gratitude you are incapable of any noble sentiment. Even animals are grateful. Oh, I see now exactly what you think of me! You were not surprised to hear me lie. To you it was something I probably did every day!

every hour!! That is how men think of women. [*She paces the room tragically*].

BLUNTSCHLI [*dubiously*]: Theres reason in everything. You said youd told only two lies in your whole life. Dear young lady: isnt that rather a short allowance? I'm quite a straightforward man myself; but it wouldnt last me a whole morning.

RAINA [*staring haughtily at him*]: Do you know, sir, that you are insulting me?

BLUNTSCHLI: I cant help it. When you strike that noble attitude and speak in that thrilling voice, I admire you; but I find it impossible to believe a single word you say.

RAINA [*superbly*]: Captain Bluntschli!

BLUNTSCHLI [*unmoved*]: Yes?

RAINA [*standing over him, as if she could not believe her senses*]: Do you mean what you said just now? Do you know what you said just now?

BLUNTSCHLI: I do.

RAINA [*gasping*]: I! I!!! [*She points to herself incredulously, meaning "I, Raina Petkoff, tell lies!" He meets her gaze unflinchingly. She suddenly sits down beside him, and adds, with a complete change of manner from the heroic to a babyish familiarity*] How did you find me out?

BLUNTSCHLI [*promptly*]: Instinct, dear young lady. Instinct, and experience of the world.

RAINA [*wonderingly*]: Do you know, you are the first man I ever met who did not take me seriously?

BLUNTSCHLI: You mean, dont you, that I am the first man that has ever taken you quite seriously?

RAINA: Yes: I suppose I do mean that. [*Cosily, quite at her ease with him*] How strange it is to be talked to in such a way! You know, Ive always gone on like that.

BLUNTSCHLI: You mean the—?

RAINA: I mean the noble attitude and the thrilling voice. [*They laugh together*]. I did it when I was a tiny child to my nurse. She believed in it. I do it before my parents. They believe in it. I do it before Sergius. He believes in it.

BLUNTSCHLI: Yes: he's a little in that line himself, isnt he?

RAINA [*startled*]: Oh! Do you think so?

BLUNTSCHLI: You know him better than I do.

RAINA: I wonder—I wonder is he? If I thought that—! [*Discouraged*] Ah, well: what does it matter? I suppose, now youve found me out, you despise me.

BLUNTSCHLI [*warmly, rising*]: No, my dear young lady, no, no, no a thousand times. It's part of your youth: part of your charm. I'm like all the rest of them: the nurse, your parents, Sergius: I'm your infatuated admirer.

RAINA [*pleased*]: Really?

BLUNTSCHLI [*slapping his breast smartly with his hand, German fashion*] Hand aufs Herz! Really and truly.

RAINA [*very happy*]: But what did you think of me for giving you my portrait?

BLUNTSCHLI [*astonished*]: Your portrait! You never gave me your portrait.

RAINA [*quickly*]: Do you mean to say you never got it?

BLUNTSCHLI: No. [*He sits down beside her, with renewed interest, and says, with some complacency*] When did you send it to me?

RAINA [*indignantly*]: I did not send it to you. [*She turns her head away, and adds, reluctantly*] It was in the pocket of that coat.

BLUNTSCHLI [*pursing his lips and rounding his eyes*]: Oh-o-oh! I never found it. It must be there still.

RAINA [*springing up*]: There still! for my father to find the first time he puts his hand in his pocket! Oh, how could you be so stupid?

BLUNTSCHLI [*rising also*]: It doesnt matter: I suppose it's only a photograph: how can he tell who it was intended for? Tell him he put it there himself.

RAINA [*bitterly*]: Yes: that is so clever! isnt it? [*Distractedly*] Oh! what shall I do?

BLUNTSCHLI: Ah, I see. You wrote something on it. That was rash.

RAINA [*vexed almost to tears*]: Oh, to have done such a thing for you, who care no more—except to laugh at me—oh! Are you sure nobody has touched it?

BLUNTSCHLI: Well, I cant be quite sure. You see, I couldnt carry it about with me all the time: one cant take much luggage on active service.

RAINA: What did you do with it?

BLUNTSCHLI: When I got through to Pirot I had to put it in safe keeping somehow. I thought of the railway cloak room; but thats the surest place to get looted in modern warfare. So I pawned it.

RAINA: Pawned it!!!

BLUNTSCHLI: I know it doesnt sound nice; but it was much the safest plan. I redeemed it the day before yesterday. Heaven only knows whether the pawnbroker cleared out the pockets or not.

RAINA [*furious: throwing the words right into his face*]: You have a low shopkeeping mind. You think of things that would never come into a gentleman's head.

BLUNTSCHLI [*phlegmatically*]: Thats the Swiss national character, dear lady. [*He returns to the table*].

RAINA: Oh, I wish I had never met you. [*She flounces away, and sits at the window fuming*].

[LOUKA *comes in with a heap of letters and telegrams on her salver, and crosses, with her bold free gait, to the table. Her left sleeve is looped up to the shoulder with a brooch, shewing her naked arm, with a broad gilt bracelet covering the bruise.*]

LOUKA [*to* BLUNTSCHLI]: For you. [*She empties the salver with a fling on to the table*]. The messenger is waiting. [*She is determined not to be civil to an enemy, even if she must bring him his letters*].

BLUNTSCHLI [*to* RAINA]: Will you excuse me: the last postal delivery that reached me was three weeks ago. These are the subsequent accumulations. Four telegrams: a week old. [*He opens one*]. Oho! Bad news!

RAINA [*rising and advancing a little remorsefully*]: Bad news?

BLUNTSCHLI: My father's dead. [*He looks at the telegram with his lips pursed, musing on the unexpected change in his arrangements.* LOUKA *crosses herself hastily*].

RAINA: Oh, how very sad!

BLUNTSCHLI: Yes: I shall have to start for home in an hour. He has left a lot of big hotels behind him to be looked after. [*He takes up a fat letter in a long blue envelope*]. Here's a whacking letter from the family solicitor. [*He pulls out the enclosures and glances over them*]. Great Heavens! Seventy! Two hundred! [*In a crescendo of dismay*] Four hundred! Four thousand!! Nine thousand six hundred!!! What on earth am I to do with them all?

RAINA [*timidly*]: Nine thousand hotels?

BLUNTSCHLI: Hotels! nonsense. If you only knew! Oh, it's too ridiculous! Excuse me: I must give my fellow orders about starting. [*He leaves the room hastily, with the documents in his hand*].

LOUKA [*knowing instinctively that she can annoy* RAINA *by disparaging* BLUNTSCHLI]: He has not much heart, that Swiss. He has not a word of grief for his poor father.

RAINA [*bitterly*]: Grief! A man who has been doing nothing but killing people for years! What does he care? What does any soldier care? [*She goes to the door, restraining her tears with difficulty*].

LOUKA: Major Saranoff has been fighting too; and he has plenty of heart left. [RAINA, *at the door, draws herself up haughtily and goes* out]. Aha! I thought you wouldn't get much feeling out of your soldier. [*She is following* RAINA *when* NICOLA *enters with an armful of logs for the stove*].

NICOLA [*grinning amorously at her*]: Ive been trying all the afternoon to get a minute alone with you, my girl. [*His countenance changes as he notices her arm*]. Why, what fashion is that of wearing your sleeve, child?

LOUKA [*proudly*]: My own fashion.

NICOLA: Indeed! If the mistress catches you, she'll talk to you. [*He puts the logs down, and seats himself comfortably on the ottoman*].

LOUKA: Is that any reason why you should take it on yourself to talk to me?

NICOLA: Come! dont be so contrairy with me. Ive some good news for you. [*She sits down beside him. He takes out some paper money.* LOUKA, *with an eager gleam in her eyes, tries to snatch it; but he shifts it quickly to his left hand, out of her reach*]. See! a twenty leva bill! Sergius gave me that, out of pure swagger. A fool and his money are soon parted. Theres ten levas more. The Swiss gave me that for backing up the mistress's and Raina's lies about him. He's no fool, he isnt. You should have heard old Catherine downstairs as polite as you please to me, telling me not to mind the Major being a little impatient; for they knew what a good servant I was—after making a fool and a liar of me before them all! The twenty will go to our savings; and you shall have the ten to spend if youll only talk to me so as to remind me I'm a human being. I get tired of being a servant occasionally.

LOUKA: Yes: sell your manhood for 30 levas, and buy me for 10! [*Rising scornfully*] Keep your money. You were born to be a servant. I was not. When you set up your shop you will only be everybody's servant instead of somebody's servant. [*She goes moodily to the table and seats herself regally in* SERGIUS's *chair*].

NICOLA [*picking up his logs, and going to the stove*]: Ah, wait til you see. We shall have our evenings to ourselves; and I shall be master in my own house, I promise you. [*He throws the logs down and kneels at the stove*].

LOUKA: You shall never be master in mine.

NICOLA [*turning, still on his knees, and squatting down rather forlornly on his calves, daunted by her implacable disdain*]: You have a great ambition in you, Louka. Remember: if any luck comes to you, it was I that made a woman of you.

LOUKA: You!

NICOLA [*scrambling up and going at her*]: Yes, me. Who was it made you give up wearing a couple of pounds of false black hair on your head and reddening your lips and cheeks like any other Bulgarian girl? I did. Who taught you to trim your nails, and keep your hands clean, and be dainty about yourself, like a fine Russian lady? Me: do you hear that? me! [*She tosses her head defiantly; and he turns away, adding, more coolly*] Ive often thought that if Raina were out of the way, and you just a little less of a fool and Sergius just a little more of one, you might come to be one of my grandest customers, instead of only being my wife and costing me money.

LOUKA: I believe you would rather be my servant than my husband. You would make more out of me. Oh, I know that soul of yours.

NICOLA [*going closer to her for greater emphasis*]: Never you mind my soul; but just listen to my advice. If you want to be a lady, your present behavior to me wont do at all, unless when we're alone. It's too sharp and impudent; and impudence is a sort of familiarity: it shews affection for me. And dont you try being high and mighty with me, either. Youre like all country girls: you think it's genteel to treat a servant the way I treat a stableboy. Thats only your ignorance; and dont you forget it. And dont be so ready to defy everybody. Act as if you expected to have your own way, not as if you expected to be ordered about. The way to get on as a lady is the same as the way to get on as a servant: youve got to know your place: thats the secret of it. And you may depend on me to know my place if you get promoted. Think over it, my girl. I'll stand by you: one servant should always stand by another.

LOUKA [*rising impatiently*]: Oh, I must behave in my own way. You take all the courage out of me with your cold-blooded wisdom. Go and put those logs on the fire: thats the sort of thing you understand.

[*Before NICOLA can retort, SERGIUS comes in. He checks himself a moment on seeing LOUKA; then goes to the stove.*]

SERGIUS [*to NICOLA*]: I am not in the way of your work, I hope.

NICOLA [*in a smooth, elderly manner*]: Oh no, sir: thank you kindly. I was only speaking to this foolish girl about her habit of running up here to the library whenever she gets a chance, to look at the books. Thats the worst of her education, sir: it gives her habits above her station. [*To LOUKA*] Make that table tidy, Louka, for the Major. [*He goes out sedately*].

[*LOUKA, without looking at SERGIUS, pretends to arrange the papers on the table. He crosses slowly to her, and studies the arrangement of her sleeve reflectively.*]

SERGIUS: Let me see: is there a mark there? [*He turns up the bracelet and sees the bruise made by his grasp. She stands motionless, not looking at him: fascinated, but on her guard*]. Ffff! Does it hurt?

LOUKA: Yes.

SERGIUS: Shall I cure it?

LOUKA [*instantly withdrawing herself proudly, but still not looking at him*]: No. You cannot cure it now.

SERGIUS [*masterfully*]: Quite sure? [*He makes a movement as if to take her in his arms*].

LOUKA: Dont trifle with me, please. An officer should not trifle with a servant.

SERGIUS [*indicating the bruise with a merciless stroke of his forefinger*]: That was no trifle, Louka.

LOUKA [*flinching; then looking at him for the first time*]: Are you sorry?

SERGIUS [*with measured emphasis, folding his arms*]: I am never sorry.

LOUKA [*wistfully*]: I wish I could believe a man could be as unlike a woman as that. I wonder are you really a brave man?

SERGIUS [*unaffectedly, relaxing his attitude*]: Yes: I am a brave man. My heart jumped like a woman's at the first shot; but in the charge I found that I was brave. Yes: that at least is real about me.

LOUKA: Did you find in the charge that the men whose fathers are poor like mine were any less brave than the men who are rich like you?

SERGIUS [*with bitter levity*]: Not a bit. They all slashed and cursed and yelled like heroes. Psha! the courage to rage and kill is cheap. I have an English bull terrier who has as much of that sort of courage as the whole Bulgarian nation, and the whole Russian nation at its back. But he lets my groom thrash him, all the same. Thats your soldier all over! No, Louka: your poor men can cut throats; but they are afraid of their officers; they put up with insults and blows; they stand by and see one another punished like children: aye, and help to do it when they are ordered. And the officers!!! Well [*with a short harsh laugh*] I am an officer. Oh, [*fervently*] give me the man who will defy to the death any power on earth or in heaven that sets itself up against his own will and conscience: he alone is the brave man.

LOUKA: How easy it is to talk! Men never seem to me to grow up: they all have schoolboy's ideas. You dont know what true courage is.

SERGIUS [*ironically*]: Indeed! I am willing to be instructed. [*He sits on the ottoman, sprawling magnificently*].

LOUKA: Look at me! how much am I allowed to have my own will? I have to get your room ready for you: to sweep and dust, to fetch and carry. How could that degrade me if it did not degrade you to have it done for you? But [*with subdued passion*] if I were Empress of Russia, above everyone in the world, then!! Ah then, though according to you I could shew no courage at all, you should see, you should see.

SERGIUS: What would you do, most noble Empress?

LOUKA: I would marry the man I loved, which no other queen in Europe has the courage to do. If I loved you, though you would be as far beneath me as I am beneath you, I would dare to be the equal of my inferior. Would you dare as much if you loved me? No: if you felt the beginnings of love for me you would not let it grow. You would not dare: you would marry a rich man's daughter because you would be afraid of what other people would say of you.

SERGIUS [*bounding up*]: You lie: it is not so, by all the stars! If I loved you, and I were the Czar himself, I would set you on the throne by my side. You know that I love another woman, a woman as high above you as heaven is above earth. And you are jealous of her.

LOUKA: I have no reason to be. She will never marry you now. The man I told you of has come back. She will marry the Swiss.

SERGIUS [*recoiling*]: The Swiss!

LOUKA: A man worth ten of you. Then you can come to me; and I will refuse you. You are not good enough for me. [*She turns to the door*].

SERGIUS [*springing after her and catching her fiercely in his arms*]: I will kill the Swiss; and afterwards I will do as I please with you.

LOUKA [*in his arms, passive and steadfast*]: The Swiss will kill you, perhaps. He has beaten you in love. He may beat you in war.

SERGIUS [*tormentedly*]: Do you think I believe that she—she! whose worst thoughts are higher than your best ones, is capable of trifling with another man behind my back?

LOUKA: Do you think she would believe the Swiss if he told her now that I am in your arms?

SERGIUS [*releasing her in despair*]: Damnation! Oh, damnation! Mockery! mockery everywhere! everything I think is mocked by everything I do. [*He strikes himself frantically on the breast*]. Coward! liar! fool! Shall I kill myself like a man, or live and pretend to laugh at myself? [*She again turns to go*]. Louka! [*She stops near the door*]. Remember: you belong to me.

LOUKA [*turning*]: What does that mean? An insult?

SERGIUS [*commandingly*]: It means that you love me, and that I have had you here in my arms, and will perhaps have you there again. Whether that is an insult I neither know nor care: take it as you please. But [*vehemently*] I will not be a coward and a trifler. If I choose to love you, I dare marry you, in spite of all Bulgaria. If these hands ever touch you again, they shall touch my affianced bride.

LOUKA: We shall see whether you dare keep your word. And take care. I will not wait long.

SERGIUS [*again folding his arms and standing motionless in the middle of the room*]: Yes: we shall see. And you shall wait my pleasure.

[BLUNTSCHLI, *much preoccupied, with his papers still in his hand, enters, leaving the door open for* LOUKA *to go out. He goes across to the table, glancing at her as he passes.* SERGIUS, *without altering his resolute attitude, watches him steadily.* LOUKA *goes out, leaving the door open.*]

BLUNTSCHLI [*absently, sitting at the table as before, and putting down his papers*]: Thats a remarkable looking young woman.

SERGIUS [*gravely, without moving*]: Captain Bluntschli.

BLUNTSCHLI: Eh?

SERGIUS: You have deceived me. You are my rival. I brook no rivals. At six o'clock I shall be in the drilling-ground on the Klissoura road, alone, on horseback, with my sabre. Do you understand?

BLUNTSCHLI [*staring, but sitting quite at his ease*]: Oh, thank you: thats a cavalry man's proposal. I'm in the artillery; and I have the choice of weapons. If I go, I shall take a machine gun. And there shall be no mistake about the cartridges this time.

SERGIUS [*flushing, but with deadly coldness*]: Take care, sir. It is not our custom in Bulgaria to allow invitations of that kind to be trifled with.

BLUNTSCHLI [*warmly*]: Pooh! dont talk to me about Bulgaria. You dont know what fighting is. But have it your own way. Bring your sabre along. I'll meet you.

SERGIUS [*fiercely delighted to find his opponent a man of spirit*]: Well said, Switzer. Shall I lend you my best horse?

BLUNTSCHLI: No: damn your horse! thank you all the same, my dear fellow. [RAINA *comes in, and hears the next sentence*]. I shall fight you on foot. Horseback's too dangerous: I dont want to kill you if I can help it.

RAINA [*hurrying forward anxiously*]: I have heard what Captain Bluntschli said, Sergius. You are going to fight. Why? [SERGIUS *turns away in silence, and goes to the stove, where he stands watching her as she continues, to* BLUNTSCHLI] What about?

BLUNTSCHLI: I dont know: he hasnt told me. Better not interfere, dear young lady. No harm will be done: Ive often acted as sword instructor. He wont be able to touch me; and I'll not hurt him. It will save explanations. In the morning I shall be off home; and youll never see me or hear of me again. You and he will then make it up and live happily ever after.

RAINA [*turning away deeply hurt, almost with a sob in her voice*]: I never said I wanted to see you again.

SERGIUS [*striding forward*]: Ha! That is a confession.

RAINA [*haughtily*]: What do you mean?

SERGIUS: You love that man!

RAINA [*scandalized*]: Sergius!

SERGIUS: You allow him to make love to you behind my back, just as you treat me as your affianced husband behind his. Bluntschli: you knew our relations; and you deceived me. It is for that that I call you to account, not for having received favors I never enjoyed.

BLUNTSCHLI [*jumping up indignantly*]: Stuff! Rubbish! I have received no favors. Why, the young lady doesnt even know whether I'm married or not.

RAINA [*forgetting herself*]: Oh! [*Collapsing on the ottoman*] Are you?

SERGIUS: You see the young lady's concern, Captain Bluntschli. Denial is useless. You have enjoyed the privilege of being received in her own room, late at night—

BLUNTSCHLI [*interrupting him pepperily*]: Yes, you blockhead! she received me with a pistol at her head. Your cavalry were at my heels. I'd have blown out her brains if she'd uttered a cry.

SERGIUS [*taken aback*]: Bluntschli! Raina: is this true?

RAINA [*rising in wrathful majesty*]: Oh, how dare you, how dare you?

BLUNTSCHLI: Apologize, man: apologize. [*He resumes his seat at the table*].

SERGIUS [*with the old measured emphasis, folding his arms*]: I never apologize!

RAINA [*passionately*]: This is the doing of that friend of yours, Captain Bluntschli. It is he who is spreading this horrible story about me. [*She walks about excitedly*].

BLUNTSCHLI: No: he's dead. Burnt alive.

RAINA [*stopping, shocked*]: Burnt alive!

BLUNTSCHLI: Shot in the hip in a woodyard. Couldnt drag himself out. Your fellows' shells set the timber on fire and burnt him, with half a dozen other poor devils in the same predicament.

RAINA: How horrible!

SERGIUS: And how ridiculous! Oh, war! war! the dream of patriots and heroes! A fraud, Bluntschli. A hollow sham, like love.

RAINA [*outraged*]: Like love! You say that before me!

BLUNTSCHLI: Come, Saranoff: that matter is explained.

SERGIUS: A hollow sham, I say. Would you have come back here if nothing had passed between you except at the muzzle of your pistol? Raina is mistaken about your friend who was burnt. He was not my informant.

RAINA: Who then? [*Suddenly guessing the truth*] Ah, Louka! my maid! my servant! You were with her this morning all that time after—after—Oh, what sort of god is this I have been worshipping! [*He meets her gaze with sardonic enjoyment of her disenchantment. Angered all the more, she goes closer to him, and says, in a lower, intenser tone*] Do you know that I looked out of the window as I went upstairs, to have another sight of my hero; and I saw something I did not understand then. I know now that you were making love to her.

SERGIUS [*with grim humor*]: You saw that?

RAINA: Only too well. [*She turns away, and throws herself on the divan under the centre window, quite overcome*].

SERGIUS [*cynically*]: Raina: our romance is shattered. Life's a farce.

BLUNTSCHLI [*to* RAINA, *whimsically*]: You see: he's found himself out now.

SERGIUS [*going to him*]: Bluntschli: I have allowed you to call me a blockhead. You may now call me a coward as well. I refuse to fight you. Do you know why?

BLUNTSCHLI: No; but it doesnt matter. I didnt ask the reason when you cried on; and I dont ask the reason now that you cry off. I'm a professional soldier: I fight when I have to, and am very glad to get out of it when I havnt to. Youre only an amateur: you think fighting's an amusement.

SERGIUS [*sitting down at the table, nose to nose with him*]: You shall hear the reason all the same, my professional. The reason is that it takes two men—real men—men of heart, blood and honor—to make a genuine combat. I could no more fight with you than I could make love to an ugly woman. Youve no magnetism: youre not a man: youre a machine.

BLUNTSCHLI [*apologetically*]: Quite true, quite true. I always was that sort of chap. I'm very sorry.

SERGIUS: Psha!

BLUNTSCHLI: But now that youve found that life isnt a farce, but something quite sensible and serious, what further obstacle is there to your happiness?

RAINA [*rising*]: You are very solicitous about my happiness and his. Do you forget his new love—Louka? It is not you that he must fight now, but his rival, Nicola.

SERGIUS: Rival!! [*bounding half across the room*].

RAINA: Dont you know that theyre engaged?

SERGIUS: Nicola! Are fresh abysses opening? Nicola!!

RAINA [*sarcastically*]: A shocking sacrifice, isnt it? Such beauty! such intellect! such modesty! wasted on a middle-aged servant man. Really, Sergius, you cannot stand by and allow such a thing. It would be unworthy of your chivalry.

SERGIUS [*losing all self-control*]: Viper! Viper! [*He rushes to and fro, raging*].

BLUNTSCHLI: Look here, Saranoff: youre getting the worst of this.

RAINA [*getting angrier*]: Do you realize what he has done, Captain Bluntschli? He has set this girl as a spy on us; and her reward is that he makes love to her.

SERGIUS: False! Monstrous!

RAINA: Monstrous! [*Confronting him*] Do you deny that she told you about Captain Bluntschli being in my room?

SERGIUS: No; but—

RAINA [*interrupting*]: Do you deny that you were making love to her when she told you?

SERGIUS: No; but I tell you—

RAINA [*cutting him short contemptuously*]: It is unnecessary to tell us anything more. That is quite enough for us. [*She turns away from him and sweeps majestically back to the window*].

BLUNTSCHLI [*quietly, as SERGIUS, in an agony of mortification, sinks on the ottoman, clutching his averted head between his fists*]: I told you you were getting the worst of it, Saranoff.

SERGIUS: Tiger cat!

RAINA [*running excitedly to BLUNTSCHLI*]: You hear this man calling me names, Captain Bluntschli?

BLUNTSCHLI: What else can he do, dear lady? He must defend himself somehow. Come [*very persuasively*]: dont quarrel. What good does it do?

[*RAINA, with a gasp, sits down on the ottoman, and after a vain effort to look vexedly at BLUNTSCHLI, falls a victim to her sense of humor, and actually leans back babyishly against the writhing shoulder of SERGIUS.*]

SERGIUS: Engaged to Nicola! Ha! ha! Ah well, Bluntschli, you are right to take this huge imposture of a world coolly.

RAINA [*quaintly to BLUNTSCHLI, with an intuitive guess at his state of mind*] I daresay you think us a couple of grown-up babies, dont you?

SERGIUS [*grinning savagely*]: He does: he does. Swiss civilization nursetending Bulgarian barbarism, eh?

BLUNTSCHLI [blushing]: Not at all, I assure you. I'm only very glad to get you two quieted. There! there! let's be pleasant and talk it over in a friendly way. Where is this other young lady?

RAINA: Listening at the door, probably.

SERGIUS [shivering as if a bullet had struck him, and speaking with quiet but deep indignation]: I will prove that that, at least, is a calumny. [He goes with dignity to the door and opens it. A yell of fury bursts from him as he looks out. He darts into the passage, and returns dragging in LOUKA, whom he flings violently against the table, exclaiming] Judge her, Bluntschli. You, the cool impartial man: judge the eavesdropper.

[LOUKA stands her ground, proud and silent.]

BLUNTSCHLI [shaking his head]: I mustnt judge her. I once listened myself outside a tent when there was a mutiny brewing. It's all a question of the degree of provocation. My life was at stake.

LOUKA: My love was at stake. I am not ashamed.

RAINA [contemptuously]: Your love! Your curiosity, you mean.

LOUKA [facing her and retorting her contempt with interest]: My love, stronger than anything you can feel, even for your chocolate cream soldier.

SERGIUS [with quick suspicion, to LOUKA]: What does that mean?

LOUKA [fiercely]: It means—

SERGIUS [interrupting her slightly]: Oh, I remember: the ice pudding. A paltry taunt, girl!

[MAJOR PETKOFF enters, in his shirtsleeves.]

PETKOFF: Excuse my shirtsleeves, gentlemen. Raina: somebody has been wearing that coat of mine: I'll swear it. Somebody with a differently shaped back. It's all burst open at the sleeve. Your mother is mending it. I wish she'd make haste: I shall catch cold. [He looks more attentively at them]. Is anything the matter?

RAINA: No. [She sits down at the stove, with a tranquil air].

SERGIUS: Oh no. [He sits down at the end of the table, as at first].

BLUNTSCHLI [who is already seated]: Nothing. Nothing.

PETKOFF [sitting down on the ottoman in his old place]: Thats all right. [He notices LOUKA]. Anything the matter, Louka?

LOUKA: No, sir.

PETKOFF [genially]: Thats all right. [He sneezes]. Go and ask your mistress for my coat, like a good girl, will you?

[NICOLA enters with the coat. LOUKA makes a pretence of having business in the room by taking the little table with the hookah away to the wall near the windows.]

RAINA [rising quickly as she sees the coat on NICOLA's arm]: Here it is, papa. Give it to me, Nicola; and do you put some more wood on the fire. [*She takes the coat, and brings it to the Major, who stands up to put it on.* NICOLA *attends to the fire*].

PETKOFF [*to* RAINA, *teasing her affectionately*]: Aha! Going to be very good to poor old papa just for one day after his return from the wars, eh?

RAINA [*with solemn reproach*]: Ah, how can you say that to me, father?

PETKOFF: Well, well, only a joke, little one. Come: give me a kiss. [*She kisses him*]. Now give me the coat.

RAINA: No: I am going to put it on for you. Turn your back. [*He turns his back and feels behind him with his arms for the sleeves. She dexterously takes the photograph from the pocket and throws it on the table before* BLUNTSCHLI, *who covers it with a sheet of paper under the very nose of* SERGIUS, *who looks on amazed, with his suspicions roused in the highest degree. She then helps* PETKOFF *on with his coat*]. There, dear! Now are you comfortable?

PETKOFF: Quite, little love. Thanks. [*He sits down; and* RAINA *returns to her seat near the stove*]. Oh, by the bye, Ive found something funny. Whats the meaning of this? [*He puts his hand into the picked pocket*]. Eh? Hallo! [*He tries the other pocket*]. Well, I could have sworn—! [*Much puzzled, he tries the breast pocket*]. I wonder—[*trying the original pocket*] Where can it—? [*He rises, exclaiming*] Your mother's taken it!

RAINA [*very red*]: Taken what?

PETKOFF: Your photograph, with the inscription: "Raina, to her Chocolate Cream Soldier: a Souvenir." Now you know theres something more in this than meets the eye; and I'm going to find it out. [*Shouting*] Nicola!

NICOLA [*coming to him*]: Sir!

PETKOFF: Did you spoil any pastry of Miss Raina's this morning?

NICOLA: You heard Miss Raina say that I did, sir.

PETKOFF: I know that, you idiot. Was it true?

NICOLA: I am sure Miss Raina is incapable of saying anything that is not true, sir.

PETKOFF: Are you? Then I'm not. [*Turning to the others*] Come: do you think I dont see it all? [*He goes to* SERGIUS, *and slaps him on the shoulder*]. Sergius: youre the chocolate cream soldier, arnt you?

SERGIUS [*staring up*]: I! A chocolate cream soldier! Certainly not.

PETKOFF: Not! [*He looks at them. They are all very serious and very conscious*]. Do you mean to tell me that Raina sends things like that to other men?

SERGIUS [enigmatically]: The world is not such an innocent place as we used to think, Petkoff.

BLUNTSCHLI [rising]: It's all right, Major. I'm the chocolate cream soldier. [PETKOFF and SERGIUS are equally astonished]. The gracious young lady saved my life by giving me chocolate creams when I was starving: shall I ever forget their flavour! My late friend Stolz told you the story at Pirot. I was the fugitive.

PETKOFF. You! [He gasps]. Sergius: do you remember how those two women went on this morning when we mentioned it? [SERGIUS smiles cynically. PETKOFF confronts RAINA severely]. Youre a nice young woman, arnt you?

RAINA [bitterly]: Major Saranoff has changed his mind. And when I wrote that on the photograph, I did not know that Captain Bluntschli was married.

BLUNTSCHLI [startled into vehement protest]: I'm not married.

RAINA [with deep reproach]: You said you were.

BLUNTSCHLI: I did not. I positively did not. I never was married in my life.

PETKOFF [exasperated]: Raina: will you kindly inform me, if I am not asking too much, which of these gentlemen you are engaged to?

RAINA: To neither of them. This young lady [introducing LOUKA, who faces them all proudly] is the object of Major Saranoff's affections at present.

PETKOFF: Louka! Are you mad, Sergius? Why, this girl's engaged to Nicola.

NICOLA: I beg your pardon, sir. There is a mistake. Louka is not engaged to me.

PETKOFF: Not engaged to you, you scoundrel! Why, you had twenty-five levas from me on the day of your betrothal; and she had that gilt bracelet from Miss Raina.

NICOLA [with cool unction]: We gave it out so, sir. But it was only to give Louka protection. She had a soul above her station; and I have been no more than her confidential servant. I intend, as you know, sir, to set up a shop later on in Sofia; and I look forward to her custom and recommendation should she marry into the nobility. [He goes out with impressive discretion, leaving them all staring after him].

PETKOFF [breaking the silence]: Well, I am—hm!

SERGIUS: This is either the finest heroism or the most crawling baseness. Which is it, Bluntschli?

BLUNTSCHLI: Never mind whether it's heroism or baseness. Nicola's the ablest man Ive met in Bulgaria. I'll make him manager of a hotel if he can speak French and German.

LOUKA [*suddenly breaking out at* SERGIUS]: I have been insulted by everyone here. You set them the example. You owe me an apology. [SERGIUS, *like a repeating clock of which the spring has been touched, immediately begins to fold his arms.*]

BLUNTSCHLI [*before he can speak*]: It's no use. He never apologizes.

LOUKA: Not to you, his equal and his enemy. To me, his poor servant, he will not refuse to apologize.

SERGIUS [*approvingly*]: You are right. [*He bends his knee in his grandest manner*] Forgive me.

LOUKA: I forgive you. [*She timidly gives him her hand, which he kisses*]. That touch makes me your affianced wife.

SERGIUS [*springing up*]: Ah! I forgot that.

LOUKA [*coldly*]: You can withdraw if you like.

SERGIUS: Withdraw! Never! You belong to me. [*He puts his arm about her*].

[CATHERINE *comes in and finds* LOUKA *in* SERGIUS's *arms, with all the rest gazing at them in bewildered astonishment.*]

CATHERINE: What does this mean?

[SERGIUS *releases* LOUKA.]

PETKOFF: Well, my dear, it appears that Sergius is going to marry Louka instead of Raina. [*She is about to break out indignantly at him: he stops her by exclaiming testily*] Dont blame me: Ive nothing to do with it. [*He retreats to the stove*].

CATHERINE: Marry Louka! Sergius: you are bound by your word to us!

SERGIUS [*folding his arms*]: Nothing binds me.

BLUNTSCHLI [*much pleased by this piece of common sense*]: Saranoff: your hand. My congratulations. These heroics of yours have their practical side after all. [*To* LOUKA] Gracious young lady: the best wishes of a good Republican! [*He kisses her hand, to* RAINA's *great disgust, and returns to his seat*].

CATHERINE: Louka: you have been telling stories.

LOUKA: I have done Raina no harm.

CATHERINE [*haughtily*]: Raina!

[RAINA, *equally indignant, almost snorts at the liberty.*]

LOUKA: I have a right to call her Raina: she calls me Louka. I told Major Saranoff she would never marry him if the Swiss gentleman came back.

BLUNTSCHLI [*rising, much surprised*]: Hallo!

LOUKA [*turning to* RAINA]: I thought you were fonder of him than of Sergius. You know best whether I was right.

BLUNTSCHLI: What nonsense! I assure you, my dear Major, my dear Madame, the gracious young lady simply saved my life, nothing else. She never cared two straws for me. Why, bless my heart and soul, look at the young lady and look at me. She, rich, young, beautiful, with her imagination full of fairy princes and noble natures and cavalry charges and goodness knows what! And I, a commonplace Swiss soldier who hardly knows what a decent life is after fifteen years of barracks and battles: a vagabond, a man who has spoiled all his chances in life through an incurably romantic disposition, a man—

SERGIUS [*starting as if a needle had pricked him and interrupting* BLUNTSCHLI *in incredulous amazement*]: Excuse me, Bluntschli: what did you say had spoiled your chances in life?

BLUNTSCHLI [*promptly*]: An incurably romantic disposition. I ran away from home twice when I was a boy. I went into the army instead of into my father's business. I climbed the balcony of this house when a man of sense would have dived into the nearest cellar. I came sneaking back here to have another look at the young lady when any other man of my age would have sent the coat back—

PETKOFF: My coat!

BLUNTSCHLI: —yes: thats the coat I mean—would have sent it back and gone quietly home. Do you suppose I am the sort of fellow a young girl falls in love with? Why, look at our ages! I'm thirty-four: I dont suppose the young lady is much over seventeen. [*This estimate produces a marked sensation, all the rest turning and staring at one another. He proceeds innocently*] All that adventure which was life or death to me, was only a schoolgirl's game to her—chocolate creams and hide and seek. Heres the proof! [*He takes the photograph from the table*]. Now, I ask you, would a woman who took the affair seriously have sent me this and written on it "Raina, to her Chocolate Cream Soldier: a Souvenir"? [*He exhibits the photograph triumphantly, as if it settled the matter beyond all possibility of refutation*].

PETKOFF: Thats what I was looking for. How the deuce did it get there? [*He comes from the stove to look at it, and sits down on the ottoman*].

BLUNTSCHLI [*to* RAINA, *complacently*]: I have put everything right, I hope, gracious young lady.

RAINA [*going to the table to face him*]: I quite agree with your account of yourself. You are a romantic idiot. [BLUNTSCHLI *is unspeakably taken aback*]. Next time, I hope you will know the difference between a schoolgirl of seventeen and a woman of twenty-three.

BLUNTSCHLI [*stupefied*]: Twenty-three!

> [RAINA *snaps the photograph contemptuously from his hand; tears it up; throws the pieces in his face; and sweeps back to her former place.*]

SERGIUS [*with grim enjoyment of his rival's discomfiture*]: Bluntschli: my one last belief is gone. Your sagacity is a fraud, like everything else. You have less sense than even I!

BLUNTSCHLI [*overwhelmed*]: Twenty-three! Twenty-three!! [*He considers*]. Hm! [*Swiftly making up his mind and coming to his host*] In that case, Major Petkoff, I beg to propose formally to become a suitor for your daughter's hand, in place of Major Saranoff retired.

RAINA: You dare!

BLUNTSCHLI: If you were twenty-three when you said those things to me this afternoon, I shall take them seriously.

CATHERINE [*loftily polite*]: I doubt, sir, whether you quite realize either my daughter's position or that of Major Sergius Saranoff, whose place you propose to take. The Petkoffs and the Saranoffs are known as the richest and most important families in the country. Our position is almost historical: we can go back for twenty years.

PETKOFF: Oh, never mind that, Catherine. [*To* BLUNTSCHLI] We should be most happy, Bluntschli, if it were only a question of your position; but hang it, you know, Raina is accustomed to a very comfortable establishment. Sergius keeps twenty horses.

BLUNTSCHLI: But who wants twenty horses? We're not going to keep a circus.

CATHERINE [*severely*]: My daughter, sir, is accustomed to a first-rate stable.

RAINA: Hush, mother: youre making me ridiculous.

BLUNTSCHLI: Oh well, if it comes to a question of an establishment, here goes! [*He darts impetuously to the table; seizes the papers in the blue envelope and turns to* SERGIUS]. How many horses did you say?

SERGIUS: Twenty, noble Switzer.

BLUNTSCHLI: I have two hundred horses. [*They are amazed*]. How many carriages?

SERGIUS: Three.

BLUNTSCHLI: I have seventy. Twenty-four of them will hold twelve inside, besides two on the box, without counting the driver and conductor. How many tablecloths have you?

SERGIUS: How the deuce do I know?

BLUNTSCHLI: Have you four thousand?

SERGIUS: No.

BLUNTSCHLI: I have. I have nine thousand six hundred pairs of sheets and blankets, with two thousand four hundred eider-down quilts. I have ten thousand knives and forks, and the same quantity of dessert spoons. I have three hundred servants. I have six palatial establishments, besides two livery stables, a tea gardens, and a private house. I have four medals for distinguished services; I have the rank of an officer and the standing of a gentleman; and I have three native languages. Shew me any man in Bulgaria that can offer as much!

PETKOFF [with childish awe]: Are you Emperor of Switzerland?

BLUNTSCHLI: My rank is the highest known in Switzerland: I am a free citizen.

CATHERINE: Then, Captain Bluntschli, since you are my daughter's choice—

RAINA [mutinously]: He's not.

CATHERINE [ignoring her]:—I shall not stand in the way of her happiness. [Petkoff is about to speak] That is Major Petkoff's feeling also.

PETKOFF: Oh, I shall be only too glad. Two hundred horses! Whew!

SERGIUS: What says the lady?

RAINA [pretending to sulk]: The lady says that he can keep his tablecloths and his omnibuses. I am not here to be sold to the highest bidder. [She turns her back on him].

BLUNTSCHLI: I wont take that answer. I appealed to you as a fugitive, a beggar, and a starving man. You accepted me. You gave me your hand to kiss, your bed to sleep in, and your roof to shelter me.

RAINA: I did not give them to the Emperor of Switzerland.

BLUNTSCHLI: Thats just what I say. [He catches her by the shoulders and turns her face-to-face with him]. Now tell us whom you did give them to.

RAINA [succumbing with a shy smile]: To my chocolate cream soldier.

BLUNTSCHLI [with a boyish laugh of delight]: Thatll do. Thank you. [He looks at his watch and suddenly becomes businesslike]. Time's up, Major. Youve managed those regiments so well that youre sure to be asked to get rid of some of the infantry of the Timok division. Send them home by way of Lom Palanka. Saranoff: dont get

married until I come back: I shall be here punctually at five in the
evening on Tuesday fortnight. Gracious ladies [*his heels click*] good
evening. [*He makes them a military bow, and goes*].

SERGIUS: What a man! Is he a man?

🏵 *Comments*

There is no reason, however, why I should take this haughty attitude
towards those representative critics whose complaint is that my talent,
though not unentertaining, lacks elevation of sentiment and seriousness of
purpose. They can find, under the surface-brilliancy for which they give
me credit, no coherent thought or sympathy, and accuse me, in various
terms and degrees, of an inhuman and freakish wantonness; of preoccupation with "the seamy side of life"; of paradox, cynicism, and eccentricity,
reducible, as some contend, to a trite formula of treating bad as good and
good as bad, important as trivial and trivial as important, serious as laughable and laughable as serious, and so forth. As to this formula I can only
say that if any gentleman is simple enough to think that even a good comic
opera can be produced by it, I invite him to try his hand, and see whether
anything resembling one of my plays will reward him.

I could explain the matter easily enough if I chose; but the result
would be that the people who misunderstand the plays would misunder-
stand the explanation ten times more. The particular exceptions taken are
seldom more than symptoms of the underlying fundamental disagreement
between the romantic morality of the critics and the natural morality of
the plays. For example, I am quite aware that the much criticized Swiss
officer in Arms and The Man is not a conventional stage soldier. He suffers
from want of food and sleep; his nerves go to pieces after three days under
fire, ending in the horrors of a rout and pursuit; he has found by experience
that it is more important to have a few bits of chocolate to eat in the field
than cartridges for his revolver. When many of my critics rejected these
circumstances as fantastically improbable and cynically unnatural, it was
not necessary to argue them into common sense: all I had to do was to
brain them, so to speak, with the first half dozen military authorities at
hand, beginning with the present Commander in Chief. But when it
proved that such unromantic (but all the more dramatic) facts implied
to them a denial of the existence of courage, patriotism, faith, hope, and
charity, I saw that it was not really mere matter of fact that was at issue
between us. One strongly Liberal critic, the late Moy Thomas, who had,
in the teeth of a chorus of dissent, received my first play with the most
generous encouragement, declared, when Arms and The Man was produced, that I had struck a wanton blow at the cause of liberty in the Balkan
Peninsula by mentioning that it was not a matter of course for a Bulgarian

in 1885 to wash his hands every day. He no doubt saw soon afterwards the squabble, reported all through Europe, between Stambouloff and an eminent lady of the Bulgarian court who took exception to his neglect of his fingernails. After that came the news of his ferocious assassination, with a description of the room prepared for the reception of visitors by his widow, who draped it with black, and decorated it with photographs of the mutilated body of her husband. Here was a sufficiently sensational confirmation of the accuracy of my sketch of the theatrical nature of the first apings of western civilization by spirited races just emerging from slavery. But it had no bearing on the real issue between my critic and myself, which was, whether the political and religious idealism which had inspired Gladstone to call for the rescue of these Balkan principalities from the despotism of the Turk, and converted miserably enslaved provinces into hopeful and gallant little States, will survive the general onslaught on idealism which is implicit, and indeed explicit, in Arms and The Man and the naturalist plays of the modern school. For my part I hope not; for idealism, which is only a flattering name for romance in politics and morals, is as obnoxious to me as romance in ethics or religion. In spite of a Liberal Revolution or two, I can no longer be satisfied with fictitious morals and fictitious good conduct, shedding fictitious glory on robbery, starvation, disease, crime, drink, war, cruelty, cupidity, and all the other common-places of civilization which drive men to the theatre to make foolish pretences that such things are progress, science, morals, religion, patriotism, imperial supremacy, national greatness and all the other names the newspapers call them. On the other hand, I see plenty of good in the world working itself out as fast as the idealists will allow it; and if they would only let it alone and learn to respect reality, which would include the beneficial exercise of respecting themselves, and incidentally respecting me, we should all get along much better and faster. At all events, I do not see moral chaos and anarchy as the alternative to romantic convention; and I am not going to pretend I do merely to please the people who are convinced that the world is held together only by the force of unanimous, strenuous, eloquent, trumpet-tongued lying. To me the tragedy and comedy of life lie in the consequences, sometimes terrible, sometimes ludicrous, of our persistent attempts to found our institutions on the ideals suggested to our imaginations by our half-satisfied passions, instead of on a genuinely scientific natural history. And with that hint as to what I am driving at, I withdraw and ring up the curtain.

From the preface to the second volume of Shaw's *Plays: Pleasant and Unpleasant* (1898).

———————◄◆►———————

The idea of taking two couples and causing them to exchange partners is hardly novel and, as I have said, the little tale of the coat and the portrait is Scribean in pattern. But Shaw can justifiably plead that this is no well-made play because the artifices of the plot are not what ultimately achieve the result. Here is one of the decisive turns in the action:

BLUNTSCHLI: When you strike that noble attitude and speak in that thrilling voice, I admire you; but I find it impossible to believe a single word you say.

RAINA: Captain Bluntschli!

BLUNTSCHLI: Yes?

RAINA: Do you mean what you said just now? Do you know what you said just now?

BLUNTSCHLI: I do.

RAINA: I! I!!!—How did you find me out?

With this last query, Raina passes over forever from Sergius's world to Bluntschli's: as a result of nothing in the Scribean arrangement of incidents but of words, words, words. It is here that, to many, the Shavian drama seems vulnerable. In drama, actions are supposed to speak louder than words. Writers on the subject invariably know their etymology— "drama" derives from a Greek verb meaning "to do"—and use it as a cudgel. Their error is a vulgar one: action need not be external. It can often be carried by words alone. Shaw used to remark that his plays were all words just as Raphael's paintings were all paint.

There is a degree of legerdemain in that remark, for Scribe too put down his plays in words. What was confusing to Shaw's readers and spectators half a century ago was that, after indicating unmistakably that he was playing Scribe's game, Shaw proceeded to break the rules. The fact that Bluntschli conquers by words gains its peculiar force from a context in which the opposite was to be expected. To look over *Arms and the Man* with an eye to technique would be to conclude that what we have here is Scribe most subtly interwoven with Shaw. Yet this formulation is inadequate, for who did the interweaving? There was a Scribe in Shaw, and there was a counter-Scribe in Shaw: what makes his works dramatic is the inter-action of the two.

The passion and preoccupation of Scribe was the idea of climax: to the Big Scene at the end—or, rather, a little before the end—all his arts are dedicated. In Bernard Shaw there was almost as great a predilection for anti-climax. It is the Shavian "effect" par excellence; no other playwright has come near finding so many possibilities in it. The bit I have quoted from Bluntschli and Raina is an apt example. *Arms and the Man* contains a corresponding scene between Sergius and Louka. Where, in a well-made play, Bluntschli and Louka would have to soar to the heights of Raina and Sergius, in the Shaw play Raina and Sergius drop with a bump to the level of Bluntschli and Louka. Such is resolution by anti-climax. It is dramaturgically effective, and it enforces the author's theme. But this is not all of Shaw: it is only the counter-Scribe. The dual anti-climaxes do not round off *Arms and the Man.* What does? Not the disenchantment of Raina and Sergius but the discovery that Bluntschli the realist is actually an enchanted soul whom nothing will disenchant. He has destroyed their romanticism but is himself "incurably romantic." This is another point that is made in "mere words"—"mere words stuck on at the end," if you wish—and yet stuck on very well, for they are firmly attached to that little tale of the coat and the photograph which gives the work its continuity and shape:

BLUNTSCHLI: —yes: that's the coat I mean. . . . Do you suppose I am the sort of fellow a young girl falls in love with? Why, look at our ages! I'm thirty four: I don't suppose the young lady is much over seventeen . . . All that adventure which was life or death to me was only a schoolgirl's game to her . . . Would a woman who took the affair seriously have sent me this and written on it: Raina, to her Chocolate Cream Soldier, a Souvenir?

PETKOFF: That's what I was looking for. How the deuce did it get there?

BLUNTSCHLI: I have put everything right, I hope, gracious young lady.

RAINA: I quite agree with your account of yourself. You are a romantic idiot. Next time I hope you will know the difference between a schoolgirl of seventeen and a woman of twenty three.

In this scene, plot and theme reach completion together, and the play of thesis and antithesis ends in synthesis.

Eric Bentley, "The Making of a Dramatist (1892–1903)," in *G. B. Shaw: A Collection of Critical Essays*, ed. R. J. Kaufmann (Englewood Cliffs: Prentice-Hall), pp. 62–63. Cited here by permission of the author.

———————◆◆———————

The Shavian terror consists of Shaw's insistence on the prerogative of every man to act decently, logically, and with a sense of humor, and on the obligation to act in this manner even in the face of opposition. He knows very well how much courage it takes to laugh about the ridiculous and how much seriousness it takes to discover the amusing. And, like all purposeful people, he knows, on the other hand, that the most time-consuming and distracting pursuit is a certain kind of seriousness which pervades literature but does not exist anywhere else. (Like us, the young generation, he considers it naive to write for the theater, and he does not show the slightest inclination to pretend that he is not aware of this: he makes far-reaching use of his naivete. He furnishes the theater with as much fun as it can take. And it can take a lot. What draws people to the theater is, strictly speaking, so much nonsense, which constitutes a tremendous buoyancy for those problems which really interest the progressive dramatic writer and which are the real value of his pieces. It follows that his problems must be so pertinent that he can be as buoyant about them as he wishes to be, for the buoyancy is what people want.

Probably all of his characters, in all their traits, are the result of Shaw's delight in upsetting our habitual prejudices. He knows that we have the terrible habit of forcing all the attributes of a certain kind of people into one preconceived, stereotyped concept. In our imagination the usurer is cowardly, sneaky, and brutal. We would not think of permitting him to be even a little courageous, sentimental, or soft hearted. Shaw does.

Concerning heroes, Shaw's degenerate successors have awkwardly amplified his refreshing conviction—that heroes are not exemplary scholars and that heroism is a very inscrutable, but very real conglomeration of contradictory traits—to mean that neither heroism nor heroes exist. But even this does not bother Shaw. It seems he considers it healthier to live among common people than among heroes.

Bertolt Brecht, "Ovation for Shaw" in *G. B. Shaw: A Collection of Critical Essays*, ed. R. J. Kaufmann (Englewood Cliffs: Prentice-Hall), pp. 16–17.

It is well to begin with the superficial; and this is the superficial effectiveness of Shaw; the brilliancy of bathos. But of course the vitality and value of his play does not lie merely in this. . . . This is not his message; but it is his method; it is his style. The first taste we had of it was in this play of *Arms and the Man;* but even at the very first it was evident that there was much more in the play than that. Among other things there was one thing not unimportant; there was savage sincerity. Indeed, only a ferociously sincere person can produce such effective flippancies on a matter like war; just as only a strong man could juggle with cannon-balls. It is all very well to use the word "fool" as synonymous with "jester"; but daily experience shows that it is generally the solemn and silent man who is the fool. It is all very well to accuse Mr. Shaw of standing on his head; but if you stand on your head you must have a hard and solid head to stand on. In *Arms and the Man* the bathos of form was strictly the incarnation of a strong satire in the idea. The play opens in an atmosphere of military melodrama; the dashing officer of cavalry going off to death in an attitude, the lovely heroine left in tearful rapture; the brass band, the noise of guns and the red fire. Into all this enters Bluntschli, the little sturdy crop-haired Swiss professional soldier, a man without a country but with a trade. He tells the army-adoring heroine frankly that she is a humbug; and she, after a moment's reflection, appears to agree with him. The play is like nearly all Shaw's plays, the dialogue of a conversion. By the end of it the young lady has lost all her military illusions and admires this mercenary soldier not because he faces guns, but because he faces facts.

G. K. Chesterton, *George Bernard Shaw* (New York: The Devin Adair Company). Reprinted by permission of the publisher.

🛆 *Anton Chekhov*

Anton Pavlovich Chekhov (1860–1904) was born in Taganrog, in southern Russia. His grandfather was a serf. He completed the study of medicine in 1884 at the University of Moscow, but did not practice regularly, turning to writing instead, which he had already tried at school. He began with light, comic pieces, then went on to those great stories whose naturalism was no doubt stimulated by his medical studies. His early dramatic efforts were influenced by the well-made play. His first full-length play, *Ivanov* (1887), was contrived and melodramatic, and it failed. Unhappy about this, he did not write his second play, *The Seagull*, until 1896. It was also poorly received, but was revived successfully by Stanislavsky, director of the Moscow Art Theatre. Stanislavsky's method, which sought to evoke the inner reality of the character, was exactly right for Chekhov's drama. It was a happy and famous conjunction of playwright and director. Chekhov's three masterpieces followed: *Uncle Vanya* (1899), *The Three Sisters* (1900), and *The Cherry Orchard* (1904). In these works he freed himself from the well-made play. He developed an episodic structure that perfectly suited his material: the aimlessness, boredom, and excessive self-preoccupation of his people. He avoided the excesses of romantic emotion by undercutting it with an ironic rhetoric. Unlike Shaw's linear *Arms*, in which character is gradually revealed, in Chekhov's episodic plays the total person is given at every moment, in each speech and gesture. He drew upon everyday people in everyday situations. But by catching that word and gesture which represented the total person he heightened the commonplace, gave it that significance it properly has but which we tend through familiarity to overlook. In this he was different from great moderns like Pirandello, Strindberg, and Beckett, who drew upon the unusual, or exaggerated the usual by placing it in an unusual situation.

READINGS:

BRUFORD, W. H., *Chekhov and His Russia*. New Haven: Yale University Press, 1947.
FERGUSSON, FRANCIS, *The Idea of a Theater*. Princeton: Princeton University Press, 1949.

MAGARSHACK, DAVID, *Chekhov the Dramatist.* New York: Hill and Wang, Inc., 1960.

SIMMONS, ERNEST J., *Chekhov.* Boston: Little, Brown and Company, 1962.

TOUMANOVA, PRINCESS NINA ANDRONIKOVA, *Anton Chekhov: The Voice of Twilight Russia.* New York: Columbia University Press, 1960.

🪷 The Cherry Orchard

Anton Chekhov

Translated from the Russian by Constance Garnett

CHARACTERS

MADAME RANEVSKY (LYUBOV AN-DREYEVNA), the owner of the Cherry Orchard

ANYA, her daughter, aged 17

VARYA, her adopted daughter, aged 24

GAEV (LEONID ANDREYEVITCH), brother of Madame Ranevsky

LOPAHIN (YERMOLAY ALEXEYE-VITCH), a merchant

TROFIMOV (PYOTR SERGEYEVITCH), a student

SEMYONOV-PISHTCHIK, a landowner

CHARLOTTA IVANOVNA, a governess

EPIHODOV (SEMYON PANTALEYE-VITCH), a clerk

DUNYASHA, a maid

FIRS, an old valet, aged 87

YASHA, a young valet

A WAYFARER

THE STATION MASTER

A POST-OFFICE CLERK

VISITORS, SERVANTS

The action takes place on the estate of MADAME RANEVSKY.

🪷 Act I

A room, which has always been called the nursery. One of the doors leads into ANYA's room. Dawn, sun rises during the scene. May, the cherry trees in flower, but it is cold in the garden with the frost of early morning. Windows closed.

Enter DUNYASHA with a candle and LOPAHIN with a book in his hand.

LOPAHIN: The train's in, thank God. What time is it?

DUNYASHA: Nearly two o'clock. [Puts out the candle] It's daylight already.

LOPAHIN: The train's late! Two hours, at least. [Yawns and stretches] I'm a pretty one; what a fool I've been. Came here on purpose to meet them at the station and dropped asleep. . . . Dozed off as I sat in the chair. It's annoying. . . . You might have waked me.

DUNYASHA: I thought you had gone. [*Listens*] There, I do believe they're coming!

LOPAHIN [*Listens*]: No, what with the luggage and one thing and another. [*A pause*] Lyubov Andreyevna has been abroad five years; I don't know what she is like now. . . . She's a splendid woman. A good-natured, kind-hearted woman. I remember when I was a lad of fifteen, my poor father—he used to keep a little shop here in the village in those days—gave me a punch in the face with his fist and made my nose bleed. We were in the yard here, I forget what we'd come about—he had had a drop. Lyubov Andreyevna—I can see her now—she was a slim young girl then—took me to wash my face, and then brought me into this very room, into the nursery. "Don't cry, little peasant," says she, "it will be well in time for your wedding day." . . . [*A pause*] Little peasant. . . . My father was a peasant, it's true, but here am I in a white waistcoat and brown shoes, like a pig in a bun shop. Yes, I'm a rich man, but for all my money, come to think, a peasant I was, and a peasant I am. [*Turns over the pages of the book*] I've been reading this book and I can't make head or tail of it. I fell asleep over it. [*A pause*]

DUNYASHA: The dogs have been awake all night, they feel that the mistress is coming.

LOPAHIN: Why, what's the matter with you, Dunyasha?

DUNYASHA: My hands are all of a tremble. I feel as though I should faint.

LOPAHIN: You're a spoilt soft creature, Dunyasha. And dressed like a lady too, and your hair done up. That's not the thing. One must know one's place.

[*Enter* EPIHODOV *with a nosegay; he wears a pea-jacket and highly polished creaking topboots; he drops the nosegay as he comes in*]

EPIHODOV [*Picking up the nosegay*]: Here! the gardener's sent this, says you're to put it in the dining-room. [*Gives* DUNYASHA *the nosegay*]

LOPAHIN: And bring me some kvass.

DUNYASHA: I will. [*Goes out*]

EPIHODOV: It's chilly this morning, three degrees of frost, though the cherries are all in flower. I can't say much for our climate. [*Sighs*] I can't. Our climate is not often propitious to the occasion. Yermolay Alexeyevitch, permit me to call your attention to the fact that I purchased myself a pair of boots the day before yesterday, and they creak, I venture to assure you, so that there's no tolerating them. What ought I to grease them with?

LOPAHIN: Oh, shut up! Don't bother me.

EPIHODOV: Every day some misfortune befalls me. I don't complain, I'm used to it, and I wear a smiling face.

[DUNYASHA *comes in, hands* LOPAHIN *the kvass*]

EPIHODOV: I am going. [*Stumbles against a chair, which falls over*] There! [*As though triumphant*] There you see now, excuse the expression, an accident like that among others. . . . It's positively remarkable. [*Goes out*]

DUNYASHA: Do you know, Yermolay Alexeyevitch, I must confess, Epihodov has made me a proposal.

LOPAHIN: Ah!

DUNYASHA: I'm sure I don't know. . . . He's a harmless fellow, but sometimes when he begins talking, there's no making anything of it. It's all very fine and expressive, only there's no understanding it. I've a sort of liking for him too. He loves me to distraction. He's an unfortunate man; every day there's something. They tease him about it—two and twenty misfortunes they call him.

LOPAHIN [*Listening*]: There! I do believe they're coming.

DUNYASHA: They are coming! What's the matter with me? . . . I'm cold all over.

LOPAHIN: They really are coming. Let's go and meet them. Will she know me? It's five years since I saw her.

DUNYASHA [*In a flutter*]: I shall drop this very minute. . . . Ah, I shall drop.

[*There is a sound of two carriages driving up to the house.* LOPAHIN *and* DUNYASHA *go out quickly. The stage is left empty. A noise is heard in the adjoining rooms.* FIRS, *who has driven to meet* MADAME RANEVSKY, *crosses the stage hurriedly leaning on a stick. He is wearing old-fashioned livery and a high hat. He says something to himself, but not a word can be distinguished. The noise behind the scenes goes on increasing. A voice: "Come, let's go in here." Enter* LYUBOV ANDREYEVNA, ANYA, *and* CHARLOTTA IVANOVNA *with a pet dog on a chain, all in traveling dresses.* VARYA *in an out-door coat with a kerchief over her head,* GAEV, SEMYONOV-PISHTCHIK, LOPAHIN, DUNYASHA *with bag and parasol, servants with other articles. All walk across the room*]

ANYA: Let's come in here. Do you remember what room this is, mamma?

LYUBOV [*Joyfully, through her tears*]: The nursery!

VARYA: How cold it is, my hands are numb [*To* LYUBOV ANDREYEVNA] Your rooms, the white room and the lavender one, are just the same as ever, mamma.

LYUBOV: My nursery, dear delightful room. . . . I used to sleep here when I was little. . . . [*Cries*] And here I am, like a little child. . . . [*Kisses her brother and Varya, and then her brother again*] Varya's just the same as ever, like a nun. And I knew Dunyasha. [*Kisses* DUNYASHA]

GAEV: The train was two hours late. What do you think of that? Is that the way to do things?

CHARLOTTA [*To* PISHTCHIK]: My dog eats nuts, too.

PISHTCHIK [*Wonderingly*]: Fancy that!

[*They all go out except* ANYA *and* DUNYASHA]

DUNYASHA: We've been expecting you so long. [*Takes* ANYA's *hat and coat*]

ANYA: I haven't slept for four nights on the journey. I feel dreadfully cold.

DUNYASHA: You set out in Lent, there was snow and frost, and now? My darling! [*Laughs and kisses her*] I have missed you, my precious, my joy. I must tell you . . . I can't put it off a minute. . . .

ANYA [*Wearily*]: What now?

DUNYASHA: Epihodov, the clerk, made me a proposal just after Easter.

ANYA: It's always the same thing with you. . . . [*Straightening her hair*] I've lost all my hairpins. [*She is staggering from exhaustion*]

DUNYASHA: I don't know what to think, really. He does love me, he does love me so!

ANYA [*Looking towards her door, tenderly*]: My own room, my windows just as though I had never gone away. I'm home! To-morrow morning I shall get up and run into the garden. . . . Oh, if I could get to sleep! I haven't slept all the journey, I was so anxious and worried.

DUNYASHA: Pyotr Sergeyevitch came the day before yesterday.

ANYA [*Joyfully*]: Petya!

DUNYASHA: He's asleep in the bath house, he has settled in there. I'm afraid of being in their way, says he. [*Glancing at her watch*] I was to have waked him, but Varvara Mihalovna told me not to. Don't you wake him, says she.

[*Enter* VARYA *with a bunch of keys at her waist*]

VARYA: Dunyasha, coffee and make haste. . . . Mamma's asking for coffee.

DUNYASHA: This very minute. [*Goes out*]

VARYA: Well, thank God, you've come. You're home again. [*Petting* her] My little darling has come back! My precious beauty has come back again!

ANYA: I have had a time of it!

VARYA: I can fancy.

ANYA: We set off in Holy Week—it was so cold then, and all the way Charlotta would talk and show off her tricks. What did you want to burden me with Charlotta for?

VARYA: You couldn't have traveled all alone, darling. At seventeen!

ANYA: We got to Paris at last, it was cold there—snow. I speak French shockingly. Mamma lives on the fifth floor, I went up to her and there were a lot of French people, ladies, an old priest with a book. The place smelt of tobacco and so comfortless. I felt sorry, oh! so sorry for mamma all at once, I put my arms round her neck, and hugged her and wouldn't let her go. Mamma was as kind as she could be, and she cried. . . .

VARYA [Through her tears]: Don't speak of it, don't speak of it!

ANYA: She had sold her villa at Mentone, she had nothing left, nothing. I hadn't a farthing left either, we only just had enough to get here. And mamma doesn't understand! When we had dinner at the stations, she always ordered the most expensive things and gave the waiters a whole rouble. Charlotta's just the same. Yasha too must have the same as we do; it's simply awful. You know Yasha is mamma's valet now, we brought him with us.

VARYA: Yes, I've seen the young rascal.

ANYA: Well, tell me—have you paid the arrears on the mortgage?

VARYA: How could we get the money?

ANYA: Oh, dear! Oh, dear!

VARYA: In August the place will be sold.

ANYA: My goodness!

LIPAHIN [Peeps in at the door and moos like a cow]: Moo! [Disappears]

VARYA [Weeping]: There, that's what I could do to him. [Shakes her fist]

ANYA [Embracing VARYA, softly]: Varya, has he made you an offer? [VARYA shakes her head] Why, but he loves you. Why is it you don't come to an understanding? What are you waiting for?

VARYA: I believe that there never will be anything between us. He has a lot to do, he has no time for me . . . and takes no notice of me. Bless the man, it makes me miserable to see him. . . . Everyone's talking of our being married, everyone's congratulating me, and all the while there's really nothing in it; it's all like a dream. [In another tone] You have a new brooch like a bee.

ANYA [Mournfully]: Mamma bought it. [Goes into her own room and in a light-hearted childish tone] And you know, in Paris I went up in a balloon!

VARYA: My darling's home again! My pretty is home again!

[DUNAYASHA returns with the coffee-pot and is making the coffee]

VARYA [Standing at the door]: All day long, darling, as I go about looking after the house, I keep dreaming all the time. If only we could marry you to a rich man, then I should feel more at rest. Then I would go off by myself on a pilgrimage to Kiev, to Moscow . . . and so I would spend my life going from one holy place to another. . . . I would go on and on. . . . What bliss!

ANYA: The birds are singing in the garden. What time is it?

VARYA: It must be nearly three. It's time you were asleep, darling. [Going into ANYA's room] What bliss!

[YASHA enters with a rug and a traveling bag]

YASHA [Crosses the stage, mincingly]: May one come in here, pray?

DUNYASHA: I shouldn't have known you, Yasha. How you have changed abroad.

YASHA: H'm! . . . And who are you?

DUNYASHA: When you went away, I was that high. [Shows distance from floor] Dunyasha, Fyodor's daughter. . . . You don't remember me!

YASHA: H'm! . . . You're a peach! [Looks round and embraces her: she shrieks and drops a saucer. YASHA goes out hastily]

VARYA [In the doorway, in a tone of vexation]: What now?

DUNYASHA [Through her tears]: I have broken a saucer.

VARYA: Well, that brings good luck.

ANYA [Coming out of her room]: We ought to prepare mamma: Petya is here.

VARYA: I told them not to wake him.

ANYA [Dreamily]: It's six years since father died. Then only a month later little brother Grisha was drowned in the river, such a pretty boy he was, only seven. It was more than mamma could bear, so she went away, went away without looking back. [Shuddering] . . . How well I understand her, if only she knew! [A pause] And Petya Trofimov was Grisha's tutor, he may remind her.

[Enter FIRS: he is wearing a pea-jacket and a white waistcoat]

FIRS [Goes up to the coffee-pot, anxiously]: The mistress will be served here. [Puts on white gloves] Is the coffee ready? [Sternly to Dunyasha] Girl! Where's the cream?

DUNYASHA: Ah, mercy on us! [*Goes out quickly*]

FIRS [*Fussing round the coffee-pot*]: Ech! you good-for-nothing! [*Muttering to himself*] Come back from Paris. And the old master used to go to Paris too . . . horses all the way. [*Laughs*]

VARYA: What is it, Firs?

FIRS: What is your pleasure? [*Gleefully*] My lady has come home! I have lived to see her again! Now I can die. [*Weeps with joy*]

[*Enter* LYUBOV ANDREYEVNA, GAEV *and* SEMYONOV-PISHTCHIK; *the latter is in a short-waisted full coat of fine cloth, and full trousers.* GAEV, *as he comes in, makes a gesture with his arms and his whole body, as though he were playing billiards*]

LYUBOV: How does it go? Let me remember. Cannon off the red!

GAEV: That's it—in off the white! Why, once, sister, we used to sleep together in this very room, and now I'm fifty-one, strange as it seems.

LOPAHIN: Yes, time flies.

GAEV: What do you say?

LOPAHIN: Time, I say, flies.

GAEV: What a smell of patchouli!

ANYA: I'm going to bed. Good-night, mamma. [*Kisses her mother*]

LYUBOV: My precious darling. [*Kisses her hands*] Are you glad to be home? I can't believe it.

ANYA: Good-night, uncle.

GAEV [*Kissing her face and hands*]: God bless you! How like you are to your mother! [*To his sister*] At her age you were just the same, Lyuba.

[ANYA *shakes hands with* LOPAHIN *and* PISHTCHIK, *then goes out, shutting the door after her*]

LYUBOV: She's quite worn out.

PISHTCHIK: Aye, it's a long journey, to be sure.

VARYA [*To* LOPAHIN *and* PISHTCHIK]: Well, gentlemen? It's three o'clock and time to say good-bye.

LYUBOV [*Laughs*]: You're just the same as ever, Varya. [*Draws her to her and kisses her*] I'll just drink my coffee and then we will all go and rest. [FIRS *puts a cushion under her feet*] Thanks, friend. I am so fond of coffee, I drink it day and night. Thanks, dear old man. [*Kisses* FIRS]

VARYA: I'll just see whether all the the things have been brought in. [*Goes out*]

LYUBOV: Can it really be me sitting here? [*Laughs*] I want to dance about and clap my hands. [*Covers her face with her hands*] And I could drop asleep in a moment! God knows I love my country, I love it tenderly; I couldn't look out of the window in the train, I kept crying so. [*Through her tears*] But I must drink my coffee, though. Thank you, Firs, thanks, dear old man. I'm so glad to find you still alive.

FIRS: The day before yesterday.

GAEV: He's rather deaf.

LOPAHIN: I have to set off for Harkov directly, at five o'clock. . . . It is annoying! I wanted to have a look at you, and a little talk. . . . You are just as splendid as ever.

PISHTCHIK [*Breathing heavily*]: Handsomer, indeed. . . . Dressed in Parisian style . . . completely bowled me over.

LOPAHIN: Your brother, Leonid Andreyevitch here, is always saying that I'm a low-born knave, that I'm a money-grubber, but I don't care one straw for that. Let him talk. Only I do want you to believe in me as you used to. I do want your wonderful tender eyes to look at me as they used to in the old days. Merciful God! My father was a serf of your father and of your grandfather, but you—you—did so much for me once, that I've forgotten all that; I love you as though you were my kin . . . more than my kin.

LYUBOV: I can't sit still, I simply can't. . . .

[*Jumps up and walks about in violent agitation*]

This happiness is too much for me. . . . You may laugh at me, I know I'm silly. . . . My own bookcase. [*Kisses the bookcase*] My little table.

GAEV: Nurse died while you were away.

LYUBOV [*Sits down and drinks coffee*]: Yes, the Kingdom of Heaven be hers! You wrote me of her death.

GAEV: And Anastasy is dead. Squinting Petruchka has left me and is in service now with the police captain in the town.

[*Takes a box of caramels out of his pocket and sucks one*]

PISHTCHIK: My daughter, Dashenka, wishes to be remembered to you.

LOPAHIN: I want to tell you something very pleasant and cheering. [*Glancing at his watch*] I'm going directly . . . there's no time to say much . . . well, I can say it in a couple of words. I needn't tell you your cherry orchard is to be sold to pay your debts; the 22nd of August is the date fixed for the sale; but don't you worry, dearest lady, you may sleep in peace, there is a way of saving it. . . . This is what I propose. I beg your attention! Your estate is not twenty miles from the town, the railway runs close by it, and if the cherry orchard and the land along the river bank were cut up into building plots and then let on lease for summer villas, you would make an income of at least 25,000 roubles a year out of it.

GAEV: That's all rot, if you'll excuse me.

LYUBOV: I don't quite understand you, Yermolay Alexeyevitch.

LOPAHIN: You will get a rent of at least 25 roubles a year for a three-acre plot from summer visitors, and if you say the word now, I'll bet you what you like there won't be one square foot of ground vacant by the autumn, all the plots will be taken up. I congratulate you; in fact, you are saved. It's a perfect situation with that deep river. Only, of course, it must be cleared—all the old buildings, for example, must be removed, this house too, which is really good for nothing and the old cherry orchard must be cut down.

LYUBOV: Cut down? My dear fellow, forgive me, but you don't know what you are talking about. If there is one thing interesting—remarkable indeed—in the whole province, it's just our cherry orchard.

LOPAHIN: The only thing remarkable about the orchard is that it's a very large one. There's a crop of cherries every alternate year, and then there's nothing to be done with them, no one buys them.

GAEV: This orchard is mentioned in the Encyclopædia.

LOPAHIN [Glancing at his watch]: If we don't decide on something and don't take some steps, on the 22nd of August the cherry orchard and the whole estate too will be sold by auction. Make up your minds! There is no other way of saving it, I'll take my oath on that. No, No!

FIRS: In old days, forty or fifty years ago, they used to dry the cherries, soak them, pickle them, make jam too, and they used——

GAEV: Be quiet, Firs.

FIRS: And they used to send the preserved cherries to Moscow and to Harkov by the wagon-load. That brought the money in! And the preserved cherries in those days were soft and juicy, sweet and fragrant. . . . They knew the way to do them then. . . .

LYUBOV: And where is the recipe now?

FIRS: It's forgotten. Nobody remembers it.

PISHTCHIK [To LYUBOV ANDREYEVNA]: What's it like in Paris? Did you eat frogs there?

LYUBOV: Oh, I ate crocodiles.

PISHTCHIK: Fancy that now!

LOPAHIN: There used to be only the gentlefolks and the peasants in the country, but now there are these summer visitors. All the towns, even the small ones, are surrounded, nowadays by these summer villas. And one may say for sure, that in another twenty years there'll be many more of these people and that they'll be everywhere. At present the summer visitor only drinks tea in his verandah, but maybe he'll take to working his bit of land too, and then your cherry orchard would become happy, rich and prosperous. . . .

GAEV [*Indignant*]: What rot!

[*Enter* VARYA *and* YASHA]

VARYA: There are two telegrams for you, mamma [*Takes out keys and opens an old-fashioned bookcase with a loud crack*] Here they are.

LYUBOV: From Paris [*Tears the telegrams, without reading them*] I have done with Paris.

GAEV: Do you know, Lyuba, how old that bookcase is? Last week I pulled out the bottom drawer and there I found the date branded on it. The bookcase was made just a hundred years ago. What do you say to that? We might have celebrated its jubilee. Though it's an inanimate object, still it is a *book* case.

PISHTCHIK [*Amazed*]: A hundred years! Fancy that now.

GAEV: Yes. . . . It is a thing. . . . [*Feeling the bookcase*] Dear, honored, bookcase! Hail to thee who for more than a hundred years hast served the pure ideals of good and justice; thy silent call to fruitful labor has never flagged in those hundred years, maintaining [*in tears*] in the generations of man, courage and faith in a brighter future and fostering in us ideals of good and social consciousness [*A pause*]

LOPAHIN: Yes. . . .

LYUBOV: You are just the same as ever, Leonid.

GAEV [*A little embarrassed*]: Cannon off the right into the pocket!

LOPAHIN [*Looking at his watch*]: Well, it's time I was off.

YASHA [*Handing* LYUBOV ANDREYEVNA *medicine*]: Perhaps you will take your pills now.

PISHTCHIK: You shouldn't take medicines, my dear madam . . . they do no harm and no good. Give them here . . . honored lady [*Takes the pillbox, pours the pills into the hollow of his hand, blows on them, puts them in his mouth and drinks off some kvass*] There!

LYUBOV [*In alarm*]: Why, you must be out of your mind!

PISHTCHIK: I have taken all the pills.

LOPAHIN: What a glutton! [*All laugh*]

FIRS: His honor stayed with us in Easter week, ate a gallon and a half of cucumbers. . . . [*Mutters*]

LYUBOV: What is he saying?

VARYA: He has taken to muttering like that for the last three years. We are used to it.

YASHA: His declining years!

[CHARLOTTA IVANOVNA, *a very thin, lanky figure in a white dress with a lorgnette in her belt, walks across the stage*]

LOPAHIN: I beg your pardon, Charlotta Ivanovna, I have not had time to greet you. [*Tries to kiss her hand*]

CHARLOTTA [*Pulling away her hand*]: If I let you kiss my hand, you'll be wanting to kiss my elbow, and then my shoulder.

LOPAHIN: I've no luck to-day! [*All laugh*] Charlotta Ivanovna, show us some tricks!

LYUBOV: Charlotta, do show us some tricks!

CHARLOTTA: I don't want to. I'm sleepy. [*Goes out*]

LOPAHIN: In three weeks' time we shall meet again. [*Kisses* LYUBOV ANDREYEVNA'S *hand*] Good-bye till then—I must go. [*To* GAEV] Good-bye. [*Kisses* PISHTCHIK] Good-bye. [*Gives his hand to* VARYA, *then to* FIRS *and* YASHA] I don't want to go. [*To* LYUBOV ANDREY-EVNA] If you think over my plan for the villas and make up your mind, then let me know; I will lend you 50,000 roubles. Think of it seriously.

VARYA [*Angrily*]: Well, do go, for goodness sake.

LOPAHIN: I'm going, I'm going. [*Goes out*]

GAEV: Low-born knave! I beg pardon, though . . . Varya is going to marry him, he's Varya's fiancé.

VARYA: Don't talk nonsense, uncle.

LYUBOV: Well, Varya, I shall be delighted. He's a good man.

PISHTCHIK: He is, one must acknowledge, a most worthy man. And my Dashenka . . . says too that . . . she says . . . various things. [*Snores, but at once wakes up*] But all the same, honored lady, could you oblige me . . . with a loan of 240 roubles . . . to pay the interest on my mortgage to-morrow?

VARYA [*Dismayed*]: No, no.

LYUBOV: I really haven't any money.

PISHTCHIK: It will turn up. [*Laughs*] I never lose hope. I thought everything was over, I was a ruined man, and lo and behold—the railway passed through my land and . . . they paid me for it. And something else will turn up again, if not to-day, then to-morrow . . . Dashenka'll win two hundred thousand . . . she's got a lottery ticket.

LYUBOV: Well, we've finished our coffee, we can go to bed.

FIRS [*Brushes* GAEV, *reprovingly*]: You have got on the wrong trousers again! What am I to do with you?

VARYA [*Softly*]: Anya's asleep. [*Softly opens the window*] Now the sun's risen, it's not a bit cold. Look, mamma, what exquisite trees! My goodness! And the air! The starlings are singing!

GAEV [*Opens another window*]: The orchard is all white. You've not forgotten it, Lyuba? That long avenue that runs straight, straight as an arrow, how it shines on a moonlight night. You remember? You've not forgotten?

LYUBOV [*Looking out of the window into the garden*]: Oh, my childhood, my innocence! It was in this nursery I used to sleep, from here I looked out into the orchard, happiness waked with me every morning and in those days the orchard was just the same, nothing has changed. [*Laughs with delight*] All, all white! Oh, my orchard! After the dark gloomy autumn, and the cold winter; you are young again, and full of happiness, the heavenly angels have never left you. . . . If I could cast off the burden that weighs on my heart, if I could forget the past!

GAEV: H'm! and the orchard will be sold to pay our debts; it seems strange. . . .

LYUBOV: See, our mother walking . . . all in white, down the avenue! [*Laughs with delight*] It is she!

GAEV: Where?

VARYA: Oh, don't, mamma!

LYUBOV: There is no one. It was my fancy. On the right there, by the path to the arbor, there is a white tree bending like a woman. . . .

    [*Enter* TROFIMOV *wearing a shabby student's uniform and spectacles*]

LYUBOV: What a ravishing orchard! White masses of blossom, blue sky. . . .

TROFIMOV: Lyubov Andreyevna! [*She looks round at him*] I will just pay my respects to you and then leave you at once. [*Kisses her hand warmly*] I was told to wait until morning, but I hadn't the patience to wait any longer. . . .

    [LYUBOV ANDREYEVNA *looks at him in perplexity*]

VARYA [*Through her tears*]: This is Petya Trofimov.

TROFIMOV: Petya Trofimov, who was your Grisha's tutor. . . . Can I have changed so much?

    [LYUBOV ANDREYEVNA *embraces him and weeps quietly*]

GAEV [*In confusion*]: There, there, Lyuba.

VARYA [*Crying*]: I told you, Petya, to wait till to-morrow.

LYUBOV: My Grisha . . . my boy . . . Grisha . . . my son!

VARYA: We can't help it, mamma, it is God's will.

TROFIMOV [*Softly through his tears*]: There . . . there.

LYUBOV [*Weeping quietly*]: My boy was lost . . . drowned. Why? Oh, why, dear Petya? [*More quietly*] Anya is asleep in there, and I'm talking loudly . . . making this noise. . . . But, Petya? Why have you grown so ugly? Why do you look so old?

TROFIMOV: A peasant-woman in the train called me a mangy-looking gentleman.

LYUBOV: You were quite a boy then, a pretty little student, and now your hair's thin—and spectacles. Are you really a student still? [*Goes towards the door*]

TROFIMOV: I seem likely to be a perpetual student.

LYUBOV [*Kisses her brother, then* VARYA]: Well, go to bed. . . . You are older too, Leonid.

PISHTCHIK [*Follows her*]: I suppose it's time we were asleep. . . . Ugh! my gout. I'm staying the night! Lyubov Andreyevna, my dear soul, if you could . . . to-morrow morning . . . 240 roubles.

GAEV: That's always his story.

PISHTCHIK: 240 roubles . . . to pay the interest on my mortgage.

LYUBOV: My dear man, I have no money.

PISHTCHIK: I'll pay it back, my dear . . . a trifling sum.

LYUBOV: Oh, well, Leonid will give it you. . . . You give him the money, Leonid.

GAEV: Me give it him! Let him wait till he gets it!

LYUBOV: It can't be helped, give it him. He needs it. He'll pay it back.

> [LYUBOV ANDREYEVNA, TROFIMOV, PISHTCHIK and FIRS go out.
> GAEV, VARYA and YASHA remain]

GAEV: Sister hasn't got out of the habit of flinging away her money. [*To* YASHA] Get away, my good fellow, you smell of the hen-house.

YASHA [*With a grin*]: And you, Leonid Andreyevitch, are just the same as ever.

GAEV: What's that? [*To* VARYA] What did he say?

VARYA [*To* YASHA]: Your mother has come from the village; she has been sitting in the servants' room since yesterday, waiting to see you.

YASHA: Oh, bother her!

VARYA: For shame!

YASHA: What's the hurry? She might just as well have come to-morrow. [*Goes out*]

VARYA: Mamma's just the same as ever, she hasn't changed a bit. If she had her own way, she'd give away everything.

GAEV: Yes. [*A pause*] If a great many remedies are suggested for some disease, it means that the disease is incurable. I keep thinking and racking my brains; I have many schemes, a great many, and that really means none. If we could only come in for a legacy from somebody, or marry our Anya to a very rich man, or we might go to

Yaroslavl and try our luck with our old aunt, the Countess. She's very, very rich, you know.

VARYA [Weeps]: If God would help us.

GAEV: Don't blubber. Aunt's very rich, but she doesn't like us. First, sister married a lawyer instead of a nobleman. . . .

[ANYA appears in the doorway]

GAEV: And then her conduct, one can't call it virtuous. She is good, and kind, and nice, and I love her, but, however one allows for extenuating circumstances, there's no denying that she's an immoral woman. One feels it in her slightest gesture.

VARYA [In a whisper]: Anya's in the doorway.

GAEV: What do you say? [A pause] It's queer, there seems to be something wrong with my right eye. I don't see as well as I did. And on Thursday when I was in the district Court . . .

[Enter ANYA]

VARYA: Why aren't you asleep, Anya?

ANYA: I can't get to sleep.

GAEV: My pet. [Kisses ANYA's face and hands] My child. [Weeps] You are not my niece, you are my angel, you are everything to me. Believe me, believe. . . .

ANYA: I believe you, uncle. Everyone loves you and respects you . . . but, uncle dear, you must be silent . . . simply be silent. What were you saying just now about my mother, about your own sister? What made you say that?

GAEV: Yes, yes. . . . [Puts his hand over his face] Really, that was awful! My God, save me! And to-day I made a speech to the bookcase . . . so stupid! And only when I had finished, I saw how stupid it was.

VARYA: It's true, uncle, you ought to keep quiet. Don't talk, that's all.

ANYA: If you could keep from talking, it would make things easier for you, too.

GAEV: I won't speak. [Kisses ANYA's and VARYA's hands] I'll be silent. Only this is about business. On Thursday I was in the district Court; well, there was a large party of us there and we began talking of one thing and another, and this and that, and do you know, I believe that it will be possible to raise a loan on an I.O.U. to pay the arrears on the mortgage.

VARYA: If the Lord would help us!

GAEV: I'm going on Tuesday; I'll talk of it again. [To VARYA] Don't blubber. [To ANYA] Your mamma will talk to Lopahin; of course, he won't refuse her. And as soon as you're rested you shall go to

Yaroslavl to the Countess, your great-aunt. So we shall all set to work in three directions at once, and the business is done. We shall pay off arrears, I'm convinced of it. [*Puts a caramel in his mouth*] I swear on my honor, I swear by anything you like, the estate shan't be sold. [*Excitedly*] By my own happiness, I swear it! Here's my hand on it, call me the basest, vilest of men, if I let it come to an auction! Upon my soul I swear it!

ANYA [*Her equanimity has returned, she is quite happy*]: How good you are, uncle, and how clever! [*Embraces her uncle*] I'm at peace now! Quite at peace! I'm happy!

[*Enter* FIRS]

FIRS [*Reproachfully*]: Leonid Andreyevitch, have you no fear of God? When are you going to bed?

GAEV: Directly, directly. You can go, Firs. I'll . . . yes, I will undress myself. Come, children, bye-bye. We'll go into details to-morrow, but now go to bed. [*Kisses* ANYA *and* VARYA] I'm a man of the eighties. They run down that period, but still I can say I have had to suffer not a little for my convictions in my life, it's not for nothing that the peasant loves me. One must know the peasant! One must know how. . . .

ANYA: At it again, uncle!

VARYA: Uncle dear, you'd better be quiet!

FIRS [*Angrily*]: Leonid Andreyevitch!

GAEV: I'm coming. I'm coming. Go to bed. Potted the shot—there's a shot for you! A beauty! [*Goes out,* FIRS *hobbling after him*]

AYNA: My mind's at rest now. I don't want to go to Yaroslavl, I don't like my great-aunt, but still my mind's at rest. Thanks to uncle. [*Sits down*]

VARYA: We must go to bed. I'm going. Something unpleasant happened while you were away. In the old servants' quarters there are only the old servants, as you know—Efimyushka, Polya and Yevstigney—and Karp too. They began letting stray people in to spend the night—I said nothing. But all at once I heard they had been spreading a report that I gave them nothing but pease pudding to eat. Out of stinginess, you know. . . . And it was all Yevstigney's doing. . . . Very well, I said to myself. . . . If that's how it is, I thought, wait a bit. I sent for Yevstigney. . . . [*Yawns*] He comes. . . . "How's this, Yevstigney," I said, "you could be such a fool as to? . . ." [*Looking at* ANYA] Anitchka! [*A pause*] She's asleep. [*Puts her arm around* ANYA] Come to bed . . . come along! [*Leads her*] My darling has fallen asleep! Come . . . [*They go*]

[*Far away beyond the orchard a shepherd plays on a pipe.*

TROFIMOV *crosses the stage and, seeing* VARYA *and* ANYA, *stands still*]

VARYA: 'Sh! asleep, asleep. Come, my own.

ANYA [*Softly, half asleep*]: I'm so tired. Still those bells. Uncle . . . dear . . . mamma and uncle. . . .

VARYA: Come, my own, come along.

[*They go into* ANYA's *room*]

TROFIMOV [*Tenderly*]: My sunshine! My spring.

CURTAIN.

🍁 *Act II*

The open country. An old shrine, long abandoned and fallen out of the perpendicular; near it a well, large stones that have apparently once been tombstones, and an old garden seat. The road to GAEV's house is seen. On one side rise dark poplars; and there the cherry orchard begins. In the distance a row of telegraph poles and far, far away on the horizon there is faintly outlined a great town, only visible in very fine clear weather. It is near sunset. CHARLOTTA, YASHA and DUNYASHA are sitting on the seat. EPIHODOV is standing near, playing something mournful on a guitar. All sit plunged in thought. CHARLOTTA wears an old forage cap; she has taken a gun from her shoulder and is tightening the buckle on the strap.

CHARLOTTA [*Musingly*]: I haven't a real passport of my own, and I don't know how old I am, and I always feel that I'm a young thing. When I was a little girl, my father and mother used to travel about to fairs and give performances—very good ones. And I used to dance *salto mortale* and all sorts of things. And when papa and mamma died, a German lady took me and had me educated. And so I grew up and became a governess. But where I came from, and who I am, I don't know. . . . Who my parents were, very likely they weren't married. . . . I don't know. [*Takes a cucumber out of her pocket and eats*] I know nothing at all. [*A pause*] One wants to talk and has no one to talk to. . . . I have nobody.

EPIHODOV [*Plays on the guitar and sings*]: "What care I for the noisy world! What care I for friends or foes!" How agreeable it is to play on the mandoline!

DUNYASHA: That's a guitar, not a mandoline. [*Looks in a hand-mirror and powders herself*]

488   *Anton Chekhov*

EPIHODOV: To a man mad with love, it's a mandoline. [*Sings*] "Were her heart but aglow with love's mutual flame."

[YASHA *joins in*]

CHARLOTTA: How shockingly these people sing! Foo! Like jackals!

DUNYASHA [*To* YASHA]: What happiness, though, to visit foreign lands.

YASHA: Ah, yes! I rather agree with you there. [*Yawns, then lights a cigar*]

EPIHODOV: That's comprehensible. In foreign lands everything has long since reached full complexion.

YASHA: That's so, of course.

EPIHODOV: I'm a cultivated man, I read remarkable books of all sorts, but I can never make out the tendency I am myself precisely inclined for, whether to live or to shoot myself, speaking precisely, but nevertheless I always carry a revolver. Here it is. . . . [*Shows revolver*]

CHARLOTTA: I've had enough, and now I'm going. [*Puts on the gun*] Epihodov, you're a very clever fellow, and a very terrible one too, all the women must be wild about you. Br-r-r! [*Goes*] These clever fellows are all so stupid; there's not a creature for me to speak to. . . . Always alone, alone, nobody belonging to me . . . and who I am, and why I'm on earth, I don't know. [*Walks away slowly*]

EPIHODOV: Speaking precisely, not touching upon other subjects, I'm bound to admit about myself, that destiny behaves mercilessly to me, as a storm to a little boat. If, let us suppose, I am mistaken, then why did I wake up this morning, to quote an example, and look round, and there on my chest was a spider of fearful magnitude . . . like this. [*Shows with both hands*] And then I take up a jug of kvass, to quench my thirst, and in it there is something in the highest degree unseemly of the nature of a cockroach. [*A pause*] Have you read Buckle? [*A pause*] I am desirous of troubling you, Dunyasha, with a couple of words.

DUNYASHA: Well, speak.

EPIHODOV: I should be desirous to speak with you alone. [*Sighs*]

DUNYASHA [*Embarrassed*]: Well—only bring me my mantle first. It's by the cupboard. It's rather damp here.

EPIHODOV: Certainly. I will fetch it. Now I know what I must do with my revolver. [*Takes guitar and goes off playing on it*]

YASHA: Two and twenty misfortunes! Between ourselves, he's a fool. [*Yawns*]

DUNYASHA: God grant he doesn't shoot himself! [*A pause*] I am so nervous, I'm always in a flutter. I was a little girl when I was taken into our lady's house, and now I have quite grown out of peasant ways, and my hands are white, as white as a lady's. I'm such a delicate, sensitive creature, I'm afraid of everything. I'm so frightened. And if you deceive me, Yasha, I don't know what will become of my nerves.

YASHA [*Kisses her*]: You're a peach! Of course a girl must never forget herself; what I dislike more than anything is a girl being flighty in her behavior.

DUNYASHA: I'm passionately in love with you, Yasha; you are a man of culture—you can give your opinion about anything. [*A pause*]

YASHA [*Yawns*]: Yes, that's so. My opinion is this: if a girl loves anyone, that means that she has no principles. [*A pause*] It's pleasant smoking a cigar in the open air. [*Listens*] Someone's coming this way . . . it's the gentlefolk. [DUNYASHA *embraces him impulsively*] Go home, as though you had been to the river to bathe; go by that path, or else they'll meet you and suppose I have made an appointment with you here. That I can't endure.

DUNYASHA [*Coughing softly*]: The cigar has made my head ache. . . . [*Goes off*]

> [YASHA *remains sitting near the shrine. Enter* LYUBOV ANDRE- YEVNA, GAEV *and* LOPAHIN]

LOPAHIN: You must make up your mind once for all—there's no time to lose. It's quite a simple question, you know. Will you consent to letting the land for building or not? One word in answer: Yes or no? Only one word!

LYUBOV: Who is smoking such horrible cigars here? [*Sits down*]

GAEV: Now the railway line has been brought near, it's made things very convenient. [*Sits down*] Here we have been over and lunched in town. Cannon off the white! I should like to go home and have a game.

LYUBOV: You have plenty of time.

LOPAHIN: Only one word! [*Beseechingly*] Give me an answer!

GAEV [*Yawning*]: What do you say?

LYUBOV [*Looks in her purse*]: I had quite a lot of money here yesterday, and there's scarcely any left to-day. My poor Varya feeds us all on milk soup for the sake of economy; the old folks in the kitchen get nothing but pease pudding, while I waste my money in a senseless way. [*Drops purse, scattering gold pieces*] There, they have all fallen out! [*Annoyed*]

YASHA: Allow me, I'll soon pick them up. [*Collects the coins*]

LYUBOV: Pray do, Yasha. And what did I go off to the town to lunch for? Your restaurant's a wretched place with its music and the table-cloth smelling of soap. . . . Why drink so much, Leonid? And eat so much? And talk so much? To-day you talked a great deal again in the restaurant, and all so inappropriately. About the era of the seventies, about the decadents. And to whom? Talking to waiters about decadents!

LOPAHIN: Yes.

GAEV [Waving his hand]: I'm incorrigible; that's evident. [Irritably to YASHA] Why is it you keep fidgeting about in front of us!

YASHA [Laughs]: I can't help laughing when I hear your voice.

GAEV [To his sister]: Either I or he. . . .

LYUBOV: Get along! Go away, Yasha.

YASHA [Gives LYUBOV ANDREYEVNA her purse]: Directly. [Hardly able to suppress his laughter] This minute. . . . [Goes off]

LOPAHIN: Deriganov, the millionaire, means to buy your estate. They say he is coming to the sale himself.

LYUBOV: Where did you hear that?

LOPAHIN: That's what they say in town.

GAEV: Our aunt in Yaroslavl has promised to send help; but when, and how much she will send, we don't know.

LOPAHIN: How much will she send? A hundred thousand? Two hundred?

LYUBOV: Oh, well! . . . Ten or fifteen thousand, and we must be thankful to get that.

LOPAHIN: Forgive me, but such reckless people as you are—such queer, unbusiness-like people—I never met in my life. One tells you in plain Russian your estate is going to be sold, and you seem not to understand it.

LYUBOV: What are we to do? Tell us what to do.

LOPAHIN: I do tell you every day. Every day I say the same thing. You absolutely must let the cherry orchard and the land on building leases; and do it at once, as quick as may be—the auction's close upon us! Do understand! Once make up your mind to build villas, and you can raise as much money as you like, and then you are saved.

LYUBOV: Villas and summer visitors—forgive me saying so—it's so vulgar.

GAEV: There I perfectly agree with you.

LOPAHIN: I shall sob, or scream, or fall into a fit. I can't stand it! You drive me mad! [To GAEV] You're an old woman!

GAEV: What do you say?

LOPAHIN: An old woman! [*Gets up to go*]

LYUBOV [*In dismay*]: No, don't go! Do stay, my dear friend! Perhaps we shall think of something.

LOPAHIN: What is there to think of?

LYUBOV: Don't go, I entreat you! With you here it's more cheerful, anyway. [*A pause*] I keep expecting something, as though the house were going to fall about our ears.

GAEV [*In profound dejection*]: Potted the white! It fails—a kiss.

LYUBOV: We have been great sinners. . . .

LOPAHIN: You have no sins to repent of.

GAEV [*Puts a caramel in his mouth*]: They say I've eaten up my property in caramels. [*Laughs*]

LYUBOV: Oh, my sins! I've always thrown my money away recklessly like a lunatic. I married a man who made nothing but debts. My husband died of champagne—he drank dreadfully. To my misery I loved another man, and immediately—it was my first punishment—the blow fell upon me, here, in the river . . . my boy was drowned and I went abroad—went away for ever, never to return, not to see that river again . . . I shut my eyes, and fled, distracted, and *he* after me . . . pitilessly, brutally. I bought a villa at Mentone, for *he* fell ill there, and for three years I had no rest day or night. His illness wore me out, my soul was dried up. And last year, when my villa was sold to pay my debts, I went to Paris and there he robbed me of everything and abandoned me for another woman; and I tried to poison myself. . . . So stupid, so shameful! . . . And suddenly I felt a yearning for Russia, for my country, for my little girl. . . . [*Dries her tears*] Lord, Lord, be merciful! Forgive my sins! Do not chastise me more! [*Takes a telegram out of her pocket*] I got this to-day from Paris. He implores forgiveness, entreats me to return. [*Tears up the telegram*] I fancy there is music somewhere. [*Listens*]

GAEV: That's our famous Jewish orchestra. You remember, four violins, a flute and a double bass.

LYUBOV: That still in existence? We ought to send for them one evening, and give a dance.

LOPAHIN [*Listens*]: I can't hear. . . . [*Hums softly*] "For money the Germans will turn a Russian into a Frenchman." [*Laughs*] I did see such a piece at the theater yesterday! It was funny!

LYUBOV: And most likely there was nothing funny in it. You shouldn't look at plays, you should look at yourselves a little oftener. How gray your lives are! How much nonsense you talk.

LOPAHIN: That's true. One may say honestly, we live a fool's life. [*Pause*] My father was a peasant, an idiot; he knew nothing and taught me nothing, only beat me when he was drunk, and always with his stick. In reality I am just another blockhead and idiot. I've learnt nothing properly. I write a wretched hand. I write so that I feel ashamed before folks, like a pig.

LYUBOV: You ought to get married, my dear fellow.

LOPAHIN: Yes . . . that's true.

LYUBOV: You should marry our Varya, she's a good girl.

LOPAHIN: Yes.

LYUBOV: She's a good-natured girl, she's busy all day long, and what's more, she loves you. And you have liked her for ever so long.

LOPAHIN: Well? I'm not against it. . . . She's a good girl. [Pause]

GAEV: I've been offered a place in the bank: 6,000 roubles a year. Did you know?

LYUBOV: You would never do for that! You must stay as you are.

[Enter FIRS with overcoat]

FIRS: Put it on, sir, it's damp.

GAEV [Putting it on]: You bother me, old fellow.

FIRS: You can't go on like this. You went away in the morning without leaving word. [Looks him over]

LYUBOV: You look older, Firs!

FIRS: What is your pleasure?

LOPAHIN: You look older, she said.

FIRS: I've had a long life. They were arranging my wedding before your papa was born. . . . [Laughs] I was the head footman before the emancipation came. I wouldn't consent to be set free then; I stayed on with the old master. . . . [A pause] I remember what rejoicings they made and didn't know themselves what they were rejoicing over.

LOPAHIN: Those were fine old times. There was flogging anyway.

FIRS [Not hearing]: To be sure! The peasants knew their place, and the masters knew theirs; but now they're all at sixes and sevens, there's no making it out.

GAEV: Hold your tongue, Firs. I must go to town to-morrow. I have been promised an introduction to a general, who might let us have a loan.

LOPAHIN: You won't bring that off. And you won't pay your arrears, you may rest assured of that.

LYUBOV: That's all his nonsense. There is no such general.

[Enter TROFIMOV, ANYA and VARYA]

GAEV: Here come our girls.

ANYA: There's mamma on the seat.

LYUBOV [Tenderly]: Come here, come along. My darlings! [Embraces

ANYA and VARYA] If you only knew how I love you both. Sit beside me, there, like that. [*All sit down*]

LOPAHIN: Our perpetual student is always with the young ladies.

TROFIMOV: That's not your business.

LOPAHIN: He'll soon be fifty, and he's still a student.

TROFIMOV: Drop your idiotic jokes.

LOPAHIN: Why are you so cross, you queer fish?

TROFIMOV: Oh, don't persist!

LOPAHIN [*Laughs*]: Allow me to ask you what's your idea of me?

TROFIMOV: I'll tell you my idea of you. Yermolay Alexeyevitch: you are a rich man, you'll soon be a millionaire. Well, just as in the economy of nature a wild beast is of use, who devours everything that comes in his way, so you too have your use.

[*All laugh*]

VARYA: Better tell us something about the planets, Petya.

LYUBOV: No, let us go on with the conversation we had yesterday.

TROFIMOV: What was it about?

GAEV: About pride.

TROFIMOV: We had a long conversation yesterday, but we came to no conclusion. In pride, in your sense of it, there is something mystical. Perhaps you are right from your point of view; but if one looks at it simply, without subtlety, what sort of pride can there be, what sense is there in it, if man in his physiological formation is very imperfect, if in the immense majority of cases he is coarse, dull-witted, profoundly unhappy? One must give up glorification of self. One should work, and nothing else.

GAEV: One must die in any case.

TROFIMOV: Who knows? And what does it mean—dying? Perhaps man has a hundred senses, and only the five we know are lost at death, while the other ninety-five remain alive.

LYUBOV: How clever you are, Petya!

LOPAHIN [*Ironically*]: Fearfully clever!

TROFIMOV: Humanity progresses, perfecting its powers. Everything that is beyond its ken now will one day become familiar and comprehensible; only we must work, we must with all our powers aid the seeker after truth. Here among us in Russia the workers are few in number as yet. The vast majority of the intellectual people I know, seek nothing, do nothing, are not fit as yet for work of any kind. They call themselves intellectual, but they treat their servants as inferiors, behave to the peasants as though they were animals, learn little, read nothing seriously, do practically nothing, only talk about science and know very little about art. They are all serious people, they all have severe faces, they all talk of weighty matters and air their theories, and yet the vast majority of us—ninety-nine per cent.—live like savages, at the least thing fly to blows and abuse, eat piggishly, sleep in filth and stuffiness, bugs everywhere, stench and damp and moral impurity. And it's clear all our fine talk is only to divert our attention and other people's. Show me where to find the crèches there's so much talk about, and the reading-rooms? They only exist in novels: in real life there are none of them. There is nothing but filth and vulgarity and Asiatic apathy. I fear and dislike very serious faces. I'm afraid of serious conversation. We should do better to be silent.

LOPAHIN: You know, I get up at five o'clock in the morning, and I work from morning to night; and I've money, my own and other people's, always passing through my hands, and I see what people are made of all round me. One has only to begin to do anything to see how few honest decent people there are. Sometimes when I lie awake at night, I think: "Oh! Lord, thou hast given us immense forests, boundless plains, the widest horizons, and living here we ourselves ought really to be giants."

LYUBOV: You ask for giants! They are no good except in story-books; in real life they frighten us.

[EPIHODOV *advances in the background, playing on the guitar*]

LYUBOV [*Dreamily*]: There goes Epihodov.

ANYA [*Dreamily*]: There goes Epihodov.

GAEV: The sun has set, my friends.

TROFIMOV: Yes.

GAEV [*Not loudly, but, as it were, declaiming*]: O nature, divine nature, thou art bright with eternal luster, beautiful and indifferent! Thou, whom we call mother, thou dost unite within thee life and death! Thou dost give life and dost destroy!

VARYA [*In a tone of supplication*]: Uncle!

ANYA: Uncle, you are at it again!

TROFIMOV: You'd much better be cannoning off the red!

GAEV: I'll hold my tongue, I will.

[*All sit plunged in thought. Perfect stillness. The only thing audible is the muttering of* FIRS. *Suddenly there is a sound in the distance, as it were from the sky—the sound of a breaking harp-string, mournfully dying away*]

LYUBOV: What is that?

LOPAHIN: I don't know. Somewhere far away a bucket fallen and broken in the pits. But somewhere very far away.

GAEV: It might be a bird of some sort—such as a heron.

TROFIMOV: Or an owl.

LYUBOV [Shudders]: I don't know why, but it's horrid. [A pause]

FIRS: It was the same before the calamity—the owl hooted and the samovar hissed all the time.

GAEV: Before what calamity?

FIRS: Before the emancipation. [A pause]

LYUBOV: Come, my friends, let us be going; evening is falling. [To ANYA] There are tears in your eyes. What is it, darling? [Embraces her]

ANYA: Nothing, mamma; it's nothing.

TROFIMOV: There is somebody coming.

[The WAYFARER appears in a shabby white forage cap and an overcoat; he is slightly drunk]

WAYFARER: Allow me to inquire, can I get to the station this way?

GAEV: Yes. Go along that road.

WAYFARER: I thank you most feelingly. [Coughing] The weather is superb. [Declaims] My brother, my suffering brother! . . . Come out to the Volga! Whose groan do you hear? . . . [To VARYA] Mademoiselle, vouchsafe a hungry Russian thirty kopecks.

[VARYA utters a shriek of alarm]

LOPAHIN [Angrily]: There's a right and a wrong way of doing everything!

LYUBOV [Hurriedly]: Here, take this. [Looks in her purse] I've no silver. No matter—here's gold for you.

WAYFARER: I thank you most feelingly! [Goes off]

[LAUGHTER]

VARYA [Frightened]: I'm going home—I'm going. . . . Oh, mamma, the servants have nothing to eat, and you gave him gold!

LYUBOV: There's no doing anything with me. I'm so silly! When we get home, I'll give you all I possess. Yermolay Alexeyevitch, you will lend me some more! . . .

LOPAHIN: I will.

LYUBOV: Come, friends, it's time to be going. And Varya, we have made a match of it for you. I congratulate you.

VARYA [Through her tears]: Mamma, that's not a joking matter.

LOPAHIN: "Ophelia, get thee to a nunnery!"

GAEV: My hands are trembling; it's a long while since I had a game of billiards.

LOPAHIN: "Ophelia! Nymph, in thy orisons be all my sins remember'd."

LYUBOV: Come, it will soon be supper-time.

VARYA: How he frightened me! My heart's simply throbbing.

LOPAHIN: Let me remind you, ladies and gentlemen: on the 22nd of August the cherry orchard will be sold. Think about that! Think about it!

[*All go off, except* TROFIMOV *and* ANYA]

ANYA [*Laughing*]: I'm grateful to the wayfarer! He frightened Varya and we are left alone.

TROFIMOV: Varya's afraid we shall fall in love with each other, and for days together she won't leave us. With her narrow brain she can't grasp that we are above love. To eliminate the petty and transitory which hinder us from being free and happy—that is the aim and meaning of our life. Forward! We go forward irresistibly towards the bright star that shines yonder in the distance. Forward! Do not lag behind, friends.

ANYA [*Claps her hands*]: How well you speak! [*A pause*] It is divine here to-day.

TROFIMOV: Yes, it's glorious weather.

ANYA: Somehow, Petya, you've made me so that I don't love the cherry orchard as I used to. I used to love it so dearly. I used to think that there was no spot on earth like our garden.

TROFIMOV: All Russia is our garden. The earth is great and beautiful—there are many beautiful places in it. [*A pause*] Think only, Anya, your grandfather, and great-grandfather, and all your ancestors were slave-owners—the owners of living souls—and from every cherry in the orchard, from every leaf, from every trunk there are human creatures looking at you. Cannot you hear their voices? Oh, it is awful! Your orchard is a fearful thing, and when in the evening or at night one walks about the orchard, the old bark on the trees glimmers dimly in the dusk, and the old cherry trees seem to be dreaming of centuries gone by and tortured by fearful visions. Yes! We are at least two hundred years behind, we have really gained nothing yet, we have no definite attitude to the past, we do nothing but theorize or complain of depression or drink vodka. It is clear that to begin to live in the present, we must first expiate our past; we must break with it; and we can expiate it only by suffering, by extraordinary unceasing labor. Understand that, Anya.

ANYA: The house we live in has long ceased to be our own, and I shall leave it, I give you my word.

TROFIMOV: If you have the house keys, fling them into the well and go away. Be free as the wind.

ANYA [*In ecstasy*]: How beautifully you said that!

TROFIMOV: Believe me, Anya, believe me! I am not thirty yet, I am young, I am still a student, but I have gone through so much already! As soon as winter comes I am hungry, sick, careworn, poor as a beggar, and what ups and downs of fortune have I not known! And my soul was always, every minute, day and night, full of inexplicable forebodings. I have a foreboding of happiness, Anya. I see glimpses of it already.

ANYA [*Pensively*]: The moon is rising.

> [EPIHODOV *is heard playing still the same mournful song on the guitar. The moon rises. Somewhere near the poplars* VARYA *is looking for* ANYA *and calling* "ANYA! *where are you?*"]

TROFIMOV: Yes, the moon is rising. [*A pause*] Here is happiness—here it comes! It is coming nearer and nearer; already I can hear its footsteps. And if we never see it—if we may never know it—what does it matter? Others will see it after us.

VARYA'S VOICE: Anya! Where are you?

TROFIMOV: That Varya again! [*Angrily*] It's revolting!

ANYA: Well, let's go down to the river. It's lovely there.

TROFIMOV: Yes, let's go. [*They go*]

VARYA'S VOICE: Anya! Anya!

CURTAIN.

❀ *Act III*

> A drawing-room divided by an arch from a larger drawing-room. A chandelier burning. The Jewish orchestra, the same that was mentioned in Act II, is heard playing in the ante-room. It is evening. In the larger drawing-room they are dancing the grand chain. The voice of SEMYONOV-PISHTCHIK: "Promenade à une paire!" Then enter the drawing-room in couples first PISHTCHIK and CHARLOTTA IVANOVA, then TROFIMOV and LYUBOV ANDREYEVNA, thirdly ANYA with the POST-OFFICE CLERK, fourthly VARYA with the STATION MASTER, and other guests. VARYA is quietly weeping and wiping away her tears as she dances. In the last couple is DUNYASHA. They move across the drawing-room. PISHTCHIK shouts: "Grand rond, balancez!" and "Les Cavaliers à genou et remerciez vos dames."
>
> FIRS in a swallow-tail coat brings in seltzer water on a tray. PISHTCHIK and TROFIMOV enter the drawing-room.

PISHTCHIK: I am a full-blooded man; I have already had two strokes. Dancing's hard work for me, but as they say, if you're in the pack, you must bark with the rest. I'm as strong, I may say, as a horse. My parent, who would have his joke—may the Kingdom of Heaven be his!—used to say about our origin that the ancient stock of the Semyonov-Pishtchiks was derived from the very horse that Caligula made a member of the senate. [Sits down] But I've no money, that's where the mischief is. A hungry dog believes in nothing but meat. [Snores, but at once wakes up] That's like me . . . I can think of nothing but money.

TROFIMOV: There really is something horsy about your appearance.

PISHTCHIK: Well . . . a horse is a fine beast . . . a horse can be sold.

[There is the sound of billiards being played in an adjoining room. VARYA appears in the arch leading to the larger drawing-room]

TROFIMOV [Teasing]: Madame Lopahin! Madame Lopahin!

VARYA [Angrily]: Mangy-looking gentleman!

TROFIMOV: Yes, I am a mangy-looking gentleman, and I'm proud of it!

VARYA [Pondering bitterly]: Here we have hired musicians and nothing to pay them! [Goes out]

TROFIMOV [To PISHTCHIK]: If the energy you have wasted during your lifetime in trying to find the money to pay your interest had gone to something else, you might in the end have turned the world upside down.

PISHTCHIK: Nietzsche, the philosopher, a very great and celebrated man . . . of enormous intellect . . . says in his works, that one can make forged bank-notes.

TROFIMOV: Why, have you read Nietzsche?

PISHTCHIK: What next . . . Dashenka told me. . . . And now I am in such a position, I might just as well forge banknotes. The day after to-morrow I must pay 310 roubles—130 I have procured. [Feels in his pockets, in alarm] The money's gone! I have lost my money! [Through his tears] Where's the money? [Gleefully] Why, here it is behind the lining. . . . It has made me hot all over.

[Enter LYUBOV ANDREYEVNA and CHARLOTTA IVANOVA]

LYUBOV [Hums the Lezginka]: Why is Leonid so long? What can he be doing in town? [To DUNYASHA] Offer the musicians some tea.

TROFIMOV: The sale hasn't taken place, most likely.

LYUBOV: It's the wrong time to have the orchestra, and the wrong time to give a dance. Well, never mind. [Sits down and hums softly]

CHARLOTTA [Gives PISHTCHIK a pack of cards]: Here's a pack of cards. Think of any card you like.

PISHTCHIK: I've thought of one.

CHARLOTTA: Shuffle the pack now. That's right. Give it here, my dear Mr. Pishtchik. Ein, zwei, drei—now look, it's in your breast pocket.

PISHTCHIK [*Taking a card out of his breast pocket*]: The eight of spades! Perfectly right! [*Wonderingly*] Fancy that now!

CHARLOTTA [*Holding pack of cards in her hands, to* TROFIMOV]: Tell me quickly which is the top card.

TROFIMOV: Well, the queen of spades.

CHARLOTTA: It is! [*To* PISHTCHIK] Well, which card is uppermost?

PISHTCHIK: The ace of hearts.

CHARLOTTA: It is! [*Claps her hands, pack of cards disappears*] Ah! what lovely weather it is to-day!

> [*A mysterious feminine voice which seems coming out of the floor answers her.* "Oh, yes, it's magnificent weather, madam"]

CHARLOTTA: You are my perfect ideal.

VOICE: And I greatly admire you too, madam.

STATION MASTER [*Applauding*]: The lady ventriloquist—bravo!

PISHTCHIK [*Wonderingly*]: Fancy that now! Most enchanting Charlotta Ivanovna. I'm simply in love with you.

CHARLOTTA: In love? [*Shrugging shoulders*] What do you know of love, guter Mensch, aber schlechter Musikant.

TROFIMOV [*Pats* PISHTCHIK *on the shoulder*]: You dear old horse. . . .

CHARLOTTA: Attention, please! Another trick! [*Takes a traveling rug from a chair*] Here's a very good rug; I want to sell it. [*Shaking it out*] Doesn't anyone want to buy it?

PISHTCHIK [*Wonderingly*]: Fancy that!

CHARLOTTA: *Ein, zwei, drei!* [*Quickly picks up rug she has dropped; behind the rug stands* ANYA; *she makes a curtsey, runs to her mother, embraces her and runs back into the larger drawing-room amidst general enthusiasm*]

LYUBOV [*Applauds*]: Bravo! Bravo!

CHARLOTTA: Now again! *Ein, zwei, drei!* [*Lifts up the rug; behind the rug stands* VARYA, *bowing*]

PISHTCHIK [*Wonderingly*]: Fancy that now!

CHARLOTTA: That's the end. [*Throws the rug at* PISHTCHIK, *makes a curtsey, runs into the larger drawing-room*]

PISHTCHIK [*Hurries after her*]: Mischievous creature! Fancy! [*Goes out*]

LYUBOV: And still Leonid doesn't come. I can't understand what he's doing in the town so long! Why, everything must be over by now. The estate is sold, or the sale has not taken place. Why keep us so long in suspense?

VARYA [*Trying to console her*]: Uncle's bought it. I feel sure of that.

TROFIMOV [*Ironically*]: Oh, yes!

VARYA: Great-aunt sent him an authorization to buy it in her name, and transfer the debt. She's doing it for Anya's sake, and I'm sure God will be merciful. Uncle will buy it.

LYUBOV: My aunt in Yaroslavl sent fifteen thousand to buy the estate in her name, she doesn't trust us—but that's not enough even to pay the arrears. [*Hides her face in her hands*] My fate is being sealed to-day, my fate. . . .

TROFIMOV [*Teasing* VARYA]: Madame Lopahin.

VARYA [*Angrily*]: Perpetual student! Twice already you've been sent down from the University.

LYUBOV: Why are you angry, Varya? He's teasing you about Lopahin. Well, what of that? Marry Lopahin if you like, he's a good man, and interesting; if you don't want to, don't! Nobody compels you, darling.

VARYA: I must tell you plainly, mamma, I look at the matter seriously; he's a good man, I like him.

LYUBOV: Well, marry him. I can't see what you're waiting for.

VARYA: Mama. I can't make him an offer myself. For the last two years, everyone's been talking to me about him. Everyone talks; but he says nothing or else makes a joke. I see what it means. He's growing rich, he's absorbed in business, he has no thoughts for me. If I had money, were it ever so little, if I had only a hundred roubles, I'd throw everything up and go far away. I would go into a nunnery.

TROFIMOV: What bliss!

VARYA [*To* TROFIMOV]: A student ought to have sense! [*In a soft tone with tears*] How ugly you've grown, Petya! How old you look! [*To* LYUBOV ANDREYEVNA, *no longer crying*] But I can't do without work, mamma; I must have something to do every minute.

[*Enter* YASHA]

YASHA [*Hardly restraining his laughter*]: Epihodov has broken a billiard cue! [*Goes out*]

VARYA: What is Epihodov doing here? Who gave him leave to play billiards? I can't make these people out. [*Goes out*]

LYUBOV: Don't tease her, Petya. You see she has grief enough without that.

TROFIMOV: She is so very officious, meddling in what's not her busi-ness. All the summer she's given Anya and me no peace. She's afraid of a love affair between us. What's it to do with her? Besides, I have given no grounds for it. Such triviality is not in my line. We are above love!

LYUBOV: And I suppose I am beneath love. [*Very uneasily*] Why is it

Leonid's not here? If only I could know whether the estate is sold or not! It seems such an incredible calamity that I really don't know what to think. I am distracted . . . I shall scream in a minute . . . I shall do something stupid. Save me, Petya, tell me something, talk to me!

TROFIMOV: What does it matter whether the estate is sold to-day or not? That's all done with long ago. There's no turning back, the path is overgrown. Don't worry yourself, dear Lyubov Andreyevna. You mustn't deceive yourself; for once in your life you must face the truth!

LYUBOV: What truth? You see where the truth lies, but I seem to have lost my sight, I see nothing. You settle every great problem so boldly, but tell me, my dear boy, isn't it because you're young—because you haven't yet understood one of your problems through suffering? You look forward boldly, and isn't it that you don't see and don't expect anything dreadful because life is still hidden from your young eyes? You're bolder, more honest, deeper than we are, but think, be just a little magnanimous, have pity on me. I was born here, you know, my father and mother lived here, my grandfather lived here, I love this house. I can't conceive of life without the cherry orchard, and if it really must be sold, then sell me with the orchard. [Embraces TROFIMOV, kisses him on the forehead] My boy was drowned here. [Weeps] Pity me, my dear kind fellow.

TROFIMOV: You know I feel for you with all my heart.

LYUBOV: But that should have been said differently, so differently. [Takes out her handkerchief, telegram falls on the floor] My heart is so heavy to-day. It's so noisy here, my soul is quivering at every sound, I'm shuddering all over, but I can't go away; I'm afraid to be quiet and alone. Don't be hard on me, Petya . . . I love you as though you were one of ourselves. I would gladly let you marry Anya—I swear I would—only, my dear boy, you must take your degree, you do nothing—you're simply tossed by fate from place to place. That's so strange. It is, isn't it? And you must do something with your beard to make it grow somehow. [Laughs] You look so funny!

TROFIMOV [Picks up the telegram]: I've no wish to be a beauty.

LYUBOV: That's a telegram from Paris. I get one every day. One yesterday and one to-day. That savage creature is ill again, he's in trouble again. He begs forgiveness, beseeches me to go, and really I ought to go to Paris to see him. You look shocked, Petya. What am I to do, my dear boy, what am I to do? He is ill, he is alone and unhappy, and who'll look after him, who'll keep him from doing the wrong thing, who'll give him his medicine at the right time? And why hide it or be silent? I love him, that's clear. I love him! I love him! He's a millstone about my neck, I'm going to the bottom with him, but I love that stone and can't live without it. [*Presses* TROFIMOV's *hand*] Don't think ill of me, Petya, don't tell me anything, don't tell me. . . .

TROFIMOV [*Through his tears*]: For God's sake forgive my frankness: why, he robbed you!

LYUBOV: No! No! No! You mustn't speak like that. [*Covers her ears*]

TROFIMOV: He is a wretch! You're the only person that doesn't know it! He's a worthless creature! A despicable wretch!

LYUBOV [*Getting angry, but speaking with restraint*]: You're twenty-six or twenty-seven years old, but you're still a schoolboy.

TROFIMOV: Possibly.

LYUBOV: You should be a man at your age! You should understand what love means! And you ought to be in love yourself. You ought to fall in love! [*Angrily*] Yes, yes, and it's not purity in you, you're simply a prude, a comic fool, a freak.

TROFIMOV [*In horror*]: The things she's saying!

LYUBOV: I am above love! You're not above love, but simply as our Firs here says, "You are a good-for-nothing." At your age not to have a mistress!

TROFIMOV [*In horror*]: This is awful! The things she is saying! [*Goes rapidly into the larger drawing-room clutching his head*] This is awful! I can't stand it! I'm going. [*Goes off, but at once returns*] All is over between us! [*Goes off into the ante-room*]

LYUBOV [*Shouts after him*]: Petya! Wait a minute! You funny creature! I was joking! Petya! [*There is a sound of somebody running quickly downstairs and suddenly falling with a crash.* ANYA *and* VARYA *scream, but there is a sound of laughter at once*]

LYUBOV: What has happened?

ANYA [*Laughing*]: Petya's fallen downstairs! [*Runs out*]

LYUBOV: What a queer fellow that Petya is!

[*The* STATION MASTER *stands in the middle of the larger room and reads* The Magdalene, *by Alexey Tolstoy. They listen to him, but before he has recited many lines strains of a waltz are heard from the ante-room and the reading is broken off. All dance.* TROFIMOV, ANYA, VARYA *and* LYUBOV ANDREYEVNA *come in from the ante-room*]

LYUBOV: Come, Petya—come, pure heart! I beg your pardon. Let's have a dance! [*Dances with Petya*]

[ANYA *and* VARYA *dance.* FIRS *comes in, puts his stick down* near the side door. YASHA *also comes into the drawing-room and looks on at the dancing*]

YASHA: What is it, old man?

FIRS: I don't feel well. In old days we used to have generals, barons and admirals dancing at our balls, and now we send for the post-office clerk and the station master and even they're not overanxious to come. I am getting feeble. The old master, the grandfather, used to give sealing-wax for all complaints. I have been taking sealing-wax for twenty years or more. Perhaps that's what's kept me alive.

YASHA: You bore me, old man! [*Yawns*] It's time you were done with.

FIRS: Ach, you're a good-for-nothing! [*Mutters*]

    [TROFIMOV *and* LYUBOV ANDREYEVNA *dance in larger room and then on to the stage*]

LYUBOV: Merci. I'll sit down a little. [*Sits down*] I'm tired.

    [*Enter* ANYA]

ANYA [*Excitedly*]: There's a man in the kitchen has been saying that the cherry orchard's been sold to-day.

LYUBOV: Sold to whom?

ANYA: He didn't say to whom. He's gone away.

    [*She dances with* TROFIMOV, *and they go off into the larger room*]

YASHA: There was an old man gossiping there, a stranger.

FIRS: Leonid Andreyevitch isn't here yet, he hasn't come back. He has his light overcoat on, *demisaison,* he'll catch cold for sure. Ach! Foolish young things!

LYUBOV: I feel as though I should die. Go, Yasha, find out to whom it has been sold.

YASHA: But he went away long ago, the old chap. [*Laughs*]

LYUBOV [*With slight vexation*]: What are you laughing at? What are you pleased at?

YASHA: Epihodov is so funny. He's a silly fellow, two and twenty misfortunes.

LYUBOV: Firs, if the state is sold, where will you go?

FIRS: Where you bid me, there I'll go.

LYUBOV: Why do you look like that? Are you ill? You ought to be in bed.

FIRS: Yes. [*Ironically*] Me go to bed and who's to wait here? Who's to see to things without me? I'm the only one in all the house.

YASHA [*To* LYUBOV ANDREYEVNA]: Lyubov Andreyevna, permit me to make a request of you; if you go back to Paris again, be so kind as to take me with you. It's positively impossible for me to stay here. [*Looking about him; in an undertone*] There's no need to say it, you see for yourself—an uncivilized country, the people have no morals, and then the dullness! The food in the kitchen's abominable, and then Firs runs after one muttering all sorts of unsuitable words. Take me with you, please do!

[*Enter* PISHTCHIK]

PISHTCHIK: Allow me to ask you for a waltz, my dear lady. [LYUBOV ANDREYEVNA *goes with him*] Enchanting lady, I really must borrow of you just 180 roubles, [*dances*] only 180 roubles. [*They pass into the larger room*]

> [*In the larger drawing-room, a figure in a gray top hat and in check trousers is gesticulating and jumping about. Shouts of "Bravo,* CHARLOTTA IVANOVNA"]

DUNYASHA [*She has stopped to powder herself*]: My young lady tells me to dance. There are plenty of gentlemen, and too few ladies, but dancing makes me giddy and makes my heart beat. Firs, the post-office clerk said something to me just now that quite took my breath away.

[*Music becomes more subdued*]

FIRS: What did he say to you?

DUNYASHA: He said I was like a flower.

YASHA [*Yawns*]: What ignorance! [*Goes out*]

DUNYASHA: Like a flower. I am a girl of such delicate feelings, I am awfully fond of soft speeches.

FIRS: Your head's being turned.

[*Enter* EPIHODOV]

EPIHODOV: You have no desire to see me. Dunyasha. I might be an insect. [*Sighs*] Ah! life!

DUNYASHA: Undoubtedly you may be right. [*Sighs*] But, of course, if one looks at it from that point of view, if I may so express myself, you have, excuse my plain speaking, reduced me to a complete state of mind. I know my destiny. Every day some misfortune befalls me and I have long ago grown accustomed to it, so that I look upon my fate with a smile. You gave me your word, and though I—

DUNYASHA: Let us have a talk later, I entreat you, but now leave me in peace, for I am lost in reverie. [*Plays with her fan*]

EPIHODOV: I have a misfortune every day, and if I may venture to express myself, I merely smile at it, I even laugh.

[VARYA *enters from the larger drawing-room*]

VARYA: You still have not gone, Epihodov. What a disrespectful creature you are, really! [*To* DUNYASHA] Go along, Dunyasha! [*To* EPIHODOV] First you play billiards and break the cue, then you go wandering about the drawing-room like a visitor!

EPIHODOV: You really cannot, if I may so express myself, call me to account like this.

VARYA: I'm not calling you to account, I'm speaking to you. You do nothing but wander from place to place and don't do your work. We keep you as a counting-house clerk, but what use you are I can't say.

EPIHODOV [Offended]: Whether I work or whether I walk, whether I eat or whether I play billiards, is a matter to be judged by persons of understanding and my elders.

VARYA: You dare to tell me that! [Firing up] You dare! You mean to say I've no understanding. Begone from here! This minute!

EPIHODOV [Intimidated]: I beg you to express yourself with delicacy.

VARYA [Beside herself with anger]: This moment! get out! away! [He goes towards the door, she following him] Two and twenty misfortunes! Take yourself off! Don't let me set eyes on you! [EPIHODOV has gone out, behind the door his voice, "I shall lodge a complaint against you"] What! You're coming back? [Snatches up the stick FIRS has put down near the door] Come! Come! Come! I'll show you! What! you're coming? Then take that! [She swings the stick, at the very moment that LOPAHIN comes in]

LOPAHIN: Very much obliged to you!

VARYA [Angrily and ironically]: I beg your pardon!

LOPAHIN: Not at all! I humbly thank you for your kind reception!

VARYA: No need of thanks for it. [Moves away, then looks round and asks softly] I haven't hurt you?

LOPAHIN: Oh, no! Not at all! There's an immense bump coming up, though!

VOICES FROM LARGER ROOM: Lopahin has come! Yermolay Alexeyevitch!

PISHTCHIK: What do I see and hear? [Kisses LOPAHIN] There's a whiff of cognac about you, my dear soul, and we're making merry here too!

[Enter LYUBOV ANDREYEVNA]

LYUBOV: Is it you, Yermolay Alexeyevitch? Why have you been so long? Where's Leonid?

LOPAHIN: Leonid Andreyevitch arrived with me. He is coming.

LYUBOV [In agitation]: Well! Well! Was there a sale? Speak!

LOPAHIN [Embarrassed, afraid of betraying his joy]: The sale was over at four o'clock. We missed our train—had to wait till half-past nine. [Sighing heavily] Ugh! I feel a little giddy.

[Enter GAEV. In his right hand he has purchases, with his left hand he is wiping away his tears]

LYUBOV: Well, Leonid? What news? [*Impatiently, with tears*] Make haste, for God's sake!

GAEV [*Makes her no answer, simply waves his hand. To* FIRS, *weeping*]: Here, take them; there's anchovies, Kertch herrings. I have eaten nothing all day. What I have been through! [*Door into the billard room is open. There is heard a knocking of balls and the voice of* YASHA *saying "Eighty-seven."* GAEV's *expression changes, he leaves off weeping*] I am fearfully tired. Firs, come and help me change my things. [*Goes to his own room across the larger drawing-room*]

PISHTCHIK: How about the sale? Tell us, Do!

LYUBOV: Is the cherry orchard sold?

LOPAHIN: It is sold.

LYUBOV: Who has bought it?

LOPAHIN: I have bought it. [*A pause,* LYUBOV *is crushed; she would fall down if she were not standing near a chair and table*]

[VARYA *takes keys from her waistband, flings them on the floor in middle of drawing-room and goes out*]

LOPAHIN: I have bought it! Wait a bit, ladies and gentlemen, pray. My head's a bit muddled, I can't speak. [*Laughs*] We came to the auction. Deriganov was there already. Leonid Andreyevitch only had 15,000 and Deriganov bid 30,000, besides the arrears, straight off. I saw how the land lay. I bid against him. I bid 40,000, he bid 45,000, I said 55, and so he went on, adding 5 thousands and I adding 10. Well . . . So it ended. I bid 90, and it was knocked down to me. Now the cherry orchard's mine! Mine! [*Chuckles*] My God, the cherry orchard's mine! Tell me that I'm drunk, that I'm out of my mind, that it's all a dream. [*Stamps with his feet*] Don't laugh at me! If my father and my grandfather could rise from their graves and see all that has happened! How their Yermolay, ignorant, beaten Yermolay, who used to run about barefoot in winter, how that very Yermolay has bought the finest estate in the world! I have bought the estate where my father and grandfather were slaves, where they weren't even admitted into the kitchen. I am asleep, I am dreaming! It is all fancy, it is the work of your imagination plunged in the darkness of ignorance. [*Picks up keys, smiling fondly*] She threw away the keys; she means to show she's not the housewife now. [*Jingles the keys*] Well, no matter. [*The orchestra is heard tuning up*] Hey, musicians! Play! I want to hear you. Come, all of you, and look how Yermolay Lopahin will take the ax to the cherry orchard, how the trees will fall to the ground! We will build houses on it and our grandsons and great-grandsons will see a new life springing up there. Music! Play up!

[*Music begins to play.* LYUBOV ANDREYEVNA *has sunk into a chair and is weeping bitterly*]

LOPAHIN [*Reproachfully*]: Why, why didn't you listen to me? My poor friend! Dear lady, there's no turning back now. [*With tears*] Oh, if all this could be over, oh, if our miserable disjointed life could somehow soon be changed!

PISHTCHIK [*Takes him by the arm, in an undertone*]: She's weeping, let us go and leave her alone. Come. [*Takes him by the arm and leads him into the larger drawing-room*]

LOPAHIN: What's that? Musicians, play up! All must be as I wish it. [*With irony*] Here comes the new master, the owner of the cherry orchard! [*Accidentally tips over a little table, almost upsetting the candelabra*] I can pay for everything! [*Goes out with* PISHTCHIK. *No one remains on the stage or in the larger drawing-room except* LYUBOV, *who sits huddled up, weeping bitterly. The music plays softly.* ANYA *and* TROFIMOV *come in quickly.* ANYA *goes up to her mother and falls on her knees before her.* TROFIMOV *stands at the entrance to the larger drawing-room*]

ANYA: Mamma! Mamma, you're crying, dear, kind, good mamma! My precious! I love you! I bless you! The cherry orchard is sold, it is gone, that's true, that's true! But don't weep, mamma! Life is still before you, you have still your good, pure heart! Let us go, let us go, darling, away from here! We will make a new garden, more splendid than this one; you will see it, you will understand. And joy, quiet, deep joy, will sink into your soul like the sun at evening! And you will smile, mamma! Come, darling, let us go!

CURTAIN.

🌺 *Act IV*

SCENE—*Same as in First Act. There are neither curtains on the windows nor pictures on the walls: only a little furniture remains piled up in a corner as if for sale. There is a sense of desolation; near the outer door and in the background of the scene are packed trunks, traveling bags, etc. On the left the door is open, and from here the voices of* VARYA *and* ANYA *are audible.* LOPAHIN *is standing waiting.* YASHA *is holding a tray with glasses full of champagne. In front of the stage* EPIHODOV *is tying up a box. In the background behind the scene a hum of talk from the peasants who have come to say good-bye. The voice of* GAEV: "*Thanks, brothers, thanks!*"

YASHA: The peasants have come to say good-bye. In my opinion, Yermolay Alexeyevitch, the peasants are good-natured, but they don't know much about things.

> [*The hum of talk dies away. Enter across front of stage* LYUBOV ANDREYEVNA *and* GAEV. *She is not weeping, but is pale; her face is quivering—she cannot speak*]

GAEV: You gave them your purse, Lyuba. That won't do—that won't do!

LYUBOV: I couldn't help it! I couldn't help it!

> [*Both go out*]

LOPAHIN [*In the doorway, calls after them*]: You will take a glass at parting? Please do. I didn't think to bring any from the town, and at the station I could only get one bottle. Please take a glass. [*A pause*] What? You don't care for any? [*Comes away from the door*] If I'd known, I wouldn't have bought it. Well, and I'm not going to drink it. [YASHA *carefully sets the tray down on a chair*] You have a glass, Yasha, anyway.

YASHA: Good luck to the travelers, and luck to those that stay behind! [*Drinks*] This champagne isn't the real thing, I can assure you.

LOPAHIN: It cost eight roubles the bottle. [*A pause*] It's devilish cold here.

YASHA: They haven't heated the stove to-day—it's all the same since we're going. [*Laughs*]

LOPAHIN: What are you laughing for?

YASHA: For pleasure.

LOPAHIN: Though it's October, it's as still and sunny as though it were summer. It's just right for building! [*Looks at his watch; says in doorway*] Take note, ladies and gentlemen, the train goes in forty-seven minutes; so you ought to start for the station in twenty minutes. You must hurry up!

> [TROFIMOV *comes in from out of doors wearing a great-coat*]

TROFIMOV: I think it must be time to start, the horses are ready. The devil only knows what's become of my goloshes; they're lost. [*In the doorway*] Anya! My goloshes aren't here. I can't find them.

LOPAHIN: And I'm getting off to Harkov. I am going in the same train with you. I'm spending all the winter at Harkov. I've been wasting all my time gossiping with you and fretting with no work to do. I can't get on without work. I don't know what to do with my hands, they flap about so queerly, as if they didn't belong to me.

TROFIMOV: Well, we're just going away, and you will take up your profitable labors again.

LOPAHIN: Do take a glass.

TROFIMOV: No, thanks.

LOPAHIN: Then you're going to Moscow now?

TROFIMOV: Yes. I shall see them as far as the town, and to-morrow I shall go on to Moscow.

LOPAHIN: Yes, I daresay, the professors aren't giving any lectures, they're waiting for your arrival.

TROFIMOV: That's not your business.

LOPAHIN: How many years have you been at the University?

TROFIMOV: Do think of something newer than that—that's stale and flat. [*Hunts for goloshes*] You know we shall most likely never see each other again, so let me give you one piece of advice at parting: don't wave your arms about—get out of the habit. And another thing, building villas, reckoning up that the summer visitors will in time become independent farmers—reckoning like that, that's not the thing to do either. After all, I am fond of you: you have fine delicate fingers like an artist, you've a fine delicate soul.

LOPAHIN [*Embraces him*]: Good-bye, my dear fellow. Thanks for everything. Let me give you money for the journey, if you need it.

TROFIMOV: What for? I don't need it.

LOPAHIN: Why, you haven't got a half-penny.

TROFIMOV: Yes, I have, thank you. I got some money for a translation. Here it is in my pocket, [*anxiously*] but where can my goloshes be!

VARYA [*From the next room*]: Take the nasty things! [*Flings a pair of goloshes on to the stage*]

TROFIMOV: Why are you so cross, Varya? h'm! . . . but those aren't my goloshes.

LOPAHIN: I sowed three thousand acres with poppies in the spring, and now I have cleared forty thousand profit. And when my poppies were in flower, wasn't it a picture! So here, as I say, I made forty thousand, and I'm offering you a loan because I can afford to. Why turn up your nose? I am a peasant—I speak bluntly.

TROFIMOV: Your father was a peasant, mine was a chemist—and that proves absolutely nothing whatever. [LOPAHIN *takes out his pocketbook*] Stop that—stop that. If you were to offer me two hundred thousand I wouldn't take it. I am an independent man, and everything that all of you, rich and poor alike, prize so highly and hold so dear, hasn't the slightest power over me—it's like so much fluff fluttering in the air. I can get on without you. I can pass by you. I am strong and proud. Humanity is advancing towards the highest truth, the highest happiness, which is possible on earth, and I am in the front ranks.

LOPAHIN: Will you get there?

TROFIMOV: I shall get there. [A pause] I shall get there, or I shall show others the way to get there.

[In the distance is heard the stroke of an ax on a tree]

LOPAHIN: Good-bye, my dear fellow; it's time to be off. We turn up our noses at one another, but life is passing all the while. When I am working hard without resting, then my mind is more at ease, and it seems to me as though I too know what I exist for; but how many people are in Russia, my dear boy, who exist, one doesn't know what for. Well, it doesn't matter. That's not what keeps things spinning. They tell me Leonid Andreyevitch has taken a situation. He is going to be a clerk at the bank—6,000 roubles a year. Only, of course, he won't stick to it—he's too lazy.

ANYA [In the doorway]: Mamma begs you not to let them chop down the orchard until she's gone.

TROFIMOV: Yes, really, you might have the tact. [Walks out across the front of the stage]

LOPAHIN: I'll see to it! I'll see to it! Stupid fellows! [Goes out after him]

ANYA: Has Firs been taken to the hospital?

YASHA: I told them this morning. No doubt they have taken him.

ANYA [To EPIHODOV, who passes across the drawing-room]: Semyon Pantaleyevitch, inquire, please, if Firs has been taken to the hospital.

YASHA [In a tone of offence]: I told Yegor this morning—why ask a dozen times?

EPIHODOV: Firs is advanced in years. It's my conclusive opinion, no treatment would do him good; it's time he was gathered to his fathers. And I can only envy him. [Puts a trunk down on a cardboard hat-box and crushes it] There, now, of course—I knew it would be so.

YASHA [Jeeringly]: Two and twenty misfortunes!

VARYA [Through the door]: Has Firs been taken to the hospital?

ANYA: Yes.

VARYA: Why wasn't the note for the doctor taken too?

ANYA: Oh, then, we must send it after them. [Goes out]

VARYA [From the adjoining room]: Where's Yasha? Tell him his mother's come to say good-bye to him.

YASHA [Waves his hand]: They put me out of all patience! [DUNYASHA has all this time been busy about the luggage. Now, when YASHA is left alone, she goes up to him]

DUNYASHA: You might just give me one look, Yasha. You're going away. You're leaving me. [Weeps and throws herself on his neck]

YASHA: What are you crying for? [*Drinks the champagne*] In six days I shall be in Paris again. To-morrow we shall get into the express train and roll away in a flash. I can scarcely believe it! *Vive la France!* It doesn't suit me here—it's not the life for me; there's no doing anything. I have seen enough of the ignorance here. I have had enough of it. [*Drinks champagne*] What are you crying for? Behave yourself properly, and then you won't cry.

DUNYASHA [*Powders her face, looking in a pocket-mirror*]: Do send me a letter from Paris. You know how I loved you, Yasha—how I loved you! I am a tender creature, Yasha.

YASHA: Here they are coming!

[*Busies himself about the trunks, humming softly. Enter* LYUBOV ANDREYEVNA, GAEV, ANYA *and* CHARLOTTA IVANOVNA]

GAEV: We ought to be off. There's not much time now. [*Looking at* YASHA] What a smell of herrings!

LYUBOV: In ten minutes we must get into the carriage. [*Casts a look about the room*] Farewell, dear house, dear old home of our fathers! Winter will pass and spring will come, and then you will be no more; they will tear you down! How much those walls have seen! [*Kisses her daughter passionately*] My treasure, how bright you look! Your eyes are sparkling like diamonds! Are you glad? Very glad?

ANYA: Very glad! A new life is beginning, mamma.

GAEV: Yes, really, everything is all right now. Before the cherry orchard was sold, we were all worried and wretched, but afterwards, when once the question was settled conclusively, irrevocably, we all felt calm and even cheerful. I am a bank clerk now—I am a financier—cannon off the red. And you, Lyuba, after all, you are looking better; there's no question of that.

LYUBOV: Yes. My nerves are better, that's true. [*Her hat and coat are handed to her*] I'm sleeping well. Carry out my things, Yasha. It's time. [*To* AYNA] My darling, we shall soon see each other again. I am going to Paris. I can live there on the money your Yaroslavl auntie sent us to buy the estate with—hurrah for auntie!—but that money won't last long.

ANYA: You'll come back soon, mamma, won't you? I'll be working up for my examination in the high school, and when I have passed that, I shall set to work and be a help to you. We will read all sorts of things together, mamma, won't we? [*Kisses her mother's hands*] We will read in the autumn evenings. We'll read lots of books, and a new wonderful world will open out before us. [*Dreamily*] Mamma, come soon.

LYUBOV: I shall come, my precious treasure. [*Embraces her*]

[*Enter* LOPAHIN. CHARLOTTA *softly hums a song*]

GAEV: Charlotta's happy; she's singing!

CHARLOTTA [*Picks up a bundle like a swaddled baby*]: Bye, bye, my baby. [*A baby is heard crying: "Ooah! ooah!"*] Hush, hush, my pretty boy! [*Ooah! ooah!*] Poor little thing! [*Throws the bundle back*] You must please find me a situation. I can't go on like this.

LOPAHIN: We'll find you one, Charlotta Ivanovna. Don't you worry yourself.

GAEV: Everyone's leaving us. Varya's going away. We have become of no use all at once.

CHARLOTTA: There's nowhere for me to be in the town. I must go away. [*Hums*] What care I . . .

[*Enter* PISHTCHIK]

LOPAHIN: The freak of nature.

PISHTCHIK [*Gasping*]: Oh . . . let me get my breath. . . . I'm worn out . . . my most honored . . . Give me some water.

GAEV: Want some money, I suppose? Your humble servant! I'll go out of the way of temptation. [*Goes out*]

PISHTCHIK: It's a long while since I have been to see you . . . dearest lady. [*To* LOPAHIN] You are here . . . glad to see you . . . a man of immense intellect . . . take . . . here [*gives* LOPAHIN] 400 roubles. That leaves me owing 840.

LOPAHIN [*Shrugging his shoulders in amazement*]: It's like a dream. Where did you get it?

PISHTCHIK: Wait a bit . . . I'm hot . . . a most extraordinary occurrence! Some Englishmen came along and found in my land some sort of white clay. [*To* LYUBOV ANDREYEVNA] And 400 for you . . . most lovely . . . wonderful. [*Gives money*] The rest later. [*Sips water*] A young man in the train was telling me just now that a great philosopher advises jumping off a house-top. "Jump!" says he; "the whole gist of the problem lies in that." [*Wonderingly*] Fancy that, now! Water, please!

LOPAHIN: What Englishmen?

PISHTCHIK: I have made over to them the rights to dig the clay for twenty-four years . . . and now, excuse me . . . I can't stay . . . I must be trotting on. I'm going to Znoikovo . . . to Kardamanovo. . . . I'm in debt all round. [*Sips*] . . . To your very good health! . . . I'll come in on Thursday.

LYUBOV: We are just off to the town, and tomorrow I start for abroad.

PISHTCHIK: What! [*In agitation*] Why to the town? Oh, I see the furniture . . . the boxes. No matter . . . [*Through his tears*] . . .

no matter . . . men of enormous intellect . . . these Englishmen. . . . Never mind . . . be happy. God will succor you . . . no matter . . . everything in this world must have an end. [Kisses LYUBOV ANDREYEVNA's hand] If the rumor reaches you that my end has come, think of this . . . old horse, and say: "There once was such a man in the world . . . Semyonov-Pishtchik . . . the Kingdom of Heaven be his!" . . . most extraordinary weather . . . yes. [Goes out in violent agitation, but at once returns and says in the doorway] Dashenka wishes to be remembered to you. [Goes out]

LYUBOV: Now we can start. I leave with two cares in my heart. The first is leaving Firs ill. [Looking at her watch] We have still five minutes.

ANYA: Mamma, Firs has been taken to the hospital. Yasha sent him off this morning.

LYUBOV: My other anxiety is Varya. She is used to getting up early and working; and now, without work, she's like a fish out of water. She is thin and pale, and she's crying, poor dear! [A pause] You are well aware, Yermolay Alexeyevitch, I dreamed of marrying her to you, and everything seemed to show that you would get married. [Whispers to ANYA and motions to CHARLOTTA and both go out] She loves you—she suits you. And I don't know—I don't know why it is you seem, as it were, to avoid each other. I can't understand it!

LOPAHIN: I don't understand it myself, I confess. It's queer somehow, altogether. If there's still time, I'm ready now at once. Let's settle it straight off, and go ahead; but without you, I feel I shan't make her an offer.

LYUBOV: That's excellent. Why, a single moment's all that's necessary. I'll call her at once.

LOPAHIN: And there's champagne all ready too. [Looking into the glasses] Empty! Someone's emptied them already. [YASHA coughs] I call that greedy.

LYUBOV [Eagerly]: Capital! We will go out. Yasha, allez! I'll call her in. [At the door] Varya, leave all that; come here. Come along! [Goes out with YASHA]

LOPAHIN [Looking at his watch]: Yes.

　　　　[A pause. Behind the door, smothered laughter and whispering, and, at last, enter VARYA]

VARYA [Looking a long while over the things]: It is strange, I can't find it anywhere.

LOPAHIN: What are you looking for?

VARYA: I packed it myself, and I can't remember. [A pause]

LOPAHIN: Where are you going now, Varvara Mihailova?

VARYA: I? To the Ragulins. I have arranged to go to them to look after the house—as a housekeeper.

LOPAHIN: That's in Yashnovo? It'll be seventy miles away. [A pause] So this is the end of life in this house!

VARYA [Looking among the things]: Where is it? Perhaps I put it in the trunk. Yes, life in this house is over—there will be no more of it.

LOPAHIN: And I'm just off to Harkov—by this next train. I've a lot of business there. I'm leaving Epihodov here, and I've taken him on.

VARYA: Really!

LOPAHIN: This time last year we had snow already, if you remember; but now it's so fine and sunny. Though it's cold, to be sure—three degrees of frost.

VARYA: I haven't looked. [A pause] And besides, our thermometer's broken. [A pause]

[Voice at the door from the yard: "YERMOLAY ALEXEYEVITCH!"]

LOPAHIN [As though he had long been expecting this summons]: This minute!

[LOPAHIN goes out quickly. VARYA sitting on the floor and laying her head on a bag full of clothes, sobs quietly. The door opens. LYUBOV ANDREYEVNA comes in cautiously]

LYUBOV: Well? [A pause] We must be going.

VARYA [Has wiped her eyes and is no longer crying]: Yes, mamma, it's time to start. I shall have time to get to the Ragulins to-day, if only you're not late for the train.

LYUBOV [In the doorway]: Anya, put your things on.

[Enter ANYA, then GAEV and CHARLOTTA IVANOVNA. GAEV has on a warm coat with a hood. Servants and cabmen come in. EPIHODOV bustles about the luggage]

LYUBOV: Now we can start on our travels.

ANYA [Joyfully]: On our travels!

GAEV: My friends—my dear, my precious friends! Leaving this house for ever, can I be silent? Can I refrain from giving utterance at leave-taking to those emotions which now flood all my being?

ANYA [Supplicatingly]: Uncle!

VARYA: Uncle, you mustn't!

GAEV [Dejectedly]: Cannon and into the pocket . . . I'll be quiet.
. . .

[Enter TROFIMOV and afterwards LOPAHIN]

TROFIMOV: Well, ladies and gentlemen, we must start.

LOPAHIN: Epihodov, my coat!

LYUBOV: I'll stay just one minute. It seems as though I have never seen before what the walls, what the ceilings in this house were like, and now I look at them with greediness, wich such tender love.

GAEV: I remember when I was six years old sitting in that window on Trinity Day watching my father going to church.

LYUBOV: Have all the things been taken?

LOPAHIN: I think all. [*Putting on overcoat, to* EPIHODOV] You, Epihodov, mind you see everything is right.

EPIHODOV [*In a husky voice*]: Don't you trouble, Yermolay Alexeyevitch.

LOPAHIN: Why, what's wrong with your voice?

EPIHODOV: I've just had a drink of water, and I choked over something.

YASHA [*Contemptuously*]: The ignorance!

LYUBOV: We are going—and not a soul will be left here.

LOPAHIN: Not till the spring.

VARYA [*Pulls a parasol out of a bundle, as though about to hit someone with it.* LOPAHIN *makes a gesture as though alarmed*]: What is it? I didn't mean anything.

TROFIMOV: Ladies and gentlemen, let us go into the carriage. It's time. The train will be in directly.

VARYA: Petya, here they are, your goloshes, by that box. [*With tears*] And what dirty old things they are!

TROFIMOV [*Putting on his goloshes*]: Let us go, friends!

GAEV [*Greatly agitated, afraid of weeping*]: The train—the station! Double baulk, ah!

LYUBOV: Let us go!

LOPAHIN: Are we all here? [*Locks the sidedoor on left*] The things are all here. We must lock up. Let us go!

AYNA: Good-bye, home! Good-bye to the old life!

TROFIMOV: Welcome to the new life!

> [TROFIMOV *goes out with* ANYA. VARYA *looks round the room and goes out slowly.* YASHA *and* CHARLOTTA IVANOVNA, *with her dog, go out*]

LOPAHIN: Till the spring, then! Come, friends, till we meet! [*Goes out*]

> [LYUBOV ANDREYEVNA *and* GAEV *remain alone. As though they had been waiting for this, they throw themselves on each other's necks, and break into subdued smothered sobbing, afraid of being overheard*]

GAEV [*In despair*]: Sister, my sister!

LYUBOV: Oh, my orchard!—my sweet, beautiful orchard! My life, my youth, my happiness, good-bye! good-bye!

VOICE OF ANYA [*Calling gaily*]: Mamma!

VOICE OF TROFIMOV [*Gaily, excitedly*]: Aa—oo!

LYUBOV: One last look at the walls, at the windows. My dear mother loved to walk about this room.

GAEV: Sister, sister!

VOICE OF ANYA: Mamma!

VOICE OF TROFIMOV: Aa—oo!

LYUBOV: We are coming. [*They go out*]

> [*The stage is empty. There is the sound of the doors being locked up, then of the carriages driving away. There is silence. In the stillness there is the dull stroke of an ax in a tree, clanging with a mournful lonely sound. Footsteps are heard.* FIRS *appears in the doorway on the right. He is dressed as always—in a pea-jacket and white waistcoat, with slippers on his feet. He is ill*]

FIRS [*Goes up to the doors, and tries the handles*]: Locked! They have gone . . . [*Sits down on sofa*] They have forgotten me. . . . Never mind . . . I'll sit here a bit. . . . I'll be bound Leonid Andreyevitch hasn't put his fur coat on and has gone off in his thin overcoat. [*Sighs anxiously*] I didn't see after him. . . . These young people . . . [*Mutters something that can't be distinguished*] Life has slipped by as though I hadn't lived. [*Lies down*] I'll lie down a bit. . . . There's no strength in you, nothing left you—all gone! Ech! I'm good for nothing. [*Lies motionless*]

> [*A sound is heard that seems to come from the sky, like a breaking harp-string, dying away mournfully. All is still again, and there is heard nothing but the strokes of the ax far away in the orchard*]

CURTAIN

❀ Comments

A Sample of Contrasting Interpretations

The Cherry Orchard, is a drama "of pathetic motivations," a theater-poem of the suffering of change; and this mode of action and awareness is much closer to the skeptical basis of modern realism, and to the histrionic basis of all realism. Direct perception before predication is always true, says Aristotle; and the extraordinary feat of Chekhov is to predicate nothing. This he achieves by means of his plot: he selects only those incidents, those moments in his characters' lives, between their rationalized efforts, when they sense their situation and destiny most directly. So he contrives to show the action of the play as whole—the unsuccessful attempt to cling to the Cherry Orchard—in many diverse reflectors and without propounding any thesis about it.

. . . .

It is very clear, I think, that Chekhov is not trying to present us with a rationalization of social change à la Marx, or even with a subtler rationalization à la Shaw. On the other hand, he is not seeking, like Wagner, to seduce us into one passion. He shows us a moment of change in society, and he shows us a "pathos"; but the elements of his composition are always taken as objectively real. He offers us various rationalizations, various images and various feelings, which cannot be reduced either to one emotion or to one idea: they indicate an action and a scene which is "there" before the rational formulations, or the emotionally charged attitudes, of any of the characters.

The surrounding scene of *The Cherry Orchard* corresponds to the significant stage of human life which Sophocles' choruses reveal, and to the empty wilderness beyond Ibsen's little parlor. We miss, in Chekhov's scene, any fixed points of human significance, and that is why, compared with Sophocles, he seems limited and partial—a bit too pathetic even for our bewildered times. But, precisely because he subtly and elaborately develops the moments of pathos with their sad insights, he sees much more in the little scene of modern realism than Ibsen does. Ibsen's snowpeaks strike us as rather hysterical; but the "stage of Europe" which we divine behind the Cherry Orchard is confirmed by a thousand impressions derived from other sources. We may recognize its main elements in a cocktail party in Connecticut or Westchester: someone's lawn full of voluble people; a dry white clapboard church (instead of an Orthodox chapel) just visible across a field; time passing, and the muffled roar of a four-lane highway under the hill—or we may be reminded of it in the final section of *The Wasteland*, with its twittering voices, its old gravestones and deserted chapel, and its dim crowd on the horizon foreboding change. It is because Chekhov says so little that he reveals so much, providing a concrete basis for many conflicting rationalizations of contemporary social change: by accepting the immediacy and unintelligibility of modern realism so completely, he in some ways transcends its limitations, and prepares the way for subsequent developments in the modern theater.

Francis Fergusson, *The Idea of a Theater* (Princeton: Princeton University Press, 1949). Reprinted by permission of the publisher.

———————————◆◆◆———————————

For it is blindness to assume that—however it may be placed by the author—there is no didacticism in *The Cherry Orchard*. Trophimov's speech in the second act, on a theme which constantly recurs in Chekhov's plays and which seems, from his letters and conversation, to have been also a personal belief—

At present only a few men work in Russia. The vast majority of the educated people that I know seek after nothing, do nothing, and are as yet incapable of work.

—this indictment is set by design against the declaration of Lopakhin, the son of a serf, a figure of the new Russia, the man who will take over the cherry orchard and chop it down to build villas:

I work from morning till night. . . . When I work for hours without getting tired I get easy in my mind and I seem to know why I exist. But God alone knows what most of the people in Russia were born for. . . . Well, who cares?

As Chekhov constructs this microcosm for us—the stupid, sentimental, generous Madame Ranevsky, the juggling, isolated Charlotte, the ineffectual Pishtchik—we assent. Our first glance confirms the impotence and the subsequent decay. The expository method is masterly of its kind. But there grows, implacably, a profound uneasiness, an uncertainty about the emotional quality of what is at the very heart of the work. It is the process, though infinitely more complicated, of one's evaluation of Galsworthy: a mastering suspicion of the emotional integrity from which the satire proceeds, a growing conviction that the author remains attached, by strings which in performance extend to and operate on us, attached to something lovable, something childlike, something vague; attached, in the human sense, to a residue of unexamined experience which for one reason or another cannot be faced, and to which, accordingly, renouncing his control, the author must submit. But to take the play beyond naturalism, to make it something more than an entertaining, but limited, collection of human sketches, this unexamined experience would have to be faced and understood. . . .

Raymond Williams, *Drama from Ibsen to Eliot* (New York: Oxford University Press, 1953), pp. 134–135. Reprinted with permission of the publisher.

The play which most directly and clearly illustrates this fact is *The Cherry Orchard*, where the situation is simplicity itself. A group of typically feckless and typically charming Chekhovian gentry are losing their estate to an up-and-coming Man of the Future. His first act is to lay an ax to their cherry orchard in order to make way for a more economic use of the land, and "Is this good or bad?" is the only question posed in the play. Characteristically, the aesthetic effect of the play does not depend upon any answers being given. Chekhov's tone is as usual elegiac, rather than philosophical or polemic. The one indisputable thing upon which the emotional attention centers is the fact that something beautiful is being destroyed—the useless cherry orchard itself and the useless lives of the people whom it symbolized. This destruction is in itself sad and pitiful whether one resents it as an evil or accepts it as something necessary and, in the end, productive of good.

Though the play is thus not primarily a problem play, both Chekhov himself and some of the characters recognize the problem implicit. One character in particular philosophized the incidents and talks glowingly of the future, although one realizes that his talk, like that of nearly all of Chekhov's characters, will never be anything but talk. Plainly Chekhov's own answer to the question posed is simply that no clear-cut answer is possible. The thing is both good and bad. No doubt it had to happen. But the present loss is at least as certain as any future gain. Whatever may be said in favor of the new world, one thing seems clear. There will be no place for Cherry Trees in it, at least for a long time to come. One cannot stand up against the Future. But one cannot be too happy about it either.

Joseph Wood Krutch, "Modernism" in *Modern Drama* (Ithaca, New York: Cornell University Press, 1953), pp. 72–73. Cited with permission of the author.

———————————◆◆———————————

We get close to the spirit of Chekhov himself in these scenes of farewells. We could not 'break the parting word into its two significant halves adieu,' though the tenderness of his indulgence sprang from seeing life as a constant slipping from one good-bye into another. It is difficult to suggest a philosophy which is never formulated. It is a feeling rather than a thought which his work leaves behind, a feeling that though everything is brief, precarious and empty, just because that is all, there is a kind of sacredness about it which the angry cynic and impatient moralist are too stupid to feel. Get rid of enormous hopes, especially of exorbitant expectations regarding yourself and others, and you will share an emotion towards mankind in which irony and sympathy are so blended that it leads the living, too, beyond 'a value of tears.'

Desmond MacCarthy, *Humanities* (London: MacGibbon & Kee Ltd., 1953), p. 81. Cited with permission of the publisher.

✤ Luigi Pirandello

Luigi Pirandello (1867–1936) is another of the great innovators of the modern theater, yet his central theme of appearance and reality is older than Plato's treatment of it. In *Six Characters in Search of an Author* (1921) his solution of the problem is not, in fact, essentially different from Plato's. Both identified appearance with change; and, since we are always changing, our lives are illusory, only appearance. Plato identified reality with his unchanging abstractions, the Idea of the Good, the True, and the Beautiful; Pirandello identifies it with the last of the Platonic trinity, that is, the Beautiful, the unchanging work of art. Art is real, not life. So it is that the Characters in *Six Characters* are real, for they are fixed forever in their roles; the actors are unreal, for they change their roles from play to play. The experience of the theme of appearance and reality (not the only one in the play) is, of course, radically different from its discursive treatment in Plato. One experience of the theme is the shifting planes: the play the actors are rehearsing, the play the characters want to perform, and the play itself. Though Pirandello was influenced by Luigi Chiarelli's theater of the grotesque (*il teatro del grottesco*), he shaped this theater to his own genius. This is further evident in his rejection of realism and romanticism, delineated in his preface. The Father and Daughter are passionate; but their ironic objectivity prevents any romantic emotionalism. At the same time Pirandello treats the realistic situation of the characters "humorously." As he says, he is interested in something else, "their drama of being in search of an author, and rejected."

The son of a mine owner, he was born in Agrigento, in Sicily. He studied at the universities in Rome and Bonn; he did his doctoral dissertation in Bonn on his native dialect. His wife, whom he had never seen before the marriage negotiated by his parents, went mad after a few years; but Pirandello, though impoverished by his father's financial misfortunes, chose to live with her rather than place her in a public institution. No doubt the years he spent with his wife influenced his work—the rages, the near-hysteria, the grotesquerie in it. Perhaps it was Pirandello's Platonism which led him to support the fascist idea of order; though the examples of Pound, Dostoyevsky, and others are proof enough that there is no necessary carry-over of the critical spirit from art to public life. In his early years he wrote fiction and poetry as well as plays; it was not until *It Is So! If You Think So* (1917) that his genius came through. Then followed the great plays: *Six Characters in Search of An Author* (1921), *Henry IV* (1921), *Each In His Own Way* (1924). He was awarded the Nobel Prize for literature in 1934.

READINGS:

BENTLEY, ERIC, *The Playwright As Thinker* (1946). New York: Meridian Books, 1955.

FERGUSSON, FRANCIS, *The Idea of a Theater* (1949). New York: Anchor Books, 1957.

MacCLINTOCK, LANDER, *The Age of Pirandello*. Bloomington: Indiana University Press, 1953.

NELSON, ROBERT J., *Play Within a Play*. New Haven: Yale University Press, 1958

STARKIE, WALTER, *Luigi Pirandello: 1867–1936*. New York: E. P. Dutton & Company, 1937.

VITTORINI, DOMENICO, *The Drama of Luigi Pirandello* (1935). New York: Dover Publications, 1957.

WILLIAMS, RAYMOND, *Drama from Ibsen to Eliot*. London: Chatto and Windus, 1954.

Six Characters in Search of an Author

(*Sei personaggi in cerca d'autore*)

Luigi Pirandello

A Comedy in the Making
English version by Edward Storer

CHARACTERS OF THE COMEDY IN THE MAKING

THE FATHER	THE BOY
THE MOTHER	THE CHILD
THE STEP-DAUGHTER	[*The last two do not speak*]
THE SON	MADAME PACE

ACTORS OF THE COMPANY

THE MANAGER	OTHER ACTORS AND ACTRESSES
LEADING LADY	PROPERTY MAN
LEADING MAN	PROMPTER
SECOND LADY	MACHINIST
LEAD	MANAGER'S SECRETARY
L'INGÉNUE	DOOR-KEEPER
JUVENILE LEAD	SCENE-SHIFTERS

Daytime. The Stage of a Theatre.

N.B. The Comedy is without acts or scenes. The performance is interrupted once, without the curtain being lowered, when the manager and the chief characters withdraw to arrange the scenario. A second interruption of the action takes place when, by mistake, the stage hands let the curtain down.

🎭 *Act I*

The spectators will find the curtain raised and the stage as it usually is during the day time. It will be half dark, and empty, so that from the beginning the public may have the impression of an impromptu performance.

Prompter's box and a small table and chair for the manager.

Two other small tables and several chairs scattered about as during rehearsals.

The ACTORS and ACTRESSES of the company enter from the back of the stage:

first one, then another, then two together; nine or ten in all. They are about to rehearse a Pirandello play: Mixing It Up.* Some of the company move off towards their dressing rooms. The PROMPTER who has the "book" under his arm, is waiting for the manager in order to begin the rehearsal.

The ACTORS and ACTRESSES, some standing, some sitting, chat and smoke. One perhaps reads a paper; another cons his part.

Finally, the MANAGER enters and goes to the table prepared for him. His SECRETARY brings him his mail, through which he glances. The PROMPTER takes his seat, turns on a light, and opens the "book."

THE MANAGER [throwing a letter down on the table]: I can't see [to PROPERTY MAN.] Let's have a little light, please!

PROPERTY MAN: Yes sir, yes, at once. [A light comes down on to the stage.]

THE MANAGER [clapping his hands]: Come along! Come along! Second act of "Mixing It Up." [Sits down.]

> [The ACTORS and ACTRESSES go from the front of the stage to the wings, all except the three who are to begin the rehearsal.]

THE PROMPTER [reading the "book"]: "Leo Gala's house. A curious room serving as dining-room and study."

THE MANAGER [to PROPERTY MAN]: Fix up the old red room.

PROPERTY MAN [noting it down]: Red set. All right!

THE PROMPTER [continuing to read from the "book"]: "Table already laid and writing desk with books and papers. Book-shelves. Exit rear to Leo's bedroom. Exit left to kitchen. Principal exit to right."

---

* i.e. *Il giuoco delle parti.*

THE MANAGER [*energetically*]: Well, you understand: The principal exit over there; here, the kitchen. [*Turning to actor who is to play the part of* SOCRATES.] You make your entrances and exits here. [*To* PROPERTY MAN.] The baize doors at the rear, and curtains.

PROPERTY MAN [*noting it down*]: Right!

PROMPTER [*reading as before*]: "When the curtain rises, Leo Gala, dressed in cook's cap and apron is busy beating an egg in a cup. Philip, also dressed as a cook, is beating another egg. Guido Venanzi is seated and listening."

LEADING MAN [*To* MANAGER]: Excuse me, but must I absolutely wear a cook's cap?

THE MANAGER [*annoyed*]: I imagine so. It says so there anyway. [*Pointing to the "book."*]

LEADING MAN: But it's ridiculous!

THE MANAGER [*jumping up in a rage*]: Ridiculous? Ridiculous? Is it my fault if France won't send us any more good comedies, and we are reduced to putting on Pirandello's works, where nobody understands anything, and where the author plays the fool with us all? [*The* ACTORS *grin. The* MANAGER *goes to* LEADING MAN *and shouts.*] Yes sir, you put on the cook's cap and beat eggs. Do you suppose that with all this egg-beating business you are on an ordinary stage? Get that out of your head. You represent the shell of the eggs you are beating! [*Laughter and comments among the* ACTORS.] Silence! and listen to my explanations, please! [*To* LEADING MAN.] "The empty form of reason without the fullness of instinct, which is blind."—You stand for reason, your wife is instinct. It's a mixing up of the parts, according to which you who act your own part become the puppet of yourself. Do you understand?

LEADING MAN: I'm hanged if I do.

THE MANAGER: Neither do I. But let's get on with it. It's sure to be a glorious failure anyway. [*Confidentially.*] But I say, please face three-quarters. Otherwise, what with the abstruseness of the dialogue, and the public that won't be able to hear you, the whole thing will go to hell. Come on! come on!

PROMPTER: Pardon sir, may I get into my box? There's a bit of a draught.

THE MANAGER: Yes, yes, of course!

At this point, the DOOR-KEEPER *has entered from the stage door and advances towards the manager's table, taking off his braided cap. During this manoeuvre, the* SIX CHARACTERS *enter, and stop by the door at back of stage, so that when the* DOOR-KEEPER *is about to announce* their coming to the MANAGER, they are already on the stage. A tenuous light surrounds them, almost as if irradiated by them—the faint breath of their fantastic reality.

This light will disappear when they come forward towards the actors. They preserve, however, something of the dream lightness in which they seem almost suspended; but this does not detract from the essential reality of their forms and expressions.

He who is known as the FATHER is a man of about 50: hair, reddish in colour, thin at the temples; he is not bald, however; thick moustaches, falling over his still fresh mouth, which often opens in an empty and uncertain smile. He is fattish, pale; with an especially wide forehead. He has blue, oval-shaped eyes, very clear and piercing. Wears light trousers and a dark jacket. He is alternatively mellifluous and violent in his manner.

The MOTHER seems crushed and terrified as if by an intolerable weight of shame and abasement. She is dressed in modest black and wears a thick widow's veil of crêpe. When she lifts this, she reveals a wax-like face. She always keeps her eyes downcast.

The STEP-DAUGHTER, is dashing, almost impudent, beautiful. She wears mourning too, but with great elegance. She shows contempt for the timid half-frightened manner of the wretched BOY (14 years old, and also dressed in black); on the other hand, she displays a lively tenderness for her little sister, the CHILD (about four), who is dressed in white, with a black silk sash at the waist.

The SON (22) tall, severe in his attitude of contempt for the FATHER, supercilious and indifferent to the MOTHER. He looks as if he had come on the stage against his will.

DOOR-KEEPER [cap in hand]: Excuse me, sir . . .

THE MANAGER [rudely]: Eh? What is it?

DOOR-KEEPER [timidly]: These people are asking for you, sir.

THE MANAGER [furious]: I am rehearsing, and you know perfectly well no one's allowed to come in during rehearsals! [Turning to the CHARACTERS.] Who are you, please? What do you want?

THE MANAGER [half angry, half amazed]: An author? What author?

THE FATHER: Any author, sir.

THE MANAGER: But there's no author here. We are not rehearsing a new piece.

THE STEP-DAUGHTER [vivaciously]: So much the better, so much the better! We can be your new piece.

AN ACTOR [coming forward from the others]: Oh, do you hear that?

THE FATHER [to STEP-DAUGHTER]: Yes, but if the author isn't here . . .
[to MANAGER.] unless you would be willing . . .

526   *Luigi Pirandello*

THE MANAGER: You are trying to be funny.

THE FATHER: No, for Heaven's sake, what are you saying? We bring you a drama, sir.

THE STEP-DAUGHTER: We may be your fortune.

THE MANAGER: Will you oblige me by going away? We haven't time to waste with mad people.

THE FATHER [mellifluously]: Oh sir, you know well that life is full of infinite absurdities, which, strangely enough, do not even need to appear plausible, since they are true.

THE MANAGER: What the devil is he talking about?

THE FATHER: I say that to reverse the ordinary process may well be considered a madness: that is, to create credible situations, in order that they may appear true. But permit me to observe that if this be madness, it is the sole *raison d'être* of your profession, gentlemen. [*The* ACTORS *look hurt and perplexed.*]

THE MANAGER [*getting up and looking at him*]: So our profession seems to you one worthy of madmen then?

THE FATHER: Well, to make seem true that which isn't true . . . without any need . . . for a joke as it were . . . Isn't that your mission, gentlemen: to give life to fantastic characters on the stage?

THE MANAGER [*interpreting the rising anger of the* COMPANY]: But I would beg you to believe, my dear sir, that the profession of the comedian is a noble one. If today, as things go, the playwrights give us stupid comedies to play and puppets to represent instead of men, remember we are proud to have given life to immortal works here on these very boards! [THE ACTORS, *satisfied, applaud their* MANAGER.]

THE FATHER [*interrupting furiously*]: Exactly, perfectly, to living beings more alive than those who breathe and wear clothes: beings less real perhaps, but truer! I agree with you entirely. [*The* ACTORS *look at one another in amazement.*]

THE MANAGER: But what do you mean? Before, you said . . .

THE FATHER: No, excuse me, I meant it for you, sir, who were crying out that you had no time to lose with madmen, while no one better than yourself knows that nature uses the instrument of human fantasy in order to pursue her high creative purpose.

THE MANAGER: Very well,—but where does all this take us?

THE FATHER: Nowhere! It is merely to show you that one is born to life in many forms, in many shapes, as tree, or as stone, as water, as butterfly, or as woman. So one may also be born a character in a play.

THE MANAGER [*with feigned comic dismay*]: So you and these other friends of yours have been born characters?

THE FATHER: Exactly, and alive as you see! [MANAGER *and* ACTORS *burst out laughing.*]

THE FATHER [*hurt*]: I am sorry you laugh, because we carry in us a drama, as you can guess from this woman here veiled in black.

THE MANAGER [*losing patience at last and almost indignant*]: Oh, chuck it! Get away please! Clear out of here! [*To* PROPERTY MAN.] For Heaven's sake, turn them out!

THE FATHER [*resisting*]: No, no, look here, we . . .

THE MANAGER [*roaring*]: We come here to work, you know.

LEADING ACTOR: One cannot let oneself be made such a fool of.

THE FATHER [*determined, coming forward*]: I marvel at your incredulity, gentlemen. Are you not accustomed to see the characters created by an author spring to life in yourselves and face each other? Just because there is no "book" [*Pointing to the* PROMPTER's *box.*] which contains us, you refuse to believe . . .

THE STEP-DAUGHTER [*advances towards* MANAGER, *smiling and coquettish*]: Believe me, we are really six most interesting characters, sir; side-tracked however.

THE FATHER: Yes, that is the word! [*To* MANAGER *all at once.*] In the sense, that is, that the author who created us alive no longer wished, or was no longer able, materially to put us into a work of art. And this was a real crime, sir; because he who has had the luck to be born a character can laugh even at death. He cannot die. The man, the writer, the instrument of the creation will die, but his creation does not die. And to live for ever, it does not need to have extraordinary gifts or to be able to work wonders. Who was Sancho Panza? Who was Don Abbondio? Yet they live eternally because—live germs as they were—they had the fortune to find a fecundating matrix, a fantasy which could raise and nourish them: make them live for ever!

THE MANAGER: That is quite all right. But what do you want here, all of you?

THE FATHER: We want to live.

THE MANAGER [*ironically*]: For Eternity?

THE FATHER: No, sir, only for a moment . . . in you.

AN ACTOR: Just listen to him!

LEADING LADY: They want to live, in us . . . !

JUVENILE LEAD [*pointing to the* STEP-DAUGHTER]. I've no objection, as far as that one is concerned.

THE FATHER: Look here! look here! The comedy has to be made. [*To the* MANAGER.] But if you and your actors are willing, we can soon concert it among ourselves.

THE MANAGER [annoyed]: But what do you want to concert? We don't go in for concerts here. Here we play dramas and comedies!

THE FATHER: Exactly! That is just why we have come to you.

THE MANAGER: And where is the "book"?

THE FATHER: It is in us! [The ACTORS laugh.] The drama is in us, and we are the drama. We are impatient to play it. Our inner passion drives us on to this.

THE STEP-DAUGHTER [disdainful, alluring, treacherous, full of impudence]: My passion, sir! Ah, if you only knew! My passion for him! [Points to the FATHER and makes a pretence of embracing him. Then she breaks out into a loud laugh.]

THE FATHER [angrily]: Behave yourself! And please don't laugh in that fashion.

THE STEP-DAUGHTER: With your permission, gentlemen, I, who am a two months' orphan, will show you how I can dance and sing. [Sings and then dances Prenez garde à Tchou-Tchin-Tchou.]

> Les chinois sont un peuple malin,
> De Shangaî à Pekin,
> Ils ont mis des écriteaux partout:
> Prenez garde à Tchou-Tchin-Tchou.

ACTORS AND ACTRESSES: Bravo! Well done! Tip-top!

THE MANAGER: Silence! This isn't a café concert, you know! [Turning to the FATHER in consternation.] Is she mad?

THE FATHER: Mad? No, she's worse than mad.

THE STEP-DAUGHTER [to MANAGER]: Worse? Worse? Listen! Stage this drama for us at once! Then you will see that at a certain moment I . . . when this little darling here . . . [Takes the CHILD by the hand and leads her to the MANAGER.] Isn't she a dear? [Takes her up and kisses her.] Darling! Darling! [Puts her down again and adds feelingly.] Well, when God suddenly takes this dear little child away from that poor mother there; and this imbecile here [Seizing hold of the BOY roughly and pushing him forward.] does the stupidest things, like the fool he is, you will see me run away. Yes, gentlemen, I shall be off. But the moment hasn't arrived yet. After what has taken place between him and me [indicates the FATHER with a horrible wink.] I can't remain any longer in this society, to have to witness the anguish of this mother here for that fool . . . [Indicates the SON.] Look at him! Look at him! See how indifferent, how frigid he is, because he is the legitimate son. He despises me, despises him [Pointing to the BOY.], despises this baby here; because . . . we are bastards. [Goes to the MOTHER and embraces her.] And he doesn't want to recognize her as his mother—she who is the common mother of us all. He looks down upon her as if she were only the mother of us three bastards. Wretch! [*She says all this very rapidly, excitedly. At the word "bastards" she raises her voice, and almost spits out the final "Wretch!"*]

THE MOTHER [*to the* MANAGER, *in anguish*]: In the name of these two little children, I beg you . . . [*She grows faint and is about to fall.*] Oh God!

THE FATHER [*coming forward to support her as do some of the* ACTORS]: Quick, a chair, a chair for this poor widow!

THE ACTORS: Is it true? Has she really fainted?

THE MANAGER: Quick, a chair! Here!

> [*One of the* ACTORS *brings a chair, the* OTHERS *proffer assistance. The* MOTHER *tries to prevent the* FATHER *from lifting the veil which covers her face.*]

THE FATHER: Look at her! Look at her!

THE MOTHER: No, no; stop it please!

THE FATHER [*raising her veil*]: Let them see you!

THE MOTHER [*rising and covering her face with her hands, in desperation*]: I beg you, sir, to prevent this man from carrying out his plan which is loathsome to me.

THE MANAGER [*dumbfounded*]: I don't understand at all. What is the situation? Is this lady your wife? [*To the* FATHER.]

THE FATHER: Yes, gentlemen: my wife!

THE MANAGER: But how can she be a widow if you are alive? [*The* ACTORS *find relief for their astonishment in a loud laugh.*]

THE FATHER: Don't laugh! Don't laugh like that, for Heaven's sake. Her drama lies just here in this: she has had a lover, a man who ought to be here.

THE MOTHER [*with a cry*]: No! No!

THE STEP-DAUGHTER: Fortunately for her, he is dead. Two months ago as I said. We are in mourning, as you see.

THE FATHER: He isn't here you see, not because he is dead. He isn't here—look at her a moment and you will understand—because her drama isn't a drama of the love of two men for whom she was incapable of feeling anything except possibly a little gratitude—gratitude not for me but for the other. She isn't a woman, she is a mother, and her drama—powerful sir, I assure you—lies, as a matter of fact, all in these four children she has had by two men.

THE MOTHER: I had them? Have you got the courage to say that I wanted them? [*To the* COMPANY] It was his doing. It was he who gave me that other man, who forced me to go away with him.

THE STEP-DAUGHTER: It isn't true.

THE MOTHER [startled]: Not true, isn't it?

THE STEP-DAUGHTER: No, it isn't true, it just isn't true.

THE MOTHER: And what can you know about it?

THE STEP-DAUGHTER: It isn't true. Don't believe it. [To MANAGER] Do you know why she says so? For that fellow there. [Indicates the SON.] She tortures herself, destroys herself on account of the neglect of that son there; and she wants him to believe that if she abandond him when he was only two years old, it was because he [Indicates the FATHER.] made her do so.

THE MOTHER [vigorously]: He forced me to it, and I call God to witness it. [To the MANAGER.] Ask him [Indicates HUSBAND.] if it isn't true. Let him speak. You [To DAUGHTER.] are not in a position to know anything about it.

THE STEP-DAUGHTER: I know you lived in peace and happiness with my father while he lived. Can you deny it?

THE MOTHER: No, I don't deny it . . .

THE STEP-DAUGHTER: He was always full of affection and kindness for you. [To the BOY, angrily.] It's true, isn't it? Tell them! Why don't you speak, you little fool?

THE MOTHER: Leave the poor boy alone. Why do you want to make me appear ungrateful, daughter? I don't want to offend your father. I have answered him that I didn't abandon my house and my son through any fault of mine, nor from any wilful passion.

THE FATHER: It is true. It was my doing.

LEADING MAN [to the COMPANY]: What a spectacle!

LEADING LADY: We are the audience this time.

JUVENILE LEAD: For once, in a way.

THE MANAGER [beginning to get really interested]: Let's hear them out. Listen!

THE SON: Oh yes, you're going to hear a fine bit now. He will talk to you of the Demon of Experiment.

THE FATHER: You are a cynical imbecile. I've told you so already a hundred times. [To the MANAGER.] He tries to make fun of me on account of this expression which I have found to excuse myself with.

THE SON]with disgust]: Yes, phrases! phrases!

THE FATHER: Phrases! Isn't everyone consoled when faced with a trouble or fact he doesn't understand, by a word, some simple word, which tells us nothing and yet calms us?

THE STEP-DAUGHTER: Even in the case of remorse. In fact, especially then.

THE FATHER: Remorse? No, that isn't true. I've done more than use words to quieten the remorse in me.

THE STEP-DAUGHTER: Yes, there was a bit of money too. Yes, yes, a bit of money. There were the hundred lire he was about to offer me in payment, gentlemen . . . [*Sensation of horror among the* ACTORS]

THE SON [*to the* STEP-DAUGHTER]: This is vile.

THE STEP-DAUGHTER: Vile? There they were in a pale blue envelope on a little mahogany table in the back of Madame Pace's shop. You know Madame Pace—one of those ladies who attract poor girls of good family into their ateliers, under the pretext of their selling *robes et manteaux*.

THE SON: And he thinks he has brought the right to tyrannize over us all with those hundred lire he was going to pay; but which, fortunately—note this, gentlemen—he had no chance of paying.

THE STEP-DAUGHTER: It was a near thing, though, you know! [*Laughs ironically.*]

THE MOTHER [*protesting*]: Shame, my daughter, shame!

THE STEP-DAUGHTER: Shame indeed! This is my revenge! I am dying to live that scene . . . The room . . . I see it . . . Here is the window with the mantles exposed, there the divan, the looking-glass, a screen, there in front of the window the little mahogany table with the blue envelope containing one hundred lire. I see it. I see it. I could take hold of it . . . But you, gentlemen, you ought to turn your backs now: I am almost nude, you know. But I don't blush: I leave that to him. [*Indicating* FATHER.]

THE MANAGER: I don't understand this at all.

THE FATHER: Naturally enough. I would ask you, sir, to exercise your authority a little here, and let me speak before you believe all she is trying to blame me with. Let me explain.

THE STEP-DAUGHTER: Ah yes, explain it in your own way.

THE FATHER: But don't you see that the whole trouble lies here. In words, words. Each one of us has within him a whole world of things, each man of us his own special world. And how can we ever come to an understanding if I put in the words I utter the sense and value of things as I see them; while you who listen to me must inevitably translate them according to the conception of things each one of you has within himself. We think we understand each other, but we never really do. Look here! This woman [*Indicating the* MOTHER.] takes all my pity for her as a specially ferocious form of cruelty.

THE MOTHER: But you drove me away.

THE FATHER: Do you hear her? I drove her away! She believes I really sent her away.

THE MOTHER: You know how to talk, and I don't; but, believe me, sir [To MANAGER.], after he had married me . . . who knows why? . . . I was a poor insignificant woman . . .

THE FATHER: But, good Heavens! it was just for your humility that I married you. I loved this simplicity in you. [He stops when he sees she makes signs to contradict him, opens his arms wide in sign of desperation, seeing how hopeless it is to make himself understood.] You see she denies it. Her mental deafness, believe me, is phenomenal, the limit: [Touches his forehead.] deaf, deaf, mentally deaf! She has plenty of feeling. Oh yes, a good heart for the children; but the brain—deaf, to the point of desperation——!

THE STEP-DAUGHTER: Yes, but ask him how his intelligence has helped us.

THE FATHER: If we could see all the evil that may spring from good, what should we do? [At this point the LEADING LADY who is biting her lips with rage at seeing the LEADING MAN flirting with the STEP-DAUGHTER, comes forward and says to the MANAGER.]

LEADING LADY: Excuse me, but are we going to rehearse today?

MANAGER: Of course, of course; but let's hear them out.

JUVENILE LEAD: This is something quite new.

L'INGÉNUE: Most interesting!

LEADING LADY: Yes, for the people who like that kind of thing. [Casts a glance at LEADING MAN.]

THE MANAGER [to FATHER]: You must please explain yourself quite clearly. [Sits down.]

THE FATHER: Very well then: listen! I had in my service a poor man, a clerk, a secretary of mine, full of devotion, who became friends with her. [Indicating the MOTHER.] They understood one another, were kindred souls in fact, without, however, the least suspicion of any evil existing. They were incapable even of thinking of it.

THE STEP-DAUGHTER: So he thought of it—for them!

THE FATHER: That's not true. I meant to do good to them—and to myself, I confess, at the same time. Things had come to the point that I could not say a word to either of them without their making a mute appeal, one to the other, with their eyes. I could see them silently asking each other how I was to be kept in countenance, how I was to be kept quiet. And this, believe me, was just about enough of itself to keep me in a constant rage, to exasperate me beyond measure.

THE MANAGER: And why didn't you send him away then—this secretary of yours?

THE FATHER: Precisely what I did, sir. And then I had to watch this poor woman drifting forlornly about the house like an animal without a master, like an animal one has taken in out of pity.

THE MOTHER: Ah yes . . . !

THE FATHER [suddenly turning to the MOTHER]: It's true about the son anyway, isn't it?

THE MOTHER: He took my son away from me first of all.

THE FATHER: But not from cruelty. I did it so that he should grow up healthy and strong by living in the country.

THE STEP-DAUGHTER [pointing to him ironically]: As one can see.

THE FATHER [quickly]: Is it my fault if he has grown up like this? I sent him to a wet nurse in the country, a peasant, as she did not seem to me strong enough, though she is of humble origin. That was, anyway, the reason I married her. Unpleasant all this may be, but how can it be helped? My mistake possibly, but there we are! All my life I have had these confounded aspirations towards a certain moral sanity. [At this point the STEP-DAUGHTER bursts into a noisy laugh.] Oh, stop it! Stop it! I can't stand it.

THE MANAGER: Yes, please stop it, for Heaven's sake.

THE STEP-DAUGHTER: But imagine moral sanity from him, if you please—the client of certain ateliers like that of Madame Pace!

THE FATHER: Fool! That is the proof that I am a man! This seeming contradiction, gentlemen, is the strongest proof that I stand here a live man before you. Why, it is just for this very incongruity in my nature that I have had to suffer what I have. I could not live by the side of that woman [Indicagint the MOTHER.] any longer; but not so much for the boredom she inspired me with as for the pity I felt for her.

THE MOTHER: And so he turned me out—.

THE FATHER: —well provided for! Yes, I sent her to that man, gentlemen . . . to let her go free of me.

THE MOTHER: And to free himself.

THE FATHER: Yes, I admit it. It was also a liberation for me. But great evil has come of it. I meant well when I did it; and I did it more for her sake than mine. I swear it. [Crosses his arms on his chest; then turns suddenly to the MOTHER.] Did I ever lose sight of you until that other man carried you off to another town, like the angry fool he was? And on account of my pure interest in you . . . my pure interest, I repeat, that had no base motive in it . . . I watched with the tenderest concern the new family that grew up around her. She can bear witness to this. [*Points to the* STEP-DAUGHTER.]

THE STEP-DAUGHTER: Oh yes, that's true enough. When I was a kiddie, so so high, you know, with plaits over my shoulders and knickers longer than my skirts, I used to see him waiting outside the school for me to come out. He came to see how I was growing up.

THE FATHER: This is infamous, shameful!

THE STEP-DAUGHTER: No. Why?

THE FATHER: Infamous! infamous! [*Then excitedly to* MANAGER *explaining.*] After she [*Indicating* MOTHER.] went away, my house seemed suddenly empty. She was my incubus, but she filled my house. I was like a dazed fly alone in the empty rooms. This boy here [*Indicating the Son.*] was educated away from home, and when he came back, he seemed to me to be no more mine. With no mother to stand between him and me, he grew up entirely for himself, on his own, apart, with no tie of intellect or affection binding him to me. And then—strange but true—I was driven, by curiosity at first and then by some tender sentiment, towards her family, which had come into being through my will. The thought of her began gradually to fill up the emptiness I felt all around me. I wanted to know if she were happy in living out the simple daily duties of life. I wanted to think of her as fortunate and happy because far away from the complicated torments of my spirit. And so, to have proof of this, I used to watch that child coming out of school.

THE STEP-DAUGHTER: Yes, yes. True. He used to follow me in the street and smiled at me, waved his hand, like this. I would look at him with interest, wondering who he might be. I told my mother, who guessed at once. [*The* MOTHER *agrees with a nod.*] Then she didn't want to send me to school for some days; and when I finally went back, there he was again—looking so ridiculous—with a paper parcel in his hands. He came close to me, caressed me, and drew out a fine straw hat from the parcel, with a bouquet of flowers—all for me!

THE MANAGER: A bit discursive this, you know!

THE SON [*contemptuously*]: Literature! Literature!

THE FATHER: Literature indeed! This is life, this is passion!

THE MANAGER: It may be, but it won't act.

THE FATHER: I agree. This is only the part leading up. I don't suggest this should be staged. She [*Pointing to the* STEP-DAUGHTER] as you see, is no longer the flapper with plaits down her back—

THE STEP-DAUGHTER: —and the knickers showing below the skirt!

THE FATHER: The drama is coming now, sir; something new, complex, most interesting.

THE STEP-DAUGHTER: As soon as my father died . . .

THE FATHER: —there was absolute misery for them. They came back here, unknown to me. Through her stupidity! [*Pointing to the* MOTHER] It is true she can barely write her own name; but she could anyhow have got her daughter to write to me that they were in need . . .

THE MOTHER: And how was I to divine all this sentiment in him?

THE FATHER: That is exactly your mistake, never to have guessed any of my sentiments.

THE MOTHER: After so many years apart, and all that had happened . . .

THE FATHER: Was it my fault if that fellow carried you away? It happened quite suddenly; for after he had obtained some job or other, I could find no trace of them; and so, not unnaturally, my interest in them dwindled. But the drama culminated unforeseen and violent on their return, when I was impelled by my miserable flesh that still lives . . . Ah! what misery, what wretchedness is that of the man who is alone and disdains debasing *liaisons!* Not old enough to do without women, and not young enough to go and look for one without shame. Misery? It's worse than misery; it's a horror; for no woman can any longer give him love; and when a man feels this . . . One ought to do without, you say? Yes, yes, I know. Each of us when he appears before his fellows is clothed in a certain dignity. But every man knows what unconfessable things pass within the secrecy of his own heart. One gives way to the temptation, only to rise from it again, afterwards, with a great eagerness to re-establish one's dignity, as if it were a tombstone to place on the grave of one's shame, and a monument to hide and sign the memory of our weaknesses. Everybody's in the same case. Some folks haven't the courage to say certain things, that's all!

THE STEP-DAUGHTER: All appear to have the courage to do them though.

THE FATHER: Yes, but in secret. Therefore, you want more courage to say these things. Let a man but speak these things out, and folks at once label him a cynic. But it isn't true. He is like all the others, better indeed, because he isn't afraid to reveal with the light of the intelligence the red shame of human bestiality on which most men close their eyes so as not to see it.

Woman—for example, look at her case! She turns tantalizing inviting glances on you. You seize her. No sooner does she feel herself in your grasp than she closes her eyes. It is the sign of her mission, the sign by which she says to man: "Blind yourself, for I am blind."

THE STEP-DAUGHTER: Sometimes she can close them no more: when she no longer feels the need of hiding her shame to herself, but dry-eyed and dispassionately, sees only that of the man who has blinded himself without love. Oh, all these intellectual complications make me sick, disgust me—all this philosophy that uncovers the beast in man, and then seeks to save him, excuse him . . . I can't stand it, sir. When a man seeks to "simplify" life bestially, throwing aside every relic of humanity, every chaste aspiration, every pure feeling, all sense of ideality, duty, modesty, shame . . . then nothing is more revolting and nauseous than a certain kind of remorse—crocodiles' tears, that's what it is.

THE MANAGER: Let's come to the point. This is only discussion.

THE FATHER: Very good, sir! But a fact is like a sack which won't stand up when it is empty. In order that it may stand up, one has to put into it the reason and sentiment which have caused it to exist. I couldn't possibly know that after the death of that man, they had decided to return here, that they were in misery, and that she [*Pointing to the* MOTHER] had gone to work as a modiste, and at a shop of the type of that of Madame Pace.

THE STEP-DAUGHTER: A real high-class modiste, you must know, gentlemen. In appearance, she works for the leaders of the best society; but she arranges matters so that these elegant ladies serve her purpose . . . without prejudice to other ladies who are . . . well . . . only so so.

THE MOTHER: You will believe me, gentlemen, that is never entered my mind that the old hag offered me work because she had her eye on my daughter.

THE STEP-DAUGHTER: Poor mamma! Do you know, sir, what that woman did when I brought her back the work my mother had finished? She would point out to me that I had torn one of my frocks, and she would give it back to my mother to mend. It was I who paid for it, always I; while this poor creature here believed she was sacrificing herself for me and these two children here, sitting up at night sewing Madame Pace's robes.

THE MANAGER: And one day you met there . . .

THE STEP-DAUGHTER: Him, him. Yes sir, an old client. There's a scene for you to play. Superb!

THE FATHER: She, the Mother arrived just then . . .

THE STEP-DAUGHTER [*treacherously*]: Almost in time!

THE FATHER [*crying out*]: No, in time! in time! Fortunately I recognized her . . . in time. And I took them back home with me to my house. You can imagine now her position and mine; she, as you see her; and I who cannot look her in the face.

THE STEP-DAUGHTER: Absurd! How can I possibly be expected—after that—to be a modest young miss, a fit person to go with his confounded aspirations for "a solid moral sanity"?

THE FATHER: For the drama lies all in this—in the conscience that I have, that each one of us has. We believe this conscience to be a single thing, but it is many-sided. There is one for this person, and another for that. Diverse consciences. So we have this illusion of being one person for all, of having a personality that is unique in all our acts. But it isn't true. We perceive this when, tragically perhaps, in something we do, we are as it were, suspended, caught up in the air on a kind of hook. Then we perceive that all of us was not in that act, and that it would be an atrocious injustice to judge us by that action alone, as if all our existence were summed up in that one deed. Now do you understand the perfidy of this girl? She surprised me in a place, where she ought not to have known me, just as I could not exist for her; and she now seeks to attach to me a reality such as I could never suppose I should have to assume for her in a shameful and fleeting moment of my life. I feel this above all else. And the drama, you will see, acquires a tremendous value from this point. Then there is the position of the others . . . his . . . [*Indicating the* SON].

THE SON [*shrugging his shoulders scornfully*]: Leave me alone! I don't come into this.

THE FATHER: What? You don't come into this?

THE SON: I've got nothing to do with it, and don't want to have; because you know well enough I wasn't made to be mixed up in all this with the rest of you.

THE STEP-DAUGHTER: We are only vulgar folk! He is the fine gentleman. You may have noticed, Mr. Manager, that I fix him now and again with a look of scorn while he lowers his eyes—for he knows the evil he has done me.

THE SON [*scarcely looking at her*]: I?

THE STEP-DAUGHTER: You! you! I owe my life on the streets to you. Did you or did you not deny us, with your behaviour, I won't say the intimacy of home, but even that mere hospitality which makes guests feel at their ease? We were intruders who had come to disturb the kingdom of your legitimacy. I should like to have you witness, Mr. Manager, certain scenes between him and me. He says

I have tyrannized over everyone. But it was just his behaviour which made me insist on the reason for which I had come into the house,—this reason he calls "vile"—into his house, with my mother who is his mother too. And I came as mistress of the house.

THE SON: It's easy for them to put me always in the wrong. But imagine, gentlemen, the position of a son, whose fate it is to see arrive one day at his home a young woman of impudent bearing, a young woman who inquires for his father, with whom who knows what business she has. This young man has then to witness her return bolder than ever, accompanied by that child there. He is obliged to watch her treat his father in an equivocal and confidential manner. She asks money of him in a way that lets one suppose he must give it her, must, do you understand, because he has every obligation to do so.

THE FATHER: But I have, as a matter of fact, this obligation. I owe it to your mother.

THE SON: How should I know? When had I ever seen or heard of her? One day there arrive with her [Indicating STEP-DAUGHTER.] that lad and this baby here. I am told: "This is your mother too, you know." I divine from her manner [Indicating STEP-DAUGHTER again.] why it is they have come home. I had rather not say what I feel and think about it. I shouldn't even care to confess to myself. No action can therefore be hoped for from me in this affair. Believe me, Mr. Manager, I am an "unrealized" character, dramatically speaking; and I find myself not at all at ease in their company. Leave me out of it, I beg you.

THE FATHER: What? It is just because you are so that . . .

THE SON: How do you know what I am like? When did you ever bother your head about me?

THE FATHER: I admit it. I admit it. But isn't that a situation in itself? This aloofness of yours which is so cruel to me and to your mother, who returns home and sees you almost for the first time grown up, who doesn't recognize you but knows you are her son . . . [Pointing out the MOTHER to the MANAGER.] See, she's crying!

THE STEP-DAUGHTER [angrily, stamping her foot]: Like a fool!

THE FATHER [indicating STEP-DAUGHTER]: She can't stand him you know. [Then referring again to the SON.] He says he doesn't come into the affair, whereas he is really the hinge of the whole action. Look at that lad who is always clinging to his mother, frightened and humiliated. It is on account of this fellow here. Possibly his situation is the most painful of all. He feels himself a stranger more than the others. The poor little chap feels mortified, humiliated at being brought into a home out of charity as it were. [*In confidence.*] He is the image of his father. Hardly talks at all. Humble and quiet.

THE MANAGER: Oh, we'll cut him out. You've no notion what a nuisance boys are on the stage . . .

THE FATHER: He disappears soon, you know. And the baby too. She is the first to vanish from the scene. The drama consists finally in this: when that mother re-enters my house, her family born outside of it, and shall we say superimposed on the original, ends with the death of the little girl, the tragedy of the boy and the flight of the elder daughter. It cannot go on, because it is foreign to its surroundings. So after much torment, we three remain: I, the mother, that son. Then, owing to the disappearance of that extraneous family, we too find ourselves strange to one another. We find we are living in an atmosphere of mortal desolation which is the revenge, as he [*Indicating* SON.] scornfully said of the Demon of Experiment, that unfortunately hides in me. Thus, sir, you see when faith is lacking, it becomes impossible to create certain states of happiness, for we lack the necessary humility. Vaingloriously, we try to substitute ourselves for this faith, creating thus for the rest of the world a reality which we believe after their fashion, while, actually, it doesn't exist. For each one of us has his own reality to be respected before God, even when it is harmful to one's very self.

THE MANAGER: There is something in what you say. I assure you all this interests me very much. I begin to think there's the stuff for a drama in all this, and not a bad drama either.

THE STEP-DAUGHTER [*coming forward*]: When you've got a character like me.

THE FATHER [*shutting her up, all excited to learn the decision of the* MANAGER]: You be quiet!

THE MANAGER [*reflecting, heedless of interruption*]: It's new . . . hem . . . yes . . .

THE FATHER: Absolutely new!

THE MANAGER: You've got a nerve though. I must say, to come here and fling it at me like this . . .

THE FATHER: You will understand, sir, born as we are for the stage . . .

THE MANAGER: Are you amateur actors then?

THE FATHER: No. I say born for the stage, because . . .

THE MANAGER: Oh, nonsense. You're an old hand, you know.

THE FATHER: No sir, no. We act that rôle which we are given in life. And in my own case, passion itself, as usually happens, becomes a trifle theatrical when it is exalted.

THE MANAGER: Well, well, that will do. But you see, without an author . . . I could give you the address of an author if you like . . .

THE FATHER: No, no. Look here! You must be the author.

THE MANAGER: I? What are you talking about?

THE FATHER: Yes, you, you! Why not?

THE MANAGER: Because I have never been an author: that's why.

THE FATHER: Then why not turn author now? Everybody does it. You don't want any special qualities. Your task is made much easier by the fact that we are all here alive before you . . .

THE MANAGER: It won't do.

THE FATHER: What? When you see us live our drama . . .

THE MANAGER: Yes, that's all right. But you want someone to write it.

THE FATHER: No, no. Someone to take it down, possibly, while we play it, scene by scene! It will be enough to sketch it out at first, and then try it over.

THE MANAGER: Well . . . I am almost tempted. It's a bit of an idea. One might have a shot at it.

THE FATHER: Of course. You'll see what scenes will come out of it. I can give you one, at once . . .

THE MANAGER: By Jove, it tempts me. I'd like to have a go at it. Let's try it out. Come with me to my office. [Turning to the ACTORS.] You are at liberty for a bit, but don't step out of the theatre for long. In a quarter of an hour, twenty minutes, all back here again! [To the FATHER.] We'll see what can be done. Who knows if we don't get something really extraordinary out of it?

THE FATHER: There's no doubt about it. They [Indicating the CHAR-ACTERS.] had better come with us too, hadn't they?

THE MANAGER: Yes, yes. Come on! come on! [Moves away and then turning to the ACTORS.] Be punctual, please! [MANAGER and the SIX CHARACTERS cross the stage and go off. The other ACTORS remain, looking at one another in astonishment.]

LEADING MAN: Is he serious? What the devil does he want to do?

JUVENILE LEAD: This is rank madness.

THIRD ACTOR: Does he expect to knock up a drama in five minutes?

JUVENILE LEAD: Like the improvisers!

LEADING LADY: If he thinks I'm going to take part in a joke like this . . .

JUVENILE LEAD: I'm out of it anyway.

FOURTH ACTOR: I should like to know who they are. [Alludes to CHARACTERS].

THIRD ACTOR: What do you suppose? Madmen or rascals!

JUVENILE LEAD: And he takes them seriously!

L'INGÉNUE: Vanity! He fancies himself as an author now.

LEADING MAN: It's absolutely unheard of. If the stage has come to this . . . well I'm . . .

FIFTH ACTOR: It's rather a joke.

THIRD ACTOR: Well, we'll see what's going to happen next.

[*Thus talking, the* ACTORS *leave the stage; some going out by the little door at the back; others retiring to their dressing-rooms.*

The curtain remains up.

The action of the play is suspended for twenty minutes].

❦ *Act II*

The stage call-bells ring to warn the company that the play is about to begin again.

The STEP-DAUGHTER *comes out of the* MANAGER'S *office along with the* CHILD *and the* BOY. *As she comes out of the office, she cries:—*

Nonsense! nonsense! Do it yourselves! I'm not going to mix myself up in this mess. [*Turning to the* CHILD *and coming quickly with her on to the stage.*] Come on, Rosetta, let's run!

[*The* BOY *follows them slowly, remaining a little behind and seeming perplexed.*]

THE STEP-DAUGHTER [*stops, bends over the* CHILD *and takes the latter's face between her hands*]: My little darling! You're frightened aren't you? You don't know where we are, do you? [*Pretending to reply to a question of the* CHILD.] What is the stage? It's a place, baby, you know, where people play at being serious, a place where they act comedies. W've got to act a comedy now, dead serious, you know; and you're in it also, little one. [*Embraces her, pressing the little head to her breast, and rocking the* CHILD *for a moment.*] Oh darling, darling, what a horrid comedy you've got to play! What a wretched part they've found for you! A garden . . . a fountain . . . look . . . just suppose, kiddie, it's here. Where, you say? Why, right here in the middle. It's all pretence you know. That's the trouble, my pet: it's all make-believe here. It's better to imagine it though, because if they fix it up for you, it'll only be painted cardboard, painted cardboard for the rockery, the water, the plants . . . Ah, but I think a baby like this one would sooner have a make-believe fountain than a real one, so she could play with it. What a joke it'll be for the others! But for you, alas! not quite such a joke: you who are real, baby dear, and really play by a real fountain that is big and green and beautiful, with ever so many bamboos around it that are reflected in the water, and a whole lot of little ducks swimming about . . . No, Rosetta, no, your mother doesn't bother about you on account of that wretch of a son there. I'm in the devil of a temper, and as for that lad . . . [*Seizes* BOY *by the arm to force him to take one of his hands out of his pockets.*] What have you got there? What are you hiding? [*Pulls his hand out of his pocket, looks into it and catches the glint of a revolver.*] Ah! where did you get this? [*The* BOY, *very pale in the face, looks at her, but does not answer*]. Idiot! If I'd been in your place, instead of killing myself, I'd have shot one of those two, or both of them: father and son.

[THE FATHER *enters from the office, all excited from his work.* THE MANAGER *follows him.*]

THE FATHER: Come on, come on dear! Come here for a minute! We've arranged everything. It's all fixed up.

THE MANAGER [*also excited*]: If you please, young lady, there are one or two points to settle still. Will you come along?

THE STEP-DAUGHTER [*following him towards the office*]: Ouff! what's the good, if you've arranged everything.

[THE FATHER, MANAGER *and* STEP-DAUGHTER *go back into the office again (off) for a moment. At the same time, the* SON *followed by the* MOTHER, *comes out.*]

THE SON [*looking at the three entering office*]: Oh this is fine, fine! And to think I can't even get away!

[*The* MOTHER *attempts to look at him, but lowers her eyes immediately when he turns away from her. She then sits down. The* BOY *and the* CHILD *approach her. She casts a glance again at the* SON, *and speaks with humble tones, trying to draw him into conversation.*]

THE MOTHER: And isn't my punishment the worst of all? [*Then seeing from the* SON's *manner that he will not bother himself about her.*] My God! Why are you so cruel? Isn't it enough for one person to support all this torment? Must you then insist on others seeing it also?

THE SON [*half to himself, meaning the* MOTHER *to hear, however*]: And they want to put it on the stage! If there was at least a reason for it! He thinks he has got at the meaning of it all. Just as if each one of us in every circumstance of life couldn't find his own explanation of it! [*Pauses.*] He complains he was discovered in a place where he ought not to have been seen, in a moment of his life which ought to have remained hidden and kept out of the reach of that convention which he has to maintain for other people. And what about my case? Haven't I had to reveal what no son ought ever to reveal: how father and mother live and are man and wife for themselves quite apart from that idea of father and mother which we give them? When this idea is revealed, our life is then linked at one point only to that man and that woman; and as such it should shame them, shouldn't it?

[*The* MOTHER *hides her face in her hands. From the dressing-rooms and the little door at the back of the stage the* ACTORS *and* STAGE MANAGER *return, followed by the* PROPERTY MAN, *and the* PROMPTER. *At the same moment, the* MANAGER *comes out of his office, accompanied by the* FATHER *and the* STEP-DAUGHTER.]

THE MANAGER: Come on, come on, ladies and gentlemen! Heh! you there, machinist!

MACHINIST: Yes sir?

THE MANAGER: Fix up the white parlor with the floral decorations. Two wings and a drop with a door will do. Hurry up!

[*The* MACHINIST *runs off at once to prepare the scene, and arranges it while the* MANAGER *talks with the* STAGE MANAGER, *the* PROPERTY MAN, *and the* PROMPTER *on matters of detail.*]

THE MANAGER [*to* PROPERTY MAN]: Just have a look, and see if there isn't a sofa or divan in the wardrobe . . .

PROPERTY MAN: There's the green one.

THE STEP-DAUGHTER: No no! Green won't do. It was yellow, ornamented with flowers—very large! and most comfortable!

PROPERTY MAN: There isn't one like that.

THE MANAGER: It doesn't matter. Use the one we've got.

THE STEP-DAUGHTER: Doesn't matter? It's most important!

THE MANAGER: We're only trying it now. Please don't interfere. [*To* PROPERTY MAN.] See if we've got a shop window—long and narrowish.

THE STEP-DAUGHTER: And the little table! The little mahogany table for the pale blue envelope!

PROPERTY MAN [*to* MANAGER]: There's that little gilt one.

THE MANAGER: That'll do fine.

THE FATHER: A mirror.

THE STEP-DAUGHTER: And the screen! We must have a screen. Otherwise how can I manage?

PROPERTY MAN: That's all right, Miss. We've got any amount of them.

THE MANAGER [to the STEP-DAUGHTER]: We want some clothes pegs too, don't we?

THE STEP-DAUGHTER: Yes, several, several!

THE MANAGER: See how many we've got and bring them all.

PROPERTY MAN: All right!

[The PROPERTY MAN hurries off to obey his orders. While he is putting the things in their places, the MANAGER talks to the PROMPTER and then with the CHARACTERS and the ACTORS.]

THE MANAGER [to PROMPTER]: Take your seat. Look here: this is the outline of the scenes, act by act. [Hands him some sheets of paper.] And now I'm going to ask you to do something out of the ordinary.

PROMPTER: Take it down in shorthand?

THE MANAGER [pleasantly surprised]: Exactly! Can you do shorthand?

PROMPTER: Yes, a little.

THE MANAGER: Good! [Turning to a STAGE HAND.] Go and get some paper from my office, plenty, as much as you can find.

[The STAGE HAND goes off, and soon returns with a handful of paper which he gives to the PROMPTER.]

THE MANAGER [to PROMPTER]: You follow the scenes as we play them, and try and get the points down, at any rate the most important ones. [Then addressing the ACTORS.] Clear the stage, ladies and gentlemen! Come over here [Pointing to the left.] and listen attentively.

LEADING LADY: But, excuse me, we . . .

THE MANAGER [guessing her thought]: Don't worry! You won't have to improvise.

LEADING MAN: What have we to do then?

THE MANAGER: Nothing. For the moment you just watch and listen. Everybody will get his part written out afterwards. At present we're going to try the thing as best we can. They're going to act now.

THE FATHER [as if fallen from the clouds into the confusion of the stage]: We? What do you mean, if you please, by a rehearsal?

THE MANAGER: A rehearsal for them. [Points to the ACTORS.]

THE FATHER: But since we are the characters . . .

THE MANAGER: All right: "characters" then, if you insist on calling yourselves such. But here, my dear sir, the characters don't act. Here the actors do the acting. The characters are there, in the "book" [Pointing towards PROMPTER's box.]—when there is a "book"!

THE FATHER: I won't contradict you; but excuse me, the actors aren't the characters. They want to be, they pretend to be, don't they? Now if these gentlemen here are fortunate enough to have us alive before them . . .

THE MANAGER: Oh this is grand! You want to come before the public yourselves then?

THE FATHER: As we are . . .

THE MANAGER: I can assure you it would be a magnificent spectacle!

LEADING MAN: What's the use of us here anyway then?

THE MANAGER: You're not going to pretend that you can act? It makes me laugh! [The ACTORS laugh.] There, you see, they are laughing at the notion. But, by the way, I must cast the parts. That won't be difficult. They cast themselves. [To the SECOND LADY LEAD.] You play the MOTHER. [To the FATHER.] We must find her a name.

THE FATHER: Amalia, sir.

THE MANAGER: But that is the real name of your wife. We don't want to call her by her real name.

THE FATHER: Why ever not, if it is her name? . . . Still, perhaps, if that lady must . . . [Makes a slight motion of the hand to indicate the SECOND LADY LEAD.] I see this woman here [Means the MOTHER.] as Amalia. But do as you like. [Gets more and more confused.] I don't know what to say to you. Already, I begin to hear my own words ring false, as if they had another sound . . .

THE MANAGER: Don't you worry about it. It'll be our job to find the right tones. And as for her name, if you want her Amalia, Amalia it shall be; and if you don't like it, we'll find another! For the moment though, we'll call the characters in this way: [To JUVENILE LEAD.] You are the SON. [To the LEADING LADY.] You naturally are the STEP-DAUGHTER . . .

THE STEP-DAUGHTER [excitedly]: What? what? I, that woman there? [Bursts out laughing.]

THE MANAGER [angry]: What is there to laugh at?

LEADING LADY [indignant]: Nobody has ever dared to laugh at me. I insist on being treated with respect; otherwise I go away.

THE STEP-DAUGHTER: No, no, ercuse me . . . I am not laughing at you . . .

THE MANAGER [to STEP-DAUGHTER]: You ought to feel honored to be played by . . .

LEADING LADY [at once, contemptuously]: "That woman there" . . .

THE STEP-DAUGHTER: But I wasn't speaking of you you know. I was speaking of myself—whom I can't see at all in you! That is all. I don't know . . . but . . . you . . . aren't in the least like me . . .

THE FATHER: True. Here's the point. Look here, sir, our temperaments, our souls . . .

THE MANAGER: Temperament, soul, be hanged! Do you suppose the spirit of the piece is in you? Nothing of the kind!

THE FATHER: What, haven't we our own temperaments, our own souls?

THE MANAGER: Not at all. Your soul or whatever you like to call it takes the shape here. The actors give body and form to it, voice and gesture. And my actors—I may tell you—have given expression to much more lofty material than this little drama of yours, which may or may not hold up on the stage. But if it does, the merit of it, believe me, will be due to my actors.

THE FATHER: I don't dare contradict you, sir; but, believe me, it is a terrible suffering for us who are as we are, with these bodies of ours, these features to see . . .

THE MANAGER [cutting him short and out of patience]: Good heavens! The make-up will remedy all that, man, the make-up . . .

THE FATHER: Maybe. But the voice, the gestures . . .

THE MANAGER: Now, look here! On the stage, you as yourself, cannot exist. The actor here acts you, and that's an end to it!

THE FATHER: I understand. And now I think I see why our author who conceived us as we are, all alive, didn't want to put us on the stage after all. I haven't the least desire to offend your actors. Far from it! But when I think that I am to be acted by . . . I don't know by whom . . .

LEADING MAN [on his dignity]: By me, if you've no objection!

THE FATHER [humbly, mellifluously]: Honored, I assure you, sir. [Bows.] Still, I must say that try as this gentleman may, with all his good will and wonderful art, to absorb me into himself . . .

LEADING MAN: Oh chuck it! "Wonderful art!" Withdraw that, please!

THE FATHER: The performance he will give, even doing his best with make-up to look like me . . .

LEADING MAN: It will certainly be a bit difficult! [The ACTORS laugh.]

THE FATHER: Exactly! It will be difficult to act me as I really am. The effect will be rather—apart from the make-up—according as to how he supposes I am, as he senses me—if he does sense me—and not as I inside of myself feel myself to be. It seems to me then that account should be taken of this by everyone whose duty it may become to criticize us . . .

THE MANAGER: Heavens! The man's starting to think about the critics now! Let them say what they like. It's up to us to put on the play if we can. [Looking around.] Come on! come on! Is the stage set? [To the ACTORS and CHARACTERS.] Stand back—stand back! Let me see, and don't let's lose any more time! [To the STEP-DAUGHTER.] Is it all right as it is now?

THE STEP-DAUGHTER: Well, to tell the truth, I don't recognize the scene.

THE MANAGER: My dear lady, you can't possibly suppose that we can construct that shop of Madame Pace piece by piece here? [*To the* FATHER.] You said a white room with flowered wall paper, didn't you?

THE FATHER: Yes.

THE MANAGER: Well then. We've got the furniture right more or less. Bring that little table a bit further forward. [*The* STAGE HANDS *obey the order. To* PROPERTY MAN.] You go and find an envelope, if possible, a pale blue one; and give it to that gentleman. [*Indicates* FATHER.]

PROPERTY MAN: An ordinary envelope?

MANAGER AND FATHER: Yes, yes, an ordinary envelope.

PROPERTY MAN: At once, sir. [*Exit*]

THE MANAGER: Ready, everyone! First scene—the Young Lady. [*The* LEADING LADY *comes forward.*] No, no, you must wait. I meant her [*Indicating the* STEP-DAUGHTER.] You just watch—

THE STEP-DAUGHTER [*adding at once*]: How I shall play it, how I shall live it! . . .

LEADING LADY [*offended*]: I shall live it also, you may be sure, as soon as I begin!

THE MANAGER [*with his hands to his head*]: Ladies and gentlemen, if you please! No more useless discussions! Scene I: the young lady with Madame Pace: Oh! [*Looks around as if lost.*] And this Madame Pace, where is she?

THE FATHER: She isn't with us, sir.

THE MANAGER: Then what the devil's to be done?

THE FATHER: But she is alive too.

THE MANAGER: Yes, but where is she?

THE FATHER: One minute. Let me speak! [*Turning to the* ACTRESSES.] If these ladies would be so good as to give me their hats for a moment . . .

THE ACTRESSES [*half surprised, half laughing, in chorus*]: What?
Why?
Our hats?
What does he say?

THE MANAGER: What are you going to do with the ladies' hats? [*The* ACTORS *laugh.*]

THE FATHER: Oh nothing. I just want to put them on these pegs for a moment. And one of the ladies will be so kind as to take off her mantle . . .

THE ACTORS: Oh, what d'you think of that?
Only the mantle?

He must be mad.

SOME ACTRESSES: But why?

Mantles as well?

THE FATHER: To hang them up here for a moment. Please be so kind, will you?

THE ACTRESSES [taking off their hats, one or two also their cloaks, and going to hang them on the racks]: After all, why not?

There you are!

This is really funny.

We've got to put them on show.

THE FATHER: Exactly; just like that, on show.

THE MANAGER: May we know why?

THE FATHER: I'll tell you. Who knows if, by arranging the stage for her, she does not come here herself, attracted by the very articles of her trade? [Inviting the ACTORS to look towards the exit at back of stage.] Look! Look!

> [The door at the back of stage opens and MADAME PACE enters and takes a few steps forward. She is a fat, oldish woman with puffy oxygenated hair. She is rouged and pow-dered, dressed with a comical elegance in black silk. Round her waist is a long silver chain from which hangs a pair of scissors. The STEP-DAUGHTER runs over to her at once amid the stupor of the actors.]

THE STEP-DAUGHTER [turning towards her]: There she is! There she is!

THE FATHER [radiant]: It's she! I said so, didn't I? There she is!

THE MANAGER [conquering his surprise, and then becoming indignant]: What sort of a trick is this?

LEADING MAN [almost at the same time]: What's going to happen next?

JUVENILE LEAD: Where does she come from?

L'INGÉNUE: They've been holding her in reserve, I guess.

LEADING LADY: A vulgar trick!

THE FATHER [dominating the protests]: Excuse me, all of you! Why are you so anxious to destroy in the name of a vulgar, commonplace sense of truth, this reality which comes to birth attracted and formed by the magic of the stage itself, which has indeed more right to live here than you, since it is much truer than you—if you don't mind my saying so? Which is the actress among you who is to play Madame Pace? Well, here is Madame Pace herself. And you will allow, I fancy, that the actress who acts her will be less true than this woman here, who is herself in person. You see my daughter recog-

nized her and went over to her at once. Now you're going to witness
the scene!

> [*But the scene between the* STEP-DAUGHTER *and* MADAME
> PACE *has already begun despite the protest of the actors and
> the reply of the* FATHER. *It has begun quietly, naturally, in a
> manner impossible for the stage. So when the actors, called to
> attention by the* FATHER, *turn round and see* MADAME PACE,
> *who has placed one hand under the* STEP-DAUGHTER's *chin to
> raise her head, they observe her at first with great attention,
> but hearing her speak in an unintelligible manner their inter-
> est begins to wane.*]

THE MANAGER: Well? well?

LEADING MAN: What does she say?

LEADING LADY: One can't hear a word.

JUVENILE LEAD: Louder! Louder please!

THE STEP-DAUGHTER [*leaving* MADAME PACE, *who smiles a Sphinx-like
smile, and advancing towards the actors*]: Louder? Louder? What
are you talking about? These aren't matters which can be shouted at
the top of one's voice. If I have spoken them out loud, it was to
shame him and have my revenge. [*Indicates* FATHER.] But for
Madame it's quite a different manner.

THE MANAGER: Indeed? indeed? But here, you know, people have got
to make themselves heard, my dear. Even we who are on the stage
can't hear you. What will it be when the public's in the theatre?
And anyway, you can very well speak up now among yourselves,
since we shan't be present to listen to you as we are now. You've got
to pretend to be alone in a room at the back of a shop where no one
can hear you.

> [*The* STEP-DAUGHTER *coquettishly and with a touch of malice
> makes a sign of disagreement two or three times with her
> finger.*]

THE MANAGER: What do you mean by no?

THE STEP-DAUGHTER [*sotto voce, mysteriously*]: There's someone who
will hear us if she [*Indicating* MADAME PACE.] speaks out loud.

THE MANAGER [*in consternation*]: What? Have you got someone else
to spring on us now? [*The* ACTORS *burst out laughing.*]

THE FATHER: No, no sir. She is alluding to me. I've got to be here—
there behind that door, in waiting; and Madame Pace knows it. In
fact, if you will allow me, I'll go there at once, so I can be quite
ready. [*Moves away.*]

THE MANAGER [*stopping him*]: No! Wait! wait! We must observe the
conventions of the theatre. Before you are ready . . .

THE STEP-DAUGHTER [*interrupting him*]: No, get on with it at once! I'm just dying, I tell you, to act this scene. If he's ready, I'm more than ready.

THE MANAGER [*shouting*]: But, my dear young lady, first of all, we must have the scene between you and this lady . . . [*Indicates* MADAME PACE.] Do you understand? . . .

THE STEP-DAUGHTER: Good Heavens! She's been telling me what you know already: that mamma's work is badly done again, that the material's ruined; and that if I want her to continue to help us in our misery I must be patient . . .

MADAME PACE [*coming forward with an air of great importance*]: Yes indeed, sir, I no wanta take advantage of her, I no wanta be hard . . .

> [Note. MADAME PACE *is supposed to talk in a jargon half Italian, half English.*]

THE MANAGER [*alarmed*]: What? What? She talks like that? [*The* ACTORS *burst out laughing again.*]

THE STEP-DAUGHTER [*also laughing*]: Yes yes, that's the way she talks, half English, half Italian! Most comical it is!

MADAME PACE: Itta seem not verra polite gentlemen laugha atta me eef I trya best speaka English.

THE MANAGER: *Diamine!* Of course! Of course! Let her talk like that! Just what we want. Talk just like that, Madame, if you please! The effect will be certain. Exactly what was wanted to put a little comic relief into the crudity of the situation. Of course she talks like that! Magnificent!

THE STEP-DAUGHTER: Magnificent? Certainly! When certain suggestions are made to one in language of that kind, the effect is certain, since it seems almost a joke. One feels inclined to laugh when one hears her talk about an "old signore" "who wanta talka nicely with you." Nice old signore, eh, Madame?

MADAME PACE: Not so old my dear, not so old! And even if you no lika him, he won't make any scandal!

THE MOTHER [*jumping up amid the amazement and consternation of the actors who had not been noticing her. They move to restrain her*]: You old devil! You murderess!

THE STEP-DAUGHTER [*running over to calm her* MOTHER]: Calm yourself, Mother, calm yourself! Please don't . . .

THE FATHER [*going to her also at the same time*]: Calm yourself! Don't get excited! Sit down now!

THE MOTHER: Well then, take that woman away out of my sight!

THE STEP-DAUGHTER [to MANAGER]: It is impossible for my mother to remain here.

THE FATHER [to MANAGER]: They can't be here together. And for this reason, you see: that woman there was not with us when we came . . . If they are on together, the whole thing is given away inevitably, as you see.

THE MANAGER: It doesn't matter. This is only a first rough sketch—just to get an idea of the various points of the scene, even confusedly . . . [Turning to the MOTHER and leading her to her chair.] Come along, my dear lady, sit down now, and let's get on with the scene . . .

[Meanwhile, the STEP-DAUGHTER, coming forward again, turns to MADAME PACE.]

THE STEP-DAUGHTER: Come on, Madame, come on!

MADAME PACE [offended]: No, no, grazie. I not do anything witha your mother present.

THE STEP-DAUGHTER: Nonsense! Introduce this "old signore" who wants to talk nicely to me. [Addressing the COMPANY imperiously.] We've got to do this scene one way or another, haven't we? Come on! [To MADAME PACE.] you can go!

MADAME PACE: Ah yes! I go'way! I go'way! Certainly! [Exits furious.]

THE STEP-DAUGHTER [to the FATHER]: Now you make your entry. No, you needn't go over here. Come here. Let's suppose you've already come in. Like that, yes! I'm here with bowed head, modest like. Come on! Out with your voice! Say "Good morning, Miss" in that peculiar tone, that special tone . . .

THE MANAGER: Excuse me, but are you the Manager, or am I? [To the FATHER, who looks undecided and perplexed.] Get on with it, man! Go down there to the back of the stage. You needn't go off. Then come right forward here.

[The FATHER does as he is told, looking troubled and perplexed at first. But as soon as he begins to move, the reality of the action affects him, and he begins to smile and to be more natural. The ACTORS watch intently.]

THE MANAGER [sotto voce, quickly to the PROMPTER in his box]: Ready! ready? Get ready to write now.

THE FATHER [coming forward and speaking in a different tone]: Good afternoon, Miss!

THE STEP-DAUGHTER [head bowed down slightly, with restrained disgust]: Good afternoon!

THE FATHER [looks under hat which partly covers her face. Perceiving she is very young, he makes an exclamation, partly of surprise, partly of fear lest he compromise himself in a risky adventure]: Ah . . . but . . . ah . . . I say . . . this is not the first time that you have come here, is it?

THE STEP-DAUGHTER [modestly]: No sir.

THE FATHER: You've been here before, eh? [Then seeing her nod agreement.] More than once? [Waits for her to answer, looks under her hat, smiles, and then says.] Well then, there's no need to be so shy, is there? May I take off your hat?

THE STEP-DAUGHTER [anticipating him and with veiled disgust]: No sir . . . I'll do it myself. [Takes it off quickly.]

[The MOTHER, who watches the progress of the scene with the SON and the other two children who cling to her, is on thorns; and follows with varying expressions of sorrow, indignation, anxiety, and horror the words and actions of the other two. From time to time she hides her face in her hands and sobs.]

THE MOTHER: Oh, my God, my God!

THE FATHER [playing his part with a touch of gallantry]: Give it to me! I'll put it down. [Takes hat from her hands.] But a dear little head like yours ought to have a smarter hat. Come and help me choose one from the stock, won't you?

L'INGÉNUE [interrupting]: I say . . . those are our hats you know.

THE MANAGER [furious]: Silence! silence! Don't try and be funny, if you please . . . We're playing the scene now I'd have you notice. [To the STEP-DAUGHTER.] Begin again, please!

THE STEP-DAUGHTER [continuing]: No thank you, sir.

THE FATHER: Oh, come now. Don't talk like that. You must take it. I shall be upset if you don't. There are some lovely little hats here; and then—Madame will be pleased. She expects it, anyway, you know.

THE STEP-DAUGHTER: No, no! I couldn't wear it!

THE FATHER: Oh, you're thinking about what they'd say at home if they saw you come in with a new hat? My dear girl, there's always a way round these little matters, you know.

THE STEP-DAUGHTER [all keyed up]: No, it's not that. I couldn't wear it because I am . . . as you see . . . you might have noticed . . . [Showing her black dress.]

THE FATHER: . . . in mourning! Of course: I beg your pardon: I'm frightfully sorry . . .

THE STEP-DAUGHTER [forcing herself to conquer her indignation and nausea]: Stop! Stop! It's I who must thank you. There's no need for you to feel mortified or specially sorry. Don't think any more of

what I've said. [*Tries to smile.*] I must forget that am dressed
so . . .

THE MANAGER [*interrupting and turning to the* PROMPTER]: Stop a
minute! Stop! Don't write that down. Cut out that last bit. [*Then
to the* FATHER *and* STEP-DAUGHTER.] Fine! it's going fine! [*To the*
FATHER *only.*] And now you can go on as we arranged. [*To the*
ACTORS.] Pretty good that scene, where he offers her the hat, eh?

THE STEP-DAUGHTER: The best's coming now. Why can't we go on?

THE MANAGER: Have a little patience! [*To the* ACTORS.] Of course, it
must be treated rather lightly.

LEADING MAN: Still, with a bit of go in it!

LEADING LADY: Of course! It's easy enough! [*To* LEADING MAN.] Shall
you and I try it now?

LEADING MAN: Why yes! I'll prepare my entrance. [*Exit in order to
make his entrance.*]

THE MANAGER [*to* LEADING LADY]: See here! The scene between you
and Madame Pace is finished. I'll have it written out properly after.
You remain here . . . oh, where are you going?

LEADING LADY: One minute. I want to put my hat on again. [*Goes over
to hat-rack and puts her hat on her head.*]

THE MANAGER: Good! You stay here with your head bowed down a
bit.

THE STEP-DAUGHTER: But she isn't dressed in black.

LEADING LADY: But I shall be, and much more effectively than you.

THE MANAGER [*to* STEP-DAUGHTER]: Be quiet please, and watch! You'll
be able to learn something. [*Clapping his hands.*] Come on! come
on! Entrance, please!

[*The door at rear of stage opens, and the* LEADING MAN *enters
with the lively manner of an old gallant. The rendering of the
scene by the* ACTORS *from the very first words is seen to be
quite a different thing, though it has not in any way the air of
a parody. Naturally, the* STEP-DAUGHTER *and the* FATHER, *not
being able to recognize themselves in the* LEADING LADY *and
the* LEADING MAN, *who deliver their words in different tones
and with a different psychology, express, sometimes with
smiles, sometimes with gestures, the impression they receive.*]

LEADING MAN: Good afternoon, Miss . . .

THE FATHER [*at once unable to contain himself*]: No! no!

[*The* STEP-DAUGHTER *noticing the way the* LEADING MAN
enters, bursts out laughing.]

THE MANAGER [*furious*]: Silence! And you please just stop that laughing. If we go on like this, we shall never finish.

THE STEP-DAUGHTER: Forgive me, sir, but it's natural enough. This lady [*Indicating* LEADING LADY.] stands there still; but if she is supposed to be me, I can assure you that if I heard anyone say "Good afternoon" in that manner and in that tone, I should burst out laughing as I did.

THE FATHER: Yes, yes, the manner, the tone . . .

THE MANAGER: Nonsense! Rubbish! Stand aside and let me see the action.

LEADING MAN: If I've got to represent an old fellow who's coming into a house of an equivocal character . . .

THE MANAGER: Don't listen to them, for Heaven's sake! Do it again! It goes fine. [*Waiting for the* ACTORS *to begin again.*] Well?

LEADING MAN: Good afternoon, Miss.

LEADING LADY: Good afternoon.

LEADING MAN [*imitating the gesture of the* FATHER *when he looked under the hat, and then expressing quite clearly first satisfaction and then fear*]: Ah, but . . . I say . . . this is not the first time that you have come here, is it?

THE MANAGER: Good, but not quite so heavily. Like this. [*Acts himself.*] "This isn't the first time that you have come here" . . . [*To* LEADING LADY.] And you say: "No, sir."

LEADING LADY: No, sir.

LEADING MAN: You've been here before, more than once.

THE MANAGER: No, no, stop! Let her nod "yes" first. "You've been here before, eh?" [*The* LEADING LADY *lifts up her head slightly and closes her eyes as though in disgust. Then she inclines her head twice.*]

THE STEP-DAUGHTER [*unable to contain herself*]: Oh my God! [*Puts a hand to her mouth to prevent herself from laughing.*]

THE MANAGER [*turning round*]: What's the matter?

THE STEP-DAUGHTER: Nothing, nothing!

THE MANAGER [*to* LEADING MAN]: Go on!

LEADING MAN: You've been here before, eh? Well then, there's no need to be shy, is there? May I take off your hat?

[*The* LEADING MAN *says this last speech in such a tone and with such gestures that the* STEP-DAUGHTER, *though she has her hand to her mouth, cannot keep from laughing.*]

LEADING LADY [*indignant*]: I'm not going to stop here to be made a fool of by that woman there.

LEADING MAN: Neither am I! I'm through with it!

THE MANAGER [*shouting to* STEP-DAUGHTER]: Silence! for once and all, I tell you!

THE STEP-DAUGHTER: Forgive me! forgive me!

THE MANAGER: You haven't any manners: that's what it is! You go too far.

THE FATHER [endeavouring to intervene]: Yes, it's true, but excuse her . . .

THE MANAGER: Excuse what? It's absolutely disgusting.

THE FATHER: Yes, sir, but believe me, it has such a strange effect when . . .

THE MANAGER: Strange? Why strange? Where is it strange?

THE FATHER: No, sir; I admire your actors—this gentleman here, this lady; but they are certainly not us!

THE MANAGER: I should hope not. Evidently they cannot be you, if they are actors.

THE FATHER: Just so: actors! Both of them act our parts exceedingly well. But, believe me, it produces quite a different effect on us. They want to be us, but they aren't, all the same.

THE MANAGER: What is it then anyway?

THE FATHER: Something that is . . . that is theirs—and no longer ours . . .

THE MANAGER: But naturally, inevitably. I've told you so already.

THE FATHER: Yes, I understand . . . I understand . . .

THE MANAGER: Well then, let's have no more of it! [Turning to the ACTORS.] We'll have the rehearsals by ourselves, afterwards, in the ordinary way. I never could stand rehearsing with the author present. He's never satisfied! [Turning to FATHER and STEP-DAUGHTER.] Come on! Let's get on with it again; and try and see if you can't keep from laughing.

THE STEP-DAUGHTER: Oh, I shan't laugh any more. There's a nice little bit coming for me now: you'll see.

THE MANAGER: Well then: when she says "Don't think any more of what I've said. I must forget, etc.," you [Addressing the FATHER.] come in sharp with "I understand, I understand"; and then you ask her . . .

THE STEP-DAUGHTER [interrupting]: What?

THE MANAGER: Why she is in mourning.

THE STEP-DAUGHTER: Not at all! See here: when I told him that it was useless for me to be thinking about my wearing mourning, do you know how he answered me? "Ah well," he said, "then let's take off this little frock."

THE MANAGER: Great! Just what we want, to make a riot in the theatre!

THE STEP-DAUGHTER: But it's the truth!

THE MANAGER: What does that matter? Acting is our business here. Truth up to a certain point, but no further.

THE STEP-DAUGHTER: What do you want to do then?

THE MANAGER: You'll see, you'll see! Leave it to me.

THE STEP-DAUGHTER: No sir! What you want to do is to piece together a little romantic sentimental scene out of my disgust, out of all the reasons, each more cruel and viler than the other, why I am what I am. He is to ask me why I'm in mourning; and I'm to answer with tears in my eyes, that it is just two months since papa died. No sir, no! He's got to say to me; as he did say: "Well, let's take off this little dress at once." And I; with my two months' mourning in my heart, went there behind that screen, and with these fingers tingling with shame . . .

THE MANAGER [running his hands through his hair]: For Heaven's sake! What are you saying?

THE STEP-DAUGHTER [crying out excitedly]: The truth! The truth!

THE MANAGER: It may be. I don't deny it, and I can understand all your horror; but you must surely see that you can't have this kind of thing on the stage. It won't go.

THE STEP-DAUGHTER: Not possible, eh? Very well! I'm much obliged to you—but I'm off!

THE MANAGER: Now be reasonable! Don't lose your temper!

THE STEP-DAUGHTER: I won't stop here! I won't! I can see you've fixed it all up with him in your office. All this talk about what is possible for the stage . . . I understand! He wants to get at his complicated "cerebral drama," to have his famous remorses and torments acted; but I want to act my part, my part!

THE MANAGER [annoyed, shaking his shoulders]: Ah! Just your part! But, if you will pardon me, there are other parts than yours: His [Indicating the FATHER.] and hers! [Indicating the MOTHER.] On the stage you can't have a character becoming too prominent and overshadowing all the others. The thing is to pack them all into a neat little framework and then act what is actable. I am aware of the fact that everyone has his own interior life which he wants very much to put forward. But the difficulty lies in this fact: to set out just so much as is necessary for the stage, taking the other characters into consideration, and at the same time hint at the unrevealed interior life of each. I am willing to admit, my dear young lady, that from your point of view it would be a fine idea if each character could tell the public all his troubles in a nice monologue or a regular one hour lecture. [Good humoredly.] You must restrain yourself, my dear, and in your own interest, too; because this fury of yours, this exaggerated disgust you show, may make a bad impression, you know. After you have confessed to me that there were others before him at Madame Pace's and more than once . . .

THE STEP-DAUGHTER [*bowing her head, impressed*]: It's true. But remember those others mean him for me all the same.

THE MANAGER [*not understanding*]: What? The others? What do you mean?

THE STEP-DAUGHTER: For one who has gone wrong, sir, he who was responsible for the first fault is responsible for all that follow. He is responsible for my faults, was, even before I was born. Look at him, and see if it isn't true!

THE MANAGER: Well, well! And does the weight of so much responsibility seem nothing to you? Give him a chance to act it, to get it over!

THE STEP-DAUGHTER: How? How can he act all his "noble remorses," all his "moral torments," if you want to spare him the horror of being discovered one day—after he had asked her what he did ask her—in the arms of her, that already fallen woman, that child, sir, that child he used to watch come out of school? [*She is moved.*]

[*The* MOTHER *at this point is overcome with emotion, and breaks out into a fit of crying.* ALL *are touched. A long pause.*]

THE STEP-DAUGHTER [*as soon as the* MOTHER *becomes a little quieter, adds resolutely and gravely*]: At present, we are unknown to the public. Tomorrow, you will act us as you wish, treating us in your own manner. But do you really want to see drama, do you want to see it flash out as it really did?

THE MANAGER: Of course! That's just what I do want, so I can use as much of it as possible.

THE STEP-DAUGHTER: Well then, ask that Mother there to leave us.

THE MOTHER [*changing her low plaint into a sharp cry*]: No! No! Don't permit it, sir, don't permit it!

THE MANAGER: But it's only to try it.

THE MOTHER: I can't bear it. I can't.

THE MANAGER: But since it has happened already . . . I don't understand!

THE MOTHER: It's taking place now. It happens all the time. My torment isn't a pretended one. I live and feel every minute of my torture. Those two children there—have you heard them speak? They can't speak any more. They cling to me to keep up my torment actual and vivid for me. But for themselves, they do not exist, they aren't any more. And she [*Indicating the* STEP-DAUGHTER.] has run away, she has left me, and is lost. If I now see her here before me, it is only to renew for me the tortures I have suffered for her too.

THE FATHER: The eternal moment! She [*Indicating the* STEP-DAUGH-TER.] is here to catch me, fix me, and hold me eternally in the stocks for that one fleeting and shameful moment of my life. She can't give it up! And you sir, cannot either fairly spare me it.

THE MANAGER: I never said I didn't want to act it. It will form, as a matter of fact, the nucleus of the whole first act right up to her surprise. [*Indicates the* MOTHER.]

THE FATHER: Just so! This is my punishment: the passion in all of us that must culminate in her final cry.

THE STEP-DAUGHTER: I can hear it still in my ears. It's driven me mad, that cry!—You can put me on as you like; it doesn't matter. Fully dressed, if you like—provided I have at least the arm bare; because, standing like this [*She goes close to the* FATHER *and leans her head on his breast.*] with my head so, and my arms round his neck, I saw a vein pulsing in my arm here; and then, as if that live vein had awakened disgust in me, I closed my eyes like this, and let my head sink on his breast. [*Turning to the* MOTHER.] Cry out mother! Cry out! [*Buries head in* FATHER's *breast, and with her shoulders raised as if to prevent her hearing the cry, adds in tones of intense emotion.*] Cry out as you did then!

THE MOTHER [*coming forward to separate them*]: No! My daughter, my daughter! [*And after having pulled her away from him.*] You brute! you brute! She is my daughter! Don't you see she's my daughter?

THE MANAGER [*walking backwards towards footlights*]: Fine! Fine! Damned good! And then, of course—curtain!

THE FATHER [*going towards him excitedly*]: Yes, of course, because that's the way it really happened.

THE MANAGER [*convinced and pleased*]: Oh, yes, no doubt about it. Curtain here, curtain!

[*At the reiterated cry of the* MANAGER, *the* MACHINIST *lets the curtain down, leaving the* MANAGER *and the* FATHER *in front of it before the footlights.*]

THE MANAGER: The darned idiot! I said "curtain" to show the act should end there, and he goes and lets it down in earnest. [*To the* FATHER, *while he pulls the curtain back to go on to the stage again.*] Yes, yes, it's all right. Effect certain! That's the right ending. I'll guarantee the first act at any rate.

✤ *Act III*

When the curtain goes up again, it is seen that the stage hands have shifted the bit of scenery used in the last part, and have rigged up instead at the back of the stage a drop, with some trees, and one or two wings. A portion of a fountain basin is visible. The MOTHER is sitting on the right with the two children by her side. The SON is on the same side, but away from the others. He seems bored, angry, and full of shame. The FATHER and the STEP-DAUGHTER are also seated towards the right front. On the other side (left) are the ACTORS, much in the positions they occupied before the curtain was lowered. Only the MANAGER is standing up in the middle of the stage, with his hand closed over his mouth in the act of meditating.

THE MANAGER [*shaking his shoulders after a brief pause*]: Ah yes: the second act! Leave it to me, leave it all to me as we arranged, and you'll see! It'll go fine!

THE STEP-DAUGHTER: Our entry into his house [*Indicates* FATHER.] in spite of him . . . [*Indicates the* SON.]

THE MANAGER [*out of patience*]: Leave it to me, I tell you!

THE STEP-DAUGHTER: Do let it be clear, at any rate, that it is in spite of my wishes.

THE MOTHER [*from her corner, shaking her head*]: For all the good that's come of it . . .

THE STEP-DAUGHTER [*turning towards her quickly*]: It doesn't matter. The more harm done us, the more remorse for him.

THE MANAGER [*impatiently*]: I understand! Good Heavens! I understand! I'm taking it into account.

THE MOTHER [*supplicatingly*]: I beg you, sir, to let it appear quite plain that for conscience' sake I did try in every way . . .

THE STEP-DAUGHTER [*interrupting indignantly and continuing for the* MOTHER]: . . . to pacify me, to dissuade me from spiting him. [*To* MANAGER.] Do as she wants: satisfy her, because it is true! I enjoy it immensely. Anyhow, as you can see, the meeker she is, the more she tries to get at his heart, the more distant and aloof does he become.

THE MANAGER: Are we going to begin this second act or not?

THE STEP-DAUGHTER: I'm not going to talk any more now. But I must tell you this: you can't have the whole action take place in the garden, as you suggest. It isn't possible!

THE MANAGER: Why not?

THE STEP-DAUGHTER: Because he [*Indicates the* SON *again*.] is always shut up alone in his room. And then there's all the part of that poor dazed-looking boy there which takes place indoors.

THE MANAGER: Maybe! On the other hand, you will understand—we can't change scenes three or four times in one act.

THE LEADING MAN: They used to once.

THE MANAGER: Yes, when the public was up to the level of that child there.

THE LEADING LADY: It makes the illusion easier.

THE FATHER [irritated]: The illusion! For Heaven's sake, don't say illusion. Please don't use that word, which is particularly painful for us.

THE MANAGER [astounded]: And why, if you please?

THE FATHER: It's painful, cruel, really cruel; and you ought to understand that.

THE MANAGER: But why? What ought we to say then? The illusion, I tell you, sir, which we've got to create for the audience . . .

THE LEADING MAN: With our acting.

THE MANAGER: The illusion of a reality.

THE FATHER: I understand; but you, perhaps, do not understand us. Forgive me! You see . . . here for you and your actors, the thing is only—and rightly so . . . a kind of game . . .

THE LEADING LADY [interrupting indignantly]: A game! We're not children here, if you please! We are serious actors.

THE FATHER: I don't deny it. What I mean is the game, or play, of your art, which has to give, as the gentleman says, a perfect illusion of reality.

THE MANAGER: Precisely—!

THE FATHER: Now, if you consider the fact that we [Indicates himself and the other five CHARACTERS.], as we are, have no other reality outside of this illusion . . .

THE MANAGER [astonished, looking at his ACTORS, who are also amazed]: And what does that mean?

THE FATHER [after watching them for a moment with a wan smile]: As I say, sir, that which is a game of art for you is our sole reality. [Brief pause. He goes a step or two nearer the MANAGER and adds.] But not only for us, you know, by the way. Just you think it over well. [Looks him in the eyes.] Can you tell me who you are?

THE MANAGER [perplexed, half smiling]: What? Who am I? I am myself.

THE FATHER: And if I were to tell you that that isn't true, because you and I . . .?

THE MANAGER: I should say you were mad—! [The ACTORS laugh.]

THE FATHER: You're quite right to laugh: because we are all making believe here. [To MANAGER.] And you can therefore object that it's only for a joke that that gentleman there [Indicates the LEADING MAN.], who naturally is himself, has to be me, who am on the contrary myself—this thing you see here. You see I've caught you in a trap! [The ACTORS laugh.]

THE MANAGER [annoyed]: But we've had all this over once before. Do you want to begin again?

THE FATHER: No, no! That wasn't my meaning! In fact, I should like to request you to abandon this game of art [Looking at the LEADING LADY as if anticipating her.] which you are accustomed to play here with your actors, and to ask you seriously once again: who are you?

THE MANAGER [astonished and irritated, turning to his ACTORS]: If this fellow here hasn't got a nerve! A man who calls himself a character comes and asks me who I am!

THE FATHER [with dignity, but not offended]: A character, sir, may always ask a man who he is. Because a character has really a life of his own, marked with his especial characteristics; for which reason he is always "somebody." But a man—I'm not speaking of you now—may very well be "nobody."

THE MANAGER: Yes, but you are asking these questions of me, the boss, the manager! Do you understand?

THE FATHER: But only in order to know if you, as you really are now, see yourself as you once were with all the illusions that were yours then, with all the things both inside and outside of you as they seemed to you—as they were then indeed for you. Well, sir, if you think of all those illusions that mean nothing to you now, of all those things which don't even seem to you to exist any more, while once they were for you, don't you feel that—I won't say these boards —but the very earth under your feet is sinking away from you when you reflect that in the same way this you as you feel it today—all this present reality of yours—is fated to seem a mere illusion to you tomorrow?

THE MANAGER [without having understood much, but astonished by the specious argument]: Well, well! And where does all this take us anyway?

THE FATHER: Oh, nowhere! It's only to show you that if we [Indicating the CHARACTERS.] have no other reality beyond the illusion, you too must not count overmuch on your reality as you feel it today, since, like that of yesterday, it may prove an illusion for you tomorrow.

THE MANAGER [determining to make fun of him]: Ah, excellent! Then you'll be saying next that you, with this comedy of yours that you brought here to act, are truer and more real than I am.

THE FATHER [*with the greatest seriousness*]: But of course; without doubt!

THE MANAGER: Ah, really?

THE FATHER: Why, I thought you'd understand that from the beginning.

THE MANAGER: More real than I?

THE FATHER: If your reality can change from one day to another . . .

THE MANAGER: But everyone knows it can change. It is always changing, the same as anyone else's.

THE FATHER [*with a cry*]: No, sir, not ours! Look here! That is the very difference! Our reality doesn't change: it can't change! It can't be other than what it is, because it is already fixed for ever. It's terrible. Ours is an immutable reality which should make you shudder when you approach us if you are really conscious of the fact that your reality is a mere transitory and fleeting illusion, taking this form today and that tomorrow, according to the conditions, according to your will, your sentiments, which in turn are controlled by an intellect that shows them to you today in one manner and tomorrow . . . who knows how? . . . Illusions of reality represented in this fatuous comedy of life that never ends, nor can ever end! Because if tomorrow it were to end . . . then why, all would be finished.

THE MANAGER: Oh for God's sake, will you at *least* finish with this philosophizing and let us try and shape this comedy which you yourself have brought me here? You argue and philosophize a bit too much, my dear sir. You know you seem to me almost, almost . . . [*Stops and looks him over from head to foot.*] Ah, by the way, I think you introduced yourself to me as a—what shall . . . we say—a "character," created by an author who did not afterward care to make a drama of his own creations.

THE FATHER: It is the simple truth, sir.

THE MANAGER: Nonsense! Cut that out, please! None of us believes it, because it isn't a thing, as you must recognize yourself, which one can believe seriously. If you want to know, it seems to me you are trying to imitate the manner of a certain author whom I heartily detest—I warn you—although I have unfortunately bound myself to put on one of his works. As a matter of fact, I was just starting to rehearse it, when you arrived. [*Turning to the ACTORS.*] And this is what we've gained—out of the frying-pan into the fire!

THE FATHER: I don't know to what author you may be alluding, but believe me I feel what I think; and I seem to be philosophizing only for those who do not think what they feel, because they blind themselves with their own sentiment. I know that for many people this self-blinding seems much more "human"; but the contrary is really true. For man never reasons so much and becomes so introspective as when he suffers; since he is anxious to get at the cause of his sufferings, to learn who has produced them, and whether it is just or unjust that he should have to bear them. On the other hand, when he is happy, he takes his happiness as it comes and doesn't analyze it, just as if happiness were his right. The animals suffer without reasoning about their sufferings. But take the case of a man who suffers and begins to reason about it. Oh no! it can't be allowed! Let him suffer like an animal, and then—ah yet, he is "human"!

THE MANAGER: Look here! Look here! You're off again, philosophizing worse than ever.

THE FATHER: Because I suffer, sir! I'm not philosophizing: I'm crying aloud the reason of my sufferings.

THE MANAGER [makes brusque movement as he is taken with a new idea]: I should like to know if anyone has ever heard of a character who gets right out of his part and perorates and speechifies as you do. Have you ever heard of a case? I haven't.

THE FATHER: You have never met such a case, sir, because authors, as a rule, hide the labour of their creations. When the characters are really alive before their author, the latter does nothing but follow them in their action, in their words, in the situations which they suggest to him; and he has to will them the way they will themselves —for there's trouble if he doesn't. When a character is born, he acquires at once such an independence, even of his own author, that he can be imagined by everybody even in many other situations where the author never dreamed of placing him; and so he acquires for himself a meaning which the author never thought of giving him.

THE MANAGER: Yes, yes, I know this.

THE FATHER: What is there then to marvel at in us? Imagine such a misfortune for characters as I have described to you: to be born of an author's fantasy, and be denied life by him; and then answer me if these characters left alive, and yet without life, weren't right in doing what they did do and are doing now, after they have attempted everything in their power to persuade him to give them their stage life. We've all tried him in turn, I, she [Indicating the STEP-DAUGHTER.] and she. [Indicating the MOTHER.]

THE STEP-DAUGHTER: It's true. I too have sought to tempt him, many, many times, when he has been sitting at his writing table, feeling a bit melancholy, at the twilight hour. He would sit in his armchair too lazy to switch on the light, and all the shadows that crept into his room were full of our presence coming to tempt him. [*As if she saw herself still there by the writing table, and was annoyed by the presence of the* ACTORS.] Oh, if you would only go away, go away and leave us alone—mother here with that son of hers—I wish that Child—that Boy there always alone—and then I wish him [*Just hints at the* FATHER.]—and then I alone, alone . . . in those shadows! [*Makes a sudden movement as if in the vision she has of herself illuminating those shadows she wanted to seize hold of herself.*] Ah! my life! my life! Oh, what scenes we proposed to him—and I tempted him more than any of the others!

THE FATHER: Maybe. But perhaps it was your fault that he refused to give us life: because you were too insistent, too troublesome.

THE STEP-DAUGHTER: Nonsense! Didn't he make me so himself? [*Goes close to the* MANAGER *to tell him as if in confidence.*] In my opinion he abandoned us in a fit of depression, of disgust for the ordinary theatre as the public knows it and likes it.

THE SON: Exactly what it was, sir; exactly that!

THE FATHER: Not at all! Don't believe it for a minute. Listen to me! You'll be doing quite right to modify, as you suggest, the excesses both of this girl here, who wants to do too much, and of this young man, who won't do anything at all.

THE SON: No, nothing!

THE MANAGER: You too get over the mark occasionally, my dear sir, if I may say so.

THE FATHER: I? When? Where?

THE MANAGER: Always! Continuously! Then there's this insistence of yours in trying to make us believe you are a character. And then too, you must really argue and philosophize less, you know, much less.

THE FATHER: Well, if you want to take away from me the possibility of representing the torment of my spirit which never gives me peace, you will be suppressing me: that's all. Every true man, sir, who is a little above the level of the beasts and plants does not live for the sake of living, without knowing how to live; but he lives so as to give a meaning and a value of his own to life. For me this is everything. I cannot give up this, just to represent a mere fact as she [*Indicating the* STEP-DAUGHTER.] wants. It's all very well for her, since her "vendetta" lies in the "fact." I'm not going to do it. It destroys my raison d'être!

THE MANAGER: Your *raison d'être*! Oh, we're going ahead fine! First she starts off, and then you jump in. At this rate, we'll never finish.

THE FATHER: Now, don't be offended! Have it your way—provided, however, that within the limits of the parts you assign us each one's sacrifice isn't too great.

THE MANAGER: You've got to understand that you can't go on arguing at your own pleasure. Drama is action, sir, action and not confounded philosophy.

THE FATHER: All right. I'll do just as much arguing and philosophizing as everybody does when he is considering his own torments.

THE MANAGER: If the drama permits! But for Heaven's sake, man, let's get along and come to the scene.

THE STEP-DAUGHTER: It seems to me we've got too much action with our coming into his house. [*Indicating* FATHER.] You said, before, you couldn't change the scene every five minutes.

THE MANAGER: Of course not. What we've got to do is to combine and group up all the facts in one simultaneous, close-knit, action. We can't have it as you want, with your little brother wandering like a ghost from room to room, hiding behind doors and meditating a project which—what did you say it did to him?

THE STEP-DAUGHTER: Consumes him, sir, wastes him away!

THE MANAGER: Well, it may be. And then at the same time, you want the little girl there to be playing in the garden . . . one in the house, and the other in the garden: isn't that it?

THE STEP-DAUGHTER: Yes, in the sun, in the sun! That is my only pleasure: to see her happy and careless in the garden after the misery and squalor of the horrible room where we all four slept together. And I had to sleep with her—I, do you understand?—with my vile contaminated body next to hers; with her folding me fast in her loving little arms. In the garden, whenever she spied me, she would run to take me by the hand. She didn't care for the big flowers, only the little ones; and she loved to show me them and pet me.

THE MANAGER: Well then, we'll have it in the garden. Everything shall happen in the garden; and we'll group the other scenes there. [*Calls a* STAGE HAND.] Here, a backcloth with trees and something to do as a fountain basin. [*Turning round to look at the back of the stage.*] Ah, you've fixed it up. Good! [*To* STEP-DAUGHTER.] This is just to give an idea, of course. The Boy, instead of hiding behind the doors, will wander about here in the garden, hiding behind the trees. But it's going to be rather difficult to find a child to do that scene with you where she shows you the flowers. [*Turning to the* BOY.] Come forward a little, will you please? Let's try it now! Come along! come along! [*Then seeing him come shyly forward, full of fear and looking lost.*] It's a nice business, this lad here. What's the matter with him? We'll have to give him a word or two to say. [Goes close to him, puts a hand on his shoulders, and leads him behind one of the trees.] Come on! come on! Let me see you a little! Hide here . . . yes, like that. Try and show your head just a little as if you were looking for someone . . . [Goes back to observe the effect, when the BOY at once goes through the action.] Excellent! fine! [Turning to STEP-DAUGHTER.] Suppose the little girl there were to surprise him as he looks round, and run over to him, so we could give him a word or two to say?

THE STEP-DAUGHTER: It's useless to hope he will speak, as long as that fellow there is here . . . [Indicates the SON.] You must send him away first.

THE SON [jumping up]: Delighted! Delighted! I don't ask for anything better. [Begins to move away.]

THE MANAGER [at once stopping him]: No! No! Where are you going? Wait a bit!

[THE MOTHER gets up alarmed and terrified at the thought that he is really about to go away. Instinctively she lifts her arms to prevent him, without, however, leaving her seat.]

THE SON [to MANAGER who stops him]: I've got nothing to do with this affair. Let me go please! Let me go!

THE MANAGER: What do you mean by saying you've got nothing to do with this?

THE STEP-DAUGHTER [calmly, with irony]: Don't bother to stop him: he won't go away.

THE FATHER: He has to act the terrible scene in the garden with his mother.

THE SON [suddenly resolute and with dignity]: I shall act nothing at all. I've said so from the very beginning. [To the MANAGER.] Let me go!

THE STEP-DAUGHTER [going over to the MANAGER]: Allow me? [Puts down the MANAGER's arm which is restraining the SON.] Well, go away then, if you want to! [The SON looks at her with contempt and hatred. She laughs and says.] You see, he can't, he can't go away! He is obliged to stay here, indissolubly bound to the chain. If I, who fly off when that happens which has to happen, because I can't bear him—if I am still here and support that face and expression of his, you can well imagine that he is unable to move. He has to remain here, has to stop with that nice father of his, and that mother whose only son he is. [Turning to the MOTHER.] Come on, mother, come along! [Turning to MANAGER to indicate her.] You see, she was getting up to keep him back. [To the MOTHER, beckoning her with her hand.] Come on! come on! [*Then to* MANAGER.] You can imagine how little she wants to show these actors of yours what she really feels; but so eager is she to get near him that . . . There, you see? She is willing to act her part. [*And in fact, the* MOTHER *approaches him; and as soon as the* STEP-DAUGHTER *has finished speaking, opens her arms to signify that she consents.*]

THE SON [*suddenly*]: No! no! If I can't go away, then I'll stop here; but I repeat: I act nothing!

THE FATHER [*to* MANAGER *excitedly*]: You can force him, sir.

THE SON: Nobody can force me.

THE FATHER: I can.

THE STEP-DAUGHTER: Wait a minute, wait . . . First of all, the baby has to go to the fountain . . . [*Runs to take the* CHILD *and leads her to the fountain.*]

THE MANAGER: Yes, yes of course; that's it. Both at the same time.

[*The second* LADY LEAD *and the* JUVENILE LEAD *at this point separate themselves from the group of* ACTORS. *One watches the* MOTHER *attentively; the other moves about studying the movements and manner of the* SON *whom he will have to act.*]

THE SON [*to* MANAGER]: What do you mean by both at the same time? It isn't right. There was no scene between me and her. [*Indicates the* MOTHER.] Ask her how it was!

THE MOTHER: Yes, it's true. I had to come into his room . . .

THE SON: Into my room, do you understand? Nothing to do with the garden.

THE MANAGER: It doesn't matter. Haven't I told you we've got to group the action?

THE SON [*observing the* JUVENILE LEAD *studying him*]: What do you want?

THE JUVENILE LEAD: Nothing! I was just looking at you.

THE SON [*turning towards the second* LADY LEAD]: Ah! she's at it too: to re-act her part! [*Indicating the* MOTHER.]

THE MANAGER: Exactly! And it seems to me that you ought to be grateful to them for their interest.

THE SON: Yes, but haven't you yet perceived that it isn't possible to live in front of a mirror which not only freezes us with the image of ourselves, but throws our likeness back at us with a horrible grimace?

THE FATHER: That is true, absolutely true. You must see that.

THE MANAGER [*to second* LADY LEAD *and* JUVENILE LEAD]: He's right! Move away from them!

THE SON: Do as you like. I'm out of this!

THE MANAGER: Be quiet, you, will you? And let me hear your mother! [*To* MOTHER] You were saying you had entered . . .

THE MOTHER: Yes, into his room, because I couldn't stand it any longer. I went to empty my heart to him of all the anguish that tortures me . . . But as soon as he saw me come in . . .

THE SON: Nothing happened! There was no scene. I went away, that's all! I don't care for scenes!

THE MOTHER: It's true, true. That's how it was.

THE MANAGER: Well now, we've got to do this bit between you and him. It's indispensable.

THE MOTHER: I'm ready . . . when you are ready. If you could only find a chance for me to tell him what I feel here in my heart.

THE FATHER [*going to* SON *in a great rage*]: You'll do this for your mother, for your mother, do you understand?

THE SON [*quite determined*]: I do nothing!

THE FATHER [*taking hold of him and shaking him*]: For God's sake, do as I tell you! Don't you hear your mother asking you for a favor? Haven't you even got the guts to be a son?

THE SON [*taking hold of the* FATHER]: No! No! And for God's sake stop it, or else . . . [*General agitation. The* MOTHER, *frightened, tries to separate them.*]

THE MOTHER [*pleading*]: Please! please!

THE FATHER [*not leaving hold of the* SON]: You've got to obey, do you hear?

THE SON [*almost crying from rage*]: What does it mean, this madness you've got? [*They separate.*] Have you no decency, that you insist on showing everyone our shame? I won't do it! I won't! And I stand for the will of our author in this. He didn't want to put us on the stage, after all!

THE MANAGER: Man alive! You came here . . .

THE SON [*indicating* FATHER]: He did! I didn't!

THE MANAGER: Aren't you here now?

THE SON: It was his wish, and he dragged us along with him. He's told you not only the things that did happen, but also things that have never happened at all.

THE MANAGER: Well, tell me then what did happen. You went out of your room without saying a word?

THE SON: Without a word, so as to avoid a scene!

THE MANAGER: And then what did you do?

THE SON: Nothing . . . walking in the garden . . . [*Hesitates for a moment with expression of gloom.*]

THE MANAGER [*coming closer to him, interested by his extraordinary reserve*]: Well, well . . . walking in the garden . . .

THE SON [*exasperated*]. Why on earth do you insist? It's horrible! [*The* MOTHER *trembles, sobs, and looks towards the fountain.*]

THE MANAGER [*slowly observing the glance and turning towards the* SON *with increasing apprehension*]: The baby?

THE SON: There in the fountain . . .

THE FATHER [*pointing with tender pity to the* MOTHER]: She was following him at the moment . . .

THE MANAGER [*to the* SON *anxiously*]: And then you . . .

THE SON: I ran over to her; I was jumping in to drag her out when I saw something that froze my blood . . . the boy standing stock still, with eyes like a madman's, watching his little drowned sister, in the fountain! [*The* STEP-DAUGHTER *bends over the fountain to hide the* CHILD. *She sobs.*] Then . . . [*A revolver shot rings out behind the trees where the* BOY *is hidden.*]

THE MOTHER [*with a cry of terror runs over in that direction together with several of the* ACTORS *amid general confusion*]: My son! My son! [*Then amid the cries and exclamations one hears her voice.*] Help! Help!

THE MANAGER [*pushing the* ACTORS *aside while* THEY *lift up the* BOY *and carry him off.*]: Is he really wounded?

SOME ACTORS: He's dead! dead!

OTHER ACTORS: No, no, it's only make believe, it's only pretence!

THE FATHER [*with a terrible cry*]: Pretence? Reality, sir, reality!

THE MANAGER: Pretence? Reality? To hell with it all! Never in my life has such a thing happened to me. I've lost a whole day over these people, a whole day!

CURTAIN

🍁 *Preface to*

Six Characters in Search of an Author (1925)

It seems like yesterday but is actually many years ago that a nimble little maidservant entered the service of my art. However, she always comes fresh to the job.

She is called Fantasy.

A little puckish and malicious, if she likes to dress in black no one will wish to deny that she is often positively bizarre and no one will wish to believe that she always does everything in the same way and in earnest. She sticks her hand in her pocket, pulls out a cap and bells, sets it on her head, red as a cock's comb, and dashes away. Here today, there tomorrow. And she amuses herself by bringing to my house—since I derive stories and novels and plays from them—the most disgruntled tribe in the world, men, women, children, involved in strange adventures which they can find no way out of; thwarted in their plans; cheated in their hopes; with whom, in short, it is often torture to deal.

Well, this little maidservant of mine, Fantasy, several years ago, had the bad inspiration or ill-omened caprice to bring a family into my house. I wouldn't know where she fished them up or how, but, according to her, I could find in them the subject for a magnificent novel.

I found before me a man about fifty years old, in a dark jacket and light trousers, with a frowning air and ill-natured, mortified eyes; a poor woman in widow's weeds leading by one hand a little girl of four and by the other a boy of rather more than ten; a cheeky and "sexy" girl, also clad in black but with an equivocal and brazen pomp, all atremble with a lively, biting contempt for the mortified old man and for a young fellow of twenty who stood on one side closed in on himself as if he despised them all. In short, the six characters who are seen coming on stage at the beginning of the play. Now one of them and now another—often beating down one another—embarked on the sad story of their adventures, each shouting his own reasons, and projecting in my face his disordered passions, more or less as they do in the play to the unhappy Manager.

What author will be able to say how and why a character was born in his fantasy? The mystery of artistic creation is the same as that of birth. A woman who loves may desire to become a mother; but the desire by itself, however intense, cannot suffice. One day she will find herself a mother without having any precise intimation when it began. In the same way an artist imbibes very many germs of life and can never say how and why, at a certain moment, one of these vital germs inserts itself into his fantasy, there to become a living creature on a plane of life superior to the changeable existence of every day.

I can only say that, without having made any effort to seek them out, I found before me, alive—you could touch them and even hear them breathe —the six characters now seen on the stage. And they stayed there in my presence, each with his secret torment and all bound together by the one common origin and mutual entanglement of their affairs, while I had them enter the world of art, constructing from their persons, their passions, and their adventures a novel, a drama, or at least a story.

Born alive, they wished to live.

To me it was never enough to present a man or a woman and what is special and characteristic about them simply for the pleasure of presenting them; to narrate a particular affair, lively or sad, simply for the pleasure of narrating it; to describe a landscape simply for the pleasure of describing it.

There are some writers (and not a few) who do feel this pleasure and, satisfied, ask no more. They are, to speak more precisely, historical writers.

But there are others who, beyond such pleasure, feel a more profound spiritual need on whose account they admit only figures, affairs, landscapes which have been soaked, so to speak, in a particular sense of life and acquire from it a universal value. These are, more precisely, philosophical writers.

I have the misfortune to belong to these last.

I hate symbolic art in which the presentation loses all spontaneous movement in order to become a machine, an allegory—a vain and misconceived effort because the very fact of giving an allegorical sense to a presentation clearly shows that we have to do with a fable which by itself has no truth either fantastic or direct; it was made for the demonstration of some moral truth. The spiritual need I speak of cannot be satisfied—or seldom, and that to the end of a superior irony, as for example in Ariosto—by such allegorical symbolism. This latter starts from a concept, and from a concept which creates or tries to create for itself an image. The former on the other hand seeks in the image—which must remain alive and free throughout—a meaning to give it value.

Now, however much I sought, I did not succeed in uncovering this meaning in the six characters. And I concluded therefore that it was no use making them live.

I thought to myself: "I have already afflicted my readers with hundreds and hundreds of stories. Why should I afflict them now by narrating the sad entanglements of these six unfortunates?"

And, thinking thus, I put them away from me. Or rather I did all I could to put them away.

But one doesn't give life to a character for nothing.

Creatures of my spirit, these six were already living a life which was their own and not mine any more, a life which it was not in my power any more to deny them.

Thus it is that while I persisted in desiring to drive them out of my spirit, they, as if completely detached from every narrative support, characters from a novel miraculously emerging from the pages of the book that contained them, went on living on their own, choosing certain moments of the day to reappear before me in the solitude of my study and coming—now one, now the other, now two together—to tempt me, to propose that I present or describe this scene or that, to explain the effects that could be secured with them, the new interest which a certain unusual situation could provide, and so forth.

For a moment I let myself be won over. And this condescension of mine, thus letting myself go for a while, was enough, because they drew from it a new increment of life, a greater degree of clarity and addition, consequently a greater degree of persuasive power over me. And thus as it became gradually harder and harder for me to go back and free myself from them, it became easier and easier for them to come back and tempt me. At a certain point I actually became obsessed with them. Until, all of a sudden, a way out of the difficulty flashed upon me.

"Why not," I said to myself, "present this highly strange fact of an author who refuses to let some of his characters live though they have been born in his fantasy, and the fact that these characters, having by now life in their veins, do not resign themselves to remaining excluded from the world of art? They are detached from me; live on their own; have acquired voice and movement; have by themselves—in this struggle for existence that they have had to wage with me—become dramatic characters, characters that can move and talk on their own initiative; already see themselves as such; have learned to defend themselves against me; will even know how to defend themselves against others. And so let them go where dramatic characters do go to have life: on a stage. And let us see what will happen."

That's what I did. And, naturally, the result was what it had to be: a mixture of tragic and comic, fantastic and realistic, in a humorous situation that was quite new and infinitely complex, a drama which is conveyed by means of the characters, who carry it within them and suffer it, a drama, breathing, speaking, self-propelled, which seeks at all costs to find the means of its own presentation; and the comedy of the vain attempt at an improvised realization of the drama on stage. First, the surprise of the poor actors in a theatrical company rehearsing a play by day on a bare stage (no scenery, no flats). Surprise and incredulity at the sight of the six characters announcing themselves as such in search of an author. Then, immediately afterward, through that sudden fainting fit of the Mother veiled in black, their instinctive interest in the drama of which they catch a glimpse in her and in the other members of the strange family, an obscure, ambiguous drama, coming about so unexpectedly on a stage that is empty and unprepared to receive it. And gradually the growth of this interest to the bursting forth of the contrasting passions of Father, of Stepdaughter, of Son, of that poor Mother, passions seeking, as I said, to overwhelm each other with a tragic, lacerating fury.

And here is the universal meaning at first vainly sought in the six characters, now that, going on stage of their own accord, they succeed in finding it within themselves in the excitement of the desperate struggle which each wages against the other and all wage against the Manager and the actors, who do not understand them.

Without wanting to, without knowing it, in the strife of their bedeviled souls, each of them, defending himself against the accusations of the others, expresses as his own living passion and torment the passion and torment which for so many years have been the pangs of my spirit: the deceit of mutual understanding irremediably founded on the empty abstraction of the words, the multiple personality of everyone corresponding to the possibilities of being to be found in each of us, and finally the inherent tragic conflict between life (which is always moving and changing) and form (which fixes it, immutable).

Two above all among the six characters, the Father and the Stepdaughter, speak of that outrageous unalterable fixity of their form in which he and she see their essential nature expressed permanently and immutably, a nature that for one means punishment and for the other revenge; and they defend it against the factitious affectations and unaware volatility of the actors, and they try to impose it on the vulgar Manager who would like to change it and adapt it to the so-called exigencies of the theatre.

If the six characters don't all seem to exist on the same plane, it is not because some are figures of first rank and others of the second, that is, some are main characters and others minor ones—the elementary perspective necessary to all scenic or narrative art—nor is it that any are not completely created—for their purpose. They are all six at the same point of artistic realization and on the same level of reality, which is the fantastic level of the whole play. Except that the Father, the Stepdaughter, and also the Son are realized as mind; the Mother as nature; the Boy as a presence watching and performing a gesture and the Baby unaware of it all. This fact creates among them a perspective of a new sort. Unconsciously I had had the impression that some of them needed to be fully realized (artistically speaking), others less so, and others merely sketched in as elements in a narrative or presentational sequence: the most alive, the most completely created, are the Father and the Stepdaughter who naturally stand out more and lead the way, dragging themselves along beside the almost dead weight of the others—first, the Son, holding back; second, the Mother, like a victim resigned to her fate, between the two children who have hardly any substance beyond their appearance and who need to be led by the hand.

And actually! actually they had each to appear in that stage of creation which they had attained in the author's fantasy at the moment when he wished to drive them away.

If I now think about these things, about having intuited that necessity, having unconsciously found the way to resolve it by means of a new perspective, and about the way in which I actually obtained it, they seem like miracles. The fact is that the play was really conceived in one of those spontaneous illuminations of the fantasy when by a miracle all the elements of the mind answer to each other's call and work in divine accord. No human brain, working "in the cold," however stirred up it might be, could ever have succeeded in penetrating far enough, could ever have been in a position to satisfy all the exigencies of the play's form. Therefore the reasons which I will give to clarify the values of the play must not be thought of as intentions that I conceived beforehand when I prepared myself for the job and which I now undertake to defend, but only as discoveries which I have been able to make afterward in tranquillity.

I wanted to present six characters seeking an author. Their play does not manage to get presented—precisely because the author whom they seek is missing. Instead is presented the comedy of their vain attempt with all that it contains of tragedy by virtue of the fact that the six characters have been rejected.

But one can present a character while rejecting him? Obviously, to present him one needs, on the contrary, to receive him into one's fantasy before one can express him. And I have actually accepted and realized the six characters: I have, however, accepted and realized them as rejected: in search of *another* author.

What have I rejected of them? Not themselves, obviously, but their drama, which doubtless is what interests them above all but which did not interest me—for the reasons already indicated.

And what is it, for a character—his drama?

Every creature of fantasy and art, in order to exist, must have his drama, that is, a drama in which he may be a character and for which he *is* a character. This drama is the character's *raison d'être*, his vital function, necessary for his existence.

In these six, then, I have accepted the "being" without the reason for being. I have taken the organism and entrusted to it, not its own proper function, but another more complex function into which its own function entered, if at all, only as a datum. A terrible and desperate situation especially for the two—Father and Stepdaughter—who more than the others crave life and more than the others feel themselves to be characters, that is, absolutely need a drama and therefore their own drama—the only one which they can envisage for themselves yet which meantime they see rejected: an "impossible" situation from which they feel they must escape at whatever cost; it is a matter of life and death. True, I have given them another *raison d'être*, another function: precisely that "impossible" situation, the drama of being in search of an author and rejected. But that this should be a *raison d'être*, that it should have become their real function, that it should be necessary, that it should suffice, they can hardly suppose; for they have a life of their own. If someone were to tell them, they wouldn't believe him. It is not possible to believe that the sole reason for our living should lie in a torment that seems to us unjust and inexplicable.

I cannot imagine, therefore, why the charge was brought against me that the character of the Father was not what it should have been because it stepped out of its quality and position as a character and invaded at times the author's province and took it over. I who understand those who don't quite understand me see that the charge derives from the fact that the character expresses and makes his own a torment of spirit which is recognized as mine. Which is entirely natural and of absolutely no significance. Aside from the fact that this torment of spirit in the character of the Father derives from causes, and is suffered and lived for reasons that have nothing to do with the drama of my personal experience, a fact which alone removes all substance from the criticism, I want to make it clear that the inherent torment of my spirit is one thing, a torment which I can legitimately—provided that it be organic—reflect in a character, and that the activity of my spirit as revealed in the realized work, the activity that succeeds in forming a drama out of the six characters in search of an author is another thing. If the Father participated in this latter activity, if he competed in forming the drama of the six characters without an author, then and only then would it by all means be justified to say that he was at times the author himself and therefore not the man he should be. But the Father suffers and does not create his existence as a character in search of an author. He suffers it as an inexplicable fatality and as a situation which he tries with all his powers to rebel against, which he tries to remedy; hence it is that he is a character in search of an author and nothing more, even if he expresses as his own the torment of my spirit. If he, so to speak, assumed some of the author's responsibilities, the fatality would be completely explained. He would, that is to say, see himself accepted, if only as a rejected character, accepted in the poet's heart of hearts, and he would no longer have any reason to suffer the despair of not finding someone to construct and affirm his life as a character. I mean that he would quite willingly accept the raison d'être which the author gives him and without regrets would forgo his own, throwing over the Manager and the actors to whom in fact he runs as his only recourse.

There is one character, that of the Mother, who on the other hand does not care about being alive (considering being alive as an end in itself). She hasn't the least suspicion that she is not alive. It has never occurred to her to ask how and why and in what manner she lives. In short, she is not aware of being a character inasmuch as she is never, even for a moment, detached from her role. She doesn't know she has a role.

This makes her perfectly organic. Indeed, her role of Mother does not of itself, in its natural essence, embrace mental activity. And she does not exist as a mind. She lives in an endless continuum of feeling, and therefore she cannot acquire awareness of her life—that is, of her existence as a character. But with all this, even she, in her own way and for her own ends, seeks an author, and at a certain stage seems happy to have been brought before the Manager. Because she hopes to take life from him, perhaps? No: because she hopes the Manager will have her present a scene with the Son in which she would put so much of her own life. But it is a scene which does not exist, which never has and never could take place. So unaware is she of being a character, that is, of the life that is possible to her, all fixed and determined, moment by moment, in every action, every phrase.

She appears on stage with the other characters but without understanding what the others make her do. Obviously, she imagines that the itch for life with which the husband and the daughter are afflicted and for which she herself is to be found on stage is no more than one of the usual incomprehensible extravagances of this man who is both tortured and torturer and—horrible, most horrible—a new equivocal rebellion on the part of that poor erring girl. The Mother is completely passive. The events of her own life and the values they assume in her eyes, her very character, are all things which are "said" by the others and which she only once contradicts, and that because the maternal instinct rises up and rebels within her to make it clear that she didn't at all wish to abandon either the son or the husband: the Son was taken from her and the husband forced her to abandon him. She is only correcting data; she explains and knows nothing.

In short, she is nature. Nature fixed in the figure of a mother.

This character gave me a satisfaction of a new sort, not to be ignored. Nearly all my critics, instead of defining her, after their habit, as "un-human"—which seems to be the peculiar and incorrigible characteristic of all my creatures without exception—had the goodness to note "with real pleasure" that at last a very *human* figure had emerged from my fantasy. I explain this praise to myself in the following way: since my poor Mother is entirely limited to the natural attitude of a Mother with no possibility of free mental activity, being, that is, little more than a lump of flesh completely alive in all its functions—procreation, lactation, caring for and loving its young—without any need therefore of exercising her brain, she realizes in her person the true and complete "human type." That must be how it is, since in a human organism nothing seems more superfluous than the mind.

But the critics have tried to get rid of the Mother with this praise without bothering to penetrate the nucleus of poetic values which the character in the play represents. A very human figure, certainly, because mindless, that is, unaware of being what she is or not caring to explain it to herself. But not knowing that she is a character doesn't prevent her from being one. That is her drama in my play. And the most living expression of it comes spurting out in her cry to the Manager, who wants her to think all these things have happened already and therefore cannot now be a reason for renewed lamentations: "No, it's happening now, it's happening always! My torture is not a pretense, signore! I am alive and present, always, in every moment of my torture: it is renewed, alive, and present always!" This she *feels*, without being conscious of it, and feels it therefore as something inexplicable: but she feels it so terribly that she doesn't think it *can* be something to explain either to herself or to others. She feels it and that is that. She feels it as pain and this pain is immediate; she cries it out. Thus she reflects the growing fixity of life in a form—the same thing, which in another way, tortures the Father and the Stepdaughter. In them, mind. In her, nature. The mind rebels and, as best it may, seeks an advantage; nature, if not aroused by sensory stimuli, weeps.

Conflict between life-in-movement and form is the inexorable condition not only of the mental but also of the physical order. The life which in order to exist has become fixed in our corporeal form little by little kills that form. The tears of a nature thus fixed lament the irreparable, continuous aging of our bodies. Hence the tears of the Mother are passive and perpetual. Revealed in three faces, made significant in three distinct and simultaneous dramas, this inherent conflict finds in the play its most complete expression. More: the Mother declares also the particular value of artistic form—a form which does not delimit or destroy its own life and which life does not consume—in her cry to the Manager. If the Father and Stepdaughter began their scene a hundred thousand times in succession, always, at the appointed moment, at the instant when the life of the work of art must be expressed with that cry, it would always be heard, unaltered and unalterable in its form, not as a mechanical repetition, not as a return determined by external necessities, but, on the contrary, alive every time and as new, suddenly born *thus forever!* embalmed alive in its incorruptible form. Hence, always, as we open the book, we shall find Francesca alive and confessing to Dante her sweet sin, and if we turn to the passage a hundred thousand times in succession, a hundred thousand times in succession Francesca will speak her words, never repeating them mechanically, but saying them as though each time were the first time with such living and sudden passion that Dante every time will turn faint. All that lives, by the fact of living, has a form, and by the same token must die—except the work of art which lives forever in so far as it *is* form.

The birth of a creature of human fantasy, a birth which is a step across the threshold between nothing and eternity, can also happen suddenly, occasioned by some necessity. An imagined drama needs a character who does or says a certain necessary thing; accordingly this character is born and is precisely what he had to be. In this way Madame Pace is born among the six characters and seems a miracle, even a trick, realistically portrayed on the stage. It is no trick. The birth is real. The new character is alive not because she was alive already but because she is now happily born as is required by the fact of her being a character—she is obliged to be as she is. There is a break here, a sudden change in the level of reality of the scene, because a character can be born in this way only in the poet's fancy and not on the boards of a stage. Without anyone's noticing it, I have all of a sudden changed the scene: I have gathered it up again into my own fantasy without removing it from the spectator's eyes. That is, I have shown them, instead of the stage, my own fantasy in the act of creating—my own fantasy in the form of this same stage. The sudden and uncontrollable changing of a visual phenomenon from one level of reality to another is a miracle comparable to those of the saint who sets his own statue in motion: it is neither wood nor stone at such a moment. But the miracle is not arbitrary. The stage—a stage which accepts the fantastic reality of the six characters—is no fixed, immutable datum. Nothing in this play exists as given and preconceived. Everything is in the making, is in motion, is a sudden experiment: even the place in which this unformed life, reaching after its own form, changes and changes again contrives to shift position organically. The level of reality changes. When I had the idea of bringing Madame Pace to birth right there on the stage, I felt I could do it and I did it. Had I noticed that this birth was unhinging and silently, unnoticed, in a second, giving another shape, another reality to my scene, I certainly wouldn't have brought it about. I would have been afraid of the apparent lack of logic. And I would have committed an ill-omened assault on the beauty of my work. The fervor of my mind saved me from doing so. For, despite appearances, with their specious logic, this fantastic birth is sustained by a real necessity in mysterious, organic relation with the whole life of the work.

That someone now tells me it hasn't all the value it could have because its expression is not constructed but chaotic, because it smacks of romanticism, makes me smile.

I understand why this observation was made to me: because in this work of mine the presentation of the drama in which the six characters are involved appears tumultuous and never proceeds in an orderly manner. There is no logical development, no concatenation of the events. Very true. Had I hunted it with a lamp I couldn't have found a more disordered, crazy, arbitrary, complicated, in short, romantic way of presenting "the drama in which the six characters are involved." Very true. But I have not presented that drama. I have presented another—and I won't undertake to say again what!—in which, among the many fine things that everyone, according to his tastes, can find, there is a discreet satire on romantic procedures: in the six characters thus excited to the point where they stifle themselves in the roles which each of them plays in a certain drama while I present them as characters in another play which they don't know and don't suspect the existence of, so that this inflammation of their passions— which belongs to the realm of romantic procedures—is humorously "placed," located in the void. And the drama of the six characters presented not as it would have been organized by my fantasy had it been accepted but in this way, as a rejected drama, could not exist in the work except as a "situation," with some little development, and could not come out except in indications, stormily, disorderedly, in violent foreshortenings, in a chaotic manner: continually interrupted, sidetracked, contradicted (by one of its characters), denied, and (by two others) not even seen.

There is a character indeed—he who denies the drama which makes him a character, the Son—who draws all his importance and value from being a character not of the comedy in the making—which as such hardly appears—but from the presentation that I made of it. In short, he is the only one who lives solely as "a character in search of an author"— inasmuch as the author he seeks is not a dramatic author. Even this could not be otherwise. The character's attitude is an organic product of my conception, and it is logical that in the situation it should produce greater confusion and disorder and another element of romantic contrast.

But I had precisely to present this organic and natural chaos. And to present a chaos is not at all to present chaotically, that is, romantically. That my presentation is the reverse of confused, that it is quite simple, clear, and orderly, is proved by the clarity which the intrigue, the characters, the fantastic and realistic, dramatic and comic levels of the work have had for every public in the world and by the way in which, for those with more searching vision, the unusual values enclosed within it come out.

Great is the confusion of tongues among men if criticisms thus made find words for their expression. No less great than this confusion is the intimate law of order which, obeyed in all points, makes this work of mine classical and typical and at its catastrophic close forbids the use of words. Though the audience eventually understands that one does not create life by artifice and that the drama of the six characters cannot be presented without an author to give them value with his spirit, the Manager remains vulgarly anxious to know how the thing turned out, and the "ending" is remembered by the Son in its sequence of actual moments, but without any sense and therefore not needing a human voice for its expression. It happens stupidly, uselessly, with the going off of a mechanical weapon on stage. It breaks up and disperses the sterile experiment of the characters and the actors, which has apparently been made without the assistance of the poet.

The poet, unknown to them, as if looking on at a distance during the whole period of the experiment, was at the same time busy creating—with it and of it—his own play.

🎭 *Bertolt Brecht*

Bertolt Brecht (1898–1956) rejected the aims of the bourgeois realistic theater: the illusion of reality created by middle class characters engaged by middle class problems in a middle class parlor; emotional identification with characters; and the idea that characters have an unchanging human nature. He substituted the "epic" theater. This theater broke up the old illusion of reality by a "narrative" structure made up of episodes whose seeming disconnectedness reduced rather than built up tension; by devices to stop the action, divert us and shut off emotions, devices like a narrator, captions on a backdrop, film projections, pantomime, and songs. Brecht wanted the spectator to know at all times that he was watching a play, not an imitation or illusion of real life. He did not want an emotional response; this would have the effect of a catharsis, that cleansing of pity and fear Aristotle spoke of in his *Poetics*. As a Marxist Brecht wanted his audience tense, frustrated, prepared to cleanse itself emotionally in society by correcting the wrongs perceived.

But Brecht's work is a classic example of the discrepancy between theory and practice. Though his devices do tend to keep us somewhat detached, we are nonetheless absorbed by Mother Courage and Kattrin, and we are moved by Mother Courage's fate. The word fate is appropriate, for despite the randomness in the chronicle, episodic form we still feel the relentless, inevitable grinding down of Mother Courage; the action has that air of fatality we feel in *Oedipus Rex*. Brecht was born in Augsburg, Germany, the son of a factory executive. In the first World War he served in a hospital where he witnessed the contradiction between the official slogans justifying and glorifying war and the actual horror. He in turn contradicted communist doctrine by becoming a pacifist. The moral and economic confusion in post-war Germany confirmed his judgment of capitalistic society. This is reflected in his masterpiece of the period, *Threepenny Opera* (1928), which owes its literary inspiration to John Gay's early eighteenth century *Beggar's Opera*. Exiled by the Nazis, he spent time in various European countries and the United States, doing scenarios for a while in Hollywood. He wrote steadily though unevenly. His work at this time included the unsuccessful *Private Life of the Master Race*

(1938), and some of his best plays: *Mother Courage* (1939), *The Good Woman of Setzuan* (1940), and *The Caucasian Chalk Circle* (1945). He returned to communist East Germany after the war, where he continued his contradictory life of the individualist artist and the collectivist ideologist.

READINGS:

BENTLEY, ERIC, *The Playwright As Thinker* (1946). New York: Meridian Books, 1955.

BORNEMAN, ERNEST, "Credo Quia Absurdum: An Epitaph for Bertolt Brecht," *Kenyon Review*, XXI (Spring 1959), 189–198.

Brecht Issue, *Tulane Drama Review*, VI (September, 1961).

DEMETZ, PETER, ed., *Brecht, A Collection of Critical Essays*. Englewood Cliffs, N.J.: Prentice-Hall, 1962.

ESSLIN, MARTIN, *Brecht: The Man and His Work*. New York: Doubleday & Company, 1960.

GRAY, RONALD, *Bertolt Brecht*. New York: Grove Press, 1961.

LÜTHY, HERBERT, "Of Poor Brecht," *Encounter*, XXXIV (1956), 33–63.

WILLETT, JOHN, *The Theatre of Bertolt Brecht*. New York: New Directions, 1959.

🎭 Mother Courage and Her Children

Bertolt Brecht

A Chronicle of the Thirty Years' War
English version by Eric Bentley

CHARACTERS

MOTHER COURAGE
KATTRIN, her dumb daughter
EILIF, her elder son
SWISS CHEESE, her younger son
RECRUITING OFFICER
SERGEANT
COOK
SWEDISH COMMANDER
CHAPLAIN
ORDNANCE OFFICER
YVETTE POTTIER
MAN WITH THE BANDAGE
ANOTHER SERGEANT
OLD COLONEL
CLERK
YOUNG SOLDIER
OLDER SOLDIER
PEASANT
PEASANT WOMAN
YOUNG MAN
OLD WOMAN
ANOTHER PEASANT
ANOTHER PEASANT WOMAN
YOUNG PEASANT
LIEUTENANT
VOICE

🌼 Scene I

SPRING, 1624. IN DALARNA, THE SWEDISH COMMANDER OXENSTIERNA IS RECRUITING FOR THE CAMPAIGN IN POLAND. THE CANTEEN WOMAN ANNA FIERLING, COMMONLY KNOWN AS MOTHER COURAGE, LOSES A SON.

[Highway outside a town. A SERGEANT and a RECRUITING OFFICER stand shivering.]

THE RECRUITING OFFICER: How the hell can you line up a squadron in a place like this? You know what I keep thinking about, Sergeant? Suicide. I'm supposed to knock four platoons together by the twelfth—four platoons the Chief's asking for! And they're so friendly around here, I'm scared to go to sleep at night. Suppose I do get my hands on some character and squint at him so I don't notice he's pigeon-chested and has varicose veins. I get him drunk and relaxed, he signs on the dotted line. I pay for the drinks, he steps outside for a minute. I have a hunch I should follow him to the door, and am I right? Away he's gone like a louse from a scratch. You can't take a man's word any more, Sergeant. There's no loyalty left in the world, no trust, no faith, no sense of honor. I'm losing my confidence in mankind, Sergeant.

THE SERGEANT: What they could use around here is a good war. What else can you expect with peace running wild all over the place? You know what the trouble with peace is? No organization. And when do you get organization? In a war. Peace is one big waste of equipment. Anything goes, no one gives a damn. See the way they eat? Cheese on pumpernickel, bacon on the cheese? Disgusting! How many horses have they got in this town? How many young men? Nobody knows! They haven't bothered to count 'em! That's peace for you! I've been in places where they haven't had a war for seventy years and you know what? The people haven't even been given names! They don't know who they are! It takes a war to fix that. In a war, everyone registers, everyone's name's on a list. Their shoes are stacked, their corn's in the bag, you count it all up—cattle, men, et cetera—and you take it away! That's the story: no organization, no war!

THE RECRUITING OFFICER: It's the God's truth.

THE SERGEANT: Of course, a war's like any good deal: hard to get going. But when it does get moving, it's a pisser, and they're all scared of peace, like a dice player who can't stop—'cause when peace comes they have to pay up. Of course, until it gets going, they're just as scared of war, it's such a novelty!

THE RECRUITING OFFICER: Hey, look, here's a canteen wagon. Two women and a couple of fellows. Stop the old lady, Sergeant. And if there's nothing doing this time, you won't catch me freezing my ass in the April wind any longer.

[A harmonica is heard. A canteen wagon rolls on, drawn by two young fellows. MOTHER COURAGE is sitting on it with her dumb daughter, KATTRIN.]

MOTHER COURAGE: A good day to you, Sergeant!

THE SERGEANT [*barring the way*]: Good day to you! Who d'you think you are?

MOTHER COURAGE: Tradespeople.

[*She sings:*]

> Stop all the troops: here's Mother Courage!
> Hey, Captain, let them come and buy!
> For they can get from Mother Courage
> Boots they will march in till they die!
> Your marching men do not adore you
> (Packs on their backs, lice in their hair)
> But it's to death they're marching for you
> And so they need good boots to wear!
> > Christians, awake! Winter is gone!
> > The snows depart! Dead men sleep on!
> > Let all of you who still survive
> > Get out of bed and look alive!
>
> Your men will walk till they are dead, sir,
> But cannot fight, sir, unless they eat.
> The blood they spill for you is red, sir,
> What fires that blood, sir, is my red meat.
> Cannon is rough on empty bellies:
> First with my meat they should be crammed.
> Then let them go and find where hell is
> And give my greetings to the damned!
> > Christians, awake! Winter is gone!
> > The snows depart! Dead men sleep on!
> > Let all of you who still survive
> > Get out of bed and look alive!

THE SERGEANT: Halt! Where are you from, riffraff?

EILIF: Second Finnish Regiment!

THE SERGEANT: Where are your papers?

MOTHER COURAGE: Papers?

SWISS CHEESE: But this is Mother Courage!

THE SERGEANT: Never heard of her. Where'd she get a name like that?

MOTHER COURAGE: They call me Mother Courage 'cause I was afraid I'd be ruined, so I drove through the bombardment of Riga like a madwoman, with fifty loaves of bread in my cart. They were going moldy, what else could I do?

THE SERGEANT: No funny business! Where are your papers?

MOTHER COURAGE [*rummaging among papers in a tin box and clambering down from her wagon*]: Here, Sergeant! Here's a missal—I got it in Altötting to wrap my cucumbers in. Here's a map of Moravia—God knows if I'll ever get there—the birds can have it if I don't. And here's a document saying my horse hasn't got hoof and mouth disease—pity he died on us, he cost fifteen guilders, thank God I didn't pay it. Is that enough paper?

THE SERGEANT: Are you pulling my leg? Well, you've got another guess coming. You need a license and you know it.

MOTHER COURAGE: Show a little respect for a lady and don't go telling these grown children of mine I'm pulling anything of yours. What would I want with you? My license in the Second Protestant Regiment is an honest face. If you wouldn't know how to read it, that's not my fault, I want no rubber stamp on it anyhow.

THE RECRUITING OFFICER: Sergeant, we have a case of insubordination on our hands. Do you know what we need in the army? Discipline!

MOTHER COURAGE: I was going to say sausages.

THE SERGEANT: Name?

MOTHER COURAGE: Anna Fierling.

THE SERGEANT: So you're all Fierlings.

MOTHER COURAGE: I was talking about me.

THE SERGEANT: And I was talking about your children.

MOTHER COURAGE: Must they all have the same name? [*Pointing to the elder son:*] This fellow, for instance, I call him Eilif Noyocki. Why? He got the name from his father who told me he was called Koyocki. Or was it Moyocki? Anyhow, the lad remembers him to this day. Only the man he remembers is someone else, a Frenchman with a pointed beard. But he certainly has his father's brains—that man could whip the breeches off a farmer's backside before he could turn around. So we all have our own names.

THE SERGEANT: You're all called something different?

MOTHER COURAGE: Are you pretending you don't understand?

THE SERGEANT [*pointing at the younger son*]: He's Chinese, I suppose.

MOTHER COURAGE: Wrong again. Swiss.

THE SERGEANT: After the Frenchman?

MOTHER COURAGE: Frenchman? What Frenchman? Don't confuse the issue, Sergeant, or we'll be here all day. He's Swiss, but he happens to be called Feyos, a name that has nothing to do with his father, who was called something else—a military engineer, if you please, and a drunkard.

[SWISS CHEESE *nods, beaming; even* KATTRIN *smiles.*]

THE SERGEANT: Then how come his name's Feyos?

MOTHER COURAGE: Oh, Sergeant, you have no imagination. Of course he's called Feyos: when he came, I was with a Hungarian. He didn't mind. He had a floating kidney, though he never touched a drop. He was a very *honest* man. The boy takes after him.

THE SERGEANT: But that wasn't his father!

MOTHER COURAGE: I said: he took after him. I call him Swiss Cheese. Why? Because he's good at pulling wagons. [*Pointing to her daughter:*] And that is Kattrin Haupt, she's half German.

THE SERGEANT: A nice family, I must say!

MOTHER COURAGE: And we've seen the whole wide world together—this wagonload and me.

THE SERGEANT: We'll need all that in writing. [*He writes.*] You're from Bamberg in Bavaria. What are you doing *here?*

MOTHER COURAGE: I can't wait till the war is good enough to come to Bamberg.

THE RECRUITING OFFICER: And you two oxen pull the cart. Jacob Ox and Esau Ox! D'you ever get out of harness?

EILIF: Mother! May I smack him in the puss? I'd like to.

MOTHER COURAGE: I'd like you to stay where you are. And now, gentlemen, what about a brace of pistols? Or a belt? Sergeant? Yours is worn clean through.

THE SERGEANT: It's something else *I'm* looking for. These lads of yours are straight as birch trees, strong limbs, massive chests. . . . What are such fine specimens doing out of the army?

MOTHER COURAGE [*quickly*]: A soldier's life is not for sons of mine!

THE RECRUITING OFFICER: Why not? It means money. It means fame. Peddling shoes is woman's work. [*To* EILIF:] Step this way and let's see if that's muscle or chicken fat.

MOTHER COURAGE: It's chicken fat. Give him a good hard look, and he'll fall right over.

THE RECRUITING OFFICER: Yes, and kill a calf in the falling!

[*He tries to hustle* EILIF *away.*]

MOTHER COURAGE: Let him alone! He's not for you!

THE RECRUITING OFFICER: He called my face a puss. That is an insult. The two of us will now go and settle the affair on the field of honor.

EILIF: Don't worry, Mother, I can handle him.

MOTHER COURAGE: Stay here. You're never happy till you're in a fight. He has a knife in his boot and he knows how to use it.

THE RECRUITING OFFICER: I'll draw it out of him like a milk tooth. Come on, young fellow!

MOTHER COURAGE: Officer, I'll report you to the Colonel, and he'll throw you in jail. His lieutenant is courting my daughter.

THE SERGEANT: Go easy. [To MOTHER COURAGE:] What have you got against the service, wasn't his own father a soldier? Didn't you say he died a soldier's death?

MOTHER COURAGE: This one's just a baby. You'll lead him like a lamb to the slaughter. I know you, you'll get five guilders for him.

THE RECRUITING OFFICER [to EILIF]: First thing you know, you'll have a lovely cap and high boots, how about it?

EILIF: Not from you.

MOTHER COURAGE: "Let's you and me go fishing" said the angler to the worm. [To SWISS CHEESE:] Run and tell everybody they're trying to steal your brother! [She draws a knife.] Yes, just you try, and I'll cut you down like dogs! We sell cloth, we sell ham, we are peaceful people!

THE SERGEANT: You're peaceful all right: your knife proves that. Why, you should be ashamed of yourself. Give me that knife, you hag! You admit you live off the war, what else could you live off? Now tell me, how can we have a war without soldiers?

MOTHER COURAGE: Do they have to be mine?

THE SERGEANT: So that's the trouble. The war should swallow the peach stone and spit out the peach, hm? Your brood should get fat off the war, but the poor war must ask nothing in return, it can look after itself, can it? Call yourself Mother Courage and then get scared of the war, your breadwinner? Your sons aren't scared, I know that much.

EILIF: Takes more than a war to scare me.

THE SERGEANT: Correct! Take me. The soldier's life hasn't done me any harm, has it? I enlisted at seventeen.

MOTHER COURAGE: You haven't reached seventy.

THE SERGEANT: I will, though.

MOTHER COURAGE: Above ground?

THE SERGEANT: Are you trying to rile me, telling me I'll die?

MOTHER COURAGE: Suppose it's the truth? Suppose I see it's your fate? Suppose I know you're just a corpse on furlough?

SWISS CHEESE: She can look into the future. Everyone says so.

THE RECRUITING OFFICER: Then by all means look into the sergeant's future. It might amuse him.

THE SERGEANT: I don't believe in that stuff.

MOTHER COURAGE: Helmet!

[The SERGEANT gives her his helmet.]

THE SERGEANT: It means less than a crap in the grass. Anything for a laugh.

MOTHER COURAGE [taking a sheet of parchment and tearing it in two]: Eilif, Swiss Cheese, Kattrin! So shall we all be torn in two if we let ourselves get too deep into this war! [To the SERGEANT:] I'll give you the bargain rate, and do it free. Watch! Death is black, so I draw a black cross.

SWISS CHEESE: And the other she leaves blank, see?

MOTHER COURAGE: I fold them, put them in the helmet, and mix 'em up together, the way we're all mixed up together from our mother's womb on. Now draw!

[The SERGEANT hesitates.]

THE RECRUITING OFFICER [to EILIF]: I don't take just anybody. I'm choosy. And you've got guts, I like that.

THE SERGEANT [fishing around in the helmet]: It's silly. Means as much as blowing your nose.

SWISS CHEESE: The black cross! Oh, his number's up!

THE RECRUITING OFFICER: Don't let them get under your skin. There aren't enough bullets to go around.

THE SERGEANT [hoarsely]: You cheated me!

MOTHER COURAGE: You cheated yourself the day you enlisted. And now we must drive on. There isn't a war every day in the week, we must get to work.

THE SERGEANT: Hell, you're not getting away with this! We're taking that bastard of yours with us!

EILIF: I'd like that, Mother.

MOTHER COURAGE: Quiet—you Finnish devil, you!

EILIF: And Swiss Cheese wants to be a soldier, too.

MOTHER COURAGE: That's news to me. I see I'll have to draw lots for all three of you. [She goes to the back to draw the crosses on bits of paper.]

THE RECRUITING OFFICER [to EILIF]: People've been saying the Swedish soldier is religious. That kind of loose talk has hurt us a lot. One verse of a hymn every Sunday—and then only if you have a voice . . .

MOTHER COURAGE [returning with the slips and putting them in the SERGEANT's helmet]: So they'd desert their old mother, would they, the scoundrels? They take to war like a cat to cream. But I'll consult these slips, and they'll see the world's no promised land, with a "Join up, son, you're officer material!" Sergeant, I'm afraid for them, very afraid they won't get through this war. They have terrible qualities, all three. [*She holds the helmet out to* EILIF.] There. Draw your lot. [EILIF *fishes in the helmet, unfolds a slip. She snatches it from him.*] There you have it: a cross. Unhappy mother that I am, rich only in a mother's sorrows! He dies. In the springtime of his life, he must go. If he's a soldier, he must bite the dust, that's clear. He's too brave, like his father. And if he doesn't use his head, he'll go the way of all flesh, the slip proves it. [*Hectoring him:*] Will you use your head?

EILIF: Why not?

MOTHER COURAGE: It's using your head to stay with your mother. And when they make fun of you and call you a chicken, just laugh.

THE RECRUITING OFFICER: If you're going to wet your pants, I'll try your brother.

MOTHER COURAGE: I told you to laugh. Laugh! Now it's your turn, Swiss Cheese. You should be a better bet, you're honest. [*He fishes in the helmet.*] Why are you giving that slip such a funny look? You've drawn a blank for sure. It can't be there's a cross on it. It can't be I'm going to lose you. [*She takes the slip.*] A cross? Him too! Could it be 'cause he's so simple? Oh, Swiss Cheese, you'll be a goner too, if you aren't honest, honest, honest the whole time, the way I always brought you up to be, the way you always bring me all the change when you buy me a loaf. It's the only way you can save yourself. Look, Sergeant, if it isn't a black cross!

THE SERGEANT: It's a cross! I don't understand how *I* got one. I always stay well in the rear. [*To the* OFFICER:] But it can't be a trick: it gets *her* children too.

SWISS CHEESE: It gets me too. But I don't accept it!

MOTHER COURAGE [*to* KATTRIN]: And now all I have left for certain is you, you're a cross in yourself, you have a good heart. [*She holds the helmet up high toward the wagon but takes the slip out herself.*] Oh, I could give up in despair! There must be some mistake, I didn't mix them right. Don't be too kind, Kattrin, just don't, there's a cross in your path too. Always be very quiet, it can't be hard, you can't speak. Well, so now you know, all of you: be careful, you'll need to be. Now let's climb on the wagon and move on. [*She returns the helmet to the* SERGEANT *and climbs on the wagon.*]

THE RECRUITING OFFICER [*to the* SERGEANT]: Do something!

THE SERGEANT: I don't feel very well.

THE RECRUITING OFFICER: Maybe you caught a chill when you handed over your helmet in this wind. Get her involved in a business transaction! [*Aloud:*] That belt, Sergeant, you could at least take a look at it. These good people live by trade, don't they? Hey, all of you, the sergeant wants to buy the belt!

MOTHER COURAGE: Half a guilder. A belt like that is worth two guilders. [*She clambers down again from the wagon.*]

THE SERGEANT: It isn't new. But there's too much wind here. I'll go and look at it behind the wagon. [*He does so.*]

MOTHER COURAGE: I don't find it windy.

THE SERGEANT: Maybe it's worth half a guilder at that. There's silver on it.

MOTHER COURAGE [*following him behind the wagon*]: A solid six ounces worth!

THE RECRUITING OFFICER [*to* EILIF]: And we can have a drink, just us men. I'll advance you some money to cover it. Let's go.

[EILIF *stands undecided.*]

MOTHER COURAGE: Half a guilder, then.

THE SERGEANT: I don't understand it. I always stay in the rear. There's no safer spot for a sergeant to be. You can send the others on ahead in quest of fame. My appetite is ruined. I can tell you right now: I won't be able to get anything down.

MOTHER COURAGE: You shouldn't take on so, just because you can't eat. Just stay in the rear. Here, take a slug of brandy, man. [*She gives him brandy.*]

THE RECRUITING OFFICER [*taking* EILIF *by the arm and making off toward the back*]: Ten guilders in advance and you're a soldier of the king and a stout fellow and the women will be mad about you. And you can give me a smack in the puss for insulting you.

[*Both leave.*]

[*Dumb* KATTRIN *jumps down from the wagon and lets out harsh cries.*]

MOTHER COURAGE: Coming, Kattrin, coming! The sergeant's just paying up. [*She bites the half guilder.*] I'm suspicious of all money, I've been badly burned, Sergeant. But this money's good. And now we'll be going. Where's Eilif?

SWISS CHEESE: Gone with the recruiting officer.

MOTHER COURAGE [*standing quite still, then*]: Oh, you simpleton! [*To* KATTRIN:] You can't speak, I know. You are innocent.

THE SERGEANT: That's life. Take a slug yourself, Mother. Being a soldier isn't the worst that could happen. You want to live off the war and keep you and yours out of it, do you?

MOTHER COURAGE: You must help your brother now, Kattrin.

[*Brother and sister get into harness together and pull the wagon.* MOTHER COURAGE *walks at their side. The wagon gets under way.*]

THE SERGEANT [*looking after them*]:
When a war gives you all you earn
One day it may claim something in return!

⚙ *Scene II*

IN THE YEARS 1625 AND 1626 MOTHER COURAGE JOURNEYS THROUGH
POLAND IN THE BAGGAGE TRAIN OF THE SWEDISH ARMY. SHE MEETS HER
SON AGAIN BEFORE WALLHOF CASTLE.—OF THE SUCCESSFUL SALE OF A
CAPON AND GREAT DAYS FOR THE BRAVE SON.

[*Tent of the Swedish Commander. Kitchen next to it. Thunder of cannon. The* COOK *is quarreling with* MOTHER COURAGE, *who is trying to sell him a capon.*]

THE COOK: Sixty hellers for that miserable bird?

MOTHER COURAGE: Miserable bird? This fat fowl? Your Commander is a glutton. Woe betide you if you've nothing for him to eat. This capon is worth sixty hellers to you.

THE COOK: They're ten hellers a dozen on every corner.

MOTHER COURAGE: A capon like this on every corner! With a siege going on and people all skin and bones? Maybe you can get a field rat! I said maybe. Because we're all out of *them* too. Don't you see the soldiers running five deep after one hungry little field rat? All right then, in a siege, my price for a giant capon is fifty hellers.

THE COOK: But we're not "in a siege," we're doing the besieging, it's the other side that's "in a siege," when will you get this into your head?

MOTHER COURAGE: A fat lot of difference that makes, we haven't got a thing to eat either. They took everything into the town with them before all this started, and now they've nothing to do but eat and drink, I hear. It's us I'm worried about. Look at the farmers around here, they haven't a thing.

THE COOK: Certainly they have. They hide it.

MOTHER COURAGE [*triumphant*]: They have not! They're ruined, that's what. They're so hungry I've seen 'em digging up roots to eat. I could boil your leather belt and make their mouths water with it.

That's how things are around here. And I'm expected to let a capon go for forty hellers!

THE COOK: Thirty. Not forty. I said thirty hellers.

MOTHER COURAGE: I say this is no ordinary capon. It was a talented animal, so I hear. It would only feed to music—one march in particular was its favorite. It was so intelligent it could count. Forty hellers is too much for all this? I know your problem: if you don't find something to eat and quick, the Chief will—cut—your—fat—head—off!

THE COOK: All right, just watch. [*He takes a piece of beef and lays his knife on it.*] Here's a piece of beef, I'm going to roast it. I give you one more chance.

MOTHER COURAGE: Roast it, go ahead, it's only one year old.

THE COOK: One day old! Yesterday it was a cow. I saw it running around.

MOTHER COURAGE: In that case it must have started stinking before it died.

THE COOK: I don't care if I have to cook it for five hours. We'll see if it's still hard after that. [*He cuts into it.*]

MOTHER COURAGE: Put plenty of pepper in, so the Commander won't smell the smell.

[*The* SWEDISH COMMANDER, *a* CHAPLAIN, *and* EILIF *enter the tent.*]

THE COMMANDER [*clapping* EILIF *on the shoulder*]: In the Commander's tent with you, my son! Sit at my right hand, you happy warrior! You've played a hero's part, you've served the Lord in his own Holy War, *that's* the thing! And you'll get a gold bracelet out of it when we take the town if *I* have any say in the matter! We come to save their souls and what do they do, the filthy, shameless peasant pigs? Drive their cattle away from us, while they stuff their priests with beef at both ends! But you showed 'em. So here's a can of red wine for you, we'll drink together! [*They do so.*] The chaplain gets the dregs, he's pious. Now what would you like for dinner, my hearty?

EILIF: How about a slice of meat?

THE COMMANDER: Cook, meat!

THE COOK: Nothing to eat, so he brings company to eat it!

[MOTHER COURAGE *makes him stop talking; she wants to listen.*]

EILIF: Tires you out, skinning peasants. Gives you an appetite.

MOTHER COURAGE: Dear God, it's my Eilif!

THE COOK: Who?

MOTHER COURAGE: My eldest. It's two years since I saw him, he was stolen from me in the street. He must be in high favor if the Commander's invited him to dinner. And what do you have to eat? Nothing. You hear what the Commander's guest wants? Meat! Better take my advice, buy the capon. The price is one guilder.

[The COMMANDER has sat down with EILIF and the CHAPLAIN.]

THE COMMANDER [roaring]: Cook! Dinner, you pig, or I'll have your head!

THE COOK: This is blackmail. Give me the damn thing!

MOTHER COURAGE: A miserable bird like this?

THE COOK: You were right. Give it here. It's highway robbery, fifty hellers.

MOTHER COURAGE: I said one guilder. Nothing's too high for my eldest, the Commander's guest of honor.

THE COOK [giving her the money]: Well, you might at least pluck it till I have a fire going.

MOTHER COURAGE [sitting down to pluck the capon]: I can't wait to see his face when he sees me. This is my brave and clever son. I have a stupid one as well but he's honest. The daughter is nothing. At least, she doesn't talk: we must be thankful for small mercies.

THE COMMANDER: Have another glass, my son, it's my favorite Falernian. There's only one cask left—two at the most—but it's worth it to meet a soldier that still believes in God! The shepherd of our flock here just looks on, he only preaches, he hasn't a clue how anything gets done. So now, Eilif, my son, give us the details: tell us how you fixed the peasants and grabbed the twenty bullocks. And let's hope they'll soon be here.

EILIF: In one day's time. Two at the most.

MOTHER COURAGE: Now that's considerate of Eilif—to bring the oxen tomorrow—otherwise my capon wouldn't have been so welcome today.

EILIF: Well, it was like this. I found out that the peasants had hidden their oxen and—on the sly and chiefly at night—had driven them into a certain wood. The people from the town were to pick them up there. I let them get their oxen in peace—they ought to know better than me where they are, I said to myself. Meanwhile I made my men crazy for meat. Their rations were short and I made sure they got shorter. Their mouths'd water at the sound of any word beginning with MEA . . . , like measles.

THE COMMANDER: Smart fella.

EILIF: Not bad. The rest was a snap. Only the peasants had clubs and outnumbered us three to one and made a murderous attack on us. Four of them drove me into a clump of trees, knocked my good sword from my hand, and yelled, "Surrender!" What now, I said to myself, they'll make mincemeat of me.

THE COMMANDER: What did you do?

EILIF: I laughed.

THE COMMANDER: You what?

EILIF: I laughed. And so we got to talking. I came right down to business and said: "Twenty guilders an ox is too much, I bid fifteen." Like I wanted to buy. That foxed 'em. So while they were scratching their heads, I reached for my good sword and cut 'em to pieces. Necessity knows no law, huh?

THE COMMANDER: What do you say, shepherd of the flock?

THE CHAPLAIN: Strictly speaking, that saying is not in the Bible. Our Lord made five hundred loaves out of five so that no such necessity would arise. When he told men to love their neighbors, their bellies were full. Things have changed since his day.

THE COMMANDER [laughing]: Things have changed! A swallow of wine for those wise words, you pharisee! [To EILIF:] You cut 'em to pieces in a good cause, our fellows were hungry and you gave 'em to eat. Doesn't it say in the Bible "Whatsoever thou doest to the least of these my children, thou doest unto me?" And what did you do for 'em? You got 'em the best steak dinner they ever tasted. Moldy bread is not what they're used to. They always ate white bread, and drank wine in their helmets, before going out to fight for God.

EILIF: I reached for my good sword and cut 'em to pieces.

THE COMMANDER: You have the making of Julius Ceasar, why, you should be presented to the King!

EILIF: I've seen him—from a distance of course. He seemed to shed a light all around. I must try to be like him!

THE COMMANDER: I think you're succeeding, my boy! Oh, Eilif, you don't know how I value a brave soldier like you! I treat such a chap as my very own son. [He takes him to the map.] Take a look at our position, Eilif, it isn't all it might be, is it?

[MOTHER COURAGE has been listening and is now plucking angrily at her capon.]

MOTHER COURAGE: He must be a very bad Commander.

THE COOK: Just a gluttonous one. Why bad?

MOTHER COURAGE: Because he needs brave soldiers, that's why. If his plan of campaign was any good, why would he need brave soldiers, wouldn't plain, ordinary soldiers do? Whenever there are great virtues, it's a sure sign something's wrong.

THE COOK: You mean, it's a sure sign something's right.

MOTHER COURAGE: I mean what I say. Why? When a general or a king is stupid and leads his soldiers into a trap, they need this virtue of courage. When he's tightfisted and hasn't enough soldiers, the few he does have need the heroism of Hercules—another virtue. And if he's slovenly and doesn't give a damn about anything, they have to be as wise as serpents or they're finished. Loyalty's another virtue and you need plenty of it if the king's always asking too much of you. All virtues which a well-regulated country with a good king or a good general wouldn't need. In a good country virtues wouldn't be necessary. Everybody could be quite ordinary, middling, and, for all I care, cowards.

THE COMMANDER: I bet your father was a soldier.

EILIF: I've heard he was a great soldier. My mother warned me. I know a song about that.

THE COMMANDER: Sing it to us. [Roaring:] Bring that meat!

EILIF: It's called The Song of the Wise Woman and the Soldier.

> [He sings and at the same time does a war dance with his saber:]

A shotgun will shoot and a jackknife will knife,
If you wade in the water, it will drown you,
Keep away from the ice, if you want my advice,
Said the wise woman to the soldier.

But that young soldier, he loaded his gun,
And he reached for his knife, and he started to run:
For marching never could hurt him!
From the north to the south he will march through the land
With his knife at his side and his gun in his hand:
That's what the soldiers told the wise woman.

Woe to him who defies the advice of the wise!
If you wade in the water, it will drown you!
Don't ignore what I say or you'll rue it one day,
Said the wise woman to the soldier.

But that young soldier, his knife at his side
And his gun in his hand, he steps into the tide:
For water never could hurt him!
When the new moon is shining on yonder church tower

We are all coming back: go and pray for that hour:
That's what the soldiers told the wise woman.

[MOTHER COURAGE *continues the song from her kitchen,*
beating on a pan with a spoon:]

Then the wise woman spoke: you will vanish like smoke
Leaving nothing but cold air behind you!
Just watch the smoke fly! Oh God, don't let him die!
Said the wise woman to the soldier.

EILIF: What's that?

[MOTHER COURAGE, *singing on:*]

And the lad who defies the wise woman's advice,
When the new moon shone, floated down with the ice:
He waded in the water and it drowned him.

The wise woman spoke, and they vanished like smoke,
And their glorious deeds did not warm us.
Your glorious deeds do not warm us!

THE COMMANDER: What a kitchen I've got! There's no end to the liberties they take!

[EILIF *has entered the kitchen and embraced his mother.*]

EILIF: To see you again! Where are the others?
MOTHER COURAGE [*in his arms*]: Happy as ducks in a pond. Swiss Cheese is paymaster with the Second Regiment, so at least he isn't in the fighting. I couldn't keep him out altogether.
EILIF: Are your feet holding up?
MOTHER COURAGE: I've a bit of trouble getting my shoes on in the morning.

[*The* COMMANDER *has come over.*]

THE COMMANDER: So you're his mother! I hope you have more sons for me like this fellow.
EILIF: If I'm not the lucky one: to be feasted by the Commander while you sit listening in the kitchen!
MOTHER COURAGE: Yes. I heard all right. [*She gives him a box on the ear.*]
EILIF [*his hand to his cheek*]: Because I took the oxen?
MOTHER COURAGE: No. Because you didn't surrender when the four

Mother Courage and Her Children **597**

peasants let fly at you and tried to make mincemeat of you! Didn't I teach you to take care of yourself? You Finnish devil, you!

[The COMMANDER and the CHAPLAIN stand laughing in the doorway.]

🌼 Scene III

THREE YEARS PASS AND MOTHER COURAGE, WITH PARTS OF A FINNISH REGIMENT, IS TAKEN PRISONER. HER DAUGHTER IS SAVED, HER WAGON-LIKEWISE, BUT HER HONEST SON DIES.

[A camp. The regiment flag is flying from a pole. Afternoon. All sorts of wares hanging on the wagon. MOTHER COURAGE's clothesline is tied to the wagon at one end, to a cannon at the other. She and KATTRIN are folding the washing on the cannon. At the same time she is bargaining with an ORDNANCE OFFICER over a bag of bullets. SWISS CHEESE, in paymaster's uniform, looks on. YVETTE POTTIER, a very good-looking young person, is sewing at a colored hat, a glass of brandy before her. She is in stocking feet. Her red boots are near by.]

THE OFFICER: I'm letting you have the bullets for two guilders. Dirt cheap. 'Cause I need the money. The Colonel's been drinking with the officers for three days and we're out of liquor.

MOTHER COURAGE: They're army property. If they find 'em on me, I'll be court-martialed. You sell your bullets, you bastards, and send your men out to fight with nothing to shoot with.

THE OFFICER: Oh, come on, you scratch my back, and I'll scratch yours.

MOTHER COURAGE: I won't take army stuff. Not at *that* price.

THE OFFICER: You can resell 'em for five guilders, maybe eight, to the Ordnance Officer of the Fourth Regiment. All you have to do is to give him a receipt for twelve. He hasn't a bullet left.

MOTHER COURAGE: Why don't you do it yourself?

THE OFFICER: I don't trust him. We're friends.

MOTHER COURAGE [taking the bag]: Give it here. [To KATTRIN:] Take it around to the back and pay him a guilder and a half. [As the OFFICER protests:] I said a guilder and a half! (KATTRIN drags the bag away. The OFFICER follows. MOTHER COURAGE speaks to SWISS CHEESE:] Here's your underwear back, take care of it; it's October

598   *Bertolt Brecht*

now, autumn may come at any time; I purposely don't say it must come, I've learned from experience there's nothing that must come, not even the seasons. But your books *must* balance now you're regimental paymaster. *Do* they balance?

SWISS CHEESE: Yes, Mother.

MOTHER COURAGE: Don't forget they made you paymaster because you're honest and so simple you'd never think of running off with the cash. Don't lose that underwear.

SWISS CHEESE: No, Mother. I'll put it under the mattress. [*He starts to go.*]

THE OFFICER: I'll go with you, paymaster.

MOTHER COURAGE: Don't teach him any monkey business.

[*Without a good-by the* OFFICER *leaves with* SWISS CHEESE.]

YVETTE [*waving to him*]: You might at least say good-by!

MOTHER COURAGE [*to* YVETTE]: I don't like that. *He's* no sort of company for my Swiss Cheese. But the war's not making a bad start. Before all the different countries get into it, four or five years'll have gone by like nothing. If I look ahead and make no mistakes, business will be good. Don't you know you shouldn't drink in the morning with your illness?

YVETTE: Who says I'm ill? That's libel!

MOTHER COURAGE: They all say so.

YVETTE: They're all liars. I'm desperate, Mother Courage. They all avoid me like a stinking fish. Because of those lies. So what am I arranging my hat for? [*She throws it down.*] That's why I drink in the morning. I never used to, it gives you crow's feet. But what's the difference? Every man in the regiment knows me. I should have stayed at home when my first was unfaithful. But pride isn't for the likes of us, you eat dirt or down you go.

MOTHER COURAGE: Now don't you start again with your friend Peter and how it all happened—in front of my innocent daughter.

YVETTE: She's the one that should hear it. So she'll get hardened against love.

MOTHER COURAGE: That's something no one ever gets hardened against.

YVETTE: I'll tell you about it, and get it off my chest. I grew up in Flanders' fields, that's where it starts, or I'd never have caught sight of him and I wouldn't be here in Poland today. He was an army cook, blond, a Dutchman, but thin. Kattrin, beware of thin men! I didn't. I didn't even know he'd had another girl before me and she called him Peter Piper because he never took his pipe out of his mouth the whole time, it meant so little to him.

[*She sings "The Fraternization Song":*]

> When I was almost seventeen
> The foe came to our land
> And laying aside his saber
> He took me gently by the hand.
>
> > First came the May Day Rite
> > Then came the May Day night.
> > The pipes played and the drums did beat.
> > The foe paraded down the street.
> > And then with us they took their ease
> > And fraternized behind the trees.
>
> Our foes they came in plenty.
> A cook was my own foe.
> I hated him by daylight
> But in the dark I loved him so.
>
> > First comes the May Day Rite
> > Then comes the May Day night.
> > The pipes play and the drums do beat.
> > The foe parades down every street.
> > And then with us they take their ease
> > And fraternize behind the trees.
>
> The heavens seemed to open
> Such passion did I feel.
> But my people never understood
> The love I felt was real.
>
> > One day the sun rose slow
> > On all my pain and woe.
> > My loved one, with the other men,
> > Presented arms and stood at ease
> > Then marched away past all those trees
> > And never did he come back again.

I made the mistake of running after him, I never found him. It's five years ago now. [*With swaying gait she goes behind the wagon.*]

MOTHER COURAGE: You've left your hat.

YVETTE: For the birds.

MOTHER COURAGE: Let this be a lesson to you, Kattrin, never start anything with a soldier. The heavens do seem to open, so watch out!

Even with men who're not in the army life's no honeypot. He tells you he'd like to kiss the ground under your feet—did you wash 'em yesterday, while we're on the subject?—and then if you don't look out, your number's up, you're his slave for life. Be glad you're dumb, Kattrin: you'll never contradict yourself, you'll never want to bite your tongue off because you spoke out of turn. Dumbness is a gift from God. Here comes the Commander's cook, what's bothering him?

[Enter the COOK and the CHAPLAIN.]

THE CHAPLAIN: I bring a message from your son Eilif. The cook came with me. You've made, ahem, an impression on him.

THE COOK: I thought I'd get a little whiff of the balmy breeze.

MOTHER COURAGE: You're welcome to that if you behave yourself, and even if you don't I think I can handle you. But what does Eilif want? I don't have any money.

THE CHAPLAIN: Actually, I have something to tell his brother, the paymaster.

MOTHER COURAGE: He isn't here. And he isn't anywhere else either. He's not his brother's paymaster, and I won't have him led into temptation. Let Eilif try it on with someone else! [She takes money from the purse at her belt.] Give him this. It's a sin. He's speculating in mother love, he ought to be ashamed of himself.

THE COOK: Not for long. He has to go with his regiment now—to his death maybe. Send some more money, or you'll be sorry. You women are hard—and sorry afterward. A glass of brandy wouldn't cost very much, but you refuse to provide it, and six feet under goes your man and you can't dig him up again.

THE CHAPLAIN: All very touching, my dear cook, but to fall in this war is not a misfortune, it's a blessing. This is a war of religion. Not just any old war but a special one, a religious one, and therefore pleasing unto God.

THE COOK: Correct. In one sense it's a war because there's fleecing, bribing, plundering, not to mention a little raping, but it's different from all other wars because it's a war of religion. That's clear. All the same, it makes you thirsty.

THE CHAPLAIN [to MOTHER COURAGE, pointing at the COOK]: I tried to hold him off but he said you'd bewitched him. He dreams about you.

THE COOK [lighting a clay pipe]: Brandy from the fair hand of a lady, that's for me. And don't embarrass me any more: the stories the chaplain was telling me on the way over still have me blushing.

MOTHER COURAGE: A man of his cloth! I must get you both something to drink or you'll be making improper advances out of sheer boredom.

THE CHAPLAIN: That is indeed a temptation, said the court chaplain, and gave way to it. [*Turning toward* KATTRIN *as he walks:*] And who is this captivating young person?

MOTHER COURAGE: She's not a captivating young person, she's a respectable young person.

[*The* CHAPLAIN *and the* COOK *go with* MOTHER COURAGE *behind the cart, and one hears them talk politics.*]

MOTHER COURAGE: The trouble here in Poland is that the Poles would keep meddling. It's true our King moved in on them with man, beast, and wagon, but instead of keeping the peace the Poles attacked the Swedish King when he was in the act of peacefully withdrawing. So they were guilty of a breach of the peace and their blood is on their own heads.

THE CHAPLAIN: Anyway, our King was thinking of nothing but freedom. The Kaiser enslaved them all, Poles and Germans alike, so our King had to liberate them.

THE COOK: Just what I think. Your health! Your brandy is first-rate, I'm never mistaken in a face.

[KATTRIN *looks after them, leaves the washing, goes to the hat, picks it up, sits down, and takes up the red boots.*]

And the war is a war of religion. [*Singing while* KATTRIN *puts the boots on:*] "A mighty fortress is our God . . ." [*He sings a verse or so of Luther's hymn.*] And talking of King Gustavus, this freedom he tried to bring to Germany cost him a pretty penny. Back in Sweden he had to levy a salt tax, the poorer folks didn't like it a bit. Then, too, he had to lock up the Germans and even cut their heads off, they clung so to slavery and their Kaiser. Of course, if no one had wanted to be free, the King wouldn't have had any fun. First it was just Poland he tried to protect from bad men, especially the Kaiser, then his appetite grew with eating, and he ended up protecting Germany too. Now Germany put up a pretty decent fight. So the good King had nothing but worries in return for his outlay and his goodness, and of course he had to get his money back with taxes, which made bad blood, but he didn't shrink even from that. For he had one thing in his favor anyway, God's Holy Word, which was all to the good, because otherwise they could have said he did it for profit. That's how he kept his conscience clear. He always put conscience first.

MOTHER COURAGE: It's plain you're no Swede, or you'd speak differently of the Hero King.

THE CHAPLAIN: What's more, you eat his bread.

THE COOK: I don't eat his bread. I bake his bread.

MOTHER COURAGE: He's unbeatable. Why? His men believe in him. [*Earnestly:*] To hear the big fellows talk, they wage war from fear of God and for all things bright and beautiful, but just look into it, and you'll see they're not so silly; they want a good profit out of it, or else the little fellows like you and me wouldn't back 'em up.

THE COOK: That's right.

THE CHAPLAIN: And as a Dutchman you'd do well to see which flag's flying here before you express an opinion!

MOTHER COURAGE: All good Protestants forever!

THE COOK: A health!

> [KATTRIN *has begun to strut about with* YVETTE's *hat on, copying* YVETTE's *sexy walk. Suddenly cannon and shots. Drums.* MOTHER COURAGE, *the* COOK, *and the* CHAPLAIN *rush around to the front of the cart, the last two with glasses in their hands. The* ORDNANCE OFFICER *and a* SOLDIER *come running to the cannon and try to push it along.*]

MOTHER COURAGE: What's the matter? Let me get my washing off that gun, you slobs! [*She tries to do so.*]

THE OFFICER: The Catholics! Surprise attack! We don't know if we can get away! [*To the* SOLDIER:] Get that gun! [*He runs off.*]

THE COOK: For heaven's sake! I must go to the Commander. Mother Courage, I'll be back in a day or two—for a short conversation. [*He rushes off.*]

MOTHER COURAGE: Hey, you've left your pipe!

THE COOK [*off*]: Keep it for me, I'll need it!

MOTHER COURAGE: This *would* happen just when we were making money.

THE CHAPLAIN: Well, I must be going too. Yes, if the enemy's so close, it can be dangerous. "Blessed are the peace-makers," a good slogan in war time! If only I had a cloak.

MOTHER COURAGE: I'm lending no cloaks. Not even to save a life, I'm not. I've had experience in that line.

THE CHAPLAIN: But I'm in special danger. Because of my religion.

MOTHER COURAGE [*bringing him a cloak*]: It's against my better judgment. Now run!

THE CHAPLAIN: I thank you, you're very generous, but maybe I'd better stay and sit here. If I run, I might attract the enemy's attention, I might arouse suspicion.

MOTHER COURAGE [*to the* SOLDIER]: Let it alone, you dolt, who's going to pay you for this? It'll cost you your life, let me hold it for you.

THE SOLDIER [*running away*]: You're my witness: I tried!

MOTHER COURAGE: I'll swear to it! [*Seeing* KATTRIN *with the hat:*] What on earth are you up to—with a whore's hat! Take it off this minute! Are you mad? With the enemy coming? [*She tears the hat off her head.*] Do you want them to find you and make a whore of you? And she has the boots on too, straight from Babylon. I'll soon settle that. [*She tries to get them off.*] Oh God, Chaplain, help me with these boots, I'll be right back. [*She runs to the wagon.*]

YVETTE [*entering and powdering her face*]: What's that you say: the Catholics are coming? Where's my hat? Who's been trampling on it? I can't run around in that, what will they think of me? And I don't even have a mirror. [*To the* CHAPLAIN:] How do I look—too much powder?

THE CHAPLAIN: Just, er, right.

YVETTE: And where are my red boots? [*She can't find them because* KATTRIN *is hiding her feet under her skirt.*] I left them here! Now I've got to go barefoot to my tent, it's a scandal! [*Exit.*]

[SWISS CHEESE *comes running in carrying a cash box.*]

[MOTHER COURAGE *enters with her hands covered with ashes.*]

MOTHER COURAGE [*to* KATTRIN]: Ashes! [*To* SWISS CHEESE:] What have you got there?

SWISS CHEESE: The regimental cash box.

MOTHER COURAGE: Throw it away! Your paymastering days are over!

SWISS CHEESE: It's a trust! [*He goes to the back.*]

MOTHER COURAGE [*to the* CHAPLAIN]: Off with your pastor's coat, Chaplain, or they'll recognize you, cloak or no cloak. [*She is rubbing ashes into* KATTRIN's *face.*] Keep still. A little dirt, and you're safe. A calamity! The sentries were drunk. Well, one must hide one's light under a bushel, as they say. When a soldier sees a clean face, there's one more whore in the world. Especially a Catholic soldier. For weeks on end, no grub. Then, when the plundering starts and they steal some, they jump on top of the womenfolk. That should do. Let me look at you. Not bad. Looks like you've been rolling in muck. Don't tremble. Nothing can happen to you now. [*To* SWISS CHEESE:] Where've you left the cash box?

SWISS CHEESE: I thought I'd just put it in the wagon.

MOTHER COURAGE [*horrified*]: What! In my wagon? God punish you for a prize idiot! If I just look away for a moment! They'll hang all three of us!

SWISS CHEESE: Then I'll put it somewhere else. Or escape with it.

MOTHER COURAGE: You'll stay where you are. It's too late.

THE CHAPLAIN [*still changing his clothes*]: For heaven's sake: the flag!

MOTHER COURAGE [*taking down the flag*]: God in heaven! I don't notice it any more. I've had it twenty-five years.

[*The thunder of cannon grows.*]

[*Three days later. Morning. The cannon is gone.* MOTHER COURAGE, KATTRIN, *the* CHAPLAIN, *and* SWISS CHEESE *sit anxiously eating.*]

SWISS CHEESE: This is the third day I've been sitting here doing nothing, and the Sergeant, who's always been patient with me, may be slowly beginning to ask, "Where on earth is Swiss Cheese with that cash box?"

MOTHER COURAGE: Be glad they're not on the trail.

THE CHAPLAIN: What about me? I can't hold a service here or I'll be in hot water. It is written, "Out of the abundance of the heart, the tongue speaketh." But woe is me if *my* tongue speaketh!

MOTHER COURAGE: That's how it is. Here you sit—one with his religion, the other with his cash box, I don't know which is more dangerous.

THE CHAPLAIN: We're in God's hands now!

MOTHER COURAGE: I hope we're not *that* desperate, but it *is* hard to sleep nights. 'Course it'd be easier if you weren't here, Swiss Cheese, all the same I've not done badly. I told them I was against the Antichrist, who's a Swede with horns on his head. I told them I noticed his left horn's a bit threadbare. When they cross-examined me, I always asked where I could buy holy candles a bit cheaper. I know these things because Swiss Cheese's father was a Catholic and made jokes about it. They didn't quite believe me but they needed a canteen, so they turned a blind eye. Maybe it's all for the best. We're prisoners. But so are lice in fur.

THE CHAPLAIN: The milk is good. As far as quantity goes, we may have to reduce our Swedish appetites somewhat. We are defeated.

MOTHER COURAGE: Who's defeated? The defeats and victories of the fellows at the top aren't always defeats and victories for the fellows at the bottom. Not at all. There've been cases where a defeat is a victory for the fellows at the bottom, it's only their honor that's lost, nothing serious. In Livonia once, our Chief took such a knock from the enemy, in the confusion I got a fine gray mare out of the baggage train, it pulled my wagon seven months—till we won and there was an inventory. But in general both defeat and victory are a costly business for us that haven't got much. The best thing is for politics to get stuck in the mud. [To SWISS CHEESE:] Eat!

SWISS CHEESE: I don't like it. How will the sergeant pay his men?

MOTHER COURAGE: Soldiers in flight don't get paid.

SWISS CHEESE: Well, they could claim to be. No pay, no flight. They can refuse to budge.

MOTHER COURAGE: Swiss Cheese, your sense of duty worries me. I've brought you up to be honest because you're not very bright. But don't overdo it. And now I'm going with the chaplain to buy a Catholic flag and some meat. There's no one can hunt out meat like him, sure as a sleepwalker. He can tell a good piece of meat from the way his mouth waters. A good thing they let me stay in the business. In business you ask what price, not what religion. And Protestant trousers keep you just as warm.

THE CHAPLAIN: As the mendicant monk said when there was talk of the Lutherans turning the whole world upside down: Beggars will always be needed. [MOTHER COURAGE disappears into the wagon.] She's worried about the cash box. Up to now they've ignored us— as if we were part of the wagon—but can it last?

SWISS CHEESE: I can get rid of it.

THE CHAPLAIN: That's almost more dangerous. Suppose you're seen. They have spies. Yesterday morning one jumped out of the very hole I was relieving myself in. I was so scared I almost broke out in prayer—that would have given me away all right! I believe their favorite way of finding a Protestant is smelling his excrement. The spy was a little brute with a bandage over one eye.

MOTHER COURAGE [clambering out of the wagon with a basket]: I've found you out, you shameless hussy! [She holds up YVETTE's red boots in triumph.] Yvette's red boots! She just swiped them—because you went and told her she was a captivating person. [She lays them in the basket.] Stealing Yvette's boots! But she disgraces herself for money, you do it for nothing—for pleasure! I told you, you must wait for the peace. No soldiers! Save your proud peacock ways for peacetime!

THE CHAPLAIN: I don't find her proud.

MOTHER COURAGE: Prouder than she can afford to be. I like her when people say "I never noticed the poor thing." I like her when she's a stone in Dalarna, where there's nothing but stones. [To SWISS CHEESE:] Leave the cash box where it is, do you hear? And pay attention to your sister, she needs it. Between the two of you, you'll be the death of me yet. I'd rather take care of a bag of fleas.

[*She leaves with the* CHAPLAIN. KATTRIN *clears the dishes away.*]

SWISS CHEESE: Not many days more when you can sit in the sun in your shirtsleeves. [KATTRIN *points to a tree.*] Yes, the leaves are yellow already. [*With gestures,* KATTRIN *asks if he wants a drink.*] I'm not drinking, I'm thinking. [*Pause.*] She says she can't sleep. So I should take the cash box away. I've found a place for it. I'll keep it in the mole hole by the river till the time comes. I might get it tonight before sunrise and take it to the regiment. How far can they have fled in three days? The Sergeant's eyes'll pop out of his head. "You've disappointed me most pleasantly, Swiss Cheese," he'll say, "I trust you with the cash box and you bring it back!" Yes, Kattrin, I *will* have a glass now!

[*When* KATTRIN *reappears behind the wagon two men confront her. One of them is a* SERGEANT. *The other doffs his hat and flourishes it in a showy greeting. He has a bandage over one eye.*]

THE MAN WITH THE BANDAGE: Good morning, young lady. Have you seen a man from the Second Protestant Regiment?

[*Terrified,* KATTRIN *runs away, spilling her brandy. The two men look at each other and then withdraw after seeing* SWISS CHEESE.]

SWISS CHEESE [*starting up from his reflection*]: You're spilling it! What's the matter with you, have you hurt your eye? I don't understand. Yes, and I must be going, too. I've decided it's the thing to do. [*He stands up. She does all she can to make him aware of the danger he is in. He only pushes her away.*] I'd like to know what you mean. I know you mean well, poor thing, you just can't get it out. And don't trouble yourself about the brandy, I'll live to drink so much of it, what's one glass? [*He takes the cash box out of the wagon and puts it under his coat.*] I'll be back right away. But don't hold me up or I'll have to scold you. Yes, I know you mean well. If you could only speak!

[*When she tries to hold him back he kisses her and pulls himself free. Exit. She is desperate and runs up and down, emitting little sounds.* MOTHER COURAGE *and the* CHAPLAIN *return.* KATTRIN *rushes at her mother.*]

MOTHER COURAGE: What is it, what is it, Kattrin? Control yourself! Has someone done something to you? Where is Swiss Cheese? [*To the* CHAPLAIN:] Don't stand around, get that Catholic flag up! [*She takes a Catholic flag out of her basket and the* CHAPLAIN *runs it up the pole.*]

THE CHAPLAIN [*bitterly*]: All good Catholics forever!

MOTHER COURAGE: Now, Kattrin, calm down and tell all about it, your mother understands you. What, that little bastard of mine's taken the cash box away? I'll box his ears for him, the rascal! Now take your time and don't try to talk, use your hands. I don't like it when you howl like a dog, what'll the chaplain think of you? You're giving him the creeps. A man with one eye was here?

THE CHAPLAIN: That fellow with one eye is an informer! Have they caught Swiss Cheese? [KATTRIN *shakes her head, shrugs her shoulders.*] This is the end.

[*Voices off. The two men bring in* SWISS CHEESE.]

SWISS CHEESE: Let me go. I've nothing on me. You're breaking my shoulder! I am innocent.

THE SERGEANT: This is where he comes from. These are his friends.

MOTHER COURAGE: Us? Since when?

SWISS CHEESE: I don't even know 'em. I was just getting my lunch here. Ten hellers it cost me. Maybe you saw me sitting on that bench. It was too salty.

THE SERGEANT: Who are you people, anyway?

MOTHER COURAGE: Law-abiding citizens! It's true what he says. He bought his lunch here. And it was too salty.

THE SERGEANT: Are you pretending you don't know him?

MOTHER COURAGE: I can't know all of them, can I? I don't ask, "What's your name and are you a heathen?" If they pay up, they're not heathens to me. Are you a heathen?

SWISS CHEESE: Oh, no!

THE CHAPLAIN: He sat there like a law-abiding fellow and never once opened his mouth. Except to eat. Which is necessary.

THE SERGEANT: Who do you think you are?

MOTHER COURAGE: Oh, he's my barman. And you're thirsty, I'll bring you a glass of brandy. You must be footsore and weary!

THE SERGEANT: No brandy on duty. [*To* SWISS CHEESE:] You were carrying something. You must have hidden it by the river. We saw the bulge in your shirt.

MOTHER COURAGE: Sure it was him?

SWISS CHEESE: I think you mean another fellow. There was a fellow with something under his shirt, I saw him. I'm the wrong man.

MOTHER COURAGE: I think so too. It's a misunderstanding. Could happen to anyone. Oh, I know what people are like, I'm Mother Courage, you've heard of me, everyone knows about me, and I can tell you this: he looks honest.

THE SERGEANT: We're after the regimental cash box. And we know what the man looks like who's been keeping it. We've been looking for him two days. It's you.

SWISS CHEESE: No, it's not!

THE SERGEANT: And if you don't shell out, you're dead, see? Where is it?

MOTHER COURAGE [urgently]: 'Course he'd give it to you to save his life. He'd up and say, *I've got it, here it is, you're stronger than me.* He's not *that* stupid. Speak, little stupid, the sergeant's giving you a chance!

SWISS CHEESE: What if I *haven't* got it?

THE SERGEANT: Come with us. We'll get it out of you. [*They take him off.*]

MOTHER COURAGE [*shouting after them*]: He'd tell you! He's not *that* stupid! And don't you break his shoulder! [*She runs after them.*]

[*The same evening. The* CHAPLAIN *and* KATTRIN *are rinsing glasses and polishing knives.*]

THE CHAPLAIN: Cases of people getting caught like this are by no means unknown in the history of religion. I am reminded of the Passion of Our Lord and Savior. There's an old song about it.

[*He sings "The Song of the Hours":*]

> In the first hour of the day
> Simple Jesus Christ was
> Presented as a murderer
> To the heathen Pilate.
>
> Pilate found no fault in him
> No cause to condemn him
> So he sent the Lord away.
> Let King Herod see him!

Hour the third: the Son of God
Was with scourges beaten
And they set a crown of thorns
On the head of Jesus.

And they dressed him as a king
Joked and jested at him
And the cross to die upon
He himself must carry.

Six: they stripped Lord Jesus bare.
To the cross they nailed him.
When the blood came gushing, he
Prayed and loud lamented.

Each upon his cross, two thieves
Mocked him like the others.
And the bright sun crept away
Not to see such doings.

Nine: Lord Jesus cried aloud
That he was forsaken!
In a sponge upon a pole
Vinegar was fed him.

Then the Lord gave up the ghost
And the earth did tremble.
Temple curtain split in twain.
Cliffs fell in the ocean.

Evening: they broke the bones
Of the malefactors.
Then they took a spear and pierced
The side of gentle Jesus.

And the blood and water ran
And they laughed at Jesus.
Of this simple son of man
Such and more they tell us.

MOTHER COURAGE [*entering, excited*]: It's life and death. But the
Sergeant will still listen to us. The only thing is, he mustn't
know it's our Swiss Cheese, or they'll say we helped him. It's only
a matter of money, but where can we get money? Isn't Yvette here
yet? I talked to her on the way over. She's picked up a Colonel who
may be willing to buy her a canteen business.

THE CHAPLAIN: You'd sell the wagon, everything?

MOTHER COURAGE: Where else would I get the money for the Sergeant?

THE CHAPLAIN: What are you to live off?

MOTHER COURAGE: That's just it.

[*Enter* YVETTE *with a hoary old* COLONEL.]

YVETTE [*embracing* MOTHER COURAGE]: Dear Mistress Courage, we meet again. [*Whispering:*] He didn't say no. [*Aloud:*] This is my friend, my, um, business adviser. I happened to hear you might sell your wagon. Due to special circumstances, I'd like to think about it.

MOTHER COURAGE: I want to pawn it, not sell it. And nothing hasty. In war time you don't find another wagon like that so easy.

YVETTE [*disappointed*]: Only pawn it? I thought you wanted to sell. I don't know if I'm interested. [*To the* COLONEL:] What do you think, my dear?

THE COLONEL: I quite agree with you, bunny.

MOTHER COURAGE: It's only for pawn.

YVETTE: I thought you *had* to have the money.

MOTHER COURAGE [*firmly*]: I do have to have it. But I'd rather wear my feet off looking for an offer than just sell. Why? We live off the wagon. It's an opportunity for you, Yvette. Who knows when you'll have another such? Who knows when you'll find another business adviser?

THE COLONEL: Take it, take it!

YVETTE: My friend thinks I should go ahead, but I'm not sure, if it's only for pawn. You think we should buy it outright, don't you?

THE COLONEL: I do, bunny, I do!

MOTHER COURAGE: Then you must go and find something that's for sale. Maybe you'll find it—if you have the time, and your friend goes with you, let's say in about a week, or two weeks, you may find the right thing.

YVETTE: Yes, we can certainly look around for something. I love going around looking, I love going around with you, Poldy . . .

THE COLONEL: Really? Do you?

YVETTE: Oh, it's lovely! I could take two weeks of it!

THE COLONEL: Really, could you?

YVETTE: If you get the money, when are you thinking of paying it back?

MOTHER COURAGE: In two weeks. Maybe one.

YVETTE: I can't make up my mind. Poldy, advise me, chéri! [*She takes the* COLONEL *to one side.*] She'll have to sell, don't worry. That Lieutenant—the blond one, you know the one I mean—he'll lend

me the money. He's *mad* about me, he says I remind him of someone. What do you advise?

THE COLONEL: Oh, I have to warn you against *him*. He's no good. He'll
exploit the situation. I told you, bunny, I told you *I'd* buy you
something, didn't I tell you that?

YVETTE: I simply can't let you!

THE COLONEL: Oh, please, please!

YVETTE: Well, if you think the Lieutenant might exploit the situation
I *will* let you!

THE COLONEL: I do think so.

YVETTE: So you advise me to?

THE COLONEL: I do, bunny, I do!

YVETTE [*returning to* MOTHER COURAGE]: My friend says all right. Write
me out a receipt saying the wagon's mine when the two weeks are up
—with everything in it. I'll just run through it all now, the two
hundred guilders can wait. [*To the* COLONEL:] You go ahead to the
camp, I'll follow, I must go over all this so nothing'll be missing
later from *my* wagon!

THE COLONEL: Wait, I'll help you up! [*He does so.*] Come soon, honey
bun! [*Exit.*]

MOTHER COURAGE: Yvette, Yvette!

YVETTE: There aren't many boots left!

MOTHER COURAGE: Yvette, this is no time to go through the wagon,
yours or not yours. You promised you'd talk to the Sergeant about
Swiss Cheese. There isn't a minute to lose. He's up before the
court-martial one hour from now.

YVETTE: I just want to count these shirts again.

MOTHER COURAGE [*dragging her down the steps by the skirt*]: You
hyena, Swiss Cheese's life's at stake! And don't say who the money
comes from. Pretend he's your sweetheart, for heaven's sake, or
we'll all get it for helping him.

YVETTE: I've arranged to meet One Eye in the bushes. He must be
there by now.

THE CHAPLAIN: And don't hand over all two hundred, a hundred and
fifty's sure to be enough.

MOTHER COURAGE: Is it your money? I'll thank you to keep your nose
out of this, I'm not doing you out of your porridge. Now run, and
no haggling, remember his life's at stake. [*She pushes* YVETTE *off.*]

THE CHAPLAIN: I didn't want to talk you into anything, but what are
we going to live on? You have an unemployable daughter around
your neck.

MOTHER COURAGE: I'm counting on that cash box, smart aleck. They'll pay his expenses out of it.

THE CHAPLAIN: You think she can work it?

MOTHER COURAGE: It's in her own interest: I pay the two hundred and she gets the wagon. She knows what she's doing, she won't have her Colonel on the string forever. Kattrin, go and clean the knives, use pumice stone. And don't you stand around like Jesus in Gethsemane. Get a move on, wash those glasses. There'll be over fifty cavalrymen here tonight, and you'll be saying you're not used to being on your feet. "Oh my poor feet, in church I never had to run around like this!" I think they'll let us have him. Thanks be to God they're corruptible. They're not wolves, they're human and after money. God is merciful, and men are bribable, that's how His will is done on earth as it is in Heaven. Corruption is our only hope. As long as there's corruption, there'll be merciful judges and even the innocent may get off.

[YVETTE comes in panting.]

YVETTE: They'll do it for two hundred if you make it snappy—these things change from one minute to the next. I'd better take One Eye to my Colonel at once. He confessed he had the cash box, they put the thumbscrews on him. But he threw it in the river when he noticed them coming up behind him. So it's gone. Shall I run and get the money from my Colonel?

MOTHER COURAGE: The cash box gone? How'll I ever get my two hundred back?

YVETTE: So you thought you could get it from the cash box? I would have been sunk. Not a hope, Mother Courage. If you want your Swiss Cheese, you'll have to pay. Or should I let the whole thing drop, so you can keep your wagon?

MOTHER COURAGE: I wasn't figuring on this. But you needn't hound me, you'll get the wagon, it's yours already, and it's been mine seventeen years. I need a minute to think it over, it's all so sudden. What can I do? I can't pay two hundred. You should have haggled with them. I must hold on to something, or any passer-by can kick me in the ditch. Go and say I'll pay a hundred and twenty or the deal's off. Even then I lose the wagon.

YVETTE: They won't do it. And anyway, One Eye's in a hurry. He keeps looking over his shoulder all the time, he's so worked up. Hadn't I better give them the whole two hundred?

MOTHER COURAGE [desperate]: I can't pay it! I've been working thirty years. She's twenty-five and still no husband. I have her to think of. So leave me alone. I know what I'm doing. A hundred and twenty or no deal.

YVETTE: You know best. [*She runs off.*]

> [MOTHER COURAGE *turns away and slowly walks a few paces to the rear. Then she turns around, looks neither at the* CHAPLAIN *nor her daughter, and sits down to help* KATTRIN *polish the knives.*]

MOTHER COURAGE: Don't break the glasses, they're not ours. Watch what you're doing, you're cutting yourself. Swiss Cheese will be back, I'll give two hundred, if I have to. You'll get your brother back. With eighty guilders we could pack a hamper with goods and begin again. It wouldn't be the end of the world.

THE CHAPLAIN: The Bible says: the Lord will provide.

MOTHER COURAGE: Rub them dry, I said.

> [*They clean the knives in silence.*]

They say the war will stop soon. How would it? I ask. And no one can answer me. [*Slowly.*] The King and the Pope are mortal enemies, their Faith is different. They must go for each other till one of them drops dead, neither of them can relax till then. Even so they can't get on with it. Why not? The Emperor is in the way, and they both have something against him. They're not going to fight each other to the death with the Emperor lurking about till they're half dead so he can fall on both of 'em! No, they're banding together against the Emperor so he'll drop dead first and they can go for each other.

> [*Suddenly* KATTRIN *runs sobbing behind the wagon.*]

Someone once offered me five hundred guilders for the wagon. I didn't take it. My Eilif, wherever he may be, thought I'd taken it and cried all night.

> [YVETTE *comes running in.*]

YVETTE: They won't do it. I warned you. One Eye was going to drop it then and there. There's no point, he said. He said the drums would roll any second now and that's the sign a verdict has been reached. I offered a hundred and fifty, he didn't even shrug. I could hardly get him to stay there while I came here.

MOTHER COURAGE: Tell him I'll pay two hundred. Run!

> [YVETTE *runs.* MOTHER COURAGE *sits, silent. The* CHAPLAIN *has stopped doing the glasses.*]

I believe—I've haggled too long.

[*In the distance, a roll of drums. The* CHAPLAIN *stands up and walks toward the rear.* MOTHER COURAGE *remains seated. It grows dark. It gets light again.* MOTHER COURAGE *has not moved.* YVETTE *appears, pale.*]

YVETTE: Now you've done it—with your haggling. You can keep the wagon now. He got eleven bullets in him. I don't know why I still bother about you, you don't deserve it, but I just happened to learn they don't think the cash box is really in the river. They suspect it's here, they think you're connected with him. I think they're going to bring him here to see if you'll give yourself away when you see him. You'd better not know him or we're in for it. And I'd better tell you straight, they're just behind me. Shall I keep Kattrin away? [MOTHER COURAGE *shakes her head.*] Does she know? Maybe she never heard the drums or didn't understand.

MOTHER COURAGE: She knows. Bring her.

[YVETTE *brings* KATTRIN, *who walks over to her mother and stands by her.* MOTHER COURAGE *takes her hand. Two men come on with a stretcher; there is a sheet on it and something underneath. Beside them, the* SERGEANT. *They put the stretcher down.*]

THE SERGEANT: Here's a man we can't identify. But he has to be registered to keep the records straight. He bought a meal from you. Look at him, see if you know him. [*He pulls back the sheet.*] Do you know him? [MOTHER COURAGE *shakes her head.*] What? You never saw him before he took that meal? [MOTHER COURAGE *shakes her head.*] Lift him up. Throw him in the carrion pit. He has no one that knows him.

[*They carry him off.*]

Scene IV

MOTHER COURAGE SINGS THE SONG OF THE GREAT CAPITULATION

[*Outside an officer's tent.* MOTHER COURAGE *waits. A* CLERK *looks out of the tent.*]

THE CLERK: I know you. You had a Protestant paymaster with you, he was hiding out with you. Better make no complaint.

MOTHER COURAGE: But I'm innocent and if I give up it'll look as if I have a bad conscience. They cut everything in my wagon to ribbons with their sabers and then claimed a fine of five thalers for nothing and less than nothing.

THE CLERK: For your own good, keep your trap shut. We haven't many canteens, so we let you stay in business, especially if you've a bad conscience and have to pay a fine now and then.

MOTHER COURAGE: I'm going to file a complaint.

THE CLERK: As you wish. Wait here till the Captain has time.

[*He withdraws into the tent.*]

[*A* YOUNG SOLDIER *comes storming in.*]

THE YOUNG SOLDIER: Screw the Captain! Where *is* the son of a bitch? Swiping my reward, spending it on brandy for his whores, I'll rip his belly open!

AN OLDER SOLDIER [*coming after him*]: Shut your hole, you'll wind up in the stocks.

THE YOUNG SOLDIER: Come out, you thief, I'll make lamb chops out of you! I was the only one in the squad who swam the river and *he* grabs my money, I can't even buy myself a beer. Come on out! And let me slice you up!

THE OLDER SOLDIER: Holy Christ, he'll destroy himself!

THE YOUNG SOLDIER: Let me go or I'll run you down too. This has got to be settled!

THE OLDER SOLDIER: Saved the Colonel's horse and didn't get the reward. He's young, he hasn't been at it long.

MOTHER COURAGE: Let him go. He doesn't have to be chained, he's not a dog. Very reasonable to want a reward. Why else should he want to shine?

THE YOUNG SOLDIER: He's in there pouring it down! You're all nice. I've done something special, I want the reward!

MOTHER COURAGE: Young man, don't scream at *me*, I have my own troubles. And go easy with your voice, you may need it when the Captain comes. The Captain'll come and you'll be hoarse and can't make a sound, so he'll have to deny himself the pleasure of sticking you in the stocks till you pass out. The screamers don't scream long, only half an hour, after which they have to be sung to sleep, they're all in.

THE YOUNG SOLDIER: I'm not all in, and sleep's out of the question. I'm hungry. They're making their bread out of acorns and hempseed, and not even much of that. He's whoring on my money, and I'm hungry. I'll murder him!

MOTHER COURAGE: I understand: you're hungry. Last year your Commander ordered you people out of the streets and into the fields. So the crops got trampled down. I could have got ten guilders for boots, if anyone'd had ten guilders, and if I'd had any boots. He didn't expect to be around this year, but he is, and there's famine. I understand: you're angry.

THE YOUNG SOLDIER: It's no use your talking. I won't stand for injustice!

MOTHER COURAGE: You're quite right. But how long? How long won't you stand for injustice? One hour? Or two? you haven't asked yourself that, have you? And yet it's the main thing. It's pure misery to sit in the stocks. Especially if you leave it till then to decide you do stand for injustice.

THE YOUNG SOLDIER: I don't know why I listen to you. Screw that Captain! Where is he?

MOTHER COURAGE: You listen because you know I'm right. Your rage has calmed down already. It was a short one and you'd need a long one. But where would you find it?

THE YOUNG SOLDIER: Are you trying to say it's not right to ask for the money?

MOTHER COURAGE: Just the opposite. I only say, your rage won't last. You'll get nowhere with it, it's a pity. If your rage was a long one, I'd urge you on. Slice him up, I'd advise you. But what's the use if you don't slice him up because you can feel your tail between your legs? You stand there and the Captain lets you have it.

THE OLDER SOLDIER: You're quite right, he's crazy.

THE YOUNG SOLDIER: All right, we'll see whether I slice him up or not. [He draws his sword.] When he comes out, I slice him up!

THE CLERK [looking out]: The Captain will be out in a minute. [In the tone of military command:] Be seated!

[The YOUNG SOLDIER sits.]

MOTHER COURAGE: And he is seated. What did I tell you? You are seated. They know us through and through. They know how they must work it. Be seated! And we sit. And in sitting there's no revolt. Better not stand up again—not the way you did before—don't stand up again. And don't be embarrassed in front of me, I'm no better, not a scrap. They've drawn our teeth, haven't they? If we say boo, it's bad for business. Let me tell you about the great capitulation.

[She sings "The Song of the Great Capitulation":]

Long ago when I was a green beginner
I believed I was a special case.

(None of your ordinary run of the mill girls, with my looks and my talent, and my love of the higher things in life!)

And if I picked a hair out of my dinner
I would put the cook right in his place.

(All or nothing. Anyhow, never the second best. I am the master of my Fate. I'll take no orders from no one.)

Then a little bird whispered in my ear:
"That's all very well, but wait a year
And you will join the big brass band
And with your trumpet in your hand
You'll march in lockstep with the rest.
Then one day, look! The battalions wheel!
The whole thing swings from east to west!
And falling on your knees, you'll squeal:
The Lord God, He knows best!
(But don't give me that!)"

And a month or two before that year was over
I had learned to drink their cup of tea.

(Two children round your neck, and the price of bread and what all!)

And the day soon came when I was to discover
They had me just where they wanted me.

(You must get in good with people. If you scratch my back, I'll scratch yours. Don't stick your neck out.)

And that little bird whispered in my ear:
"You didn't even take a year!
And you have joined the big brass band
And with your trumpet in your hand
You marched in lockstep with the rest.
But one day, look! The battalions wheeled!
The whole thing swung from east to west!
And falling on your knees, you squealed:
The Lord God, He knows best!
(But don't give me that!)"

Yes, our hopes are high, our plans colossal!
And we hitch our wagon to a star!

(Where there's a will there's a way. One can't hold a good man down.)

> We can move mountains, says St. Paul the great
> > Apostle
> And yet: how heavy one cigar!

(We must cut our coat according to our cloth.)

> For that little bird whispers in your ear:
> "That's all very well but wait a year
> And we will join the big brass band
> And with our trumpet in our hand
> We march in lockstep with the rest.
> But one day, look! The battalions wheel!
> The whole thing swings from east to west!
> And falling on our knees, we squeal:
> The Lord God, He knows best!
> (But don't give me that!)"

And so I think you should stay here with your sword drawn if you're set on it and your anger is big enough. You have good cause, I admit. But if your anger is a short one, you'd better go.

THE YOUNG SOLDIER: Kiss my ass. [*He stumbles off, the other* SOLDIER *following him.*]

THE CLERK [*sticking his head out*]: The Captain is ready now. You can file your complaint.

MOTHER COURAGE: I've thought better of it. I'm not complaining. [*Exit.*]

[*The* CLERK *looks after her, shaking his head.*]

❀ Scene V

TWO YEARS HAVE PASSED. THE WAR COVERS WIDER AND WIDER TER-
RITORY. FOREVER ON THE MOVE, THE LITTLE WAGON CROSSES POLAND,
MORAVIA, BAVARIA, ITALY, AND AGAIN BAVARIA. 1631. TILLY'S VICTORY
AT MAGDEBURG COSTS MOTHER COURAGE FOUR OFFICERS' SHIRTS.

[*The wagon stands in a war-ravaged village. Faint military music from the distance. Two* SOLDIERS *are being served at a counter by* KATTRIN *and* MOTHER COURAGE. *One of them has a woman's fur coat about his shoulders.*]

MOTHER COURAGE: What, you can't pay? No money, no brandy! They can play victory marches, they should pay their men.

THE FIRST SOLDIER: I want my brandy! I arrived too late for plunder. The Chief allowed one hour to plunder the town, it's a swindle. He's not inhuman, he says. So I suppose they bought him off.

THE CHAPLAIN [*staggering in*]: There are more in the farmhouse. A family of peasants. Help me someone. I need linen!

[*The second* SOLDIER *goes with him.* KATTRIN *is getting very excited. She tries to get her mother to bring linen out.*]

MOTHER COURAGE: I have none. I sold all my bandages to the regiment. I'm not tearing up my officers' shirts for these people.

THE CHAPLAIN [*calling over his shoulder*]: I said I need linen!

MOTHER COURAGE [*stopping* KATTRIN *from entering the wagon*]: Not a thing! They can't pay, and why? They have nothing and they pay nothing!

THE CHAPLAIN [*to a* WOMAN *he is carrying in*]: Why did you stay out there in the line of fire?

THE WOMAN: Our farm—

MOTHER COURAGE: Think they'd ever let go of *anything?* And now I'm supposed to pay. Well, I won't!

THE FIRST SOLDIER: They're Protestants, why should they be Protestants?

MOTHER COURAGE: Protestant, Catholic, what do *they* care? Their farm's gone, that's what.

THE SECOND SOLDIER: They're not Protestants anyway, they're Catholics.

THE FIRST SOLDIER: In a bombardment we can't pick and choose.

A PEASANT [*brought on by the* CHAPLAIN]: My arm's gone.

THE CHAPLAIN: Where's that linen?

[*All look at* MOTHER COURAGE, *who does not budge.*]

MOTHER COURAGE: I can't give you any. With all I have to pay out— taxes, duties, bribes. . . . [KATTRIN *takes up a board and threatens her mother with it, emitting gurgling sounds.*] Are you out of your mind? Put that board down or I'll let you have one, you lunatic! I'm giving nothing, I don't dare, I have myself to think of. [*The* CHAPLAIN *lifts her bodily off the steps of the wagon and sets her down on the ground. He takes out shirts from the wagon and tears them in strips.*] My shirts, my officers' shirts!

[*From the house comes the cry of a child in pain.*]

THE PEASANT: The child's still in there.

[KATTRIN *runs in.*]

THE CHAPLAIN [*to the* WOMAN]: Stay where you are. She's getting it for you.

MOTHER COURAGE: Hold her back, the roof may fall in!

THE CHAPLAIN: I'm not going back in there!

MOTHER COURAGE [*pulled in both directions*]: Go easy on my expensive linen.

[*The* SECOND SOLDIER *holds her back.* KATTRIN *brings a baby out of the ruins.*]

MOTHER COURAGE: Another baby to drag around, you must be pleased with yourself. Give it to its mother this minute! Or do I have to fight you again for hours till I get it from you? Are you deaf? [*To the* SECOND SOLDIER:] Don't stand about gawking, go back there and tell 'em to stop that music, I can see their victory without it. I have nothing but losses from your victory!

THE CHAPLAIN [*bandaging*]: The blood's coming through.

[KATTRIN *is rocking the child and half humming a lullaby.*]

MOTHER COURAGE: There she sits, happy as a lark in all this misery. Give the baby back, the mother is coming to! [*She sees the* FIRST SOLDIER. *He had been handling the drinks, and is now trying to make off with the bottle.*] God's truth! You beast! You want another victory, do you? Then pay for it!

THE FIRST SOLDIER: I have nothing.

MOTHER COURAGE [*snatching the fur coat back*]: Then leave this coat, it's stolen goods anyhow.

THE CHAPLAIN: There's still someone in there.

⚜ *Scene VI*

BEFORE THE CITY OF INGOLSTADT IN BAVARIA MOTHER COURAGE IS PRESENT AT THE FUNERAL OF THE FALLEN COMMANDER, TILLY. CONVERSATIONS TAKE PLACE ABOUT WAR HEROES AND THE DURATION OF THE WAR. THE CHAPLAIN COMPLAINS THAT HIS TALENTS ARE LYING FALLOW AND KATTRIN GETS THE RED BOOTS. THE YEAR IS 1632.

[*The inside of a canteen tent. The inner side of a counter at the rear. Rain. In the distance, drums and funeral music. The* CHAPLAIN *and the regimental* CLERK *are playing draughts.* MOTHER COURAGE *and her daughter are taking an inventory.*]

THE CHAPLAIN: The funeral procession is just starting out.

MOTHER COURAGE: Pity about the Chief—twenty-two pairs of socks— getting killed that way. They say it was an accident. There was a fog over the fields that morning, and the fog was to blame. The Chief called up another regiment, told 'em to fight to the death, rode back again, missed his way in the fog, went forward instead of back, and ran smack into a bullet in the thick of the battle—only four lanterns left. [*A whistle from the rear. She goes to the counter. To a* SOLDIER:] It's a disgrace the way you're all skipping your Commander's funeral! [*She pours a drink.*]

THE CLERK: They shouldn't have handed the money out before the funeral. Now the men are all getting drunk instead of going to it.

THE CHAPLAIN [*to the* CLERK]: Don't you have to be there?

THE CLERK: I stayed away because of the rain.

MOTHER COURAGE: It's different for you, the rain might spoil your uniform. I hear they wanted to ring the bells for his funeral, which is natural, but it came out that the churches had been shot up by his orders, so the poor Commander won't be hearing any bells when they lower him in his grave. Instead, they'll fire off three shots so the occasion won't be *too* sober—sixteen leather belts.

A VOICE FROM THE COUNTER: Service! One brandy!

MOTHER COURAGE: Your money first. No, you *can't* come inside the tent, not with those boots on. You can drink outside, rain or no rain. I only let officers in here. [*To the* CLERK:] The Chief had his troubles lately, I hear. There was unrest in the Second Regiment because he didn't pay 'em but he said it was a war of religion and they must fight it free of charge.

[*Funeral march. All look toward the rear.*]

THE CHAPLAIN: Now they're filing past the body.

MOTHER COURAGE: I feel sorry for a Commander or an Emperor like that—when he might have had something special in mind, something they'd talk about in times to come, something they'd raise a statue to him for. The conquest of the world now, *that's* a goal for a Commander, he wouldn't know any better. . . . Lord, worms have got into the biscuits. . . . In short, he works his hands to the bone and then it's all spoiled by the common riffraff that only wants a jug of beer or a bit of company, not the higher things in life. The finest plans have always been spoiled by the littleness of them that should carry them out. Even Emperors can't do it all by themselves. They count on support from their soldiers and the people round about. Am I right?

THE CHAPLAIN [laughing]: You're right, Mother Courage, till you come to the soldiers. They do what they can. Those fellows outside, for example, drinking their brandy in the rain, I'd trust 'em to fight a hundred years, one war after another, two at a time if necessary. And I wasn't trained as a commander.

MOTHER COURAGE: . . . Seventeen leather belts. . . . Then you don't think the war might end?

THE CHAPLAIN: Because a commander's dead? Don't be childish, they're a dime a dozen. There are always heroes.

MOTHER COURAGE: Well, I wasn't asking for the sake of argument. I was wondering if I should buy up a lot of supplies. They happen to be cheap just now. But if the war ended, I might just as well throw them away.

THE CHAPLAIN: I realize you are serious, Mother Courage. Well, there've always been people going around saying some day the war will end. I say, you can't be sure the war will ever end. Of course it may have to pause occasionally—for breath, as it were—it can even meet with an accident—nothing on this earth is perfect—a war of which we could say it left nothing to be desired will probably never exist. A war can come to a sudden halt—from unforeseen causes—you can't think of everything—a little oversight, and the war's in the hole, and someone's got to pull it out again! The someone is the Emperor or the King or the Pope. They're such friends in need, the war has really nothing to worry about, it can look forward to a prosperous future.

A SOLDIER [singing at the counter]:

> One schnapps, mine host, make haste!
> We have no time to waste:
> We must be shooting, shooting, shooting
> Our Emperor's foes uprooting!

Make it a double. This is a holiday.

MOTHER COURAGE: If I was sure you're right . . .

THE CHAPLAIN: Think it out for yourself: how could the war end?

THE SOLDIER [off-stage]:

Two breasts, mine host, make haste!
For we have no time to waste:
We must be hating, hating, hating
We cannot keep our Emperor waiting!

THE CLERK [*suddenly*]: What about peace? Yes, peace. I'm from Bohemia. I'd like to get home once in a while.

THE CHAPLAIN: Oh, you would, would you? Dear old peace! What happens to the hole when the cheese is gone?

THE SOLDIER [*off-stage*]:

Your blessing, priest, make haste!
For we have no time to waste:
We must be dying, dying, dying
Our Emperor's greatness glorifying!

THE CLERK: In the long run you can't live without peace!

THE CHAPLAIN: Well, I'd say there's peace even in war, war has its islands of peace. For war satisfies *all* needs, even those of peace, yes, they're provided for, or the war couldn't keep going. In war—as in the very thick of peace—you can take a crap, and between one battle and the next there's always a beer, and even on the march you can snatch a nap—on your elbow maybe, in a gutter—something can always be managed. Of course you can't play cards during an attack, but neither can you while ploughing the fields in peace time: it's when the victory's won that there are possibilities. You have your leg shot off, and at first you raise quite an outcry as if it was something, but soon you calm down or take a swig of brandy, and you end up hopping about, and the war is none the worse for your little misadventure. And can't you be fruitful and multiply in the thick of slaughter—behind a barn or somewhere? Nothing can keep you from it very long in any event. And so the war has your off-spring and can carry on. War is like love, it always finds a way. Why *should* it end?

[KATTRIN *has stopped working. She stares at the* CHAPLAIN.]

MOTHER COURAGE: Then I *will* buy those supplies, I'll rely on you. [KATTRIN *suddenly bangs a basket of glasses down on the ground and runs out.* MOTHER COURAGE *laughs.*] Kattrin! Lord, Kattrin's still going to wait for peace. I promised her she'll get a husband—when it's peace. [*She runs after her.*]

THE CLERK [*standing up*]: I win. You were talking. You pay.

MOTHER COURAGE [*returning with* KATTRIN]: Be sensible, the war'll go on a bit longer, and we'll make a bit more money, then peace'll be all the nicer. Now you go into the town, it's not ten minutes walk, and bring the things from the Golden Lion, just the more expensive ones, we can get the rest later in the wagon. It's all arranged, the clerk will go with you, most of the soldiers are at the Commander's funeral, nothing can happen to you. Do a good job, don't lose anything, Kattrin, think of your trousseau!

[KATTRIN *ties a cloth around her head and leaves with the* CLERK.]

THE CHAPLAIN: You don't mind her going with the clerk?

MOTHER COURAGE: She's not so pretty anyone would want to ruin her.

THE CHAPLAIN: The way you run your business and always come through is highly commendable, Mother Courage—I see how you got your name.

MOTHER COURAGE: The poor need courage. Why? They're lost. That they even get up in the morning is something—in their plight. Or that they plough a field—in war time. Even their bringing children into the world shows they have courage, for they have no prospects. They have to hang each other one by one and slaughter each other in the lump, so if they want to look each other in the face once in a while, well, it takes courage. That they put up with an Emperor and a Pope, that takes an unnatural amount of courage, for they cost you your life. [*She sits, takes a small pipe from her pocket and smokes it.*] You might chop me a bit of firewood.

THE CHAPLAIN [*reluctantly taking his coat off and preparing to chop wood*]: Properly speaking, I'm a pastor of souls, not a woodcutter.

MOTHER COURAGE: But I don't have a soul. And I do need wood.

THE CHAPLAIN: What's that little pipe you've got there?

MOTHER COURAGE: Just a pipe.

THE CHAPLAIN: I think it's a very particular pipe.

MOTHER COURAGE: Oh?

THE CHAPLAIN: The cook's pipe in fact. The cook from the Oxenstierna Regiment.

MOTHER COURAGE: If you know, why beat about the bush?

THE CHAPLAIN: Because I don't know if you've been aware that's what you've been smoking. It was possible you just rummaged among your belongings and your fingers just lit on a pipe and you just took it. In pure absent-mindedness.

MOTHER COURAGE: How do you know that's not it?

THE CHAPLAIN: It isn't. You are aware of it. [*He brings the ax down on the block with a crash.*]

MOTHER COURAGE: What if I was?

THE CHAPLAIN: I must give you a warning, Mother Courage, it's my duty. You are unlikely to see the gentleman again but that's no pity, you're in luck. Mother Courage, he did not impress me as trustworthy. On the contrary.

MOTHER COURAGE: Really? He was such a nice man.

THE CHAPLAIN: Well! So that's what you call a nice man. I do not. [The ax falls again.] Far be it from me to wish him ill, but I cannot —cannot—describe him as nice. No, no, he's a Don Juan, a cunning Don Juan. Just look at that pipe if you don't believe me. You must admit it tells all.

MOTHER COURAGE: I see nothing special in it. It's been used, of course.

THE CHAPLAIN: It's bitten halfway through! He's a man of great violence! It is the pipe of a man of great violence, you can see that if you've any judgment left! [He deals the block a tremendous blow.]

MOTHER COURAGE: Don't bite my chopping block halfway through!

THE CHAPLAIN: I told you I had no training as a woodcutter. The care of souls was my field. Around here my gifts and capabilities are grossly misused. In physical labor my God-given talents find no—um —adequate expression—which is a sin. You haven't heard me preach. Why, I can put such spirit into a regiment with a single sermon that the enemy's a mere flock of sheep to them and their own lives no more than smelly old shoes to be thrown away at the thought of final victory! God has given me the gifts of tongues. I can preach you out of your senses!

MOTHER COURAGE: I need my senses. What would I do without them?

THE CHAPLAIN: Mother Courage, I have often thought that—under a veil of plain speech—you conceal a heart. You are human, you need warmth.

MOTHER COURAGE: The best way of warming this tent is to chop plenty of firewood.

THE CHAPLAIN: You're changing the subject. Seriously, my dear Courage, I sometimes ask myself how it would be if our relationship should be somewhat more firmly cemented. I mean, now the wild wind of war has whirled us so strangely together.

MOTHER COURAGE: The cement's pretty firm already. I cook your meals. And you lend a hand—at chopping firewood, for instance.

THE CHAPLAIN [going over to her, gesturing with the ax]: You know what I mean by a close relationship. It has nothing to do with eating and woodcutting and such base necessities. Let your heart speak!

MOTHER COURAGE: Don't come at me like that with your ax, that'd be too close a relationship!

THE CHAPLAIN: This is no laughing matter, I am in earnest. I've thought it all over.

MOTHER COURAGE: Dear Chaplain, be a sensible fellow. I like you, and I don't want to heap coals of fire on your head. All I want is to bring me and my children through in that wagon. It isn't just mine, the wagon, and anyway I've no mind to start any adventures. At the moment I'm taking quite a risk buying these things when the Commander's fallen and there's all this talk of peace. Where would you go, if I was ruined? See? You don't even know. Now chop some firewood and it'll be warm of an evening, which is quite a lot in times like these. What was that? [She stands up. KATTRIN enters, breathless, with a wound across the eye and forehead. She is dragging all sorts of articles, parcels, leather goods, a drum, etc.] What is it, were you attacked? On the way back? She was attacked on the way back! I'll bet it was that soldier who got drunk on my liquor. I should never have let you go. Dump all that stuff! It's not bad, the wound is only a flesh wound. I'll bandage it for you, it'll all be healed up in a week. They're worse than animals. [She bandages the wound.]

THE CHAPLAIN: I reproach them with nothing. At home they never did these shameful things. The men who start the wars are responsible, they bring out the worst in people.

MOTHER COURAGE: Didn't the clerk walk you back home? That's because you're a respectable girl, he thought they'd leave you alone. The wound's not at all deep, it will never show. There: all bandaged up. Now, I've got something for you, rest easy. I've been keeping them secret. [She digs YVETTE's red boots out of a bag.] Well, what do you see? You always wanted them. Now you have them. [She helps her to put the boots on.] Put them on quick, before I change my mind. It will never show, though it wouldn't bother me if it did. The ones they like fare worst. They drag them around till they're finished. Those they don't care for they leave alone. I've seen so many girls, pretty as they come in the beginning, then all of a sudden they're so ugly they'd scare a wolf. They can't even go behind a tree on the street without having something to fear from it. They lead a frightful life. Like with trees: the tall, straight ones are cut down for roof timber, and the crooked ones can enjoy life. So this wound here is really a piece of luck. The boots have kept well. I gave them a good cleaning before I put them away.

[KATTRIN leaves the boots and creeps into the wagon.]

THE CHAPLAIN [when she's gone]: I hope she won't be disfigured?

MOTHER COURAGE: There'll be a scar. She needn't wait for peace now.

THE CHAPLAIN: She didn't let them get any of the stuff.

MOTHER COURAGE: Maybe I shouldn't have made such a point of it. If only I ever knew what went on inside her head. Once she stayed out all night, once in all the years. Afterward she seemed much the same, except that she worked harder. I could never get out of her what happened. I worried about it for quite a while. [*She picks up the things* KATTRIN *spilled and sorts them angrily.*] This is war. A nice source of income, I must say!

[*Cannon shots.*]

THE CHAPLAIN: Now they're lowering the Commander into his grave! A historic moment.

MOTHER COURAGE: It's a historic moment to me when they hit my daughter over the eye. She's all but finished now, she'll never get a husband, and she's so mad about children! Even her dumbness comes from the war. A soldier stuck something in her mouth when he was little. I'll never see Swiss Cheese again, and where my Eilif is the Good Lord knows. Curse the war!

❦ Scene VII

MOTHER COURAGE AT THE HEIGHT OF HER BUSINESS CAREER

[*A highway. The* CHAPLAIN, MOTHER COURAGE, *and her daughter* KATTRIN *pull the wagon, and new wares are hanging from it.* MOTHER COURAGE *wears a necklace of silver coins.*]

MOTHER COURAGE: I won't let you spoil my war for me. Destroys the weak, does it? Well, what does peace do for 'em, huh? War feeds its people better.

[*She sings:*]

> If war don't suit your disposition
> When victory comes, you will be dead.
> War is a business proposition:
> But not with cheese, with steel instead!
>   Christians, awake! Winter is gone!
>   The snows depart! Dead men sleep on!
>   Let all of you who still survive
>   Get out of bed and look alive!

And staying in one place won't help either. Those who stay at home are the first to go.

[*She sings:*]

> Too many seek a bed to sleep in:
> Each ditch is taken, and each cave
> And he who digs a hole to creep in
> Finds he has dug an early grave.
> And many a man spends many a minute
> In hurrying toward some resting place.
> You wonder, when at last he's in it
> Just why the fellow forced the pace.

[*The wagon proceeds.*]

❀ Scene VIII

1632. IN THIS SAME YEAR GUSTAVUS ADOLPHUS FELL IN THE BATTLE OF LÜTZEN. THE PEACE THREATENS MOTHER COURAGE WITH RUIN. HER BRAVE SON PERFORMS ONE HEORIC DEED TOO MANY AND COMES TO A SHAMEFUL END.

[*A camp. A summer morning. In front of the wagon, an* OLD WOMAN *and her son. The son is dragging a large bag of bedding.*]

MOTHER COURAGE [*from inside the wagon*]: Must you come at the crack of dawn?

THE YOUNG MAN: We've been walking all night, twenty miles it was, we have to be back today.

MOTHER COURAGE [*still inside*]: What do I want with bed feathers? People don't even have houses.

THE YOUNG MAN: At least wait till you see 'em.

THE OLD WOMAN: Nothing doing here either, let's go.

THE YOUNG MAN: And let 'em sign away the roof over our heads for taxes? Maybe she'll pay three guilders if you throw in that bracelet. [*Bells start ringing.*] You hear, Mother?

VOICES [*from the rear*]: It's peace! The King of Sweden's been killed!

[MOTHER COURAGE *sticks her head out of the wagon. She hasn't done her hair yet.*]

MOTHER COURAGE: Bells! What are the bells for, middle of the week?

THE CHAPLAIN [*crawling out from under the wagon*]: What's that they're shouting?

THE YOUNG MAN: It's peace.

THE CHAPLAIN: Peace!

MOTHER COURAGE: Doesn't tell me peace has broken out—when I've just gone and bought all these supplies!

THE CHAPLAIN [*calling, toward the rear*]: Is it peace?

VOICE [*from a distance*]: They say the war stopped three weeks ago. I've only just heard.

THE CHAPLAIN [*to* MOTHER COURAGE]: Or why would they ring the bells?

VOICE: A great crowd of Lutherans have just arrived with wagons—they brought the news.

THE YOUNG MAN: It's peace, Mother. [*The* OLD WOMAN *collapses.*] What's the matter?

MOTHER COURAGE [*back in the wagon*]: Kattrin, it's peace! Put on your black dress, we're going to church, we owe it to Swiss Cheese! Can it be true?

THE YOUNG MAN: The people here say so too, the war's over. Can you stand up? [*The* OLD WOMAN *stands up, dazed.*] I'll get the harness shop going again now, I promise you. Everything'll be all right, father will get his bed back. . . . Can you walk? [*To the* CHAPLAIN:] She felt ill, it was the news. She didn't believe there'd ever be peace again. Father always said there would. We're going home. [*They leave.*]

MOTHER COURAGE [*off*]: Give her some brandy.

THE CHAPLAIN: They've left already.

MOTHER COURAGE [*still off*]: What's going on in the camp over there?

THE CHAPLAIN: They're all getting together. I think I'll go over. Shall I put my pastor's coat on again?

MOTHER COURAGE: Better get the exact news first, and not risk being taken for the Antichrist. I'm glad about the peace even though I'm ruined. At least I've got two of my children through the war. Now I'll see my Eilif again.

THE CHAPLAIN: And who may this be coming down from the camp? Well, if it isn't our Swedish Commander's cook!

THE COOK [*somewhat bedraggled, carrying a bundle*]: Who's here? The chaplain!

THE CHAPLAIN: Mother Courage, a visitor!

[MOTHER COURAGE *clambers out.*]

THE COOK: Well, I promised I'd come over for a brief conversation as soon as I had time. I didn't forget your brandy, Mrs. Fierling.

MOTHER COURAGE: Jesus, the Commander's cook! After all these years! Where is Eilif, my eldest?

THE COOK: Isn't he here yet? He went on ahead yesterday, he was on his way over.

THE CHAPLAIN: I will put my pastor's coat on. I'll be back. [He goes behind the wagon.]

MOTHER COURAGE: He may be here any minute then. [She calls toward the wagon:] Kattrin, Eilif's coming! Bring a glass of brandy for the cook, Kattrin! [KATTRIN doesn't come.] Just pull your hair over it. Mr. Lamb is no stranger. [She gets the brandy herself.] She won't come out. Peace is nothing to her, it was too long coming. They hit her right over the eye. You can hardly see it now. But she thinks people stare at her.

THE COOK: Ah yes, war! [He and MOTHER COURAGE sit.]

MOTHER COURAGE: Cook, you come at a bad time: I'm ruined.

THE COOK: What? That's terrible!

MOTHER COURAGE: The peace has broken my neck. On the chaplain's advice I've gone and bought a lot of supplies. Now everybody's leaving and I'm holding the baby.

THE COOK: How could you listen to the chaplain? If I'd had time—but the Catholics were too quick for me—I'd have warned you against him. He's a windbag. Well, so now he's the big man round here!

MOTHER COURAGE: He's been doing the dishes for me and helping with the wagon.

THE COOK: With the wagon—him! And I'll bet he's told you a few of his jokes. He has a most unhealthy attitude to women. I tried to influence him but it was no good. He isn't sound.

MOTHER COURAGE: Are you sound?

THE COOK: If I'm nothing else, I'm sound. Your health!

MOTHER COURAGE: Sound! Only one person around here was ever sound, and I never had to slave as I did then. He sold the blankets off the children's beds in the spring, and he called my harmonica unchristian. You aren't recommending yourself if you admit you're sound.

THE COOK: You fight tooth and nail, don't you? I like that.

MOTHER COURAGE: Don't tell me you've been dreaming of my teeth and nails.

THE COOK: Well, here we sit, while the bells of peace do ring, and you pouring your famous brandy as only you know how!

MOTHER COURAGE: I don't think much of the bells of peace at the moment. I don't see how they can hand out all this pay that's in arrears. And then where shall I be with my famous brandy? Have you all been paid?

THE COOK [hesitating]: Not exactly. That's why we disbanded. In the circumstances, I thought, why stay? For the time being, I'll look up a couple of friends. So here I sit—with you.

MOTHER COURAGE: In other words, you're broke.

THE COOK [annoyed by the bells]: It's about time they stopped that racket! I'd like to set myself up in some business. I'm fed up with being their cook. I'm supposed to make do with tree roots and shoe leather, and then they throw my hot soup in my face! Being a cook nowadays is a dog's life. I'd sooner be a soldier, but of course, it's peace now. [As the CHAPLAIN turns up, wearing his old coat:] We'll talk it over later.

THE CHAPLAIN: The coat's pretty good. Just a few moth holes.

THE COOK: I don't know why you take the trouble. You won't find another pulpit. Who could you incite now to earn an honest living or risk his life for a cause? Besides, I have a bone to pick with you.

THE CHAPLAIN: Have you?

THE COOK: I have. You advised a lady to buy superfluous goods on the pretext that the war would never end.

THE CHAPLAIN [hotly]: I'd like to know what business it is of yours?

THE COOK: It's unprincipled behavior! How can you give unwanted advice? And interfere with the conduct of other people's business?

THE CHAPLAIN: Who's interfering now, I'd like to know? [To MOTHER COURAGE:] I had no idea you were such a close friend of this gentleman and had to account to him for everything.

MOTHER COURAGE: Now don't get excited. The cook's giving his personal opinion. You can't deny your war was a flop.

THE CHAPLAIN: You have no respect for peace, Courage. You're a hyena of the battlefield!

MOTHER COURAGE: A what?

THE COOK: Who insults my girl friend insults me!

THE CHAPLAIN: I am not speaking to you, your intentions are only too transparent! [To MOTHER COURAGE:] But when I see you take peace between finger and thumb like a snotty old hanky, my humanity rebels! It shows that you want war, not peace, for what you get out of it. But don't forget the proverb: he who sups with the devil must use a long spoon!

MOTHER COURAGE: Remember what one fox said to another that was caught in a trap? "If you stay there, you're just asking for trouble!"

There isn't much love lost between me and the war. And when it comes to calling me a hyena, you and I part company.

THE CHAPLAIN: Then why all this gumbling about the peace just as everyone's heaving a sigh of relief? Is it for the junk in your wagon?

MOTHER COURAGE: My goods are not junk. I live off them. You've been living off them.

THE CHAPLAIN: You live off the war. Exactly.

THE COOK [to the CHAPLAIN]: As a grown man, you should know better than to go around advising people. [To MOTHER COURAGE:] Now, in your situation you'd be smart to get rid of certain goods at once—before the prices sink to nothing. Get ready and get going, there isn't a moment to lose!

MOTHER COURAGE: That's sensible advice, I think I'll take it.

THE CHAPLAIN: Because the cook says so.

MOTHER COURAGE: Why didn't you say so? He's right, I must get to the market. [She climbs into the wagon.]

THE COOK: One up for me, Chaplain. You have no presence of mind. You should have said, "I gave you advice? Why, I was just talking politics!" And you shouldn't take me on as a rival. Cockfights are not becoming to your cloth.

THE CHAPLAIN: If you don't shut your trap, I'll murder you, cloth or no cloth!

THE COOK [taking his boots off and unwinding the wrappings on his feet]: If you hadn't degenerated into a godless tramp, you could easily get yourself a parsonage, now it's peace. Cooks won't be needed, there's nothing to cook, but there's still plenty to believe, and people will go right on believing it.

THE CHAPLAIN: Mr. Lamb, please don't drive me out! Since I became a tramp, I'm a somewhat better man. I couldn't preach to 'em any more.

[YVETTE POTTIER enters, decked out in black, with a stick. She is much older, fatter, and heavily powdered. Behind her, a SERVANT.]

YVETTE: Hullo, everybody! Is this Mother Courage's establishment?

THE CHAPLAIN: Quite right. And with whom have we the pleasure?

YVETTE: I am Madame Colonel Starhemberg, good people. Where's Mother Courage?

THE CHAPLAIN [calling to the wagon]: Madame Colonel Starhemberg wants to speak to you!

MOTHER COURAGE [from inside]: Coming!

YVETTE [*calling*]: It's Yvette!

MOTHER COURAGE [*inside*]: Yvette!

YVETTE: Just to see how you're getting on! [*As the* COOK *turns around in horror:*] Peter!

THE COOK: Yvette!

YVETTE: Of all things! How did you get here?

THE COOK: On a cart.

THE CHAPLAIN: Well! You know each other? Intimately?

YVETTE: I'll say. [*Scrutinizing the* COOK:] You're fat.

THE COOK: For that matter, you're no beanpole.

YVETTE: Anyway, nice meeting you, tramp. Now I can tell you what I think of you.

THE CHAPLAIN: Do so, tell him all, but wait till Mother Courage comes out.

THE COOK: Now don't make a scene . . .

MOTHER COURAGE [*coming out, laden with goods*]: Yvette! [*They embrace.*] But why are you in mourning?

YVETTE: Doesn't it suit me? My husband, the colonel, died several years ago.

MOTHER COURAGE: The old fellow that nearly bought my wagon?

YVETTE: His elder brother.

MOTHER COURAGE: So you're not doing badly. Good to see one person who got somewhere in the war.

YVETTE: I've had my ups and downs.

MOTHER COURAGE: Don't let's speak ill of colonels. They make money like hay.

THE CHAPLAIN [*to the* COOK]: If I were you, I'd put my shoes on again. [*To* YVETTE:] You promised to give us your opinion of this gentleman.

THE COOK: Now, Yvette, don't make a stink!

MOTHER COURAGE: He's a friend of mine, Yvette.

YVETTE: He's—Peter Piper, that's who.

MOTHER COURAGE: What!

THE COOK: Cut the nicknames. My name's Lamb.

MOTHER COURAGE [*laughing*]: Peter Piper? Who turned the women's heads? And I've been keeping your pipe for you.

THE CHAPLAIN: And smoking it.

YVETTE: Lucky I can warn you against him. He's a bad lot. You won't find worse on the whole coast of Flanders. He got more girls in trouble than . . .

THE COOK: That's a long time ago, it isn't true any more.

YVETTE: Stand up when you talk to a lady! Oh, how I loved that man; and all the time he was having a little bowlegged brunette. He got *her* into trouble too, of course.

THE COOK: I seem to have brought you luck!

YVETTE: Shut your trap, you hoary ruin! And you take care, Mother Courage, this type is still dangerous even in decay!

MOTHER COURAGE [to YVETTE]: Come with me, I must get rid of this stuff before the prices fall.

YVETTE [concentrating on the COOK]: Miserable cur!

MOTHER COURAGE: Maybe you can help me at army headquarters, you have contacts.

YVETTE: Seducer!

MOTHER COURAGE [shouting into the wagon]: Kattrin, church is all off, I'm going to market!

YVETTE: Whore hunter!

MOTHER COURAGE [still to KATTRIN]: When Eilif comes, give him something to drink!

YVETTE: That a man like him should have been able to turn me from the straight and narrow! I have my own star to thank that I rose none the less to the heights! But I've put an end to your tricks, Peter Piper, and one day—in a better life than this—the Lord God will reward me! Come, Mother Courage! [*She leaves with* MOTHER COURAGE.]

THE CHAPLAIN: As our text this morning let us take the saying: the mills of God grind slowly. And you complain of my jokes!

THE COOK: I never have any luck. I'll be frank, I was hoping for a good hot dinner, I'm starving. And now they'll be talking about me, and she'll get a completely wrong picture. I think I should go before she comes back.

THE CHAPLAIN: I think so too.

THE COOK: Chaplain, peace makes me sick. Mankind must perish by fire and sword, we're born and bred in sin! Oh, how I wish I was roasting a great fat capon for the Commander—God knows where he's got to—with mustard sauce and those little yellow carrots . . .

THE CHAPLAIN: Red cabbage—with capon, red cabbage.

THE COOK: You're right. But he always wanted yellow carrots.

THE CHAPLAIN: He never understood a thing.

THE COOK: You always put plenty away.

THE CHAPLAIN: Under protest.

THE COOK: Anyway, you must admit, those were the days.

THE CHAPLAIN: Yes, that I might admit.

THE COOK: Now you've called her a hyena, there's not much future for you here either. What are you staring at?

THE CHAPLAIN: It's Eilif!

[*Followed by two soldiers with halberds,* EILIF *enters. His hands are fettered. He is white as chalk.*]

THE CHAPLAIN: What's happened to you?

EILIF: Where's Mother?

THE CHAPLAIN: Gone to town.

EILIF: They said she was here. I was allowed a last visit.

THE COOK [*to the* SOLDIERS]: Where are you taking him?

A SOLDIER: For a ride.

[*The other* SOLDIER *makes the gesture of throat cutting.*]

THE CHAPLAIN: What has he done?

THE SOLDIER: He broke in on a peasant. The wife is dead.

THE CHAPLAIN: Eilif, how could you?

EILIF: It's no different. It's what I did before.

THE COOK: That was in war time.

EILIF: Shut your hole. Can I sit down till she comes?

THE SOLDIER: No.

THE CHAPLAIN: It's true. In war time they honored him for it. He sat at the Commander's right hand. It was bravery. Couldn't we speak with the provost?

THE SOLDIER: What's the use? Stealing cattle from a peasant, what's brave about that?

THE COOK: It was just stupid.

EILIF: If I'd been stupid, I'd have starved, smarty.

THE COOK: So you were bright and paid for it.

THE CHAPLAIN: At least we must bring Kattrin out.

EILIF: Let her alone. Just give me some brandy.

THE SOLDIER: No.

THE CHAPLAIN: What shall we tell your mother?

EILIF: Tell her it was no different. Tell her it was the same. Oh, tell her nothing.

[*The* SOLDIERS *take him away.*]

THE CHAPLAIN: I'll come with you, I'll . . .

EILIF: I don't need a priest!

THE CHAPLAIN: You don't know—yet. [*He follows him.*]

THE COOK [*calling after him*]: I'll have to tell her, she'll want to see him!

THE CHAPLAIN: Better tell her nothing. Or maybe just that he was here, and he'll return, maybe tomorrow. Meantime I'll be back and can break the news. [*He leaves quickly.*]

[*The* COOK *looks after him, shakes his head, then walks about uneasily. Finally, he approaches the wagon.*]

THE COOK: Hello! Won't you come out? You want to sneak away from the peace, don't you? Well, so do I! I'm the Swedish Commander's cook, remember me? I was wondering if you've got anything to eat in there—while we're waiting for your mother. I wouldn't mind a bit of bacon—or even bread—just to pass the time. [*He looks in.*] She's got a blanket over her head.

[*The thunder of cannon.*]

[MOTHER COURAGE *runs in, out of breath, still carrying the goods.*]

MOTHER COURAGE: Cook, the peace is over, the war's on again, has been for three days! I didn't get rid of this stuff after all, thank God! There's a shooting match in the town already—with the Lutherans. We must get away with the wagon. Pack, Kattrin! What's on your mind? Something the matter?

THE COOK: Nothing.

MOTHER COURAGE: But there is. I see it in your face.

THE COOK: Because the war's on again, most likely. May it last till tomorrow evening, so I can get something in my belly!

MOTHER COURAGE: You're not telling me.

THE COOK: Eilif was here. Only he had to go away again.

MOTHER COURAGE: He was here? Then we'll see him on the march. I'll be with our side this time. How'd he look?

THE COOK: The same.

MOTHER COURAGE: He'll never change. And the war couldn't get *him*, he's bright. Help me with the packing. [*She starts it.*] Did he tell you anything? Is he well in with the Captain? Did he tell you about his heroic deeds?

THE COOK [*darkly*]: He's done one of them again.

MOTHER COURAGE: Tell me about it later. [KATTRIN *appears.*] Kattrin, the peace is over, we're on the move again. [*To the* COOK:] What *is* the matter with you?

THE COOK: I'll enlist.

MOTHER COURAGE: A good idea. Where's the Captain?

THE COOK: In the town. With Eilif.

MOTHER COURAGE: Stay with us a while, Lamb, I need a bit of help.

THE COOK: This matter of Yvette . . .

MOTHER COURAGE: Hasn't done you any harm at all in my eyes. Just the opposite. Where there's smoke, there's fire, they say. You'll come?

THE COOK: I may as well.

MOTHER COURAGE: The Twelfth Regiment's under way. Into harness with you! Maybe I'll see Eilif before the day is out, just think! That's what I like best. Well, it wasn't such a long peace, we can't grumble. Let's go!

[The COOK and KATTRIN are in harness.]

MOTHER COURAGE [sings]:

> From Ulm to Metz, past dome and steeple
> My wagon always moves ahead.
> The war can care for all its people
> So long as there is steel and lead.
> Though steel and lead are stout supporters
> A war needs human beings too.
> Report today to your headquarters!
> If it's to last, this war needs you!

❧ Scene IX

THE GREAT WAR OF RELIGION HAS LASTED SIXTEEN YEARS AND GERMANY HAS LOST HALF ITS INHABITANTS. THOSE WHO ARE SPARED IN BATTLE DIE BY PLAGUE. OVER ONCE BLOOMING COUNTRYSIDE HUNGER RAGES. TOWNS ARE BURNED DOWN. WOLVES PROWL THE EMPTY STREETS. IN THE AUTUMN OF 1634 WE FIND MOTHER COURAGE IN THE FICHTEL-GEBIRGE NOT FAR FROM THE ROAD THE SWEDISH ARMY IS TAKING. WINTER HAS COME EARLY AND IS HARD. BUSINESS IS BAD. ONLY BEGGING REMAINS. THE COOK RECEIVES A LETTER FROM UTRECHT AND IS SENT PACKING.

[In front of a half-ruined parsonage. Early winter. A gray morning. Gusts of wind. MOTHER COURAGE and the COOK at the wagon in shabby clothes.]

THE COOK: There are no lights on. No one's up.

MOTHER COURAGE: But it's a parsonage. The parson'll have to leave his feather bed and ring the bells. Then he'll have some hot soup.

THE COOK: Where'll he get it from? The whole village is starving.

MOTHER COURAGE: The house is lived in. There was a dog barking.

THE COOK: If the parson has anything, he'll hang on to it.

MOTHER COURAGE: Maybe if we sang him something . . .

THE COOK: I've had enough. [Suddenly:] I didn't tell you, a letter came from Utrecht. My mother's died of cholera, the inn is mine. There's the letter, if you don't believe me. I'll show it to you, though my aunt's railing about me and my ups and downs is none of your business.

MOTHER COURAGE [reading]: Lamb, I'm tired of wandering, too. I feel like a butcher's dog taking meat to my customers and getting none myself. I've nothing more to sell and people have nothing to pay with. In Saxony someone tried to force a chestful of books on me in return for two eggs. And in Württemberg they would have let me have their plough for a bag of salt. Nothing grows any more, only thorn bushes. In Pomerania I hear the villagers have been eating their younger children. Nuns have been caught commiting robbery.

THE COOK: The world's dying out.

MOTHER COURAGE: Sometimes I see myself driving through hell with this wagon and selling brimstone. And sometimes I'm driving through heaven handing our provisions to wandering souls! If only we could find a place where there's no shooting, me and my children —what's left of 'em—we might rest a while.

THE COOK: We could open this inn together. Think about it, Courage. My mind's made up. With or without you, I'm leaving for Utrecht. And today too.

MOTHER COURAGE: I must talk to Kattrin, it's a bit sudden, and I don't like to make my decisions in the cold on an empty stomach [KATTRIN emerges from the wagon.] Kattrin, I've something to tell you. The cook and I want to go to Utrecht, he's been left an inn. You'd be able to stay put and get to know some people. Many a man'd be prepared to take on a girl with a position. Looks aren't everything. I like the idea. I get on well with the cook. I'll say this for him: he has a head for business. We'd be sure of our dinner, that would be all right, wouldn't it? You'd have your own bed, what do you think of that? In the long run, this is no life, on the road. You might be killed any time. You're eaten up with lice as it is. And we must decide now, because otherwise we go north with the Swedes. They must be over there somewhere. [She points left.] I think we'll decide to go, Kattrin.

THE COOK: Anna, I must have a word with you alone.

MOTHER COURAGE: Go back inside, Kattrin.

[KATTRIN *does so.*]

THE COOK: I'm interrupting because there's a misunderstanding, Anna.
I thought I wouldn't have to say it right out, but I see I must. If
you're bringing her, it's all off. Do we understand each other?

[KATTRIN *has her head out of the back of the wagon and is
listening.*]

MOTHER COURAGE: You mean I leave Kattrin behind?

THE COOK: What do you think? There's no room in the inn, it isn't
one of those places with three counters. If the two of us look lively
we can earn a living, but three's too many. Let Kattrin keep your
wagon.

MOTHER COURAGE: I was thinking we might find her a husband in
Utrecht.

THE COOK: Don't make me laugh. With that scar? And old as she is?
And dumb?

MOTHER COURAGE: Not so loud!

THE COOK: Loud or soft, what is, is. That's another reason I can't have
her in the inn. Customers don't like having something like that
always before their eyes. You can't blame them.

MOTHER COURAGE: Shut up. I told you not to talk so loud.

THE COOK: There's a light in the parsonage, we can sing now!

MOTHER COURAGE: Cook, how could she pull the wagon by herself?
The war frightens her. She can't bear it. She has terrible dreams.
I hear her groan at night, especially after battles. What she sees in
her dreams I don't know. She suffers from sheer pity. The other day
I found her with a hedgehog that we'd run over.

THE COOK: The inn's too small. [*Calling:*] Worthy Sir, menials, and all
within! We now present the song of Solomon, Julius Caesar, and
other great souls who came to no good, so you can see we're law-
abiding folk too, and have a hard time getting by, especially in
winter.

[*He sings "The Song of the Great Souls of this Earth":*]

King Solomon was very wise,
So what's his history?
He came to view this life with scorn,
Yes, he came to regret he ever had been born
Declaring: all is vanity.
King Solomon was very wise,

But long before the day was out
The consequence was clear, alas:
His wisdom 'twas that brought him to this pass.
A man is better off without.

For the virtues are dangerous in this world, as our fine song tells.
You're better off without, you have a nice life, breakfast included—
some good hot soup maybe . . . I'm an example of a man who's not
had any, and I'd like some, I'm a soldier, but what good did my
bravery do me in all those battles? None at all. I might just as well
have wet my pants like a poltroon and stayed at home. For why?

Old Julius Caesar, he was brave.
His fame shall never cease.
He sat like a god on an altar piece.
Yet they tore brave old Julius limb from valiant limb
And Brutus helped to slaughter him.
Old Julius was very brave
But long before the day was out
The consequence was clear, alas:
His bravery 'twas that brought him to this pass.
A man is better off without.

[*Under his breath:*] They don't even look out. [*Aloud:*] Worthy Sir,
menials, and all within! You could say, no, courage isn't the thing
to fill a man's belly, try honesty, that should be worth a dinner, at
any rate it must have some effect. Let's see.

You all know honest Socrates
Who always spoke the truth.
They owed him thanks for that, you'd think,
But what happened? Why, they put hemlock in his
    drink
And swore that he misled the youth.
How honest was this Socrates!
Yet long before the day was out
The consequence was clear, alas:
His honesty had brought him to this pass.
A man is better off without.

Yes, we're told to be unselfish and share what we have, but what if
we have nothing? And those who do share it don't have an easy time
either, for what's left when you're through sharing? Unselfishness is
a very rare virtue—it doesn't pay.

Mother Courage and Her Children   **641**

Unselfish Martin could not bear
His fellow creatures' woes.
He met a poor man in the snows
And he gave this poor fellow half his cloak to wear:
So both of them fell down and froze.
His brothers' woes he could not bear,
So long before the day was out
The consequence was clear, alas:
Unselfishness had brought him to this pass.
A man is better off without.

That's how it is with us. We're law-abiding folk, we keep to ourselves, don't steal, don't kill, don't burn the place down. And in
this way we sink lower and lower and the song proves true and
there's no soup going. And if we were different, if we were thieves
and killers, maybe we could eat our fill! For virtues bring no reward,
only vices. Such is the world, need it be so?

God's ten commandments we have kept
And acted as we should.
It has not done us any good.
All you people who sit beside a roaring fire
O help us in our need so dire!
The ten commandments we have kept
And long before the day was out
The consequence was clear, alas:
Our godliness has brought us to this pass.
A man is better off without.

VOICE [from above]: You there! Come up! There's some soup here
for you!
MOTHER COURAGE: Lamb, I couldn't swallow a thing. I don't say what
you said is unreasonable, but was it your last word? We've always
understood each other.
THE COOK: Yes, Anna. Think it over.
MOTHER COURAGE: There's nothing to think over. I'm not leaving her
here.
THE COOK: You're going to be silly, but what can I do? I'm not inhuman, it's just that the inn's a small one. And now we must go up,
or there'll be nothing doing here too, and we've been singing in the
cold for nothing.

MOTHER COURAGE: I'll fetch Kattrin.

THE COOK: Better stick something in your pocket for her. If there are three of us, they'll get a shock.

[Exeunt.]

[KATTRIN clambers out of the wagon with a bundle. She makes sure they are both gone. Then, on a wagon wheel, she lays out a skirt of her mother's and a pair of the cook's trousers side by side and easy to see. She has just finished, and has picked up her bundle, when MOTHER COURAGE returns.]

MOTHER COURAGE [with a plate of soup]: Kattrin! Stay where you are, Kattrin! Where do you think you're going with that bundle? [She examines the bundle.] She's packed her things. Were you listening? I told him there was nothing doing, he can have Utrecht and his lousy inn, what would we want with a lousy inn? [She sees the skirt and trousers.] Oh, you're a stupid girl, Kattrin, what if I'd seen that and you gone? [She takes hold of KATTRIN who is trying to leave.] And don't think I've sent him packing on your account. It was the wagon. You can't part us, I'm too used to it, you didn't come into it, it was the wagon. Now we're leaving, and we'll put the cook's things here where he'll find 'em, the stupid man. [She clambers up and throws a couple of things down to go with the trousers.] There! He's fired. The last man I'll take into this business! Now let's be going, you and me. This winter'll pass, like all the others. Get into harness, it looks like snow.

[They harness themselves to the wagon, turn it around, and start out. A gust of wind. Enter the COOK, still chewing. He sees his things.]

🏵 Scene X

DURING THE WHOLE OF 1635 MOTHER COURAGE AND KATTRIN PULL THE WAGON ALONG THE ROADS OF CENTRAL GERMANY IN THE WAKE OF THE EVER MORE TATTERED ARMIES.

[On the highway. MOTHER COURAGE and KATTRIN are pulling the wagon. They come to a prosperous farmhouse. Someone inside is singing.]

THE VOICE:

> In March a bush we planted
> To make the garden gay.
> In June we were enchanted:
> A lovely rose was blooming ·
> The balmy air perfuming!
> Blest are they
> Who have gardens gay!
> In June we were enchanted.
>
> When snow falls helter-skelter
> And loudly blows the storm
> Our farmhouse gives us shelter.
> The winter's in a hurry
> But we've no cause to worry.
> We are warm
> In the midst of the storm!
> Our farmhouse gives us shelter.

[MOTHER COURAGE and KATTRIN have stopped to listen. Then they start out again.]

✤ Scene XI

JANUARY, 1636. CATHOLIC TROOPS THREATEN THE PROTESTANT TOWN OF HALLE. THE STONE BEGINS TO SPEAK. MOTHER COURAGE LOSES HER DAUGHTER AND JOURNEYS ONWARD ALONE. THE WAR IS NOT YET NEAR ITS END.

[The wagon, very far gone now, stands near a farmhouse with a straw roof. It is night. Out of the woods come a LIEUTENANT and three SOLDIERS in full armor.]

THE LIEUTENANT: And there mustn't be a sound. If anyone yells, cut him down.

THE FIRST SOLDIER: But we'll have to knock—if we want a guide.

THE LIEUTENANT: Knocking's a natural noise, it's all right, could be a cow hitting the wall of the cowshed.

[The SOLDIERS knock at the farmhouse door. An OLD PEASANT WOMAN opens. A hand is clapped over her mouth. Two SOLDIERS enter.]

A MAN'S VOICE: What is it?

[*The* SOLDIERS *bring out an* OLD PEASANT *and his son.*]

THE LIEUTENANT [*pointing to the wagon on which* KATTRIN *has appeared*]: There's one. [*A* SOLDIER *pulls her out.*] Is this everybody that lives here?

THE PEASANTS [*alternating*]: That's our son. And that's a girl that can't talk. Her mother's in town buying up stocks because the shopkeepers are running away and selling cheap. They're canteen people.

THE LIEUTENANT: I'm warning you. Keep quiet. One sound and we'll crack you over the head with a pike. And I need someone to show us the path to the town. [*He points to the* YOUNG PEASANT.] You! Come here!

THE YOUNG PEASANT: I don't know any path!

THE SECOND SOLDIER [*grinning*]: He don't know any path!

THE YOUNG PEASANT: I don't help Catholics.

THE LIEUTENANT [*to the* SECOND SOLDIER]: Let him feel your pike in his side.

THE YOUNG PEASANT [*forced to his knees, the pike at his throat*]: I'd rather die!

THE SECOND SOLDIER [*again mimicking*]: He'd rather die!

THE FIRST SOLDIER: I know how to change his mind. [*He walks over to the cowshed.*] Two cows and a bull. Listen, you. If you aren't going to be reasonable, I'll saber your cattle.

THE YOUNG PEASANT: Not the cattle!

THE PEASANT WOMAN [*weeping*]: Spare the cattle, Captain, or we'll starve!

THE LIEUTENANT: If he must be pigheaded!

THE FIRST SOLDIER: I think I'll start with the bull.

THE YOUNG PEASANT [*to the old one*]: Do I have to? [*The older one nods.*] I'll do it.

THE PEASANT WOMAN: Thank you, thank you, Captain, for sparing us, for ever and ever, Amen.

[*The* OLD MAN *stops her going on thanking him.*]

THE FIRST SOLDIER: I knew the bull came first all right!

[*Led by the* YOUNG PEASANT, *the* LIEUTENANT *and the* SOLDIERS *go on their way.*]

THE OLD PEASANT: I wish we knew what it was. Nothing good, I suppose.

THE PEASANT WOMAN: Maybe they're just scouts. What are you doing?

THE OLD PEASANT [*setting a ladder against the roof and climbing up*]: I'm seeing if they're alone. [*On the roof.*] Things are moving—all over. I can see armor. And a cannon. There must be more than a regiment. God have mercy on the town and all within!

THE PEASANT WOMAN: Are there lights in the town?

THE OLD PEASANT: No, they're all asleep. [*He climbs down.*] There'll be an attack, and they'll all be slaughtered in their beds.

THE PEASANT WOMAN: The watchman'll give warning.

THE OLD PEASANT: They must have killed the watchman in the tower on the hill or he'd have sounded his horn before this.

THE PEASANT WOMAN: If there were more of us . . .

THE OLD PEASANT: But being that we're alone with that cripple . . .

THE PEASANT WOMAN: There's nothing we can do, is there?

THE OLD PEASANT: Nothing.

THE PEASANT WOMAN: We can't get down there. In the dark.

THE OLD PEASANT: The whole hillside's swarming with 'em.

THE PEASANT WOMAN: We could give a sign?

THE OLD PEASANT: And be cut down for it?

THE PEASANT WOMAN: No, there's nothing we can do. [*To* KATTRIN:] Pray, poor thing, pray! There's nothing we can do to stop this bloodshed, so even if you can't talk, at least pray! He hears, if no one else does. I'll help you. [*All kneel,* KATTRIN *behind.*] Our Father, which art in Heaven, hear our prayer, let not the town perish with all that lie therein asleep and fearing nothing. Wake them, that they rise and go to the walls and see the foe that comes with fire and sword in the night down the hill and across the fields. [*Back to* KATTRIN:] God protect our mother and make the watchman not sleep but wake ere it's too late. And save our son-in-law too, O God, he's there with his four children, let them not perish, they're innocent, they know nothing—[*To* KATTRIN, *who groans:*]—one of them's not two years old, the eldest is seven. [KATTRIN *rises, troubled.*] Heavenly Father, hear us, only Thou canst help us or we die, for we are weak and have no sword nor nothing; we cannot trust our own strength but only Thine, O Lord; we are in Thy hands, our cattle, our farm, and the town too, we're all in Thy hands, and the foe is nigh unto the walls with all his power.

[KATTRIN, *unperceived, has crept off to the wagon, has taken something out of it, put it under her apron, and has climbed up the ladder to the roof.*]

Be mindful of the children in danger, especially the little ones, be mindful of the old folk who cannot move, and of all Christian souls, O Lord.

THE OLD PEASANT: And forgive us our trespasses as we forgive them that trespass against us. Amen.

[*Sitting on the roof,* KATTRIN *takes a drum from under her apron and starts to beat it.*]

THE PEASANT WOMAN: Heavens, what's she doing?

THE OLD PEASANT: She's out of her mind!

THE PEASANT WOMAN: Get her down, quick.

[*The* OLD PEASANT *runs to the ladder but* KATTRIN *pulls it up on the roof.*]

She'll get us in trouble.

THE OLD PEASANT: Stop it this minute, you silly cripple!

THE PEASANT WOMAN: The soldiers'll come!

THE OLD PEASANT [*looking for stones*]: I'll stone you!

THE PEASANT WOMAN: Have you no pity, have you no heart? We have relations there too, four grandchildren, but there's nothing we can do. If they find us now, it's the end, they'll stab us to death!

[KATTRIN *is staring into the far distance, toward the town. She goes on drumming.*]

THE PEASANT WOMAN [*to the* PEASANT]: I told you not to let that riffraff in your farm. What do they care if we lose our cattle?

THE LIEUTENANT [*running back with* SOLDIERS *and the* YOUNG PEASANT]: I'll cut you all to bits!

THE PEASANT WOMAN: We're innocent, sir, there's nothing we can do. She did it, a stranger!

THE LIEUTENANT: Where's the ladder?

THE OLD PEASANT: On the roof.

THE LIEUTENANT [*calling*]: Throw down the drum. I order you! [KAT-TRIN *goes on drumming.*] You're all in this, but you won't live to tell the tale.

THE OLD PEASANT: They've been cutting down fir trees around here. If we bring a tall enough trunk we can knock her off the roof . . .

THE FIRST SOLDIER [*to the* LIEUTENANT]: I beg leave to make a suggestion. [*He whispers something to the* LIEUTENANT, *who nods.*]

Listen, you! We have an idea—for your own good. Come down and go with us to the town. Show us your mother and we'll spare her.

[KATTRIN goes on drumming.]

THE LIEUTENANT [pushing him away]: She doesn't trust you, no wonder with your face. [He calls up to KATTRIN:] Hey, you! Suppose I give you my word? I'm an officer, my word's my bond!

[KATTRIN drums harder.]

Nothing is sacred to her.

THE YOUNG PEASANT: Sir, it's not just because of her mother!

THE FIRST SOLDIER: This can't go on, they'll hear it in the town as sure as hell.

THE LIEUTENANT: We must make another noise with something. Louder than that drum. What can we make a noise with?

THE FIRST SOLDIER: But we mustn't make a noise!

THE LIEUTENANT: A harmless noise, fool, a peacetime noise!

THE OLD PEASANT: I could start chopping wood.

THE LIEUTENANT: That's it! [The PEASANT brings his ax and chops away.] Chop! Chop harder! Chop for your life!

[KATTRIN has been listening, beating the drum less hard. Very upset, and peering around, she now goes on drumming.]

It's not enough. [To the FIRST SOLDIER:] You chop too!

THE OLD PEASANT: I've only one ax. [He stops chopping.]

THE LIEUTENANT: We must set fire to the farm. Smoke her out.

THE OLD PEASANT: That's no good, Captain. When they see fire from the town, they'll know everything.

[During the drumming KATTRIN has been listening again. Now she laughs.]

THE LIEUTENANT: She's laughing at us, that's too much, I'll have her guts if it's the last thing I do. Bring a musket!

[Two SOLDIERS off. KATTRIN goes on drumming.]

THE PEASANT WOMAN: I have it, Captain. That's their wagon over there, Captain. If we smash that, she'll stop. It's all they have, Captain.

THE LIEUTENANT [to the YOUNG PEASANT]: Smash it! [Calling:] If you don't stop that noise, we'll smash your wagon!

[The YOUNG PEASANT deals the wagon a couple of feeble blows with a board.]

THE PEASANT WOMAN [*to* KATTRIN]: Stop, you little beast!

> [KATTRIN *stares at the wagon and pauses. Noises of distress come out of her. But she goes on drumming.*]

THE LIEUTENANT: Where are those sons of bitches with that gun?

THE FIRST SOLDIER: They can't have heard anything in the town or we'd hear their cannon.

THE LIEUTENANT [*calling*]: They don't hear you. And now we're going to shoot you. I'll give you one more chance: throw down that drum!

THE YOUNG PEASANT [*dropping the board, screaming to* KATTRIN]: Don't stop now! Or they're all done for. Go on, go on, go on . . .

> [*The* SOLDIER *knocks him down and beats him with his pike.* KATTRIN *starts crying but goes on drumming.*]

THE PEASANT WOMAN: Not in the back, you're killing him!

> [*The* SOLDIERS *arrive with the musket.*]

THE SECOND SOLDIER: The Colonel's foaming at the mouth. We'll be court-martialed.

THE LIEUTENANT: Set it up! Set it up! [*Calling while the musket is set up on forks:*] Once and for all: stop that drumming!

> [*Still crying,* KATTRIN *is drumming as hard as she can.*]

Fire!

> [*The* SOLDIERS *fire.* KATTRIN *is hit. She gives the drum another feeble beat or two, then slowly collapses.*]

THE LIEUTENANT: That's an end to the noise.

> [*But the last beats of the drum are lost in the din of cannon from the town. Mingled with the thunder of cannon, alarm bells are heard in the distance.*]

THE FIRST SOLDIER: She made it.

❧ *Scene XII*

TOWARD MORNING. *The drums and pipes of troops on the march, receding. In front of the wagon* MOTHER COURAGE *sits by* KATTRIN's *body. The* PEASANTS *of the last scene are standing near.*

THE PEASANTS: You must leave, woman. There's only one regiment to go. You can never get away by yourself.

MOTHER COURAGE: Maybe she's fallen asleep.

[She sings:]

Lullaby, baby, what's that in the hay?
The neighbor's kids cry but mine are gay.
The neighbor's kids are dressed in dirt:
Your silks are cut from an angel's skirt.
They are all starving: you have a pie.
If it's too stale, you need only cry.
Lullaby, baby, what's rustling there?
One lad fell in Poland. The other is—where?

You shouldn't have told her about the children.

THE PEASANTS: If you hadn't gone off to the town to get your cut, maybe it wouldn't have happened.

MOTHER COURAGE: She's asleep now.

THE PEASANTS: She's not asleep, it's time you realized. She's gone. You must get away. There are wolves in these parts. And the bandits are worse.

MOTHER COURAGE: That's right.

[She goes and fetches a cloth from the wagon to cover up the body.]

THE PEASANT WOMAN: Have you no one now? Someone you can go to?

MOTHER COURAGE: There's one. My Eilif.

THE PEASANT [while MOTHER COURAGE covers the body]: Find him then. Leave her to us. We'll give her a proper burial. You needn't worry.

MOTHER COURAGE: Here's money for the expenses.

[She pays the PEASANT. The PEASANT and his son shake her hand and carry KATTRIN away.]

THE PEASANT WOMAN [also taking her hand, and bowing, as she goes away]: Hurry!

MOTHER COURAGE [harnessing herself to the wagon]: I hope I can pull the wagon by myself. Yes, I'll manage, there's not much in it now. I must get back into business.

[Another regiment passes at the rear with pipe and drum.]

[MOTHER COURAGE starts pulling the wagon.]

MOTHER COURAGE: Hey! Take me with you!

[*Soldiers are heard singing:*]

> With all its luck, with all its danger,
> The war moves on, but will not quit.
> And even if it lasts forever,
> We shall get nothing out of it.
> Starvation, filth, and cold enslave us.
> The army robs us of our pay.
> But God may yet come down and save us:
> His holy war won't end today.
> > Christians, awake! Winter is gone!
> > The snows depart! Dead men sleep on!
> > Let all of you who still survive
> > Get out of bed and look alive!

EDITORIAL NOTES

Mother Courage and Her Children was copyrighted in the U.S. in 1940, and first published here, not in German, but in English, in 1941: the translation was by H. R. Hays, and the play appeared in an anthology of new writing entitled *New Directions, 1941*, published by New Directions. An Eric Bentley version of the play, with the cuts made by Brecht for the German production, appeared in *The Modern Theatre*, volume two (Doubleday, Anchor, 1955). A second Bentley version, even more heavily cut for a projected American production, appeared in *Seven Plays by Bertolt Brecht* (Grove Press, 1961).

The world première of the play (and this was in German) took place in 1941 at the Zürich Schauspielhaus; the director was Leopold Lindtberg.

The now famous production of the Berlin Ensemble dates back to 1949 (though the Ensemble did not yet exist) when Erich Engel and Bertolt Brecht put the play on at the Deutsches Theater in Berlin with Helene Weigel (Mrs. Bertolt Brecht) in the title role. Frau Weigel is today (1963) one of the few actors from the original cast who are still in the show.

The first Broadway production of *Mother Courage and Her Children*, in a version by Eric Bentley, opened at the Martin Beck Theatre, New York City, on March 28, 1963. Produced by Cheryl Crawford and Jerome Robbins, directed by Jerome Robbins, and with the music of Paul Dessau, it featured Anne Bancroft, Zohra Lampert, and Barbara Harris. Other professional productions of the play, adapted by Eric Bentley, have been staged in London, Bristol, Dublin, Cleveland, and San Francisco. It has also been presented by BBC-TV.

The music to the world première in Zürich was by Paul Burkhard, and there is an as yet unused score by Darius Milhaud, composed expressly for English lyrics of Eric Bentley, but the music generally associated with the play is that of Paul Dessau, for which the lyrics in the present text were written. Part of Dessau's score can be heard, with the words in French, on a Vanguard Record (VRS-9022); part with the words sung in German by the Berlin cast, on East German records usually available from Deutsche Schallplatten, Deutscher Buch Export, Lenin-strasse 16, Leipzig C.I. Two lyrics from the play, one set by Dessau, the other by Hanns Fisler, are to be found on *Bentley on Brecht* (Riverside Records, RM 7017).

AUTHOR'S NOTES TO *Mother Courage and Her Children*

The world première of *Mother Courage and Her Children* in Zürich during the Hitler War, with the outstanding Therese Giehse in the title role, made it possible, despite the antifascist and pacifist stand of the Zürich Schauspielhaus (mainly staffed with German emigrants), for the bourgeois press to speak of a Niobe tragedy and of the overwhelming vital strength of the mother animal. Duly warned, the playwright made some changes for the Berlin production. The original text follows.

From Scene One, pages 590–591

MOTHER COURAGE: . . . all of you: be careful, you'll need to be. Now let's climb on the wagon and move on.
SERGEANT: I don't feel very well.
RECRUITING OFFICER: Maybe you caught a chill when you handed over your helmet in all this wind.

[*The* SERGEANT *grabs his helmet.*]

MOTHER COURAGE: And you give me my papers. Someone else might ask for them and I'll be without. [*She collects them in her tin.*]
RECRUITING OFFICER [*to* EILIF]: You can at least take a look at the boots. And we can have a drink, just us men. I can advance you money: come behind the wagon, and I'll prove it.

[*They go behind the wagon.*]

SERGEANT: I don't understand. I always stay in the rear. There's no safer spot for a sergeant to be. You can send the others on ahead in quest of fame. My appetite is ruined. I can tell you right now, I won't be able to get anything done.

MOTHER COURAGE [*going over to him*]: You shouldn't take on so, just because you can't eat. Just stay in the rear. Here, take a slug of brandy, man, and no offence. [*She gives him something to drink from the wagon.*]

RECRUITING OFFICER [*who has taken* EILIF's *arm and is making off toward the back*]: You die anyway. You drew a cross, so what? Ten guilders in advance and you're a soldier of the king and a stout fellow and the women will be mad about you. And you can give me a smack in the kisser for insulting you.

[*Both leave. Dumb* KATTRIN *lets out harsh cries, for she has seen the abduction.*]

MOTHER COURAGE: Coming, Kattrin, coming. The Sergeant isn't well, he's superstitious, I didn't know that. And now we'll be going. Where's Eilif?

SWISS CHEESE: He must have gone with the recruiting officer. He was talking with him the whole time.

From Scene Five, pages 620–621

MOTHER COURAGE: What, you can't pay? No money, no brandy! They can play victory marches, they should pay their men!

SOLDIER [*threateningly*]: I want my brandy! I arrived too late for plunder. The Chief allowed one hour for plunder. He's not inhuman, he says. So I suppose they bought him off.

[*The* CHAPLAIN *staggers in.*]

CHAPLAIN: There are more in the farmhouse. A family of peasants. Help me, someone, I need linen!

[*The* SECOND SOLDIER *goes off with him.*]

MOTHER COURAGE: I have none. I sold all my bandages to the regiment. I'm not tearing up my officers' shirts for these people.

CHAPLAIN [*calling back*]: I said I need linen!

MOTHER COURAGE [*rummaging around in her wagon*]: Not a thing! They have nothing, and they pay nothing!

[*The* CHAPLAIN *stoops over a* WOMAN *whom he has brought on.*]

CHAPLAIN: Why did you stay out there in the line of fire?

WOMAN [*weakly*]: Our farm . . .

MOTHER COURAGE: Expect them to leave? My beautiful shirts. My officers will be coming tomorrow, and I won't have a thing for them. [*She throws some stuff down.* KATTRIN *takes it to the* PEASANT WOMAN.] What am I doing, giving stuff away? I didn't start the war.

FIRST SOLDIER: They're Protestants. Why should they be Protestants?

MOTHER COURAGE: Protestant, Catholic, what do they care? Their farm's gone, that's what.

SECOND SOLDIER: They're not Protestants anyway: they're Catholics.

FIRST SOLDIER: In a bombardment we can't pick and choose.

[*A* PEASANT *is brought in by the* CHAPLAIN.]

PEASANT: My arm's gone.

[*From the house comes the cry of a child in pain.*]

CHAPLAIN [*to the* PEASANT WOMAN]: Don't get up.

MOTHER COURAGE: Get the child out of there.

[KATTRIN *runs off.*]

MOTHER COURAGE [*tearing up shirts*]: Half a guilder a shirt. I'm ruined. Don't move her when you're bandaging, it may be her back. [*To* KATTRIN *who has brought a young baby out of the ruins and is rocking it as she walks around:*] Another baby to drag around—you must be pleased with yourself! Give it to its mother this minute. Or do I have to fight you again for hours till I get it from you? Are you deaf? [KATTRIN *ignores all this.*] I have nothing but losses from your victories. Now, make do with this, Chaplain, don't waste any of my linen, do you hear?

CHAPLAIN: I need more. The blood's coming through.

MOTHER COURAGE [*referring to* KATTRIN]: There she sits, happy as a lark in all this misery. Give the baby back, the mother is coming to! [*As* KATTRIN *finally and reluctantly gives the child back to the* PEASANT WOMAN, MOTHER COURAGE *rips up a new shirt.*] I'm giving nothing, I can give nothing, I have myself to think of. [*To the* SECOND SOLDIER:] Don't stand around gawking, go back there and tell them to stop that music, I can see their victory without it. Have yourself a glass of brandy, Chaplain, don't say no, I have enough to cope with. [*She has to get down from the wagon to snatch her daughter from the* FIRST SOLDIER, *who is drunk.*] You beast! You want another victory, do you? Well, you don't get away from me without paying up! [*To the* PEASANT:] Your child is all right. [*Pointing to the* WOMAN:] Get something down her. [*To the* FIRST SOLDIER:] Then leave this coat. It's stolen goods anyhow.

[FIRST SOLDIER *staggers away.* MOTHER COURAGE *goes on ripping shirts.*]

CHAPLAIN: There's still someone in there.

MOTHER COURAGE: Don't worry, I'll tear up all I have.

From Scene Seven, pages 628–629

[*A highway. The* CHAPLAIN, MOTHER COURAGE, *and* KATTRIN *pull the wagon. It is dirty and neglected, but new wares are hanging from it.*]

MOTHER COURAGE [*sings*]:

> So many seek a bed to sleep in:
> Each ditch is taken, and each cave,
> And he who seeks a hole to creep in
> Finds he has dug an early grave.
> And many a man spends many a minute
> In hurrying toward some resting place.
> You wonder, when at last he's in it,
> Just why the fellow forced the pace.

[*She plays the refrain, "Christians, awake!" on the harmonica.*]

From Scene Twelve, page 650

PEASANTS: You must leave, woman. There's only one regiment to go. You can never get away by yourself.

MOTHER COURAGE: She's still breathing. Maybe she's fallen asleep.

Of the Peasants' War, which was the greatest misfortune of German history, one may say that, socially considered, it pulled the teeth of the Reformation. Its legacy was cynicism and business as usual. Mother Courage (let it be said to help performances in the theatre) recognizes, as do her friends and guests and nearly everyone, the purely commercial character of the war: this is precisely what attracts her. She believes in the war to the end. It never occurs to her that one must have a big pair of scissors to take one's cut out of a war. Those who look on at catastrophes wrongly expect those involved to learn something. So long as the masses are the *object* of politics they cannot regard what happens to them as an experiment but only as a fate. They learn as little from catastrophe as a scientist's rabbit learns of biology. It is not incumbent on the playwright to give Mother Courage insight at the end—she sees something, around the middle of the play, at the close of the sixth scene, then loses again what she has seen—his concern is that the spectator should see.

B.B.

🎋 Comments

Mother Courage is the tale of a woman of the people who, with three illegitimate children, follows the troops during the Thirty Years' War to sell them liquor and sundry other articles soldiers crave. The play shows us how she is slowly deprived of everything she cherishes: her children, her trade, her reason for being. This woman who takes no sides, who seeks only to live and let live in the most friendly fashion, is swept along by the currents of life in a war period until nothing remains of her native honesty, good nature, moral or material possessions.

There are very funny scenes in the play, dramatic scenes and scenes which for all their brevity give us a remarkably sharp view of the epoch. But what is most important to bear in mind is that, though Brecht always endeavors to keep his writing and presentation dispassionate and rather matter-of-factly quiet—effects of climax, suspense, mood, being systematically avoided—what is ultimately achieved is indelibly vivid and emotionally telling. One leaves the theatre with the unalterable conviction that war is nothing less than the greatest scourge of man's making.

In his staging, Brecht doesn't attempt picturesqueness; yet his stage has a constant visual interest. Everything is apparently being done to destroy illusion—the light, for instance, is always bright white, and the electric apparatus always in view; the revolving stage by which Mother Courage's endless wanderings are shown is plainly a stage mechanism. Songs interrupt the action arbitrarily. They sharpen the play's points like epigrams of instruction. (Splendid songs they are, too.)

The purpose of all this is to tell the audience that the play is a conscious device to present what the dramatist and his colleagues want the audience to understand—the play's moral point. But—and it cannot be repeated too often—all this does not make the play any the less moving. Everything seems congruous and right. One rarely gets any feeling of a stylistic mannerism, of a trick, labored "modernism."

Brecht is a classicist. He seeks that form of artistic truth which allows the spectator to appreciate the play with that repose and refinement of attention which liberate the spirit without drugging the senses. Brecht's programmatic antiromanticism is against art as magic as it is against faith as superstition. But, more deeply, Brecht's technique is a form of discipline undertaken by the artist to convey as devotedly and self-abnegatingly as possible his perception of reality. The goal is wisdom rather than excitement. It has always been the aspiration of the highest art.

———————————◆◆———————————

What is a performance of *Mother Courage And Her Children* primarily meant to show? That in wartime big business is not conducted by small people. That war is a continuation of business by other means, making the human virtues fatal even to those who exercise them. That no sacrifice is too great for the struggle against war.

We felt that the tradeswoman's voluntary and active participation in the war was made clear enough by showing the great distance which she has travelled to get into it. From a number of press notices, however, and a lot of discussions with members of the audience it appeared that many people see Courage as the representative of the "little people" who get "caught up" in the war because "there's nothing they can do about it," they are "powerless in the hands of fate," etc. Deep-seated habits lead theatre audiences to pick on the characters' more emotional utterances and forget all the rest. Business deals are accepted with the same boredom as descriptions of landscape in a novel. The "business atmosphere" is simply the air we breathe and pay no special attention to. In our discussions war was always cropping up in this way as a timeless abstraction, however hard we might try to present it as the sum of everybody's business operations.

.   .   .   .

Experience shows that many actresses playing Courage find it easier and more congenial to play this final scene simply for its tragedy. This is no service to the playwright. He doesn't want to detract from the tragedy, but there is something that he wants to add: the warning that Courage has learnt *nothing*.

———————————◆◆———————————

The narrower a political creed, the less it corresponds to the real complexities of the world and the more difficult it will be for a creative writer to obey its dictates. Marxist dogma, in its mid-twentieth-century communist form, is so far removed from reality that it is practically impossible to make any literary work aiming at poetic truth conform to it.

Hence Brecht's inability to keep his work even remotely in line with the requirements of the party.

On the other hand, Brecht's commitment to Marxism and to the party did have a beneficial effect on his writing: it gave his anarchic and nihilistic tendencies a rigid framework of intellectual discipline. The inner tension created by this discipline, by the effort to repress the amorphous forces of his subconscious mind, gave Brecht's work its own peculiar spell, its tautness, poetic ambiguity, and depth. Had he set out by a conscious effort to make Mother Courage a latter-day Niobe, he would have succeeded only in producing a sentimental character—for Brecht had his sentimental, self-pitying side. But by following his rationalist, behaviorist conception, which denied the very existence of the deeper levels of human character and saw man as merely the product of the social environment he finds himself in at any moment, Brecht made Mother Courage a battlefield of contra-dictory impulses. Behind the rigid sociological framework the human side constantly reasserted itself; while the politician in Brecht piled on the social villainy, the poet in him drew on the subconscious feeling he had for the archetypal mother-figure, on his fund of pity—and sentiment—and cun-ningly smuggled these elements into the language, loading it with the subtlest overtones. And so in spite of Brecht's conscious and often declared intention of producing one-dimensional social schemata, the character he created has all the depth of a great tragic figure. And it is to this that the audience responds.

🕮 *Samuel Beckett*

Samuel Beckett (1906–) is probably the classic dramatist of the post-war period. His style is generally austere and rigorous; this was in part owing to the fact that he first wrote his plays in French. He felt that writing in a foreign language would act to restrain stylistic excesses. Born in Dublin of Protestant parents, he was an outsider there as well as in France, where he settled in 1937. He first went to Paris in 1928, teaching English in the École Normale for two years. He joined James Joyce's circle, and contributed to the famous symposium on *Finnegans Wake*, *Our Exagmination round his Factification for Incamination of Work in Progress*. In his essay he attacked those who read merely for ideas, who separated form from content. It was a defense of difficulty in art. The artist's first obligation was to use that form—no matter how difficult—which was appropriate to the content. It was a defense of Joyce and, by anticipation, his own work. It was equally a rejection of the idea that we can understand each other through the abstractions of discursive language. Language given body through action was another matter, though. Before the war he wrote poems, stories, novels (notably *Murphy*, 1938), and essays; his genius matured after the war in a trilogy of novels (*Molloy*, 1951; *Malone Dies*, 1951; *The Unnamable*, 1953), and the plays which have made him world-famous (*Waiting for Godot*, 1952; *Endgame*, 1957; *Krapp's Last Tape*, 1960; and *Happy Days*, 1961). The form of the novel suited his introspection; the drama forced him out of himself, but only to restate in another form the difficulty of relating to another person. He never married, though Joyce's daughter Lucia and the art patron Peggy Guggenheim were both in love with him.

Happy Days deals with the fundamental Beckett situation, the isolated pair in a barren setting. Here, though, one character, Winnie, does most of the talking, so that the play is largely a monologue, appropriate to Beckett's introspection. It is as absolute as *Godot* in its rejection of the idea of civilization; like that play it is a tragi-comedy of our non-relation to each other and to God, a parody on the ways of Providence and the middle-class clichés which justify those ways.

READINGS:

COHN, RUBY, *Samuel Beckett*. New Brunswick: Rutgers University Press, 1962.

ESSLIN, MARTIN, *The Theatre of the Absurd*. New York: Doubleday and Company, 1961.

FOWLIE, WALLACE, *Dionysus in Paris*. New York: Meridian Books, 1959.

HOFFMAN, FREDERICK J., *Samuel Beckett*. Carbondale: University of Southern Illinois Press, 1962.

KENNER, HUGH, *Samuel Beckett*. New York: Grove Press, 1961.

❧ Happy Days

Samuel Beckett

A Play in Two Acts

The world première of Happy Days was presented by Theatre 1962 (Messrs. Richard Barr and Clinton Wilder) at the Cherry Lane Theatre, New York, on September 17, 1961, with the following cast:

WINNIE, a woman about fifty   Ruth White
WILLIE, a man about sixty   John C. Becher

❦ Act I

EXPANSE of scorched grass rising centre to low mound. Gentle slopes down to front and either side of the stage. Back an abrupter fall to stage level. Maximum of simplicity and symmetry.

Blazing light.

Very pompier trompe-l'oeil backcloth to represent unbroken plain and sky receding to meet in far distance.

Imbedded up to above her waist in exact centre of mound, WINNIE. About fifty, well preserved, blond for preference, plump, arms and shoulders bare, low bodice, big bosom, pearl necklet. She is discovered sleeping, her arms on the ground before her, her head on her arms. Beside her on ground to her left a capacious black bag, shopping variety, and to her right a collapsible collapsed parasol, break of handle emerging from sheath.

To her right and rear, lying asleep on ground, hidden by mound, WILLIE.

Long pause. A bell rings piercingly, say ten seconds, stops. She does not move. Pause. Bell more piercingly, say five seconds. She wakes. Bell

stops. *She raises her head, gazes front. Long pause. She straightens up,
lays her hands flat on ground, throws back her head and gazes at
zenith. Long pause.*

WINNIE [*gazing at zenith*]: Another heavenly day. [*Pause. Head back
level, eyes front, pause. She clasps hands to breast, closes eyes. Lips
move in inaudible prayer, say ten seconds. Lips still. Hands remain
clasped. Low.*] For Jesus Christ sake Amen. [*Eyes open, hands
unclasp, return to mound. Pause. She clasps hands to breast again,
closes eyes, lips move again in inaudible addendum, say five seconds.
Low.*] World without end Amen. [*Eyes open, hands unclasp,
return to mound. Pause.*] Begin, Winnie. [*Pause.*] Begin your day,
Winnie. [*Pause. She turns to bag, rummages in it without moving it
from its place, brings out toothbrush, rummages again, brings out
flat tube of toothpaste, turns back front, unscrews cap of tube, lays
cap on ground, squeezes with difficulty small blob of paste on brush,
holds tube in one hand and brushes teeth with other. She turns
modestly aside and back to her right to spit out behind mound. In
this position her eyes rest on* WILLIE. *She spits out. She cranes a little
further back and down. Loud.*] Hoo-oo! [*Pause. Louder.*] Hoo-oo!
[*Pause. Tender smile as she turns back front, lays down brush.*]
Poor Willie—[*examines tube, smile off*]—running out—[*looks for
cap*]—ah well—[*finds cap*]—can't be helped—[*screws on cap*]—
just one of those old things—[*lays down tube*]—another of those
old things—[*turns towards bag*]—just can't be cured—[*rummages
in bag*]—cannot be cured—[*brings out small mirror, turns back
front*]—ah yes—[*inspects teeth in mirror*]—poor dear Willie—
[*testing upper front teeth with thumb, indistinctly*]—good Lord!
—[*pulling back upper lip to inspect gums, do.*]—good God!—[*pulling
back corner of mouth, mouth open, do.*]—ah well—[*other corner,
do.*]—no worse—[*abandons inspection, normal speech*]—no better,
no worse—[*lays down mirror*]—no change—[*wipes fingers on
grass*]—no pain—[*looks for toothbrush*]—hardly any—[*takes up
toothbrush*]—great thing that—[*examines handle of brush*]—
nothing like it—[*examines handle, reads*]—pure . . . what?—
[*pause*]—what?—[*lays down brush*]—ah yes—[*turns towards bag*]
—poor Willie—[*rummages in bag*]—no zest—[*rummages*]—for
anything—[*brings out spectacles in case*]—no interest—[*turns back
front*]—in life—[*takes spectacles from case*]—poor dear Willie—
[*lays down case*]—sleep for ever—[*opens spectacles*]—marvellous
gift—[*puts on spectacles*]—nothing to touch it—[*looks for toothbrush*]—in my opinion—[*takes up toothbrush*]—always said so—

[examines handle of brush]—wish I had it—[examines handle, reads]—genuine . . . pure . . . what?—[lays down brush]—blind next—[takes off spectacles]—ah well—[lays down spectacles]—seen enough—[feels in bodice for handkerchief]—I suppose—[takes out folded handkerchief]—by now—[shakes out handkerchief]—what are those wonderful lines—[wipes one eye]—woe woe is me—[wipes the other]—to see what I see—[looks for spectacles]—ah yes—[takes up spectacles]—wouldn't miss it—[starts polishing spectacles, breathing on lenses]—or would I?—[polishes]—holy light—[polishes]—bob up out of dark—[polishes]—blaze of hellish light. [Stops polishing, raises face to sky, pause, head back level, resumes polishing, stops polishing, cranes back to her right and down.] Hoo-oo! [Pause. Tender smile as she turns back front and resumes polishing. Smile off.] Marvellous gift—[stops polishing, lays down spectacles]—wish I had it—[folds handkerchief]—ah well—[puts handkerchief back in bodice]—can't complain—[looks for spectacles]—no no—[takes up spectacles]—mustn't complain—[holds up spectacles, looks through lens]—so much to be thankful for—[looks through other lens]—no pain—[puts on spectacles]—hardly any—[looks for toothbrush]—wonderful thing that—[takes up toothbrush]—nothing like it—[examines handle of brush]—slight headache sometimes—[examines handle, reads]—guaranteed . . . genuine . . . pure . . . what?—[looks closer]—genuine pure . . . —[takes handkerchief from bodice]—ah yes—[shakes out handkerchief]—occasional mild migraine—[starts wiping handle of brush]—it comes—[wipes]—then goes—[wiping mechanically]—ah yes—[wiping]—many mercies—[wiping]—great mercies—[stops wiping, fixed lost gaze, brokenly]—prayers perhaps not for naught—[pause, do.]—first thing—[pause, do.]—last thing—[head down, resumes wiping, stops wiping, head up, calmed, wipes eyes, folds handkerchief, puts it back in bodice, examines handle of brush, reads]—fully guaranteed . . . genuine pure . . . —[looks closer]—genuine pure . . . [Takes off spectacles, lays them and brush down, gazes before her.] Old things. [Pause.] Old eyes. [Long pause.] On, Winnie. [She casts about her, sees parasol, considers it at length, takes it up and develops from sheath a handle of surprising length. Holding butt of parasol in right hand she cranes back and down to her right to hang over WILLIE.] Hoo-oo! [Pause.] Willie! [Pause.] Wonderful gift. [She strikes down at him with beak of parasol.] Wish I had it. [She strikes again. The parasol slips from her grasp and falls behind mound. It is immediately restored to her by WILLIE's invisible hand.] Thank you, dear. [She transfers parasol to *left hand, turns back front and examines right palm.*] Damp. [*Returns parasol to right hand, examines left palm.*] Ah well, no worse. [*Head up, cheerfully.*] No better, no worse, no change. [*Pause. Do.*] No pain. [*Cranes back to look down at* WILLIE, *holding parasol by butt as before.*] Don't go off on me again now dear will you please, I may need you. [*Pause.*] No hurry, no hurry, just don't curl up on me again. [*Turns back front, lays down parasol, examines palms together, wipes them on grass.*] Perhaps a shade off colour just the same. [*Turns to bag, rummages in it, brings out revolver, holds it up, kisses it rapidly, puts it back, rummages, brings out almost empty bottle of red medicine, turns back front, looks for spectacles, puts them on, reads label.*] Loss of spirits . . . lack of keenness . . . want of appetite . . . infants . . . children . . . adults . . . six level . . . tablespoonfuls daily—[*head up, smile*]—the old style!—[*smile off, head down, reads*]—daily . . . before and after . . . meals . . . instantaneous . . . [*looks closer*] . . . improvement. [*Takes off spectacles, lays them down, holds up bottle at arm's length to see level, unscrews cap, swigs it off head well back, tosses cap and bottle away in* WILLIE's *direction. Sound of breaking glass.*] Ah that's better! [*Turns to bag, rummages in it, brings out lipstick, turns back front, examines lipstick.*] Running out. [*Looks for spectacles.*] Ah well. [*Puts on spectacles, looks for mirror.*] Musn't complain. [*Takes up mirror, starts doing lips.*] What is that wonderful line? [*Lips.*] Oh fleeting joys—[*lips*]—oh something lasting woe. [*Lips. She is interrupted by disturbance from* WILLIE. *He is sitting up. She lowers lipstick and mirror and cranes back and down to look at him. Pause. Top back of* WILLIE's *bald head, trickling blood, rises to view above slope, comes to rest.* WINNIE *pushes up her spectacles. Pause. His hand appears with handkerchief, spreads it on skull, disappears. Pause. His hand appears with boater, club ribbon, settles it on head, rakish angle, disappears. Pause.* WINNIE *cranes a little further back and down.*] Slip on your drawers, dear, before you get singed. [*Pause.*] No? [*Pause.*] Oh I see, you still have some of that stuff left. [*Pause.*] Work it well in, dear. [*Pause.*] Now the other. [*Pause. She turns back front, gazes before her. Happy expression.*] Oh this is going to be another happy day! [*Pause. Happy expression off. She pulls down spectacles and resumes lips.* WILLIE *opens newspaper, hands invisible. Tops of yellow sheets appear on either side of his head.* WINNIE *finishes lips, inspects them in mirror held a little further away.*] Ensign crimson. [WILLIE *turns page.* WINNIE *lays down lipstick and mirror, turns towards bag.*] Pale flag.

[WILLIE *turns page.* WINNIE *rummages in bag, brings out small ornate brimless hat with crumpled feather, turns back front, straightens hat, smooths feather, raises it towards head, arrests gesture as* WILLIE *reads.*]

WILLIE: His Grace and Most Reverend Father in God Dr Carolus Hunter dead in tub.

[*Pause.*]

WINNIE [*gazing front, hat in hand, tone of fervent reminiscence*]: Charlie Hunter! [*Pause.*] I close my eyes—[*she takes off spectacles and does so, hat in one hand, spectacles in other,* WILLIE *turns page*] —and am sitting on his knees again, in the back garden at Borough Green, under the horse-beech. [*Pause. She opens eyes, puts on spectacles, fiddles with hat.*] Oh the happy memories!

[*Pause. She raises hat towards head, arrests gesture as* WILLIE *reads.*]

WILLIE: Opening for smart youth.

[*Pause. She raises hat towards head, arrests gesture, takes off spectacles, gazes front, hat in one hand, spectacles in other.*]

WINNIE: My first ball! [*Long pause.*] My second ball! [*Long pause. Close eyes.*] My first kiss! [*Pause.* WILLIE *turns page.* WINNIE *opens eyes.*] A Mr Johnson, or Johnston, or perhaps I should say Johnstone. Very bushy moustache, very tawny. [*Reverently.*] Almost ginger! [*Pause.*] Within a toolshed, though whose I cannot conceive. We had no toolshed and he most certainly had no toolshed. [*Closes eyes.*] I see the piles of pots. [*Pause.*] The tangles of bast. [*Pause.*] The shadows deepening among the rafters.

[*Pause. She opens eyes, puts on spectacles, raises hat towards head, arrests gesture as* WILLIE *reads.*]

WILLIE: Wanted bright boy.

[*Pause.* WINNIE *puts on hat hurriedly, looks for mirror.* WILLIE *turns page.* WINNIE *takes up mirror, inspects hat, lays down mirror, turns towards bag. Paper disappears.* WINNIE *rummages in bag, brings out magnifying-glass, turns back front, looks for toothbrush. Paper reappears, folded, and begins to fan* WILLIE'S *face, hand invisible.* WINNIE *takes up toothbrush and examines handle through glass.*]

WINNIE: Fully guaranteed . . . [WILLIE *stops fanning*] . . . genuine
pure . . . [*Pause.* WILLIE *resumes fanning.* WINNIE *looks closer,*
reads.] Fully guaranteed . . . [WILLIE *stops fanning*] . . . genuine
pure . . . [*Pause.* WILLIE *resumes fanning.* WINNIE *lays down glass*
and brush, takes handkerchief from bodice, takes off and polishes
spectacles, puts on spectacles, looks for glass, takes up and polishes
glass, lays down glass, looks for brush, takes up brush and wipes
handle, lays down brush, puts handkerchief back in bodice, looks for
glass, takes up glass, looks for brush, takes up brush and examines
handle through glass.] Fully guaranteed . . . [WILLIE *stops fan-*
ning] . . . genuine pure . . . [*pause,* WILLIE *resumes fanning*]
. . . hog's [WILLIE *stops fanning, pause*] . . . setae. [*Pause.*
WINNIE *lays down glass and brush, paper disappears,* WINNIE *takes*
off spectacles, lays them down, gazes front.] Hog's setae. [*Pause.*]
That is what I find so wonderful, that not a day goes by—[*smile*]—to
speak in the old style—[*smile off*]—hardly a day, without some
addition to one's knowledge however trifling, the addition I mean,
provided one takes the pains. [WILLIE's *hand reappears with a post-*
card which he examines close to eyes.] And if for some strange
reason no further pains are possible, why then just close the eyes—
[*she does so*]—and wait for the day to come—[*opens eyes*]—the
happy day to come when flesh melts at so many degrees and the
night of the moon has so many hundred hours. [*Pause.*] That is
what I find so comforting when I lose heart and envy the brute
beast. [*Turning towards* WILLIE.] I hope you are taking in—[*She*
sees postcard, bends lower.] What is that you have there, Willie,
may I see? [*She reaches down with hand and* WILLIE *hands her card.*
The hairy forearm appears above slope, raised in gesture of giving,
the hand open to take back, and remains in this position till card is
returned. WINNIE *turns back front and examines card.*] Heavens
what are they up to! [*She looks for spectacles, puts them on and*
examines card.] No but this is just genuine pure filth! [*Examines*
card.] Make any nice-minded person want to vomit! [*Impatience of*
WILLIE's *fingers. She looks for glass, takes it up and examines card*
through glass. Long pause.] What does that creature in the background think he's doing? [*Looks closer.*] Oh no really! [*Impatience*
of fingers. Last long look. She lays down glass, takes edge of card
between right forefinger and thumb, averts head, takes nose between
left forefinger and thumb.] Pah! [*Drops card.*] Take it away!
[WILLIE's *arm disappears. His hand reappears immediately, holding*
card. WINNIE *takes off spectacles, lays them down, gazes before her.*
During what follows WILLIE *continues to relish card, varying angles*

and distance from his eyes]. Hog's setae. [Puzzled expression.] What exactly is a hog? [Pause. Do.] A sow of course I know, but a hog. . . [Puzzled expression off.] Oh well what does it matter, that is what I always say, it will come back, that is what I find so wonderful, all comes back. [Pause.] All? [Pause.] No, not all. [Smile.] No no. [Smile off.] Not quite. [Pause.] A part. [Pause.] Floats up, one fine day, out of the blue. [Pause.] That is what I find so wonderful. [Pause. She turns towards bag. Hand and card disappear. She makes to rummage in bag, arrests gesture.] No. [She turns back front. Smile.] No no. [Smile off.] Gently Winnie. [She gazes front. WILLIE's hand reappears, takes off hat, disappears with hat.] What then? [Hand reappears, takes handkerchief from skull, disappears with handkerchief. Sharply, as to one not paying attention.] Winnie! [WILLIE bows head out of sight.] What is the alternative? [Pause.] What is the al—[WILLIE blows nose loud and long, head and hands invisible. She turns to look at him. Pause. Head reappears. Pause. Hand reappears with handkerchief, spreads it on skull, disappears. Pause. Hand reappears with boater, settles it on head, rakish angle, disappears. Pause.] Would I had let you sleep on. [She turns back front. Intermittent plucking at grass, head up and down, to animate following.] Ah yes, if only I could bear to be alone, I mean prattle away with not a soul to hear. [Pause.] Not that I flatter myself you hear much, no Willie, God forbid. [Pause.] Days perhaps when you hear nothing. [Pause.] But days too when you answer. [Pause.] So that I may say at all times, even when you do not answer and perhaps hear nothing, Something of this is being heard, I am not merely talking to myself, that is in the wilderness, a thing I could never bear to do—for any length of time. [Pause.] That is what enables me to go on, go on talking that is. [Pause.] Whereas if you were to die—[smile]—to speak in the old style— [smile off]—or go away and leave me, then what would I do, what could I do, all day long, I mean between the bell for waking and the bell for sleep? [Pause.] Simply gaze before me with compressed lips. [Long pause while she does so. No more plucking.] Not another word as long as I drew breath, nothing to break the silence of this place. [Pause.] Save possibly, now and then, every now and then, a sigh into my looking-glass. [Pause.] Or a brief . . . gale of laughter, should I happen to see the old joke again. [Pause. Smile appears, broadens and seems about to culminate in laugh when suddenly replaced by expression of anxiety.] My hair! [Pause.] Did I brush and comb my hair? [Pause.] I may have done. [Pause.] Normally I do. [Pause.] There is so little one can do. [Pause.] One does it all.

[*Pause.*] All one can. [*Pause.*] Tis only human. [*Pause.*] Human nature. [*She begins to inspect mound, looks up.*] Human weakness. [*She resumes inspection of mound, looks up.*] Natural weakness. [*She resumes inspection of mound.*] I see no comb. [*Inspects.*] Nor any hairbrush. [*Looks up. Puzzled expression. She turns to bag, rummages in it.*] The comb is here. [*Back front. Puzzled expression. Back to bag. Rummages.*] The brush is here. [*Back front. Puzzled expression.*] Perhaps I put them back, after use. [*Pause. Do.*] But normally I do not put things back, after use, no, I leave them lying about and put them back all together, at the end of the day. [*Smile.*] To speak in the old style. [*Pause.*] The sweet old style. [*Smile off.*] And yet . . . I seem . . . to remember . . . [*Suddenly careless.*] Oh well, what does it matter, that is what I always say, I shall simply brush and comb them later on, purely and simply, I have the whole—[*Pause. Puzzled.*] Them? [*Pause.*] Or it? [*Pause.*] Brush and comb it? [*Pause.*] Sounds improper somehow. [*Pause. Turning a little towards* WILLIE.] What would you say, Willie? [*Pause. Turning a little further.*] What would you say, Willie, speaking of your hair, them or it? [*Pause.*] The hair on your head, I mean. [*Pause. Turning a little further.*] The hair on your head, Willie, what would you say speaking of the hair on your head, them or it?

[*Long pause.*]

WILLIE: It.

WINNIE [*turning back front, joyful*]: Oh you are going to talk to me today, this is going to be a happy day! [*Pause. Joy off.*] Another happy day. [*Pause.*] Ah well, where was I, my hair, yes, later on, I shall be thankful for it later on. [*Pause.*] I have my—[*raises hands to hat*]—yes, on, my hat on—[*lowers hands*]—I cannot take it off now. [*Pause.*] To think there are times one cannot take off one's hat, not if one's life were at stake. Times one cannot put it on, times one cannot take it off. [*Pause.*] How often I have said, Put on your hat now, Winnie, there is nothing else for it, take off your hat now, Winnie, like a good girl, it will do you good, and did not. [*Pause.*] Could not. [*Pause. She raises hand, frees a strand of hair from under hat, draws it towards eye, squints at it, lets it go, hand down.*] Golden you called it, that day, when the last guest was gone—[*hand up in gesture of raising a glass*]—to your golden . . . may it never. . . . [*voice breaks*] . . . may it never . . . [*Hand down. Head down. Pause. Low.*] That day. [*Pause. Do.*] What day? [*Pause. Head up. Normal voice.*] What now? [*Pause.*] Words fail, there are times when even they fail. [*Turning a little towards*

WILLIE.] Is that not so, Willie? [*Pause. Turning a little further.*] Is not that so, Willie, that even words fail, at times? [*Pause. Back front.*] What is one to do then, until they come again? Brush and comb the hair, if it has not been done, or if there is some doubt, trim the nails if they are in need of trimming, these things tide one over. [*Pause.*] That is what I mean. [*Pause.*] That is all I mean. [*Pause.*] That is what I find so wonderful, that not a day goes by— [*smile*]—to speak in the old style—[*smile off*]—without some blessing—[WILLIE *collapses behind slope, his head disappears,* WINNIE *turns towards event*]—in disguise. [*She cranes back and down.*] Go back into your hole now, Willie, you've exposed yourself enough. [*Pause.*] Do as I say, Willie, don't lie sprawling there in this hellish sun, go back into your hole. [*Pause.*] Go on now, Willie. [WILLIE *invisible starts crawling left towards hole.*] That's the man. [*She follows his progress with her eyes.*] Not head first, stupid, how are you going to turn? [*Pause.*] That's it . . . right round . . . now . . . back in. [*Pause.*] Oh I know it is not easy, dear, crawling backwards, but it is rewarding in the end. [*Pause.*] You have left your vaseline behind. [*She watches as he crawls back for vaseline.*] The lid! [*She watches as he crawls back towards hole. Irritated.*] Not head first, I tell you! [*Pause.*] More to the right. [*Pause.*] The *right*, I said. [*Pause. Irritated.*] Keep your tail down, can't you! [*Pause.*] Now. [*Pause.*] There! [*All these directions loud. Now in her normal voice, still turned towards him.*] Can you hear me? [*Pause.*] I beseech you, Willie, just yes or no, can you hear me, just yes or nothing.

[*Pause.*]

WILLIE: Yes.

WINNIE [*turning front, same voice*]: And now?

WILLIE [*irritated*]: Yes.

WINNIE [*less loud*]: And now?

WILLIE [*more irritated*]: Yes.

WINNIE [*still less loud*]: And now? [*A little louder.*] And now?

WILLIE [*violently*]: Yes!

WINNIE [*same voice*]: Fear no more the heat o' the sun. [*Pause.*] Did you hear that?

WILLIE [*irritated*]: Yes.

WINNIE [*same voice*]: What? [*Pause.*] What?

WILLIE [*more irritated*]: Fear no more.

[*Pause.*]

WINNIE [*same voice*]: No more what? [*Pause.*] Fear no more what?

WILLIE [*violently*]: Fear no more!

WINNIE [*normal voice, gabbled*]: Bless you Willie I do appreciate your goodness I know what an effort it costs you, now you may relax I shall not trouble you again unless I am obliged to, by that I mean unless I come to the end of my own resources which is most unlikely, just to know that in theory you can hear me even though in fact you don't is all I need, just to feel you there within earshot and conceivably on the qui vive is all I ask, not to say anything I would not wish you to hear or liable to cause you pain, not to be just babbling away on trust as it is were not knowing and something gnawing at me. [*Pause for breath.*] Doubt. [*Places index and second finger on heart area, moves them about, brings them to rest.*] Here. [*Moves them slightly.*] Abouts. [*Hand away.*] Oh no doubt the time will come when before I can utter a word I must make sure you heard the one that went before and then no doubt another come another time when I must learn to talk to myself a thing I could never bear to do such wilderness. [*Pause.*] Or gaze before me with compressed lips. [*She does so.*] All day long. [*Gaze and lips again.*] No. [*Smile.*] No no. [*Smile off.*] There is of course the bag. [*Turns towards it.*] There will always be the bag. [*Back front.*] Yes, I suppose so. [*Pause.*] Even when you are gone, Willie. [*She turns a little towards him.*] You are going, Willie, aren't you? [*Pause. Louder.*] You will be going soon, Willie, won't you? [*Pause. Louder.*] Willie! [*Pause. She cranes back and down to look at him.*] So you have taken off your straw, that is wise. [*Pause.*] You do look snug, I must say, with your chin on your hands and the old blue eyes like saucers in the shadows. [*Pause.*] Can you see me from there I wonder, I still wonder. [*Pause.*] No? [*Back front.*] Oh I know it does not follow when two are gathered together—[*faltering*]—in this way—[*normal*]—that because one sees the other the other sees the one, life has taught me that . . . too. [*Pause.*] Yes, life I suppose, there is no other word. [*She turns a little towards him.*] Could you see me, Willie, do you think, from where you are, if you were to raise your eyes in my direction? [*Turns a little further.*] Lift up your eyes to me, Willie, and tell me can you see me, do that for me, I'll lean back as far as I can. [*Does so. Pause.*] No? [*Pause.*] Well never mind. [*Turns back painfully front.*] The earth is very tight today, can it be I have put on flesh, I trust not. [*Pause. Absently, eyes lowered.*] The great heat possibly. [*Starts to pat and stroke ground.*] All things expanding, some more than others. [*Pause. Patting and stroking.*] Some less. [*Pause. Do.*] Oh I can well imagine what is passing through your mind, it is not enough to have to listen to the woman, now I must look at her as well. [*Pause. Do.*] Well it is very understandable. [*Pause. Do.*] Most understandable. [*Pause. Do.*] One does not appear to be asking a great deal, indeed at times it would seem hardly possible—[*voice breaks, falls to a murmur*]—to ask less—of a fellow-creature—to put it mildly—whereas actually—when you think about it—look into your heart—see the other—what he needs—peace—to be left in peace— then perhaps the moon—all this time—asking for the moon. [*Pause. Stroking hand suddenly still. Lively.*] Oh I say, what have we here? [*Bending head to ground, incredulous.*] Looks like life of some kind! [*Looks for spectacles, puts them on, bends closer. Pause.*] An emmet! [*Recoils. Shrill.*] Willie, an emmet, a live emmet! [*Seizes magnifying-glass, bends to ground again, inspects through glass.*] Where's it gone? [*Inspects.*] Ah! [*Follows its progress through grass.*] Has like a little white ball in its arms. [*Follows progress. Hand still. Pause.*] It's gone in. [*Continues a moment to gaze at spot through glass, then slowly straightens up, lays down glass, takes off spectacles and gazes before her, spectacles in hand. Finally.*] Like a little white ball.

[*Long pause. Gesture to lay down spectacles.*]

WILLIE: Eggs.

WINNIE [*arresting gesture*]: What?

[*Pause.*]

WILLIE: Eggs. [*Pause. Gesture to lay down glasses.*] Formication.

WINNIE [*arresting gesture*]: What?

[*Pause.*]

WILLIE: Formication.

[*Pause. She lays down spectacles, gazes before her. Finally.*]

WINNIE [*murmur*]: God. [*Pause.* WILLIE *laughs quietly. After a moment she joins in. They laugh quietly together.* WILLIE *stops. She* laughs on a moment alone. WILLIE joins in. They laugh together. She stops. WILLIE laughs on a moment alone. He stops. Pause. Normal voice.] Ah well what a joy in any case to hear you laugh again, Willie, I was convinced I never would, you never would. [Pause.] I suppose some people might think us a trifle irreverent, but I doubt it. [Pause.] How can one better magnify the Almighty than by sniggering with him at his little jokes, particularly the poorer ones? [Pause.] I think you would back me up there, Willie. [Pause.] Or were we perhaps diverted by two quite different things? [Pause.] Oh well, what does it matter, that is what I always say, so long as one . . . you know . . . what is that wonderful line . . . laughing wild . . . something something laughing wild amid sever-est woe. [Pause.] And now? [Long pause.] Was I lovable once, Willie? [Pause.] Was I ever lovable? [Pause.] Do not misunder-stand my question, I am not asking you if you loved me, we know all about that, I am asking you if you found me lovable—at one stage. [Pause.] No? [Pause.] You can't? [Pause.] Well I admit it is a teaser. And you have done more than your bit already, for the time being, just lie back now and relax, I shall not trouble you again unless I am compelled to, just to know you are there within hearing and conceivably on the semi-alert is . . . er . . . paradise enow. [Pause.] The day is now well advanced. [Smile.] To speak in the old style. [Smile off.] And yet it is perhaps a little soon for my song. [Pause.] To sing too soon is a great mistake, I find. [Turning towards bag.] There is of course the bag. [Looking at bag.] The bag. [Back front.] Could I enumerate its contents? [Pause.] No. [Pause.] Could I, if some kind person were to come along and ask, What all have you got in that big black bag, Winnie? give an exhaustive answer? [Pause.] No. [Pause.] The depths in particular, who knows what treasures. [Pause.] What comforts. [Turns to look at bag.] Yes, there is the bag. [Back front.] But something tells me, Do not overdo the bag, Winnie, make use of it of course, let it help you . . . along, when stuck, by all means, but cast your mind forward, something tells me, cast your mind forward, Winnie, to the time when words must fail—[she closes eyes, pause, opens eyes]—and do not overdo the bag. [Pause. She turns to look at bag.] Perhaps just one quick dip. [She turns back front, closes eyes, throws out left arm, plunges hand in bag and brings out revolver. Disgusted.] You again! [She opens eyes, brings revolver front and contemplates it. She weighs it in her palm.] You'd think the weight of this thing would bring it down among the . . . last rounds. But no. It doesn't. Ever uppermost, like Browning. [Pause.] Brownie

[Margin annotations, handwritten: Time / Old Style / Freedom / Perpetual Hell]

. . . [*Turning a little towards* WILLIE.] Remember Brownie, Willie? [*Pause.*] Remember how you used to keep on at me to take it away from you? Take it away, Winnie, take it away, before I put myself out of my misery. [*Back front. Derisive.*] Your misery! [*To revolver.*] Oh I suppose it's a comfort to know you're there, but I'm tired of you. [*Pause.*] I'll leave you out, that's what I'll do. [*She lays revolver on ground to her right.*] There, that's your home from this day out. [*Smile.*] The old style! [*Smile off.*] And now? [*Long pause.*] Is gravity what it was, Willie, I fancy not. [*Pause.*] Yes, the feeling more and more that if I were not held—[*gesture*]—in this way, I would simply float up into the blue. [*Pause.*] And that perhaps some day the earth will yield and let me go, the pull is so great, yes, crack all round me and let me out. [*Pause.*] Don't you ever have that feeling, Willie, of being sucked up? [*Pause.*] Don't you have to cling on sometimes, Willie? [*Pause. She turns a little towards him.*] Willie.

[*Pause.*]

WILLIE: Sucked up?

WINNIE: Yes love, up into the blue, like gossamer. [*Pause.*] No? [*Pause.*] You don't? [*Pause.*] Ah well, natural laws, natural laws, I suppose it's like everything else, it all depends on the creature you happen to be. All I can say is for my part is that for me they are not what they were when I was young and . . . foolish and . . . [*faltering, head down*] . . . beautiful . . . possibly . . . lovely . . . in a way . . . to look at. [*Pause. Head up.*] Forgive me, Willie, sorrow keeps breaking in. [*Normal voice.*] Ah well what a joy in any case to know you are there, as usual, and perhaps awake, and perhaps taking all this in, some of all this, what a happy day for me . . . it will have been. [*Pause.*] So far. [*Pause.*] What a blessing nothing grows, imagine if all this stuff were to start growing. [*Pause.*] Imagine. [*Pause.*] Ah yes, great mercies. [*Long pause.*] I can say no more. [*Pause.*] For the moment. [*Pause. Turns to look at bag. Back front. Smile.*] No no. [*Smile off. Looks at parasol.*] I suppose I might—[*takes up parasol*]—yes, I suppose I might . . . hoist this thing now. [*Begins to unfurl it. Following punctuated by mechanical difficulties overcome.*] One keeps putting off—putting up—for fear of putting up—too soon—and the day goes by—quite by—without one's having put up—at all. [*Parasol now fully open. Turned to her right she twirls it idly this way and that.*] Ah yes, so little to say, so little to do, and the fear so great, certain days, of finding oneself . . . left, with hours still to run, before the bell for sleep, and nothing more to say, nothing more to do, that the days go by, certain days go by, quite by, the bell goes, and little or nothing said, little or nothing done. [*Raising parasol.*] That is the danger. [*Turning front.*] To be guarded against. [*She gazes front, holding up parasol with right hand. Maximum pause.*] I used to perspire freely. [*Pause.*] Now hardly at all. [*Pause.*] The heat is much greater. [*Pause.*] The perspiration much less. [*Pause.*] That is what I find so wonderful. [*Pause.*] The way man adapts himself. [*Pause.*] To changing conditions. [*She transfers parasol to left hand. Long pause.*] Holding up wearies the arm. [*Pause.*] Not if one is going along. [*Pause.*] Only if one is at rest. [*Pause.*] That is a curious observation. [*Pause.*] I hope you heard that, Willie, I should be grieved to think you had not heard that. [*She takes parasol in both hands. Long pause.*] I am weary, holding it up, and I cannot put it down. [*Pause.*] I am worse off with it up than with it down, and I cannot put it down. [*Pause.*] Reason says, Put it down, Winnie, it is not helping you, put the thing down and get on with something else. [*Pause.*] I cannot. [*Pause.*] I cannot move. [*Pause.*] No, something must happen, in the world, take place, some change, I cannot, if I am to move again. [*Pause.*] Willie. [*Mildly.*] Help. [*Pause.*] No? [*Pause.*] Bid me put this thing down, Willie, I would obey you instantly, as I have always done, honoured and obeyed. [*Pause.*] Please, Willie. [*Mildly.*] For pity's sake. [*Pause.*] No? [*Pause.*] You can't? [*Pause.*] Well I don't blame you, no, it would ill become me, who cannot move, to blame my Willie because he cannot speak. [*Pause.*] Fortunately I am in tongue again. [*Pause.*] That is what I find so wonderful, my two lamps, when one goes out the other burns brighter. [*Pause.*] Oh yes, great mercies. [*Maximum pause. The parasol goes on fire. Smoke, flames if feasible. She sniffs, looks up, throws parasol to her right behind mound, cranes back to watch it burning. Pause.*] Ah earth you old extinguisher. [*Back front.*] I presume this has occurred before, though I cannot recall it. [*Pause.*] Can you, Willie? [*Turns a little towards him.*] Can you recall this having occurred before? [*Pause. Cranes back to look at him.*] Do you know what has occurred, Willie? [*Pause.*] Have you gone off on me again? [*Pause.*] I do not ask if you are alive to all that is going on, I merely ask if you have not gone off on me again. [*Pause.*] Your eyes appear to be closed, but that has no particular significance we know. [*Pause.*] Raise a finger, dear, will you please, if you are not quite senseless. [*Pause.*] Do that for me, Willie please, just the little finger, if you are still conscious. [*Pause. Joyful.*] Oh all five, you are a darling today, now I may continue with an easy mind. [Back front.] Yes, what ever occurred that did not occur before and yet . . . I wonder, yes, I confess I wonder. [Pause.] With the sun blazing so much fiercer down, and hourly fiercer, is it not natural things should go on fire never known to do so, in this way I mean, spontaneous like. [Pause.] Shall I myself not melt perhaps in the end, or burn, oh I do not mean necessarily burst into flames, no, just little by little be charred to a black cinder, all this—[ample gesture of arms]—visible flesh. [Pause.] On the other hand, did I ever know a temperate time? [Pause.] No. [Pause.] I speak of temperate times and torrid times, they are empty words. [Pause.] I speak of when I was not yet caught—in this way—and had my legs and had the use of my legs, and could seek out a shady place, like you, when I was tired of the sun, or a sunny place when I was tired of the shade, like you, and they are all empty words. [Pause.] It is no hotter today than yesterday, it will be no hotter tomorrow than today, how could it, and so on back into the far past, forward into the far future. [Pause.] And should one day the earth cover my breasts, then I shall never have seen my breasts, no one ever seen my breasts. [Pause.] I hope you caught something of that, Willie, I should be sorry to think you had caught nothing of all that, it is not every day I rise to such heights. [Pause.] Yes, something seems to have occurred, something has seemed to occur, and nothing has occurred, nothing at all, you are quite right, Willie. [Pause.] The sunshade will be there again tomorrow, beside me on this mound, to help me through the day. [Pause. She takes up mirror.] I take up this little glass, I shiver it on a stone—[does so]—I throw it away—[does so far behind her]—it will be in the bag again tomorrow, without a scratch, to help me through the day. [Pause.] No, one can do nothing. [Pause.] That is what I find so wonderful, the way things . . . [voice breaks, head down] . . . things . . . so wonderful. [Long pause, head down. Finally turns, still bowed, to bag, brings out unidentifiable odds and ends, stuffs them back, fumbles deeper, brings out finally musical-box, winds it up, turns it on, listens for a moment holding it in both hands, huddled over it, turns back front, straightens up and listens to tune, holding box to breast with both hands. It plays the Waltz Duet "I love you so" from The Merry Widow. Gradually happy expression. She sways to the rhythm. Music stops. Pause. Brief burst of hoarse song without words—musical-box tune—from WILLIE. Increase of happy expression. She lays down box.] Oh this will have been a happy day! [She claps hands.] Again, Willie, again! [Claps.] Encore, Willie, please!

[*Pause. Happy expression off.*] No? You won't do that for me? [*Pause.*] Well it is very understandable, very understandable. One cannot sing just to please someone, however much one loves them, no, song must come from the heart, that is what I always say, pour out from the inmost, like a thrush. [*Pause.*] How often I have said, in evil hours, Sing now, Winnie, sing your song, there is nothing else for it, and did not. [*Pause.*] Could not. [*Pause.*] No, like the thrush, or the bird of dawning, with no thought of benefit, to oneself or anyone else. [*Pause.*] And now? [*Long pause. Low.*] Strange feeling. [*Pause. Do.*] Strange feeling that someone is looking at me. I am clear, then dim, then gone, then dim again, then clear again, and so on, back and forth, in and out of someone's eye. [*Pause. Do.*] Strange? [*Pause. Do.*] No, here all is strange. [*Pause. Normal voice.*] Something says, Stop talking now, Winnie, for a minute, don't squander all your words for the day, stop talking and do something for a change, will you? [*She raises hands and holds them open before her eyes. Apostrophic.*] Do something! [*She closes hands.*] What claws! [*She turns to bag, rummages in it, brings out finally a nailfile, turns back front and begins to file nails. Files for a time in silence, then the following punctuated by filing.*] There floats up—into my thoughts—a Mr Shower—a Mr and perhaps a Mrs Shower—no—they are holding hands—his fiancée then more likely—or just some—loved one. [*Looks closer at nails.*] Very brittle today. [*Resumes filing.*] Shower—Shower—does the name mean anything—to you, Willie—evoke any reality, I mean— for you, Willie—don't answer if you don't—feel up to it—you have done more—than your bit—already—Shower—Shower. [*Inspects filed nails.*] Bit more like it. [*Raises head, gazes front.*] Keep yourself nice, Winnie, that's what I always say, come what may, keep yourself nice. [*Pause. Resumes filing.*] Yes—Shower—Shower— [*stops filing, raises head, gazes front, pause*]—or Cooker, perhaps I should say Cooker. [*Turning a little towards* WILLIE.] Cooker, Willie, does Cooker strike a chord? [*Pause. Turns a little further. Louder.*] Cooker, Willie, does Cooker ring a bell, the name Cooker? [*Pause. She cranes back to look at him. Pause.*] Oh really! [*Pause.*] Have you no handkerchief, darling? [*Pause.*] Have you no delicacy? [*Pause.*] Oh, Willie, you're not eating it! Spit it out, dear, spit it out! [*Pause. Back front.*] Ah well, I suppose it's only natural. [*Break in voice.*] Human. [*Pause. Do.*] What is one to do? [*Head down. Do.*] All day long. [*Pause. Do.*] Day after day. [*Pause. Head up. Smile. Calm.*] The old style! [*Smile off. Resumes nails.*] No, done him. [*Passes on to next.*] Should have put on my glasses.

[*Pause.*] Too late now. [*Finishes left hand, inspects it.*] Bit more human. [*Starts right hand. Following punctuated as before.*] Well anyway—this man Shower—or Cooker—no matter—and the woman—hand in hand—in the other hands bags—kind of big brown grips—standing there gaping at me—and at last this man Shower—or Cooker—ends in er anyway—stake my life on that— What's she doing? he says—What's the idea? he says—stuck up to her diddies in the bleeding ground—coarse fellow—What does it mean? he says—What's it meant to mean?—and so on—lot more stuff like that—usual drivel—Do you hear me? he says—I do, she says, God help me—What do you mean, he says, God help you? [*Stops filing, raises head, gazes front.*] And you, she says, what's the idea of you, she says, what are you meant to mean? It is because you're still on your two flat feet, with your old ditty full of tinned muck and changes of underwear, dragging me up and down this fornicating wilderness, coarse creature, fit mate—[*with sudden violence*]—let go of my hand and drop for God's sake, she says, drop! [*Pause. Resumes filing.*] Why doesn't he dig her out? he says— referring to you, my dear—What good is she to him like that? —What good is he to her like that?—and so on—usual tosh—Good! she says, have a heart for God's sake—Dig her out, he says, dig her out, no sense in her like that—Dig her out with what? she says—I'd dig her out with my bare hands, he says—must have been man and—wife. [*Files in silence.*] Next thing they're away—hand in hand—and the bags—dim—then gone—last human kind—to stray this way. [*Finishes right hand, inspects it, lays down file, gazes front.*] Strange thing, time like this, drift up into the mind. [*Pause.*] Strange? [*Pause.*] No, here all is strange. [*Pause.*] Thankful for it in any case. [*Voice breaks.*] Most thankful. [*Head down. Pause. Head up. Calm.*] Bow and raise the head, bow and raise, always that. [*Pause.*] And now? [*Long pause. Starts putting things back in bag, toothbrush last. This operation, interrupted by pauses as indicated, punctuates following.*] It is perhaps a little soon—to make ready—for the night—[*stops tidying, head up, smile*]—the old style! —[*smile off, resumes tidying*]—and yet I do—make ready for the night—feeling it at hand—the bell for sleep—saying to myself— Winnie—it will not be long now, Winnie—until the bell for sleep. [*Stops tidying, head up.*] Sometimes I am wrong. [*Smile.*] But not often. [*Smile off.*] Sometimes all is over, for the day, all done, all said, all ready for the night, and the day not over, far from over, the night not ready, far, far from ready. [*Smile.*] But not often. [*Smile off.*] Yes, the bell for sleep, when I feel it at hand, and so make ready for the night—[gesture]—in this way, sometimes I am wrong —[smile]—but not often. [Smile off. Resumes tidying.] I used to think—I say I used to think—that all these things—put back into the bag—if too soon—put back too soon—could be taken out again—if necessary—if needed—and so on—indefinitely—back into the bag—back out of the bag—until the bell—went. [Stops tidying, head up, smile] But no. [Smile broader.] No no. [Smile off. Resumes tidying.] I suppose this—might seem strange—this—what shall I say—this what I have said—yes—[she takes up revolver]— strange—[she turns to put revolver in bag]—were it not—[about to put revolver in bag she arrests gesture and turns back front]—were it not—[she lays down revolver to her right, stops tidying, head up]—that all seems strange. [Pause.] Most strange. [Pause.] Never any change. [Pause.] And more and more strange. [Pause. She bends to mound again, takes up last object, i.e. toothbrush, and turns to put it in bag when her attention is drawn to disturbance from WILLIE. She cranes back and to her right to see. Pause.] Weary of your hole, dear? [Pause.] Well I can understand that. [Pause.] Don't forget your straw. [Pause.] Not the crawler you were, poor darling. [Pause.] No, not the crawler I gave my heart to. [Pause.] The hands and knees, love, try the hands and knees. [Pause.] The knees! The knees! [Pause.] What a curse, mobility! [She follows with eyes his progress towards her behind mound, i.e. towards place he occupied at beginning of act.] Another foot, Willie, and you're home. [Pause as she observes last foot.] Ah! [Turns back front laboriously, rubs neck.] Crick in my neck admiring you. [Rubs neck.] But it's worth it, well worth it. [Turning slightly towards him.] Do you know what I dream sometimes? [Pause.] What I dream sometimes, Willie. [Pause.] That you'll come round and live this side where I could see you. [Pause. Back front.] I'd be a different woman. [Pause.] Unrecognizable. [Turning slightly towards him.] Or just now and then, come round this side just every now and then and let me feast on you. [Back front.] But you can't, I know. [Head down.] I know. [Pause. Head up.] Well anyway— [looks at toothbrush in her hand]—can't be long now—[looks at brush]—until the bell. [Top back of WILLIE's head appears above slope. WINNIE looks closer at brush.] Fully guaranteed . . . [head up] . . . what's this it was? [WILLIE's hand appears with handker-chief, spreads it on skull, disappears.] Genuine pure . . . fully guaranteed . . . [WILLIE's hand appears with boater, settles it on head, rakish angle, disappears] . . . genuine pure . . . ah! hog's setae. [Pause.] What is a hog exactly? [Pause. Turns slightly towards WILLIE.] What exactly is a hog, Willie, do you know, I can't remember. [Pause. Turning a little further, pleading.] What is a hog, Willie, please!

[Pause.]

WILLIE: Castrated male swine. [Happy expression appears on WINNIE's face.] Reared for slaughter.

[Happy expression increases. WILLIE opens newspaper, hands invisible. Tops of yellow sheets appear on either side of his head. WINNIE gazes before her with happy expression.]

WINNIE: Oh this is a happy day! This will have been another happy day! [Pause.] After all. [Pause.] So far.

[Pause. Happy expression off. WILLIE turns page. Pause. He turns another page. Pause.]

WILLIE: Opening for smart youth.

[Pause. WINNIE takes off hat, turns to put it in bag, arrests gesture, turns back front. Smile.]

WINNIE: No. [Smile broader.] No no. [Smile off. Puts on hat again, gazes front, pause.] And now? [Pause.] Sing. [Pause.] Sing your song, Winnie. [Pause.] No? [Pause.] Then pray. [Pause.] Pray your prayer, Winnie.

[Pause. WILLIE turns page. Pause.]

WILLIE: Wanted bright boy.

[Pause. WINNIE gazes before her. WILLIE turns page. Pause. Newspaper disappears. Long pause.]

WINNIE: Pray your old prayer, Winnie.

[Long pause.]

CURTAIN

❀ *Act II*

SCENE as before.

WINNIE imbedded up to neck, hat on head, eyes closed. Her head, which she can no longer turn, nor bow, nor raise, faces front motionless through act. Movements of eyes as indicated.

Bag and parasol as before. Revolver conspicuous to her right on mound.

Long pause.

Bell rings loudly. She opens eyes at once. Bell stops. She gazes front. Long pause.

WINNIE: Hail, holy light. [*Long pause. She closes her eyes. Bell rings loudly. She opens eyes at once. Bell stops. She gazes front. Long smile. Smile off. Long pause.*] Someone is looking at me still. [*Pause.*] Caring for me still. [*Pause.*] This is what I find so wonderful. [*Pause.*] Eyes on my eyes. [*Pause.*] What is that unforgettable line? [*Pause. Eyes right.*] Willie. [*Pause. Louder.*] Willie. [*Pause. Eyes front.*] May one still speak of time? [*Pause.*] Say it is a long time now, Willie, since I saw you. [*Pause.*] Since I heard you. [*Pause.*] May one? [*Pause.*] One does. [*Smile.*] The old style! [*Smile off.*] There is so little one can speak of. [*Pause.*] One speaks of it all. [*Pause.*] All one can. [*Pause.*] I used to think . . . [*Pause.*] . . . I say I used to think that I would learn to talk alone. [*Pause.*] By that I mean to myself, the wilderness. [*Smile.*] But no. [*Smile broader.*] No no. [*Smile off.*] Ergo you are there. [*Pause.*] Oh no doubt you are dead, like the others, no doubt you have died, or gone away and left me, like the others, it doesn't matter, you are there. [*Pause. Eyes left.*] The bag too is there, the same as ever, I can see it. [*Pause. Eyes right. Louder.*] The bag is there, Willie, as good as ever, the one you gave me that day . . . to go to market. [*Pause. Eyes front.*] That day. [*Pause.*] What day? [*Pause.*] I used to pray. [*Pause.*] I say I used to pray. [*Pause.*] Yes, I must confess I did. [*Smile.*] Not now. [*Smile broader.*] No no. [*Smile off. Pause.*] Then . . . now . . . what difficulties here, for the mind. [*Pause*] To have been always what I am—and so changed from what I was. [*Pause.*] I am the one, I say the one, then the other. [*Pause.*] Now the one, then the other. [*Pause.*] There is so little one can say, one says it all. [*Pause.*] All one can. [*Pause.*] And no truth in it anywhere. [*Pause.*] My arms. [*Pause.*] My breasts. [*Pause.*] What arms? [*Pause.*] What breasts? [*Pause.*] Willie. [*Pause.*] What Willie? [*Sudden vehement affirmation.*] My Willie! [*Eyes right, calling.*] Willie! [*Pause. Louder.*] Willie! [*Pause. Eyes front.*] Ah well, not to know, not to know for sure, great mercy, all I ask. [*Pause.*] Ah yes . . . then . . . now . . . beechen green . . . this . . . Charlie . . . kisses . . . this . . . all that . . . deep trouble for the mind. [*Pause.*] But it does not trouble mine. [*Smile.*] Not now. [*Smile broader.*] No no. [*Smile off. Long pause. She closes eyes. Bell rings loudly. She opens eyes. Pause.*] Eyes float up that seem to close in peace . . . to see . . . in peace. [*Pause.*] Not mine. [*Smile.*] Not now. [*Smile broader.*] No no. [*Smile off. Long pause.*] Willie. [*Pause.*] Do you think the earth has lost its atmosphere, Willie? [*Pause.*] Do you, Willie? [*Pause.*] You have no opinion? [*Pause.*] Well that is like you, you never had any opinion about anything. [*Pause.*] It's understandable. [*Pause.*] Most. [*Pause.*] The earthball. [*Pause.*] I sometimes wonder. [*Pause.*] Perhaps not quite all. [*Pause.*] There always remains something. [*Pause.*] Of everything. [*Pause.*] Some remains. [*Pause.*] If the mind were to go. [*Pause.*] It won't of course. [*Pause.*] Not quite. [*Pause.*] Not mine. [*Smile.*] Not now. [*Smile broader.*] No no. [*Smile off. Long pause.*] It might be the eternal cold. [*Pause.*] Everlasting perishing cold. [*Pause.*] Just chance, I take it, happy chance. [*Pause.*] Oh yes, great mercies, great mercies. [*Pause.*] And now? [*Long pause.*] The face. [*Pause.*] The nose. [*She squints down.*] I can see it . . . [*squinting down*] . . . the tip . . . the nostrils . . . breath of life . . . that curve you so admired . . . [*pouts*] . . . a hint of lip . . . [*pouts again*] . . . if I pout them out . . . [*sticks out tongue*] . . . the tongue of course . . . you so admired . . . if I stick it out . . . [*sticks it out again*] . . . the tip . . . [*eyes up*] . . . suspicion of brow . . . eyebrow . . . imagination possibly . . . [*eyes left*] . . . cheek . . . no . . . [*eyes right*] . . . no . . . [*distends cheeks*] . . . even if I puff them out . . . [*eyes left, distends cheeks again*] . . . no . . . no damask. [*Eyes front.*] That is all. [*Pause.*] The bag of course . . . [*eyes left*] . . . a little blurred perhaps . . . but the bag. [*Eyes front. Offhand.*] The earth of course and sky. [*Eyes right.*] The sunshade you gave me . . . that day . . . [*pause*] . . . the lake . . . the reeds. [*Eyes front. Pause.*] What day? [*Pause.*] What reeds? [*Long pause. Eyes close. Bell rings loudly. Eyes open. Pause. Eyes right.*] Brownie of course. [*Pause.*] You remember Brownie, Willie, I can see him. [*Pause.*] Brownie is there, Willie, beside me. [*Pause.*

Loud.] Brownie is there, Willie. [Pause. Eyes front.] That is all. [Pause.] What would I do without them? [Pause.] What would I do without them, when words fail? [Pause.] Gaze before me, with compressed lips. [Long pause while she does so.] I cannot. [Pause.] Ah yes, great mercies, great mercies. [Long pause. Low.] Sometimes I hear sounds. [Listening expression. Normal voice.] But not often. [Pause.] They are a boon, sounds are a boon, they help me . . . through the day. [Smile.] The old style! [Smile off.] Yes, those are happy days, when there are sounds. [Pause.] When I hear sounds. [Pause.] I used to think . . . [pause] . . . I say I used to think they were in my head. [Smile.] But no. [Smile broader.] No no. [Smile off.] That was just logic. [Pause.] Reason. [Pause.] I have not lost my reason. [Pause.] Not yet. [Pause.] Not all. [Pause.] Some remains. [Pause.] Sounds. [Pause.] Like little . . . sunderings, little falls . . . apart. [Pause. Low.] It's things, Willie. [Pause. Normal voice.] In the bag, outside the bag. [Pause.] Ah yes, things have their life, that is what I always say, things have a life. [Pause.] Take my looking-glass, it doesn't need me. [Pause.] The bell. [Pause.] It hurts like a knife. [Pause.] A gouge. [Pause.] One cannot ignore it. [Pause.] How often . . . [pause] . . . I say how often I have said, Ignore it, Winnie, ignore the bell, pay no heed, just sleep and wake, sleep and wake, as you please, open and close the eyes, as you please, or in the way you find most helpful. [Pause.] Open and close the eyes, Winnie, open and close, always that. [Pause.] But no. [Smile.] Not now. [Smile broader.] No no. [Smile off. Pause.] What now? [Pause.] What now, Willie? [Long pause.] There is my story of course, when all else fails. [Pause.] A life. [Smile.] A long life. [Smile off.] Beginning in the womb, where life used to begin, Mildred has memories, she will have memories, of the womb, before she dies, the mother's womb. [Pause.] She is now four or five already and has recently been given a big waxen dolly. [Pause.] Fully clothed, complete outfit. [Pause.] Shoes, socks, undies, complete set, frilly frock, gloves. [Pause.] White mesh. [Pause.] A little white straw hat with a chin elastic. [Pause.] Pearly necklet. [Pause.] A little picture-book with legends in real print to go under her arm when she takes her walk. [Pause.] China blue eyes that open and shut. [Pause. Narrative.] The sun was not well up when Milly rose, descended the steep . . . [pause] . . . slipped on her nightgown, descended all alone the steep wooden stairs, backwards on all fours, though she had been forbidden to do so, entered the . . . [pause] . . . tiptoed down the silent passage, entered the nursery and began to undress Dolly. [Pause.] Crept under the table and began to undress

Dolly. [*Pause.*] Scolding her . . . the while. [*Pause.*] Suddenly a mouse—[*Long pause.*] Gently, Winnie. [*Long pause. Calling.*] Willie! [*Pause. Louder.*] Willie! [*Pause. Mild reproach.*] I sometimes find your attitude a little strange, Willie, all this time, it is not like you to be wantonly cruel. [*Pause.*] Strange? [*Pause.*] No. [*Smile.*] Not here. [*Smile broader.*] Not now. [*Smile off.*] And yet . . . [*Suddenly anxious.*] I do hope nothing is amiss. [*Eyes right, loud.*] Is all well, dear? [*Pause. Eyes front. To herself.*] God grant he did not go in head foremost! [*Eyes right, loud.*] You're not stuck, Willie? [*Pause. Do.*] You're not jammed, Willie? [*Eyes front, distressed.*] Perhaps he is crying out for help all this time and I do not hear him! [*Pause.*] I do of course hear cries. [*Pause.*] But they are in my head surely. [*Pause.*] Is it possible that . . . [*Pause. With finality.*] No no, my head was always full of cries. [*Pause.*] Faint confused cries. [*Pause.*] They come. [*Pause.*] Then go. [*Pause.*] As on a wind. [*Pause.*] That is what I find so wonderful. [*Pause.*] They cease. [*Pause.*] Ah yes, great mercies, great mercies. [*Pause.*] The day is now well advanced. [*Smile. Smile off.*] And yet it is perhaps a little soon for my song. [*Pause.*] To sing too soon is fatal, I always find. [*Pause.*] On the other hand it is possible to leave it too late. [*Pause.*] The bell goes for sleep and one has not sung. [*Pause.*] The whole day has flown—[*smile, smile off*]—flown by, quite by, and no song of any class, kind or description. [*Pause.*] There is a problem here. [*Pause.*] One cannot sing . . . just like that, no. [*Pause.*] It bubbles up, for some unknown reason, the time is ill chosen, one chokes it back. [*Pause.*] One says, Now is the time, it is now or never, and one cannot. [*Pause.*] Simply cannot sing. [*Pause.*] Not a note. [*Pause.*] Another thing, Willie, while we are on this subject. [*Pause.*] The sadness after song. [*Pause.*] Have you run across that, Willie? [*Pause.*] In the course of your experience. [*Pause.*] No? [*Pause.*] Sadness after intimate sexual intercourse one is familiar with of course. [*Pause.*] You would concur with Aristotle there, Willie, I fancy. [*Pause.*] Yes, that one knows and is prepared to face. [*Pause.*] But after song . . . [*Pause.*] It does not last of course. [*Pause.*] That is what I find so wonderful. [*Pause.*] It wears away. [*Pause.*] What are those exquisite lines? [*Pause.*] Go forget me why should something o'er that something shadow fling . . . go forget me . . . why should sorrow . . . brightly smile . . . go forget me . . . never hear me . . . sweetly smile . . . brightly sing . . . [*Pause. With a sigh.*] One loses one's classics. [*Pause.*] Oh not all. [*Pause.*] A part. [*Pause.*] A part remains. [*Pause.*] That is what I find so wonderful, a part remains, of one's classics, to help one through the day. [*Pause.*] Oh yes, many mercies, many mercies. [*Pause.*] And now? [*Pause.*] And now, Willie? [*Long pause.*] I call to the eye of the mind . . . Mr. Shower—or Cooker. [*She closes her eyes. Bell rings loudly. She opens her eyes. Pause.*] Hand in hand, in the other hands bags. [*Pause.*] Getting on . . . in life. [*Pause.*] No longer young, not yet old. [*Pause.*] Standing there gaping at me. [*Pause.*] Can't have been a bad bosom, he says, in its day. [*Pause.*] Seen worse shoulders, he says, in my time. [*Pause.*] Does she feel her legs? he says. [*Pause.*] Is there any life in her legs? he says. [*Pause.*] Has she anything on underneath? he says. [*Pause.*] Ask her, he says, I'm shy. [*Pause.*] Ask her what? she says. [*Pause.*] Is there any life in her legs. [*Pause.*] Has she anything on underneath. [*Pause.*] Ask her yourself, she says. [*Pause. With sudden violence.*] Let go of me for Christ sake and drop! [*Pause. Do.*] Drop dead! [*Smile.*] But no. [*Smile broader.*] No no. [*Smile off.*] I watch them recede. [*Pause.*] Hand in hand—and the bags. [*Pause.*] Dim. [*Pause.*] Then gone. [*Pause.*] Last human kind—to stray this way. [*Pause.*] Up to date. [*Pause.*] And now? [*Pause. Low.*] Help. [*Pause. Do.*] Help, Willie. [*Pause. Do.*] No? [*Long pause. Narrative.*] Suddenly a mouse . . . [*Pause.*] Suddenly a mouse ran up her little thigh and Mildred, dropping Dolly in her fright, began to scream—[WINNIE *gives a sudden piercing scream*]—and screamed and screamed— [WINNIE *screams twice*]—screamed and screamed and screamed and screamed till all came running, in their night attire, papa, mamma, Bibby and . . . old Annie, to see what was the matter . . . [*pause*] . . . what on earth could possibly be the matter. [*Pause.*] Too late. [*Pause.*] Too late. [*Long pause. Just audible.*] Willie. [*Pause. Normal voice.*] Ah well, not long now, Winnie, can't be long now, until the bell for sleep. [*Pause.*] Then you may close your eyes, then you must close your eyes—and keep them closed. [*Pause.*] Why say that again? [*Pause.*] I used to think . . . [*pause.*] . . . I say I used to think there was no difference between one fraction of a second and the next. [*Pause.*] I used to say . . . [*pause*] . . . I say I used to say, Winnie, you are changeless, there is never any difference between one fraction of a second and the next. [*Pause.*] Why bring that up again? [*Pause.*] There is so little one can bring up, one brings up all. [*Pause.*] All one can. [*Pause.*] My neck is hurting me. [*Pause. With sudden violence.*] My neck is hurting me! [*Pause.*] Ah that's better. [*With mild irritation.*] Everything within reason. [*Long pause.*] I can do no more. [*Pause.*] Say no more. [*Pause.*] But I must say more. [*Pause.*] Problem here.

[Pause.] No, something must move, in the world, I can't any more. [Pause.] A zephyr. [Pause.] A breath. [Pause.] What are those immortal lines? [Pause.] It might be the eternal dark. [Pause.] Black night without end. [Pause.] Just chance, I take it, happy chance. [Pause.] Oh yes, abounding mercies. [Long pause.] And now? [Pause.] And now, Willie? [Long pause.] That day. [Pause.] The pink fizz. [Pause.] The flute glasses. [Pause.] The last guest gone. [Pause.] The last bumper with the bodies nearly touching. [Pause.] The look. [Long pause.] What day? [Long pause.] What look? [Long pause.] I hear cries. [Pause.] Sing. [Pause.] Sing your old song, Winnie.

> [Long pause. Suddenly alert expression. Eyes switch right. WILLIE's head appears to her right round corner of mound. He is on all fours, dressed to kill—top hat, morning coat, striped trousers, etc., white gloves in hand. Very long bushy white Battle of Britain moustache. He halts, gazes front, smooths moustache. He emerges completely from behind mound, turns to his left, halts, looks up at WINNIE. He advances on all fours towards centre, halts, turns head front, gazes front, strokes moustache, straightens tie, adjusts hat, advances a little further, halts, takes off hat and looks up at WINNIE. He is now not far from centre and within her field of vision. Unable to sustain effort of looking up he sinks head to ground.

WINNIE [mondaine]: Well this is an unexpected pleasure! [Pause.] Reminds me of the day you came whining for my hand. [Pause.] I worship you, Winnie, be mine. [He looks up.] Life a mockery without Win. [She goes off into a giggle.] What a get up, you do look a sight! [Giggles.] Where are the flowers? [Pause.] That smile today. [WILLIE sinks head.] What's that on your neck, an anthrax? [Pause.] Want to watch that, Willie, before it gets a hold on you. [Pause.] Where were you all this time? [Pause.] What were you doing all this time? [Pause.] Changing? [Pause.] Did you not hear me screaming for you? [Pause.] Did you get stuck in your hole? [Pause. He looks up.] That's right, Willie, look at me. [Pause.] Feast your old eyes, Willie. [Pause.] Does anything remain? [Pause.] Any remains? [Pause.] No? [Pause.] I haven't been able to look after it, you know. [He sinks his head.] You are still recognizable, in a way. [Pause.] Are you thinking of coming to live this side now . . . for a bit maybe? [Pause.] No? [Pause.] Just a brief call? [Pause.] Have you gone deaf, Willie? [Pause.] Dumb? [Pause.]

Oh I know you were never one to talk, I worship you Winnie be mine and then nothing from that day forth only titbits from Reynolds' News. [*Eyes front. Pause.*] Ah well, what matter, that's what I always say, it will have been a happy day, after all, another happy day. [*Pause.*] Not long now, Winnie. [*Pause.*] I hear cries. [*Pause.*] Do you ever hear cries, Willie? [*Pause.*] No? [*Eyes back on* WILLIE.] Willie. [*Pause.*] Look at me again, Willie. [*Pause.*] Once more, Willie. [*He looks up. Happily.*] Ah! [*Pause. Shocked.*] What ails you, Willie, I never saw such an expression! [*Pause.*] Put on your hat, dear, it's the sun, don't stand on ceremony, I won't mind. [*He drops hat and gloves and starts to crawl up mound towards her. Gleeful.*] Oh I say, this is terrific! [*He halts, clinging to mound with one hand, reaching up with the other.*] Come on, dear, put a bit of jizz into it, I'll cheer you on. [*Pause.*] Is it me you're after, Willie . . . or is it something else? [*Pause.*] Do you want to touch my face . . . again? [*Pause.*] Is it a kiss you're after, Willie . . . or is it something else? [*Pause.*] There was a time when I could have given you a hand. [*Pause.*] And then a time before that again when I did give you a hand. [*Pause.*] You were always in dire need of a hand, Willie. [*He slithers back to foot of mound and lies with face to ground.*] Brrum! [*Pause. He rises to hands and knees, raises his face towards her.*] Have another go, Willie, I'll cheer you on. [*Pause.*] Don't look at me like that! [*Pause. Vehement.*] Don't look at me like that! [*Pause. Low.*] Have you gone off your head, Willie? [*Pause. Do.*] Out of your poor old wits, Willie?

  [*Pause.*]

WILLIE [*just audible*]: Win.

  [*Pause.* WINNIE's *eyes front. Happy expression appears, grows.*

WINNIE: Win! [*Pause.*] Oh this *is* a happy day, this will have been another happy day! [*Pause.*] After all. [*Pause.*] So far.

  [*Pause. She hums tentatively beginning of song, then sings softly, musical-box tune.*

> Though I say not
> What I may not
> Let you hear,
> Yet the swaying
> Dance is saying,
> Love me dear!

Every touch of fingers
Tells me what I know,
Says for you,
It's true, it's true,
You love me so!

[Pause. *Happy expression off. She closes her eyes. Bell rings loudly. She opens her eyes. She smiles, gazing front. She turns her eyes, smiling, to* WILLIE, *still on his hands and knees looking up at her. Smile off. They look at each other. Long pause.*

CURTAIN

🏵 *Comments*

Hers (Winnie's) is the ultimate impasse. Having rotated its several elements at varying speeds, so that some pass before us twice, some three or four a dozen times, the play closes in a long tableau of mutual interrogation: Winnie's head alone protruding from the sand, Willie on all fours gazing into her eyes, and thinking perhaps of her, or perhaps of the revolver beside her, and if the latter, then planning to use it perhaps on her (out of pity, or else because she has threatened to sing) or perhaps on himself out of despair, or weariness with her babble). The rotation of the earth is very slow now, the days very long and very hot, space very empty, memories very remote. To utter the mere word "day" is to "speak in the old style," for the light seems interminable; but some power, interceding on behalf of human metabolism, has furnished a bell for waking and a bell for sleep. The beneficence of this power is questionable, though, since the waking bell clangs imperiously whenever Winnie illicitly closes her eyes. She looks forward, first fondling possessions and then memories, to "the happy day to come when the flesh melts at so many hundred degrees and the night of the moon has so many hundred hours." And it breaks upon us suddenly that the play is not really the lunatic fantasy it seems, but perhaps an H-bomb explosion rendered in extreme slow motion, the blazing instant stretched into an evening's theatre time.

Hugh Kenner, *Flaubert, Joyce and Beckett, The Stoic Comedians* (Boston: The Beacon Press, 1962), p. 100.

In *Happy Days* Beckett has discovered a new stage metaphor for the old human condition—burial in a dying earth, exposure under a ruthless sun. Although Winnies's resolute cheerfulness is suspect, her happy smiles and words nevertheless lighten the atmosphere. Not only does she insist upon the happiness of her day—"old style" though it may be—but she is constantly, busily counting her blessings. Her most frequently repeated refrain, "That is what I find so wonderful," and the ability to smile remain with her almost to the final curtain of Act II. In two of her quotations about Woe, there is also mention of "joys" and "laughing." In the scene from which the *Romeo* and *Juliet* phrases are taken, Juliet is not actually dead, and in *Cymbeline* Imogen does not die at all.

But for all Winnie's resources of good cheer, whose "end . . . is most unlikely," it is mainly to Willie that she owes her happy days. In spite of his limitations as a conversationalist, his presence protects her from becoming Hamm, whose final words are spoken into the silence, or Krapp, who speaks only to his tape recorder. Intermittently but dependably, Willie protects Winnie from the solipsistic self she calls her "wilderness."

Ruby Cohn, *Samuel Beckett, The Comic Gamut* (New Brunswick: Rutgers University Press, 1962), p. 257.

Whatever temptation a more complex person may provide for Beckett, it must be noted that *Happy Days* (1961) resists that temptation and, dramatically, marks time. The play toys for a while with the human assertion, but rejects it for a statement of the usual paralysis by the innocent: Winnie, a woman about fifty, is imbedded up to her waist in a mound. The Eleatic argument of immobility is still expressed by Beckett's version of Achilles and the tortoise—death is forever on the way but never arrives. In Act II, Winnie is imbedded up to her neck, but the play continues.

The monologue is familiar. The social tropism persists in spite of irrefutable evidence that existence is a mockery. Like the other characters of Beckett's drama, Winnie is fluent. And she also commands, as once did Pozzo, the elaborate paraphernalia of the social ritual, a literal bagful of tricks. These are the social level of her self-deception, the gestures that are rendered grotesque through the failure of any meaningful reference. In the face of annihilation, toothbrushing is nearly obscene. Beckett underscores the futility of this preoccupation by having Winnie interrupt her metaphysical commentary in her concern to find out what it is about the toothbrush that is referred to as "genuine pure. . . ." At the nonsocial level of her speculation, she shares in the literary deception already noted in other plays of Beckett, the belief that as a poetized fiction life can be rendered more endurable or meaningful. Winnie is kept ecstatic by instances of "the old style . . . the sweet old style" and its cliches, some of which are deliberately literary. . . .

Winnie has a husband, Willie—one of Beckett's congenital cripples whose debility needs no props for its evidence. Once again, names show these people to be the complements of a monologue. The "happy days" to which the title refers ironically are the moments when the illusion of communication is indulged. But Willie's occasional monosyllables serve only to emphasize Winnie's isolation. Yet *Happy Days* is a comedy. The consciousness of death is a truth sufficiently intimate to link in a single reality character and spectator; it is out of this awareness that tragedy develops. When blindness cancels the unpleasant awareness, not only does a lighter mood settle on the stage, but also the spectator is separate from the incomplete character. The stage is set for comedy. In *Happy Days*, the title and the mechanical pursuits of Winnie outweigh her moments of awareness and tip the scales on the side of comedy. Furthermore, the physical stage is less sordid; and for once in a Beckett play, the human being is seen prior to decomposition—the heroine is an attractive woman. Puns are still there, but less frequent; laughter is not meant to break against the gloom. The pervasive irony of the play suggests humor of another sort, less violent and more sustained—the death rattle is now merely the patter of a silly woman whose fun and meaning derive from the disparity between what she says and the world in which she says it. Still, those critics who have seen in the play a departure from the old Beckett are referred to the final tableau: *Pause. Happy expression off. She closes her eyes. Bell rings loudly. She opens her eyes. She smiles, gazing front. She turns her eyes, smiling, to Willie, still on his hands and knees looking up at her. Smile off. They look at each other. Long pause. Curtain.*

The final note is one of awareness that reduces Winnie's previous actions and words to nought. She ends as one of the conscious spinners of sounds and gestures before a familiar doom.

Beckett had a choice. In the feminine reality of Winnie, in the endurance of her social tropisms, Beckett could have seen a human assertion and a persistency that is its own justification and significance. But Beckett reduces the femininity of Winnie's empty gestures, the kinematics of the object. Winnie's plumpness, her bare arms and shoulders, her "low bodice, big bosom," are buried in Act II; if she is "well preserved," it is a mere irony, the author's view of her present situation. Her human reality, the brief glimmer of her sexuality, is extinguished in the thing which she becomes, the gestures that have no meaning, the hopelessness of her words. The spectator is reminded that even though the play escapes from the confining womb, the ash cans, and the wheel chairs and is set in the open, the grass is "scorched," the landscape is artificial ("maximum of simplicity and symmetry"), and the unbroken plain and sky are "pompier trompe l'oeil." This world is as dead as the objects which its people have become. Even the unusual light is deceptive—it burns Winnie's parasol to a crisp. We are indeed close to hell, a feeling intensified by the customary references to a malevolent divinity: "How can one better magnify the Almighty than by sniggering with him at his little jokes."

From *Four Playwrights and a Postscript: Brecht, Ionesco, Beckett, Genet* by David I. Grossvogel (Ithaca: Cornell University Press), pp. 128–31. © 1962 by Cornell University. Used by permission of Cornell University Press.

———◆—————

In Beckett's most recent play, *Happy Days*, he presents a woman buried in the ground up to her waist. Just as much of her is gone as is present when the curtain rises. The action of the play consists in her sinking deeper into the ground, so that when the curtain falls, only her head is visible. In the meantime, there is nothing for her to do but to recall what is absent from the stage and to play with her husband, who circles about her on all fours. Is he like a dog on the scent, trying to find the trail of all that is gone?

Why are time and its effects so important to Beckett? Because, I suspect, of his nostalgia for eternity. Should we not be, at the very least, the playthings of eternity and not merely the playthings of time? Such is the question Beckett poses in his plays, thus suggesting that the actual characters are themselves the scenes of an invisible action: the action of time, which might be eternal itself, or the surrogate, although we cannot be sure of this, for eternity.

But these plays cannot be understood or appreciated fully unless we recognize that for all their special content, oddity, and purely personal lyricism, they conform to the kind of dramatic work I have designated as metatheatre: what makes them so special is that life in these plays has been theatricalized, not by any attitudes taken by the characters, not by any tricks of dramaturgy, and not by the author's intent to demonstrate any propositions about the world, but by the mere passage of time, that drastic fact of ordinary life.

From *Metatheatre* by Lionel Abel (New York: Hill & Wang, Inc., 1963), pp. 84–85. Reprinted by permission of Hill & Wang, Inc.